Adult Eyewitness Testimony

Adult Eyewitness Testimony: Current Trends and Developments provides an overview of current empirical research on eyewitness testimony and identification accuracy, covering both theory and application. The volume is organized to address three important issues: First, what are the cognitive, social, and physical factors that influence the accuracy of eyewitness reports? Second, how should lineups be constructed and verbal testimony be taken to improve the chances of obtaining accurate information? And third, whose testimony should be believed? Are there differences between accurate and inaccurate witnesses, and can jurors make such a distinction? *Adult Eyewitness Testimony: Current Trends and Developments* is crucial reading for memory researchers, as well as police officers, judges, lawyers, and other members of the criminal justice system.

Adult Eyewitness Testimony

Current trends and developments

Edited by

DAVID FRANK ROSS

J. DON READ

MICHAEL P. TOGLIA

CAMBRIDGE
UNIVERSITY PRESS

Published by the Press Syndicate of the University of Cambridge
The Pitt Building, Trumpington Street, Cambridge CB2 1 RP
40 West 20th Street, New York, NY 10011-4211, USA
10 Stamford Road, Oakleigh, Melbourne 3166, Australia

© Cambridge University Press 1994

First published 1994

Printed in the United States of America

Library of Congress Cataloging-in-Publication Data
Adult eyewitness testimony : current trends and developments / edited
by David Frank Ross, J. Don Read, Michael P. Toglia.
p.   cm.
ISBN 0-521-43255-3 (hardback)
1. Eyewitness identification.   2. Evidence, Criminal.
3. Psychology, Forensic.   I. Ross, David F., 1959–   .   II. Read,
J. Don.   III. Toglia, Michael P.
K5483.A73   1994
345.73'066–dc20
[347.30566]   93-8004

A catalog record for this book is available from the British Library.

ISBN 0–521–43255–3 hardback

Contents

Part II   Lineup construction and collection of testimony

**Part III   Whom to believe? Distinguishing accurate from inaccurate
eyewitnesses**

Contributors

Garrett L. Berman
Florida International University
Department of Psychology
College of Arts and Sciences
North Miami, Florida

John C. Brigham
Florida State University
Department of Psychology
Tallahassee, Florida

Stephen J. Ceci
Department of Human Development
   and Family Studies
Cornell University
Ithaca, New York

Brian L. Cutler
Florida International University
Department of Psychology
College of Arts and Sciences
North Miami, Florida

David Dunning
Department of Psychology
Cornell University
Ithaca, New York

Ronald P. Fisher
Florida International University
Department of Psychology
College of Arts and Sciences
North Miami, Florida

Jason N. Frowley
University of St. Andrews
Department of Psychology
St. Andrews, Fife
Scotland, U.K.

R. Edward Geiselman
Department of Psychology
University of California, Los Angeles
Los Angeles, California

Harmon Hosch
Department of Psychology
University of Texas at El Paso
El Paso, Texas

Michael R. Leippe
Adelphi University
Department of Psychology
Garden City, Long Island, New York

D. Stephen Lindsay
Department of Psychology
University of Victoria
Victoria, British Columbia
Canada

R.C.L. Lindsay
Queen's University
Department of Psychology
Kingston, Ontario
Canada

Elizabeth F. Loftus
University of Washington
Department of Psychology
Seattle, Washington

C.A. Elizabeth Luus
Department of Psychology
University of Victoria
Victoria, British Columbia
Canada

Malcolm D. MacLeod
University of St. Andrews
Department of Psychology
St. Andrews, Fife
Scotland, U.K.

Michelle R. McCauley
Florida International University
Department of Psychology
College of Arts and Sciences
North Miami, Florida

Steven Penrod
University of Minnesota
Minneapolis, Minnesota

Jeffrey E. Pfeifer
Department of Psychology
University of Regina
Regina, Saskatchewan
Canada

J. Don Read
Department of Psychology
University of Lethbridge
Lethbridge, Alberta
Canada

David F. Ross
Boise State University
Department of Psychology
Boise, Idaho

Sheila M. Rydell
Department of Psychology
Iowa State University
Ames, Iowa

Eric P. Seelau
Department of Psychology
Iowa State University
Ames, Iowa

John W. Shepherd
Department of Psychology
University of Aberdeen
Aberdeen, Scotland, U.K.

Siegfried Ludwig Sporer
School of Law and Criminology
Marburg, Germany

Lisa B. Stern
Department of Psychology
Cornell University
Ithaca, New York

M.P. Toglia
Department of Psychology
State University of New York–Cortland
Cortland, New York

H. Kelly Toland
University of Washington
Department of Psychology
Seattle, Washington

Patricia A. Tollestrup
Department of Psychology
University of British Columbia
Vancouver, Canada

John W. Turtle
Atkinson College, York University
North York, Ontario, Canada

Kenneth R. Weingardt
University of Washington
Department of Psychology
Seattle, Washington

Gary L. Wells
Department of Psychology
Iowa State University
Ames, Iowa

A. Daniel Yarmey
Department of Psychology
University of Guelph
Guelph, Ontario
Canada

John C. Yuille
Department of Psychology
University of British Columbia
Vancouver, Canada

Preface

The impetus for this book was a symposium that was presented at the American Psychological Society meeting in Washington, D.C. in June of 1991. Following the symposium there was a general agreement among the six symposium contributors of the need for an edited volume directed at surveying the wide range of topics on eyewitness testimony that were being investigated. As many observers have noted, the field of psychology and the law has seen enormous growth within the last decade and within this broad field the topic of eyewitness testimony has received a great deal of attention. Because there had not been a volume dedicated to adult eyewitness testimony since the 1984 classic, *Eyewitness Testimony: Psychological Perspectives,* edited by Gary Wells and Elizabeth Loftus and published by Cambridge University Press, we embarked on this project to fill a void in the literature. We chose topics that are representative of the diversity of research currently being conducted in the field.

In the history of the legal system, there are numerous examples of individuals who have been accused, tried, and convicted of crimes they did not commit. These unfortunate events can follow the misidentification of an innocent person from a police lineup by an eyewitness when the court has accepted and weighted the identification evidence heavily in its decision. The present volume is designed to provide an overview of current empirical research on adult eyewitness testimony and identification accuracy, providing insight into theory and application. The volume contains eighteen chapters written by psycholegal researchers from the United States, Canada, Scotland, and Germany. It is organized to address three basic issues in eyewitness testimony that should be of interest to memory researchers as well as police officers, judges, lawyers, and other members of the judicial system. First, what are the cognitive, social, and physical factors or processes that influence the accuracy of eyewitness reports? Second, how should lineups be constructed and verbal testimony taken to improve the chances of obtaining accurate information? Third, whose testimony should be believed? Are there differences between accurate and inaccurate witnesses, and can jurors make such a distinction?

Part I   Cognitive, physical, and social processes and factors influencing eyewitness recall and identification

This section contains seven chapters and examines a variety of factors and processes involved in eyewitness testimony. To begin with, Kenneth Weingardt, Kelly Toland, and Beth Loftus present research on the impact on eyewitness memory of misleading or suggestive questions. This research investigates the much debated issue of whether misleading questions change or distort eyewitness memory, and to what extent witnesses believe in their "suggested" memories. Providing further insight on the issue, Steve Lindsay provides both a broad review of the literature on "source monitoring" relevant to eyewitness reports, and a critique of several topics within eyewitness testimony from a source-monitoring perspective. Among others, these include the impairment of memory by misleading questions, and bystander misidentification. Lindsay's own research makes use of Jacoby's "logic of opposition" (also described in the previous chapter) and with it he reports reliable memory impairment effects.

In the next several chapters a number of issues and problems are explored that have only recently emerged in the field. For example, Don Read investigates some of the cognitive processes involved when witnesses make a lineup identification. That is, how does a witness move from simply recognizing someone in a lineup as familiar, to selecting that person as the perpetrator? What additional information is needed for a positive identification to be made? This research is relevant to misidentifications in general, and to the misidentification of the "innocent but familiar" persons described in the next chapter. Specifically, David Ross, Steve Ceci, David Dunning, and Michael Toglia investigate the little known or understood phenomenon referred to as unconscious transference that occurs when a witness misidentifies a familiar but innocent person from a police lineup. Ross and his colleagues present one of the first empirical demonstrations of this phenomenon and offer an explanation by comparing several theoretical approaches.

Although the psycholegal literature has given a great deal of attention to facial identification, in many criminal cases the witness does not have the opportunity to see the face of the perpetrator because a disguise was used or the environment afforded little opportunity for proper viewing. As a result, the witness is asked to identify the perpetrator using other physical characteristics such as voice, body size, or shape. This is an important issue yet one that has received relatively little attention from psycholegal researchers. The next two chapters begin to fill this void. Earwitness memory, or the ability to identify a perpetrator's voice, is described in the chapter by Daniel Yarmey who presents a program of research that examines a variety of factors influencing or related to earwitness memory accuracy including: retention interval, witness confidence, telephone voice identification, verbal descriptions of voices, show-ups, and the impact of stereotypes on voice identification. The chapter by Malcolm MacLeod, Jason Frowley, and John Shepherd, on the other hand, presents research on "whole body identification" examining the accuracy of eyewitness memory for body characteristics such as weight, shape, gait, and movement. In particular, a number of theoretical and practical issues central to whole body identification are examined. These include, for example, the impact of social stereotypes about body characteristics (for example, beliefs about people who are over- or underweight, or tall versus short) on memory and perception, the reliability of weight and height judgments and how these are related to the height and weight of the witness, and the role of clothing in lineup identification and witness memory.

In the final chapter in this section, Patricia Tollestrup, John Turtle, and John Yuille report an archival analysis of police files investigating over 120 actual cases of robbery and 60 cases of fraud. This is a highly innovative and informative procedure rarely undertaken in the past. The chapter provides an ecologically meaningful look at lineups used by police in actual criminal cases, and discusses the ability of actual victims of crime to make accurate lineup identifications, report accurately the physical characteristics of perpetrators, and recall events they witnessed. This chapter will provide an interesting contrast to the many laboratory studies of eyewitness testimony presented in this volume.

Part II Lineup construction and collection of testimony

This section contains five chapters and investigates the difference between fair and unfair lineups in terms of characteristics such as foil selection, the measurement of lineup fairness, as well as the procedures suggested within the "cognitive interview" technique for enhancing the amount and accuracy of verbal testimony. In the first of these chapters, Brian Cutler, Garrett Berman, Steven Penrod, and Ronald Fisher examine the impact of the modality of the lineup identification test. Specifically, a series of meta-analyses of previous research studies are presented that compare the effect of live lineups, videotape lineups, and photo lineups on witness identification accuracy. Because of its focus on the question of whether the type of identification test medium affects the successful identification rate, the chapter by Cutler and his colleagues assumes the use of fair or unbiased lineups by investigating officers. There have been a number of criminal cases, however, in which biased or unfair lineups have been used. In a famous Minnesota case, a lineup that contained a black suspect and four white distractors was presented to a witness. The police claimed that the lineup was fair because it reflected the proportion of blacks to whites that lived in the town. Rod Lindsay examines the origin of these kinds of bad or unfair lineups. That is, when a lineup is clearly unfair what is the source of the problem? Is it ignorance – the police not knowing how to construct a lineup – sloppiness or not taking the time to do it correctly, or intentional to lead witnesses to identify a particular individual from the lineup? On the basis of a series of laboratory studies, Lindsay reaches the controversial conclusion that highly biased lineups reflect intentional behavior of police officers.

In the following chapter John Brigham and Jeffrey Pfeifer extend the question by assessing various measures for the empirical evaluation of lineup fairness as reflected in lineup size and bias. Their chapter includes a study on how police officers evaluate the fairness of lineups: Brigham and Pfeifer's research-generated measures appear to match well the factors considered by experienced law enforcement officers in their own evaluations of lineups.

The next chapter examines how lineups should be constructed to ensure lineup fairness and maximize witness accuracy. Gary Wells, Eric Seelau, Sheila Rydell, and Elizabeth Luus recommend guidelines for the construction of a fair lineup. In particular, it describes a two-step procedure for selecting lineup distractors and a series of experiments on this procedure, and discusses the theoretical and practical implications. The intended effect of one procedure in lineup construction advocated by Wells and his colleagues is to increase what they refer to as "propitious heterogeneity," the extent to which lineup foils or distractors differ from the suspect in features not included in the witness's verbal description. This controversial suggestion runs counter to the view that, insofar as is possible, lineup foils should match the suspect in all features.

The final chapter in this section by Ronald Fisher, Michelle McCauley, and Edward Geiselman presents research on how to improve the accuracy of eyewitness verbal testimony using the Cognitive Interview – a technique designed to assist the witness to retrieve a memory during an interview conducted by police. In this chapter, Fisher and his colleagues document the development of this procedure (including research on its use with actual victims of crime), present a new series of studies on the most recent version of this procedure, and describe both its effectiveness with different types of eyewitness memory (recall versus facial identification) and the resulting practical implications.

Part III   Who to believe?
Distinguishing accurate from inaccurate eyewitnesses

Historically, psycholegal researchers have been unable to identify the characteristics or behaviors of eyewitnesses that could be used to distinguish those who are accurate from those who are inaccurate. The next three chapters provide exciting new developments on this topic. In the chapter by Lisa Stern and David Dunning, several studies are reported that identify qualitative differences in the memory processes of witnesses who make accurate versus inaccurate lineup identifications. Moreover, when mock jurors were taught what to look for in judging the accuracy of eyewitness reports, they showed a dramatic improvement in their ability to distinguish accurate from inaccurate witnesses. Siegfried Sporer uses the length of time it takes a witness to make a lineup identification as a predictor of witness accuracy. Briefly, accurate identifications are made significantly faster than are inaccurate decisions. And the chapter by Harmon Hosch provides a series of studies identifying individual differences in personality (for example, self-monitoring, cognitive styles) that are related to the accuracy of eyewitness memory and facial recognition ability. In some cases, as with Sporer's research, accurate and inaccurate witnesses were differentiated by their decision times but the direction of these differences depended on the level of personality variable under consideration.

Elizabeth Luus and Gary Wells next present research that demonstrates how social and cognitive factors interact to influence the confidence eyewitnesses have in their reports. In a series of experiments, the confidence of a witness was found to be influenced by information regarding the identification from a fellow eyewitness to the crime. For example, the news that a co-eyewitness identified the same or a different person from a lineup was found to have a dramatic impact on the confidence of the witness in his or her identification. As we shall see, witness confidence is the criterion mock jurors most frequently use in deciding whose testimony is to be believed, and, the Luus and Wells research has potentially important implications for trial outcomes.

The final two chapters investigate how jurors evaluate eyewitness testimony. That is, what factors do jurors use in making judgments about the accuracy of eyewitness testimony? How accurate are their judgments? Can jurors tell the difference between accurate and inaccurate eyewitnesses? First, Rod Lindsay presents a series of mock jury studies that focus on the factors jurors use in judging witness accuracy. Consistent with the findings of past research, Lindsay reports that witness confidence consistently influenced juror verdicts and perceptions of witness accuracy, whereas a variety of other factors had little or no effect. Several additional findings suggest that mock jurors make a determination of guilt or innocence by distorting the evidence to conform to their decisions.

In the final chapter of the section and the volume, Michael Leippe presents several lines of research that culminate in a theory that views eyewitness testimony as a "persuasive communication" whereby the witness attempts to persuade the jury that his or her testimony is accurate. Leippe's theory incorporates research on nonverbal communication, metamemory, and persuasion, and explains how a variety of factors influence the believability of eyewitness testimony, including witness attributes, witness behavior and speech, consistency of testimony, witnessing conditions, and juror characteristics. Leippe also addresses the issue of whether jurors can discern the accuracy of eyewitness memory, and reports that under certain conditions jurors are capable of distinguishing accurate from inaccurate eyewitnesses (as seen in the Stern and Dunning chapter). Finally an evaluation is made regarding the effectiveness of using different types of witness cues (confidence, hesitations in speech, for example) to judge witness accuracy. Leippe's chapter integrates many of the themes and issues discussed within the volume, and we hope thus provides the reader with a sense of closure.

David F. Ross
J. Don Read
Michael P. Toglia

Part I

Cognitive, physical, and social processes and factors influencing eyewitness recall and identification

1 Reports of suggested memories: Do people truly believe them?

*Kenneth R. Weingardt, H. Kelly Toland, and
Elizabeth F. Loftus*

A true case, described using pseudonyms in *Witness for the Defense* (Loftus and Ketcham, 1991), provides a powerful anecdote showing just how strongly witnesses can believe in their memories – even when their memories are false. The case arose out of an incident that happened early one morning in the spring of 1979 when Sally Blackwell awoke to find an intruder at the foot of her bed. As she raised her head to speak to the man, he put a gun to her head and told her that if she made any noise, he would kill her children. What followed was a two hour ordeal in which both Ms. Blackwell and her teenage daughter Janet were bound, blindfolded, and systematically raped and sodomized by their assailant.

The following morning Sally called Lois Williams, a co-worker, to explain that she would not be coming to work that day. Several hours later, Sally's irate boyfriend began urging her to come up with a name for the man who had assaulted her. He thought the rapist must have been someone she knew, or why else would the man have been so careful to conceal his identity? As Ms. Blackwell testified, he kept saying "It's got to be somebody you know. You've seen him in the neighborhood, you've seen him somewhere before. Just think where you've seen him. You saw him at the grocery store or at church; you've seen him somewhere. You've seen him at a party somewhere." As he said "party," according to Ms. Blackwell, a name flashed with the face.

The name she connected with the face of her rapist was Clarence Von Williams. Williams was the forty-two-year-old husband of Lois Williams, the co-worker Sally had called earlier that morning. Sally and her boyfriend had attended a party with the Von Williamses several weeks earlier, and the two couples had spent several hours together.

With this connection made, Sally found someone to blame for the nightmare that she and her family had been forced to endure. Criminal charges were filed against Von Williams. As the date of the trial grew near, Ms. Blackwell's repeated assertions that "I know what I saw in my mind" made her increas-

Significant portions of the research described in this chapter were supported by a grant from the National Institute of Mental Health to E. F. Loftus. We wish to thank D. S. Lindsay for his helpful comments on portions of this chapter.

ingly confident that Von Williams was the man who had raped her and her daughter.

Ms. Blackwell's positive identification of her attacker during the trial was obviously quite convincing. Despite Von Williams' emotional denials of the accusations, and the lack of any corroborating physical evidence, he was convicted of aggravated rape and sentenced to fifty years in prison.

Two months after his conviction, there was a new development in the Von Williams case: A thirty-two-year-old man named Jon Simonis was picked up by the Louisiana State Police. He confessed to over seventy crimes in seven different states, including the rapes for which Clarence Von Williams had been convicted. Simonis' entire confession was videotaped. When the prosecutors responsible for Von Williams' conviction had the opportunity to watch the tape, they immediately dismissed all charges against him.

The fact that charges against Von Williams were dropped suggests something about the compelling quality of Simonis' confession. Yet the reaction of Sally Blackwell to this videotape was one of stunned shock and disbelief. When she first saw the confession, she was only able to stare at the man on the tape, shake her head back and forth, and with her voice rising over the sound of the videotape, repeated "No, no, no, no, *no no.*"

Sally Blackwell believed so fully in the validity of her memory for her assailant, that even when presented with concrete evidence contradicting that recollection, she refused to budge. Loftus and Ketcham (1991) explained: "The victim made her choice – Clarence Von Williams – and later, even with the real criminal staring her in the face, confessing to the rape, and bringing up details that only he could have known, she couldn't accept it. . . . Once Von Williams's face merged with her memory of the rapist's face, and once she committed herself to that memory by stating in court that Von Williams was her rapist, it became impossible to separate the two memories. They were, in a very real sense, permanently fused together" (p. 208).

As this story exemplifies, discussion after witnessing an event can influence people's recollections of that event. If this discussion is misleading (as were the suggestions of Ms. Blackwell's boyfriend), it can cause errors in a person's eyewitness account. And, as Clarence Von Williams would undoubtedly agree, these errors can have enormous consequences.

This phenomenon, by which new information leads to errors in eyewitness reports, has been well documented empirically, and is often referred to as the "misinformation effect" (Loftus and Hoffman, 1989). Most of the research on the impact of misinformation (for example, Lindsay, 1990; Loftus, Donders, Hoffman, and Schooler, 1989; Loftus, Miller, and Burns, 1978; Mc-Closkey and Zaragoza, 1985; Tversky and Tuchin, 1989) has employed a three-stage procedure in which subjects first witness an event by means of a slide sequence or videotape. Then subjects receive new information about the event, often in the form of a written narrative or embedded in questions.

Finally, subjects take a test of their memory for the event. Typically, people in such studies report that they have seen objects or actions as part of an event, when in fact those objects or actions came from other sources.

The issue of "true belief"

Although the misinformation effect has been well established as a psychological phenomenon, and many of the factors associated with it have been identified, there has been little consensus regarding its interpretation. An issue that has inspired considerable debate concerns whether subjects who have received misleading suggestions about an item (item being loosely defined here as a person, object, or action) come to genuinely believe, as did Sally Blackwell, that they had actually seen the item which had only been suggested to them.

Many researchers have demonstrated that subjects exposed to misleading postevent information are likely confidently to report such misinformation on subsequent memory tests. For example, Loftus, Donders, Hoffman, and Schooler (1989) tested subjects for their memories of what they saw in a series of slides depicting a burglary, and measured their reaction times and confidence levels. When subjects were administered a recognition memory test that required them to choose between the event item and the misinformation item (often referred to as the "standard test"), misled subjects responded as quickly and confidently when choosing the incorrect misinformation response as they did when they chose correctly.

Although this result indicates that misled subjects are confident about their incorrect responses, and that they do not spend much time deliberating about them, it does not conclusively establish that subjects who base their test responses on memories of suggested items actually truly believe that they saw the suggested items as part of the event. In fact, other researchers (for example, McCloskey and Zaragoza, 1985; Zaragoza and Koshmider, 1989) contend that misinformation-based responses are in no way indicative of "true belief." For example, Zaragoza and Koshmider (1989) argued that because "subjects in the typical misinformation experiment are not encouraged to distinguish between what they believe happened in the original event and what they specifically remember seeing in the original event" (p. 246), the results of experiments that use the standard test are uninterpretable with respect to the issue of true belief.

How can one empirically address the issue of "true belief"? One obvious approach is to come right out and ask subjects to report the source of their memory for each test item. This is exactly what Zaragoza and Koshmider did by administering a memory test that forced their subjects to indicate the source of their memory for each test item. Specifically, subjects were shown slides depicting the critical items, either in the event form or in the postevent form, and subjects were required to indicate the source of their memory by choosing among the following four response options: the SAW option if subjects were absolutely sure they had seen the test item in the slides; READ if they did not remember seeing the item but did remember reading about it in the narrative; the CONSISTENT option if the item in the slides were consistent with what they remembered about the event, but did not know where it came from; INCONSISTENT if the item in the test slide contradicted what they remembered about the event.

The proportion of SAW responses to the misleading test slide in the misled condition was not statistically greater than the proportion of SAW responses in the control condition. The misleading test slide contained misleading or false information that was provided in the postevent narrative that was given to subjects in the misled condition. Control subjects were not exposed to this misleading information in the narrative they were given. Consequently, the authors argued that exposure to misleading information did not lead subjects to falsely remember seeing the misinformation items, that is, they did not come to genuinely believe that they had seen the misinformation items.

Zaragoza and Koshmider were neither the first nor the last investigators to utilize such a "source monitoring test" in an attempt to address the issue of true belief. Lindsay and Johnson have conducted numerous studies in which subjects were required to identify the source of their memories for each test item (Johnson and Lindsay, 1986; Lindsay and Johnson, 1987, 1989a). Although Lindsay and Johnson's earlier experiments obtained results that were essentially the same as those obtained by Zaragoza and Koshmider, their interpretation of them was considerably different. Zaragoza and Koshmider interpreted the pattern of results mentioned above as evidence that subjects were aware that their memories of the suggested details were derived from the narrative. That is, subjects are typically presented the original event using slides and the narrative is given after the event in the form of a document that subjects read. Lindsay and Johnson argued that subjects taking an old/ new recognition test may well have experienced source monitoring confusions (that is, said "yes" to suggested items because they thought they had seen those items in the slide) because they were using lax source monitoring criteria.

This interpretive debate was superseded by findings in both laboratories of suggestibility effects among subjects tested with source monitoring tests. For example, Lindsay and Johnson's most recent (1989a) source monitoring data showed that although misled subjects were capable of identifying the source of their memories of misleading suggestions, they nonetheless sometimes misidentified them as memories derived from the original event. Similarly, Zaragoza's most recent experimentation (Zaragoza and Muench, 1989) also indicates that misled subjects really do experience recollections of suggestions as recollections of details seen in the event.

Though the evidence from some source monitoring studies indicates that misled subjects "truly believe" that they have seen suggested items in the event, the results of such studies are subject to alternative explanations. For example, misled subjects may perform more poorly than their control counterparts because they base their test responses on information they know was obtained from the narrative.

McCloskey and Zaragoza (1985) convincingly argued that subjects are led to believe that the narrative is accurate (in some experiments, subjects are informed that the narrative was written by a professor who had watched the slides very closely). Consequently, subjects may base their responses on information they know was obtained from the narrative because they wish to show that they are attentive and remember details from both the event and the narrative. This explanation is often referred to as a "demand characteristic" interpretation.

As in studies employing standard recognition tests, subjects in misinformation studies that use source monitoring tests are led to believe that the narrative is accurate, and may wish to show their attentiveness by reporting details that they actually only remember from the narrative but that they assume or infer were also present in the visual event (Lindsay, 1990). Because of the demand characteristics inherent in source monitoring tests, experiments that contain such tests are unable to establish conclusively whether subjects truly believe that they saw the suggested details. For these reasons, Lindsay (1990) looked for an entirely new procedure to preclude the demand characteristic interpretation: He adapted Jacoby, Woloshyn, and Kelley's (1989) "logic of opposition" paradigm.

The logic of opposition

The demand characteristic interpretation of the results of typical misinformation studies suggests that subjects who base their test responses on memories of suggested items do not really remember seeing such items in the event. Rather, it is argued that subjects choose the misinformation response (suggested details) because they believe in the accuracy of the narrative and wish to appear observant. By instructing his subjects that any information contained in the narrative was wrong and should not be reported on the test, Lindsay set the tendency to report suggested details in opposition to the ability to remember the source of the details. Under such opposition instructions, demand characteristics work against the hypothesis of genuine memory effects. If subjects continue to base their test responses on suggested items, despite explicit instructions against doing so, one can more confidently infer that such subjects genuinely believe that they saw the suggested items in the slides.

A more concrete example of the logic of opposition may help the reader attain a fuller understanding of this concept. Suppose that Gene Siskell and Roger Ebert, the independent minded film critics who appear weekly on the syndicated television show "At the Movies," are about to review a movie that you are considering seeing. From the promotional materials, it is clear that *Halloween Part VI* is a somewhat stereotypical horror picture. Further suppose that it is widely known that Ebert is a big fan of films of this genre, while Siskell detests them. The logic of opposition dictates that if you want to determine whether the movie is actually worth today's exorbitant price of admission, you should attend to Siskell's opinion. If Siskell, who has been known to deride virtually all films of this genre, gives *Halloween Part VI* a "thumbs-up," you know that it must be an excellent film indeed.

Analogously, when Lindsay's subjects based their test responses on information contained in the narrative, despite being informed that any such information was incorrect, he could confidently conclude that misled subjects truly believed they saw the suggested details in the slide sequence. In addition to establishing that some misled subjects come to truly believe that they saw suggested items, Lindsay's logic of opposition study provided evidence that misinformation impairs subject's ability to remember event details. Before explaining how he came about this last piece of evidence, it is necessary to become familiar with several aspects of the design he used.

Lindsay's use of Jacoby's Logic of Opposition: "If you read it, don't report it"

Lindsay employed the standard three-stage misinformation paradigm. First, subjects saw a sequence of color slides depicting an incident in which a maintenance man steals some money and a calculator from an office. Following the slide presentation, subjects read a detailed description of the events depicted in the slides. This narrative included misleading suggestions about some critical details in the slide sequence and neutral terms for three other details. For example, subjects in the misled condition saw a screwdriver, and then read about a wrench, whereas subjects in the control condition also saw a screwdriver, but read about a tool. Finally, subjects took a test of their memory for the event depicted in the slides.

The innovative character of the test he used, and the manner in which it was administered, allowed Lindsay to observe situations in which subjects' memories for the original event were impaired by exposure to misinformation. Lindsay's unique design also allowed him to observe situations in which subjects appeared to truly believe that they saw items which were only suggested to them.

The test of memory that Lindsay used consisted of one cued recall question about each critical detail. Questions were of the following form: "The man had a pack of CIGARETTES. What BRAND OF CIGARETTES was shown in the slides?" (p. 1080). As was mentioned earlier, this test was accompanied by "logic of opposition" instructions, as follows:

> For some of the questions, the detail in question was not mentioned in the story at all (that is, you saw the correct answer in the slide show, but the detail in question was not mentioned in the story). For other questions, the detail was mentioned, but it was described inaccurately (that is, you saw the correct answer in the slide show, but an incorrect answer was mentioned in the story). **There is no question on this test for which the correct answer was mentioned in the story.**

Subjects were always tested in a second session, forty-eight hours after viewing the slides. In the low-discriminability condition, subjects viewed a slide sequence and studied a postevent narrative in session one, and completed a test of memory when they returned to the laboratory two days later. In the high-discriminability condition, subjects only viewed the slide sequence in the first session, and read the postevent narrative and took the memory test in the second session.

In addition to presenting the event and suggested details in the different experimental sessions, other factors were manipulated in an effort to increase the differences between memories of the slides and memories of the postevent narrative in the high-discriminability condition.

> The presentation of the postevent narrative differed in several ways from the low discriminability condition: Subjects listened to the postevent narrative while standing in the fully lit classroom, they were instructed to mentally repeat each word of the narrative as they heard it . . . and the tape recording (which accompanied the narrative) was of a male voice (distinctly different from the female voice which accompanied the presentation of the slide sequence). (p. 1080)

The overall design can thus be viewed as a 2×2 mixed factorial, with acquisition condition (high versus low discriminability) as the between-subjects factor and item type (misled versus control) as the within-subjects factor.

The first finding of interest addresses the issue of true belief. Did subjects genuinely believe that they saw the suggested details in the event? Lindsay's results indicate that, for some subjects, the answer is yes. In his low-discriminability condition, subjects who received misinformation more often claimed that they had seen suggested items than subjects who were not misinformed. Whereas misled subjects based their responses on suggested items 27 percent of the time, control subjects based their responses on suggested items only 9 percent of the time.

Another of Lindsay's findings suggests that exposure to misleading suggestions impairs subjects' memories for the original event. In the low-discriminability condition, Lindsay found that the proportion of correct responses for subjects who had received misinformation (.45) was significantly less than the proportion of correct responses for subjects who received no misinformation (.51). More interesting, even in the high-discriminability condition, misinformation seemed to impair the subject's ability to correctly recall event items. In Lindsay's words, "Although subjects in the high-discriminability condition were able to identify the source of their memories of suggested details (and so did not report seeing them more often on misled than control items), the misleading suggestions nonetheless hampered their ability to report the event details" (p. 1081). This impairment is evident when one compares proportion of correct responses for misled and control subjects in the high-discriminability condition (.39 and .48 respectively).

Logic of opposition revisited: "If you saw it, don't report it"

In an effort to provide convergent evidence on the issue of true belief, we recently conducted in collaboration with Stephen Lindsay a series of experiments at the University of Washington that utilized the logic of opposition paradigm (Weingardt, Loftus, & Lindsay, forthcoming). These studies, two of which are briefly described here, extend and generalize Lindsay's findings. In these new studies, the means by which the logic of opposition paradigm was operationalized was considerably different than Lindsay's original method. Recall that Lindsay administered a cued-recall test and informed subjects that "There is no question on the test for which the correct answer was mentioned in the story." We, on the other hand, asked subjects to generate category exemplars, and informed them that if they remembered a particular item from the slide sequence, they should not include it on their list. In essence, whereas Lindsay told his subjects; "If you read it, don't report it," we instructed our subjects, "If you saw it, don't report it."

Aside from the novel memory test described above, this experiment followed the typical misinformation paradigm. Specifically, subjects saw a slide sequence depicting a complex event. Following the slides they read a narrative containing some items of misinformation. Finally subjects were asked to list a number of items belonging in each specified category with the prohibition that they exclude items seen in the slides.

Our prediction for the results of this study was twofold. First, we predicted that subjects who read about a suggested item (misled subjects) would include that suggested item on their category lists *less* often than control subjects. Why? If some misled subjects think they actually saw the suggested item as the literature suggests, they would heed the opposition instruction forbidding them to list what they saw, and would thus exclude the suggested item from their list. Thus, the proportion of suggested items that were listed by misled subjects would be lower than the proportion of these same items listed by control subjects. Our second prediction was that misled subjects would include the event item on their category lists *more* often than controls. Why? If some misled subjects are induced to think that they actually saw the suggested item, then they would consequently believe they did not see the event item. If they then heeded the logic of opposition instruction that forbids them to list what they saw, they would not hesitate to list the event item. Thus the proportion of event items listed by misled subjects would be greater than the proportion of event items listed by control subjects.

Method. At the outset of the experimental session, subjects were told that the experiment involved assessment of the relative effectiveness of visual versus verbal modes of presentation. Subjects were therefore instructed to pay close attention to both the slide sequence and subsequent written narrative because they would be asked to evaluate them later.

The two hundred undergraduate subjects watched a sequence of sixty-eight color slides. The sequence depicts a male college student visiting a university bookstore. While shopping, he examines various items, slips several of them into his pack, and watches a handyman in the store doing some maintenance work. There were two versions each of the critical slides, for soft drink (7-Up or Coke), magazine (*Esquire* or *GQ*), and tool (screwdriver or wrench). Half of the subjects in each condition saw each version of the slide sequence. A tape-recorded narrative accompanied the slide sequence. This narrative commented only on the most salient aspects of each slide, and each critical item was mentioned at a generic level (for example, "The handyman picked up a *tool* and began fixing a damaged display case").

After a four-minute filler activity, subjects read a narrative describing the events depicted in the slides. The postevent narrative was a detailed verbal description of the event. For each subject, the narrative inaccurately described three of the six critical items, while describing the remaining three critical items in neutral terms. The items described inaccurately in the narrative served as "misled" items, whereas those items described neutrally served as "control" items. All items were counterbalanced across subject groups: For each item, half the subjects received misinformation about that item in the narrative and the other half received neutral information.

Finally, the subjects entered the test phase of the experiment. On the test of memory, subjects were asked to list five different exemplars of each specified category, but were given explicit instructions against listing items that they had seen in the slides. For example, subjects were asked to generate five different types of magazines, but were prohibited from including on their list any magazines they had seen in the slides. The most important part of these instructions was as follows:

For each question, you will be asked to list five different items that belong within a given category. For example, you may be asked to "Please list five different types of fruit." When making these lists, please refrain from including any items that you remember seeing in the slides. In other words, if you saw a certain item in the slide sequence, do not include it in your list.

These instructions were repeated and rephrased several times, and an example was provided to ensure that subjects understood them.

Results. For each critical item, each subject was asked to list five different exemplars that could be included within the specified categories. For each category list, we recorded whether or not the subject included the item in the slides (the event item) and whether or not the subject included the item suggested in the narrative (the suggested item) on the list. We could then compare lists that were produced when subjects had received misinformation, to lists that were produced when subjects had not.

Recall that our first prediction for this experiment was that the proportion of suggested items listed by misled subjects would be lower than the proportion of suggested items listed by control subjects. In accordance with this expectation, misled subjects included the suggested items on the category list significantly less often than subjects in the control condition (28 percent versus 43 percent, $t(199) = 5.49, p < .001$).

Also recall our second prediction, that misled subjects would include the event item on their category lists more often than controls. The data analysis also confirmed this prediction. Whereas control subjects included the event item on their lists 26 percent of the time, misled subjects listed the event item 33 percent of the time, significantly more often than control subjects ($t(199) = 2.38, p = .02$).

Discussion. The primary results from this study can be easily summarized. When subjects were given a logic of opposition instruction to list category members but exclude any items that they saw in the slides, they responded differently in the face of misinformation. When given misinformation, they were less likely than controls to put suggested items on their list, and more likely to include the event items.

Why are misled subjects refraining from putting the suggested items on their list? One possibility is that subjects genuinely believe they saw the suggested item, and, given the logic instructions, they do not list it. However, another possibility is that subjects adopt a strategy for responding to the request to produce category members that involve avoiding any exemplar presented in the experiment. For example, say a subject correctly remembers seeing a hammer in the slides, and reading about a screwdriver in the narrative. However, when asked to "Please list five different types of tools," the subject, eager to obey instructions against listing items seen in the slides, fills up each of the available slots with tools that did not appear anywhere in the experiment (for example, shovel, drill, rake, etc.). This strategy could account for the lowered frequency of suggested items in the category lists produced by misled subjects.

We think that this explanation is unlikely. One reason is that misled subjects did not also avoid the event item. Put another way, they were more likely than controls to list the event item in the category list. This brings us to the second major finding of this experiment, that misinformation increased the frequency of listing event items, even though subjects were explicitly instructed not to list what they remembered seeing.

Why were misled subjects more likely to list the event item than controls? One possibility is that misinformation impaired their memory for the event item, making subjects fail to remember seeing it, and thus leaving them free to list it. There are several other plausible explanations for this finding, however, all of which have nothing to do with memory impairment.

One possibility is that the result is due to limitations placed on subjects as to the number of category exemplars that were required. Recall that subjects in this experiment were asked to produce five different exemplars of each specified category, with the prohibition that they not list items that they remembered seeing in the slides. The requirement to produce five, and only five, members of each category limits the conclusions that can be drawn from the results. Perhaps, when asked to list five different types of soft drink, for example, misinformed subjects first thought of 7-Up (that is, the suggested item). They would then include 7-Up on their list of soft drinks, because they correctly remembered that they read about 7-Up, and did not see it. In thinking about 7-Up, subjects might then be induced to think of other light-colored soft drinks (Sprite, ginger ale, seltzer, etc.). Because subjects start thinking about light-colored soft drinks, it is possible they fill in the remaining four slots on their lists with members of this subcategory of drinks thereby leaving no slots for an event item that is not a member of the subcategory (Coca-Cola). Thus, subjects who did not remember seeing the event item may nonetheless have excluded it from the list, for reasons having nothing to do with impairment of event memory.

Another possible reason for the finding that misled subjects were more likely than controls to list the event item (Coca-Cola) is based on sheer probability. We have already seen that misinformation reduces reports of the suggested item. This alone could cause reports of the event item (Coca-Cola) to rise. Misled subjects who refrained from listing 7-Up would have five slots to fill with other items, whereas control subjects who did not refrain from listing 7-Up would have only four slots.

These concerns motivated a second logic of opposition study. In this second study, we made sure that subjects had more slots for listing category members than there were category members to list. This was accomplished in the following way. Subjects again saw slides, received misinformation on some critical items, and then were tested. The test again asked subjects to generate exemplars for each of the specified categories. However, rather than ask subjects to think up five exemplars for each category, as they did in the first experiment, we gave all subjects in the second experiment a list of two hundred words including both the suggested and event items. The list consisted of ten exemplars for each of twenty categories. Four were categories that included the critical items (magazines, tools, cartoon characters, and soft drinks), and sixteen were filler categories. Subjects were asked to include in their test booklet all possible category members from the attached list, except for those seen in the slides. The test booklet contained many more spaces for possible category members than there were members on the list of two hundred words. Again, subjects were instructed to exclude from their lists those category members that they had seen in the slides. If we still find more listings of the event item for misled subjects, the result cannot be an artifact of having a limited number of slots to fill.

Providing subjects with a long list of category members from which they were to select is one way to ensure that subjects have more slots on the test booklet than they have category members to fill the slots. But this feature of the experiment has an added advantage. In the first study, 28 percent of misled subjects listed the suggested item (thus 72 percent did not), and 33 percent of misled subjects listed the event item (thus 67 percent did not). Does this mean that 72 percent of subjects think that they saw the suggested item, and 67 percent think they saw the event item? Of course not. Subjects could fail to report an item because that item simply did not occur to them at the time they compiled their category lists. By providing subjects with a list of exemplars from which to choose, we ensure that each critical category member is contemplated. By forcing subjects to contemplate the items in this manner, we have greater confidence that when an item is left off the list, it is because a subject remembers seeing it and has deliberately excluded it. Any instances in which items appear on the lists suggest that the subject did not remember seeing it.

With two exceptions, the stimuli, design, and procedure employed in the second experiment in this series were virtually identical to those used in the first. One exception was the modification of the final memory test. Remember, subjects in this experiment were required to select category exemplars from a list of two hundred words that was provided, rather than simply being asked to list five different exemplars of each specified category as was the case in the first experiment. The second, relatively minor modification made to the procedure for the second logic of opposition study was the provision of a prize to the participant who compiled the most complete word lists that did not include any event items. This modification was intended to provide subjects with an incentive for good performance.

Results of second "logic" study. We again analyzed the category lists provided for each of the critical categories. For each critical category, we noted whether subjects included the event item on their list, and whether they included the suggested item. We then compared lists that were produced when subjects had received misinformation, and when they had not.

Our first prediction was that subjects who received misleading suggestions would include fewer suggested items on their category lists than control subjects. An analysis of the data provided support for this expectation. Although control subjects included the suggested item on their lists 83 percent of the time, misled subjects listed the suggested item 68 percent of the time, significantly less often than controls ($t(204) = 5.37, p < .001$).

Second, we predicted that subjects who received misinformation about an item seen in the slides would include that event item on their category lists more often than subjects who were not misled. A comparison of the number of instances of event item generation for control and misled subjects did not, however, garner support for this prediction. Those who were misinformed about the event item listed that event item 44 percent of the time, but those who were not misinformed about the event item listed it 42 percent of the time. Although this difference was in the predicted direction, it did not approach statistical significance.

Discussion of second "logic" study. The chief results from this study are readily summarized. When subjects were given a logic of opposition instruction to list category members but exclude any items that they saw in the slides from their lists, they responded differently in the face of misinformation. When given misinformation, they were less likely than controls to put suggested items on their list. This result replicates that found in Experiment 1, but tells us more. Recall that in Experiment 1, 28 percent of misled subjects listed the suggested item, implying that they believed they did not see it. What about the other 72 percent who refrained from listing the suggested item? We cannot conclude that these subjects all believe they saw the suggested item. Many of them may not have contemplated the item at all, or at least not among the first five that came to mind. In the second experiment, however, all subjects were forced to contemplate the suggested item, and the percentage of subjects who listed it rose dramatically – to 68 percent. This number indicates that two thirds of our subjects do not believe they saw the suggested item. One third, however, still refrain from listing the suggested item, and we have more confidence that at least these subjects may genuinely believe they saw that item.

What have we learned from the logic of opposition? Lindsay's original study, and our extensions, were attempts to eliminate demand characteristics as an explanation for reports of suggested memories. The results of these studies indicate that when the demand characteristic interpretation is ruled out, subjects still often embrace the misinformation. This is at least consistent with the hypothesis that they genuinely believe in the suggested memories that they are reporting.

Betting as a measure of "true belief"

How is it possible to determine when a subject truly believes he or she has seen a suggested memory? One way is to prohibit the subject from basing test responses on suggested items, and see if he or she does so anyway (as in Lindsay's [1990] application of the logic of opposition). Another way of assessing a subject's degree of true belief is to prohibit him or her from listing items seen in the slides. The inclusion of event details and the exclusion of suggested details can then be interpreted as a measure of true belief (as in our logic of opposition experiments). A third way of determining whether a subject truly believes in a suggested memory is to have him or her bet money on it. The more strongly one believes in a memory, the more money one should be willing to bet on its accuracy. Assuming willingness to bet money reflects true belief, true belief would be demonstrated to the extent that the subject would be willing to bet as much money on suggested memories as they would on real memories.

Toland's betting study

As a means of assessing true belief as outlined above, Toland (1990) employed a typical three-stage misinformation paradigm, with subjects viewing a slide presentation and subsequently receiving misleading postevent information about several critical items. The betting measure was incorporated into a Yes/ No recognition test for the event and postevent critical items. We describe the experiment below in some detail to give the flavor of how this was conducted.

Method. One hundred and thirty-five University of Washington undergraduate subjects viewed a sequence of sixty-six color slides. This sequence, a longer version of which we also used for our logic of opposition studies, depicts a student who visits a college bookstore, looks at various items, and slips several into his pack. Among the items with which he comes in contact are eight critical items, presented in one of two versions to each subject. The critical items were a candle (blue or yellow), a notebook (red or green), a stapler (red or blue), a textbook (computer science or chemistry), a sweatshirt (Mickey Mouse or Minnie Mouse), a magazine (*Vogue* or *Esquire*), an elevator (open or closed), and a towel (black or light blue). Other than the two versions of the critical slides, the two slide sequences were identical.

After viewing the slide sequence, subjects read a written narrative. This postevent narrative was a detailed description of the event depicted in the slide sequence. For each subject, four of the eight critical items were described inaccurately, serving as misled items; the other four critical items were described neutrally, serving as control items. All items were counterbalanced across subject groups such that for each item, half of all subjects would receive misinformation about that item in the narrative and the other half would receive neutral information.

After subjects finished reading the written narrative, they were given a final memory test. This recognition test of memory for the critical items was a two-alternative, forced-choice test consisting of sixteen statements to which subjects had to respond "Yes" or "No." The statements were like "The textbook that Jim picked up was a Computer Science book." Half of the statements mentioned one of the critical items, whereas the other half were filler statements. Every subject answered eight critical test items. Of these eight test statements, four referred to items that were actually seen in the slides, and four referred to items that were not seen in the slides.

Subjects were also required to bet money on their memories. They were allowed to bet a maximum of ten dollars on each memory. If correct on a given bet, they received double the amount bet. They were instructed that the person accumulating the most money would win a prize. Finally, they were debriefed and dismissed, and the winner was later contacted to receive the prize.

Results: Recognition Accuracy. Were subjects less accurate in the face of misinformation? For ease of exposition, assume that the event item was Mickey Mouse and that misled subjects were given Minnie Mouse as misinformation. Two measures of performance reveal a strong misinformation effect. First, when asked about the event item, Mickey Mouse, misled subjects responded significantly less accurately than control subjects. Whereas 73 percent of control subjects correctly said "yes" to the event item, only 60 percent of misled subjects said "yes" to the event item ($t(134) = 3.73$, $p < .001$). Second, when asked about the misinformation item, Minnie Mouse, misled subjects incorrectly responded "yes" significantly more often than subjects who did not receive misinformation. Forty-three percent of subjects who received misinformation incorrectly said "yes" to the misinformation item, whereas only 21 percent of control subjects made such errors ($t(134) = 5.46$, $p < .001$). Thus, there was a strong misinformation effect as evidenced in recognition accuracy.

Betting. Subjects bet on four different types of memories. To appreciate these four types of memories, assume that subjects saw the event item, Mickey Mouse. If they had earlier received no misinformation on this item, they would now be betting on a "real" memory. Since that real memory was in the control condition, we refer to it as a "Real-control" memory. If they

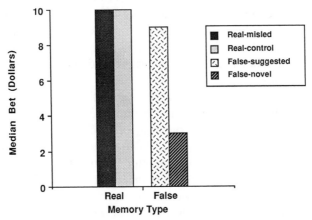

Figure 1.1: Median bet for each of the four memory conditions.

had earlier received misinformation on the item, they would still be betting on a "real" memory. But since they had received misinformation, we refer to it as a "Real-misled" memory.

Suppose further that after seeing Mickey Mouse, half the subjects got misinformation about Minnie Mouse. If we test subjects with a statement about Minnie Mouse, and they bet money on this memory, they are obviously betting on a false memory. If misled subjects are tested with a statement about Minnie Mouse, they are being asked about an item that was never seen, but only suggested. We call this a "False-suggested" memory. The subjects who never got misinformation about Minnie Mouse were also tested on this item. Because these subjects had never encountered Minnie Mouse before, they are asked to bet on a completely novel memory that we refer to as a "False-novel" memory.

Figure 1.1 shows the median bets for the four different types of memories. Notice that subjects bet a median of ten dollars on their real memories, regardless of whether these were in the control or misled condition. The median bet on the suggested memories was slightly, but not significantly less (nine dollars). This is shown in Figure 1.1 in the column labeled "False-suggested." Notice also that the bets on the "False-novel" memories (three dollars) were significantly lower than the "False-suggested" memories.

Examination of the median bets conceals important information that is revealed when one examines the distribution of bets. Consider first the distribution of "False-suggested" bets shown in Figure 1.2. Notice that the percentage of people who bet the maximum possible amount on these memories was 48 percent. The maximum amount possible (ten dollars) was the modal response on the "False-suggested" memories. Thus if our measure of "true belief" is the willingness on the part of the subject to bet the maximum, then a sizable proportion of subjects displayed this willingness.

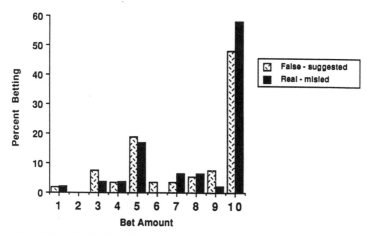

Figure 1.2: Distribution of bets on real memories in the misled condition, with the distribution of bets on the suggested item.

How does this compare to subjects' bets on their real memories? Figure 1.2 shows the distribution of bets on the "False-suggested" memories along with the distribution of bets on the real memories ("Real-Misled") so a comparison can be made. Notice that subjects do bet the maximum more often when it is a real memory than a suggested one (58 percent versus 48 percent) but notice how similar the two distributions are. (The same conclusion is reached if we use real memory bets in the control condition.)

The bets on suggested memories thus look very similar to bets on real memories, but they look completely different from the bets on novel memories. In Figure 1.3, we show the distribution of bets on the "False-suggested" memories (previously displayed) with the distribution of bets on "False-novel" memories. Notice that subjects do not very often bet the maximum on their novel memories (18 percent versus the figure of 48 percent for suggested memories). Moreover, the modal bet for the novel memories is one dollar and the distributions look completely different.

In conclusion, we find the bets on the suggested memories are more similar to bets on real memories than they are to bets on novel memories. And, nearly half the time, subjects were willing to bet the maximum of ten dollars on their suggested memories.

Discussion. If the amount one bets on a memory reflects true belief in that memory, the results of this experiment suggest that when misled subjects report postevent items, they do so because they believe they saw the items in the original event. The average bets of misled subjects on their suggested memories did not differ significantly from the average bets control subjects placed on their actual memories. Nor did the average bets placed by misled

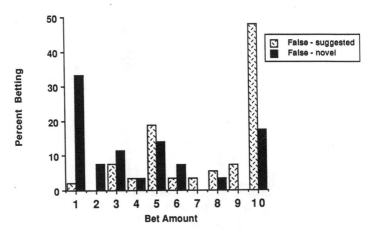

Figure 1.3: Distribution of bets on novel false memories, with the distribution of bets on suggested item.

subjects on their suggested memories differ from the bets those same misled subjects placed on their actual memories. Overall, 48 percent of all subjects who responded "yes" when presented with a postevent item at test were willing to place a bet of ten dollars on these suggested memories. Assuming a bet of ten dollars reflects true belief in a memory, close to half of all subjects who reported suggested memories truly believe those reports. There are, however, two caveats which preclude reaching strong conclusions on the basis of these results.

First, the betting scale used may not be a measure of true belief in memories. In placing a bet, rational bettors might tend to use the ends of the scale more than the middle values. If a subject (call her Georgette) thinks there is a good probability of getting an answer correct, she may opt to take a risk and bet the maximum amount allowed. On the other hand, if another subject, Rolf, has low confidence in a response, he may opt to take no risk and might bet the minimum. If this type of reasoning were occurring, the betting scale would not be a measure of true belief and bets would reflect people's betting strategies rather than true belief.

Second, although the instructions clearly stated that they were to place bets on the accuracy of their memories for what they saw in the slides, some subjects may have assumed that the narrative was accurate and therefore may not have responded to the test questions based exclusively on their memories for the slides. Rather, subjects may have reported their postevent memories, and placed high bets on their responses, because they wanted to show that they are attentive and remember details from both the event and the narrative. This alternative explanation for the misinformation effect, first pointed out by McCloskey and Zaragoza in 1985, has been referred to as the demand characteristic interpretation.

A second betting experiment attempted to address the two caveats described above. The first modification anchored the endpoints of the betting scale. This alteration was expected to increase the likelihood that different subjects would use the betting scale in the same manner, and decrease the probability that subjects would use the ends of the scale, thereby making the scale less of a reflection of individual betting strategies, and more of a reflection of the degree of true belief in individual memories.

Another modification in this second betting study was designed to preclude demand characteristic interpretations using a procedure modeled after one of the conditions of Lindsay's (1990) logic of opposition experiments. Recall that Lindsay employed the discriminability of the event and postevent information by manipulating the similarity between encoding conditions for event and postevent information. In the high-discriminability condition, in which the event and postevent information were presented under dissimilar conditions in different experimental sessions, subjects were able to follow the logic of opposition instructions and avoid reporting the postevent information on a recall test. However, in the low-discriminability condition in which the event and postevent information were similar, and presented in close temporal proximity, subjects were more likely to base their responses on information contained in the narrative despite receiving instructions against doing so.

The second betting experiment employed the same basic procedure that Lindsay used in his low-discriminability condition. The experiment was conducted in two sessions. In the first session subjects viewed the event depicted in a slide sequence and listened to a postevent narrative containing some misleading information about the event. When subjects returned for the second session forty-eight hours later, they were tested on their memory for several critical details from the slide presentation.

The test was a six-item cued-recall test. For each item, subjects were given the category cue (for example, "Recall the tool that you saw") and asked to recall the critical item from the slides. Before completing the recall test, Toland's subjects received a logic of opposition instruction identical to that used by Lindsay (1990), informing them that "There is no question on this test for which the correct answer was mentioned in the story." Subjects could respond with either the event item, the item presented as misinformation in the misled condition, or with some other item.

The test in the second experiment included a betting scale similar to that used previously, the only change being that subjects in the current study were given instructions that served to anchor the endpoints of the betting scale. Specifically, subjects were told to place a bet of ten dollars on a response only if they were as sure of their response as they were that the wall in the front of the room was white. They were instructed to place a bet of one dollar only if they had no idea what the correct answer was, and were responding with a pure guess.

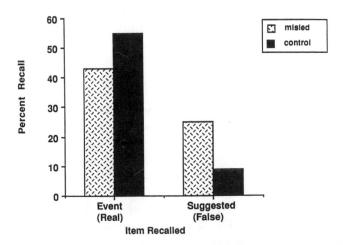

Figure 1.4: Percentage of misled and control subjects who correctly recalled items seen in the slides (event), and incorrectly recalled items suggested in the narrative (suggested), Recall of items other than the event and suggested items have been excluded from this figure, thus percentages do not sum to one hundred.

Results of betting study with logic of opposition instructions: Accuracy. A clear misinformation effect was observed in these data. We found that when given misinformation, subjects correctly recalled the event item significantly less often than subjects who did not receive misinformation ("Real-Misled": 43 percent versus "Real-Control": 55 percent, $t(79) = 3.54$, $p < .001$), and they incorrectly recalled the postevent item significantly more often than those who did not receive misinformation ("False-suggested": 25 percent versus "False-novel": 9 percent, $t(79) = 4.97$, $p < .001$). These relationships are depicted graphically in Figure 1.4

Betting. Under the more stringent conditions of this study, how were subjects' bets affected? The median bets associated with the reports produced on the cued recall test are shown in Figure 1.5. Notice that the bets in general are not so high as they were before. On their real memories, subjects are betting a median of approximately eight-fifty to nine dollars. They bet much less on their suggested memories (three to five dollars). They still bet more on their suggested memories, however, than they did on their novel memories. (There are three kinds of "novel" memories shown in this figure. The recall of the postevent item in the control condition is one type, leading to a median bet of three dollars. The production of the "other" items leads to median bets that are even lower (a dollar thirty-three to two dollars).

Next, we examined the distribution of bets on the different memory items. The distribution of bets on the real items indicates that subjects were willing to bet the full ten dollars on their real memories 48 percent of the time.

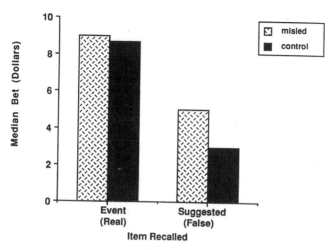

Figure 1.5: Median bet for misled and control subjects who correctly recalled items seen in the slides (event), and incorrectly recalled items suggested in the narrative (suggested). Recall of items other than the event and suggested items have been excluded from this figure, thus percentages do not sum to one hundred.

Subjects bet the maximum on the suggested item significantly less often (18 percent of the time). Although subjects bet the maximum on their memories for the suggested item almost one-fifth of the time, however, they never bet the maximum on their memories for completely novel items (novel–false memories). Thus, although subjects exhibited less confidence in their memories for the suggested item than for real items, they exhibited more confidence in their memories for suggested–false items than they did for their memories of novel–false items.

Discussion. The accuracy results from this experiment demonstrate a clear misinformation effect. Subjects displayed an impaired ability to recall the event item and an increased tendency to recall the postevent item in the misled condition relative to the control condition. As predicted, this inaccuracy replicates the result Lindsay obtained in his low-discriminability condition. In light of the fact that the instructions clearly stated that critical details in the postevent narrative were incorrect, it can be argued that any reports of postevent information reflect some degree of belief.

In terms of the betting measure, if a median bet reflects the average true belief across all memories of a certain type, then the betting measure indicates that subjects do not, on the average, believe their postevent memories to the same extent that they believe their event memories. However, some belief in suggested memories is demonstrated by the fact that subjects placed higher bets, on the average, on their postevent item responses than they did on their other-item responses. In addition, across all postevent-item responses, 18 percent received the maximum bet of ten dollars. Given that the scale was anchored so a bet of ten dollars should only reflect absolute certainty in the veridicality of a response, this proportion of maximum bets clearly indicates that many subjects truly believe they saw the postevent information.

In sum, the betting measure indicates that the postevent item responses were not believed as strongly as real memories, but they were believed more than novel memories. This is not a surprising result. If a subject, Kim, was aware of the source of a postevent memory, she would not have reported it in the first place (note that Kim received logic of opposition instructions in this study). Therefore, if Kim reports a postevent item, this indicates that she has confused its source with the original event. Losing the source of information would obviously render most postevent memories more believable than other-item responses because other-item responses are guesses.

What do these betting studies tell us about true belief?

The results of the first betting experiment show that subjects who reported misleading suggestions were willing to bet as much, on the average, as they did on their real memories. Moreover, close to 50 percent of all suggested-memory reports received a bet of ten dollars, the maximum allowed. Taken together, these results suggest that memories derived from postevent suggestions are truly believed by the subjects who report them – at least if one uses this fairly liberal criterion for true belief.

With a stricter criterion in place, as in the second betting study, it appears that subjects believe their suggested memories, on the average, less than their real memories. Yet the results still give an indication of true belief in some nontrivial proportion of suggested memories. Some proportion of subjects indicated the truest belief possible by betting the maximum amount on their suggested memories. Considering the stricter criterion for reporting postevent information, induced by the logic of opposition instructions and the anchoring of the betting scale, the fact that any suggested items were reported and given a maximum bet is convincing evidence of true belief in those instances. In conclusion, the results of the second betting study demonstrate that, in many instances, subjects do believe misleading information when they report it.

Reports of suggested memories: Do people truly believe them?

In many cases, the answer is an unequivocal yes. Lindsay demonstrated this by showing that subjects continue to base test responses on suggested items, even when explicitly informed that any information contained in the narrative was incorrect. Using a different operationalization of the logic of opposition paradigm, Weingardt, Loftus, and Lindsay found additional evidence that subjects sometimes come to believe they saw items in the event that in reality were only suggested to them. Specifically, we found that when instructed to refrain from including items seen in the slide sequence on several category lists, subjects continued to include event items on their lists (indicating confusion about the source of their memory for the event items), and to exclude suggested items from their lists (thereby indicating true belief in their reports of suggested details). Finally, the betting studies show that some nontrivial proportion of subjects bet the maximum amount possible on their suggested memories, providing convincing evidence of true belief in the accuracy of their false memories. In sum, the empirical evidence seems to be in accordance with the anecdotal evidence that served to introduce this topic: Witnesses can exhibit strong belief in their memories, even when those memories are verifiably false.

References

Jacoby, L. L., Woloshyn, V., & Kelley, C. M. (1989). Becoming famous without being recognized: Unconscious influences of memory produced by divided attention. *Journal of Experimental Psychology, General, 118*, 115–125.

Johnson, M. K., & Lindsay, D. S. (1986). *Despite McCloskey and Zaragoza, suggestibility effects may reflect memory impairment.* Unpublished manuscript.

Lindsay, D. S. (1990). Misleading suggestions can impair eyewitnesses' ability to remember event details. *Journal of Experimental Psychology: Learning, Memory and Cognition, 16*, 1077–1083.

Lindsay, D. S., & Johnson, M. K. (1987). Reality monitoring and suggestibility: Children's ability to discriminate among memories for different sources. In S. J. Ceci, M. P. Toglia, & D. F. Ross (Eds.), *Children's eyewitness memory* (pp. 92–121). New York: Springer-Verlag.

Lindsay, D. S., & Johnson, M. K. (1989a). The eyewitness suggestibility effect and memory for source. *Memory & Cognition, 17*, 349–358.

Loftus, E. F., Donders, K., Hoffman, H., & Schooler, J. W. (1989). Creating new memories that are quickly accessed and confidently held. *Memory & Cognition, 17*, 607–616

Loftus, E. F., & Hoffman, H. (1989). Misinformation and memory: The creation of new memories. *Journal of Experimental Psychology: General, 118*, 100–104.

Loftus, E. F., & Ketcham, K. (1991) *Witness for the defense: The accused, the eyewitness, and the expert who puts memory on trial.* New York: St Martin's Press.

Loftus, E. F., Miller, D. G., & Burns, H. J. (1978). Semantic integration of verbal information into a visual memory. *Journal of Experimental Psychology: Human Learning & Memory, 4*, 19–31.

McCloskey, M., & Zaragoza, M. (1985). Misleading postevent information and memory for events: Arguments and evidence against memory impairment hypotheses. *Journal of Experimental Psychology: General, 114*, 1–16.

Toland, H. K. (1990). *True belief in misleading postevent information.* Unpublished Masters Thesis, University of Washington.

Tversky, B., & Tuchin, M. (1989). A reconciliation of the evidence of eyewitness testimony: Comments on McCloskey & Zaragoza (1985). *Journal of Experimental Psychology: General, 118*, 86–91.

Zaragoza, M. S., & Koshmider, J. W. III. (1989). Misled subjects may know more than their performance implies. *Journal of Experimental Psychology: Learning, Memory & Cognition,* 15, 246–255.

Zaragoza, M. S., & Meunch, J. (1989, November). *Source confusion following exposure to misleading postevent information.* Paper presented at the annual meeting of the Psychonomic Society, Atlanta, GA.

2   Memory source monitoring and eyewitness testimony

D. Stephen Lindsay

When called upon to testify, eyewitnesses must distinguish between memories of their experience of the event in question and memories of other sources of information about that event. The latter might include memories of their own or other people's descriptions of the event, memories of thoughts and fantasies related to the event (before or after its occurrence), and general knowledge and beliefs. Thus a question such as "Tell me what happened on the afternoon of Wednesday, June 24th, 1992" might serve as a retrieval cue for a wealth of memories in addition to those of the witness's own experience that fateful afternoon.

"Source monitoring" refers to the hypothetical cognitive processes by which people identify the sources of their recollections. Understanding such processes will allow us to specify the factors that lead people to misidentify memories from one source as memories from another (for example, mistake memories of postevent suggestions as memories of the event itself). This chapter begins with a summary of the source monitoring approach in general terms, followed by a review of evidence concerning the factors that affect the likelihood of source monitoring errors (see Johnson, Hashtroudi, & Lindsay, 1992, for a more extended treatment of these ideas). The next, and largest, section discusses research Johnson and I and others have conducted on the role of source monitoring processes in studies of eyewitness suggestibility. Subsequent sections examine related issues such as bystander misidentification and age-related changes in source monitoring skills.

Memory source monitoring

Aspects of memory for source have been studied for many years in a variety of domains, such as list differentiation (for example, Winograd, 1968; for review, see Abra, 1972), memory for surface details (for example, Craik & Kirsner, 1974; Geiselman & Belleza, 1976; Hintzman, Block, & Inskeep, 1972; Kolers, 1976), and context reinstatement effects (for example, Godden & Baddeley, 1975). Moreover, cognitive psychologists have long known that memory for source plays an important role in *all* direct tests of memory –

that is, all tests in which subjects are directly asked to remember particular prior events. For example, Anderson and Bower (1972, 1974) pointed out that in word-list recognition studies subjects cannot respond solely on the basis of familiarity, because in such studies *all* the test items are familiar words. Likewise, on a recall test subjects are not asked simply to recall whatever comes to mind, but rather to recall items or events from a particular source in their past experience (e.g., items from a study list).

Anderson and Bower (1972, 1974) proposed that memories for studied items be tagged with labels that specify their sources. For example, if FISH were a word on the first list in a multilist experiment, then the memory representation of that encounter with FISH would be tagged with a "List 1" label. This approach to the problem was in keeping with the zeitgeist of the time, which emphasized memory for abstract, propositionlike information and the rapid forgetting of surface-level characteristics. More recently, the pendulum has swung back, with many theorists emphasizing memory for specific perceptual details (Alba & Hasher, 1983; Jacoby & Brooks, 1984; Johnson & Hasher, 1987; Kolers, 1976; Masson, 1984). A wealth of data demonstrates remarkable memory for finely detailed perceptual information (for example, long-lasting effects of type face on priming) (see Richardson-Klavehn & Bjork, 1988, for a review). From today's vantage point, it seems odd that memory theorists ever argued that surface-level perceptual details are poorly retained in memory.

In the source monitoring approach, following Johnson's Multiple-entry Modular (MEM) model of memory (for example, Johnson, 1983; Johnson & Hirst, in press), memory is viewed as a record of the cognitive processes that give rise to and constitute ongoing experience. Memory is not a "place" for storing specially prepared traces that encapsulate abstract descriptions of past events (Watkins, 1990). Memory is not separate from other cognitive processes, but rather is a history of their past operation and a shaper of their current operation (as in connectionist models). One implication of this view is that only those ongoing processes that are abstract and propositionlike (for example, explicitly naming objects, reflecting on the relations between events, planning future actions, etc.) are recorded in memory in an abstract, propositionlike form. Information that is tacit and implicit in ongoing experience is tacit and implicit in memory. Thus, for example, as you listen to a friend tell a joke you do not continuously and explicitly note your friend's name, the date and place, and so forth, so the memory records of hearing that joke would not include abstract tags or labels fully specifying its source. Those memory records would, however, include a wealth of cues to source – for example, memory information about the sound of your friend's voice, his or her appearance, perceptual characteristics of the surroundings, the semantic content of the joke, and your thoughts and feelings at the time.[1]

According to the source monitoring account, the perceptual and semantic content of an activated memory record is used to identify the source of that memory at retrieval. The idea is that identifying and labeling remembered objects is analogous in some ways to identifying and labeling objects in ongoing perceptual experience. When a person looks, say, at his or her living room, the pattern of sensory information is recognized as a particular known room. This process does not rely on tags – that is, the room need not be festooned with banners proclaiming "This is Joe's living room" in order for Joe to recognize it as such. Instead, knowledge about the room is evoked in the process of perceiving the sensory array. Likewise, an event memory includes information about various properties of the past experience, and that information can be recognized and identified in the process of retrieval.

The perceptual and semantic content of a memory record of a past experience can be used to identify the source of that memory only if knowledge about the characteristics of that source can be accessed. For example, a vivid auditory memory of the sound of a speaker's voice can be used to identify the speaker only if knowledge relating those vocal qualities to a particular person is accessed. If such knowledge is not accessible, one remembers (in this example) the sound of the voice but is unable to say whose voice it is. The retrieval and use of such knowledge itself involves judgment processes (see Johnson et al., 1992).

Most of the time, source monitoring attributions are performed very rapidly and without phenomenal awareness of decision making. Sometimes, however, these rapid, nonreflective processes fail to identify one or more dimensions of source. When this occurs, one has the subjective experience of recollecting some aspects of an event without fully specifying its source (for example, you might remember a joke that someone told at the office, but not remember who told it – in this case, automatic source monitoring processes have identified some aspects of the source of the memory but have failed to identify the joke teller). Often we don't care about fully specifying the source of a recollection – in a particular situation it may be sufficient simply to remember the joke (provided one isn't about to tell it to the person from whom one initially learned it – Allen & Jacoby, 1990). Further, when we do care, the source of a recollection can often be more fully identified by strategic and effortful searches of memory and inferences. Of course, people are sometimes unable to remember aspects of source despite the most arduous attempts – indeed, as Neisser (1982) pointed out, inability to remember the source of an otherwise clear recollection (as when one remembers an anecdote but not its author) is among the most common of everyday memory failures. Finally, and perhaps most forensically relevant, people sometimes misidentify the sources of their recollections. Such source misidentifications may reflect errors in rapid, automatic source monitoring processes or errors in more consciously mediated source attributions. The following section examines the factors that affect the likelihood of such source monitoring confusions.

Source monitoring confusions

As noted above, according to the source monitoring approach, knowledge about the characteristic properties of particular sources is used to interpret the source-relevant information accessed from an event memory, much as knowledge about the characteristic properties of particular objects is used to identify those objects in ongoing perceptual experience. A number of factors affect the ease with which the source of a memory is identified, including (a) the amount and nature of source-relevant information in the activated memory record; (b) the amount and nature of accessible knowledge about the characteristic properties of the source; (c) the extent to which the attributes of the memory in question are uniquely specific to memories from its source; and (d) the stringency and appropriateness of the decision-making processes and criteria employed during remembering. These factors may be clarified by analogy to ongoing perception: Perceptual errors are relatively likely when stimuli are degraded or unfamiliar, when targets are similar to distractors, and when decision criteria are low or inappropriate. All other things being equal, source monitoring errors are also relatively likely when memories are vague or incomplete, when the source is unfamiliar, when more than one source characteristically gives rise to memories with properties similar to the memory in question, or when the attribution is made quickly and automatically rather than with careful deliberation.

Empirical support for some of these hypotheses comes from studies in which subjects are exposed to information from two or more different sources and are later asked to identify the source (for example, source A, source B, or new) of particular pieces of information (see Johnson et al., 1992, for a review). Such experiments have shown that source monitoring errors are more frequent when potential memory sources are similar to one another in terms of their perceptual properties, modality of presentation, semantic content, or cognitive operations (orienting tasks). For example, subjects are more likely to misremember which of two people had talked about a particular event if the two storytellers were similar looking than if they were dissimilar (Lindsay, Johnson, & Kwon, 1991). Hasher and Griffin (1978) and Raye, Johnson, and Taylor (1980) reported studies demonstrating the role of decision-making criteria in determining the likelihood of source monitoring errors. Source discrimination has also been shown to improve with the amount of time subjects are given to respond to the test probe (Kounios & Johnson, in preparation) and with full as opposed to divided attention at study (Jacoby & Kelley, 1992; Jacoby, Woloshyn, & Kelley, 1989) and at test (Jacoby, 1991).

Systematic biases in source monitoring responses provide further evidence for the hypothesis that recollections are attributed to particular sources via decision-making processes. For example, in a study in which subjects were to discriminate between memories of their own actions and memories of a confederate's actions, subjects more often misidentified distractor (new) items as actions the confederate had performed than as actions they themselves had performed (the "it-had-to-be-you" effect) (Johnson, Raye, Foley, & Foley, 1981). Presumably, the pre-experimental familiarity of the action led subjects to misidentify it as something done in the course of the experiment, and the paucity of memory information occasioned by the fact that the action had not really been performed during the experiment led them to identify it as something they had merely seen another person do rather than as something they had done themselves. Similarly, if the discrimination is between memories of actions that were actually performed and memories of actions that were imagined, subjects tend to identify falsely recognized distractor items as imagined rather than as actual actions (Johnson & Raye, 1981).

Source monitoring and eyewitness suggestibility: Empirical work

Subjects who receive misleading suggestions about details in a previously witnessed event often perform more poorly than control subjects when later asked to remember those event details (for example, Loftus, 1979; Weingardt et al., this volume). This well established empirical phenomenon raises two related but separable issues. First, do misleading suggestions impair subjects' memory for the corresponding event details? We know that subjects who receive misleading suggestions perform more poorly than control subjects on a variety of memory measures, but, as McCloskey and Zaragoza (1985a) pointed out, this does not necessarily mean that the misleading suggestions impaired memory for the event details. For example, it might be that misled subjects remember the event detail just as well as control subjects, but also remember the suggested detail and rely on it at test. Although debates about whether or not misinformation effects reflect memory impairment have been the focus of attention in the years since McCloskey and Zaragoza's (1985a) critique was published, the second issue raised by misinformation effects is equally important: Whether or not misled subjects sometimes believe they are remembering *seeing* something in the event when they retrieve memories of a postevent suggestion.

Loftus's theoretical approach (especially her earlier work, for example, Loftus, 1979, 1981; Loftus, Miller, & Burns, 1978) treated these two issues as inseparable. She proposed a mechanism, termed "destructive updating" or "overwriting," whereby the suggested detail is incorporated into an integrated memory representation of the original event. Memory for the original event detail is thereby destroyed, and the memory for the suggested detail becomes an integral part of the memory of the event itself. Thus subjects experience retrieval of the memory of the suggested detail as remembering something seen in the event because the underlying memory representation of the suggested detail has become part of the memory trace of seeing the event.

The source monitoring approach also suggests that illusory recollections of eyewitnessing can occur, but proposes a different mechanism. According to the source monitoring approach, memory records of postevent suggestions are not stored as integral parts of the earlier memory of the event itself. Rather, as in Bekerian and Bowers (1983) and Christiaansen and Ochalek (1983), memory representations of the postevent information are assumed to coexist with (rather than replace) those of the event. The source monitoring hypothesis holds that at test memory records of the postevent suggestions are sometimes misidentified as memories of the event itself (either quickly and automatically or after conscious deliberation). The procedures typically employed in studies of suggestibility create very good conditions for illusory memories of eyewitnessing – that is, subjective experiences of remembering suggested details as things seen in the event. The event and the postevent information concern the same topic, and are usually presented close together in time, in the same environment, by the same experimenter, etc. These similarities and other characteristics of the procedures, to be discussed below, may lead subjects to later misidentify memories derived from the postevent information as memories derived from the original event. Thus people may experience compelling illusory memories of eyewitnessing.

The reversed suggestibility effect

One implication of the source monitoring account of illusory memories of eyewitnessing is that memories of pre-event information may later be misidentified as memories of the event, just as memories of postevent information may be. That is, suggestibility effects should occur even when the misleading suggestions are given before the visual event that subjects are later asked to remember. Consistent with this idea, Lindsay and Johnson (1989b) reported a study in which subjects first read a narrative description of a scene (with or without inaccurate descriptions of details in the scene) and then viewed the scene to which that narrative referred. As in the standard procedure, subjects were later tested on their memory for the visual scene. Subjects who had received misleading pre-event suggestions were much more likely to indicate that they had seen the suggested details in the scene than were controls. Lindsay and Johnson (1989b) argued that this reversed suggestibility effect is incompatible with Loftus's overwriting mechanism, in which new information replaces old information.

Although the reversed suggestibility effects cannot be explained in terms of destructive updating, the finding is not inconsistent with the more general idea that information from different sources can give rise to memories in which that information is integrated (blended). For one thing, suggestibility effects would be unlikely to occur if subjects did not understand that the postevent information refers to the witnessed event. Thus, although there is no reason to assume that the original memory records are destroyed in the process, postevent information must in some way be mentally associated with existing memories of the event. Additional integration or blending could occur when people consciously reflect on memories from different sources without specifically attending to or focusing on the sources of those memories. People often review their knowledge and beliefs about past events in their lives, drawing on information from multiple sources. Episodes of such mental reviews are themselves recorded in memory and may serve as the basis for future recollections (that is, one may retrieve memory records of one's thoughts about a past event rather than, or as well as, memory records of perceiving the event itself). Mentally reviewing information garnered from different sources may make it difficult to later specify the sources of particular details, because the most accessible memories may be those of reflective episodes in which information from different sources was integrated irrespective of source (see Hastie, Landsman, & Loftus, 1978, for related research on the effects of repeated questioning).

Source monitoring criteria

According to the source monitoring hypothesis, the criteria subjects use to identify the sources of their memories may vary depending on the purpose of the remembering (Johnson, 1988). The term "criteria" refers to the characteristics of a memory that the person takes as evidence that it came from a particular source, as well as to the amount of evidence required to make an attribution. Under some conditions it might be enough for an item to be familiar and not contradict other information remembered from a source for subjects to attribute it to that source. Under other circumstances further information, such as a perceptually detailed recollection, might be required. For example, people are likely to use much more lax source monitoring criteria when exchanging anecdotes at a cocktail party than when testifying on the witness stand.

The recognition tests typically used in studies of eyewitness suggestibility may lead subjects to use lax source monitoring criteria. In the standard procedure, subjects receive a lengthy series of recognition test trials consisting of items from the original event and new distractor items (either in the form of forced-choice pairs or individual yes/no items). The critical test items, in which the suggested details appear, are embedded among these old/new filler items. Because most of the test items require subjects to discriminate between objects presented in the visual event and completely new distractors, subjects may adopt a familiarity criterion (Atkinson & Juola, 1973) early on in the test, and stop attending to potentially useful information about the sources of their memories (for example, the amount and nature of perceptual detail). When a critical item is encountered, subjects may recognize the suggested detail as something presented during the experimental session and, because they are using a familiarity criterion, select that item as something seen in the original event. On a forced-choice test, the suggested item in a test pair may seem more familiar than the original item due to its relative recency and salience. Thus standard testing procedures with both yes/no and forced-choice recognition tests may lead subjects to base judgments on familiarity and hence to ignore memory information about the source of an item's familiarity.

In support of these ideas, Lindsay and Johnson (1989a) reported two experiments in which a suggestibility effect was obtained among subjects tested with a recognition test but not among subjects tested with a source monitoring test that oriented them toward discriminating between memories derived from the event and memories derived from the postevent narrative. The two tests consisted of the same list of items: Subjects given the recognition test were to respond "yes" to items they remembered seeing in the visual event and "no" to all other items, whereas subjects given the source monitoring test were to indicate, for each item, whether they remembered seeing that item only in the event, only in the postevent information, in both sources, or in neither. As is typically found, subjects tested with the recognition test often claimed to have seen suggested items in the event (that is, responded "yes" to suggested details). In contrast, those tested with the source monitoring test correctly attributed their memories of suggested details to the postevent information.

Details of Lindsay and Johnson's (1989a) results shed further light on the nature of the errors subjects made. Subjects given the recognition test more often said "yes" to items presented in both the scene and the narrative than to items presented only in the scene. In contrast, subjects given the source monitoring test more often claimed that items were in the scene if those items had been presented only in the scene than if they had been presented in both the scene and the narrative. This interaction supports our hypothesis that subjects given the yes/no test tended to base their judgments on familiarity (and hence responded "yes" most often to items presented in both sources because they were most familiar) whereas subjects given the source monitoring test based their responses on source-relevant memory information (and hence sometimes attributed memories of items presented in both sources to the text, because their recollections of those items contained source information specific to reading).

We viewed these findings as evidence that subjects tested with recognition tests sometimes misidentify memories from the postevent narrative as memories of the event because they are using lax source monitoring criteria. The source monitoring instructions led subjects to use more stringent criteria and thereby correctly attribute memories of suggested details to the postevent information. In independent research, Zaragoza and Koshmider (1989) obtained analogous results using a similar procedure, but they interpreted the finding as evidence that even subjects tested with recognition tests are aware of the source of suggested items and respond "yes" to them simply because they assume or infer that they were also present in the event. That is, they argued that the source monitoring test merely reduced demand characteristics to claim that suggested details had been seen in the event. More recent research from both labs demonstrates that this is not always the case; Lindsay (unpublished) and Zaragoza and Muench (1989) obtained suggestibility effects among subjects tested with source monitoring tests. Several aspects of these procedures made it relatively difficult for subjects to discriminate between memories of the visual event and memories of the postevent narrative. For example, in the Lindsay study, subjects viewed the McCloskey and Zaragoza (1985a) slide sequence and then listened to a tape-recorded postevent narrative that included misleading suggestions about some event details and neutral control information about other event details (a within-subjects design), and the source monitoring test was administered after a twenty-four hour delay. At test subjects were to indicate, for each test item, whether they remembered that item only from the slides, only from the narrative, from both sources, or not at all. Under these conditions subjects showed a reliable tendency to indicate that they had seen suggested details in the slides. That is, even though subjects were explicitly oriented toward discriminating between memories from different sources, they nonetheless sometimes misidentified memories of things they had merely read about as memories of things they had seen in the slides as well as read about in the narrative.

Zaragoza and her coworkers have recently reported several interesting experiments using source monitoring tests to explore factors that affect the likelihood of source misattributions in the eyewitness suggestibility paradigm. Carris, Zaragoza, and Lane (1992), for example, found that subjects were more likely to indicate later that they remembered seeing suggested details in the event if they had been instructed to form visual images of the postevent narrative when it was presented. Presumably, visualizing misleading suggestions makes memories of them more similar to memories of seeing things in the event. Zaragoza and Lane (1991) reported that subjects were more likely to claim to have seen suggested details in the event if they were required to make their test responses quickly than if they were given more time to respond. These findings are consistent with the source monitoring approach.

Cued recall measures

Source monitoring tests do not altogether eliminate the possibility that demand characteristics might contribute to apparent source monitoring confusions. Subjects are led to believe that the narrative is accurate, and they may wish to show that they are attentive subjects who remember the suggested details from both the event and the narrative. Consistent with this demand characteristics explanation, subjects in the studies described in the preceding section very rarely attributed suggested details to the event alone. Rather, either they correctly attributed suggested details only to the narrative or they attributed them to both the narrative and the event. Perhaps subjects knew that their memories of those details were from the narrative alone, but assumed that those details had also been present in the event. Wishing to show themselves to be bright and attentive people, subjects would be motivated to indicate that they remember the suggested details in both sources. Thus demand characteristics may affect performance on source monitoring tests.

Another recent set of experiments (Belli, Lindsay, Gales, & McCarthy, 1992; see also Zaragoza & Lane, 1992) obtained evidence of a misinformation effect and illusory memories of eyewitnessing using a cued recall test in which subjects were warned that the narrative had included misleading suggestions and were instructed to recall both what they had seen in the slide and what they had read in the narrative. Thus subjects knew that the narrative was not a reliable source of information about the event, and were given an opportunity to display their knowledge of the suggested details without having to claim that they saw them in the event. Subjects first viewed the McCloskey and Zaragoza (1985a) slides, then read a postevent narrative that included misleading suggestions about some event details. At test, subjects were informed that the narrative had included misleading suggestions about some details in the event. Each test item asked subjects to indicate what they had seen in the slides and what they had heard in the narrative.

There were two major findings in these studies. First, correct recall of event details was lower on items for which misleading suggestions had been given. Thus, even though subjects were warned about the presence of misleading suggestions, were not required to guess (unlike a forced-choice recognition test), and could report a misleading suggestion and the corresponding event detail if they remembered both, a misinformation effect was nonetheless obtained. Second, subjects quite often recalled suggested details as things they had seen in the slides – that is, illusory memories of eyewitnessing were obtained using this cued recall procedure.

Jacoby's "logic of opposition"

More compelling evidence that subjects sometimes mistake memories of postevent suggestions as memories of the event itself comes from a study using Jacoby's (for example, Jacoby, Woloshyn, & Kelley, 1989) "opposition" procedure (Lindsay, 1990). In this experiment, conditions were set up such that the effect of remembering that a particular detail had been presented in the postevent narrative would be opposite to the effect of genuine memory source confusions. To do this, we correctly informed subjects at test that the post-event information did not include any correct answers to the test questions. Thus, if subjects remembered that a particular detail had been mentioned in the postevent narrative, they would know it was wrong and should not be reported. Acquisition conditions were manipulated such that remembering the misleading suggestions and their source would be very easy for some subjects and relatively difficult for others. In the easy condition, subjects received the misleading suggestions two days after viewing the event, minutes before taking the test, and under conditions that differed from those in which they viewed the event. Subjects in the difficult condition, on the other hand, received the misleading suggestions minutes after viewing the event, under very similar conditions, two days before taking the test. At test, subjects were correctly informed that anything mentioned in the postevent narrative that was relevant to any test question was wrong. This instruction was repeated and rephrased several times. That is, subjects were explicitly and emphatically told not to report anything they remembered from the postevent narrative. Subjects in the easy condition showed no tendency to report suggested details at above-baseline rates, indicating that subjects understood and attempted to follow the injunction against reporting information from the postevent narrative. Subjects in the difficult condition quite often reported the suggested details as things they recalled seeing in the event. Even though subjects were specifically trying to avoid using memories of the postevent narrative, they sometimes did so. These findings indicate that illusory memories of eyewitnessing sometimes occur even when subjects are explicitly oriented toward avoiding them, provided that the memories of the misleading suggestions are sufficiently similar to the memories of the event itself.

Memory impairment

The opposition study described above also provided important evidence that misleading postevent suggestions can impair subjects' ability to remember event details. Although subjects in the easy condition were able to identify the source of their memories of suggested details (and so did not report seeing them more often on misled items than control items), the misleading suggestions nonetheless hampered their ability to report the event details. That is, although they did not report the suggested details, they failed to report the event details (that is, left the answer blank or guessed) more often on misled items than on control items. Correct recall of event details was 9 percent lower on misled items than on control items.

Given the opposition instructions, response biases such as differential rates of correct guessing or differential response criteria for control and misled items (McCloskey & Zaragoza, 1985a) would occur only when subjects cannot identify the source of a remembered suggested detail. This is because if the source of a recollected suggested detail is identified then subjects will know that that detail is wrong, and so will not use it in lieu of a guess or in favor of a concurrently remembered detail. Thus, under opposition instructions, differential guessing rates and response criteria will contribute to suggestibility effects only when subjects fail to identify the sources of recollected suggested details. It is clear that subjects in the easy condition correctly identified the source of their recollections of suggested details, because they showed no tendency more often to report seeing suggested details on misled than control items. Moreover, a subanalysis revealed that correct recall was significantly impaired even among a subgroup of subjects in the easy condition who never reported any suggested details. Thus it is clear that neither differential rates of correct guessing nor differential response criteria account for the lower level of recall of event details on misled than control items in the easy condition. These findings are powerful evidence of memory impairment.

How can the findings of this opposition study be reconciled with the repeated failure to detect memory impairment effects using McCloskey and Zaragoza's modified test (that is, with adults, six experiments in McCloskey & Zaragoza, 1985a; two experiments in Loftus, Donders, Hoffman, & Schooler, 1989; one experiment in Bonto & Payne, 1991, and Lord knows how many unpublished studies; with children, two experiments in Zaragoza, 1987, three experiments in Zaragoza, 1991, and one experiment in Zaragoza, Dahlgren, & Muench, in press)? First, as discussed below, some investigators have found effects on the modified test. As Belli (Belli, in press; Belli, Windschitl, McCarthy, & Winfrey, 1992) has argued, it may be that memory impairment effects can only be detected on the modified test under ideal conditions. Second, a number of critics have pointed out that the modified test may be insensitive to certain forms of memory impairment (for example, Belli, 1989; Johnson & Lindsay, 1986; Loftus et al., 1989; Tversky & Tuchin, 1989). For example, although failure to detect memory impairment on the modified test indicates that misleading suggestions did not impair memory for the event detail beyond the presumably minimal level of memory required to discriminate between the event detail and a completely new distractor, this does not mean that no trace degradation occurred. For example, it might be that misleading suggestions can reduce the strength of the memory for the event detail but cannot altogether eliminate that memory. This is analogous to many cases in the natural world; for example, a large percentage of a blob of ketchup can be removed from a tablecloth with a napkin, but it is quite difficult to eliminate the stain altogether. To speak in somewhat more sophisticated terms, the modified test may also be insensitive to memory impairing effects that are more subtle or complex than a reduction in the overall strength of the memory (for example, reduction of contextual cues). We know from phenomena such as recognition failure of recallable items (Tulving & Thomson, 1973), dissociations between direct and indirect tests of memory

(Richardson-Klavehn & Bjork, 1988), and dissociations between mere familiarity and recollection (Jacoby, 1991), that the determinants of memory performance are complex and multifaceted rather than unidimensional. Factors that affect memory performance on one measure may not alter performance on another. For example, the modified test may be insensitive to retrieval-based coexistence forms of memory impairment that play larger roles in recall than in recognition (for example, blocking).

The question of whether misleading postevent information actually alters memory traces or merely reduces their retrievability may not be soluble by cognitive psychology (Watkins, 1990). From an applied perspective, the important issue is determining what conditions are likely to impair performance. In practical, functionalist terms, the evidence suggests that effects of misleading suggestions on ability to remember event details are likely to be small and nonreliable when appropriate recognition probes are used (as in the modified test), but may be considerably larger and more robust when appropriate recall measures are used (as in the opposition test). This is consistent with what we know about retroactive inhibition (see Crowder, 1976, for review) and reconstructive memory errors (see Alba & Hasher, 1983, for review). Such effects are generally much larger when memory is tested with recall rather than with recognition measures.

Critiques of other evidence of memory impairment

In my view, the memory impairment effect obtained with the opposition procedure (Lindsay, 1990; Toland, 1990, cited in Weingardt et al., this volume) is the only evidence published to date that is not susceptible to alternative explanations such as demand characteristics, differential response criteria on misled and control items, or differential guessing rates on misled and control items (see McCloskey & Zaragoza, 1985a, 1985b, and Zaragoza & McCloskey, 1989, for critiques of earlier claims). My point is not that memory impairment did not occur in the other experiments, but merely that those experiments are susceptible to alternative explanations that the opposition procedure avoids. Without reviewing this literature exhaustively, the following critiques some recent claims of evidence of memory impairment.

Chandler (1989, 1991) obtained impairment effects on a version of McCloskey and Zaragoza's (1985a) modified test procedure. In Phase 1, subjects viewed a set of nature pictures (for example, a portion of a photograph of the surface of a pond). In Phase 2, they viewed a second set of pictures, some of which were closely related to some of the Phase 1 pictures (for example, another portion of the same photograph of the pond). At test, subjects were to indicate which picture they had seen in Phase 1, choosing between the Phase 1 picture and a different closely related picture (for example, a third portion of that same photograph of the pond). Performance was poorer on items for which a related picture had been presented in Phase 2.

Chandler's (1989, 1991) findings are consistent with the memory impairment hypothesis, but they may afford another interpretation as well. Consider two subjects who saw picture A of the pond in the first phase, one of whom also saw picture B of the pond in the second phase. Assume that the A–C test pair acts, in part, as a retrieval cue for memory information about recently viewed photos of ponds (a view of recognition processes that has been proposed before – for example, Kintsch, 1974). Suppose further that both subjects recollect exactly the same amount of information derived from seeing A in the first phase, but that the misled subject also recollects some information derived from seeing B (for example, that there was a particularly large lily pad in the upper right-hand corner). Independent of any memory impairment effect, one might expect better performance on an A–C test pair among subjects who recollect only something about A than among subjects who recollect something about A and something about B. This is because B and C are likely to share properties that are not present in A (for example, it might be that both B and C have a large lily pad in the upper right-hand corner, whereas A does not). This effect would not involve memory impairment (for example, trace degradation or blocking) because subjects retrieve the same amount of information about the Phase 1 pictures in the misled and control conditions.

Chandler (1991) argued against this sort of account by presenting three experiments in which no reliable proactive interference was observed (that is, performance on an A–C test pair was not impaired when subjects saw B in Phase 1 and A in Phase 2). She argued that if the retroactive interference effect of exposure to B after A were due to retrieval at test of information about B (rather than to memory impairment for A), then the effect would also be observed when subjects see B before A. As Chandler noted, however, there are reasons one might expect retroactive effects to be greater than proactive ones (for example, the recency and distinctiveness of the materials presented in Phase 2). Chandler argued that such factors cannot explain the failure to observe proactive interference, and supported this argument by showing that proactive interference did not occur even when there was a forty-eight hour retention interval between Phases 2 and 3 (that is, when neither A nor B would be particularly recent or distinctive). However, Chandler's own experiments also show that there is little or no retroactive interference with a forty-eight hour retention interval, a finding that is consistent with the account offered here.

Chandler's (1989, 1991) research is first-rate, it adds substantially to our understanding of misinformation effects, and it provides powerful evidence that interpolated material can impair memory performance even when demand characteristics and guessing biases are eliminated. Further, many of the considerations mentioned above are clearly laid out in her 1991 paper. The point of my argument is that, if the reasoning presented above is correct, her studies do not provide unequivocable evidence of memory impairment per se.

We turn now to a critique of evidence for memory impairment among subjects tested with McCloskey and Zaragoza's (1985a) modified test. Ceci, Ross, and Toglia (1987) and Toglia, Ross, and Ceci (in press) obtained evidence of memory impairment among children tested with the modified test after receiving suggestions about details in a story. Belli et al. (1992) also obtained an effect on the modified test with undergraduate subjects. First, it should be noted that Zaragoza (1987, 1991; Zaragoza, Dahlgren, & Muench, in press) failed to replicate the Ceci et al. (1987) and Toglia et al. (in press) results in several reasonably close replications of the procedure, and that Belli et al. (1992) obtained the effect in only two of four experiments. Further, Toglia et al. presented evidence that the prestige or authority of the source of the misleading suggestions plays a role in the impairment effect they obtained on the modified test. This suggests that demand characteristics may contribute to effects of misleading suggestions on the modified test. Specifically, it could be that what subjects learn from the misinformation is that what they remember from the event is wrong. Suppose, for example, that a subject first hears a story in which a clown is said to have red balloons; when those balloons are later described as blue the subject may think, "Gee, I mistakenly thought they were red. I guess those balloons were not red." At test, when the subject is asked whether the balloons were green or red, he or she may no longer be able to recall what was seen in the event (due to spontaneous forgetting) but remember that the experimenter had indicated that the balloons were not red. Or subjects might still recollect seeing red balloons, but also remember that the postevent narrative indicated that they were not red. That is, misled subjects (and perhaps especially misled children) may err on the modified test not because of memory impairment per se but because they remember that they had been told that the event detail was wrong.

It should be noted that if this demand characteristics mechanism does influence performance on the modified test, its effects are neither large nor common – after all, effects of misleading suggestions are rarely observed when the modified test is used. It should also be noted that my point here is not to claim that memory impairment does not contribute to effects of misleading suggestions on the modified test (although it is clear that those effects are, at most, small and unreliable), but rather to raise the possibility that demand characteristics may also contribute to such effects.

Finally, I will turn to a critique of research using a variant of the opposition procedure. Weingardt et al. (this volume) report two studies in which, after viewing a slide sequence and reading a postevent narrative including misleading suggestions, subjects were instructed to generate category exemplars (for example, a list of tools). Subjects were told not to include any exemplars shown in the slides – that is, if they remembered seeing a particular object in the slides, they should not write that object as a category exemplar. Weingardt et al. argued that if misled subjects sometimes think they had seen suggested items in the slides, then subjects who had received misleading suggestions should be less likely to include the suggested objects in their lists of exemplars, and that if misleading suggestions impair memory for event details, then subjects who received misleading suggestions should be more likely to include the corresponding event details in their lists of exemplars (because they would be unable to remember that they had seen those objects in the slides and so think it all right to write them down). The results provide some support for these claims. Unfortunately, these studies, like those using the standard Loftus test procedure, cannot distinguish between cases in which subjects assume that a misleading suggestion that they correctly remember as something from the postevent information was also present in the event (for example, "I don't remember what tool was in the event, but the narrative said wrench, so I assume that it was a wrench") and cases in which subjects really think that they saw a suggested item in the event itself ("I remember seeing a wrench in the event"). The former case does not involve an effect of suggestions on memory for event details or any memory source confusion. This does not reduce to a matter of confidence; one could be 100 percent confident in the veridicality of something that one knows is remembered from the narrative rather than the event. Thus although memory impairment and/ or source monitoring confusions may well have occurred in these studies, the procedures do not entirely eliminate alternative explanations.

Source monitoring and eyewitness suggestibility: Summary

It is clear that a sizable proportion of the large and dramatic misinformation effect typically obtained with the standard Loftus procedure (for example, Loftus et al., 1978) is due to aware uses of memory for the postevent information, of the sort proposed by McCloskey and Zaragoza (1985a). For example, some subjects may fail to notice the critical detail in the event but remember what the postevent information said about that detail; given that the narrative is presented as a reliable source of information, such subjects would quite reasonably rely upon it when tested.

On the other hand, there is mounting evidence that subjects sometimes do experience retrieval of memories of details they read or heard about in the postevent information as recollections of seeing those details in the event. These source monitoring errors may range from vague "sourceless" recollections (for example, "I think I remember something about a stop sign.") to vivid and compelling illusory memories of eyewitnessing of the sort described by Schooler, Gerhard, and Loftus (1986).

Taken together, three points are clear from the studies reviewed in the preceding section. First, source confusions are more common when two or more potential sources give rise to highly similar memory records. Second, the likelihood of source misattributions also depends on the criteria subjects adopt in making source monitoring judgments. Finally, source misattributions sometimes occur even under very stringent criteria – even when subjects are deliberating trying to avoid making such errors – provided the memories of the suggestions are sufficiently similar to the memories of the event itself.

There is also mounting evidence that misleading suggestions can impair subjects' ability to remember event details (Ceci et al., 1987; Chandler, 1989, 1991; Belli et al., 1992; Lindsay, 1990; Toglia et al., in press). My reading of these studies is that, as Ceci (1992) has also argued, memory impairment effects are small and unreliable when memory is tested with recognition probes (as in the McCloskey & Zaragoza, 1985a, modified test), but may be considerably larger and more robust when appropriate recall measures are used (as in Lindsay, 1990).

The source monitoring issue is distinct from the memory impairment issue: Even if misleading suggestions do not impair ability to remember event details, the question of whether or not subjects sometimes misremember suggestions as things they had seen in the event is an important one. Indeed, from a forensic point of view the consequences of source monitoring confusions may well be more ominous than those of memory impairment. That is, the possibility that misleading suggestions may lead witnesses to believe that they saw something they did not (for example, that an assailant had a gun) may have more serious implications than the possibility that suggestions may impair the ability of witnesses to remember what they did see.

Although the source monitoring issue is distinct from the memory impairment issue, source monitoring processes and memory impairment mechanisms may interact (Lindsay, 1990; Zaragoza & Moore, 1990). For example, subjects who retrieve memory records of a suggested detail before they retrieve memory records of the corresponding event detail may be less likely to continue searching memory (and hence fail to retrieve memories of the event detail) if they misidentify their memory of the suggested detail as a memory of the event itself. That is, source monitoring confusions may contribute to retrieval impairment. Conversely, subjects may be more likely to make source monitoring errors if they retrieve only the suggested detail than if they retrieve both the suggested detail and the event detail (because in the latter case they may be more likely to deliberate consciously about the sources of those memories).

Bystander misidentification in lineup identification

Bystander misidentification (also known as "unconscious transference") occurs when a witness misidentifies an innocent bystander (that is, a person the witness has seen before, but who was not seen committing the crime) as the perpetrator of a crime (for example, Read, Tollestrup, Hammersley, Mc-Fadzen, & Christensen, 1990; Read, this volume; Ross, Ceci, Dunning, & Toglia, this volume). The source monitoring approach provides a straight-forward way to describe some of the processes that may underlie such errors. Specifically, the source monitoring approach suggests that the likelihood of bystander misidentification is influenced by factors that affect the discrimin-ability of the two sources of memories (for example, similarity of the bystander and perpetrator and of the spatial and temporal contexts in which they were seen, the amount and kind of ongoing elaborative processing, etc.) and factors that affect source monitoring attributions at test (for example, stringency and appropriateness of the judgment criteria, time given for responses, full versus divided attention, etc.).

Ross et al. (this volume) used the term "source monitoring" in a more narrow sense than Johnson and I have. Ross used the term to refer to cases in which subjects are consciously aware of discriminating between two dif-ferent potential sources of a memory (for example, at test, subjects recognize the bystander as familiar and consciously deliberate about whether the by-stander was seen committing the crime or elsewhere). Ross contrasts this kind of source monitoring process with cases in which at test subjects misidentify the bystander as the perpetrator without recollecting the prior exposure to the bystander (that is, they automatically misidentify memories of seeing the bystander as memories of seeing the perpetrator). From the perspective de-scribed here, both of these would be examples of source monitoring errors – the former involves consciously mediated source monitoring decisions and the latter involves more rapid and automatic source attribution processes.

The primary focus in the work of Ross et al. is on a third mechanism that may contribute to bystander misidentification: cases in which at test subjects correctly recollect seeing the perpetrator and seeing the bystander, but had incorrectly inferred at the time of encoding that the same person was seen in both events. Ross et al. reported a series of studies in which subjects viewed a multiscene video. One scene depicted a man reading a story to a group of children, and a later scene depicted a very similar looking man stealing a wallet in a cafeteria. At test, subjects were shown a set of mug shots that included the bystander but not the perpetrator. Compared to a control con-dition, subjects who had seen the bystander were nearly three times more likely to select him in the mug shot test.

Follow-up measures and experiments reported by Ross et al. suggest that this effect is due to misidentification during witnessing: That is, when the perpetrator appeared on the screen, subjects thought he was the same person as the bystander in the earlier scene ("There's that story-reader guy again – wow, he's stealing her wallet!"). Therefore it is not surprising that subjects later selected the bystander from the lineup ("There's that guy I saw reading the story, the one who later stole the wallet"). In this case, selecting the bystander from the mug shots does not represent a memory error but rather accurate memory of an inaccurate identification made when the perpetrator was initially seen in the video.

Interestingly, and consistent with the results of several of the studies described above, Ross et al. found that subjects did not tend to misidentify the bystander as the perpetrator if they were informed at test that the bystander and the perpetrator were in fact two different people. This indicates that memory records of seeing the perpetrator coexisted with (rather than were irrevocably blended into) memories of seeing the bystander; informing subjects that the two were different people enabled them to use existing differences in the memory records of the two events to identify the person in the lineup as the bystander rather than the perpetrator.

The research reported by Read et al. (1990) and Read (this volume) suggests that bystander misidentifications may be relatively rare. Read's studies were conducted in everyday settings (for example, subjects were store clerks and the target and bystander pretended to be customers). Subjects rarely misidentified the bystander when later asked to select the target from a lineup. Perhaps this is partly because live interactions with another person usually give rise to memory records with myriad cues to source, and hence to accurate source monitoring performance. Consistent with the source monitoring approach, Read et al. did obtain a bystander misidentification effect when the bystander was similar to the perpetrator (more similar than any of the other people in the lineup). Read (this volume) presents evidence that bystander misidentifications, when they do occur, may reflect conscious inferences rather than "unconscious transference" (compare Ross et al., this volume). Source monitoring suggests that both mechanisms could give rise to bystander misidentifications under the appropriate conditions. Obviously, further research is needed to explore the conditions under which various mechanisms are likely to produce bystander misidentification. Stern and Dunning's interesting chapter in this volume, reporting research in which they analyzed the decision processes typical of accurate and inaccurate decisions in lineup tests, suggests one promising approach to this issue.

Verbal and nonverbal overshadowing in lineup identification

Schooler and Engstler-Schooler (1990) reported a fascinating series of studies in which they demonstrated that requiring eyewitnesses to provide a verbal description of a perpetrator can impair their performance on a subsequent lineup identification test. It is important to note that when subjects were required to make their lineup selections very quickly, there was no effect of having verbally described the robber's face. This result indicates that providing the verbal description did not alter the memory records of seeing the robber's face, but rather gave rise to additional memory records of the verbalizations; provided subjects were given sufficient time to respond, their selection on the test was influenced by these memories of their own verbalizations. Because faces are inherently difficult to verbalize, the subjects' performances were impaired when they were influenced by memories of such verbalizations. Schooler and Engstler-Schooler referred to this effect as "verbal overshadowing."

In earlier work, Comish (1987) showed that subjects who attempted to create an Identi-kit rendition of a suspect performed more poorly than control subjects on a subsequent lineup identification task. Presumably, the mechanisms that underlie this effect are similar to those involved in Schooler and Engstler-Schooler's (1990) verbal overshadowing; memories of the thoughts and images produced during the Identi-kit session are retrieved during the lineup test, and because some of those memories do not accurately map on to the suspect performance is impaired. Consistent with this account, Comish found that subjects were particularly likely to make false identifications if the foils were modified to resemble their own errors on the Identi-kit reconstruction.

Both these effects can be described in terms of source monitoring processes: Memory information derived from describing the face is retrieved and used when subjects attempt to match their memories of seeing the face with the photos in the lineup. The interpolated material is retrieved because of its similarity and relevance to the to-be-retrieved memories of actually seeing the face, and subjects may not be aware that they are in fact drawing on memories from different sources at test. One implication of this view is that subjects might be able to avoid such effects if they were warned about them, and so tightened their source monitoring criteria during the lineup test.

Age-related developments in source monitoring

The competence of children as eyewitnesses is a very controversial topic at present. Testifying draws on a multitude of cognitive, linguistic, and social skills, so it comes as no surprise that the relationship between age and competence is complex and situation specific (Ceci & Bruck, in press). For example, Foley, Johnson, and Raye (1983) reported that, compared to older children and adults, six-year-old children had difficulty discriminating between memories of words they had actually said aloud and memories of words they had imagined saying during an acquisition phase, but that they were as accurate as adults when discriminating between memories of words they had imagined saying and memories of words they had heard another person say, or when remembering which of two other people had said particular words. Foley and Johnson (1985) reported a similar pattern of results with tasks involving memories for actual and imagined actions (for example, "Did you

really touch your nose, or did you just imagine yourself touching your nose?").
Relative to adults, young children were more likely to be confused about
which things they had actually done and which they had merely imagined,
but children were not more likely to mistake memories of what they had done
as memories of what another person had done, nor did they more often
misidentify which of two other people had performed particular actions (see
also Foley et al., 1991, and Foley et al., 1989).

Findings such as these led Foley and her colleagues (for example, Foley et
al., 1989; 1991) to propose that young children have special difficulty discriminating between actual and imagined self-generations ("Realization Judgments"). Lindsay et al. (1991) broadened this hypothesis and argued that
young children may be more likely than adults to confuse memories from
different sources whenever those sources are highly similar to one another.
Consistent with this hypothesis, Lindsay et al. (Experiment 3) found that
compared to adults eight-year-old children were more likely to mistake memories of actions they had imagined another person performing as memories
of actions they had merely imagined that same person performing. Presumably, the fact that the same person was involved in the witnessed and imagined
actions made the memories for the two types of events relatively similar and
hence confusable, especially for the children.

Questions concerning children's competence as eyewitnesses have occupied
center stage in recent years, but the future is likely to bring an increasing
focus on the elderly eyewitness. A rapidly increasing proportion of the North
American population is over sixty-five years of age. Further, the elderly are
vulnerable to crime and, like children, are not infrequently the sole witness
to criminal acts. Older adults are also similar to children in that they are often
said to have poor attention and poor memory.

Elderly adults demonstrate a complex pattern of preserved and impaired
cognitive capacities (for example, Hultsch & Dixon, 1991). There is considerable evidence that the elderly often have particular difficulty remembering
source-specifying, contextual information (for example, Burke & Light, 1981;
McIntyre & Craik, 1987; see Johnson et al., 1992, for review). For example,
Hashtroudi, Johnson, and Chrosniak (1989, 1990) report several studies in
which younger and older adults were exposed to information from different
sources and later asked to remember the sources of particular pieces of information. In one study subjects performed some naturalistic, everyday actions (for example, having coffee and cookies; wrapping a package) and
imagined others. Subjects were later tested on their ability to remember which
actions had actually been performed and which merely imagined. As in the
studies of children's source monitoring, whether or not the older subjects
were more likely than the younger ones to confuse memories of actual and
imagined events depended on the particulars of the situation.

These findings indicate that under some but not all conditions older adults may be more vulnerable than young adults to misleading suggestions. There is evidence that this is sometimes the case. Cohen and Faulkner (1989) reported a study in which young and older adults participated in a standard Loftus misinformation procedure. As predicted, misleading suggestions had a greater detrimental effect on the memory performance of the older subjects. We know that the elderly do not always demonstrate such deficits, and further research is needed to refine our understanding of the conditions under which older witnesses are likely to perform more poorly than younger ones.

Source attributions and the construction of subjective experience

The research described above has focused on the processes by which people identify the source of their memories. A more general question is how people differentiate between different kinds of mental events – for example, how people differentiate between images that are retrieved from memory (remembering) and images that are generated anew (imaging or fantasizing) (for example, Jacoby, Kelley, & Dywan, 1989). The source monitoring argument is that remembering always involves both retrieval and judgment processes, even when the subjective experience is one of directly recollecting rather than of inferring. Ongoing thinking also always involves both new thinking and memory retrieval, even when the subjective experience is one of inferring or creating rather than of remembering.

This constructivist perspective harkens back to "schema" theories of memory (for example, Bartlett, 1932). This should come as no surprise, considering Marcia Johnson's pivotal role both in research on reconstructive memory (for example, Bransford & Johnson, 1972) and in the development of the source monitoring approach (for example, Johnson & Raye, 1981). Schema theory lost popularity among memory researchers in the early eighties, partly because of mounting evidence of (and interest in) memory for surface-level details (Alba & Hasher, 1983). Source monitoring reconciles these approaches by describing remembering as an interplay between activated memory records (which might well include exquisite perceptual detail) and automatic and controlled reconstructive processes.

Recent theoretical and empirical work by Jacoby and his coworkers has shed new light on the reconstructive and attribution-making processes that underlie the subjective experience of cognitive events (for example, Jacoby, Kelley, & Dywan, 1989; Jacoby, Lindsay, & Toth, 1992). One line of research has shown that when subjects are oriented toward making memory judgments, certain manipulations of current conditions can give rise to illusory experiences of remembering. Specifically, factors that facilitate processing of nonstudied items on a memory test can increase the likelihood that subjects will falsely "remember" those items. For example Jacoby and Whitehouse (1989) showed that briefly flashing a word immediately before its presentation as a recognition probe increases the likelihood that subjects will judge that the word had appeared in the study list; presumably the flashed preview of the word facilitates processing of the recognition probe, and that fluent processing is taken as evidence of having previously encountered the word on the study list. Thus under some conditions new ideas can be experienced as memories.

For present purposes, the important point is that the eyewitness must not only discriminate between memory records of the event itself and memory records of related episodes that occurred before and after that event, but must also discriminate between veridical and nonveridical products of ongoing reconstructive processes while testifying. Because all remembering involves judgment and inference processes, the eyewitness cannot simply "read off" memory records, but rather must interpret them. These unconscious interpretation processes can give rise to inaccurate recollections.

Conclusions

The core idea underlying the source monitoring approach is a simple one: That we can name, in remembering, things that went unnamed during the event itself; that we can feel, in reminiscence, emotions that were not experienced when the event occurred; and that we can perceive in our recollections shapes and colors to which we were blind in the past. In short, that activated memory records can serve as input to ongoing cognitive processes, and that all remembering is a blend of reactivating and interpreting, retrieving and constructing. People are sometimes aware of using inference to fill in missing details in their recollections, but more often these judgment processes are performed rapidly and without conscious reflection as an integral part of remembering. That is, remembering naturally and necessarily involves judgment and inference processes akin to those by which we perceive and understand and label aspects of ongoing external events. Thus not only is external reality transformed and interpreted in our ongoing experience, but our remembrance of things past requires an additional layer of transformation and interpretation.

For the most part, this synthesis of retrieval and inference works marvelously well – we are able to report a great deal about our past experiences, most of what we remember proves to be accurate, and we can often differentiate between accurate recollections and iffy inferences (at least when motivated to do so). Sometimes, however, the same mechanisms that generally serve us well can give rise to compelling source monitoring confusions in which memory information from one source is remembered as memory information from another source.

With important exceptions, the majority of the studies described in this chapter tested memory for relatively artificial laboratory tasks (for instance, remembering which of two people had uttered particular words on a word list, or remembering which of two storytellers had talked about a particular event). It is difficult to predict, a priori, whether the results of such studies exaggerate or underestimate source monitoring confusions in everyday life. On the one hand, the richness and complexity of naturalistic events imbues memory for them with many cues to source. On this basis, one would predict highly accurate source monitoring in everyday life. On the other hand, the sterility of the laboratory materials may reduce the probability that subjects spontaneously reminiscence about them, thereby potentially reducing the likelihood of subsequent source confusions. Furthermore, the formality of the laboratory testing situation may increase the stringency of source monitoring criteria at retrieval, and the short retention intervals typical of such studies likely support highly accurate source monitoring.

Both controlled studies and anecdotal accounts suggest that inability to remember source is a common memory failure, and that source confusions do indeed occur in everyday life (for example, Brown & Murphy, 1989; Linton, 1982; Neisser, 1982). Obviously, a great deal of additional research is needed to provide insights into source monitoring errors in complex and naturalistic settings such as those that are of concern to forensic psychologists. For the present, it is reasonable to conclude that people do sometimes confuse memories from different sources, and that such errors have important practical and theoretical implications. A witness asked to describe "what happened on the afternoon of Wednesday, June 24th, 1992" may well include in his or her reply information suggested by others, memories of past thoughts or fantasies about the event in question, and ideas based on general knowledge and beliefs that come to mind in response to the question. Future research will help us understand the factors that affect the likelihood of such errors and develop procedures that may allow us to detect or avoid them.

Note

1 The source monitoring approach is similar to Brainerd and Reyna's (in press) "fuzzy trace theory" in that the distinction between perceptual and reflective processes in MEM is akin to the distinction between "verbatim" and "gist" traces in fuzzy trace theory. Unlike fuzzy trace theory, however, the source monitoring approach treats these as end points on a continuum; no cognitive process is purely perceptual or purely reflective.

References

Abra, J. C. (1972). List differentiation and forgetting. In C. P. Duncan, L. Sechrest, & A. W. Melton (Eds.), *Human memory: Festschrift in honor of Benton J. Underwood.* New York: Appleton-Century-Crofts.

Alba, J. W., & Hasher, L. (1983). Is memory schematic? *Psychological Bulletin, 93,* 203–231.

Allen, S. W., & Jacoby, L. L. (1990). Reinstating study context produces unconscious influences of memory. *Memory and Cognition, 18,* 270–278.

Anderson, J. R., & Bower, G. H. (1972). Recognition and retrieval processes in free recall. *Psychological Review, 79,* 97–123.

Anderson, J. R., & Bower, G. H. (1974). A propositional theory of recognition memory. *Memory and Cognition, 2,* 406–412.

Atkinson, R. C., & Juola, J. F. (1973). Factors influencing speed and accuracy of word recognition. In S. Kornblum (Ed.), *Attention and performance IV* (pp. 583–612). New York: Academic Press.

Bartlett, F. C. (1932). *Remembering: A study in experimental and social psychology.* London: Cambridge University Press.

Bekerian, D. A., & Bowers, J. M. (1983). Eyewitness testimony: Were we misled? *Journal of Experimental Psychology: Learning, Memory, and Cognition, 9,* 139–145.

Belli, R. F. (1989). Influences of misleading postevent information: Misinformation interference and acceptance. *Journal of Experimental Psychology: General, 118,* 72–85.

Belli, R. F. (in press). Failures of interpolated tests in inducing memory impairment with final modified tests: Evidence unfavorable to the blocking hypothesis. *American Journal of Psychology.*

Belli, R. F., Lindsay, D. S., Gales, M. S., & McCarthy, T. T. (1992). *Memory impairment and source misattribution in postevent misinformation experiments with short retention intervals.* Manuscript in preparation.

Belli, R. F., Windschitl, P. D., McCarthy, T. T., & Winfrey, S. E. (1992). Detecting memory impairment with a modified test procedure. *Journal of Experimental Psychology: Learning, Memory, and Cognition, 18,* 356–367.

Bonto, M. A., & Payne, D. G. (1991). Role of environmental context in eyewitness memory. *American Journal of Psychology, 104,* 117–134.

Brainerd, C. J., & Reyna, V. F. (1993). Memory independence and memory interference in cognitive development. *Psychological Review, 100,* 42–67.

Bransford, J. D., & Johnson, M. K. (1972). Contextual prerequisites for understanding: Some investigations of comprehension and recall. *Journal of Verbal Learning and Verbal Behavior, 11,* 717–726.

Brown, A. S., & Murphy, D. R. (1989). Cryptomnesia: Delineating inadvertent plagiarism. *Journal of Experimental Psychology: Learning, Memory, and Cognition, 15,* 432–442.

Burke, D. M., & Light, L. L. (1981). Memory and aging: The role of retrieval processes. *Psychological Bulletin, 90,* 513–546.

Carris, M., Zaragoza, M., & Lane, S. (1992). *The role of visual imagery in source misattribution errors.* Paper presented at the annual meeting of the Midwestern Psychological Society, Chicago, IL.

Ceci, S. J. (1992, May). The Suggestibility of the Child Witness. Paper presented at the NATO Advanced Study Institute on Child Witnesses, Italy.

Ceci, S. J., & Bruck, M. (in press). The suggestibility of the child witness: A historical review and synthesis. *Psychological Bulletin.*

Ceci, S. J., Ross, D. R., & Toglia, M. P. (1987). Age differences in suggestibility: Narrowing the uncertainties. In S. J. Ceci, M. P. Toglia, & D. F. Ross (Eds.), *Children's eyewitness memory* (pp. 79–91). New York: Springer-Verlag.

Chandler, C. C. (1989). Specific retroactive interference in modified recognition tests: Evidence for an unknown cause of interference. *Journal of Experimental Psychology: Learning, Memory, and Cognition, 15,* 256–265.

Chandler, C. C. (1991). How memory for an event is influenced by related events: Interference in modified recognition tests. *Journal of Experimental Psychology: Learning, Memory, and Cognition, 17,* 11–125.

Christiaansen, R. E., & Ochalek, K. (1983). Editing misleading information from memory: Evidence for the coexistence of original and post-event information. *Memory and Cognition, 11,* 467–475.

Cohen, G., & Faulkner, D. (1989). Age differences in source forgetting: Effects on reality monitoring and on eyewitness testimony. *Psychology and Aging, 4,* 10–17.

Comish, S. E. (1987). Recognition of facial stimuli following an intervening task involving the Identi-kit. *Journal of Applied Psychology, 72,* 488–491.

Craik, F. I. M., & Kirsner, K. (1974). The effects of speaker's voice on word recognition. *Quarterly Journal of Experimental Psychology, 26,* 284.

Crowder, R. G. (1976). *Principles of learning and memory.* Hillsdale, NJ: Erlbaum.

Foley, M. A., Durso, F. T., Wilder, A., & Friedman, R. (1991). Developmental comparisons of explicit versus implicit imagery and reality monitoring. *Journal of Experimental Child Psychology, 51,* 1–13.

Foley, M. A., & Johnson, M. K. (1985). Confusion between memories for performed and imagined actions. *Child Development, 56,* 1145–1155.

Foley, M. A., Johnson, M. K., & Raye, C. L. (1983). Age-related changes in confusion between memories for thoughts and memories for speech. *Child Development, 54,* 51–60.

Foley, M. A., Santini, C., & Sopasakis, M. (1989). Discriminating between memories: Evidence for children's spontaneous elaborations. *Journal of Experimental Child Psychology, 48,* 146–169.

Geiselman, R. E., & Belleza, F. S. (1976). Long-term memory for speaker's voice and source location. *Memory and Cognition, 4,* 483–489.

Godden, D., & Baddeley, A. D. (1975). Context-dependent memory in two natural environments: On land and under water. *British Journal of Psychology, 66,* 325–331.

Hasher, L., & Griffin, M. (1978). Reconstructive and reproductive processes in memory. *Journal of Experimental Psychology, 4,* 318–330.

Hashtroudi, S., Johnson, M. K., & Chrosniak, L. D. (1989). Aging and source monitoring. *Psychology and Aging, 4,* 106–112.

Hashtroudi, S., Johnson, M. K., & Chrosniak, L. D. (1990). Aging and qualitative characteristics of memories for perceived and imagined complex events. *Psychology and Aging, 5,* 119–126.

Hastie, R., Landsman, R., & Loftus, E. F. (1978). Eyewitness testimony: The dangers of guessing. *Jurimetrics Journal, 19,* 1–8.

Hintzman, D. L., Block, R. A., & Inskeep, N. R. (1972). Memory for mode of input. *Journal of Verbal Learning and Verbal Behavior, 11,* 741–749.

Hultsch, D. F., & Dixon, R. A. (1991). Learning and memory and aging. In J. E. Birren & K. W. Schaie (Eds.), *Handbook of the psychology of aging* (3rd ed.). San Diego: Academic Press.

Jacoby, L. L. (1991). A process dissociation framework: Separating automatic from intentional uses of memory. *Journal of Memory and Language, 30,* 513–541.

Jacoby, L. L., & Brooks, L. R. (1984). Nonanalytic cognition: Memory, perception, and concept learning. In G. H. Bower (Ed.), *The psychology of learning and motivation: Advances in research and theory* (Vol. 18, pp. 1–47). New York: Academic Press.

Jacoby, L. L., & Kelley, C. M. (1992). Unconscious influences of memory: Dissociations and automaticity. In D. Milner & M. Rugg (Eds.), *The neuropsychology of consciousness* (pp. 201–233). New York: Academic Press.

Jacoby, L. L., Kelley, C. M., & Dywan, J. (1989). Memory attributions. In H. L. Roediger & F. I. M. Craik (Eds.), *Varieties of memory and consciousness: Essays in honour of Endel Tulving* (pp. 391–422). Hillsdale, NJ: Erlbaum.

Jacoby, L. L., Lindsay, D. S., & Toth, J. P. (in press). Unconscious processes revealed: A question of control. *American Psychologist.*

Jacoby, L. L., & Whitehouse, K. (1989). An illusion of memory: False recognition influenced by unconscious perception. *Journal of Experimental Psychology: General, 118,* 126–135.

Jacoby, L. L., Woloshyn, V., & Kelley, C. M. (1989). Becoming famous without being recognized: Unconscious influences of memory produced by dividing attention. *Journal of Experimental Psychology: General, 118,* 115–125.

Johnson, M. K. (1983). A multiple-entry, modular memory system. In G. H. Bower (Ed.), *The psychology of learning and motivation* (Vol. 17, pp. 81–123). New York: Academic Press.

Johnson, M. K. (1988). Discriminating the origin of information. In T. F. Oltmanns & B. A. Maher (Eds.), *Delusional beliefs: Interdisciplinary perspectives* (pp. 34–65). New York: John Wiley & Sons.

Johnson, M. K., & Hasher, L. (1987). Human learning and memory. *Annual Review of Psychology, 38*, 631–668.

Johnson, M. K., Hashtroudi, S., & Lindsay, D. S. (1992). *Source monitoring.* Manuscript submitted for publication.

Johnson, M. K., & Hirst, W. (1991). Processing subsystems of memory. In H. J. Weingartner & R. G. Lister (Eds.), *Cognitive neuroscience* (pp. 197–217). New York: Oxford University Press.

Johnson, M. K., & Lindsay, D. S. (1986). *Despite McCloskey and Zaragoza, suggestibility effects may reflect memory impairment.* Unpublished manuscript, Princeton University, Princeton, NJ.

Johnson, M. K., & Raye, C. L. (1981). Reality monitoring. *Psychological Review, 88*, 67–85.

Johnson, M. K., Raye, C. L., Foley, H. J., & Foley, M. A. (1981). Cognitive operations and decision bias in reality monitoring. *American Journal of Psychology, 94*, 37–64.

Kintsch, W. (1974). *The representation of meaning in memory.* Hillsdale, NJ: Erlbaum.

Kolers, P. A. (1976). Reading a year later. *Journal of Experimental Psychology: Human Learning and Memory, 2*, 554–565.

Kounios, J., & Johnson, M. K. (in preparation). *Revival functions for reality monitoring and recognition.*

Lindsay, D. S. (1989). [A suggestibility effect obtained among subjects tested with a source monitoring test.] Unpublished raw data.

Lindsay, D. S. (1990). Misleading suggestions can impair eyewitnesses' ability to remember event details. *Journal of Experimental Psychology: Learning, Memory, and Cognition, 16*, 1077–1083.

Lindsay, D. S., & Johnson, M. K. (1989a). Eyewitness suggestibility and memory for source. *Memory and Cognition, 17*, 349–358.

Lindsay, D. S., & Johnson, M. K. (1989b). The reversed eyewitness suggestibility effect. *Bulletin of the Psychonomic Society, 27*, 111–113.

Lindsay, D. S., Johnson, M. K., & Kwon, P. (1991). Developmental changes in memory source monitoring. *Journal of Experimental Child Psychology, 52*, 297–318.

Linton, M. (1982). Transformations of memory in everyday life. In U. Neisser (Ed.), *Memory observed: Remembering in natural contexts* (pp. 77–91). San Francisco: Freeman.

Loftus, E. F. (1979). *Eyewitness testimony.* Cambridge, MA: Harvard University Press.

Loftus, E. F. (1981). Mentalmorphosis: Alterations in memory produced by the mental bonding of new information to old. In J. Long & A. Baddeley (Eds.), *Attention and performance IX* (pp. 417–434). Hillsdale, NJ: Erlbaum.

Loftus, E. F., Donders, K., Hoffman, H. G., & Schooler, J. W. (1989). Creating new memories that are quickly accessed and confidently held. *Memory and Cognition, 17*, 607–616.

Loftus, E. F., Miller, D. G., & Burns, H. J. (1978). Semantic integration of verbal information into a visual memory. *Journal of Experimental Psychology: Human Learning and Memory, 4*, 19–31.

Masson, M. E. J. (1984). Memory for the surface structure of sentences: Remembering with and without awareness. *Journal of Verbal Learning and Verbal Behavior, 23*, 579–592.

McCloskey, M., & Zaragoza, M. (1985a). Misleading postevent information and memory for events: Arguments and evidence against memory impairment hypotheses. *Journal of Experimental Psychology: General, 114*, 1–16.

McCloskey, M., & Zaragoza, M. (1985b). Postevent information and memory: Reply to Loftus, Schooler, and Wagenaar. *Journal of Experimental Psychology: General, 114*, 381–387.

McIntyre, J. S., & Craik, F. I. M. (1987). Age differences in memory for item and source information. *Canadian Journal of Psychology, 41,* 175–192.

Neisser, U. (1982). Memory: What are the important questions? In U. Neisser (Ed.), *Memory observed: Remembering in natural contexts.* San Francisco: Freeman.

Raye, C. L., Johnson, M. K., & Taylor, T. H. (1980). Is there something special about memory for internally-generated information? *Memory and Cognition, 8,* 141–148.

Read, J. D. (this volume). Understanding bystander misidentifications: The role of familiarity and contextual knowledge. In D. F. Ross, J. D. Read, & M. P. Toglia (Eds.), *Adult eyewitness testimony: Current trends and developments* (pp. 56–79). New York: Cambridge University Press.

Read, J. D., Tollestrup, P., Hammersley, R., McFadzen, E., & Christensen, A. (1990). The unconscious transference effect: Are innocent bystanders ever misidentified? *Applied Cognitive Psychology, 4,* 3–31.

Richardson-Klavehn, A., & Bjork, R. A. (1988). Measures of memory. *Annual Review of Psychology, 39,* 475–543.

Ross, D. F., Ceci, S. J., Dunning, D., & Toglia, M. P. (this volume). Unconscious transference and lineup identification: Toward a memory blending approach. In D. F. Ross, J. D. Read, & M. P. Toglia (Eds.), *Adult eyewitness testimony: Current trends and developments* (pp. 80–100). New York: Cambridge University Press.

Schooler, J. W., & Engstler-Schooler, T. Y. (1990). Verbal overshadowing of visual memories: Some things are better left unsaid. *Cognitive Psychology, 22,* 36–71.

Schooler, J. W., Gerhard, D., & Loftus, E. F. (1986). Qualities of the unreal. *Journal of Experimental Psychology: Learning, Memory, and Cognition, 12,* 171–181.

Toglia, M. P., Ross, D. F., & Ceci, S. J. (in press). The suggestibility of children's memory: A cognitive and social-psychological interpretation. In M. L. Howe, C. J. Brainerd, & V. F. Reyna (Eds.), *The development of long-term retention.* New York: Springer-Verlag.

Tulving, E., & Thomson, D. M. (1973). Encoding specificity and retrieval processes in episodic memory. *Psychological Review, 80,* 352–373.

Tversky, B., & Tuchin, M. (1989). A reconciliation of the evidence on eyewitness testimony: Comments on McCloskey and Zaragoza (1985). *Journal of Experimental Psychology: General, 118,* 86–91.

Watkins, M. J. (1990). Mediationism and the obfuscation of memory. *American Psychologist, 45,* 328–335.

Weingardt, K. R., Toland, H. K., & Loftus, E. F. (this volume). Reports of suggested memories: Do people truly believe them? In D. F. Ross, J. D. Read, & M. P. Toglia (Eds.), *Adult eyewitness testimony: Current trends and developments* (pp. 3–26). New York: Cambridge University Press.

Winograd, E. (1968). List differentiation, recall, and category similarity. *Journal of Experimental Psychology, 78,* 510–515.

Zaragoza, M. S. (1987). Memory, suggestibility, and eyewitness testimony in children and adults. In S. J. Ceci, M. P. Toglia, & D. F. Ross (Eds.), *Children's eyewitness memory* (pp. 79–91). New York: Springer-Verlag.

Zaragoza, M. S. (1991). Preschool children's susceptibility to memory impairment. In J. Doris (Ed.), *The suggestibility of children's memory (with special reference to the child witness).* Washington, D.C.: American Psychological Association.

Zaragoza, M. S., Dahlgren, D., & Muench, J. (in press). The role of memory impairment in children's suggestibility. In M. L. Howe, C. J. Brainerd, & V. F. Reyna (Eds.), *The development of long-term retention.* New York: Springer-Verlag.

Zaragoza, M. S., & Koshmider, J. W., III. (1989). Misled subjects may know more than their performance implies. *Journal of Experimental Psychology: Learning, Memory, and Cognition, 15,* 246–255.

Zaragoza, M. S., & Lane, S. (1991, November). *The role of attentional resources in suggestibility and source monitoring.* Paper presented at the annual meeting of the Psychonomic Society, San Francisco, CA.

Zaragoza, M. S., & Lane, S. (1992). *Misinformation and memory impairment: Evidence from a modified free recall test.* Manuscript in preparation.

Zaragoza, M. S., & McCloskey, M. (1989). Misleading postevent information and the memory impairment hypothesis: Comment on Belli and reply to Tversky and Tuchin. *Journal of Experimental Psychology: General, 118,* 92–99.

Zaragoza, M. S., & Muench, J. (1989, November). *Source confusion following exposure to misleading postevent information.* Paper presented at the meeting of the Psychonomic Society, Atlanta, GA.

3   Understanding bystander misidentifications: The role of familiarity and contextual knowledge

J. Don Read

Misidentifications of innocent individuals in photospread lineups may arise from faulty assessments by eyewitnesses of their levels of perceptual or contextual knowledge about a target person. Eyewitness memory research has generally placed the burden of the responsibility for misidentifications on the first of these; that is, when witnesses have inadequate levels of perceptual knowledge. In contrast, for the "unconscious transference" type of misidentification it has been argued that an innocent bystander has been misidentified, not because perceptual knowledge or the sense of familiarity that arose from it was inadequate, but because the witness relied on this knowledge to the neglect of other, contextual, information. As a result, a level of perceived familiarity normally adequate for a *recognition* decision alone also served as the basis for an *identification* decision.

The present chapter maintains this distinction between recognition and identification decisions and asks what additional information accompanies the witness' shift from a recognition to an identification decision, and to what extent perceived familiarity is the basis for one or both of these decisions. Analyses of our subjects' responses collected prior to an identification task suggested that their misidentifications were based on a combination of perceived familiarity, contextual recall, and the use of conscious inferential processes that provided a rationale for the selection of the most plausible lineup member. In short, the identification task was perhaps seen by our subject-witnesses as a problem to be solved, one in which a decision was arrived at by assessing the relative plausibility as well as the relative similarity (compare Lindsay & Johnson, 1989; Wells, 1984; 1992) of each lineup member. As a result, the present research emphasizes the role of

This research was supported by grants to the author from the Alberta Law Foundation and the National Sciences and Engineering Research Council of Canada. The author wishes to thank Eileen McFadzen, Blaine Mohninger, and Laura Mensch for assistance in data tabulation and analysis, Troy Geisinger and Todd Schultz for serving as target and bystander, respectively, and to Steve Lindsay and David Ross for their valuable and constructive comments on an earlier draft of this chapter. Professor Robert Arms kindly allowed access to his class for experimental manipulations and testing.

retrieval as opposed to encoding processes in the misidentification of innocent bystanders.

The phenomenon of unconscious transference refers to a misidentification of an innocent person ("bystander") who had been previously seen by witnesses to a crime in a context different from the crime itself. However, in a series of field studies (Read, Tollestrup, Hammersley, McFadzen & Christensen, 1990) we concluded that oft-cited fears within the eyewitness testimony literature about this type of error may have been exaggerated (compare Kassin, Ellsworth, & Smith, 1989). Our arguments centered on our failure to produce the phenomenon in real world settings when the characteristics of the settings should have favored such misidentifications and should have closely resembled those forensic situations for which researchers have argued that unconscious transference is relevant. Specifically, in four of five studies, we failed to obtain such misidentifications despite high perpetrator–bystander similarity, identical physical environments, memorable interactions between perpetrator and witnesses, forensically reasonable retention intervals, and photospread lineups in which the bystander was the only previously seen member. In the final study, the frequency of bystander misidentifications was significantly higher for those participants who had previously seen the bystander (the Transference Condition) than for those who had not (Control Condition). However, even here the result was qualified by the fact that it occurred in only one type of lineup, one that was characterized by a relatively low level of similarity between the remaining foils and the perpetrator. In other words, the bystander was noticeably the most similar lineup member to the absent perpetrator, creating, in effect, a lineup of low functional size (see Brigham, this volume; Malpass & Devine, 1983; Wells, 1992). On the other hand, in a lineup that provided a higher overall level of similarity between foils and perpetrator and, therefore, a fairer lineup, misidentifications of the bystander were not elevated by prior exposure to him.

Nonetheless, an unconscious transference effect was obtained in the Read et al. research, a result that provided support for the anecdotal cases in the legal literature. The central concern of the present chapter is with the theoretical explanations that have been offered for the occurrence of unconscious transference errors. Historically, those explanations have focused on the notion of "unconscious" transfer of a person from one context to a different context or time. However, apart from recent work by Ross and his associates (Ross, 1990; Ross, this volume, 1992; Ross, Ceci, Dunning, & Toglia, 1991) and Read et al., there has been no discussion of what is intended by "unconscious." Williams (1955), who coined the term "unconscious transference," had little to say about whether witnesses were aware of any bases of their decisions. However, in discussions of the error since Williams, other writers appear to have assumed that at the time of a corporeal or photo lineup the witness responds on the basis of a sense of familiarity for any lineup member who has been previously seen (for example, Loftus, 1976, 1979; Shepherd, Ellis, & Davies, 1982). That is, prior exposure presumably produces resemblance knowledge from which a sense of familiarity arises. That experience and assessment of familiarity are then used, solely it would seem from the accounts, to make a lineup selection. Read et al. took exception to this model because it failed to distinguish between the processes of recognition and identification, at least as used by most cognitive psychologists and, as a result, allowed the inclusion of many laboratory recognition studies in the data base for what are identification decisions. The distinction is one that has been particularly well made by Mandler (1980) and highlights the difference between the responses of "have seen this person before" and "who this person is."

To argue that witnesses respond entirely on the basis of familiarity minimizes any role of the retrieval of contextual information (the circumstances and environments in which someone was observed) or the retrieval of any other information that the witness may have encoded with the perpetrator, for example, information about the uniqueness of some facial feature, the judgments the witness made of the perpetrator's voice and personality. However, current theory in cognitive psychology incorporates dual-process models of identification wherein a fast nonanalytic decision, based on familiarity or perceptual fluency, is accompanied or followed by an analytic, active retrieval search for some type of additional information to verify that this person is who we think it is (for example, Jacoby, Kelley, & Dywan, 1989; Mandler, 1980; Tiberghien, 1986). Similarly, current models of person identification explicitly make this argument, and anecdotal as well as systematic diary studies of face recognition failures make the same point (for example, Bruce, 1988; Bruce & Young, 1986; Young, Hay & Ellis, 1985). In short, most theoretical and empirical work on these kinds of decisions assumes cognitive processes beyond simple assessments of familiarity. However, a reading of the discussions of unconscious transference prior to Read et al. (1990) would lead one to conclude that witnesses respond entirely in a nonanalytic fashion. The inclusion of face-recognition research wherein multiple targets are presented in continuous yes/no recognition tests in discussions of person misidentification simply reinforced the view that familiarity assessments were all that mattered.

In no small way has the unfortunate labeling of a particular kind of misidentification as an error of "unconscious transference" contributed to the confusion. Because this label explicitly offers an explanation of cognitive process (that is, both unconscious and dynamic transfer of identity across contexts) this hypothesized process has often been considered synonymous with the simple observation of misidentification errors. To minimize such confusion, misidentifications of previously seen, hence familiar, but innocent persons will hereafter be called simply "bystander misidentifications."

In Experiment 5 of Read et al. several analyses were brought to bear on the issue of whether the participants' decisions could be seen to be the direct results of simple responses to familiarity or the result of more cognitively based decision processes. For one, familiarity judgments were collected to determine whether there might be a differential sense of familiarity experienced for a bystander and, if so, whether it was reliably related to his eventual identification as the perpetrator. This was indeed the case: Significant relationships existed between the identification–nonidentification decisions and the familiarity judgments assigned lineup members. A second analysis focused on the subjects' retrospective thoughts as to where the bystander might have been previously seen, whether identified as from the same or different context than the perpetrator. Subjects in the Transference Condition significantly more frequently recalled a context for the bystander than did the Control Condition subjects. Unfortunately, the tasks from which both of these types of information were collected, familiarity judgments and recall of contexts, always followed the identification task. As a result, Read et al. argued that the judgments and comments might well have been influenced by the prior identification decision; that is, perhaps subjects justified their commitments to their choices (compare Wells, 1984; Wells, Seelau, Rydell, & Luus, this volume) by such judgments. In keeping with this line of thought, Read et al. argued that bystander misidentifications might better be thought of as the results of a process of conscious inference than of unconscious transference.

To remedy the shortcomings of the earlier research and to clarify further the relationships between familiarity and identification decisions and between explicit retrieval processes and identification decisions, information should be collected on these matters prior to and, insofar as possible, independent of the identification decision. The present research thus extends our earlier work and asks a more general question: Given that a witness has a sense of familiarity for a person depicted in a lineup, *what additional information, if any, accompanies the witness' shift from a simple recognition "have seen before" response to an identification decision of the "that's the perpetrator" type?* A reading of the literature on bystander misidentification would suggest that the second follows inexorably from the first. In an exploration of the relationship between these two decisions, data relevant to the several explanations of the bystander misidentification effect offered by Ross (this volume) are also presented.

The experiment

The design closely followed Experiment 5 of Read et al. wherein student subjects were first exposed to a "perpetrator" and three weeks later received an identification test for him. However, for one half ($n = 85$) of the subjects (Transference Condition) exposure to a second individual was also arranged. This second individual, seen in one of their other university classes, was the "bystander." For the remaining Control Condition subjects ($n = 92$), exposure to the bystander was not arranged. The subjects were students in two large introductory psychology courses ($N = 177$) who, on the occasion of a midterm examination (same day, adjacent class hours), were introduced to a young male as the class assistant who would be, in part, responsible for marking examinations and course organization. This introduction and the perpetrator's activities were designed to capture the students' full attention. Over the next three weeks a second young man (the bystander) of similar general description attended other classes of approximately one-half of these students. At those classes, as in Read et al., the bystander engaged in a variety of activities from announcing the late arrival of an instructor to serving as a proctor and examination distributor. Of course, we could not guarantee that the bystander would be observed by every subject in these alternative classes because of attendance variability. Nor could we be assured that he would not be observed by Control Condition subjects in other situations on or off campus. With respect to the perpetrator, however, there were no other opportunities for him to be seen because he attended the university only on the day he was introduced and he then immediately departed for his home two hundred kilometers away. He was the identical perpetrator used in Read et al.'s Experiment 5 some eighteen months earlier. Unfortunately, the bystander from Read et al. was no longer available and a different bystander was obtained. He worked on campus but in a service facility unlikely to be visited by students and he had not attended school in the city. The classes of the remaining, Control Condition, students were not visited by the bystander.

Two assessments of the level of physical similarity between perpetrator and bystander were completed, one absolute, the other relative. For the first, fourteen students not enrolled in the introductory class rated on a five-point scale the level of similarity between the target or perpetrator and each foil, including the bystander. The scale ranged from "not at all similar" to "highly similar." Of the five members, the bystander received intermediate ratings ($M = 2.07$) among the five photos; however, none was considered more than marginally similar and differences between the five were nonsignificant by analysis of variance, $F (4, 52) = 1.52$. For the second, relative, assessment, each of eighteen subjects ranked the five lineup members in terms of their similarity to the perpetrator. Although the members differed significantly in their relative similarity rankings, three of the members including the bystander tied for being the "most" similar. In short, the bystander was judged to be neither highly similar nor most similar to the perpetrator.

On the identification test all students received first a six-choice (five foils plus a "not present" option) target-absent lineup in which the bystander was present but the target absent. Ross refers to this lineup construction as a bystander-present lineup. A second target-present lineup followed the first and included the perpetrator as well as four new foils. None of the remaining four foils in either lineup resided in the city of Lethbridge (site of the experiments) and thus would not have been seen previously by our subjects. For both lineups the option "not present in the lineup" was available and so indicated to subjects in the instructions. Choices made from both lineups were followed by judgments of confidence on five-point rating scales (from "not at all" to "very confident"). Apart from the replacement of the original bystander of Read et al. with the current bystander's photo, the lineups were identical to those used in the successful demonstration of bystander misidentification errors reported by Read et al.

What was unique about the test procedure however, was the collection of familiarity ratings and retrieval information prior to the identification tasks and prior to the instruction that the purpose of the task was to attempt an identification of the perpetrator, the class assistant introduced three weeks earlier. Specifically, three weeks after exposure, students were asked to take part in a research project. They were shown the target-absent lineup projected on a screen and asked to study the photos of the five people depicted. Two tasks followed. In the first, the familiarity judgment task, subjects assigned a rating of familiarity on a five-point scale ranging from "unfamiliar" to "very familiar" to each of the five faces. This task was prefaced by instructions that suggested that faces, regardless of prior exposure, can often evoke a sense of familiarity and that their job was to indicate the levels of any such senses of familiarity. Similar instructions have been used successfully by Vokey and Read (1988, 1992) to assess the structural or "context-free" familiarity of previously unseen male and female faces. The second task required subjects to indicate for each lineup member whether he had been "seen before" by a yes/no decision. If the answer was yes, subjects then provided on an adjacent line details of the context ("where seen?"), if known, in which the person had been seen. The identification task immediately followed these rating tasks and it was not until this time that the students were reminded of the class assistant's appearance three weeks earlier and were instructed to attempt an identification of him.

Finally, an additional between-subjects variable was used to partition the subjects in the Transference and Control Conditions. Because we reasoned that any kind of real world event witnessed by someone for which an identification test or lineup might follow would also be an event that would likely receive further thought and rehearsal by a witness, we added opportunities for the perpetrator and perpetrator event to be rehearsed or thought about during the retention interval (compare Read, Hammersley, Cross-Calvert, & McFadzen, 1989; Read, 1992; Turtle & Yuille, 1989). We predicted that if students were provided additional contextual information about the perpetrator during the retention interval, these students would be more likely to choose someone from a target-absent lineup. The notion here is that subjects might misattribute a sense of familiarity that arises from enhanced contextual knowledge to their perceptual or resemblance knowledge (see Jacoby et al., 1989) and, as a result, more frequently choose someone from a target-absent lineup. To enhance such contextual knowledge one class of students received information about the perpetrator from the instructor on four occasions: These comments often represented the perpetrator as an example of a particular psychological process discussed in class (for example, absent-mindedness) and, on occasion, he was the brunt of light humor. Because we assumed that such mentioning would in some way reinstate or call up memories of the perpetrator, this condition was referred to as the Retrieval Condition. In the Non-Retrieval condition the perpetrator was never mentioned during the retention interval. The success of this manipulation was abundantly evident at the time of the actual identification test because Retrieval Condition subjects knowingly nodded when the perpetrator's name was mentioned whereas the Non-Retrieval Condition subjects asked "who?" We save discussion of this variable until the end of our primary results.

Results

Misidentifications of the bystander and other foils

The 177 subjects made 81 misidentifications of a person in the target-absent lineup for the class assistant or perpetrator. This false identification rate of 45.8 percent corresponds well with that reported by other investigators in field identification studies (for example, Malpass & Devine, 1983; Read et al., 1990; Shapiro & Penrod, 1985). As a result, we obtained a corpus of misidentification errors that may be analyzed as to source: the four other foils or the bystander. Plotted in Figure 3.1 are the mean misidentifications of these two categories of lineup members. It is clear that the bystander was misidentified about four times as frequently as any of the foils. Analysis of this overall difference in selection frequency was significant, $F (1, 173) = 24.56$, $MSe = 0.109$, $p < .05$, the alpha level used throughout this research. As may be seen, there were significantly more misidentification responses in the Control ($M = 0.52$) than in the Transference ($M = 0.38$) Condition, $F (1, 173) = 3.98$, $MSe = 0.225$. The lower rate of bystander selections in the Transference ($M = 0.20$) than Control ($M = 0.26$) Condition did not, however, reach significance, $F = 1.01$. In short, we did not obtain evidence that our contrived observations of the bystander by the Transference Condition subjects selectively increased their rates of misidentification, a difference required to demonstrate unambiguously the bystander misidentification effect. Instead, subjects in the Transference Condition actually chose the bystander and foils less frequently than the Control Condition. This enhanced accuracy of the Transference Condition has also been previously reported by

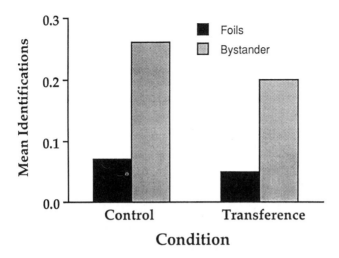

Figure 3.1: Mean misidentifications of foils and bystanders by subjects in the Control and Transference Conditions.

Read et al. and may reflect enhanced, rather than decreased discrimination of bystander and perpetrator in the Transference Condition.

Nonetheless, the large difference in the selection rates for bystander and foils shown in Figure 3.1 reveals an obvious and statistically reliable preference for the bystander that may well have been the result of both his experimental and uncontrolled nonexperimental appearances in and around campus. That is, perhaps he was seen by subjects in both conditions within many campus and community contexts including those that we arranged. We believe this explanation to be reasonable for three reasons: First, as we shall see, both conditions significantly more frequently recalled observing the bystander in campus and community contexts than any of the foils. Second, as described earlier, separate groups of subjects had not rated him most similar in appearance to the perpetrator and, therefore, his high selection rate is unlikely to be an artifact of physical similarity to the perpetrator. In fact, given the objectively low similarity ratings of all lineup members including the bystander, the conclusion of Read et al. that high similarity between target and bystander is important to the occurrence of bystander misidentification was not supported. It also occurred to us after the fact that the bystander may have been chosen because he perhaps best fit the nonphysical or physiognomic attributes of the perpetrator. That is, perhaps the bystander looked most like someone who could be a class assistant.[1] To assess this possibility an additional group of thirty-five students were asked to rank the lineup members in terms of the likelihood that they might serve as a class assistant, responsible for exam distribution and some marking of examination papers. Analyses of these data revealed no significant differences between the five members. Finally, a retrospective investigation of the bystander's activities before and during the three-week retention interval suggested that, despite our attempts to prevent it, he had in fact circulated rather widely through the small campus and community environments. Considering the rating data and the bystander's activities, we suggest that his high selection rate resulted from his greater familiarity to both Transference and Control Condition students by virtue of both his controlled and uncontrolled appearances on campus. As a result, we make no further distinction between the two experimental conditions and assume that both conditions had opportunities to observe the bystander. Before doing so, however, it is worth noting that the patterns of data within each of the subsequent analyses were highly similar across Control and Transference Conditions and in no cases were significant differences between them obtained. Indeed, more than we had originally thought, the research speaks to the misidentifications of previously seen and hence, familiar, persons. Whether the transference manipulation was successful is, in our view, not critical because what we have for analysis is a large corpus of misidentification errors that allows an investigation of the bases for their selection independent of the success of the experimental manipulation.

Relationships between familiarity, recognition, and identification judgments

The focus of the study was on the fate of lineup members in the bystander-present lineup for whom a sense of familiarity had been reported and, more important, on the fate of those members for whom a recognition or "seen before" decision had been made. For Ross (this volume), bystander misidentifications occur because an innocent person is confused with a perpetrator at the time of the event or encoding, forming a "blended" memory, one that is "coherent, but flawed." A misperception occurs whereby the witness believes that the two people are one and the same; this confusion occurs prior to an identification test (see Experiment 3, this volume). The result is a "blended" memory. Because our perpetrator and bystander had similar roles within highly similar contexts, such blending may perhaps occur and, as a result, bystander misidentifications would result. Indeed, if the bystander misidentifications are initially accompanied by reports that he had been seen in the classroom context, strong support for Ross's memory blending hypothesis of bystander misidentifications would be gained. If, however, this is not the case, the bystander misidentification error in our research might more logically be attributed to decision processes or problem solving at the time of retrieval as compared to blending of memories at the time of the encoding. There is no reason why under different and separate circumstances, both hypotheses might not be valid. First, we look at the overall relationships between the three tasks.

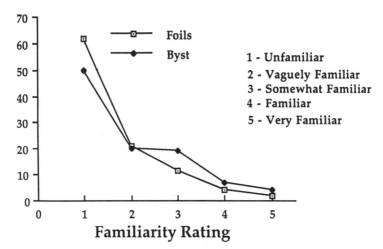

Figure 3.2: Distribution of familiarity ratings for foils and bystander in the bystander-present lineup.

In what follows data have been averaged and mean values presented for the four foils; however, these foils received familiarity and recognition judgments that demonstrated significant variability. Whereas all subjects responded to the various tasks, two subjects provided only partial data, having failed to rate each and every face. For this reason, the total numbers of observations on the rating tasks described later do not in every case match the number of subjects. First, for familiarity ratings, the distribution of responses on the five-point scale are presented in Figure 3.2 separately for the bystander and foils. As may be seen, the two distributions are highly similar in overall shape. However, a chi-square analysis of the frequency distributions revealed a significant difference [X^2 (4, $N = 877$) = 14.28].[2] This result was supported by analysis of variance across all subjects in which the bystander received a significantly higher overall mean familiarity rating ($M = 1.95$) than that given to the other foils ($M = 1.66$), F (1, 171) = 11.4, $MSe = 0.642$. When subjects were separated by their eventual identification responses (chose or did not choose someone), the bystander received higher familiarity ratings both by subjects who chose no one [F (1, 92) = 4.89, $MSe = 0.577$] and by those who chose him. In contrast, subjects who chose a foil gave approximately equivalent ratings to the bystander and the foil chosen, leading to a significant interaction term in the analysis of these "choosers," F (1, 171) = 6.40, $MSe = 0.722$. In line with the failure of the transference manipulation to produce more bystander misidentifications in the Transference than Control Condition, the mean familiarity ratings assigned the bystander by these conditions (1.83 and 2.00, respectively) were also not significantly different, F (1, 171) = 1.67.

Responses to the "Seen Before" or recognition task revealed that of the

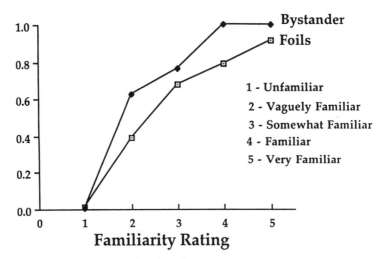

Figure 3.3: Relationships between familiarity rating and recognition ("seen before?") decisions for foil and bystander lineup members.

877 responses to photos, 221 or 25.2 percent received a yes response. With respect to the bystander face, 38.29 percent of the total subject sample responded yes whereas each of the other foils received an average of only 5.48 percent recognition responses. Thus, the bystander was positively recognized about seven times as frequently as other foils, on average. The average rate of the false recognitions of foils well matches that reported by Vokey and Read (1988, 1992). In agreement with their lower overall misidentification rate on the identification test, Transference Condition subjects also less frequently, but not significantly so, recognized the bystander (0.35) than subjects in the Control (0.41) Condition, $F < 1$. Across subjects, 33.3 percent of the total sample "recognized" no lineup members, 24.3 percent recognized one lineup member, 27.7 percent two members, 11.9 percent three, 2.8 percent four, and no subjects recognized all five members.

To assess the relationship between the familiarity ratings and recognition decisions, faces were separated as to whether they had or had not received a yes response to the "seen before" question. In Figure 3.3 are presented, for each rating, the proportions of total ratings that were followed by a positive recognition decision. The relationships are obvious and significant. When, for example, a face received a rating of "vaguely familiar" the overall probability of recognizing (that is, saying "have seen before") was about .5. On the other hand, a rating of "very familiar" virtually always meant a subsequent positive recognition decision. Based on group data, the correlation coefficients for the foil and bystanders were $r = .96$ and $r = .91$ (dfs = 4), respectively for these familiarity–recognition relationships. It would be surprising indeed if it were otherwise. Later, we look at the more controversial relationship between familiarity ratings and identification decisions.

Of those students who reported having seen a lineup member previously (a total of 221 such "recognitions" were reported) their responses to the subsequent "Where seen?" question were assigned to one of a number of categories including reports that the person had been seen in their introductory psychology class or some other class within the university. However, for only one foil and by only one subject was the context reported as the introductory psychology class: for the bystander, never. Similarly, in only two instances were foils recalled from another university class: the bystander, never. In these three instances, the subjects were members of the Control rather than Transference Condition. In short, despite our certainty that the majority of Transference Condition subjects had actually seen the bystander in one or more of their classes, he was never recalled from the psychology class context. At this point in the procedure, subjects were still unaware that the rating tasks were related to the class assistant seen twenty-one days earlier. Further, because no subjects placed the bystander within the psychology class context, a "memory blending" theory of misidentification gains little support from these data. Any subsequent assignment of the bystander to the psychology class itself on the identification task may be interpreted as an inference of plausibility made by subjects rather than a recollection from a blended memory. The virtual nonexistence of psychology class recalls is all the more striking given the physical retrieval environment: the same psychology class and classroom.

Figure 3.4 presents the total numbers of responses to the "where seen?" component of the recognition task for the bystander and the mean total numbers for the foils for all subjects who initially responded yes to the "seen before?" question. Overall, of all the foil "recognitions," only 13.63 percent were not accompanied by contextual recall. The comparable figure for the bystander was 16.47 percent. Thus, when a subject indicated that a lineup member had been previously seen, it was typically the case that a context was recalled in which the subject thought the person had been seen. As only the bystander had been available for observation within the university or community, the absolute rate of fallacious recalls is striking: On average, every subject "remembered" one context in which they reported seeing someone they could not have seen. The subjects' written responses were assigned to one of four "context" categories and were ordered in terms of decreasing specificity and/or increasing distance from the psychology class itself: within the university, within the community, external to the city of Lethbridge, or on television, etc., and finally, no context recalled. A chi-square analysis of these frequencies revealed no difference in the two distributions of the frequencies presented in Figure 3.4 [X^2 (3, $N = 105$) = 1.55].

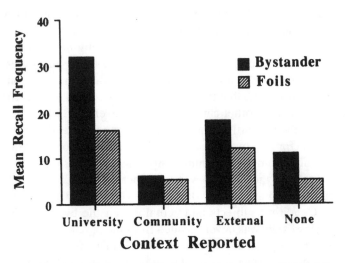

Figure 3.4: Mean frequency of different types of contexts recalled for foils and bystander. The four context categories are university, community, external to city or on television, and no information recalled.

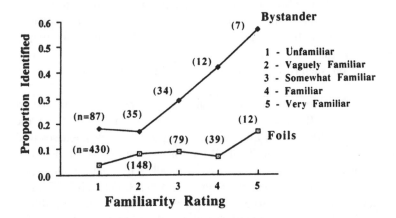

Figure 3.5. Proportion of lineup members subsequently identified as the perpetrator in the target-absent lineup. Proportions are presented as a function of prior familiarity rating and type of lineup member (foil or bystander). Values in brackets reflect the frequencies of persons rated at each level of familiarity.

Familiarity and identification. To assess the relationship between a familiarity rating assigned to a lineup member and his eventual likelihood of being identified, the proportion of times that an identification decision followed a specific familiarity rating was calculated separately for foils and bystander. The advantage of separating judgments in this way is that any overall difference in perceived familiarity for the foils and bystander is controlled. These data are presented in Figure 3.5. Also presented in the figure are the numbers of face ratings on which the identification rates are based. It is clear that the subjects treated foils and bystander very differently at the time of the identification task, regardless of familiarity rating. There was, as mentioned, a large and significant difference in favor of the bystander. As well, at every level of familiarity rating, the bystander was significantly more likely to be identified than a foil, $ts \geq 2.0$ (by significance tests of correlated proportions). Further, as familiarity ratings increased from unfamiliar to very familiar, bystander identifications diverged significantly from foil identifications, as tested by chi-square, X^2 (4, $N = 51$) = 12.20. This pattern is striking and, perhaps to a greater degree than any other data, suggests that the bystander was not selected merely because he was familiar: Foils rated as highly familiar were very rarely selected.

In other words, we did find misidentifications of a previously seen person (bystander) to be more frequent than those of previously unseen persons and, as a result, one may argue that the research provides support for a large bystander misidentification effect. Surprisingly, the greater likelihood of bystander over foil identification was not reflected in differential confidence ratings following identifications of the bystander ($M = 2.59$) and foils ($M = 2.43$), $F < 1$. Confidence ratings in identification did, however, increase significantly from faces rated low in familiarity ($M = 2.12$) to those rated highest ($M = 3.33$) in familiarity, F (4, 171) = 4.00, $MSe = 0.808$.

Among choosers the familiarity rating given to a subsequently identified person was significantly higher ($M = 2.20$) than to a face not identified ($M = 1.78$), F (1, 75) = 10.21, $MSe = 0.662$. When the familiarity ratings assigned a face were correlated with the identify/nonidentify decisions the point-biserial correlation coefficients were all weak ($-.10 \leq r$ values $\geq .21$) but achieved statistical reliability for one of the foils [r (df $= 176$) $= .20$] and the bystander, [r (df $= 176$) $= .21$]. The foil for whom this relationship held received the second highest mean familiarity rating but it did not differ significantly from the other foil means. It is noteworthy that all these correlations were consistently and substantially lower than those reported by Read et al. (that is, $.34 \leq r$ values $\geq .56$) which supports the argument that prior identification decisions likely inflated the relationship between the two variables in their study.

Recognition and identification. As mentioned, 221 of the 877 recognition opportunities were answered in the affirmative. Of these, only 36 (or 16.29 percent) were subsequently identified as the perpetrator. Of the 656 nonrecognitions, 45 (or 6.86 percent) were nonetheless subsequently identified. Although the difference in these proportions was significant [t (876) = 3.03] and a statistically reliable overall correlation between recognition and identification was obtained [r (df $= 876$) $= .07$], the predictability of this relationship is trivially small. Such unpredictability was also well demonstrated

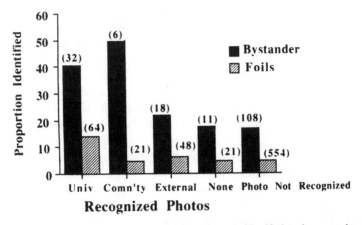

Recognized Photos

Figure 3.6: Proportion of "recognized" faces that were identified on the target-absent lineup. Proportions are provided as a function of type of contextual information recalled. The final data points represent the proportions of "nonrecognized" faces that were subsequently identified. Values in brackets reflect the frequencies of persons described by each form of contextual recall.

by the absence of significant correlations between these recognition and identification judgments calculated separately for each of the five lineup members. Only one was significant: for the bystander, r (176) = .18. Thus, when identification decisions are considered in the light of either prior familiarity ratings or prior recognition responses, they are related substantially to neither. Because familiarity ratings do predict recognition but not identification decisions, the relevance of face recognition studies to those of person identification may be questioned (compare Read et al., 1990).

Figure 3.6 presents the proportion of subjects who identified either the bystander or a foil as the perpetrator after having reported that they "recognized" the person. Once again, the preference for the bystander over the foils is evident. The identification rates are provided as a function of the context in which subjects recalled having seen the person in question: in the university, within the larger community, external to the community or no context recalled. At the right is the proportion of subjects who identified a foil or the bystander after they had first indicated that he had not been recognized. For the bystander, a positive identification was made following nonrecognition about 20 percent of the time. For a foil identification this occurred only about 5 percent of the time. Whereas these rates may appear low, their impact on the total number of misidentifications was substantial: As described, of the eighty-one total misidentifications, 55.6 percent followed subjects' responses that the identified lineup member had not, in fact, been previously seen. However, these weak relationships notwithstanding, when an identification was made, the mean confidence assigned the previously recognized lineup members (M = 2.81) was significantly higher than the confidence assigned faces that had not been previously recognized ($M =$ 2.25), $F (1, 76) = 6.73$, $MSe = 0.859$. At a minimum, despite their numerically more frequent identifications of persons they claimed not to have seen than those they had seen previously, subjects did discriminate between these two types of false positives (recognized versus not recognized) in their confidence ratings.

We saw earlier that a trivial but reliable relationship existed between familiarity and identification when all recognition judgments were included. If we consider only recognized persons, however, rated familiarity was significantly related to overall identification rates of bystander and foils [$F (2, 197) = 3.87$, $MSe = 0.124$]: Identifications increased with increased familiarity. This relationship was most obvious for the bystander, whose identification rate rose from .08 at low to .35 at intermediate, and to .47 at high familiarity (one cell with zero entries required a collapsing of the original five-point scale to a three-point familiarity scale). The comparable figures for the foils were .06, .12, and .10, and these different relationships led to a marginally significant interaction term, $F (2, 197) = 2.38$, $MSe = 0.124$, $p < .10$.

Many subjects ($n = 36$) did follow a positive recognition response with an identification decision. As indicated earlier most, but not all, recognitions were accompanied by the recall of contextual information so it is no surprise that contextual recall usually also preceded identification. Indeed, of those foils who were recognized and identified, only one of fourteen identifications (7.14 percent) had *not* been preceded by contextual recall. The comparable figure for the bystander was two of twenty-two (9.10 percent). These data are in agreement with the arguments of Read et al. that person identification is usually accompanied by recollection of context. This certainly appears to be the case when preceded by a recognition decision.

However, because 55.6 percent of the identifications followed nonrecognitions the argument may take one of two directions. On the one hand, the identification task and its instructions may have served as effective retrieval cues for contextual recall and, as a result, these identification responses perhaps similarly followed the retrieval, albeit covert, of contextual information. Alternatively, subjects may have responded simply to the demand characteristics of the testing situation and chosen someone in the absence of any contextual recall. Inspection of Figure 3.6 suggests that the true situation may be somewhere between these positions, because 20 percent of bystander nonrecognitions were followed by identification but only 5 percent of foil nonrecognitions were so followed, a rate difference between bystander and foils that matches approximately that found for both recognition and identification responses. Given the greater availability in memory of contextual information about the bystander than foils (because he had been present in the campus and community environment prior to and during the three-week retention interval), the difference in these rates suggests that subsequent access to such information may have contributed to identification for at least some subjects who initially failed to recognize the bystander.

Was the recall of contextual information critical to the identification of recognized persons? As may be seen in Figure 3.6, the identification rates following contextual recall were generally higher than the rates following no recall. Summing foils and bystander, these proportions were .18 and .08, respectively. The difference between these correlated proportions was significant by a one-tailed test [t (220) = 1.83]. Whereas the comparable comparison for the bystander alone (.36 and .18, respectively) was similarly significant [t (66) = 1.75], it was not for the foils [t (153) = 0.71]. In short, when a person who had been previously seen was recognized, identification was twice as likely when contextual information was recalled as when it was not.

Inspection of Figure 3.6 also reveals the large differences in the likelihood of making an identification for a lineup member (given his recognition) as a function of the type of contextual information recalled. Both chi-square and t-tests of differences between correlated proportions revealed that whereas the bystander was identified significantly more frequently than foils following contextual recall of university and community information [X^2s (1) $\geq$ 7.30; ts $\geq$ 2.54], the difference was only marginally significant when external information was recalled [X^2 (1, N = 66), $p < .10$], and nonsignificant when no information was recalled. Of interest is the pattern of declining identification rates as a function of decreasing specificity of context and increasing distance from the psychology class. In short, subjects were much less likely to identify a recognized person as the class assistant if the recalled context suggested a less plausible or, perhaps implausible, basis for his appearance in an introductory psychology class.

Finally, we also assessed the amount of contextual information retrieved by subjects about bystander and foils. To do so, the numbers of words provided in the answers to the "where seen?" question were tabulated on the simple (but, no doubt, questionable) assumption that the more specific a recalled context was, the greater the number of words required to describe it. For example, instead of responding "the university" to the "where seen?" question, some students may have said "in the gymnastics area of the university." Our hypothesis was that, in general, because he had actually been available for observation but the foils had not, the bystander would elicit more descriptive words than foils. Although the difference was small, this hypothesis was supported statistically because the mean number of words elicited by the bystander ($M = 2.21$) significantly exceeded that elicited by the foils ($M = 1.81$), t (220) = 2.10. Thus, not only were significantly more contexts recalled for the bystander than the foil, but as an imprecise index of contextual knowledge, more words were also recalled. Thus, whereas both the type and amount of contextual information were predictive of the likelihood of identification for the bystander, neither was predictive of identification for the foils.

To summarize, we obtained significantly more bystander than foil misidentifications and significantly higher identification rates at each level of familiarity and type of recalled context for bystander than foils. These results conflict with the claims of many earlier writers on bystander misidentification that perceived familiarity is the critical variable for determining whether someone is identified as the perpetrator. We saw from the correlational data that judged familiarity did not account for overall identification rates, and from Figure 3.5 it is clear that it also does not account for the large differences in identification rates of bystander and foils when familiarity is held constant. Read et al. argued that the retrieval of context is critical. We see in Figure 3.6 that the variable is indeed related to bystander identifications. On the other hand, recall of context apparently had little to do with foil identifications. For example, if a university context was recalled for the bystander, the identification rate was about .40. For the foils, however, the comparable identification rate was about .12 and this was about the same as for foils recalled from different contexts. In short, as was the case for familiarity, bystander identifications were related to the context recall variable but the foil identifications were not. Further comparisons of the proportions identified of the bystander and foil recognitions as a function of both familiarity rating and contextual retrieval considered together revealed no differences between the two kinds of lineup members.

Retrievability manipulation

The Transference and Control conditions had each been partitioned into two groups, one which received reminders about the class assistant and the other which received no reminders over the retention interval. The effect of this manipulation on the target-absent lineup identification was large: The Retrievability Conditions subjects were twice as likely (60 percent) to misidentify someone from the lineup as the Non-Retrieval Condition subjects (30 percent), $F(1, 73) = 18.36$, $MSe = 0.225$. The effects were not selective with regard to the bystander manipulation however. The rates of bystander choosing (as a percentage of all false positives made) were not significantly different in the Retrieval and Non-Retrieval conditions. This variable, as expected, had no impact on the three tasks preceding the identification because all the subjects were as yet unaware of the relationships between those tasks and the class assistant. However, the Retrieval manipulation did reduce the relationship between accuracy and confidence. Specifically, whereas the Non-Retrieval subjects demonstrated an overall significant relationship between accuracy and confidence on the target-absent lineup [r (df $= 85) = .35$], the Retrieval subjects did not [r (df $= 90) = .05$]. In contrast, there was no difference in the strength of this relationship between Transference [r (df = 84) = .26] and Control [r (df = 91) = .25] conditions. Thus, the rehearsal or retrieval manipulation increased their willingness to identify someone from the lineup but apparently reduced the extent to which the subjects' confidence ratings reflected their accuracy. Further analysis revealed that the Retrieval and Non-Retrieval conditions did not differ in the mean confidence ratings assigned their misidentifications (Ms = 2.46 and 2.53, respectively), F (1,92) = 7.52, MSe = 1.74. Read (1992) presents an extended discussion of the effects of similar "retrievability" manipulations on identification performance in a series of field studies.

Target-present lineup performance

Given the frequent misidentifications made by subjects in this study, it is reasonable to ask whether subjects had sufficient perceptual knowledge or resemblance information to identify the class assistant when he was actually present. Overall, the correct performance (hit rates) on the second, target-present, lineup were 65, 71, 60, and 69 percent for those subjects who selected on the first lineup, respectively, anyone, only the bystander, any foil, or none. As may be seen, overall performance was about 65 percent, a level that suggests neither a particularly easy nor a particularly difficult lineup decision. These figures match closely those reported in Experiment 5 of Read et al. with the identical perpetrator, retention interval, and target-present lineup. Finally, the results similarly mimic those of the earlier study with highest performance on the second lineup by those who originally chose none from the first lineup and lowest by those who chose a foil. In contrast, however, those who initially chose the bystander performed as well as those who chose none.

Discussion

The interpretation given to the misidentification errors in this research relies heavily on retrieval rather than encoding processes. Ross has offered three explanations for the bystander misidentification effect: automatic processing of events, difficulties in "source monitoring," and "memory blending" of the two people involved. Of these, the last two hold most promise. The first, automatic processing, suggests that bystander misidentifications occur because a witness's interactions with a bystander were encoded without effort or awareness but are elicited later from memory by the retrieval cue of the bystander at the identification test. In other words, the bystander is judged familiar but the witness can provide no retrieval information as to why the he might seem familiar. The anecdotal evidence lends little support to the automatic processing interpretation because it implies that witnesses would be unable to recall the circumstances of their prior encounters with the bystander, even when prompted to do so. There is simply no evidence as to whether they could or couldn't, did or didn't.

Of the remaining two explanations, however, Ross offers convincing evidence that memory blending can account for bystander misidentifications in his experimental paradigm. Specifically, Ross's subjects undoubtedly did confuse (or "blend") the bystander and perpetrator at the time of encoding because they were highly similar to one another in physical appearance, presented in a continuous video format (three minutes between exposures to bystander and perpetrator), and the video's story line supported such confusion. As a result, many subjects thought at the time of observing the perpetrator that he was the same person as the bystander seen with some children three minutes earlier. For Ross, "blending" appears to mean the conscious, intentional combination of two or more sources of information at the time of encoding but not necessarily a synthesis and amalgamation of those two memory representations with corresponding loss of their separate identities. Consequently, in his Experiment 4, given appropriate instructions, subjects were able to "unblend" the two sources when tested immediately after viewing the video clip. It would be particularly informative if this manipulation were attempted on a delayed test.

However, as compelling as these results are, Ross's experimental paradigm does not well simulate the circumstances and timing of real world events in which bystander misidentifications have been alleged to occur and for which the unconscious transference explanation has been invoked. At odds with these real world events are the durations separating the various encounters between witness and perpetrator and between witness and bystander, durations that would support independent memory and distinctive representations or traces of perpetrator and bystander and, accordingly, would reduce the likelihood that one person might be misperceived for another. From our perspective, bystander misidentifications in real world environments, as in the present research, are more likely to be generally interpretable from a source monitoring than memory blending position. According to a source monitoring perspective (for example, Lindsay, this volume, 1990; Lindsay & Johnson, 1989) identification errors occur because witnesses have difficulty discerning the source of one or more memory representations. More specifically, two memories may be difficult to distinguish one from the other if they are similar in quality (accessibility and vividness), or in content because they arose from similar sources, or because the objects, events, and persons to which they refer have similar characteristics. Against this backdrop of poor discriminability reflective cognitive processes are brought to bear on the problem. If a lineup member produces an above-threshold experience of familiarity and if his general physical characteristics match those of the perpetrator and if recalled contextual information provides a plausible basis for his selection, the subjects' experience of familiarity may be misattributed to the crime event (and viewing of the perpetrator). The bystander is then misidentified. A less active or reflective cognitive process could also be hypothesized that places all the responsibility for misidentification errors directly on source-monitoring difficulties (Lindsay, 1990). That is, we might assume that errors are made not because subjects consciously infer or reason their ways to the most plausible choices but are made instead because subjects' decisions simply reflect the difficulties of distinguishing memories from the same or highly similar sources. Because memories of persons recalled from university contexts (as indexed by the written contextual recall responses) were most similar to the subjects' memories of the perpetrator within the psychology class, subjects should have had greatest difficulty in making this discrimination and, accordingly, they chose persons remembered from a university context more frequently than persons remembered from outside that context. Although we cannot at this point distinguish between the more from the lesser inferential process, source monitoring has been assumed to include assessments of plausibility as well as similarity of content (Lindsay, this volume; Lindsay & Johnson, 1989, 1991). The plausibility of a particular person would be enhanced by his simple presence in a lineup.

In our view, the strongest evidence for such an inferential interpretation are some simple observations of the subjects' responses in the familiarity, recognition, and context recall tasks. First, whereas virtually all subjects reported that they had recognized at least one of the lineup members, for only one of these 221 recognitions was the introductory psychology class recalled as the location of the observation. If bystander misidentifications were the result of a memory blending process, one would expect that the bystander would serve as a retrieval cue for the context in which the blending had taken place. The absence of such recalls is all the more striking when it is remembered that the class itself served as the retrieval environment in which the tasks were completed and stands in contrast to the subjects' frequent "recalls" of these same persons in a variety of other contexts.

Further, of all those subjects who eventually identified someone as the class assistant, 55.6 percent did so after first failing even to recognize the person they chose. These identification responses were often given with mild confidence ($M = 2.25$, on a five-point scale, among those who did not first recognize the person) despite their seeming contradiction with the subject's performance on the immediately preceding tasks. It seems clear, therefore, that the introduction of identification test instructions defines the parameters within which a choice can be made and subjects readily adopt a decision strategy that results in a choice. That subjects were not simply responding to their assessments of familiarity alone seems certain, given the weak relationship noted earlier between familiarity rating and identification. Instead, the recalls of contextual information and an assessment of plausibility, not some unconscious response to familiarity, appear to have influenced their decisions. If this kind of memory performance is characteristic of target-absent lineups in the real world, the potential for a misidentification is indeed considerable and a source of real concern (see also Goldstein, Chance & Schneller, 1989; Wells, 1992). This fear would be reduced substantially, however, if investigatory procedures were developed that could make use of recognition information prior to identification decisions on the assumption that those witnesses who first failed to recognize a suspect would have greatly reduced credibility on the subsequent identification test. Obviously, the circumstances in which such a recognition test might occur would be infrequent but perhaps akin to a disguised showup procedure (Brooks, 1983). Similarly, altered lineup presentation procedures that reduce the role of relative judgments (of both similarity and plausibility) have shown dramatic reductions in misidentification rates (for example, Lindsay, Lea, & Fulford, 1991) and could be used in real world investigations.

In summary, we have argued that subjects approach the lineup identification as a problem to be solved. Problem solution appears to involve information gathered from a number of sources (that is, perceived familiarity, type and amount of recalled information) and an assessment of plausibility of a match between a particular lineup member and what little is known about the perpetrator. Perhaps Wells's (1984; 1992) notion of the "relative judgment" heuristic of physical similarity in lineup identifications should be extended to "relative plausibility," a judgment that can certainly weight relative similarity along with other information. From this perspective our retrievability manipulation may have been successful in generating more misidentifications because it provided subjects with more information (although not more accurate information) about the perpetrator by which a match could be made. In this vein as well, Ross's testing procedure is seen to provide each and every subject with a critical piece of information: the context in which the bystander was seen. Based on our results, his high rates of bystander misidentifications are not surprising. With the identification test's provision of contextual information, the problem became considerably easier to solve for subjects in the transference condition. In any event, the idea that bystander misidentifications reflect an unconscious transference of identities or of unconscious responses to familiarity has gained no support from the present research.

Notes

1 Steven Lindsay and Michael Masson suggested this useful analysis.
2 Because more than one data point was provided by subjects the assumption of independence of observations for chi-square has been violated by these tests. Accordingly, their outcomes should be treated with caution. Where appropriate, the use of *t*-tests of differences between correlated proportions were used to assess differences in identification rates for bystanders

and foils to reflect the frequent, but not consistent, contribution of the same subjects to both proportions.

References

Brigham, J. C., & Pfeifer, J. E. (1992). Evaluating the fairness of lineups. In D. F. Ross, J. D. Read, & M. P. Toglia (Eds.), *Adult eyewitness testimony: Current trends and developments.* New York: Cambridge University Press.

Brooks, N. (1983). *Police guidelines: Pretrial identification procedures.* Ottawa: Law Reform Commission.

Bruce, V. (1988). *Recognising faces.* Hove, Sussex: Lawrence Erlbaum Associates.

Bruce, V., & Young, A. (1986). Understanding face recognition. *British Journal of Psychology, 77,* 305–327.

Goldstein, A. G., Chance, J. E., & Schneller, G. R. (1989). Frequency of eyewitness identification in criminal cases. *Bulletin of the Psychonomic Society, 27,* 71–74.

Jacoby, L. L., Kelley, C. M., & Dywan, J. (1989). Memory attributions. In H. L. Roediger & F. I. M. Craik (Eds.), *Varieties of memory and consciousness: Essays in honour of Endel Tulving.* Hillsdale, N.J.: Erlbaum.

Kassin, S., Ellsworth, P. C., & Smith, V. L. (1989). The "General Acceptance" of psychological research on eyewitness testimony: A survey of the experts. *American Psychologist, 44,* 1089–1098.

Lindsay, D. S. (1992). Memory source monitoring and eyewitness testimony. In D. F. Ross, J. D. Read, & M. P. Toglia (Eds.). *Adult eyewitness testimony: Current trends and developments.* New York: Cambridge University Press.

Lindsay, D. S. (1990). Misleading suggestions can impair eyewitnesses' ability to remember event details. *Journal of Experimental Psychology: Learning, Memory and Cognition, 16,* 1077–1083.

Lindsay, D. S., & Johnson, M. K. (1989). The eyewitness suggestibility effect and memory for source. *Memory & Cognition, 17,* 349–358.

Lindsay, D. S., & Johnson, M. K. (1991). Recognition memory and source monitoring. *Bulletin of the Psychonomic Society, 29,* 203–205.

Lindsay, R. C. L., Lea, J. A., & Fulford, J. A. (1991). Sequential lineup presentation: Technique matters. *Journal of Applied Psychology, 76,* 741–745.

Loftus, E. F. (1976). Unconscious transference in eyewitness identification. *Law and Psychology Review, 2,* 93–98.

Loftus, E. F. (1979). *Eyewitness testimony.* Cambridge, MA: Harvard University Press.

Malpass, R. S., & Devine, P. G. (1983). Measuring the fairness of eyewitness identification lineups. In S. M. A. Lloyd-Bostock & B. Clifford (Eds.), *Evaluating witness evidence* (pp. 81–102). London: Wiley.

Mandler, G. (1980). Recognising: The judgement of previous occurrence. *Psychological Review, 87,* 252–271.

Read, J. D. (1992). The availability heuristic in eyewitness memory: The misleading consequences of enhanced contextual information. In preparation.

Read, J. D., Hammersley, R. H., Cross-Calvert, S., & McFadzen, E. (1989). Rehearsal of faces and details in action events. *Applied Cognitive Psychology, 3,* 295–311.

Read, J. D., Tollestrup, P., Hammersley, R., McFadzen, E., & Christensen, A. (1990). The unconscious transference effect: Are innocent bystanders ever misidentified? *Applied Cognitive Psychology, 4,* 3–31.

Ross, D. V., Ceci, S. J., Dunning, D., & Toglia, M. P. (1992). Unconscious transference and lineup identification: Toward a memory blending approach. In D. F. Ross, J. D. Read, & M. P. Toglia (Eds.), *Adult eyewitness testimony: Current trends and developments.* New York: Cambridge University Press.

Ross, D. F. (1990). Unconscious transference and mistaken identity: When a witness misidentifies a familiar but innocent person from a lineup. Unpublished doctoral dissertation, Cornell University, January.

Ross, D. F., Ceci, S. J., Dunning, D., & Toglia, M. P. (1991). Unconscious transference and mistaken identity: When a witness misidentifies a familiar but innocent person from a lineup. Paper presented at the American Psychological Society, Washington, D.C., June.

Shapiro, P. N., & Penrod, S. (1986). Meta-analysis of facial identification studies. *Psychological Bulletin, 100,* 139–156.

Shepherd, J. W., Ellis, H. D., & Davies, G. M. (1982). *Identification evidence: A psychological evaluation.* Aberdeen: Aberdeen University Press.

Tiberghien, G. (1986). Context effects in recognition memory of faces: Some theoretical problems. In H. D. Ellis, M. A. Jeeves, F. Newcombe, & A. Young (Eds.), *Aspects of face processing* (pp. 88–104). NATO ISI Series, Series D: Behavioural and Social Sciences–No. 28, Dordrecht: Nijhoff.

Turtle, J. W., & Yuille, J. C. (1989). Can repeatedly remarking on an event lead to a "remarkable" eyewitness memory? Paper presented at the Canadian Psychological Association, Halifax, June.

Vokey, J. R., & Read, J. D. (1988). Typicality, familiarity and the recognition of male and female faces. *Canadian Journal of Psychology, 42,* 489–495.

Vokey, J. R., & Read, J. D. (1992) Familiarity, memorability and the effect of typicality on the recognition of faces. *Memory & Cognition, 20,* 291–302.

Wells, G. L. (1984). The psychology of lineup identifications. *Journal of Applied Social Psychology, 14,* 89–103.

Wells, G. L. (1993). What do we know about eyewitness identification? *American Psychologist, 48,* 553–571.

Williams, G. (1955). *The proof of guilt: a study of the English criminal trial.* London: Stevens and Sons.

Young, A. W., Hay, D. C., & Ellis, H. D. (1985). The faces that launched a thousand slips: Everyday difficulties and errors in recognizing people. *British Journal of Psychology, 76,* 495–523.

4 Unconscious transference and lineup identification: Toward a memory blending approach

David F. Ross, Stephen J. Ceci, David Dunning, and
Michael P. Toglia

In 1983 Lenell Geter was given a life sentence for a series of armed robberies that he did not commit. After serving eighteen months in prison, he was released when new evidence revealed that another man committed the crimes. An investigation into the case showed that the prosecution's key witness had made a tragic error. The police had shown the witness a photo lineup shortly after the crime occurred. At that time the witness reported that the assailant was not present in the lineup. Several months later the same witness was shown another lineup. It contained five photographs, four new photographs, and one photograph that had been present in the first lineup. The witness selected the "old" or "familiar" photograph, and the person in the photograph was Lenell Geter. Apparently the witness did not remember having seen Geter's photograph in the first lineup, and as a result she incorrectly associated its familiarity with the crime, and made a false identification (Buckhout, 1984). In a similar case, a ticket agent in a railroad station was the victim of an armed robbery (Houts, 1963; Loftus, 1976; Read, Tollestrup, Hammersley, McFadzen, & Christensen, 1990). From a police lineup the ticket agent identified a sailor who had proof that he could not have been at the station at the time of the robbery. When questioned as to why he misidentified the sailor, the ticket agent claimed the sailor looked familiar to him. An investigation discovered that the sailor lived near the train station, and had purchased tickets from the agent at three different times prior to the robbery. The ticket agent had clearly seen the sailor before but did not remember him as a customer.

The above cases illustrate "unconscious transference" (Buckhout, 1974; Houts, 1956; Loftus, 1976; Read et al., 1990; Ross, Ceci, Dunning, & Toglia, 1991; Williams, 1963) which is defined as the inability of an eyewitness to distinguish between a familiar but innocent person and an assailant observed at the scene of a crime or in some other context. When presented with a lineup that contains a familiar person, frequently a bystander, a witness may incorrectly associate the familiarity of the bystander with the crime, and make a false identification. The term "unconscious" implies that the witness has no conscious recollection of prior exposure to the bystander (Ross et al., 1991). Read et al. (1990) define the concept as "the transfer of one person's identity to that of another person from a different setting, time, or context" (p. 3).

The purpose of this chapter is fourfold. First, to review the literature on unconscious transference. Second, to provide three different theoretical perspectives on how unconscious transference occurs. Third, to report five experiments that we conducted to demonstrate the existence of unconscious transference and to explain how it occurs. Fourth, to respond to Don Read's (this volume) view of this phenomenon.

Unconscious transference: A review of past research

To date, there are only a handful of studies on unconscious transference and the findings are mixed, providing weak and inconsistent support for the existence of unconscious transference. In the first known study on this topic, college students were exposed to a staged assault on a professor (Buckhout, 1974). Seven weeks later subjects were asked to identify the attacker from a photo lineup that contained the attacker, a bystander who was observed by the subjects at the crime scene but who was not involved in the attack, and four unfamiliar foils. Only 40 percent of the subjects correctly identified the attacker. Of the 60 percent who were incorrect in their identification, 41 percent misidentified the bystander revealing a potentially provocative tendency toward unconscious transference. These results are difficult to interpret, however, because of the failure to include a control group who saw the same crime and were given the same lineup, but were not exposed to the innocent bystander.

In another study college students listened to an audiotape of a crime (Loftus, 1976). Photographs taken from a high school yearbook were used to illustrate the characters in the story. Three days later subjects were asked to identify the assailant from one of two lineups that contained the assailant and four unfamiliar faces, or four unfamiliar faces and one face of an innocent bystander who was seen in the story. When the assailant was in the lineup, 84 percent of the subjects correctly identified him. However when the bystander was in the lineup, 76 percent of the subjects were incorrect in their identification, and 60 percent of these subjects misidentified the familiar bystander. One problem with the study is that facial photographs were used to illustrate the characters in the story. Because the characters were not seen engaged in a behavior or activity, this denied subjects exposure to contextual information, that if available, may have increased recognition accuracy and perhaps eliminated the effect. Research has shown that contextual information is often incorporated into our memories of others, and used in the identification process (Davies & Milne, 1982; Memon & Bruce, 1985; Read et al., 1990; Davies & Thompson, 1988).

More direct support for unconscious transference was found in a study in which an electrician (the assailant) interrupted a class to fix an electrical problem (Read et al., 1990, Experiment 5). Prior to the event, transference subjects were exposed to a bystander who was seen in a context outside the classroom (distributing exam material in another class); control subjects were not exposed to the bystander. Two weeks later subjects were asked to identify the assailant from a photo lineup that contained the bystander and four unfamiliar foils. Twenty-five percent of the transference subjects misidentified the bystander, as compared with only 12 percent of the control subjects. Moreover, 13 percent of the transference subjects who had seen the bystander and misidentified him thought the bystander and the assailant were the same person seen in two different places, a process Read refers to as "conscious inference." Although a conscious inference process may explain why a small percentage (6/26 or 23 percent) of the transference subjects misidentified the bystander, it is not apparent what caused the remaining subjects in the transference condition to misidentify him.

In a study with similar results two "criminals" handed out a test or answer sheet to college students on a day of an examination (Brown, Deffenbacher, Sturgill, 1977). Three days after the exam students were asked to identify the criminals from eleven mug shots containing one criminal and ten unfamiliar foils. Four days later subjects were shown a live lineup containing four people: *criminal with a mug shot* – this person handed out exam materials and was seen in the first lineup; *criminal without a mug shot* – this person handed out exam materials but was not seen in the first lineup; *bystander with mug shot* – this person was not a criminal, but was seen in the first lineup; and *lineup only* – foils who were seen only in the second lineup. Subjects were accurate at identifying the criminal whose mug shot was seen in the first line up. Even if subjects were able to identify the criminal, however, they were performing at chance in reporting whether the criminal handed out the exam or answer sheet. More important, the innocent bystander whose mug shot was seen in the first lineup was as likely to be identified in the second lineup as the criminal whose mug shot was not shown previously. Also, the familiar bystander was misidentified more often than the lineup-only foils who were unfamiliar to the subjects. Brown et al. (1977) concluded from this work that "we would tend to distrust indictments in situations such as those where witnesses had previously seen the suspects' mug shots" (p 316). The idea is that once a mug shot has been seen the witness is likely to recognize the same mug shot if it is presented in another lineup, and its familiarity should increase the likelihood it will be misidentified. Similar results are reported by Peters (1985).

Another problem facing the bystander is that, once he or she is misidentified it is unlikely that witnesses will change their identification even if they are later shown a lineup that contains the actual assailant (Gorenstein & Ellsworth, 1980). For example, in a study by Loftus and Greene (1980) subjects were shown a photograph of a group of people at a party and read a narrative about the picture that contained misleading information (indicating the main character in the picture had a mustache when he did not), or no misleading information (the same narrative with no reference made to the mustache). Subjects were asked to identify the main character or "assailant" from a lineup that contained several foils, each with a mustache. Because the assailant was not present in the lineup subjects were forced to make a misidentification. Several days later subjects who received misleading information and earlier had misidentified a foil with a mustache, were shown another lineup that contained the person they misidentified from the first lineup, the main character or "assailant," and other foils. Approximately 89 percent of the misled subjects selected the same mug shot that they misidentified in the first lineup, even though the assailant was in the lineup.

In a similar study an "assailant" interrupted a college class claiming her wallet was left in the room, and she wanted to come in and look for it (Gorenstein & Ellsworth, 1980). Twenty-five minutes after the event some of the students in the class were asked to identify the assailant from a lineup. Because the assailant was not in the lineup subjects were forced to make a misidentification. Five days later subjects were asked to identify the assailant from another lineup that contained the person they misidentified from the first lineup, the assailant, two individuals who were seen in the first lineup but were not selected, and two unfamiliar foils. The results showed that 44 percent of the subjects misidentified the same person they selected in the first lineup, even though the assailant was in the lineup. Only 17 percent of the control subjects, who were in the class but not given the first lineup, misidentified these same lineup foils.

Why does this occur? Why do witnesses continue to misidentify a familiar bystander when they are later shown a lineup that contains the assailant? First, witnesses may be reluctant to change their identification because they feel obligated to be consistent in their testimony, a tendency referred to as a "commitment effect" (Gorenstein & Ellsworth, 1980; Wells, 1984). Second, once witnesses misidentify the bystander, the memory of the bystander may overwrite, impair, or render inaccessible the original memory of the assailant (Loftus, 1981).

There are, however, researchers who have gone in search of unconscious transference and found no evidence for the phenomenon. In sharp contrast to the findings described above, in a series of studies Read et al. (1990, Experiments 1–4) found little or no support for unconscious transference. In several studies clerks working in a shopping mall interacted with an "assailant" who requested twenty quarters in change for a five dollar bill. Clerks assigned to the transference condition also interacted with a bystander who asked, for example, if the clerk had seen his wife and child. Clerks assigned to the control condition interacted with the assailant, but did not interact with the bystander. When asked to identify the assailant from a lineup that contained the bystander and four unfamiliar foils, transference clerks who had seen the bystander were less likely to misidentify him than control clerks who had not seen the bystander. Apparently the clerks in the transference condition remembered the bystander all too well and quickly eliminated him as an option in the lineup. Although these findings were weak in magnitude they held regardless of retention interval (five levels were examined ranging from twenty minutes to two weeks), and timing of the exposure to the bystander (in some conditions the bystander and assailant were seen on the same day, whereas in other conditions the bystander was seen before or after exposure to the assailant).

Read et al. (1990) concluded on the basis of their research that it is very unlikely that unconscious transference will occur in actual criminal trials for a number of reasons. First, unconscious transference was not observed when aspects of the study closely resembled those found in real cases, for example, when the assailant and witness interact directly. Second, it is unlikely that a witness would recognize a bystander without recalling where the bystander was encountered, thus immediately rejecting the bystander as a potential lineup choice. Read et al. (1990) argued this point on the basis of the Encoding Specificity Principle (Tulving & Thompson, 1973) and several reviews of the face recognition literature (Davies & Milne, 1982; Memon & Bruce, 1985) that indicate contextual information, such as where we encountered someone we meet for the first time, is automatically encoded into memory and used in the face identification process.

Although the findings of Read et al. contradict those reported earlier, they can be explained in terms of a Trace Strength Model of Memory (Ceci, Ross & Toglia, 1987; Ceci, Toglia, & Ross, 1988). The idea is that unconscious transference is unlikely to occur when the strength of the memory trace for the bystander and the assailant is very weak or very strong. First, if the bystander and the assailant are seen by the witness for a long period of time, a misidentification is unlikely because the memory for both individuals is very strong, and the witness should be able to distinguish one from the other. This may have occurred in the Read et al. study when the shopping mall clerks remembered the context in which the bystander was encountered and quickly determined that he was familiar but innocent, and therefore rejected him as a potential lineup choice. Second, if the bystander and the assailant are seen for a short period of time, a misidentification is unlikely because the memory trace for the bystander may be too weak to support subsequent retrieval when the bystander is seen in the lineup, and as a result, the bystander may not appear familiar to the witness. Third, one of several situations in which unconscious transference is very likely to occur is when the memory trace for the bystander and the assailant is moderate and equal in strength. In this case the witness should recognize the bystander when seen in the lineup, but the memory is not sufficiently detailed and is void of contextual tags, thus allowing the possibility that the witness may incorrectly associate the familiarity of the bystander with the crime. Therefore the strength of the memory trace for the bystander and the assailant appears to be critical to understanding when unconscious transference will and will not occur.

In summary the literature provides mixed support and somewhat weak support for the existence of unconscious transference. Laboratory studies constitute the bulk of research in this area. These studies, which are convincing yet lacking in ecological validity, indicate that when witnesses are shown a lineup that contains a familiar bystander, the bystander is more likely to be recognized than any other innocent but unfamiliar individual. If the bystander is seen as familiar, but not so familiar that witnesses can remember the original encoding context, a misidentification is probable, in part because witnesses assume that the assailant is in the lineup and the familiarity of the bystander is used to confirm their expectation.

In support of this contention Wells and Turtle (1986) report that police rarely, if ever, intentionally construct a blank lineup that does not contain a suspect. Perhaps witnesses are aware of this fact. In the mind of a witness, why would police have a lineup unless a suspect is present? Therefore a misidentification is likely to occur because witnesses are placed in a situation where they think the assailant is present in the lineup; they search for information to confirm their expectation (Nisbett & Ross, 1980); and there is an implicit demand on them to make an identification. Consistent with this view are findings from studies that present blank lineups (where the assailant is absent) to adults. These studies typically report very high rates of false identifications, ranging from 81 to 93 percent (Malpass & Devine, 1981; Egan, Pittner, & Goldstein, 1977; Buckhout, Alper, Chern, Silverberg, & Slomovits, 1974; Loftus, 1976; Wells & Turtle, 1986). Moreover once a misidentification does take place it is unlikely that witnesses will change their lineup identification, even if later shown a lineup that contains the assailant. This may happen because witnesses feel obligated to be consistent in their testimony (Wells, 1984; Gorenstein & Ellsworth, 1980), and because, as a result of repeated exposure, the memory for the bystander may overwrite, replace, distort, or render inaccessible the memory for the assailant (Loftus, 1981).

What is not clear from this line of research is what causes a sense of familiarity for the bystander, and how it leads to a misidentification. To answer these questions, we outline below three theoretical approaches that explain how unconscious transference might occur, and then examine these accounts in a series of five experiments.

Theoretical approaches to unconscious transference

Three theoretical approaches can be articulated to account for unconscious transference: automatic processing, source monitoring, and memory blending.

Automatic processing

Historically, the unconscious component of this phenomenon refers to the witness having no awareness of the previous encounter with the innocent bystander prior to misidentifying him or her in the lineup (Loftus, 1976; Read et al., 1990; Ross et al., 1991). The memory of the bystander is presumably formed automatically or incidentally, with little or no effort on behalf of the witness (Hasher & Zacks, 1979; Posner & Snyder, 1975). As seen in the case described above, the ticket agent made three sales to the sailor, observed him in passing as just another customer, and paid no special attention to him. The ticket agent had no conscious memory that the sailor was one of his customers. The presence of the sailor in the lineup, however, served to evoke the unconsciously stored memory, making him appear familiar to the ticket agent and thus enhancing the likelihood that he would be misidentified.

According to Hasher and Zacks (1979) automatic processing is responsible for the encoding of basic information central to our ability to monitor everyday experience, including temporal sequence, spatial location, and the frequency with which events occur. It takes place continually without attention or awareness; it does not disrupt conscious memorial processes such as rehearsal; it is thought to be hard-wired or genetically based and therefore not varying by age; and it is not influenced by environmental factors such as stress or practice. Information acquired through automatic processing can be called into consciousness and used in a variety of ways, thereby acting as a retrieval cue to enhance recognition and recall memory. Hasher and Zacks (1979) give a common example of losing one's keys. In an attempt to find the keys we retrace our steps to the last place where the keys were seen, and the mental map we follow is thought to have been encoded automatically because no conscious effort was made to remember the sequence of events at the time they were experienced. In sum, this approach argues that past experience (such as exposure to an innocent bystander) can influence memory and behavior without conscious awareness of the past experience (see Richardson-Klavehn, 1988 for an excellent review). One difficulty in applying this conceptualization to the ticket agent example is that facial processing may not be as completely under the control of automatic processing as are frequency information, temporal order, and spatial lay outs.

Source monitoring

A source monitoring approach is based on the work of Marcia Johnson, Steve Lindsay, and their colleagues (Johnson & Raye, 1981; Lindsay & Johnson, 1989; 1990; Lindsay, Johnson, & Kwon, 1991; Lindsay, this volume). This approach suggests that a more deliberate or conscious memorial process could also explain how a witness could misidentify a familiar bystander from a lineup. For example, a witness may consciously remember having encountered the bystander and the assailant and is aware that they are two different individuals who look alike, but he or she may confuse the two memories at the time of retrieval when asked to identify the assailant from the lineup. This is referred to as a source monitoring problem because the witness recognizes the bystander in the lineup, but then attributes his familiarity to the memory of the crime (the wrong source), and misidentifies the bystander.

The misattribution of the bystander's familiarity occurs because the memory for the assailant and the bystander share many attributes in terms of contextual features (perhaps both individuals were seen in the same general area) and physical features (perhaps both individuals look very similar in appearance), thus making the two memories difficult to distinguish (Lindsay & Johnson, 1990). Applied to the case described above, one possible scenario is that the ticket agent informs the police that the assailant looks very similar in appearance to one of his customers, and that he has doubts whether he can distinguish one from the other. Nonetheless, the ticket agent agrees to view the lineup and subsequently misidentifies the innocent sailor.

Steve Lindsay (this volume) points out that our use of the term "source monitoring" is more narrow and specific than his use of the term. Moreover, Lindsay suggests (personal communication) that perhaps the term "deliberate source monitoring" is a more adequate description for the source monitoring approach to unconscious transference that is described here.

Memory blending

A third explanation for how an eyewitness could misidentify a familiar bystander from a lineup is that the witness remembers having seen the assailant and the bystander, but thinks that they are the same person. This approach is based on the work of Beth Loftus and her colleagues (Loftus, Donders, Hoffman, & Schooler, 1989). For example, in the ticket agent case, one possible scenario is that the robber may have appeared highly familiar to the ticket agent at the time of the robbery because of his similarity to the sailor whom he had seen several times prior to the robbery. If the ticket agent had a conscious memory of the sailor, he could easily infer that the sailor and the robber were the same person. The robber's face may serve as an effective retrieval cue for the memory of the sailor. As a result, the ticket agent could have told the police that the robber was a former customer who had bought tickets from him on three occasions prior to the robbery. This approach to unconscious transference is referred to as memory blending because the witness uses new information (the image of the assailant) and old information (the memory of the bystander) to form a coherent, but flawed, memory of the crime (see Loftus and Doyle, 1989, for a review of research in memory blending).

In sum, the traditional automatic processing approach argues that the witness is unaware of the previous encounter with the bystander. However, the presence of the bystander in the lineup serves to evoke the unconsciously stored memory of the bystander, making him or her appear familiar to the witness, thus enhancing the likelihood that he or she will be misidentified. A source monitoring approach argues that the witness consciously remembers the bystander and the assailant as different individuals, but confuses the two memories because they share many of the same physical attributes. Finally, a memory blending approach argues that the witness remembers having seen both the assailant and the bystander, but thinks they are the same person.

To understand how unconscious transference occurs, witnesses can be asked contextual questions such as "who did what and where" to determine whether a bystander misidentification is due to automatic processing (that is, the witness reports having no conscious memory for the encounter with the bystander, yet misidentifies him or her in the lineup), source monitoring (that is, the witness reports having a separate memory for the bystander and the assailant, but confuses the memory of one with the other), or memory blending (that is, the witness thinks the assailant and the bystander are the same person seen in two different places). We take this approach in the five studies outlined below. Only a limited number of the experimental conditions are reported due to space limitations. For a more detailed description of these experiments, see Ross et al. (1992).

EXPERIMENT 1

In Experiment 1 college students were asked to watch and give their reactions to a film on teacher education. The film consisted of a number of short segments showing teachers interacting with children. At the end of the film a female teacher enters a cafeteria to take a break, and while in the cafeteria she is robbed. Everyone in the study saw the same film with one exception. Subjects assigned to the transference condition saw a male bystander reading a story to a group of children several minutes before the robbery scene. Subjects assigned to the control condition did not see the bystander; they saw the female teacher who was the victim of the robbery reading to the children. Therefore, everyone in the study saw the crime and the assailant, but only

Table 4.1. *Identification accuracy by condition and lineup instruction: Bystander in Lineup*

Condition	Byst	Foil	Nil	D.K.
Transference	60.9%*	5.4%	33.7%*	0.0%*
Control	21.9%	8.2%	64.4%	5.5%

$\chi^2(3) = 27.7, p < .05$
*Percentage of subjects who picked the bystander (Byst), another foil (Foil), indicated not in lineup (Nil), or said don't know (D.K.) when presented with a lineup with the bystander and four unfamiliar foils.
Sample size: Transference = 92, Control = 73.

the transference subjects saw the bystander. For subjects in the transference and control condition the assailant and the bystander were both seen for approximately thirty-four seconds. Moreover, the bystander was seen only once in the preschool reading to the children, and the assailant was seen only once in the cafeteria where the crime took place.

The film ended immediately after the crime scene and the experimenter explained that the study was really about eyewitness memory and how well people can recall crimes they have observed unexpectedly. Approximately three to five minutes later subjects were asked to identify the assailant from a lineup that contained the bystander and four unfamiliar foils. With this design it is possible to determine whether subjects in the transference condition, who saw the bystander in the film reading to the children, are more likely to misidentify the bystander than subjects in the control condition, who did not see the bystander in the film.

As seen in Table 4.1, when asked to identify the assailant from a target-absent lineup that contained the bystander and four other foils, transference subjects who saw the bystander reading to the children in the preschool were nearly three times more likely to misidentify the bystander than control subjects, who did not see the bystander in the film (60.9 percent versus 21.9 percent, $z = 5.0, p < .001$). As a result, transference subjects were also less likely than control subjects to respond correctly that the assailant was not in the lineup (33.7 percent versus 64.4 percent, $z = 3.9, p < .001$).

To understand how unconscious transference occurs, after viewing the lineup subjects were asked three context questions concerning "who did what and where in the film." First, was the assailant seen in any place in the film other than in the cafeteria where the crime took place? And if so, where and what was he doing? Second, were any male preschool teachers shown in the film? If so, state how many, describe their appearance, and indicate what they were doing. Third, is there any person in the lineup who was in the film but was not the assailant? If so, indicate what numerical position that person has in the lineup, and indicate what he was doing in the film. This last question was included in the event that unconscious transference does not occur, to measure whether transference subjects correctly remembered the bystander as the familiar but innocent preschool teacher.

According to an automatic processing view, transference subjects should misidentify the bystander without having any conscious recollection of a bystander reading to the children in the preschool because the memory for the bystander was formed automatically or incidentally, without conscious awareness. A source monitoring approach argues that transference subjects should remember both the assailant and the bystander, accurately report that they are two different individuals, but then confuse the memory of one with the other. Finally, a memory blending approach argues that transference subjects will remember the assailant and the bystander, but think that they are the same person seen in two different places.

Based on subjects' responses to the context questions, the unconscious transference effect reported above appeared to be due to memory blending. The first context question asked subjects whether the assailant was seen in any place in the film other than in the cafeteria where the crime took place. The correct response to this question is no, because in both conditions the assailant is seen only in the cafeteria. Transference and control subjects differed significantly in their response to this question. Sixty-six percent of the transference subjects incorrectly responded that the assailant was seen in a context outside the cafeteria. When further probed as to where the assailant was seen, 95 percent of these subjects indicated that the assailant was seen reading to the children in the preschool (the role played by the bystander). A majority of the subjects in the transference condition thought the assailant and the bystander were the same person. In sharp contrast, a majority of the control subjects (95.9 percent) did not make this error, and were accurate in responding that the assailant was seen only in the cafeteria, $X^2(1) = 66.31$, $p < .001$.

Second, when subjects were asked whether any male preschool teachers were shown in the film, and if so, to describe their appearance and state what they were doing, 91 percent of the transference subjects recalled the bystander reading to the children in the preschool. As an aside, approximately 27 percent of these subjects referred to the bystander as the "robber" when answering this question, and many of the subjects' descriptions of the bystander's behavior in the preschool reflected memory blending even though this question was not designed to elicit it. For example, one subject described the bystander as "the robber – brown hair and eyes, good skin but had nervous and shifting eyes. Looked displeased with the job of reading the story to the children. When he stole the money from the wallet, he still had a nervous look in his eyes." Therefore, it is clear from the two measures described thus far that most of the transference subjects had a vivid memory for the bystander, but thought the bystander and the assailant were the same person.

Third, subjects were asked whether there was any one in the lineup who was in the film but was not the assailant. For transference subjects the correct answer to this question is yes, because the familiar bystander is in the lineup. For control subjects the correct answer is no, because none of the individuals in the lineup was in the film. Although the correct response to this question differs by condition, the findings indicate that a majority of subjects in the transference and control condition answered no to the question (76.7 percent versus 84.9 percent, respectively), $X^2(1) = 1.75$, $p > .10$.

This finding is consistent with those reported above as well as with a "memory blending" interpretation. Transference subjects report that no one in the lineup is familiar but innocent, because the only familiar person they recognize (who is actually the bystander) is thought to be the assailant. The majority of control subjects answered no to the question, because none of the individuals in the lineup was in the film they watched. Therefore, although transference and control subjects gave the same response to this question, they did so for very different reasons.

In sum, subjects in the transference condition were significantly more likely to misidentify the bystander than control subjects. Moreover, transference subjects engaged in memory blending, believing that the assailant and the bystander were the same person seen in two different places.

EXPERIMENT 2

If memory blending is causing the unconscious transference effect found in Experiment 1, we should be able to eliminate the effect by "unblending" the memory of subjects in the transference condition by informing them that the assailant and the bystander are two different people. Therefore, in Experiment 2, another group of transference subjects were administered the same procedure used in Experiment 1, except just prior to being shown the lineup the subjects were informed that the assailant was seen only once during the film, in the cafeteria where the crime took place, and that the person reading the story to the children in the preschool looked similar in appearance to the assailant but was a different individual.

The unconscious transference effect is eliminated when transference subjects are told that the assailant and the bystander are different people. In particular, as shown in Table 4.2, only 25 percent of the transference subjects misidentified the bystander, and this percentage does not differ significantly from the 21.9 percent of the control subjects (see Table 4.1) who misidentified the bystander in Experiment 1 ($z = .37$). Moreover, the percentage of transference subjects who misidentified the bystander in Experiment 2 is signifi-

Table 4.2. *Identification accuracy*

Condition	Byst	Foil	Nil	D.K.
Transference	25.0%	15.0%	57.5%	2.5%

Note: Percentage of subjects who picked the bystander (Byst), another foil (Foil), indicated not in lineup (Nil), or said don't know (D.K.) when presented a lineup with the bystander and four unfamiliar foils. Sample size = 40.

cantly less than the percentage of transference subjects who misidentified the bystander in Experiment 1 (25 percent versus 60.9 percent, $z = 3.8$, $p <$ .01). Therefore, highlighting the distinctiveness of the bystander and the assailant prevented transference subjects from misidentifying the bystander.

The findings from Experiment 2 indicate that although transference subjects thought the assailant and the bystander were the same person at the time the crime occurred, it was possible for them to make a distinction between the two individuals if given the opportunity to do so. Therefore, transference subjects may have misidentified the bystander, in part because the memory blending effect at the time of retrieval prevented subjects from engaging in a source monitoring process that, if employed, would have allowed them to distinguish the bystander from the assailant. Our interpretation of these findings is that transference subjects had two separate memories (one for the assailant and another for the bystander) that are connected by a contextual tag (the inference that the bystander and the assailant were the same person seen in two different places). If the contextual tag is removed, as in Experiment 2, by informing transference subjects that the bystander and the assailant were not the same individual, they were capable of making a distinction between the two individuals. When the contextual tag remains intact, however (that is, they are not given information about the bystander and the assailant), transference subjects misidentified the bystander. Moreover, we predict that once the bystander is misidentified, if he were to appear in another lineup at a later point in time, transference subjects would continue to misidentify the bystander (even if the assailant were also present in the lineup): The memory for the bystander should be stronger than the memory for the assailant because it is more recent, vivid, and more likely to be retrieved, and because the subjects would want to appear to be consistent in their lineup identification.

Experiment 3

Experiments 3 to 5 were designed to determine when the memory blending effect takes place. According to a memory blending approach the effect occurs at encoding or shortly after transference subjects observed the assailant at the scene of the crime. The idea is that transference subjects misperceived the assailant as the bystander at the time the crime was observed. When transference subjects observed the assailant they inferred he was the bystander because they were similar in appearance, and were seen in close temporal continuity. Thus the image of the assailant served as an effective retrieval cue for the memory of the bystander. Therefore, subjects formed what Schooler and Tanaka (1991) referred to as a "composite" memory – a memory formed by using information that is omnipresent (the image of the assailant), and information that had been previously stored in memory (the memory for the bystander).

An alternative hypothesis is that the memory blending occurs at retrieval as a function of actually completing the lineup identification task, and that subjects see the assailant and the bystander as the same person in an attempt to justify their identification of the bystander. We tested these competing hypotheses in Experiments 3 to 5.

In Experiment 3 we employed the same procedure and method used in the transference condition in Experiment 1. In particular, two groups of transference subjects were shown the film about teacher education; we varied when we asked the context question that provided our primary measure of memory blending in Experiment 1: "Was the robber seen in any place in the film other than in the cafeteria where the crime occurred—yes/no? And if yes, where was he seen and what was he doing?" Subjects in the "before lineup condition" were asked the context question immediately after the crime occurred at the end of the film but before the lineup was shown (the lineup contained the bystander without the assailant). Subjects in the "after lineup condition" were asked the same context question but after completing the lineup identification. This was done as a between-subjects manipulation. If memory blending occurs at encoding, the level of memory blending should not vary as a function of when the question is asked. Conversely, if memory blending occurs as a result of actually performing the lineup identification task, subjects should display memory blending after the lineup task but not before.

The results indicated, as predicted, that memory blending occurs at encoding. That is, approximately 72 percent of the subjects in the "before lineup condition" reported that the assailant was seen in a context other than in the cafeteria, and 95 percent of these subjects further reported that the assailant was seen in the preschool reading a story to the children – the role played by the bystander. In a similar vein, 82 percent of the subjects in the "after lineup" condition reported that the assailant was seen in a context other than in the cafeteria, and 91.3 percent of these subjects further reported that the assailant was seen reading to the children in the preschool. Thus the level of memory blending observed in these two conditions is not statistically significant (72 versus 82 percent, $z = .87$).

Although Experiment 3 indicated that memory blending did not occur at the time of retrieval as a result of actually completing the lineup identification task, it did not provide conclusive evidence that subjects misperceived the assailant as the bystander at the time when the assailant was first encountered. Experiment 4 was designed to provide further and more definitive evidence that memory blending occurs at encoding.

Experiment 4

In Experiment 4, subjects in the transference and control condition were instructed to watch the videotape and stop it each time an adult male was seen more than once.[1] Several males, none of whom was the bystander or assailant, appeared in the videotape. After stopping the videotape, subjects were instructed to indicate where that person had been seen earlier and what he was doing at the time. If memory blending occurs at encoding, transference subjects should stop the videotape as soon as they see the assailant, and indicate that he was seen earlier reading to the children in the preschool. Moreover, we measured the length of time it took transference subjects to make this inference. Subjects in the control condition should not stop the videotape when the assailant is encountered because no memory blending occurs in that condition.

As predicted, the results provide further evidence that the memory blending effect occurs at encoding. First, 69.2 percent of the transference subjects stopped the film when the assailant was seen in the cafeteria where the crime occurred, and 94.4 percent of these subjects indicated that the assailant was seen reading to the children in the preschool. Conversely, only one subject (1/26) in the control condition stopped the videotape when the assailant appeared on the screen. Second, the transference subjects who engaged in memory blending did so as soon as the assailant appeared in close-up on the screen. That is, it took transference subjects an average of 3.6 seconds to stop the videotape and report that the assailant was seen earlier in the film reading to the children in the preschool. This average does not include one outlier who took twenty seconds to stop the videotape. When the outlier is included in the analysis, the average increases to 4.5 seconds.

Experiment 5

The purpose of the final experiment was to complement the previous study by providing converging evidence for memory blending. Subjects were told we were interested in the accuracy and speed with which they could monitor an event. Specifically, their task was to decide whether or not adult characters, appearing in the theft episode employed in the above experiments, had been seen previously in the videotape. Red arrows were inserted throughout the video with each one pointing to the adult for whom a decision was required. Using their dominant hand, subjects responded to each person associated with an arrow by pressing one of two reaction time (RT) keys labeled "old" and "new." Each key was paired with a distinctive tone which provided subjects with auditory feedback for each response. The tone generator was connected to a video cassette recorder such that every time a subject pressed a key the resulting tone was recorded on the videotape, which allowed us to play back each tape (one for each subject) and calculate RT as the time between the appearance of an arrow and the tone that followed. All participants were given several practice trials with an unrelated video clip to familiarize them with the task.

During the course of the robbery video subjects made eight decisions, the last of which involved responding to the assailant. In the transference condition the fourth decision concerned the male bystander shown reading to the preschoolers. At this point control subjects responded to a female teacher reading to children. For the seven nontarget decisions preceding the assailant, subjects in both conditions performed accurately and quickly. The mean proportion of correct decisions was .88 in the control group and .93 in the transference group, resulting in no statistical difference ($p > .05$). The groups also did not differ in terms of RT. When considering only correct decisions, the mean RTs were 1.21 seconds and 1.17 s for the control and transference conditions, respectively. The pattern was virtually identical (1.21 s versus 1.19 s) if incorrect responses were included in the analysis.

Only one transference subject incorrectly said "old" to the bystander, yet correctly indicated "new" for the assailant. In sharp contrast to the nontarget data, however, transference subjects were generally much poorer than controls when responding to the assailant, the target decision. Mean accuracy for this decision was only .50 for transference subjects which differed significantly ($p < .05$) from 1.00 for control subjects as they made no errors. This finding is consistent with a memory blending approach.

The considerable confusion on the part of the transference group was also reflected in the speed of response data. Although overall mean RT did not differentiate transference subjects (1.52 sec) from control subjects (1.55 sec), an examination of these data broken out by correct versus incorrect decisions was quite revealing. Transference subjects who correctly labeled the assailant as "new" took 1.78 seconds on average to do so, whereas the error-free control group responded significantly faster ($p < .05$) at 1.14 seconds. Notice that control subjects responded to the target and nontargets with approximately the same speed (1.14 and 1.21 sec). This was not the case for accurate transference subjects (1.78 and 1.31 sec, $p < .05$), strongly suggesting that for them the assailant presented a rather difficult decision. This would be expected if one assumes these subjects were comparing the bystander and the assailant, taking time with the discrimination process.

On the other hand, we would not anticipate such a comparison when transference subjects incorrectly believed the assailant was "old" and presumably the bystander, as predicted by a memory blending approach. In fact, transference subjects responded faster when they were wrong (1.32 sec) than when they were right (1.78 sec), although with limited power this difference was not significant. The memory blending position garners additional support from the fact that the RT associated with inaccurate target decisions by transference subjects was quite similar to the speed displayed by control subjects on the target trail.

Discussion

These five experiments provide evidence for the existence of unconscious transference and the memory blending approach. In Experiment 1, transference subjects were nearly three times more likely to misidentify the bystander than control subjects, and a majority of the transference subjects thought the assailant and the bystander were the same person – a process we refer to as memory blending. Presumably the prior exposure to the bystander led the transference subjects to misperceive the assailant as the bystander at the crime scene. In particular, observing the assailant may have served as a retrieval cue for the memory of the bystander, and as a result, transference subjects inferred that the assailant and the bystander were the same person seen in two different places. We refer to this as a "composite" memory (Schooler & Tanaka, 1991), formed by integrating omnipresent information (the image of the assailant) and information previously stored in memory (the memory for the bystander). Moreover, the memory blending process used to form the composite memory appeared to occur at encoding. In support of this conclusion, in Experiment 3 we found that the memory blending effect did not occur as a result of actually making the lineup identification task, and in Experiments 4 and 5, transference subjects were found to misperceive the assailant as the bystander at the time the assailant was first observed.

This "composite" memory is thought to consist of two separate memories that are connected by a contextual tag (the inference that the assailant and the bystander are the same person). When this contextual tag is broken, as seen in Experiment 2 when transference subjects were informed that the assailant and the bystander were not the same person, transference subjects were able to monitor or distinguish the source of their memories, and the unconscious transference effect was eliminated. Thus the memory blending that occurred at encoding appeared to prevent transference subjects from engaging in a source monitoring process at retrieval that would prevent the bystander misidentification from taking place. Moreover, if transference subjects were not given the warning and a high rate of misidentification of the bystander did occur (as seen in Experiment 1), we argue that from that point on transference subjects would continue to misidentify the bystander if he were seen in a subsequent lineup. This could occur through a destructive updating process whereby the memory for the bystander may overshadow, overwrite, or make less likely to retrieve the memory of the assailant once the misidentification took place.

How do our findings and conclusions compare with those concerning the existence of unconscious transference reported by Read (this volume)? The two sets of findings share a number similarities and dissimilarities. First, we agree with Read that in order to understand the basis of any lineup identification, one must pay careful attention to the role of contextual information. Indeed, our data indicate that contextual information (in the form of an inference that the assailant and the bystander are the same person seen in two different places) is a prerequisite for unconscious transference or bystander misidentification, in Read's terminology, to occur.

Second, we agree with Read that there is little or no empirical evidence (as of now) for the traditional definition of unconscious transference that involves a witness misidentifying a familiar bystander solely on the basis of familiarity without having any conscious recollection of the previous encounter with the bystander. In our studies, transference subjects had a vivid memory for the encounter with the bystander, and because this memory was conscious and appeared to be used in the identification process, we suggest that the type of bystander misidentification observed in our studies should be referred to as "conscious transference." This conclusion is striking because in a recent survey (Kassin, Ellsworth, & Smith, 1989) approximately 84.5 percent of a sample of experts in the psycholegal field indicated that there was sufficient evidence to testify in court as to the reliability of the unconscious transference phenomenon (Kassin, Ellsworth, & Smith, 1989).

Third, we agree with Read that the lineup identification process can be characterized as problem solving involving inferential processes at the time of retrieval. We argue, however, that inferential processes are also involved at the time of encoding when a witness observes a crime and attempts to determine what is happening and who is committing it. One major difference between Read's studies and our own is that in our studies subjects actually saw a crime take place (on videotape) that was totally unexpected. This led subjects to engage in inferential processing or memory blending at encoding. As seen in Experiment 4, transference subjects were quick to infer who the assailant was as soon as he was encountered at the crime scene, and in the process they assembled a composite memory in an attempt to make sense of the situation. Thus in our experiments there was a motivation for subjects to engage in memory blending at the time of encoding. In Read's studies subjects never witnessed a crime. The witnessed events involved exposing students to a class assistant (that is, the assailant) or exposing clerks working in a shopping mall to a customer (that is, the assailant) who requested change. In these situations there is little or no motivation for subjects to engage in the type of inferential processing or memory blending needed to produce unconscious transference. In fact, Read (this volume) reports that many of the subjects in his experiment had no memory of the assailant (much less the bystander) because the incident was unimportant to them. In addition, in Read's experiments there was no control of estimator variables such as exposure duration, that are critical to obtaining the effect. Therefore, given the design of Read's experiments, we are not surprised that an unconscious transference effect was not obtained. Moreover, we argue that in order to understand how unconscious transference occurs, one must first demonstrate the basic phenomenon. Because Read did not obtain an unconscious transference effect in the experiment he reported in this volume, we are somewhat skeptical of the conclusions he draws on the basis of that experiment regarding how unconscious transference occurs and whether memory blending is an appropriate explanation for this phenomenon.

Another difference between our conclusions and those reported by Read concerns the factors involved in the lineup identification process. In Read's work the focus has been on cognitive factors (the role of familiarity and the utilization of contextual information). In contrast, we argue that any lineup identification is a combination of cognitive and social factors. For example, it may be entirely possible that a witness could make a lineup identification solely on the basis of familiarity if the witness expected that the assailant were in the lineup, and if biased lineup instructions were presented that implied that the assailant was in the lineup. As stated earlier, we argue that witnesses assume that the assailant is in the lineup when asked to make an identification, because in the mind of the witness, why would police present a lineup unless a suspect had been apprehended? Therefore, a bystander misidentification could occur if a witness expects the assailant to be in the lineup, and the familiarity of the bystander is used to confirm this expectation. Consistent with this hypothesis is the finding that high rates of false identifications are obtained when "blank" lineups (those that do not contain the assailant) are presented to witnesses (Wells & Turtle, 1986). Moreover, once a witness misidentifies an innocent bystander, he or she may continue to misidentify that person in subsequent lineups in an attempt to be consistent in his or her testimony (Gorenstein & Ellsworth, 1980; Loftus & Greene, 1980; Wells, 1984). Thus unconscious transference may occur through a variety of factors both cognitive (that is, memory blending) and social (that is, expectancy and commitment effects).

In sum, the research reported here was designed to provide a theoretical basis for understanding unconscious transference and to test and contrast three competing explanations for unconscious transference in a series of five experiments. Because these experiments are laboratory studies, they do not capture the level of stress or personal involvement experienced by witnesses to real crimes. In addition, the goal of this research was to isolate several factors (that is, exposure duration and bystander–assailant similarity) that are critical to producing an unconscious transference effect. Because this research is in its infancy, it would be inappropriate to make any definitive statements regarding this phenomenon at the present time. To date, unconscious transference has received relatively little attention from psycholegal researchers. It may be entirely possible that by using different stimuli or procedures an unconscious transference effect could occur through different types of cognitive and social processes than those described here. In this light, the research reported here should be viewed as the mere beginning of an investigation into this intriguing and important topic.

Note

1 We thank R. C. L. Lindsay for giving us the idea for Experiment 4.

References

Brown, E., Deffenbacher, K., & Sturgill, W. (1977). Memory for faces and the circumstances of encounter. *Journal of Applied Psychology, 62,* 311–318.

Buckhout, R. (1974). Eyewitness testimony. *Scientific American, 231,* 23–31.

Buckhout, R. (1984). Double mistaken identification in Dallas: Texas v. Lenell Geter and Anthony Williams. *Social Action and the Law, 10,* 3–11.

Buckhout, R., Alper, A., Chern, S., Silverberg, G., & Slomovits, M. (1974). Determinants of eyewitness performance on a lineup. *Bulletin of the Psychonomic Society, 4,* 191–192.

Ceci, S. J., Ross, D. F., & Toglia, M. P. (1987). Suggestibility of children's memory: Psycholegal implications. *Journal of Experimental Psychology: General, 116,* 38–49.

Ceci, S. J., Toglia, M. P., & Ross, D. F. (1988). On remembering.... More or less: A trace strength interpretation of developmental differences in suggestibility. *Journal of Experimental Psychology: General, 117,* 201–203.

Davies, G. & Milne, A. (1982). Recognizing faces in and out of context. *Current Psychological Research, 2,* 235–246.

Davies, G., & Thompson, D. (1988). (Eds.), *Memory in context: Context in memory.* London: Wiley.

Egan, D., Pittner, M., & Goldstein, A. (1977). Eyewitness identification – photographs vs. live models. *Law and Human Behavior, 1,* 199–206.

Goldstein, A. G., Chance, J. E., & Schneller, G. R. (1989). Frequency of eyewitness identification in criminal cases: A survey of prosecutors. *Bulletin of the Psychonomic Society, 27,* 71–74.

Gorenstein, G., & Ellsworth, P. (1980). Effect of choosing an incorrect photograph on a later identification by an eyewitness. *Journal of Applied Psychology, 5,* 616–622.

Hasher, L., & Zacks, R. T. (1979). Automatic and effortful processes in memory. *Journal of Experimental Psychology: General, 108,* 356–388.

Houts, M. (1963). *From evidence to guilt.* Springfield, IL.: Charles C. Thomas

Johnson, M. K., & Raye, C. L. (1981). Reality monitoring. *Psychological Review, 88,* 67–85.

Kassin, S., Ellsworth, P., & Smith, V. (1989). The "general acceptance" of psychological research on eyewitness testimony. *American Psychologist, 44,* 1089–1098.

Lindsay, D. S. (This volume). Memory source monitoring and eyewitness testimony. In Ross, D. F., Read, J. D., & Toglia, M. P. (Eds.), *Adult eyewitness testimony: Current trends and developments* (pp. 27–55). New York: Cambridge University Press.

Lindsay, D. S., & Johnson, M. K. (1989). The eyewitness suggestibility effect and memory for source. *Memory and Cognition, 17,* 349–358.

Lindsay, D. S., & Johnson, M. K. (1990). Recognition memory and source monitoring. *Bulletin of the Psychonomic Society, 29,* 203–205.

Lindsay, D. S., Johnson, M. K., & Kwon, P. (1991). Developmental changes in memory source monitoring. *Journal of Experimental Child Psychology,* 1–22.

Loftus, E. F. (1976). Unconscious transference. *Law and Psychology Review, 2,* 93–98.

Loftus, E. F. (1979). *Eyewitness testimony.* Cambridge: Harvard University Press.

Loftus, E. F. (1981). Mentalmorphosis: Alterations in memory produced by the mental bonding of new information to old. In J. Long and A. Baddeley (Eds.), *Attention and Performance,* vol. 9, pp 417–434. Hillsdale, NJ: Erlbaum.

Loftus, E. F., Donders, K., Hoffman, H., Schooler, J. (1989). Creating new memories that are quickly accessed and confidently held. *Memory & Cognition, 17,* 607–616.

Loftus, E. F., & Doyle, J. M (1989). *Eyewitness testimony: Civil and criminal.* New York: Kluwer.

Loftus, E. F., & Greene, E. (1980). Warning: Even memory for faces may be contagious. *Law and Human Behavior, 4,* 323–334.

Malpass, R., & Devine, P. (1981). Guided memory in eyewitness identification. *Journal of Applied Psychology, 66,* 343–350.

Memon, A., & Bruce, V. (1985). Context effects in episodic studies of verbal and facial memory: A review. *Current Psychological Research,* 349–369.

Nisbett, R., & Ross, L. (1980). *Human inference: Strategies and shortcomings of social judgment.* Englewood Cliffs, N.J.: Prentice-Hall.

Peters, D. (1985). A naturalistic study of earwitness memory: Does the addition of voice to a lineup influence accuracy and/or confidence? Paper presented at the annual meeting of the Eastern Psychological Association.

Posner, M. I., & Snyder, C. R. (1975). Attention and cognitive control. In R. L. Solso (Ed.), *Information processing and cognition: The Loyola Symposium.* Hillsdale, N.J.

Read, J. D., Tollestrup, P., Hammersley, R., McFadzen, E., & Christensen, A. (1990). The unconscious transference effect: Are innocent bystanders ever misidentified? *Applied Cognitive Psychology, 4.* 3–31.

Richardson-Klavehn, A., & Bjork, R. A. (1988). Measures of memory. *Annual Review of Psychology, 39,* 475–543.

Ross, D.F., Ceci, S.J., Dunning, D., & Toglia, M. P. (1991). Unconscious transference and mistaken identity: When a witness misidentifies a familiar but innocent person from a lineup. In D. F. Ross and M. P. Toglia (Chairs), Current trends in research on adult eyewitness memory and identification accuracy. Symposium conducted at the meeting of the American Psychological Society.

Ross, D. F., Ceci, S. J., Dunning, D., & Toglia, M. P. (1992). Unconscious transference and mistaken identity: When a witness misidentifies a familiar but innocent person from a lineup. Manuscript under review.

Schooler, J., & Tanaka (1991). Composites, compromises, and CHARM: What is the evidence for blend memory representations? *Journal of Experimental Psychology: General, 120,* 96–100.

Thompson, D. M. (1988). Context and false recognition. In G. M. Davies & D. M. Thompson (Eds.), *Memory in context: Context in memory.* New York: John Wiley & Sons.

Wells, G. L. (1984). The psychology of lineup identifications. *Journal of Applied Social Psychology, 14,* 89–103.

Wells, G. L. & Turtle, J. W. (1986). Eyewitness identification: The importance of lineup models. *Psychological Bulletin, 88,* 776–784.

Williams, G. (1963). *The proof of guilt.* Springfield, IL.: Charles C. Thomas.

5 Earwitness evidence: Memory for a perpetrator's voice

A. Daniel Yarmey

Earwitness testimony, in contrast to eyewitness testimony, has not received a great amount of attention from either psycholegal researchers or the courts, possibly because of the greater reliance on information processed visually rather than orally. Some crimes may include both visual and auditory information, or may only be seen but not heard. For some crimes, however, such as those committed in darkness, or with perpetrators wearing masks, or those committed over the telephone, the sole source of identification evidence may be auditory.

Experimental research on earwitness testimony has been pursued by researchers in North America, the United Kingdom, and Europe (see reviews by Bull & Clifford, 1984; Clifford, 1983; Deffenbacher, Cross, Handkins, Chance, Goldstein, Hammersley, & Read, 1989; Hammersley & Read, in press; Kunzel, 1990). This research has had only limited impact on police practices and on the courts (see Yarmey, 1990), however, and has not been widely reported in the mass media. For example, Kleiman (1988) reported in the *New York Times* that prosecutors in a Riverhead, Long Island, trial believed their use of a voice lineup as the primary method to identify an accused serial rapist was a ground breaking procedure in criminal proceedings. English courts have accepted voice identification evidence from lay witnesses at least since 1660 (Hollien, Bennett, & Gelfer, 1983). If the *Times* article is representative of the general knowledge of officers of the court, the construction of voice lineups and judgments about the influence of selected estimator and structural factors on earwitness identifications are based on intuition or common knowledge rather than on scientific findings and theory. Common knowledge beliefs and the opinions of experts about eyewitness identification have been assessed (see, for example, Kassin, Ellsworth & Smith, 1989; Yarmey & Jones, 1983), but research on earwitness testimony remains to be done.

The purpose of this chapter is twofold. First, to describe the impact of

The author gratefully acknowledges the support of the Social Sciences and Humanities Research Council of Canada in the preparation of this chapter.

several factors on the accuracy of earwitness identification. The factors studied include: (1) assessing the fairness of a voice lineup; (2) earwitness description of voices – how do earwitnesses characterize voices they hear? (3) the impact of group discussion on earwitness recall; (4) the impact of stereotypes on earwitness memory; (5) the impact of exposure duration and retention interval on earwitness identification and confidence; (6) the accuracy of earwitness memory for voices heard over the telephone; and (7) the accuracy of earwitness and eyewitness identification when showups are used.

The second issue addressed in the chapter concerns the intuitive knowledge that laypersons have regarding the accuracy of earwitness memory and identification accuracy. That is, to what extent does the knowledge possessed by potential jurors fit with what is known in the research literature. To study this issue, the chapter presents a prediction study that asked laypersons to make judgments about the accuracy of earwitness and eyewitness memory. Thus, two major goals of the chapter are to describe research on a series of factors that influence the accuracy of earwitness memory and to compare those results with what potential jurors think about earwitness and eyewitness memory and their presumed accuracy and credibility.

STUDY 1: ASSESSING THE FAIRNESS OF A VOICE LINEUP

In 1987 I served as an expert witness in Santa Cruz County, California. The defense attorney who contacted me believed that the lineup procedures were faulty and, in particular, that the voice lineup in which his client was identified by five rape victims was biased. Two lineups were constructed by the police. The first was a video corporeal lineup in which the suspect and five foils were shown reading aloud the same message. The suspect was not identified. The second lineup was a six-person voice lineup presented by a tape recorder. The suspect was the only individual repeated in the two lineups. The defense attorney argued that the defendant may have been identified in the voice lineup because of the biasing effects of prior exposure and familiarity from the video lineup. He also cited the poor quality of the voice lineup.

In order to test the fairness of the voice identification lineup used for the Santa Cruz trial, a planned study was conducted by the author. Expert eyewitness testimony on the results of planned studies are not unusual (see Brigham, Ready, & Spier, 1990), but, to my knowledge, expert earwitness testimony based on planned studies had not previously been presented in trials. Forty female and nine male undergraduate and graduate students participated as "hearsay witnesses." All subjects were white, native English speakers. They were given a general description of the crimes committed and a description of the perpetrator based on police reports. "The suspect was described as a white male, 5'9"–5'10" tall, 170–180 lbs, and 20 to 35 years old. He had an unkempt appearance and nervous demeanor. The suspect was

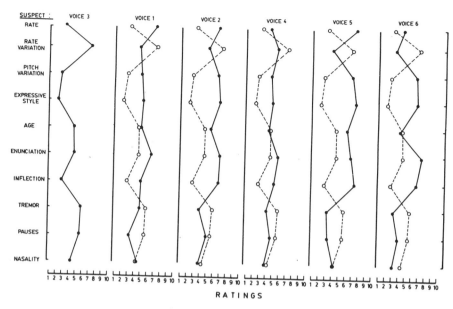

Figure 5.1: Voice profiles of the suspect and foils.

described as talkative, apologetic, and not very educated. He was described as having a quiet, slow, low pitch voice, and no accent." Participants were given the entire six-person voice tape twice in succession in the same order used by the police. The hearsay witnesses were instructed to select the person most likely to have committed the crimes. They were told to choose one voice only. After their decisions were made, the six voices were played again in random order and rated on a ten-point scale (Handkins & Cross, 1985) for: (1) rate of speech (very slow–very fast); (2) rate variation (smooth flowing and steady–halting, jerky, irregular; (3) pitch variation (monotone–highly varied); (4) expressive style (none–very much); (5) age (twenty to thirty-eight years); (6) enunciation (very poor–very good); (7) inflection (none, flat–very much); (8) tremor (very steady–very shaky); (9) pauses (very short–very long); and (10) nasality (none–very nasal).

Sixty-seven percent of the participants selected the voice of the defendant. The suspect's voice was chosen at a four to one ratio greater than chance whereas all other voices were selected just below chance (16.7 percent). Wells, Leippe, and Ostrom (1979) define the functional size of a lineup as equal to the total number of hearsay witnesses divided by the number who choose the suspect. In this case, the functional size was 49/33 = 1.48 which indicates that the lineup was closer to a one-person "showup" than it was to a six-person lineup. Figure 5.1 shows the voice profile of the suspect compared with the voice profiles of the five foils for the ten voice characteristics.

Analysis of variance conducted on subjects' ratings for each of the six voices revealed statistically significant differences for each of the ten characteristics. As the figure shows, the suspect's voice (voice number 3) is clearly dissimilar from each of the foils on most rated characteristics. In contrast, the foils (all of whom were police officers) were similar to each other on most of the rated characteristics. A reliability of ratings check was conducted by comparing the ratings for each voice for pitch variation and inflection because these two characteristics are conceptually similar. The ratings between them did not differ significantly on any of the six voices.

In my opinion the lineup procedures used in this trial were faulty and the voice lineup was biased. The ultimate decision, of course, rests with the jury. The accused was found guilty on charges related to sexual assault of two women, and not guilty on charges related to two other victims. The defendant pleaded guilty prior to trial for the rape of one other victim.

STUDY 2: EARWITNESS DESCRIPTIONS OF VOICES

One of the first things a police officer seeks from a witness is a description of the perpetrator. Unfortunately, language is one of several factors which may contribute to witness misidentification. The imprecision of language may introduce distortions and errors and may fail to capture the richness of detail of mental representations. Facial descriptions, for example, are frequently impoverished and superficial and degenerate over time (Ellis, Shepherd, & Davies, 1980). Linguistic deficiencies can interfere with verbal encoding and person identification (Sporer, 1989).

The difficulty in describing others is not limited, however, solely to facial characteristics and physical appearance. Descriptions of perpetrators' voices also are brief and imprecise (Kunzel, 1990). One way to overcome the difficulties of the imprecision of language in describing a voice, especially over time, is to use rated descriptions of the voice characteristics, such as rate of speech, tremor, pauses, and so forth (Voiers, 1964).

In a study designed to examine the rated quality of earwitnesses' descriptions of a perpetrator's voice over time, 295 undergraduate students played the role of kidnap victims in a mock crime (Yarmey, 1991a). Subjects rated either a highly distinctive speaker or a nondistinctive speaker (experimentally predetermined) on ten selected voice characteristics. Two speakers of each type were used and each target was presented on a tape recording for thirty-six seconds speaking in a normal, conversational manner. Subjects were then randomly divided into three retention conditions, an immediate test, a twenty-four-hour delay test, and a one-week delay test. Participants rated the following target voice characteristics: rate of speech, rate variation, pitch, expressive style, age, enunciation, inflection, tremor, pauses, and nasality (Handkins & Cross, 1985). A fourth group of subjects, referred to as the

Table 5.1. *Mean ratings of voice characteristics*

Voice characteristics	Delay conditions			
	Perception	Immediate	24 hour	1 week
Distinctive				
Rate	5.50	4.54	4.75	4.36
Rate variation	6.37	6.71	6.61	6.11
Pitch	4.60	3.92	3.25	3.39
Expressive style	3.80	2.62	2.60	3.82
Age	5.60	5.42	6.00	4.82
Enunciation	4.83	4.96	5.75	5.93
Inflection	4.33	3.83	4.55	3.96
Tremor	4.33	3.83	4.55	3.96
Pauses	4.97	4.62	5.50	5.61
Nasality	5.83	5.83	4.45	5.61
Nondistinctive				
Rate	5.88	6.02	5.69	4.78
Rate variation	3.04	4.67	4.19	4.63
Pitch	5.00	5.62	4.62	4.84
Expressive style	5.27	5.62	4.92	4.92
Age	4.12	3.69	4.10	4.06
Enunciation	7.48	7.04	7.29	7.02
Inflection	5.38	5.10	5.50	5.39
Tremor	2.60	3.35	3.58	4.27
Pauses	2.96	2.98	3.56	4.71
Nasality	2.69	4.62	3.79	4.94

perception condition, was allowed to listen to repetitions of the tape recording as they simultaneously completed their ratings.

Table 5.1 shows the mean ratings of voice characteristics for the distinctive and nondistinctive voices over time.

In contrast to ratings made in the immediate perception and twenty-four-hour retention conditions, descriptions of nondistinctive voices made after a one-week interval showed reliable decrements on five voice characteristics: rate of speech, rate variation, tremor, pauses, and nasality. Ratings of pitch, expressive style, age, enunciation, and inflection were similar to the ratings made by the perception group and did not change over time. Nasality of voice proved to be a very poor descriptor because the perception condition differed reliably from all three of the memory conditions, including immediate memory. For distinctive voices only rate of speech was remembered differently over time. That is, the target voices were remembered as being reliably slower in rate of speech after a one-week delay in testing. As expected, distinctive voices varied considerably from each other and from the nondistinctive voices.

These results suggest that recall of the characteristics of nondistinctive voices in contrast to distinctive voices is more adversely affected by the length of the retention interval. Over a one-week period most (rated) descriptions of distinctive voices were found to be consistent. Any generalizations made from this study, however, should be restricted to nonstressful events that are approximately a half minute in duration, and to situations in which the witness is set to try to remember the perpetrator's voice.

Study 3: Effects of Group Discussion on Earwitness Recall

In 1981 in Lethbridge, Alberta, an armed perpetrator wearing a ski mask over his face broke into a house containing two adolescent boys. The boys were held hostage for approximately two hours while the perpetrator searched through the house and intermittently returned to talk with them. While alone the boys discussed ways to remember his voice and anything that would help the police identify this man. When the parents arrived home they were assaulted and robbed by the masked perpetrator. Subsequently, all four victims identified the same man as the perpetrator from a voice lineup. Although most legal authorities support the proposition that witnesses' identification evidence should be the result of independent judgment, this Alberta case shows that it is not always possible. The question can be asked, however, whether group discussions lead to greater accuracy or greater distortion in recall of the original event.

In general, the effects of group discussion on eyewitness memory have yielded equivocal results. For example, individual eyewitness reports following group discussion are more complete and accurate than individual eyewitness reports without previous discussion. In contrast to the findings of Hollin and Clifford (1983) and Warnick and Sanders (1980), however, Alper, Buckhout, Chern, Harwood, and Slomovits (1976) found that group discussion witnesses made significantly more errors of commission (fabrications) on later individual testimony than no-discussion subjects.

There are few forensically related studies of the effects of group discussion on earwitness memory (see Stephenson, Clark, & Wade, 1986). Note that all the eyewitness memory studies and Yarmey's (1992a) earwitness study (described below) have focused on the effects of group discussion on witness reports rather than on identification memory.

Some 112 undergraduate students were blindfolded when they arrived at the laboratory and told to assume that they had just been kidnapped and were being held for ransom. Subjects, in groups of two to four persons, overheard a tape recorded telephone conversation involving a perpetrator discussing his crime and were tested for their reconstructions of the incident either ten minutes later or forty-eight hours later. They were told to try to remember as many details of the phone conversation as possible in order to facilitate the subsequent police investigation. Subjects were randomly assigned to one of three groups: (1) a dyadic-collaborative condition, subjects discussed the incident and gave a joint response at the test; (2) a dyadic-individual condition, subjects discussed the incident but individual responses were given at the test; and (3) a no-discussion individual condition, subjects did not discuss the incident with anyone else. The text of the perpetrator's dialogue was parsed into fifty-four constituent propositions or "idea units."

The results showed that dyadic discussion (both with and without a requirement to produce collaborative recall) did not increase the overall accuracy of individuals' earwitness reconstructions of the criminal incident. Subjects in the dyadic-individual condition, however, made significantly more errors of commission than subjects in the no-discussion individual condition and subjects in the dyadic-collaborative condition. Several advantages were found for earwitness recall through collaborative joint responses. Collaborative dyads were significantly less verbose in their immediate free recall of the incident, were reliably more concise in correct statements, and made significantly fewer fabrications than subjects in the discussion-individual-recall condition. Collaborative dyads also produced fewer fabrications in recall than individuals, but this difference fell short of statistical significance. Collaborative reconstructions of earwitness evidence appeared to minimize gratuitous comment and focus recall more strictly on the evidential matters at issue. This result has also been found in eyewitness studies (Stephenson, 1990) which suggests that collaborative-dyadic recall could lead to the exclusion of some "correct" evidence.

Police officers and trial courts should persist in being concerned with possible fabrications in eyewitness and earwitness reports without an independent basis in perception. The criminal justice system should not, however, automatically dismiss the evidentiary value of collaborative-dyadic recall.

STUDY 4: IMPACT OF STEREOTYPES ON EARWITNESS MEMORY

Facial stereotypes of criminals have been shown to influence eyewitness behavior (Goldstein, Chance, & Gilbert, 1984; Shoemaker, South, & Lowe, 1973; Yarmey, 1979; 1982). Listeners also attribute personality characteristics to individuals on the basis of speech characteristics. These attributions show a high degree of consensus, but are not necessarily accurate (Aronovitch, 1976). Stylistic descriptors of speech, such as "powerful" and "powerless," have been shown to be extralegal variables that influence juror sentiments and jury decisions (Erickson, Lind, Johnson, & O'Barr, 1978). Because stereotypes probably operate on all types of human decision making, it is highly likely that stereotypes have an effect on earwitnesses.

As part of our research program on earwitness memory we conducted a study that investigated stereotypic conceptions for voices and physical appearance of criminals (Yarmey, unpublished data). Two hundred and forty subjects were randomly assigned to one of three video conditions in which: (1) they saw and heard fifteen males give the identical speech; or (2) they saw the targets (nonspeaking); or (3) they heard the targets (nonvisual). Thirty young white men in their mid-twenties recruited from the university community were used as targets. To minimize stimulus sampling errors, two stimulus lists of fifteen targets each were used with half the subjects in each condition receiving list A or list B. Subjects were presented one of the video conditions for three consecutive trials during which time they were asked to complete their ratings of traits and voice characteristics. Each target was presented for thirty-seven seconds on each trial, with a five-second interstimulus interval. The presentation order for rating traits and vocal characteristics was counterbalanced across subjects. The nine seven-point bipolar traits scales were: (a) submissive–dominating, (b) vulnerable–invulnerable, (c) weak–strong, (d) scatter-brained–serious, (e) naive–worldly, (f) lazy–industrious, (g) warm–cold, (h) nurturant–not nurturant, (i) straightforward–deceitful. The six vocal characteristics in the seven-point bipolar rating scales were: (a) very high–very deep, (b) very soft–very loud, (c) relaxed–tight, (d) not clear–clear, (e) monotone–changing, (f) slow–rapid (Montepare & Zebrowitz-McArthur, 1987).

On completion of the rating stage, subjects were given one additional trial to select, if possible, the person who best represented a mass murderer, a sexual assault felon, and an armed robber (categorized collectively as "bad guys"), and a clergyman, a medical doctor, and an engineer ("good guys") (Goldstein, Chance, & Gilbert, 1984).

The last stage of the experiment consisted of a recognition memory test for the stimuli they had just rated and judged. The test featured the fifteen targets randomly mixed with fifteen foils. Each stimulus was presented for five seconds. Subjects were asked to indicate whether they were definitely sure the stimulus was a new person, moderately sure he was a new person, moderately sure he was an old person, or definitely sure he was an old person.

Because of the very large data set and the space limitations of this chapter a detailed report of the results is prohibited. Instead, a summary of selected findings is presented, with particular attention to the relationship between ratings for traits and for vocal characteristics in the face alone (nonspeaking) condition. This condition may be considered a pure stereotype since subjects had to judge vocal characteristics of the targets based only on their video appearance.

The results showed that individuals attributed specific personality traits and vocal characteristics on the basis of both speech and personal appearance stereotypes in all three video conditions. The ratings of subjects for stimulus persons categorized as bad guys and for stimulus persons categorized as good guys in the face alone condition were selected for further analysis. Correlations

Table 5.2. *Correlations of voice ratings and trait ratings for good guys: Face alone condition*

| Traits | Voice characteristics | | | | | |
	High–deep	Soft–loud	Relaxed–tight	Unclear–clear	Monotone–changing	Slow–rapid
Submissive–dominating	.45**	.40**	−.12	.14	−.12	.09
Vulnerable–invulnerable	.43**	.24*	−.25*	.25*	−.22	−.04
Weak–strong	.55**	.25*	−.37**	.12	−.19	−.15
Scatter-brained–serious	.27*	.01	−.24*	.18	−.08	−.26*
Naive–worldly	.43**	.16	−.28*	.34**	.02	−.11
Lazy–industrious	.34**	−.02	−.19	.16	.07	−.08
Warm–cold	−.04	.22	.08	−.07	−.12	.17
Nurturant–not nurturant	−.04	.13	.01	.03	−.26*	−.01
Straightforward–deceitful	−.08	−.08	.06	−.10	−.10	−.04

$**p < .01; *p < .05; df = 78.$

Table 5.3. *Correlation of voice ratings and trait ratings for bad guys: Face alone condition*

| Traits | Voice characteristics | | | | | |
	High–deep	Soft–loud	Relaxed–tight	Unclear–clear	Monotone–changing	Slow–rapid
Submissive–dominating	.27*	.28*	.06	.11	−.13	.02
Vulnerable–invulnerable	.21	.24*	.04	.19	−.04	.05
Weak–strong	.61**	.44**	−.11	.01	−.13	−.20
Scatter-brained–serious	.35**	.19	.18	.41**	−.19	−.05
Naive–worldly	.36**	.28*	.02	.17	−.10	−.07
Lazy–industrious	.25*	.27*	−.03	.33**	.12	−.14
Warm–cold	−.16	−.17	.17	−.22	−.22	.02
Nurturant–not nurturant	−.02	.01	.01	−.22	−.14	.00
Straightforward–deceitful	.04	−.10	.00	−.24	.00	.02

$*p < .05; df = 76; **p < .01.$

were computed between averaged ratings of traits and averaged ratings of vocal characteristics. Subjects systematically associated particular traits with particular vocal attributes for good guys (see Table 5.2) and for bad guys (see Table 5.3).

In general, the magnitude of the correlation coefficients tended to be moderate. As both tables show there were significant relationships between many of the personality traits and particular vocal characteristics. Thirty-four of the

Table 5.4. *Correlations of voice ratings and trait ratings for good guys: Voice alone condition*

Traits	Voice characteristics					
	High–deep	Soft–loud	Relaxed–tight	Unclear–clear	Monotone–changing	Slow–rapid
Submissive–dominating	.15	.35**	.01	.18	.23*	.16
Vulnerable–invulnerable	.10	.19	−.06	.17	.09	−.12
Weak–strong	.26*	.15	−.11	.13	−.01	.02
Scatter-brained–serious	−.09	−.12	−.28*	.28*	.29**	.04
Naive–worldly	.10	.21	.03	.19	.27*	.25*
Lazy–industrious	.00	.24*	.27*	.40**	.40**	.17
Warm–cold	.01	.15	.07	−.11	−.19	−.11
Nurturant–not nurturant	.03	.03	.12	−.29**	−.23*	−.02
Straightforward–deceitful	−.07	−.10	.10	−.07	−.36**	−.15

$*p < .05$; df = 78; $**p < .01$.

fifty-four correlations between traits and vocal characteristics were not, however, significant for either good guys or bad guys. Eight significant correlations were common to both good guys and bad guys.

The following positive relationships between traits and vocal characteristics were found only for good guys: vulnerable–invulnerable and high voice–deep voice, vulnerable–invulnerable and unclear voice–clear voice, naive–worldly and unclear voice–clear voice. The following negative relationships between traits and vocal characteristics were found only for good guys: vulnerable–invulnerable and relaxed voice–tight voice, weak–strong and relaxed voice–tight voice, scatter-brained–serious and relaxed voice–tight voice, and finally, naive–worldly and relaxed voice–tight voice.

Only four significant positive correlations were found between traits and vocal characteristics for bad guys that were not found for good guys: naive–worldly and soft voice–loud voice, lazy–industrious and soft voice–loud voice, and lazy–industrious and unclear voice–clear voice, scatter-brained–serious and unclear voice–clear voice, and finally, lazy–industrious and unclear voice–clear voice.

For purposes of comparison, Tables 5.4 and 5.5 show the relationships between rated traits and rated voice characteristics for subjects' selections of good guys and bad guys when subjects were presented only with the voices of the targets. These results show that many of the significant relationships between traits and vocal characteristics for good guys and bad guys found when the faces were observed were not evident when only the voices were observed.

The fact that several significant correlations emerged for good guys but not

Table 5.5. *Correlation of voice ratings and trait ratings for bad guys: Voice only condition*

Traits	Voice characteristics					
	High–deep	Soft–loud	Relaxed–tight	Unclear–clear	Monotone–changing	Slow–rapid
Submissive–dominating	.08	.39**	−.04	.21	.40**	.16
Vulnerable–invulnerable	.01	.33**	−.06	.03	.28*	.04
Weak–strong	.12	.40**	−.07	.29**	.49**	.10
Scatter-brained–serious	.14	.14	−.15	.14	.05	.04
Naive–worldly	.10	.09	−.12	.01	.13	.21
Lazy–industrious	.01	.27*	.10	.27*	.24*	.25*
Warm–cold	.16	.08	.36**	−.17	−.21	.13
Nurturant–not nurturant	.01	.10	.29**	−.24*	−.11	.07
Straightforward–deceitful	.21	.11	.27*	−.16	−.02	.08

*$p < .05$; df = 77; **$p < .01$.

for bad guys, and vice versa, supports the hypothesis of voice stereotypes, or high interrater reliability in the assignment of particular traits to particular voices for criminalistic and noncriminalistic types. Stereotypes of criminals and noncriminals differ in some respects when perceptions are based on physical appearance versus vocal information. Furthermore, these stereotypes may influence our recollections for person descriptions and identifications (Sporer, 1989).

Subjects' selections of persons fitting criminal types and noncriminal types were made in a nonrandom manner. Some targets were selected as a good guy or a bad guy significantly more often than others in each of the three video conditions. These results replicate Goldstein et al. (1984) who used photographs of targets as stimuli.

Recognition memory performance for the fifteen targets was relatively good in all three conditions. Recognition of target voices was, however, significantly inferior to recognition of face and voice targets and face only targets. The latter two conditions did not differ from each other. Recognition performance of targets specifically selected by each subject as good guys was superior to recognition of targets subjects judged as bad guys in each of the three presentation conditions. These results suggest that good guys are given greater attention and deeper processing than are bad guys. As a consequence, more false identifications would be expected for those persons who evoke bad guy stereotypes than for good guy stereotypes.

In sum, these results show that stereotypes exist in the relationship between physical appearance, voice characteristics, and certain personality characteristics. It is possible that subjects remembered the ratings they gave to specific faces and then chose good guys to fit certain ratings and bad guys to fit others. This is unlikely, however, given the large number of personality ratings and voice characteristic ratings to be completed in a short amount of time with fifteen different targets. Given only the physical appearance, or the voice, or both the voice and appearance of stimulus persons, subjects select individuals to fit images of bad guys and good guys in a nonrandom manner. Furthermore, processing stimulus persons into categories representing "good guys" and "bad guys" influences the accuracy of recognition memory performance.

Study 5: Impact of Exposure Duration and Retention Interval on Earwitness Accuracy and Confidence

Common knowledge and the U.S. Supreme Court (*Neil v. Biggers*, 1972) support the opinion that the longer the interval of time available to observe a perpetrator the greater the probability of accuracy of identification. The issue of how long voice sample durations should be to permit forensically useful inferences in earwitness identification, however, is uncertain. Results of experiments utilizing traditional laboratory procedures suggest that voice samples of unfamiliar people which exceed a minimum of about two seconds, or a single fifteen-word sentence, are recognized significantly better than chance on immediate tests of memory (Bull & Clifford, 1984; Clifford, 1983). Voice recognition has been shown to improve with increased speech sample lengths up to one hundred and sixty-two words and sixty-second durations (Goldstein & Chance, 1985). The only study in which adults' voice identification was tested after a relatively long listening duration involved a five-minute two-party conversation (Hammersley & Read, 1985). Identification of the partner's voice from a voice lineup after a forty-eight hour retention interval was very high (83 percent correct). In contrast, Peters (1987), using young children between the ages of three and eight, failed to find significant recognition of a stranger's voice (one that was heard for at least five minutes during active conversation in a naturalistic setting) after a twenty-four- to forty-eight-hour retention period.

Although an extended opportunity to listen to the voice of a perpetrator is highly important for identification it may be less important than hearing a suspect's voice distributed over time (Deffenbacher et al., 1989). Goldstein and Chance (1985) discovered that subjects who heard a 162-word voice sample (approximately sixty seconds of speech) distributed in equal portions over each of three consecutive days, in contrast to hearing the whole voice sample in one session, were significantly superior in identifying the speaker over a two-week retention interval.

In *Neil v. Biggers* (1972), the court also recognized the importance of the length of the retention interval on the probability of identification. Retention intervals longer than twenty-four hours appear to have significant negative effects on subsequent voice identification (Clifford, Rathborn, & Bull, 1981; Hammersley & Read, 1985). Little or no decrease in identification accuracy has been found, however, for retention intervals under a twenty-four-hour period (Saslove & Yarmey, 1980). These results suggest that the length of the retention interval, especially if it is twenty-four hours or greater, does have an effect on voice identification.

Because listening duration and length of retention are critical theoretical factors and have great practical importance, Yarmey and Matthys (in press) tested a modified version of the Goldstein and Chance (1985) study. A total of 576 subjects participated in a mock abduction study in which they heard the taped voice of their male abductor for eighteen, thirty-six, or one hundred and twenty seconds, or six minutes. One-third of all subjects heard the perpetrator's voice for one massed trial, one-third for two equal periods separated by a five-minute intertrial interval, and the remainder for three equal periods separated by five-minute intervals. Voice identification was tested immediately after observation, twenty-four hours later, or one week later. Two white adult males served as perpetrators. Two six-person suspect-present lineups and two six-person suspect-absent lineups were constructed. Voices used as foils were selected from a pool of forty-four voices and were pre-experimentally judged by a separate group of subjects to be moderately similar to each target on ten-point scales. The two foils with the highest average similarity rating to each target were selected as the innocent suspects and put in the suspect-absent lineups. The four lineups were tested for fairness by a separate panel of judges. Chi-square analyses revealed that none of the voices in any lineup was selected reliably more frequently than any other voice.

Accuracy of identification of the target voice (hits) was relatively poor with speech sample durations of thirty-six seconds or less (31 percent accuracy) compared to voice samples two minutes (55 percent accuracy) and six minutes in duration (48 percent accuracy). The false alarm rate, however exceeded the hit rate in all duration conditions except for the six-minute duration condition. False alarms in the suspect-absent lineups were consistently high (overall $M = .58$) and exceeded the overall hit rate ($M = .40$). The innocent suspect was not reliably selected any more frequently than any other foil on any of the lineups.

Hearing the voice of the perpetrator twice separated by a five minute interval improved identification relative to a single massed presentation. Hearing the perpetrator's voice three times did not, however, improve performance relative to the massed condition. It is possible that voice identification is facilitated after distributed learning of unfamiliar voices only when relatively long intertrial intervals are used, such as twenty-four-hour intervals (Goldstein & Chance, 1985). Finally, it was shown that the length of the retention period influences the false alarm rate more than the hit rate in voice identification. The hit rate was not affected by delay in testing; however, the false alarm rate in the suspect-present lineup was significantly greater after both a twenty-four-hour delay and a one-week delay in testing. These results suggest that voice identification is a difficult task even when opportunities to listen are relatively good and witnesses are prepared to study the unfamiliar voice.

The final factor investigated in this study was the relationship between subjects' level of confidence and objective accuracy in voice identification. Subjects who did not select a voice were excluded from the analysis of results. At a general level of analysis subjective confidence was not related to identification, but confidence and identification were related under specific conditions. For example, a significant negative correlation ($r = -.24$) was found with the short eighteen-second voice sample. No reliable relationship was found between confidence and identification for the thirty-six-second voice sample condition. Significant positive correlations were found with the two-minute voice sample ($r = .18$) and with the six-minute voice sample ($r = .17$). These values are very similar to the results of Yarmey (1986a) who found a zero correlation between accuracy and confidence, and Saslove and Yarmey (1980) who found a low, positive correlation of .26. Similarly, Bothwell, Deffenbacher, and Brigham (1987) in their metaanalysis of thirty-five staged event studies of visual identification found a correlation of only .25 between accuracy and confidence. As Thompson (1985) correctly emphasized, "although confidence and accuracy are related, subjects making incorrect (voice) identifications were quite confident about their choices. . . . In short, an incorrect choice is often made with complete confidence" (p. 25).

STUDY 6: THE ACCURACY OF EARWITNESS MEMORY FOR VOICES OVER THE TELEPHONE

Very few studies have been conducted on the effects of voice recognition over the telephone (see Bull & Clifford, 1984). One of the few studies having considerable forensic interest was conducted by Rathborn, Bull, and Clifford (1981). Contrary to police beliefs, Rathborn and her colleagues showed that a voice heard originally over the telephone need not be tested over the telephone in order for recognition performance to be at its highest. Voices heard originally over the telephone can be tested with a tape recorder without significant loss of recognition accuracy.

Perpetrators may use the telephone to make calls of a threatening nature, as in kidnapping and blackmail schemes. In these types of crimes, victims are aware of their victimization and may intentionally try to remember the suspect's voice. For other crimes, such as swindles or confidence games, victims lack a forensic reason to intentionally remember the speaker's voice and may be victimized after trusting the perpetrator.

This writer recently tested voice identification over the telephone as part of a larger study on the attitudes of citizens toward police and personal victimization (Yarmey, 1991b). A telephone interview conducted by two female research assistants provided participants an opportunity to learn the voice of their interviewer (Yarmey, 1991c). In order to test the subjects' incidental memory for the interviewer's voice, participants were called back by a third person immediately after hanging up the telephone, two hours later, or two or three days later and asked to take a voice lineup test presented over the telephone. One hundred and seventy-seven males and females ranging in age between eighteen and eighty-eight ($M = 39.5$) participated. Subjects were put into three voice sample duration categories (short, $M = 3.2$ min, medium, $M = 4.3$ min, and long, $M = 7.8$ min) by rank ordering the length of the interviews and dividing them into three equal groups.

Two six-person target-present lineups and two six-person target-absent lineups were used. Voices used as foils were selected from a panel of female volunteers similar in race (white), age, and educational and geographical background to the targets. The tape recorded voice lineups were tested for fairness by a separate group of judges. Subjects were told that the target may or may not be in the lineup.

Identification accuracy (hits) improved with longer opportunities to listen to the target voice, but the false alarm rate also reliably increased with longer duration in a target-present lineup. False alarms were consistently high (overall $M = .48$) in the target-absent lineup. No significant differences were found in hit scores or false alarm scores over the two- or three-day retention interval. For those subjects who chose a stimulus voice, no significant correlation was found between confidence scores and accuracy of performance in target-present lineups ($r = .10$), but a significant correlation ($r = .36$) was found for target-absent lineups.

The fact that false alarms increased with longer exposure durations to a target (see also Yarmey & Matthys, in press) is not unique to voice identification. This effect also has been found in studies of eyewitness memory (Read, 1990; 1991). Read suggested that an availability heuristic operates with long exposures to a target. Subjects may feel that they should be able to identify the target because of the relatively long exposure to the person. Consequently, there may be a high willingness to make a response even though memory for the target may not be particularly strong.

STUDY 7: THE ACCURACY OF EARWITNESS AND EYEWITNESS MEMORY
WHEN SHOWUPS ARE USED

The presentation of a single suspect, commonly referred to as a "showup," is not recommended because of the high possibility of presumed suggestibility (*Stovall v. Deno*, 1967). All showups are not necessarily suggestive, however, and even some showups that are suggestive are not necessarily unreliable (Loftus & Doyle, 1987). The courts have decided, for example, that some aspects of showups such as a short period of time (that is, 30 minutes or less) between the occurrence of an incident and the showup procedure actually contribute to accuracy (*Singletary v. United States*, 1978; *People v. Brnja*, 1980). Although this conclusion is logical and reasonable, it has been made with limited empirical support. It is also based on the assumption that all showups involve a facial photograph or personal showup which is not necessarily true. A showup could involve a tape recording of a suspected perpetrator. Furthermore, if voice showups and visual showups are used it would be important to determine if these two types of tests produce relatively equivalent identification performances.

In a study designed to examine these issues (Yarmey, 1992b), 651 white, native English speaking citizens between the ages of eighteen and sixty-five were randomly approached in public places and asked for directions. An additional 130 individuals were asked to participate in the study but were not used as subjects because they refused to cooperate, did not speak English as a first language, or were younger than eighteen or older than sixty-five years of age. The duration of exposure to one of two female targets was fifteen seconds. Two minutes later the witness was approached by an investigator and asked to participate in a study on perception and memory. Subjects were given a cued recall test for the target's physical appearance followed by an identification test. Witnesses rated their confidence on seven-point scales for overall accuracy of cued recall and their confidence in their showup identification. The showup identification test consisted of a single photograph of either the target or a highly similar foil, or a tape recording of the voice of the target or of a highly similar foil. Twenty-five judges rated a set of fifty-three photographs of individuals who resembled the targets. The photographs of the two individuals rated most similar to each of the two targets served as showup foils. Similarly, taped voice recordings of twenty-nine persons were rated by a separate group of twenty-five judges for their similarity to the voices of the targets. The two voices rated most similar to each of the targets' voices were selected as the showup voice foils.

In order to determine central details and peripheral details of the physical characteristics of the targets, another group of twenty judges were shown a videotape of a mock encounter with one of the targets. The videotape was filmed from the perspective of a witness. Subjects were given the eight physical characteristics used on the cued recall test and were asked to rate each characteristic on a four-point scale ($1 =$ very central, to $4 =$ very peripheral) for its centrality of importance for memory of that person. Mean ratings below 2.5 were used to characterize central characteristics (hair color, hair length, age plus or minus three years, height plus or minus two inches) and those rated 2.5 and above were classified as peripheral characteristics (hair style, eye color, complexion, weight plus or minus five pounds).

The results showed that young adults (eighteen to twenty-nine years of age) were significantly superior (M = 72 percent) to middle-aged witnesses (thirty to forty-four) (M = 61 percent), who in turn were significantly superior to older adults (forty-five to sixty-five) (M = 54 percent) in accuracy of cued recall of physical characteristics. Females (M = 75 percent) were significantly superior to males (M = 69 percent) in cued recall of central characteristics but did not differ in cued recall of peripheral characteristics (females M = 32 percent, males M = 31 percent).

Witnesses who were unsure in target recognition were excluded from further data analysis. There were no significant differences in the frequency of subjects who were unsure as a function of age or sex. The photograph of the foil was correctly rejected significantly more often (M = 88 percent correct rejections) than the photograph of the target was identified (M = 57 percent correct identifications). Note that chance was 50 percent. Analysis of the voice showup also yielded a significant difference for correct responses to the foil (M = 70 percent correct rejections) over the target (M = 28 percent correct identifications).

Reaction time to make a decision about the photographic foil (M = 2.91 sec) was significantly shorter than that of the target (M = 4.15 sec). There were no significant differences in decision time for recognition of the foil voice (12.5 sec) and the target voice (13.1 sec).

There were no significant differences in confidence scores in photo showup identifications or in voice showup identifications. Small but significant correlations were found between accuracy of showup identification of the target photo and confidence (r = .16, p < .05) and foil photo and confidence (r = .27, p < .01), but voice showup identifications were not related to confidence. No significant correlations were found between accuracy of showup identifications and recall of central or peripheral physical characteristics.

Although the targets were poorly identified from their photographs, the fact that a highly similar foil was significantly more often rejected than the target was identified suggests that for photo showup identifications unfamiliar foils are unlikely to be falsely accused. Voice showup performance was, however, very poor. If these results can be replicated little credibility should be attached to voice showup identifications resulting from very short interpersonal interactions of strangers in nonsignificant everyday street situations.

Summary and implications of factors influencing earwitness memory

Jurors may benefit from the presentation of expert evidence, including the use of planned studies, on earwitness memory. The role of the expert on earwitness identification does not differ from that of the expert on eyewitness identification. Furthermore, all types of expert witnesses on person identification are bound by the same considerations of ethics (Yarmey, 1986b).

Verbal descriptions of perpetrators' voices typically are imprecise and superficial. The imprecision of language in the descriptions of both distinctive voices and nondistinctive voices may be minimized by the use of ratings for selected voice characteristics. These ratings, however, should be done as soon as possible after the incident, and no longer than twenty-four hours after the incident, when the voices are nondistinctive.

Victims and witnesses to a crime act as "data-gathering sources whose construction of reality can significantly affect the fate of the alleged offender" (Levine & Tapp, 1982, p. 99). Discussion among witnesses to a crime is difficult, if not impossible, to prevent prior to the arrival of the police. Reliably more fabrications may be expected when two witnesses discuss an incident and later give individual recall than when two people discuss an incident and give a joint response, or when there is no discussion between witnesses.

Just as facial stereotypes of criminals are known to influence eyewitness behavior, voice stereotypes of criminals can influence earwitness behavior.

Accuracy of identification of unfamiliar voices increases with longer voice sample durations; the false alarm rate, however, also increases. This result has been found in both a forensically related laboratory study and in a more naturalistic field study (telephone voice identification), and has been found in studies of eyewitness memory.

The correlation between voice identification and confidence is generally low. Earwitness confidence and eyewitness confidence are not very reliable indicators of identification accuracy.

Contrary to court opinion (*Singletary v. United States,* 1978; *People v. Brnja,* 1980), showup identifications using photographs and voice recordings as stimuli only minutes after an incident do not necessarily lead to high accuracy.

STUDY 8: LAYPERSONS' INTUITIVE KNOWLEDGE ABOUT ACCURACY AND
CONFIDENCE IN EARWITNESS AND EYEWITNESS MEMORY

Trial judges and officers of the court often consider knowledge of the factors that influence eyewitness memory to be nothing more than common knowledge (for example, Yarmey & Jones, 1983). The question can be asked: Is the knowledge of factors that influence eyewitness and earwitness identifications intuitively obvious? Are the intuitions of laypersons about person identification consistent with the scientific evidence (Wells, 1984)?

The following study was conducted to examine the intuitive knowledge laypersons hold about earwitness and eyewitness showup identifications (Yarmey, 1992b). The "prediction approach" method to assess intuitive knowledge was employed (Brigham & Bothwell, 1983; Wells, 1984). That is, subjects were given a summary description of the procedures used in Study 7 and asked to predict the results.

Some 164 citizens approached in public places agreed to volunteer in a

Table 5.6. *Percent accuracy and predicted accuracy of cued recall for physical characteristics and confidence*

Characteristics	Accuracy	Predicted
Central		
Hair color	81	70*
Hair length	60	60
Age (+ or − 3 years)	66	45*
Height (+ or − 2 inches)	81	47*
Peripheral		
Hair style	54	45*
Eye color	25	25
Complexion	88	47*
Weight (+ or − 5 pounds)	48	34*
Overall mean confidence in recall (7-point scale)	4.52	4.11*

*$p < .01$.

study testing common knowledge about memory for people. Subjects ranged in age between eighteen and sixty-five and all were white, native English speakers. Summary descriptions of the earwitness and eyewitness showup conditions used in Study 7 were given. Participants were asked to predict the percentage of witnesses who would accurately recall specific physical characteristics of the target, and the percentage of witnesses who would accurately identify the target and correctly reject a highly similar foil in eyewitness and earwitness showup identifications. Subjects were also asked to predict witnesses' confidence in cued recall and showup identifications.

Table 5.6 presents the percentage of subjects who were correct in their cued recall for target characteristics from Study 7 and the prediction estimates for these characteristics. Caution should be exercised in generalizing from these percentages. Judgments of cued recall performance and showup identification performance based on percentage values from one experiment may be misleading. The table shows that all prediction scores differed significantly from accuracy scores except for hair length and eye color. Note that the laypersons' predictions tended to underestimate the mean percentage of witnesses who would be accurate in these conditions. Subjects also were significantly lower in their predictions of the overall confidence level (seven-point scale) of the accuracy of witnesses in cued recall for target descriptions.

Table 5.7 shows the percentage of witnesses who accurately identified the target or accurately rejected the foil, and the predictions for these behaviors for both eyewitness (photographs) and earwitness (tape recorded voices) showups. The mean confidence scores obtained and mean predicted confidence scores using seven-point scales also are presented.

Table 5.7. *Obtained and predicted (N = 164) mean percent accuracy of showup identifications and mean level of rated confidence (7-point scale)*

	Identification		Confidence	
Conditions	Obtained	Predicted	Obtained	Predicted[a]
Identification of photo of target (n = 138)	.57*	.64*	5.34	4.88
Correct rejection of photo of foil (n = 156)	.88**	.37**	5.56	4.03
Identification of voice of target (n = 134)	.28*	.35*	4.65	3.79
Correct rejection of voice of foil (n = 125)	.70**	.32**	4.67	3.54

[a]each predicted confidence rating differs ($p < .01$) from the obtained confidence score.
*$p < .10$.
**$p < .01$.

Subjects significantly overestimated the percentage of accurate witnesses in identification of targets in both eyewitness and earwitness showups. Subjects accurately predicted that voice identification of a target is more difficult than photographic identification. However, subjects significantly underestimated the percent accuracy of witnesses who would correctly reject the photographs and voice tapes of highly similar foils. All the predicted levels of confidence were significantly lower than the obtained confidence levels witnesses expressed in their eyewitness and earwitness showup identifications.

Although the prediction method is limited by the quality of the summary descriptions provided to subjects, and does not explain how any one witness would be evaluated, these results do provide an initial assessment of intuitive judgments about showup performances. Laypersons, in general, underestimated the percent accuracy of witnesses' cued recall of a target and overestimated the percent accuracy of showup identifications of a target seen just two minutes earlier. It is surprising that approximately two-thirds of the subjects predicted that witnesses would confuse the photograph or the voice of a highly similar foil with the target after a two-minute retention period. Laypersons' interpretations of the concept "similarity" between a foil and a target may account for this finding. The general public also underestimated the confidence levels that witnesses express in their ability to accurately recollect and identify a showup target within minutes of an incident. It may be concluded that common knowledge does not provide good insight into earwitness and eyewitness showup behaviors.

Conclusions

In many jurisdictions the claim of a single eyewitness that he or she saw the accused commit the crime is sufficient for the defendant to be found guilty. Whether or not earwitness identification reports are as incriminating as eyewitness identification reports in the conviction of defendants is uncertain. Laypersons are aware that earwitness identifications are significantly less accurate than eyewitness identifications, and that both are far from perfect. Both American and Canadian courts are aware of the dangers inherent in eyewitness testimony (*Regina v. Audy*, 1977; *United States v. Wade*, 1967). The United States Supreme Court (*Neil v. Biggers*, 1972) listed five factors to be considered in determining eyewitness identification accuracy:

(1) the opportunity of the witness to view the criminal, at the time of the crime, (2) the witness' degree of attention, (3) the accuracy of the witness' prior description of the criminal, (4) the level of certainty demonstrated by the witness at the time of confrontation, (5) the length of time between the crime and the confrontation. (p. 199)

Ten years ago Wells and Murray (1983) summarized the literature of that period and argued that the *Neil v. Biggers* advice or criteria have limited usefulness in judging the accuracy of eyewitness identification evidence. Eyewitness identification research conducted over the last decade supports Wells and Murray's conclusions. It is probable that the courts assume these criteria also apply to earwitness identification and are guided by their intent. Much more research is needed on earwitness identification both to replicate earlier studies and to investigate other factors, such as the influence of stress on memory for voices (see Kunzel, 1990; Mayor, 1985), the accuracy of identification from voice lineups versus voice and visual lineups (McAllister, 1992), and so on, before strong generalizations are warranted. The research reviewed in this chapter suggests, however, that most of the limitations of the *Neil v. Biggers* criteria directed toward eyewitness identification also apply to earwitness identification evidence.

References

Alper, A., Buckhout, R., Chern, S., Harwood, R., & Slomovits, M. (1976). Eyewitness identification: Accuracy of individual vs. composite recollections of a crime. *Bulletin of the Psychonomic Society, 8,* 147–149.

Aronovitch, C. (1976). The voice of personality: Stereotyped judgments and their relation to voice quality and sex of speaker. *Journal of Social Psychology, 99,* 207–220.

Bothwell, R. K., Deffenbacher, K. A., & Brigham, J. C. (1987). Correlation of eyewitness accuracy and confidence: Optimality hypothesis revisited. *Journal of Applied Psychology, 72,* 691–695.

Brigham, J. C., & Bothwell, R. K. (1983). The ability of prospective jurors to estimate the accuracy of eyewitness identifications. *Law and Human Behavior, 7,* 19–30.

Brigham, J. C., Ready, D. J., & Spier, S. A. (1990). Standards for evaluating the fairness of photograph lineups. *Basic and Applied Social Psychology, 11,* 149–163.

Bull, R., & Clifford, B. R. (1984). Earwitness voice recognition accuracy. In G. L. Wells and E. F. Loftus (Eds.), *Eyewitness testimony: Psychological perspectives* (pp. 92–123). New York: Cambridge University Press.

Clifford, B. R. (1983). Memory for voices: The feasibility and quality of earwitness evidence. In S. M. A. Lloyd-Bostock and B. R. Clifford (Eds.), *Evaluating witness evidence* (pp. 189–218). Toronto: Wiley.

Clifford, B. R., Rathborn, H., & Bull, R. (1981). The effects of delay on voice recognition accuracy. *Law and Human Behavior, 5,* 201–208.

Deffenbacher, K. A., Cross, J. F., Handkins, R. E., Chance, J. E., Goldstein, A. G., Hammersley, R., & Read, J. D. (1989). Relevance of voice identification research to criteria for evaluating reliability of an identification. *Journal of Psychology, 123,* 109–119.

Ellis, H. D., Shepherd, J. W., & Davies, G. M. (1980). The deterioration of verbal descriptions of faces over different delay intervals. *Journal of Police Science and Administration, 8,* 101–106.

Erickson, B., Lind, A., Johnson, C., & O'Barr, W. (1978). Speech style and impression formation in a court setting: The effects of "powerful" and "powerless" speech. *Journal of Experimental Social Psychology, 14,* 266–279.

Goldstein, A. G., & Chance, J. E. (1985), May). *Voice recognition: The effects of faces, temporal distribution of "practice," and social distance.* Paper presented at the meeting of the Midwestern Psychological Association, Chicago, IL.

Goldstein, A. G., Chance, J. E., & Gilbert, B. J. (1984). Facial stereotypes of good guys and bad guys: A replication and extension. *Bulletin of the Psychonomic Society, 22,* 549–552.

Hammersley, R., & Read. J. D. (1985). The effect of participation in a conversation on recognition and identification of the speakers' voices. *Law and Human Behavior, 9,* 71–81.

Hammersley, R., & Read, J. D. (in press). Person recognition and identification from voice. In G. Kohnken & S.L. Sporer (Eds.), *Suspect identification: Psychological knowledge, problems and perspectives.*

Handkins, R. E., & Cross, J. F. (1985, March). *Can a voice line-up be too fair?* Paper presented at the meeting of the Midwestern Psychology Association, Chicago, IL.

Hollien, H., Bennett, G., & Gelfer, M. P. (1983). Criminal identification comparison: Aural versus visual identifications resulting from a simulated crime. *Journal of Forensic Sciences, 28,* 208–221.

Hollin, C. R., & Clifford, B. R. (1983). Eyewitness testimony: The effects of discussion on recall accuracy and agreement. *Journal of Applied Social Psychology, 13,* 234–244.

Kassin, S. M., Ellsworth, P. C., & Smith, V. L. (1989). The "general acceptance" of psychological research on eyewitness testimony. *American Psychologist, 44,* 1089–1098.

Kleiman, D. (1988). In an unusual Long Island trial, one key clue: A rapist's voice. *New York Times,* April 15, pp. B1, B28.

Kunzel, H.J. (1990). *Phonetische untersuchungen zur spechererkennung durch linguistisch naive personen.* Stuttgart: Franz Steiner Verlag.

Levine, F. J., & Tapp, J. L. (1982). Eyewitness identification: Problems and pitfalls. In V.J. Konecni & E.B. Ebbesen (Eds.), *The criminal justice system: A social-psychological analysis* (pp. 99–127). San Francisco: Freeman.

Loftus, E. F., & Doyle, J. M. (1987). *Eyewitness testimony: civil and criminal.* New York: Kluwer.

Mayor, D. (1985). Subjective voice identification. *Royal Canadian Mounted Police Gazette, 47,* 6–10.

McAllister, H. A. (1992, March). *When eyewitnesses are also earwitnesses: Effects on visual and voice identifications.* Poster presentation at the meeting of the American Psychology-Law Society, San Diego, CA.

Montepare, J. M., & Zebrowitz-McArthur, L. (1987). Perceptions of adults with childlike voices in two cultures. *Journal of Experimental Social Psychology, 23,* 331–349.

Neil v. Biggers, 409 U.S. 188 (1972).

People v. Brnja, 70 A.D.2d 17, 419 N.Y.S.2d 591 (1979), aff'd, 50 N.Y.2d 366, 406 N.E.2d 1066, 429 N.Y.S.2d 173 (1980).

Peters, D. P. (1987). The impact of naturally occurring stress on children's memory. In S. J. Ceci, M. P. Toglia, & D. F. Ross (Eds.), *Children's eyewitness memory* (pp. 122–141). New York: Springer-Verlag.

Rathborn, H. A., Bull, R. H., & Clifford, B. R. (1981). Voice recognition over the telephone. *Journal of Police Science and Administration. 9,* 280–284.

Read, J. D. (1990, July). *Effects of familiarity and incidental rehearsal on eyewitness memory for natural interactions.* Paper presented at the International Congress of Applied Psychology, Kyoti, Japan.

Read, J. D. (1991, May). *Knowing who's new: From déja to jamais vu.* Paper presented at the Banff Annual Seminar in Cognitive Science. Banff, Alberta, Canada.

Regina v. Audy, 1977, 34 C.C.C. 2d 231 Ont. C.A.

Saslove, H., & Yarmey, A. D. (1980). Long-term auditory memory: Speaker identification. *Journal of Applied Psychology, 60,* 111–116.

Shoemaker, D. J., South, D. R., & Lowe, J. (1973). Facial stereotypes of deviants and judgments of guilt or innocence. *Social Forces, 51,* 427–433.

Singletary v. United States, 383 A.2d 1064 (D.C. 1978).

Sporer, S. L. (1989). Verbal and visual processes in person identification. In H. Wegener, F. Losel, & J. Haisch (Eds.), *Criminal behavior and the justice system: Psychological perspective* (pp. 303–324). New York: Springer-Verlag.

Stephenson, G. M. (1990). Should collaborative testimony be permitted in courts of law? *Criminal Law Review,* 302–314.

Stephenson, G. M., Clark, N. K., & Wade, G. S. (1986). Meetings make evidence? An experimental study of collaborative and individual recall of a simulated police interrogation. *Journal of Personality and Social Psychology, 50,* 1113–1122.

Stovall v. Denno, 388 U.S. 293, 87 S. Ct. 1967, 8 L. Ed. 2d 1199 (1967).

Thompson, C. P. (1985). Voice identification: Speaker identifiability and a correction of the record regarding sex effects. *Human Learning, 14,* 19–27.

United States v. Wade, 388 U.S. 218 (1967).

Voiers, W. D. (1964). Perceptual bases of speaker identity. *Journal of the Acoustical Society of America, 36,* 1065–1073.

Warnick, D. H., & Sanders, G. S. (1980). The effects of group discussion on eyewitness accuracy. *Journal of Applied Social Psychology, 10,* 249–259.

Wells, G. L. (1984). How adequate is human intuition for judging eyewitness testimony? In G. L. Wells & E. F. Loftus (Eds.), *Eyewitness testimony: Psychological perspectives* (pp. 256–272). Cambridge: Cambridge University Press.

Wells, G. L., Leippe, M. R., & Ostrom, T. M. (1979). Guidelines for empirically assessing the fairness of a lineup. *Law and Human Behavior, 3,* 285–293.

Wells, G. L., & Murray, D. M. (1983). What can psychology say about the Neil vs. Biggers criteria for judging eyewitness accuracy? *Journal of Applied Psychology, 68,* 347–362.

Yarmey, A. D. (1979). *The psychology of eyewitness testimony.* New York: Free Press.

Yarmey, A. D. (1982). Eyewitness identification and stereotypes of criminals. In A. Trankell (Ed.), *Reconstructing the past: The role of psychologists in criminal trials* (pp. 205–225). Deventer, The Netherlands: Kluwer.

Yarmey, A. D. (1986a). Verbal, visual, and voice identification of a rape suspect under different levels of illumination. *Journal of Applied Psychology, 71,* 363–370.

Yarmey, A. D. (1986b). Ethical responsibilities governing the statements experimental psychologists make in expert testimony. *Law and Human Behavior, 10,* 101–115.

Yarmey, A. D. (1990). *Understanding police and police work: Psychosocial issues.* New York: New York University Press.

Yarmey, A. D. (1991a). Descriptions of distinctive and nondistinctive voices over time. *Journal of the Forensic Science Society, 31,* 421–428.

Yarmey, A. D. (1991b). Retrospective perceptions of police following victimization. *Canadian Police College Journal, 15,* 137–143.

Yarmey, A. D. (1991c). Voice identification over the telephone. *Journal of Applied Social Psychology, 21,* 1868–1876.

Yarmey, A. D. (1992a). The effects of dyadic discussion on earwitness recall. *Basic and Applied Social Psychology, 13,* 251–263.

Yarmey, A. D. (1992b, March). *Accuracy of eyewitness and earwitness showup identifications in a field setting.* Poster presented at the American Psychology-Law Society conference. San Diego, CA.

Yarmey, A. D., & Jones, H. P. T. (1983). Is the psychology of eyewitness identification a matter of common sense? In S. Lloyd-Bostock & B.R. Clifford (Eds.), *Evaluating witness evidence* (pp. 13–40). Chichester, England: Wiley.

Yarmey, A. D., & Matthys, E. (1992). Voice identification of an abductor. *Applied Cognitive Psychology, 6,* 367–377.

6 Whole body information: Its relevance to eyewitnesses

Malcolm D. MacLeod, Jason N. Frowley, and John W. Shepherd

Introduction

During the past two decades, there has been a rapid increase in the number of psychological studies concerned with how we perceive and remember the human face (see Davies, Ellis, & Shepherd, 1981; Ellis, Jeeves, Newcombe, & Young, 1986; Shepherd, Ellis, & Davies, 1982; Young & Ellis, 1989, for reviews). This is perhaps unsurprising given the importance we attach to identifying other individuals and their emotions from facial information. What is surprising, however, is the relative lack of attention given to the role of nonfacial information such as body shape, dimension, and movement in person perception and recognition. The judgments we make about other people are often not based on facial information alone. Decisions such as whether a person is truthful or untruthful, happy or sad, sexy or unsexy appear to be based, at least in part, on nonfacial information (see, for example, Ekman, 1989; DePaulo & Kirkendol, 1989; Montepare & Zebrowitz-McArthur, 1988). It is also probable that general physical characteristics such as height and weight play a role in eyewitness identification (Wells, 1984), but there has been little systematic investigation of this issue.

The present chapter has two aims. The first is to review briefly the literature on the perception and recognition of body features. In doing so, we hope to point out the relevance of this work for eyewitness testimony. The second aim is to consider how nonfacial information could be incorporated into an identification system. We report on a series of studies we conducted which examine the potential of such a system. In particular, we will examine the kinds of descriptors typically used for bodies and movement, and the reliability of codings based on these descriptors.

Some of the research in this chapter was supported by the Home Office S.R.D.B. (SC/86 7/21/4). The opinions expressed are those of the authors and not necessarily those of the Home Office. We should also like to acknowledge our appreciation of Jean Shepherd for her help in conducting some of the studies reported in this chapter.

125

Perception and memory for bodies and movement

Research on eyewitness testimony for whole body features such as height and weight has indicated that a primary source of error may occur at the perceptual stage rather than during recall (see Flin & Shepherd, 1986; Tollestrup, Turtle, & Yuille, this volume). We felt, therefore, that it was important to consider some of the factors that may impinge on the perceptual processes of eye-witnesses before attempting to assess the likely accuracy of eyewitness testimony for body information. In doing so, we have also drawn parallels with some of the extensive work on how we perceive faces.

Perception of whole bodies

Our perception of body shape and dimension appears to be involved in judgments of personal characteristics similar to those that have been demonstrated to occur in face perception (see, for example, Berry & McArthur, 1985; Cash, 1981; Keating, 1985; Klatzky, Martin, & Kane, 1982a; McArthur, 1982). In face perception, value ratings of an individual appear to be influenced by whether that person is perceived to have average features or not. The further away from the average, the more deviant (from the mean rating) becomes the personality evaluation of that individual (Secord, 1958). More recent perceptual studies using sophisticated computer imaging techniques (Benson & Perrett, 1991; 1992) lend support to this idea. Ratings of facial attractiveness, for example, were found to be influenced by the extent to which facial composites approached average proportions (see also Langlois & Roggman, 1990). Similarly, we appear to have shared stereotypes as to the appearance of certain kinds of individuals based partly on previous experience and partly on cultural norms and expectations. In other words, certain body types typically have particular qualities associated with them. Lerner and Korn (1972), for example, in an examination of the development of such body stereotypes in males, found that the mesomorph was regarded as the most positive somatotype throughout three different age groups. The endomorph, in contrast, was regarded very negatively and the ectomorph less so (see also Hiller, 1982). Judgments about attractiveness (Lerner & Moore, 1974) and popularity (Janssen & Horowski, 1980) have also been shown to be positively related to subjects' judgments of height of a target person so that the taller the target is perceived to be, the more attractive and popular that person is considered. Findings from body image research (for example, Bailey, Shinedling, & Payne, 1970; Collins, 1987; Collins & Plahn, 1988) also indicate that the judgments we make about body shape and size are not only dependent on the *objective* characteristics of the target but on the target's *perceived* characteristics and the relationship that these may have to the perceiver.

Another important element of person perception is body movement information. Building on the exploratory work of Johansson (1975), Barclay, Cutting and Kozlowski (1978) have shown that we are capable of discriminating between male and female targets by means of only two moving points of light (one on each ankle). Gender recognition performance can be improved when body features such as hips and shoulders are included in the point-light displays (Kozlowski & Cutting, 1977). Movement information alone has also been shown to be a sufficient basis for recognizing oneself and familiar others (Cutting & Kozlowski, 1977) but it remains to be investigated as to its importance for recognizing unfamiliar others.

In contrast, value judgments made about other people have clearly been shown to be influenced by movement and posture information. Montepare and Zebrowitz-McArthur (1988), for example, showed videotapes of moving targets where the brightness had been adjusted so that all that remained visible were moving points of light corresponding to the points where pieces of reflective tape had been attached to the targets' bodies. They found that the ratings of the targets' traits and gaits varied with the age of the targets. Ratings of sexiness, for example, increased from children to adolescents and young adults but then decreased for older adults. Similarly, ratings of hip sway, knee bend, stride length, bounce, and loose-jointedness in the target decreased with age. It also appeared that the possession of a youthful gait (characterized by hip sway, knee bending, arm swing, loose-jointedness, and more steps per second) was strongly related to the happiness and power attributed to the targets. Even when subjects were shown the same tapes with the brightness turned up so that the subjects could see the targets walking rather than only points of light, ratings were still found to be influenced by the targets' gait. Targets with a youthful gait were rated as more powerful and happier than those with an older gait, despite the fact that other cues concerning their actual age were now available.

In addition to values attached to certain body shapes or movements, stereotypic expectations based on the physique or movement of a target may affect the way in which that person's actions are interpreted. Duncan (1976), for example, using racial categories, clearly illustrated how an ambiguous shove by a black actor could be interpreted by observers as being more violent than the same behavior performed by a white actor. It is conceivable, therefore, that people who possess certain body types may be subject to similar biases in the interpretation of ambiguous or innocuous behaviors. We have recently conducted an exploratory study that attempts to examine just this (Frowley & MacLeod, 1992).

In a paradigm similar to that employed by Duncan (1976), we manipulated the body size of the perpetrator and the victim in an incident which culminated in an ambiguous shove that could be coded by subjects as "playing around," "dramatizing," "aggressive behavior," or "violent behavior." Subjects were led to believe they were witnessing a video recording of an interaction that had taken place between two experimental subjects like themselves earlier in the week. Subjects were asked to code the behaviors they saw during the interaction using the coding scheme at a number of predetermined points in the interaction, one of which was an "ambiguous shove." We found no significant effects for objective body size conditions. When we asked subjects to rate whether they thought the two people in the film were of similar or different size, however, we found that a perceived disparity in body size could affect how the incident was interpreted. Specifically, when the protagonist was perceived to have been large and the victim small, subjects were significantly more likely to interpret the behavior as aggressive or violent than when the two people in the film were perceived as having the same body size (X^2 (3) = 18.5, p < .001). The basis for this finding is unclear although no significant effect was found for the small aggressor–large victim condition. Further research is required to examine whether perceived discrepancies in body size between two people can systematically affect the way in which behaviors are interpreted by observers.

The mechanisms underlying such judgments have also to be identified. One possibility lies in Heider's notion that such judgments are a result of our "fundamental search for causation." In an early experiment by Heider and Simmel (1944), for example, subjects were shown a film of animated geometrical shapes of various sizes that moved in such a way as to appear to move in relation to each other. Subjects reported that a large triangle was "chasing" a small circle and a small triangle rather than "following" them. If people explain the movement of geometric shapes of different sizes by attributing to them wants, desires, and intentions, it is conceivable that their explanations for the actions of people may similarly be influenced by body shape and dimension.

Another possible explanation lies in Berry and McArthur's (1986) suggestion that information directly perceptible to the perceiver such as the appearance of a target and his movements may provide useful information about a target's "affordances." In other words, body information may provide important cues about the opportunities for acting or being acted on, and this may account for the importance we attach to social information. The results reported by Montepare and Zebrowitz-McArthur (1988) appear to be consistent with this hypothesis.

Summary

Psychological research has revealed that body perception is a complex process that involves not only the objective characteristics of the target, but also the target's perceived characteristics. Information about body dimension can also affect our value judgments about other people and may also influence the way in which we interpret behavior. The importance of movement information for body recognition, however, is less clear. Although gender and familiar others can be recognized on the basis of movement information alone, it is unclear whether it plays any part in recognizing unfamiliar others save those who have unusual gaits or deformities.

Memory for body features

Unfortunately, there are few studies in the psychological literature which have assessed accuracy of memory for whole body information but those that have tend to suggest that memory for bodies, like that for many other forms of information, is susceptible to bias. Christiaansen, Sweeney, and Ochalek (1983), for example, conducted a study in which subjects encountered a male target and were subsequently told his occupation. The introduction of such postevent information was found to bias weight estimates. When the target was said to have been a truck driver, subjects gave heavier weight estimates than when he was said to have been a dancer. From a forensic perspective, however, it is perhaps of more interest to establish the effects of systematic biases on memory for body information. Flin and Shepherd's study (1986) used a range of male targets varying in weight and height. Members of the public were asked for directions by one of these targets in a busy city center. Once the target had disappeared from view, the subjects were asked by a second confederate to estimate the target's height and weight. Subjects tended to underestimate the height of the target. The greatest mean underestimate was 4.91 inches for the tallest target (78 inches). It is interesting that the one target for whom there was a mean overestimation of height (+1.05 inches) was the smallest target at 66 inches. A similar situation was found for weight estimates: The weights of the heaviest targets were consistently underestimated and the lightest targets overestimated.

Flin and Shepherd found that the second most important source of variance for these estimates was the height and weight of the subject making the estimates, particularly in the case of male subjects (for female subjects the own-anchor effect held only for height estimates). Thus, it would appear that one's own physical characteristics can affect judgments about the height and weight of other individuals: They are used as norms or anchors against which relative judgments are made. In this sample, taller subjects tended to be more accurate in their height estimates of the targets than did shorter subjects as there was a general tendency to underestimate the height of the targets. Inaccurate estimates for the tallest, lightest, and heaviest targets tended toward rather than away from the norm, perhaps indicating a general regression to the population mean (see also Tollestrup, Turtle, & Yuille, this volume).

Yuille and Cutshall (1986) also considered the kinds of information recalled by thirteen of twenty-one people who had been witness to an extraordinary robbery during which a gun battle ensued and one of the perpetrators was killed. Although Yuille and Cutshall were principally concerned with making comparisons between the accuracy of information reported during the police interview and that reported during subsequent research interviews, some interesting observations about body descriptions were made. Of the total number of classifiable details, the percentage given over to person description was 27.71 percent in the police interview and 25.27 percent in the research interview. Of these, approximately 75 percent and 72 percent respectively were correct. Most of the errors for person description details in the police interview (52 percent) and over a third of such errors (37 percent) in the research interview involved height, age, and weight estimates. When all estimates were removed from the analysis for body description details, overall accuracy increased to 82.47 percent in the police interview and 79.9 percent in the research interview. Details about the style and color of hair and the style and color of clothing comprised the bulk of the remaining person description errors.

In a more recent study by Tollestrup, Turtle, and Yuille (this volume) victims of robbery were found to have provided the most information regarding the perpetrator's physical appearance. They also found that the ability of eyewitnesses to provide accurate estimates of age, height, and weight seemed to be unaffected by the level of arousal as assessed via a comparison of victim (high arousal) and other witness (low arousal) reports. Both victims and witnesses overestimated age whereas only victims underestimated height. In a similar study by MacLeod and Shepherd (1986), the effects of arousal on eyewitness testimony were estimated by comparing witness reports for assaults that involved either physical injury or no physical injury to the victim. Of the 379 eyewitness reports analyzed, no differences were found in the kinds and amount of details reported by male and female witnesses when the victim did not sustain physical injury. Female witnesses, however, were found to report significantly fewer details about the perpetrator's appearance than did male witnesses when injury to the victim was involved.

Summary

With the exception of estimates regarding height, weight, and age, our ability to recall details about a perpetrator's physical appearance appears to be remarkably accurate. Height and weight estimates in eyewitness reports, however, appear to be susceptible to systematic biases such as the own-anchor effect which probably occur at the perception stage. Explanations for such biases tend to be couched in terms of population norms for height and weight and the subject's awareness of these population norms. Beyond that, there seems to be little theoretical understanding of how such biases work. More research needs to be conducted in this area if we are to provide law enforcement officials with practical ways of estimating a perpetrator's true height and weight from the information provided by eyewitnesses – perhaps by taking into account the witness's own age, gender, height, and weight.

Whole body information and computers

In the meantime, can psychological research on whole body information provide any practical help for law enforcement officials? One possibility is that whole body information could be used more effectively during criminal investigations by employing it in computer searches for suspects. It would seem reasonable to suppose that identification systems could be developed that use coded information from eyewitness reports regarding whole body features. This coded whole body information could then be used to retrieve coded targets previously stored within the system.

In the remainder of this chapter we report our findings from a series of studies which have sought to examine this possibility. Unfortunately, we are not yet at a stage where we can give a comprehensive answer but the work we have completed to date permits an assessment of the likely viability of such identification systems. In particular, we focus on the extent to which a data base composed of precoded body information could be set up. This precoded material must have good interrater reliability to permit the possibility of different weightings being placed on various dimensions during the matching process, similar to that developed for F.R.A.M.E. (Face Retrieval and Matching Equipment, see Shepherd, 1986). F.R.A.M.E. incorporates a data base in which a large set of images of faces has been coded to provide a retrieval system which can be searched from a description of a target provided by a witness. So far, F.R.A.M.E. has been used successfully to search from descriptions provided by witnesses working on the basis of their recall of the suspect. The studies that we report in the following section examine how such a system could be extended to use body information.

Development of a set of descriptive categories

One of the first things to establish is how the human form is typically described. We conducted a series of experiments wherein a range of static and moving targets were presented to subjects who were then asked to describe them (Shepherd, Shepherd, & MacLeod, 1990). Static targets were twelve adult males who were photographed in full length, frontal pose, dressed in normal indoor clothing (shirt or light sweater and trousers). The targets were selected to provide a wide range in height and build. Slides of the targets were projected individually on a screen producing an image approximately four feet high. Subjects were not given any time limit in which to describe each target. When all had completed the description of the target, the next slide was presented. A total of 156 slides were described, from which 687 descriptors were gen-

Table 6.1. *Percentage of total number of descriptors for which body features were mentioned in describing static and moving present targets*

Descriptor	Static (%) $n = 687$	Moving (%) $n = 1,041$
Global physique	43.5	61.6
Proportion	9.6	11.5
Height	15.9	18.1
Build/weight	9.8	25.9
Posture/stance	8.3	6.1
Head and neck	6.1	1.9
Head	2.2	0.02
Neck	3.9	1.9
Torso	25.4	18.3
Shoulders	14.3	10.8
Chest/stomach	11.1	7.5
Arms and hands	8.7	5.3
Arms	6.1	2.6
Hands	2.6	2.7
Lower body	16.3	12.7
Hips/buttocks	4.1	2.4
Legs	11.8	9.3
Feet	0.4	1.0

erated with an average of 4.4 descriptors per slide. These descriptors were subsequently coded into categories on the basis of the part of the body referred to. We found that for static targets, the greatest proportion of descriptors concerned global attributes of physique such as height, build, and general proportions (43.5 percent). A quarter of all descriptors concerned the upper body (25.45 percent), almost equally divided between the shoulders and the chest or stomach area. The lower body, in contrast, accounted for only 16.3 percent of the total number of descriptors used. Of the specific parts of the body, the height, shoulders, chest, and legs were the most frequently mentioned, and were generally described in terms of their length or thickness (see Table 6.1).

To approximate more closely naturalistic viewing conditions, we conducted a second pilot study where twelve clips, each of thirty seconds duration, showing a man in full length engaged in a variety of everyday pursuits, were employed. These were mostly taken from transmitted television broadcasts, and included competitors in golf tournaments, a hill walker, and scenes from various dramatic productions. Each clip was edited to provide a moving sequence of the target that included a number of activities (standing, walking, running, bending) and was shot from various angles (front view, rear view,

Table 6.2. *Percentage of total number of descriptors relating to aspects of movement and character attribution*

Movement & other descriptors	Percent $n = 197$
Pace	20.3
Length of stride	14.7
Smoothness of gait	39.0
Character attribution	17.8
Others	8.1

side view). The targets could thus be seen from a number of angles and performing a range of activities. Subjects were run individually and allowed as much time as they wished to play through the video tapes. After each clip, they were asked to write a general description of the person in the clip without making any comparative references to preceding clips.

A total of 264 video sequences were described, generating 1,238 descriptors, an average of 4.7 descriptors per clip. Of these, 1,041 (84.1 percent) related to aspects of physique, whereas the remainder related to the description of movement. The results are presented in Table 6.1. Even more than for static targets, the majority of descriptors used to describe moving targets referred to global attributes (61.6 percent of body descriptors), such as height (18.1 percent), build (25.9 percent) and general proportion (11.5 percent). Of the descriptors referring to specific body features, 18.3 percent were used for the torso, and 12.7 percent for hips, legs, and feet. The increase in global attributes is perhaps due to the difficulty of making more fine-grained estimates of the length or thickness of individual body features of moving targets. This particular distribution of descriptors may also be caused by increased competition for attentional resources owing to the introduction of movement or the part that movement may play in describing overall physique.

In addition to descriptions of parts of the body, 197 descriptors of movement and other nonbody references were also elicited. The greatest single category related to "smoothness of gait." These are listed in Table 6.2.

A finer grained analysis of the difference between descriptions of static and moving figures was carried out using only those attributes used to describe global physique. These were more likely to be used in describing moving targets than for describing static targets (62 percent versus 43 percent), but within the global physique category, there were differences in relative frequencies for describing specific features. In particular, references to build or weight were relatively more common for moving targets (42 percent of the category) than for static targets (22 percent of the category), whereas reference to posture was more common for static than for moving targets (19 and 10 percent of the category, respectively). At the same time, reference to bodily proportion and to height differed little between the two kinds of targets (22 versus 20 percent and 36 versus 31 percent for the two comparisons, respectively).

The explanation for these disparities is not clear. The two sets of targets differed in many ways. Not only were they different people, they were dressed differently, were photographed or filmed in different settings, and were involved in different activities. It is tempting to speculate that the general body mass (build/weight) may have been more salient in a dynamic target than in a static target, whereas posture would be more salient for a person standing still than for a moving target. Perhaps more surprising was the lack of difference between static and moving targets in the frequency with which the lower limbs were mentioned. Not only did the two kinds of targets have a similar overall frequency in the number of descriptors for the lower body (16 and 13 percent), they also showed little difference in the distribution of descriptors within the general category. Intuitively, one might have expected more comment on hips in moving targets in view of the role of hips in movement perception (Montepare & Zebrowitz-McArthur, 1988). Instead, subjects used the vocabulary of movement to describe stride and gait in moving targets (16 percent of all descriptors were related to movement), without reference to the specific parts of the body involved. Of the 197 attributes related to movement, 39 percent described "smoothness of gait."

One further observation on the comparison of moving and static targets is that in spite of the greater richness of information which might be expected from a dynamic source, descriptions of moving targets were no longer (4.7 descriptors per target) than descriptions of static targets (4.4 descriptors per target).

The mean number of physical features reported (4.7) is slightly lower than that reported by Tollestrup et al. (this volume) in their study of eyewitness reports of victims and other witnesses to crimes. At first glance this may appear surprising since in our study subjects were making descriptions with the target in view, whereas the witnesses in the Tollestrup et al. study were reporting from memory. There are other differences between the studies, however, which may explain the discrepancy. Their subjects were interacting with a police investigator who may have prompted for some key physical indicators such as height, build and age, and in their analysis, Tollestrup et al. count attributes such as age, hair color, and eyeglasses as items of physical measurement. These characteristics were excluded from our study. If these items are discounted, it may turn out that the numbers of physical characteristics reported in the two studies are quite close.

Reliability studies

Given the range, outlined earlier in the chapter, of social information that can impinge on our decision-making processes concerning the shape and size of nonfacial body features, how reliable are our judgments? We were particularly interested in this question as it related directly to the viability of a computer-based retrieval system that employs as its basis a data set of pre-coded information about targets. From the terms generated from the free descriptions of static and dynamic targets described above, a number of descriptors (incorporating those that occurred most frequently and mentioning each part of the body referred to in the descriptions) were assessed for reliability. This gave a total of twenty-three descriptors which were variously formulated as bipolar five-point scales, or as dichotomous items.

For this study a new set of target stimuli was generated on video where each target appeared first in full shot, facing the camera, then in left full length profile, right full length profile, walking at regular pace toward the camera, walking away from the camera, walking from left to right and from right to left across the field of the camera, to return to a full frontal still pose. One hundred and eight men were recorded. They ranged in age from twenty to fifty-eight, in height from five feet, three inches to six feet, eight inches, and in weight from seven stones, seven pounds (one hundred and five pounds) to nineteen stones (two hundred and sixty-six pounds).

Forty targets were selected to represent a wide range of build and height; these were randomly divided into two sets of twenty. Each set of twenty targets was edited on a video tape and displayed on a color monitor to twenty subjects who were asked to rate each target on the set of twenty-three scales. Each group of twenty subjects provided ratings on twenty-three scales for twenty targets. The reliability of the scales was estimated by dividing each group of raters into two random groups of ten, and averaging the rating for each target on each scale across the ten members of each random group. This was done for each group of twenty subjects and provided for each of the twenty-three scales a pair of means for each of forty targets based on ten raters for each mean. The product moment correlation between the two columns of means was then used as an estimate of the reliability of the scales. It is clear from these results that, on the whole, people's estimations regarding body shape and dimension show a high level of reliability. Reliabilities ranged from 0.96 to 0.58, with eight of the scales having correlations above 0.9, and a further nine above 0.8. Of the remaining scales, five have correlations above

Table 6.3. *Product moment correlation coefficients for parameters of body and movement descriptors*

Scales	Reliability (Pearson R)
General body descriptors	
1. slim–heavy (5)	.96
2. thin–fat (5)	.96
3. gangly–stocky (5)	.94
4. short–tall (5)	.94
Body parts	
5. thin–thick neck (5)	.79
6. short–long neck (5)	.90
7. narrow–broad (5)	.87
8. rounded–square (5)	.83
9. slim–barrel chest (5)	.91
10. short–long arms (5)	.75
11. thin–thick arms (5)	.85
12. narrow–broad hips (5)	.89
13. thin–thick legs (5)	.92
14. short–long legs (5)	.91
15. bowed–straight legs (5)	.85
16. upright–slouched posture (5)	.79
17. not well prop–well prop (5)	.76
Physique	
18. healthy–unhealthy (2)	.86
19. athletic–unathletic (2)	.83
20. muscular–not muscular (2)	.81
Movement	
21. short–long stride (5)	.78
22. slow–fast pace (5)	.86
23. jerky–fluid stride (5)	.58

Note: Numbers in brackets refer to the number points on each scale.

0.74, after which there is a sharp drop to the lowest correlation of 0.58 for "jerky–fluid stride." See Table 6.3.

The reliability of a scale (that is, the level of agreement among sets of raters for the same target) is one criterion on which scales for a data base for an identification system could be selected. A further means of clarifying the kinds of body and movement information that are picked up by observers is to eliminate those scales that replicate what is being measured by other scales, thereby eliminating redundancy in the coding system.

We accomplished this by conducting a factor analysis of the data (see Shepherd, Shepherd, & MacLeod, 1990, for details of the procedure employed). For this a 40×23 data matrix[1] was computed comprising the mean

Table 6.4. *Loadings of scales on rotated factors (Varimax criterion)*

Scale	F1	F2	F3	F4
		Loading (decimal omitted)		
Gangly	95			
Slim chest	95			
Thin arms	93			
Thin legs	91			
Slim	91			
Thin	89			
Thin neck	84			
Narrow hips	76			
Short arms	−75			
Narrow shoulders	75			
Short neck	−67			
Short legs	−62			58
Athletic		88		
Muscular		80		
Not well proportioned	−79			
Healthy	61	65		
Slow-paced movement			80	
Upright posture			−75	
Round shouldered			74	
Short stride			62	
Bow legged				75
Short				70
Jerky stride				66

Note: Only one pole of the scale is named, and decimal points are omitted. All loadings start at the first decimal place.

ratings for each target on each scale. The correlation matrix derived from this was subjected to a principal components analysis. This resulted in four components being extracted with eigen values greater than one accounting for 77 percent of the total variance. These components were then rotated using the Varimax criterion to give an orthogonal solution. The rotated factor matrix is listed in Table 6.4.

The first factor was identified as a "linearity" factor on which fourteen of the scales had substantial loadings. These contrasted tall thin with short thick (not necessarily fat) individuals. Thus high positive loadings were found on "gangly–stocky," "slim–barrel chested," and "thin–thick arms" and "thin–thick legs" together with "slim–heavy." The second factor was defined by high loadings relating to "physique" in the sense that proportions of the body rather than general linearity were involved. For example, the three highest loadings were on "athletic–unathletic," "muscular–not muscular," and "not well proportioned–well proportioned" (negative loading, that is, scored in

Table 6.5. *Scales selected for reliability*

Scale	Reliability	Factor	Loading
Thin–fat body shape	.96	Linearity	.93
Short–tall body shape	.94	Legs	.70
Not well–well proportioned	.77	Physique	.79
Short–long neck	.90	Linearity	.67
Thin–thick neck	.79	Linearity	.84
Rounded–square shoulders	.84	Posture & movement	.74
Slim–barrel chest	.92	Linearity	.90
Short–long arms	.76	Linearity	.75
Thin–thick arms	.86	Linearity	.93
Narrow–broad hips	.89	Linearity	.75
Short–long legs	.91	Linearity & legs	.62 & .58
Thin–thick legs	.92	Linearity	.91
Bow–straight legged	.85	Legs	.75

the opposite direction). Factor 3 had substantial loadings on four scales. These were "round shoulders" and "upright posture" (negative), and "length of stride" and "pace of stride." The interpretation of these is not altogether clear, but they seem to be best subsumed under a "posture and movement" factor. Factor 4 might best be described as a "legs" factor. The highest loadings on this factor were for "bowed–straight legged," "short–tall," "short–long legs," and "jerky–fluid stride."

The factor analysis thus seems to differentiate "height" from "build" in that no bodily descriptor is common to both factors. Of passing interest is that "healthy" appearance loads on both factors, being associated with a long, lean body as well as with muscular, athletic body. A second notable feature is that stride length (Factor 3) is distinguished from stride quality (Factor 4), the former being associated with poor posture and slow movement, whereas the latter shares loadings with short stature, short legs, and bowleggedness.

These studies indicate that it is possible to devise a set of descriptors for whole body features that will generate reliable ratings on five-point scales that can be used to describe targets presented on video monitors. The scales derived cover most aspects of the body, from general assessment of build to specific features such as the shoulders, arms, and legs. The criteria for selecting these scales were that they had a satisfactory reliability, and represented the factors that had emerged from the factor analysis (see Table 6.5). These attributes should also provide a good basis for conducting future research on whole body description.

We have not included scales which describe movement on this list. We reasoned that an individual's pattern of movement might be variable over time according to specific circumstances such as hurrying or strolling, walking on a level or down a set of stairs. This particular problem requires much further exploration. Eyewitnesses, for example, frequently view perpetrators running away from the scene of the crime. The effects of such movement on the reliability of body judgments, therefore, will have direct relevance to the viability of any retrieval system for whole body identification.

A final experiment was conducted to test the reliability of the set of scales listed in Table 6.6. An additional aim was to examine the effect of training on raters. A total of seventy-two targets was selected from the one hundred and eight who had been captured on videotape for the previous study. Of these, sixteen were selected for pretraining rating, forty for training, and sixteen for posttraining rating. The pre- and posttraining sets were matched for age, physique, and familiarity of raters with targets.

Raters were told that they would see a series of clips on a video monitor, each showing an individual moving about a room. Each clip lasted thirty seconds and raters were asked to rate the target on the set of scales as they watched. Following this, after a short break, the training session was conducted. For this, a set of exemplar targets for each scale point on the fourteen body scales was prepared. These were selected from the reliability study, and the mean rating on the parameter was adopted as the criterion. Each exemplar was shown to the raters, who rated it and compared their rating with the standard. Any discrepancies were then discussed to determine the source of disagreement. The raters then rated a set of forty targets. After each target, ratings were compared and discrepancies reconciled. After a further break, the posttraining set of targets was presented, and rated independently on the body scales.

The reliability of each scale was estimated following a procedure recommended by Winer (1971). A single factor repeated measure ANOVA was used in which the raters represent the repeated measure and the targets the subjects. For the purpose of our study, we computed two estimates of reliability. The first was the estimated reliability of a single measurement. This is the equivalent of the average correlation of the individual ratings between the raters. The second measure of reliability was for the average ratings of the targets. In this case, the estimate is of the correlation between the mean ratings one would expect if another sample of raters rated the same targets.

It should also be noted that different targets were used for the pre- and posttraining sessions, so the data in Table 6.6 are not an indication of test-retest reliability. The difference in the targets, although detracting from a clear interpretation of a training effect, does allow more confident inferences to be drawn about overall reliability, being in effect a cross-validation of the reliability of the scales.

It was clear from our results that training appeared to have little overall effect on reliability. In some cases there was an increase and in others a decrease in reliability; in the main these were fairly trivial. (See Table 6.6).

Table 6.6. *Reliabilities for body parameters*

Scale	Individual Training		Mean Training	
	Pre-	Post-	Pre-	Post-
Thin–fat body	.773	.728	.953	.941
Short–fat	.489	.687	.852	.929
Not well–well proportioned	.141	.279	.496	.398
Athletic–unathletic	.249	.058	.665	.270
Short–long neck	.570	.597	.888	.898
Thin–thick neck	.644	.411	.916	.807
Rounded–square shoulders	.166	.390	.545	.793
Slim–barrel chest	.407	.486	.742	.850
Short–long arms	.242	.357	.657	.769
Thin–thick arms	.389	.423	.793	.815
Narrow–broad hips	.648	.633	.917	.912
Short–long legs	.700	.367	.933	.777
Thin–thick legs	.798	.533	.959	.873
Bow–straight legs	.242	− .023	.657	− .156
Young–old	.884	.897	.979	.981
Weight	.701	.402	.934	.801
Height (measure)	.461	.688	.837	.929

Given the high initial reliability of many of the scales, it is perhaps not that surprising that little change was found after training. Of more importance is the apparent reliability of the selected scales. If the reliabilities in Table 6.6 are compared with those for the same scales in the reliability study, where the reliabilities were based on product moment correlations, it will be seen that they are largely of the same order. This gives added confidence to their reliability.

Conclusions

This chapter has identified, through a review of the psychological research on the perception and memory for whole body information, a number of important areas where research urgently needs to be conducted. We need to have a clearer understanding of how information about body shape and dimension can affect value judgments about other people and the extent to which these judgments affect our memories for people and for the interpretation of events. We need to design research that specifically sets out to look at the accuracy of eyewitness testimony for body information about perpetrators. In addition, much more research in this area should be conducted using archival methods as pioneered by Yuille and Cutshall (1986) and MacLeod and Shepherd (1986) in which actual eyewitness reports are used.

As far as the development of a retrieval system for whole bodies is concerned, our studies illustrate that it is possible to devise a set of descriptors for the whole body which will generate reliable ratings on five-point scales. The scales derived cover most aspects of the body, from general assessments of build to specific areas such as shoulders, arms, and legs. Admittedly, the reliability of ratings by individual raters was not so impressive but it seems likely that with more effective training, the reliability of individual raters could be greatly improved. The training aspect of the study described above was negligible, largely because of the absence of source material that minimized the number of exemplars that could be used for the various attributes on which the raters were being trained. With more time for preparation, more source material, and a longer training period, levels of reliability close to those of the average raters should be attainable.

There is thus every reason to be optimistic that the attributes we have identified regarding body shape and dimension should provide a good basis for the future development of a retrieval system that uses whole body descriptors. It is important to note, however, that this work was conducted on targets in a laboratory setting who were present on video at the time of the description. This work should be extended to examine the types and amount of body feature information that would be recalled under target-absent conditions that pertain in most eyewitness situations. Although Yuille and colleagues have already made important contributions to this area, through their examination of reports by eyewitnesses to actual crimes, this mode of research tends to be the exception rather the rule.

Our own program of research is at a stage where we are about to embark on a series of studies (both laboratory-based and archival) designed to examine the kinds of body information typically recalled under eyewitness conditions and to assess the accuracy of memory for this information. In addition, we are investigating how different conditions may affect accuracy of report for body information by eyewitnesses, especially where perpetrators have worn some form of disguise. Only through increased attention to the matters we have sought to raise in this chapter will psychologists be in a position to provide valuable advice and practical help to law enforcement officials on issues of person identification.

Note

1 In the present case, there are forty targets, each rated on twenty-three scales. Conventionally, it is recommended that the ratio of sample size to number of variables be at least 5:1, and preferably 10:1. In the present case, this requirement is clearly not met. As a means of checking the solution obtained with the average ratings with the forty targets, a further factor analysis was carried out on the individual ratings by each rater on each target. This gave a total sample

size of eight hundred (twenty raters by twenty targets by two), with ratings on twenty-three scales. This is not altogether satisfactory, since each case in the sample is not independent. Nevertheless, to the extent that the two analyses generate very similar solutions, it adds some confidence to the results of any one solution.

References

Bailey, W. L., Shinedling, M. M., & Payne, I. R. (1970). Obese individuals' perception of body image. *Perceptual & Motor Skills*, 3(2), 617–618.

Barclay, C. D., Cutting, J. E., & Kozlowski, L. T. (1978). Temporal and spatial factors in gait perception that influence gender recognition. *Perception and Psychophysics*, 23(2), 145–152.

Benson, P., & Perrett, D. (1991). Computer averaging and manipulation of faces. In P. Wombell (Ed.), *Photovideo: Photography in the Age of the Computer*. London: Rivers Oram Press.

Benson, P. & Perrett, D. (1992). Face to face with the perfect image. *New Scientist*, 133, 32–35.

Berry, D. S., & McArthur, L.Z. (1985). Some components and consequences of a babyface. *Journal of Personality and Social Psychology*, 48, 312–323.

Berry, D. S., & McArthur, L. Z. (1986). Perceiving character in faces: The impact of age-related craniofacial changes on social perception. *Psychological Bulletin*, 100, 3–18.

Cash, T. F. (1981). Physical attractiveness: An annotated bibliography of theory and research in the behavioral sciences. *JSAS Catalog of Selected Documents in Psychology*, 11, Ms. 2370.

Christiaansen, R. E., Sweeney, J. D., & Ochalek, K. (1983). Influencing eyewitness descriptions. *Law and Human Behavior*, 7, 59–65.

Collins, J. K. (1987). Methodology for the objective measurement of body image. *International Journal of Eating Disorders*, 16(3), 393–399.

Collins, J. K., & Plahn, M. R. (1988). Recognition accuracy, stereotype preference and subjective judgment of body appearance in adolescents and young adults. Unpublished manuscript, Macquarie University, School of Behavioural Sciences, Sydney.

Cutting, J. E., & Kozlowski, L. T. (1977). Recognizing friends by their walk: Gait perception without familiarity cues. *Bulletin of the Psychonomic Society*, 9, 353–356.

Davies, G. M., Ellis, H. D., & Shepherd, J. W. (Eds.), (1981). *Perceiving and Remembering Faces*. London: Academic Press.

DePaulo, B. M., & Kirkendol, S. E. (1989). The motivational impairment effect in the communication of deception. In J. C. Yuille (Ed.), *Credibility Assessment*. Dordrecht: Kluwer Press.

Duncan, B. L. (1976). Differential social perception and attribution of intergroup violence: Testing the lower limits of stereotyping of blacks. *Journal of Personality and Social Psychology*, 34, 590–598.

Ekman, P. (1989). Why lies fail and what behaviors betray a lie. In J.C. Yuille (Ed.), *Credibility Assessment*. Dordrecht: Kluwer Press.

Ellis, H. D., Jeeves, M. A., Newcombe, F., & Young, A. (1986). (Eds.), *Aspects of Face Processing*. Dordrecht: Nijhoff.

Flin, R. H., & Shepherd, J. W. (1986). Tall stories: Eyewitnesses' ability to estimate height and weight characteristics. *Human Learning*, 5, 29–38.

Frowley, J. N., & MacLeod, M. D. (1992). *Stereotypes and Eyewitness Memory*. Paper presented at the Third European Conference on Law & Psychology, Oxford.

Heider, F., & Simmel, M. (1944). An experimental study of apparent behavior. *American Journal of Psychology*, 57, 243–259.

Hiller, D. V. (1982). Overweight as master status: A replication. *Journal of Psychology*, 110(1), 107–113.

Janssen, J. P., & Horowski, A. (1980). Students' estimates of stature: Tendency to accentuate as a cognitive style in person perception. *Zeitschrift für Enteicklungspsychologie und Pädagogische Psychologie,* 12(2), 167–176.

Johansson, G. (1975). Visual motor perception. *Scientific American,* 232(6), 76–89.

Keating, C. F. (1985). Gender and the physiognomy of dominance and attractiveness. *Social Psychology Quarterly,* 48, 61–70.

Klatzky, R. L., Martin, G. L., & Kane, R. A. (1982). Influence of social-category activation on processing of visual information. *Social Cognition,* 1, 95–109.

Kozlowski, L. T., & Cutting, J. E. (1977). Recognising the sex of a walker from a dynamic point-light display. *Perception and Psychophysics,* 21, 575–580.

Langlois, J. H., & Roggman, L. A. (1990). Attractive faces are only average. *Psychological Science,* 1, 115–121.

Lerner, R. M., & Korn, S. J. (1972). The development of body-build stereotypes in males. *Child Development,* 43(3), 908–920.

Lerner, R. M., & Moore, T. (1974). Sex and status effects on perception of physical attractiveness. *Psychological Reports,* 34(3), 1047–1050.

MacLeod, M. D., & Shepherd, J. W. (1986). Sex differences in eyewitness reports of criminal assaults. *Medicine Science & Law,* 26(4), 311–318.

McArthur, L. Z. (1982). Judging a book by its cover: A cognitive analysis of the relationship between physical appearance and stereotyping. In A. Hastorf & A. Isen (Eds.), *Cognitive Social Psychology.* New York: Elsevier.

Montepare, J. M., & Zebrowitz-McArthur, L. (1988). Impressions of people created by age-related qualities of their gaits. *Journal of Personality and Social Psychology,* 55, 547–556.

Secord, P. (1958). Facial features and inference processes in interpersonal perception. In R. Taguiri & L. Petrullo (Eds.), *Person Perception and Interpersonal Behavior.* Stanford: Stanford University Press.

Shepherd, J. W. (1986). An interactive computer system for retrieving faces. In H. D. Ellis, M. A. Jeeves, F. Newcombe, & A. Young (Eds.), *Aspects of Face Processing.* Dordrecht: Nijhoff.

Shepherd, J. W., Ellis, H. D., & Davies, G. M. (1982). *Identification Evidence: A Psychological Evaluation.* Aberdeen: Aberdeen University Press.

Shepherd, J. W., Shepherd, J., & MacLeod, M. D. (1990). Interim report on the development of a database of coded whole-body descriptions obtained during observation of targets. S.R.D.B. of the Home Office SC/86 7/21/4.

Wells, G. L. (1984). The psychology of lineup identification. *Journal of Applied Social Psychology,* 14, 89–103.

Winer, B. J. (1971). *Statistical Principles in Experimental Design.* (2d ed.) New York: McGraw-Hill.

Young, A. W., & Ellis, H. D. (1989). (Eds.), *Handbook of Research on Face Processing.* North Holland: Elsevier.

Yuille, J. C., & Cutshall, J. L. (1986). A case study of eyewitness memory of a crime. *Journal of Applied Psychology,* 71(2), 291–301.

7 Actual victims and witnesses to robbery and fraud: An archival analysis

Patricia A. Tollestrup, John W. Turtle, and
John C. Yuille

Although there are some exceptions (for example, Cutshall & Yuille, 1989; Fisher, Geiselman, & Amador, 1989; Read, Tollestrup, Hammersley, McFadzen, & Christensen, 1990; Sporer, 1992; Yuille & Cutshall, 1986) most of the research in the field of eyewitness memory has been laboratory based. This overreliance on laboratory research has left the field open to challenges of the external validity of the research (for example, McCloskey & Egeth, 1983; McKenna, Treadway, & McCloskey, 1992; Yuille & Wells, 1991) and has led to the recognition of a need for more diverse methods of learning about eyewitness memory (for example, Davies, 1990; Yuille & Wells, 1991). In response to this deficit of diversity, this chapter reports the results of an inquiry into actual police case files. We realize that file research lacks the experimental control of laboratory studies. Our data from police case files, however, represent a degree of realism and a range of variables impossible to simulate in a laboratory setting. We are able to provide information on a number of important topics such as the characteristics of actual eyewitnesses, the amount of detail in eyewitnesses' descriptions of suspects, the accuracy of these descriptions, types of identification tasks employed, the prevalence and accuracy of eyewitness identification, and the weapon focus effect. We believe that the discrepancies and similarities between our results and laboratory research will be informative and serve to point out instances when research conducted in one context can apply in another.

The laboratory context has customarily cast eyewitnesses into a uniform role (Yuille & Tollestrup, in press). Most laboratory eyewitnesses watch a robbery or a car accident presented with slides, on video, or staged live. The event may be violent and gory, but it is ethically limited in the extent to which it can engage or arouse the subjects. Essentially, most laboratory eyewitnesses are in the role of unaffected observers.

This research was supported by a grant from NSERC to the third author and by a SSHRC postdoctoral fellowship to the second author.

The authors would like to thank the Royal Canadian Mounted Police, particularly the Richmond detachment, without whose cooperation this research would not have been possible.

In actual forensic contexts, eyewitnesses are cast in a multitude of roles that exhibit varying degrees of similarity to the laboratory eyewitness. For example, in the majority of violent crimes such as robbery and assault the only eyewitness is the victim, a direct participant in an arousing and threatening event (Yuille, 1986). But not all eyewitnesses are involved in arousing events. Victims of fraud, for example, probably have levels of arousal similar to the typical laboratory eyewitness. Low levels of arousal are also experienced by many secondary eyewitnesses, those who did not witness a crime, but who, police believe, interacted with a suspect and can tie him or her to the crime (for example, a store clerk who sold a piece of evidence left at the scene of a crime such as an article of clothing). The field of eyewitness memory could benefit from knowledge about actual eyewitnesses who demonstrate various degrees of similarity to the typical laboratory eyewitness. To this end, we chose to examine cases of robbery and fraud. Victims of robbery bear the least similarity to the typical laboratory eyewitness, fraud victims bear the most, and witnesses of robbery are somewhere in between.

Description of sample

The files of a Vancouver suburb serviced by the Royal Canadian Mounted Police (RCMP) were used as the data source. All cases of robbery committed between 1987 and 1989 inclusive ($n = 119$) and all fraud cases in 1989 ($n = 66$) were examined. Some cases were excluded from the analysis ($n = 42$ robbery and 45 fraud cases) because they did not contain any information regarding descriptions provided by, or identification attempts by, eyewitnesses. The excluded files largely comprised requests for assistance from other police departments to locate a suspect, unfounded cases (usually a false tip of criminal activity), or instances of fraud between business associates who knew each other. The nature of the robberies varied and included purse snatchings and armed bank robbery. Each robbery file represented a single criminal episode, although a number of criminal code offenses (for example, theft and assault) could be committed in a single episode. The majority of fraud cases were instances of passing bad checks and also included passing counterfeit bills and welfare, insurance, and credit card fraud. Each fraud file typically represented numerous separate but similar criminal acts (for example, passing bad checks at various locations) committed by an individual.

Descriptive information about each crime such as location (grocery store, bank, and so forth), date and time, number of eyewitnesses and perpetrators, and use of a weapon was collected. We also gathered demographic data, information on the relationships between those involved, and eyewitness descriptions of the perpetrator(s). Finally, we collected information about the use of preidentification procedures such as viewing mugshots, and the type of identification task (photo or live lineup, showup, and so forth), and the outcome of identification attempts.

Descriptive information

Throughout this chapter the term "eyewitness" is used when a distinction between victims and nonvictims is unnecessary. When a finer distinction is required, "victim" refers to individuals who directly interacted with the perpetrator and "witness" refers to individuals who were present during all or part of the crime but who did not directly interact with the perpetrator.

We consider the seventy-seven robbery cases first. There were one hundred and twenty-two perpetrators ($M = 1.58$; range: 1 to 6 per robbery), 81 victims ($M = 1.05$; range: 1 to 2), and 83 witnesses ($M = 1.07$; range: 0 to 33). All perpetrators of robbery were male. Police descriptions of charged individuals indicated that the average age of robbery perpetrators was 20.87 years (range: fifteen to forty years). There were thirty-five female and forty-five male victims of robbery.[1] The average age of female and male victims was 36.81 and 35.85 years respectively. The age of the female victims ranged from eighteen to seventy-eight years; males ranged from eleven to eighty-two years. There were forty-four female and twenty-eight male witnesses to robbery. The average age of female and male witnesses was 29.51 and 27.18 years respectively. Their ages ranged from 11.5 to 47 years in the case of females and from 11.5 to 58 years in the case of males.

The majority of robberies ($n = 48$; 62.3 percent of the total) involved only a single victim and no other witnesses. There were twenty-eight (36.3 percent) cases in which there was at least one other witness. Finally, one case (1.3 percent) involved two victims and no witnesses. The identity of the perpetrator was generally unknown to eyewitnesses of robbery. In only two cases were eyewitnesses (victims) able to supply the police with the identity of the perpetrator. Five robberies were committed by a perpetrator who seemed familiar to the eyewitnesses (five victims and one witness). These eyewitnesses thought the perpetrator lived in the area or had been in the vicinity prior to the robbery. Witnesses present during a robbery were frequently acquainted with the victim. Witnesses were coworkers, friends, or family members of the victim in sixteen (57.14 percent) of the twenty-eight robberies that had witnesses. These data on the typical configuration of a robbery (number of eyewitnesses, relationships between participants) replicate those found in an archival study reported by Yuille (1986).

In the twenty-one cases of fraud there were forty-four perpetrators ($M = 2.09$; range 1 to 13) and one hundred and thirty-four victims ($M = 6.38$; range: 1 to 24). All but two of the fraud cases involved a single perpetrator. The average number of perpetrators in the fraud cases was elevated by two cases in which police suspected that several perpetrators were at work. We considered each of the incidents in these cases to have been perpetrated by a different individual (n = 12 and 13).

The police charged an equal number of males and females with fraud (n = 4 each). The average age of charged suspects was 26.88 years and ranged from twenty to thirty-five years. Most victims of fraud were female (90 female, 39 male).[2] The average age of victims where recorded (n = 9 female, 5 male) was 25.86 years and ranged from seventeen to fifty-eight years.

Unlike robbery, any potential eyewitnesses present during the commission of a fraud (including the victim) are usually unaware that a crime is taking place. Hence they do not have a reason to attend to the event or remain on the scene like witnesses to robbery. Once the crime has been detected, it is difficult to locate eyewitnesses unless they work in the store or place of business where the frauds most often occurred. The fraud files we examined involved only victims. Most fraud victims within a case were involved in separate instances, and it is assumed that within a case the victims were strangers to one another. By virtue of our selection, no victims of fraud knew the identity of the perpetrator and unlike robbery victims, no fraud victims reported feeling a sense of familiarity with the perpetrator.

Amount and accuracy of eyewitness descriptions of perpetrators

We recorded eyewitness descriptions of the perpetrator(s) and tabulated the amount of detail according to the protocol described in Yuille and Cutshall (1989). Briefly, the details of the descriptions were categorized as either physical (for example, age, height, complexion, need for glasses, facial hair, and so forth) or clothing. Each unit of information in these categories was assigned a point. For example the phrase, "Caucasian male about 25 years old, wearing jeans and boots" contains three units of physical description and two units of clothing description.

Most eyewitnesses to robbery were able to provide some information about the appearance of the perpetrator. This was not the case, however, for fraud victims. Because some cases involved more than a single perpetrator [n = 27 robbery, 2 fraud], there were 116 possible descriptions from victims of robbery, 100 from witnesses of robbery, and 136 from fraud victims. Nine and one-half percent of possible descriptions from robbery victims (n = 11), 11 percent from robbery witnesses (n = 11), and 71.3 percent of possible descriptions from fraud victims (n = 97) offered no information regarding the appearance of the perpetrator. Whereas some fraud files suggested that the victim was unable to describe the perpetrator (for example the clerk didn't even remember the transaction), there generally was no consistent indication regarding whether fraud victims could not describe the perpetrator or were not asked to.

One-way ANOVAs indicated a significant effect of type of eyewitness on

P.A. TOLLESTRUP, J.W. TURTLE, & J.C. YUILLE

Table 7.1. *Mean number of descriptive details provided by eyewitnesses who provided at least four details regarding the suspect's physical appearance*

| Type of detail | Type of Eyewitness | | |
	Robbery victims ($n = 73$)	Robbery witnesses ($n = 48$)	Fraud victims ($n = 28$)
Clothing details			
Mean	4.94	6.41	1.53
S.D.	3.91	4.30	2.28
Physical appearance details			
Mean	9.76	8.38	7.57
S.D.	3.54	3.21	1.71
Total details			
Mean	14.71	14.79	9.11
S.D.	5.94	5.92	3.17

S.D. = Standard deviation.

the total amount recalled, amount of clothing and physical appearance details [all F's $(2, 349) > 54$; p's $< .0001$]. Scheffé tests at $p = .05$ were conducted. Fraud victims provided an overall average of 2.11 details which was significantly less than the 10.96 provided by victims of robbery and the 9.37 offered by robbery witnesses. Fraud victims also offered fewer details regarding the clothing of the perpetrator (0.34) than victims (4.03) and witnesses (4.35) of robbery. Victims of robbery offered more details regarding the physical appearance of the perpetrator (6.9) than both robbery witnesses (5.02) and fraud victims (1.76).

The previous analyses included eyewitnesses who were unable or were not asked to provide a description of the perpetrator as well as eyewitnesses who provided descriptions so scant that they could not have been very useful. A description of only two details regarding physical appearance (for example, that the suspect is a white male) does not radically reduce the population of suspects and thus does not offer much helpful information to the police. A description of four units regarding physical appearance (for example, the suspect is a white male with brown hair and a mustache) is a bit more useful. We repeated the above analysis on a reduced sample of eyewitnesses who provided a minimum of four details regarding the physical appearance of the perpetrator. The results are presented in Table 7.1.

In this sample victims and witnesses of robbery offered an average total of 14.71 and 14.79 details respectively and fraud victims offered an average total of 9.11 details. One-way ANOVAs indicated a significant effect of type of eyewitness on the total amount recalled, amount of clothing, and amount of physical appearance details [all F's (2, 146) > 5.80; p's < .01]. Post hoc multiple comparisons (Scheffé at p = .05) indicated that victims and witnesses of robbery offered more total details than fraud victims. Victims and witnesses of robbery also provided more clothing details (4.94 and 6.41) than fraud victims (1.54) and victims of robbery offered more details (9.76) regarding the physical appearance of the perpetrator than fraud victims (7.57).

Our results are similar to an earlier analysis of one hundred descriptions provided by victims of murder, assault, rape, and armed robbery conducted by Kuehn (1974). Those victims provided an average of 7.2 traits regarding the physical appearance of the perpetrator, compared to the 6.93 details provided by all victims of robbery in the present study. Although Kuehn could only caution that "a victim might provide an erroneous although full description to the police" (p. 1161), our analysis permits an examination of the accuracy of some eyewitness accounts.

In cases where a suspect was charged, his or her age, height, weight, and hair and eye color were recorded by the police. This permitted a comparison between the eyewitness descriptions of these attributes and the measured values obtained from the charged suspect(s). Difference scores were calculated for age, height, and weight by subtracting the measured value of the charged suspect from the estimated value provided by eyewitnesses. Recall of hair color and presence or absence of facial hair was scored as accurate if it was consistent with what was recorded at the time of arrest. The accuracy of hair color was conservatively scored such that a comparison between blonde and light brown was scored as incorrect. Too few (n = 3) eyewitnesses offered information regarding eye color of the suspect to draw any conclusions regarding accuracy. No eyewitnesses reported a different sex or race of the perpetrator than was recorded by police at the time of arrest.

Because the sample of charged suspects might contain some innocent suspects, we present only those cases in which the suspect confessed his or her guilt. The pattern of results obtained on the entire sample of charged suspects does not differ from that based on confession cases alone. The police laid charges in 23 percent of robbery cases (n = 18 cases involving 27 perpetrators) and 38 percent of fraud cases (n = 8 cases involving eight perpetrators). Of those cases where charges were laid, 67 percent of robbery cases (n = 12 cases involving twenty perpetrators) and 50 percent of fraud cases (n = 4 cases involving four perpetrators) saw a confession offered. Too few fraud victims gave descriptions to analyze the accuracy of their estimates in either the sample based on suspects who confessed, or in the sample based on all charged suspects. Table 7.2 depicts the accuracy of age, height, and weight estimates provided by victims. These estimates were significantly different from zero and they did not differ from each other. Two z-tests on proportions were conducted for descriptions of hair color and facial hair. Hair color was

Table 7.2. *Mean difference scores for robbery eyewitnesses' estimates of age, height, and weight of perpetrators who confessed*

	Type of eyewitness	
Estimate	Victim	Witness
Age		
avg.	2.87	3.40
median	2.75	2.25
S.D.	3.48	4.05
min	−1.00	−4.00
max	10.00	10.00
n	12	24
Height		
avg.	−1.90	−0.476
median	−1.50	−0.450
S.D.	1.56	2.27
min	−5.50	−6.40
max	0.00	3.00
n	11	38
Weight		
Avg.	−7.56	−4.78
median	−5.15	−11.80
S.D.	14.93	14.35
min	−31.60	−36.40
max	25.40	25.40
n	10	24

Note: Difference scores are calculated by subtracting the estimate provided by the eyewitness from the measured value obtained by the police. Negative values represent underestimates.
Age = years; height = inches; weight = pounds.
S.D. = Standard deviation; n = sample size.

consistent with what was recorded at the time of arrest in 38.46 percent of victim's and 48.28 percent of witnesses' descriptions. These proportions do not significantly differ ($z = -.59$). Victims and witnesses did differ significantly ($z = -2.25$) in description of facial hair. Sixty percent of victims' and 100 percent of witnesses' descriptions of facial hair were consistent with what was recorded at the time of arrest.

In amount of detail offered, comparable numbers of victims and witnesses of robbery were unable to describe the perpetrator. Victims, who presumably had the best view of the perpetrator but also higher levels of arousal, provided more information regarding the perpetrator's physical appearance than witnesses. With respect to the accuracy of the descriptions, victims and witnesses did not differ from each other in their estimates of age and weight. Witnesses' estimates of height were more accurate than those of victims who tended to underestimate. All eyewitnesses in the present study (including the few fraud victims who offered a description) presented the same pattern, albeit not significant in all comparisons, of overestimating age and underestimating height and weight. A similar pattern was reported by Flin and Shepherd (1986), who found that people underestimated the height and weight of a person they interacted with in a nonthreatening manner.

Identification procedures

The negative effects of biased lineup instructions and suggestive lineup construction on eyewitness identification have been well documented. For example, not clarifying that the real offender may not be present (Malpass & Devine, 1981) or using a lineup where everyone is a suspect (Wells & Turtle, 1986) can dramatically inflate false identifications of innocent suspects. Most discussions of the negative effects of biased lineups have centered on lineups that do not contain the actual perpetrator and the possibility of drastic consequences for an innocent person falsely identified under these circumstances. If the perpetrator is present in a biased lineup, the bias generally acts to secure his or her positive identification. Defense lawyers are well versed in the effects of biased lineups, however, and can easily discredit an identification made with such lineups. Thus, bias in target-present lineups has drastic real world consequences for the prosecution of the case. The officers in this police detachment had considered the legal consequences of biased lineups and had taken steps to eliminate suggestion in the construction and administration of lineups. Most photo spreads in our sample contained eight photographs. The photo arrays viewed by the authors were well constructed; in all cases, the foils resembled the suspect and there was nothing in the construction of the array that suggested the identity of the police suspect. One officer was well aware of the tactics employed by defense lawyers to discredit an eyewitness identification. In anticipation, therefore, he first showed his lineups to other officers who knew nothing about the case and asked them to select the suspect and to look for bias in his lineups. This is precisely the procedure used by Wells, Leippe, and Ostrom (1979) to assess the fairness of a lineup and we feel it is a reasonable way to avoid at least some problems of using lineups.

There were 170 identification attempts. Of these, 90.58 percent ($n = 154$) were with photo spreads. It appears that live lineups have fallen out of favor due to the cost and the difficulty in constructing a fair one, particularly for suspects from ethnic minorities. Only ten identification attempts were made with traditional physical or live lineups. In an additional four identification attempts, the police either brought the suspect to the victim, or the victim to the suspect (that is, showups). One identification attempt involved a fraud victim viewing a videotape of the bank activities on the day of the crime. In one case a victim of robbery encountered her assailant while out shopping and alerted the police.

Identification outcomes

There is a well established literature describing case studies in which wrongful conviction and imprisonment resulted from eyewitness misidentifications (for example, Brandon & Davies, 1973; Borchard, 1932; Wall, 1965). To our knowledge, however, the present project represents the first large-scale analysis of eyewitness identification in actual police cases. We are able to address several important topics in the area, such as the effects of arousal and delay on identification accuracy. Perhaps the simplest feature of our identification data concerns the question raised by Konecni and Ebbesen (1986) regarding the frequency of eyewitness identification evidence in real cases. Those researchers estimated that only a very small proportion of cases making it to court concerned the identification of the offender and suggested that the efforts of eyewitness researchers are therefore out of proportion to the actual role identification evidence plays in real cases. Without resorting to actual data, Goldstein, Chance, and Schneller (1989) have pointed out that even a conservative estimate that only 3 percent of cases involve identification of the offender indicates approximately seventy-seven thousand such cases in a typical year in the United States. And although we do not dispute Ebbesen and Konecni's estimate, our research suggests that eyewitness identification is important in the investigatory phase of a case if not in the cases that actually come to trial. Almost 40 percent ($n = 30$) of all robbery cases and two-thirds ($n = 14$) of fraud cases included an identification attempt. The police suspect was identified in sixteen cases of robbery and ten cases of fraud. Thus, in our sample the police had a positive eyewitness identification in 20.8 percent of robberies and 47.6 percent of frauds. Presumably, these cases would be prosecuted, but the weight of the eyewitness identifications remains unknown because police records seldom include information regarding the fate of a case once it is turned over to the prosecution. It is possible that a positive identification leads to the collection of more evidence that carries the case in court, or that the accused is encouraged to plea bargain and the case is closed at that point. Either way, our admittedly small sample suggests that identification is an important issue in many cases and that continued research is warranted.

Our examination of identification outcomes faced two obstacles. The first was to determine whether or not the lineup contained the actual perpetrator. This obstacle was overcome by classifying cases according to the degree of certainty that a photo spread contained a picture of the perpetrator. We recorded the nature of any evidence that pointed to the identity of a perpetrator. In a large proportion of cases, there was no evidence recorded in the file. Some cases had evidence such as fingerprints, or in fraud cases, returned checks with a driver's license number which implicated the suspect. In a smaller proportion of cases, a suspect confessed. These three evidence conditions (no evidence, implicating evidence, and confession) reflect degrees of certainty regarding the presence of the perpetrator. We can be most certain that the suspect is the perpetrator in a lineup when the suspect has confessed. Even in these situations, there is some risk that an innocent person might confess. Lineups from cases in which there is implicating evidence regarding the identity of the perpetrator represent a reduced degree of certainty. Finally, we can be least certain of the presence of a perpetrator in lineups in cases in which there was no evidence. Some of the lineups in this category were collections of photos of people known to commit certain types of crimes. In these types of fishing expeditions the police generally do not have a particular suspect in mind and the lineup is an attempt to generate one, much like a mug shot inspection or computer-assisted look at likely suspects.

The second obstacle could not be removed and thus served to limit the analyses. It was difficult to distinguish reliably between false alarms and rejection of photo spreads. Identification outcomes were entered in the files in a variety of ways such as "negative results," "unable to identify police suspect," "not in the lineup," "pointed out suspect and one other as looking like perpetrator," "positive ID," and "weak ID." Sometimes it was clear from comments made by an eyewitness at the time of the identification attempt that he or she had rejected the photo spread entirely (for example, "There's not even one close") but for the most part, we could not distinguish reliably between outcomes in which an eyewitness rejected the photo spread and those in which he or she failed to select the police suspect. Identification attempts in which an eyewitness selected only the police suspect are labeled "positive." All other outcomes had to be labeled "negative," and these include false alarms and rejections. This recording procedure suggests that police do not consider the lack of an identification distinct from a misidentification and certainly not as informative as a positive ID, despite Wells and Lindsay's (1980) argument suggesting that nonidentifications can be just as informative as positive identifications.

Table 7.3 presents the proportion of positive identification outcomes by evidence condition and type of eyewitness. Identification attempts in cases involving no evidence yielded the lowest proportion of positive identifications (17.5 percent) and attempts in cases involving a confession yielded the highest (47.7 percent). Victims of robbery identified the police suspect most often (46.5 percent). The police suspect was selected in 33.3 percent of identification attempts by witnesses to robbery and in 25.5 percent of attempts by victims of fraud. A chi-square test of association across evidence conditions revealed

Table 7.3. *Proportion of positive identification by type of evidence and eyewitness*

	Type of Evidence			Total row percentage
Eyewitness	None	Implicating	Confession	
Robbery victims	21.7	57.1	84.6	46.5
	(n = 23)	(n = 7)	(n = 13)	
Robbery witnesses	11.0	—	55.5	33.3
	(n = 9)		(n = 9)	
Fraud victims	16.7	38.9	22.7	25.47
	(n = 48)	(n = 36)	(n = 22)	
Total column percentage	17.5	41.9	47.7	

a significant association (χ^2 (2, n = 167) = 6.25; p < .05) between the three types of eyewitness and identification outcomes. Post hoc multiple comparisons (Marascuilo, 1966) did not reveal any significant differences between eyewitness types.

Considering only cases in which a suspect confessed, a second chi-square test again revealed a significant association (χ^2 (2, n = 44) = 12.82; p < .05) between type of eyewitness and identification outcome. The police suspect was selected in 84.6 percent of identification attempts made by victims of robbery, 55.5 percent of attempts made by witnesses to robbery, and in 22.7 percent of attempts made by fraud victims. Subsequent multiple comparisons demonstrated a significant difference between victims of robbery and fraud (χ^2 (2, n = 17) = 5.99; p < .05).

Victims of robbery may owe part of their performance to the fact that they faced the shortest delay between exposure and identification (M = 31.11 days). Witnesses of robbery waited an average of 44.39 days and fraud victims waited an average of 107.87 days. In addition, the period of delay was shortest in cases involving a confession (M = 8.77 days) and longest in cases in which there was no evidence (M = 88.25 days).

One of the clearest findings to emerge from this analysis is that the proportion of positive identifications dropped dramatically with time. Table 7.4 presents this information. Eyewitnesses to robbery and fraud who faced the shortest delays made roughly the same high proportion of positive identifications despite a difference in average delay of over a month. One possible factor that might account for this is the difference in the extent to which eyewitnesses to robbery and fraud interacted with the perpetrator. The robberies in our sample were brief and the eyewitnesses may not have been exposed to the perpetrator for very long. The frauds in our sample were

Table 7.4. *Range and average delay in days between exposure to perpetrator and identification attempt in cases of robbery and fraud*

Delay	Average	Sample size	Proportion positive IDs (percent)
Robbery			
0–1	0.5	14	71.43
3–5	3.6	15	46.67
7–34	18.9	21	33.33
38–191	120.21	14	14.29
Fraud			
7–62	32.94	18	77.78
70–90	74.4	18	5.55
107–154	131.67	15	20.0
170–382	200.42	17	17.65

generally brief as well, consisting of a routine purchase or deposit, but there were exceptions. Thirty-two fraud victims (35.9 percent) had a relatively extensive interaction with the perpetrator such as selling expensive items (over $1,000) like furniture, a car, or stereo equipment, handling a suspect's application for welfare benefits, or instructing a suspect on the use of automated teller machines. These interactions were more involved and lasted longer than the routine transactions that characterized the majority of the fraud interactions. Seventy-four percent of victims who selected the police suspect had an extensive interaction with the perpetrator, whereas only 19.3 percent of victims who failed to select the police suspect had such an interaction with the perpetrator.

Presence of a weapon

According to the notion of weapon focus, eyewitnesses direct most of their attention to the weapon resulting in poor memory for the face. The laboratory studies that have examined this topic have found support for weapon focus in terms of the greater attention paid to the weapon (Loftus, Loftus & Messo, 1987) and the predicted effects on both recognition and recall (Kramer, Buckhout, & Eugenio, 1990; Maass & Kohnken, 1989; Tooley, Brigham, Maass, & Bothwell, 1987). More recently a meta-analysis has demonstrated that the presence of a weapon has significant detrimental effect on identification and description (Steblay, 1992).

The analysis of weapon effects in our project is limited to robbery cases. Of the seventy-seven robbery cases, forty-three (55.84 percent) were committed with an actual (thirty-eight cases) or implied (five cases) weapon. Table

Table 7.5. *Average number of details by eyewitness type and presence versus absence of weapon*

	Weapon in case		No weapon used	
	Victim	Witness	Victim	Witness
Clothing	5.07	4.89	2.96	2.20
Physical appearance	7.92	5.16	5.91	4.45
Total	12.98	10.05	8.88	6.65
N	59	80	57	20

N = sample size.

7.5 reports the average amount of information recalled as a function of presence or absence of a weapon. Separate two by two ANOVAs (victim versus witness by weapon versus no weapon) were conducted for each of the three categories of details (clothing, physical appearance, and total). Despite the fact that we should expect victims to suffer the most from the weapon-focus phenomenon, no interaction between weapon presence and eyewitness role was found in any of the three analyses. There were, however, significant main effects for weapon presence and eyewitness role. There was a significant effect of weapon presence in all three analyses. Eyewitnesses in crimes involving a weapon provided more total details ($M = 11.29$) compared to those involved in weaponless crimes [($M = 8.3$); $F(1, 212) = 13.19$; $p < 0.001$]. Eyewitnesses in weaponless crimes provided an average of 2.77 clothing and 5.53 physical appearance details, significantly fewer than the 4.96 clothing and 6.33 physical appearance details provided by eyewitnesses to crimes committed with a weapon [F's$(1, 212) = 15.07$, $p < 0.001$ for clothing and 5.42, $p < .01$ for physical appearance details].

Victims provided significantly more total details ($M = 10.97$) than witnesses [($M = 9.37$), $F(1, 212) = 7.11$, $p < 0.01$], as well as more physical appearance details [(Ms = 6.93 and 5.02, respectively), $F(1, 212) = 14.04$, $p < 0.001$].

On the basis of these findings, it appears that the presence of a weapon did not hinder the ability of eyewitnesses to offer a detailed description. Eyewitnesses in crimes involving a weapon provided more detailed descriptions than those in weaponless crimes and victims offered more detailed descriptions than witnesses.

We turn to the effect of a weapon on accuracy of descriptions. The police charged a suspect in fourteen cases committed with a weapon and in six weaponless cases. The sample of perpetrators who confessed was too small to examine weapon presence effects in these cases alone so these results are based on all suspects charged by police. The tendency to overestimate age and to underestimate height remains, regardless of the presence or absence of a weapon. Separate two by two ANOVAs (victim versus witness by weapon versus no weapon) were conducted for each of the three estimates (age, height, and weight). There were no interactions and no significant main effects of either weapon presence or eyewitness role. There was a marginally significant difference between the average errors in the estimates of height of victims ($M = -1.72$) and witnesses [($M = -0.48$), $F(1, 55) = 3.24$, $p < 0.10$].

Laboratory research has generally found that the presence of a weapon impairs the ability of eyewitnesses to describe the weapon holder. There are many differences between the actual forensic context and the laboratory that might account for this difference. Most laboratory studies of the weapon focus effect have employed slide sequences (only Maass & Kohnken, 1989, employed a live event). The laboratory eyewitnesses would probably not feel personally threatened by a person holding a weapon in a slide. In addition, all the studies employed some sort of a cued recall test of eyewitness memory that varied from a multiple choice test (Loftus, Loftus, & Messo, 1987) to a set of open-ended questions (Maass & Kohnken, 1989). In contrast, the eyewitnesses in our study usually provided a free recall and answered some open-ended questions. The actual eyewitnesses often offered information that many of the laboratory studies did not seek such as the complexion, odor, or gait of the perpetrator. Whereas laboratory scores of eyewitness accuracy are generally a compound of attributes such as hair color, age, and clothing description, our accuracy scores are for separate estimates of age, height, and weight.

Less than a quarter ($n = 8$, 23 percent) of weaponless cases and over half of crimes committed with a weapon ($n = 22$, 51 percent) resulted in an identification attempt. Only 30.61 percent of identification attempts made by eyewitnesses to crimes committed with a weapon resulted in selection of the police suspect. In weaponless crimes, 73.33 percent of identification attempts resulted in selection of the police suspect. Eyewitnesses in weaponless crimes, however, made their identification attempts after a much shorter period of time than eyewitnesses in crimes committed with a weapon ($M = 7.33$ versus 41.47 days).

All but one identification attempt in weaponless crimes were made after only seventeen days. Almost half ($n = 22$; 44.8 percent) of identification attempts in crimes committed with a weapon were made at delays greater than seventeen days. We tried to control for the different delays between weapon conditions by examining only identification attempts made at delays of seventeen days or less. In this consideration, the average delays were 5.15 and 4.5 days for crimes committed with and without a weapon. Even with similar delays between exposure and identification attempt, the police suspect was selected in 44.44 percent of identification attempts made by eyewitnesses to crimes involving a weapon and in 71.42 percent of identification attempts made by eyewitnesses to weaponless crimes. An analysis of covariance with identification outcome as the dependent measure, presence or absence of a weapon as a factor, and delay as covariate demonstrated a marginally significant effect of weapon [F (1, 126) = 3.578, p = .061].[3]

On the basis of these findings from actual eyewitnesses it would seem that the presence of a weapon has complex effects. The presence of a weapon does not appear to have a detrimental influence on the amount of descriptive information or accuracy of that information provided by actual eyewitnesses. This would indicate that eyewitnesses are able to encode information about the perpetrator's appearance. Yet the presence of a weapon does act as a detriment to subsequent recognition of the person holding the weapon. It is possible that descriptions are more vigorously pursued from eyewitnesses, particularly victims, of crimes involving a weapon. And although the presence of a weapon led to more detailed descriptions, it may be that the type or quality of information encoded was not useful at a subsequent recognition task. The negative effect of weapon presence on identification appears to be relatively robust. The effects have been demonstrated in the laboratory where the level of arousal is low, the target person is on a two-dimensional slide, and recognition is tested after short delays. The negative effects of weapon presence were also demonstrated in our sample of robberies where the level of arousal was higher, the target person was real, and may have been very close, and recognition was tested after an average delay of over a month.

General discussion

This analysis of actual police cases has revealed variability in case characteristics between and within crime types in actual forensic contexts. For example, frauds typically take longer to reach the identification stage than robberies, but more frauds involve an identification attempt than robberies. Within robberies, many factors vary, such as presence or absence of a weapon, presence or absence of witnesses, and the relationships that witnesses have with the victim. Within frauds, the nature of the interaction between the victim and the perpetrator varies. The forensic contexts that we studied also revealed natural confounds such as victim's closer proximity to the perpetrator and (presumably) subsequent higher arousal. The present results demonstrated that these differences can affect eyewitness recall or recognition. Consequently researchers of eyewitness memory must be cautious about generalizing results from one context to another. This caution should be exercised not only when applying laboratory or field simulation findings to actual eyewitnesses, but also when applying findings based on actual eyewitnesses to other eyewitnesses. The forensic context is clearly multifaceted and different performances are found in different situations. This conclusion ought to be trite but the eyewitness literature has frequently treated all eye-witness contexts as if they were the same.

No simple research type can effectively deal with all the issues related to eyewitness memory. A combination of laboratory studies, field simulations, and archival and case studies is needed. An overdependence on laboratory research and field simulations has left this field with a potentially distorted rather than comprehensive picture of eyewitnesses. The present results have confirmed the complexity of this field. There is a clear and pressing need for more research, as well as more direct studies of actual eyewitnesses of crime. This study needs replication and extension so that the extensive laboratory literature can be appropriately and properly applied.

Notes

1 There were no demographic data on twelve robbery eyewitnesses (one victim and eleven witnesses). The age of twenty-eight robbery eyewitnesses was not recorded in the files.
2 There were no demographic data on five fraud victims. The age of one hundred and fifteen fraud victims was not recorded in the files.
3 Citing a marginally significant finding is appropriate in this case because although the assumption of homogeneity of variance is not met, the data are in the positive condition (larger variances associated with larger n's) and therefore, the F-test is conservative.

References

Borchard, E. M. (1932). *Convicting the innocent: Errors of criminal justice.* New Haven: Yale University Press.

Brandon R., & Davies, C. (1973). *Wrongful imprisonment: Mistaken convictions and their consequences.* London: George Allen and Unwin.

Cutshall, J. L., & Yuille, J. C. (1989). Field studies of eyewitness memory of actual crimes. In D. C. Raskin (Ed.), *Psychological methods in criminal investigation and evidence* (pp. 97–124). New York: Springer.

Davies, G. (1990, September). *Influencing public policy on eyewitnessing: Problems and possibilities.* Paper presented at the Second European Law and Psychology Conference, Nuremberg, Germany.

Fisher, R. P., Geiselman, R. E., & Amador, M. (1989). Field test of the cognitive interview: Enhancing the recollection of actual victims and witnesses of crime. *Journal of Applied Psychology, 74*(5), 722–727.

Flin, R. H., & Shepherd, J. W. (1986). Tall stories: Eyewitnesses' ability to estimate height and weight characteristics. *Human Learning, 5,* 29–38.

Goldstein, A. G., Chance, J. E., & Schneller, G. R. (1989). Frequency of eyewitness identification in criminal cases: A survey of prosecutors. *Bulletin of the Psychonomic Society, 27*(11), 71–74.

Konecni, V. J., & Ebbesen, E. B. (1986). Courtroom testimony by psychologists on eyewitness identification issues: Critical notes and reflections. *Law and Human Behavior, 10*(½), 117–126.

Kramer, T. H., Buckhout, R., & Eugenio, P. (1990). Weapon focus, arousal, and eyewitness memory: Attention must be paid. *Law and Human Behavior, 14,* 167–184.

Kuehn, L. L. (1974). Looking down a gun barrel: Person perception and violent crime. *Perceptual and Motor Skills, 39,* 1159–1164.

Loftus, E. F., Loftus, G. R., & Messo, J. (1987). Some facts about "weapon focus." *Law and Human Behavior, 11*(1), 55–62.

Maass, A., & Kohnken, G. (19). Eyewitness identification: Simulating the "weapon effect." *Law and Human Behavior, 13*(4), 397–408.

Malpass, R. S., & Devine, P. G. (1981). Eyewitness identification: Lineup instructions and absence of the offender. *Journal of Applied Psychology, 66,* 482–489.

Marascuilo, L. A. (1966). Large-sample multiple comparisons. *Psychological Bulletin, 65,* 280–290.

McCloskey, M., & Egeth, H. E. (1983). Eyewitness identification: What can a psychologist tell a jury? *American Psychologist, 38,* 550–563.

McKenna, J., Treadway, M., & McCloskey, M. E. (1992). Expert psychological testimony on eyewitness reliability: Selling psychology before its time. In P. Suedfeld & P. E. Tetlock (Eds.), *Psychology and Social Policy* (pp. 283–293). New York: Hemisphere Publishing Corporation.

Read, J. D., Tollestrup, P., Hammersley, R., McFadzen, E., & Christensen, A. (1990). The unconscious transference effect: Are innocent bystanders ever misidentified? *Applied Cognitive Psychology, 4,* 3–31.

Sporer, S. L. (March, 1992). Person descriptions in an archival analysis of criminal cases. Paper presented at the Biennial meeting of the American Psychology and Law Society, San Diego.

Steblay, N. M. (1992). A meta-analytic review of the weapon focus effect. *Law and Human Behavior, 16* (4), 413–424.

Tooley, V., Brigham, J. C., Maass, A., & Bothwell, R. K. (1987). Facial recognition: Weapon effect and attentional focus. *Journal of Applied Social Psychology, 17,* 845–859.

Wall, P. M. (1965). *Eyewitness identification in criminal cases.* Springfield, IL: Charles C. Thomas.

Wells, G. L., Leippe, M. R., & Ostrom, T. M. (1979). Guidelines for empirically assessing the fairness of a lineup. *Law and Human Behavior, 3,* 285–293.

Wells, G. L., & Lindsay, R. C. L. (1980). On estimating the diagnosticity of eyewitness non-identifications. *Psychological Bulletin, 88,* 776–784.

Wells, G. L., & Turtle, J. W. (1986). Eyewitness identification: The importance of lineup models. *Psychological Bulletin, 99,* 320–329.

Yuille, J. C. (1986). Meaningful research in the police context. In Yuille, J. C. (Ed.), *Police selection and training: The role of psychology.* Dordrecht, The Netherlands: Nijhoff.

Yuille, J. C., & Cutshall, J. L. (1986). A case study of eyewitness memory of a crime. *Journal of Applied Psychology, 71*(2), 291–301.

Yuille, J. C., & Cutshall, J. L. (1989). Analysis of the statements of victims, witnesses and suspects. In J. C. Yuille (Ed.), *Credibility Assessment* (pp. 175–191). Dordrecht, The Netherlands: Kluwer Academic.

Yuille, J. C., & Tollestrup, P. A. (in press). A model of the diverse effects of emotion on eyewitness memory. In S. A. Christianson (Ed.), *The handbook of emotion and memory.* Hillsdale, NJ: Erlbaum.

Yuille, J. C., & Wells, G. L. (1991). Concerns about the application of research findings: The issue of ecological validity. In J. Doris (Ed.), *The suggestibility of children's recollections: Implications for eyewitness testimony* (pp. 118–128). Washington, D. C.: American Psychological Association.

Part II

Lineup construction and collection of testimony

8   Conceptual, practical, and empirical issues associated with eyewitness identification test media

Brian L. Cutler, Garrett L. Berman, Steven Penrod, and Ronald P. Fisher

Introduction

In our attempts to devise methods for improving the accuracy of eyewitness identification, a considerable portion of our research has focused on the role of the identification test medium (ITM), that is, whether the identification test consists of a live lineup, videotaped lineup, or photo array. Traditionally, identification tests have consisted of live lineups or photo arrays, but videotaped lineups have become more prevalent, due to the accessibility of high quality, inexpensive, and user-friendly audiovisual technology. This chapter reviews the conceptual distinctions pertaining to the ITM, the practical considerations associated with ITM, and empirical studies that directly compare identification performance as a function of ITM. In addressing the latter, we quantitatively review a large body of literature within which ITM was manipulated between or across experiments. Our goal is to draw conclusions about the role of ITM based on existing research and to clarify the practical implications arising from those findings. Despite the considerable number of experiments addressing ITM, we find many important questions unanswered, and we therefore discuss directions for further research.

Conceptual distinctions among identification test media

An inherent distinction between various ITMs is *image quality*. Common sense tells us that live lineups produce the clearest image; reproducing these images, in any manner, can only lead to poorer quality. Live lineups would therefore be expected to produce identification performance superior to both videotaped lineups and photo arrays. Whether inherent differences in image quality affect identification performance in eyewitness cases is open to debate. The influence of image quality on identification performance might depend on a practical consideration, *reproduction quality*. Professional film producers and photographers can produce images that show little degradation from the actual

163

object or person. In contrast, anyone who has viewed police mug shots is aware that they are of discernibly lower quality. Although they vary considerably across history and precinct, it is not difficult to find poorly focused, monochrome snapshots taken under inadequate lighting conditions. Quality of videotaping or filming can vary similarly. Thus, the conceptual hypothesis is that quality of image, as influenced by quality of reproduction, significantly influences identification performance.

The second distinction inherent in ITM is content of physical characteristic cues (henceforth referred to as "cues"). By cues, we mean all a person's physical features that potentially contribute to recognition. An eyewitness has the potential to encode a perpetrator's facial characteristics, height, weight, body type, hair color, gait, posture, voice, skin color, and many other cues. In addition, the eyewitness can be expected to encode features of the environment (compare Tulving & Thomson, 1973), such as weather conditions, scenery, objects at the scene of the crime, other people, and so forth. This review focuses on identification accuracy as a function of the number of personal cues present at test. As mentioned above, ITM poses limits on the available cues. In theory, photo arrays cannot provide cues concerning gait or other forms of body movement or voice. In practice, they may contain even fewer cues. Mug shots showing only front views of the head and shoulders not only lack cues regarding body movement and voice, but also cues that would be available from a profile, three-quarter, or full-body view. Monochrome photo arrays also lack cues associated with skin color and tone. Videotaped lineups potentially contain most of the cues associated with live lineups, but in practice they might not. The first author once witnessed a demonstration of a videotaped police lineup as part of an instruction program for police officers on the use of videotaping equipment in criminal investigations. The videotaped lineup showed eight lineup members sitting on chairs, as still as can be. Functionally, this videotaped lineup was no different than a photo array!

Given that ITMs differ in available cues, either by design or as a function of inherent limits imposed by the medium, can we expect them to produce differences in identification performance? This question is addressed at length below. The answer has important implications not only for choosing an appropriate ITM, but also for planning the behavior of the lineup members within the ITM. Prior to examining the empirical literature, we raise the question of why we should be concerned with differences in performance. If, in theory, live lineups contain the most cues, why not always use live lineups? We devote the next section to practical considerations associated with ITM.

Practical issues in choosing the identification test medium

Until recently, eyewitness identification tests have consisted exclusively of live lineups or photo arrays. Live lineups tend to be preferred over photo arrays, presumably because they produce more accurate identification judgments and provide more convincing evidence in court (although we know of no studies examining how ITM influences jury decisions). Even when photo array identification tests are conducted, they are often followed up with identification tests from live lineups. Why are photo arrays used? They are important at the beginning stage of an investigation to identify or rule out suspects, before anyone is taken into custody. The major advantage of photo arrays over live lineups is convenience. Summarized below are some of these convenience factors.

Immediate availability and selection of foils

Live lineups are time-consuming to construct. If an investigator chooses to use other officers and/or inmates to form a lineup, time is required to find people who share physical characteristics with the suspect or the suspect's description. Use of photo arrays obviates this necessity. Photo arrays also provide a greater data base from which to choose people who resemble the suspect or perpetrator in physical appearance.

Portability

In some cases it is difficult for eyewitnesses to visit the police station, and the lineup must therefore be brought to the eyewitness's home or workplace. Such cases preclude the use of a live lineup. Police therefore use photo arrays which are easily transported.

Control over behavior of lineup members and viewing time

In a live lineup there is always a danger that a suspect will act out in a deliberate attempt to draw the eyewitness's attention. Such behavior can invalidate a lineup. Photo arrays eliminate this problem. In addition, they can be examined repeatedly and for extended lengths of time – benefits not afforded by live lineups.

Changes in appearance

A suspect can deliberately change his or her appearance between the time of the crime and the identification test. Photos of the suspect may be available from prior arrests, however, or the photo taken when he or she is taken into custody can be used in photo arrays, even if the identification test takes place long after the crime.

Eyewitness anxiety

Confronting a perpetrator face-to-face can cause the eyewitness to become anxious, especially if the perpetrator has harmed the eyewitness or the eyewitness is a child who has been assaulted by an adult. Photo arrays might be less threatening.

An alternative to both the live lineup and the photo array is the videotaped lineup. The availability of inexpensive, high quality, user-friendly videotaping equipment has led police officers increasingly to use this medium. Videotaped lineups can reproduce many of the physical characteristic cues inherent in live lineups. If conducted like live lineups, videotaped lineups should produce accuracy rates comparable to those of live lineups. They also exhibit many of the benefits of photo arrays. They require less personnel and less time to construct; they are portable; with sufficient preparation (that is, creating a bank of videotaped mug shots), selection of foils is enhanced; the behavior of lineup members and viewing time are controlled; changes in suspect appearance are minimized; and eyewitness anxiety may be reduced. Videotaped lineups combine the advantages of live lineups with those of photo arrays.

Videotape is becoming increasingly popular in police departments. Among other things, it is used for surveillance, interrogations and confessions, drunk driving assessments, and crime scene investigations. The videotaped lineup is a natural and logical extension of this trend.

From a practical standpoint, there are thus strong arguments for the use of videotaped lineups. We hypothesize that, because videotaped lineups and live lineups contain comparable cues, they should produce comparable identification performance, and that both should be superior to photo arrays, because they reproduce more cues. Next we review the available empirical literature that addresses these and related questions.

Empirical research on identification test medium

We shall discuss three sets of studies that examine the impact of ITM and cues. The first is Shapiro and Penrod's (1986) meta-analysis of facial recognition studies. Shapiro and Penrod's "study characteristics" analysis tests whether studies that use different ITMs (and presumably quantitatively and qualitatively different cues) produce different overall rates of face recognition accuracy; thus, in this analysis, cues are manipulated between studies and between ITMs. For example, the recognition accuracy rates from studies using photo arrays are compared with those from studies using live lineups (with other factors statistically controlled for). The second set of studies holds ITMs constant and manipulates the quantity and/or quality of cues; thus, cues are manipulated within the study and within the ITM. For example, Cutler and Penrod (1988) used only videotaped lineups but manipulated the cues available (voice, motion) within the lineup. The third set of experiments manipulates ITMs within the study; thus, cues are manipulated within the study and between ITMs. For example, Cutler and Fisher (1990) had some subjects attempt identifications from live lineups and others from photo arrays or videotaped lineups. Live and videotaped lineups differed from photo arrays with respect to the cues available. Besides addressing the overall effects of ITM, these experiments also explore the qualifying conditions of cues and ITM (that is, interactions with other eyewitnessing and identification conditions).

Cues manipulated between ITM and between studies

In Shapiro and Penrod's (1986) "study characteristics" analysis, 960 experimental cells (from 128 studies, 16,950 subjects) were coded for a variety of study characteristics including ITM. ITM was scored as a linear variable, ranging from ITM containing the most embellished cues to ITM containing the most impoverished cues: live lineup versus videotaped lineup versus photo array versus line drawing. The 960 cells were factor analyzed, and the variables retained (including ITM) served as predictors in separate regression models for hits, false alarms, and d' (a measure of sensitivity that takes into consideration both hits and false alarms). Because the study characteristics tend to be confounded with one another, both zero-order correlations and partial correlations were examined.

Hit rate. At the zero-order level, ITM (referred to as "mode of presentation" in the meta-analysis) correlated − .16 with hit rate, meaning that higher hit rates were associated with ITMs containing impoverished cues. When entered into the regression analysis together with the other subject characteristics, however, ITM failed to account for unique variance in hit rate.

False alarm rate. Unexpectedly, ITMs correlated .21 with false alarm rate, meaning that ITMs containing embellished cues were associated with higher false alarm rates. This relation held in the regression analysis as well (partial $r = .11$).

Sensitivity. Consistent with the results from the false alarm data, analysis of d' scores showed that ITMs correlated − .17 with sensitivity. Subjects who attempted identification tests from ITMs containing embellished physical characteristic cues performed more poorly than subjects who attempted identifications from ITMs containing impoverished physical characteristic cues. This relation accounted for unique variance in the regression analysis as well (partial $r = -.06$).

Summary. The above analysis is contrary to our prediction. We expected better person recognition performance from studies that use ITMs containing embellished cues (live or videotaped lineups) than from studies that use ITMs containing impoverished cues (photo arrays or line drawings). The analysis of false alarm rates and sensitivity showed just the opposite. It is difficult to explain this counterintuitive pattern of results. Perhaps it is due to confounded variables not included in the meta-analysis.

Cues manipulated within ITM and within studies

These experiments held ITM constant (videotape) but manipulated the cues available in the ITM. These experiments thus provide the most controlled tests of the influence of cues on identification performance. All the experiments used both target-present and target-absent identification tests so the results can be examined separately for hits and false alarms.*

Cutler, Penrod, and Martens (1987). In this experiment, 290 participants viewed one of two videotaped crimes and then attempted to identify the robber two or fourteen days after initial viewing. The types of physical characteristic cues available in the identification test and presence or absence of the target were two of several additional variables that were manipulated. Subjects in the embellished cues condition attempted identification from videotaped lineups showing each suspect walking (cues to gait and posture) and speaking (each suspect provided a voice sample). Subjects in the impoverished cues condition attempted identification from a videotaped lineup showing each suspect's head and shoulders from a front and full profile. Results are summarized in Table 8.1. Embellished cues produced slightly more hits (d, the standardized difference between means = .10), fewer false alarms (d = .12), and a greater proportion of correct judgments (d = .12) than did impoverished cues. Neither the main effect of cues nor its interaction with lineup type (target-present versus target-absent) were significant. Several significant interactions emerged, however. With proportion correct as the dependent variable, cues interacted significantly with lineup composition (*t*, from the regression equation = 2.35, *p* < .05). Cues had a larger effect on

---

*Hit rates and false alarm rates were not reported separately in the Cutler and Penrod (1988), Cutler, Penrod, and Martens (1987), Cutler, Penrod, O'Rourke, and Martens (1986), and O'Rourke, Penrod, Cutler, and Stuve (1989) experiments because interactions between the relevant independent variables and lineup type (target-present versus target-absent) were nonsignificant in those studies. They are reported here for exploratory purposes. The effect-sizes reported here may differ slightly from those reported in the original reports. Effect-sizes reported in the original reports were computed from the regression output, whereas effect-sizes reported here were computed from the raw data. In no case was the difference substantial.

Table 8.1. *Cutler, Penrod, and Martens, 1987*

	Proportion hits (*n*)	Proportion false alarms (*n*)	Proportion correct (*n*)
Main effect of lineup cues			
Impoverished cues	.62 (68)	.74 (77)	.43 (145)
Embellished cues	.67 (72)	.68 (73)	.49 (145)
d	.10	.12	.12
Lineup similarity X cues			
Low similarity lineups			
Impoverished cues	.62 (34)	.61 (36)	.50 (70)
Embellished cues	.65 (37)	.77 (40)	.43 (77)
d	.06	− .32	− .14
High similarity lineups			
Impoverished cues	.62 (34)	.85 (41)	.36 (75)
Embellished cues	.69 (35)	.58 (33)	.56 (68)
d	.14	.54	.40
Retention interval X cues			
2-day retention interval			
Impoverished cues	.70 (33)	.70 (43)	.47 (76)
Embellished cues	.56 (34)	.79 (38)	.38 (72)
d	− .28	− .18	− .18
14-day retention interval			
Impoverished cues	.54 (35)	.79 (34)	.38 (69)
Embellished cues	.76 (38)	.57 (35)	.60 (73)
d	.44	.44	.44

proportion correct in high similarity lineups, where the lineup foils had a stronger resemblance to the target (d = .40), as opposed to low similarity lineups, where the resemblance was weaker (d = − .14). Although the three-way interaction with lineup type was nonsignificant, the pattern described above appears to be more pronounced in the false alarm data. Embellished cues decreased false alarms (d = .54) in high similarity lineups but increased false alarms (d = − .32) in low similarity lineups. With proportion correct as the dependent variable, retention interval interacted significantly with cues ($t = 2.91, p < .01$). Embellished cues had a stronger impact among subjects who attempted identifications after two weeks (*d* = .44) than among subjects who attempted identifications after two days (d = − .18). Again, the three-way interaction with lineup type was nonsignificant and the pattern of means seemed comparable for hits and false alarms. In summary, Cutler, Penrod, and Martens (1987) demonstrated that embellished cues have a greater impact in longer retention intervals and when the lineup members bear a closer physical resemblance to the target. The main effect for cues, however, was nonsignificant.

Table 8.2. *Cutler & Penrod, 1988*

	Proportion hits (n)	Proportion false alarms (n)	Proportion correct (n)
Main effect of lineup cues			
Impoverished cues	.72 (36)	.33 (48)	.69 (84)
Embellished cues	.82 (45)	.26 (46)	.78 (91)
d	.23	.16	.18
Presentation X cues			
Simultaneous presentation			
Impoverished cues	.70 (20)	.54 (26)	.57 (46)
Embellished cues	.81 (21)	.24 (25)	.78 (46)
d	.25	.68	.48
Sequential presentation			
Impoverished cues	.75 (16)	.09 (22)	.84 (38)
Embellished cues	.83 (24)	.29 (21)	.78 (45)
d	.18	− .46	− 14

Cutler and Penrod (1988). This experiment used the same stimulus materials and cue conditions described above and roughly the same experimental procedures. A videotaped robbery was viewed by 175 subjects and identifications were attempted after one week. In addition to manipulating cues and lineup type, this experiment also manipulated lineup presentation. Lineup members were shown simultaneously (as in the traditional police lineup) or sequentially. In a sequentially presented lineup, members are shown one at a time. As each lineup member is presented, witnesses decide whether or not the lineup member is the perpetrator. Subjects view each lineup member only once, and when a positive identification is made, the lineup procedure ceases. Lindsay and Wells (1985) found that sequential presentation of lineups produced significantly fewer false identifications than did simultaneous presentation, a pattern of results that has been replicated repeatedly (Cutler & Penrod, 1988; Lindsay, Lea, & Fulford, 1991). Cutler and Penrod's (1988) data are summarized in Table 8.2. Embellished cues, as compared to impoverished cues, produced slightly more hits (d = .23), fewer false alarms (d = .16), and a greater proportion correct (d = .18). Neither the main effect for cues nor the interaction between cues and lineup type was significant. Cues interacted significantly with lineup presentation ($t = 2.06, p < .05$). Embellished cues produced a higher proportion of correct judgments among subjects exposed to simultaneous presentation (d = .48) than among subjects exposed to sequential presentation (d = − .14). Although the three-way interaction with lineup type was nonsignificant, the pattern of the two-way interaction appears more pronounced in false alarms than in hits. Embellished cues decreased false alarm rate among subjects exposed to simultaneous presentation (d =

Table 8.3. *O'Rourke, Penrod, Cutler, and Stuve, 1989*

	Proportion hits (n)	Proportion false alarms (n)	Proportion correct (n)
Main effect of lineup cues			
Impoverished cues	.44 (27)	.60 (30)	.42 (57)
Embellished cues	.38 (53)	.36 (22)	.45 (75)
d	−.12	.48	.06

.68), as expected, but increased false alarm rate among subjects exposed to sequential presentation (d = −.46). This latter finding is contrary to the results of previous research and warrants replication. In summary, the Cutler and Penrod (1988) experiment demonstrated that embellished cues are more beneficial for traditional, simultaneously presented lineups.

O'Rourke, Penrod, Cutler, and Stuve (1989). The Cutler and Penrod (1988) manipulation of cues was tested again on a sample of 120 college students and community residents. One goal of this experiment was to demonstrate that findings observed in earlier studies, such as those previously discussed, are not idiosyncratic to college student populations. Subjects viewed the videotaped crime and participated in an identification test one week later. Data from this experiment are summarized in Table 8.3. The main effect of cues was nonsignificant. Embellished cues, as compared to impoverished cues, produced somewhat fewer hits (d = −.12), fewer false alarms (d = .48), and a somewhat higher proportion correct (d = .06). Cues did not interact significantly with lineup type nor with any of the other variables manipulated in this experiment. Because other main effects and interactions were significant, insensitivity of the data to the cue manipulation is an unlikely explanation for the pattern of effects.

Cutler, Penrod, O'Rourke, and Martens (1986). In the three experiments described above all the physical characteristic context cues were combined, as opposed to manipulated separately, in order to form a manipulation with high impact. Combined cues were expected to have a greater influence on recognition performance than cues manipulated separately. Thus, the previous experiments confounded quantity with quality of cues. The experiment we are now discussing attempted to separate quantity from quality by manipulating cues independently. Subjects were 287 students who viewed one of two videotaped crimes and, in the same experimental session, attempted identifications. In a fractional factorial design we independently manipulated

Body movement (lineup members shown walking versus standing still)
Three-quarter pose (shown versus not shown)

Table 8.4. *Cutler, Penrod, O'Rourke, and Martens, 1986*

	Proportion hits (n)	Proportion false alarms (n)	Proportion correct (n)
Main effect of motion			
No motion	.39 (76)	.63 (73)	.38 (149)
Motion	.36 (88)	.61 (83)	.37 (171)
d	− .06	.04	− .02
Main effect of ¾ pose			
No ¾ pose	.39 (87)	.64 (77)	.38 (164)
¾ pose	.36 (77)	.61 (79)	.38 (156)
d	− .06	.06	.00
Main effect of full body view			
Closeup only	.35 (84)	.60 (80)	.37 (164)
Closeup and full body view	.41 (80)	.64 (76)	.38 (156)
d	.12	− .08	.02
Main effect of voice samples			
No voice samples	.41 (80)	.65 (79)	.38 (159)
Voice samples	.35 (84)	.60 (77)	.37 (161)
d	− .12	.10	− .02
Main effect of color			
Black & white	.38 (81)	.59 (75)	.40 (156)
Color	.37 (83)	.65 (81)	.36 (164)
d	− .02	− .12	− .08

View (closeup of head and shoulders versus closeup and full body)
Voice samples (provided versus not provided)
Color (lineups shown in black and white versus color)

As Table 8.4 shows, each of these five cues produced trivial effects on hits (ds ranged from − .12 to .12), false alarms (ds ranged from − .12 to .10), and proportion correct (ds ranged from − .08 to .02). Interactions among these cues and between these cues and other independent variables were nonsignificant. Again, the presence of other main effects argues against the explanation that our dependent variables lacked sensitivity. In summary, as the previous research demonstrates, combined cues have mixed effects on eyewitness identification accuracy. As this study showed, cues, when manipulated separately, have no effect on identification performance.

Cues manipulated between ITM and within studies

These experiments manipulate ITMs. Each experiment contains at least two of the following: photo arrays, videotaped lineups, or live lineups. We assume that live and videotaped lineups contain more cues than do photo arrays. Although cues are not manipulated independently of ITM (indeed, they are confounded with ITM) these studies more closely estimate the differences in

Table 8.5. *Cutler, Fisher, and Chicvara, 1989*

	Proportion hits (n)	Proportion false alarms (n)	Proportion correct (n)
Live versus videotaped lineups			
Videotaped lineups	.69 (16)	.38 (8)	.67 (24)
Live lineups	.65 (17)	.11 (9)	.73 (26)
d	−.09	.59	.13

identification performance that are likely to be obtained from the three different ITMs.

Cutler, Fisher, and Chicvara (1989). In this experiment fifty students witnessed a staged theft of a professor's wallet during class. Five days later subjects attempted an identification from a live lineup or a videotaped lineup. Both lineups were embellished with the same physical characteristic cues; lineup members were shown in various poses, walking and speaking. The data are summarized in Table 8.5. No differences were statistically significant. Videotaped lineups produced slightly more hits than did live lineups (d = −.09). Although the magnitude of the effect of ITM on false alarms appears large (d = .59), the cell sizes are quite small, so the reliability of this difference is questionable. In summary, live and videotaped lineups produced comparable hit rates and proportions correct.

Cutler and Fisher (1990). Subjects in this experiment were seventy-two students who also witnessed a staged theft in which a male student and a female student stole videotaping equipment from a classroom. Sixteen days later subjects attempted to identify both thieves from live lineups, videotaped lineups, or photo arrays (manipulated between subjects). The live and videotaped lineups were designed to exploit their advantages. They showed the lineup members walking, exhibiting some typical behaviors, and speaking. The photo arrays were front view snapshots of each person (and one of the full lineup). The male thief was present in his lineup and the female thief was absent from her lineup. Results are summarized in Table 8.6. Because lineup type and target were confounded, data from the lineup type were not treated as a factor in the analysis. Target-present and target-absent data were analyzed separately, and no conclusion can be drawn about the relative magnitudes of the effects. Live and videotaped lineups produced comparable identification performance. Live lineups produced somewhat fewer hits (d = −.16), fewer false alarms (d = .08), and fewer correct judgments (d = −.08). These differences were not statistically significant. Data from live and videotaped

Table 8.6. *Cutler and Fisher, 1990*

	Proportion hits (n)	Proportion false alarms (n)	Proportion correct (n)
Live versus videotaped lineups			
Videotaped lineups	.31 (26)	.19 (26)	.56 (26)
Live lineups	.23 (26)	.15 (26)	.54 (26)
d	−.16	.08	−.08
Photo arrays versus lineups			
Photo arrays	.29 (21)	.43 (21)	.43 (21)
Live or videotaped lineups	.27 (52)	.17 (52)	.55 (52)
d	−.04	.52	.24

lineups were therefore combined and tested against photo arrays. The difference in hits was small ($d = -.04$) and nonsignificant. Live and videotaped lineups, however, produced fewer false alarms ($d = .52$) than photo arrays, and this difference was marginally significant ($t = 1.92, p < .06$). In summary, data from this experiment support the contention that live and videotaped lineups produce comparable identification performance. They also provide support for the importance of physical characteristic cues, as live and videotaped lineups produced fewer false alarms than did photo arrays.

Egan, Pittner, and Goldstein (1977). Subjects, in small groups, witnessed two targets act out a robbery. Subjects attempted identification tests from target-present lineups two, twenty-one, or fifty-six days after the robbery. Subjects attempted identifications from live lineups or photo arrays. Each lineup or photo array contained only one target (manipulated between subjects). Results are summarized in Table 8.7. Live lineups produced significantly more hits than did photo arrays ($d = .45$). ITMs did not interact significantly with retention interval or target. This study supports the contention that ITMs containing embellished physical characteristic cues have beneficial effects on

Table 8.7. *Egan, Pittner, and Goldstein, 1977*

	Proportion hits (n)
Photo arrays versus live lineups	
Photo arrays	.85 (43)
Live lineups	.98 (43)
d	.45

Table 8.8. *Shepherd, Ellis, and Davies, 1982*

	Proportion hits (n)	Matrix of mean differences (d)		
		Color	Video	Live
Identification test medium				
Black & white slides	.81 (16)	.29	.45	.26
Color slides	.92 (13)		.10	−.10
Videotaped lineups	.95 (20)			−.19
Live lineups	.89 (19)			
Slides versus lineups				
Slides (B&W and color)	.86 (29)			
Lineups (live and video)	.82 (39)			
d	−.13			

identification performance in comparison to ITMs containing impoverished cues.

Shepherd, Ellis, and Davies (1982). In this experiment subjects viewed to-be-recognized persons but not in the context of a crime simulation. Each subject was exposed to one of two targets (manipulated between subjects). At encoding, targets were shown live, on videotape, or via a monochrome or color slide presentation of to-be-recognized targets. The same four ITM conditions were manipulated in the recognition test. We review the data from the live presentation at encoding, because those data are most relevant to crime simulations. They are summarized in Table 8.8. Cross-tabulation produced nonsignificant differences among the four conditions (chi-square = 1.94). We tested the mean of the live and videotaped lineup conditions against the mean of the slide conditions. Live and videotaped lineups produced comparable hit rates (d = −.13), as in earlier research. The importance of cues was not supported in these data.

Summary of research described above

First, the data appear to be consistent in showing that live and videotaped lineups produce comparable identification accuracy. Less clear are the results for embellished versus impoverished cues, whether manipulated within ITM (that is, videotaped lineups containing embellished versus impoverished cues), between ITM and within studies (that is, live lineups containing embellished cues versus photo arrays containing impoverished cues), and between ITM and between studies (for example, studies using live lineups versus studies using photo arrays).

Shapiro and Penrod's (1986) "study characteristics" meta-analysis examines the influence of cues manipulated between ITM and between studies. The meta-analysis convincingly shows no support for the cue hypothesis. Studies using live or videotaped lineups do not show superior face recognition in comparison to studies using photo arrays or line drawings, even when many other variables are controlled for.

Where cues are manipulated within study and between ITMs the following conclusions obtain. Cutler and Fisher (1990) found that live and videotaped lineups produced significantly fewer false alarms than did photo arrays but the ITMs did not differ in proportion of hits. In contrast, Egan, Pittner, and Goldstein (1977) found that live lineups produced significantly more hits than did photo arrays. In contrast to Egan et al. (1977) but consistent with Cutler and Fisher (1990), Shepherd, Ellis, and Davies (1982) found no differences in hits as a function of live lineups, videotaped lineups, or slides.

Studies that manipulated cues within ITMs reached the following conclusions. A main effect of cues on identification performance emerged only in Shapiro and Penrod's meta-analysis of manipulated variables. This effect was small. Cues, when manipulated separately, had trivial effects (Cutler, Penrod, O'Rourke, & Martens, 1986). When cues were combined in an effort to create a manipulation of substantial impact, they had no effect in one study (O'Rourke, Penrod, Cutler, & Stuve, 1989), and their effects were qualified in other studies by mode of presentation of lineup members (Cutler & Penrod, 1988), retention interval, and physical resemblance of the lineup foils to the target (Cutler, Penrod, & Martens, 1987). Embellished cues seemed most effective when the lineup members resembled the target in physical appearance, when lineup members were presented simultaneously, or when there was a longer retention interval.

A major point of Shapiro and Penrod's (1986) meta-analysis, however, is that statistical significance should not be the only metric against which consistency of findings and importance of effects should be measured. Magnitude of effects is important. In an effort to address this issue, we first consulted Shapiro and Penrod's (1986) meta-analysis of "manipulated studies" and then updated this meta-analysis with the studies cited above. Note that the meta-analyses examine only the main effect of cues; they do not take into consideration the interactions between cues and other variables, such as those cited above.

Shapiro and Penrod's (1986) meta-analysis. Whereas Shapiro and Penrod's "study characteristics" analysis examined the influence of ITMs manipulated between studies, the "manipulated studies" analysis included only those studies that manipulated either ITMs or cues. For each study a single effect-size (*d*) was computed, and this effect-size was averaged across studies. The average was then tested for statistical significance. Hits and false alarms were analyzed separately. In both analyses, the effect-sizes represent the difference

Table 8.9. *Shapiro and Penrod, 1986*

	Proportion hits (n)	Proportion false alarms (n)	d'	B''
Main effect of lineup cues				
Impoverished cues	.50	.30	.10	.14
Embellished cues	.50	.26	.10	.09
d (based on full sample)	.07	.17		
N of studies	11	7		

in identification performance for live and videotaped lineups versus photo arrays or line drawings. The live and videotaped lineup conditions presumably reflect embellished cues, whereas the photo array and line drawing conditions presumably contain impoverished cues. Only one of the studies described above (Cutler, Penrod, O'Rourke, & Martens, 1986) was included in Shapiro and Penrod's (1986) meta-analysis. Thirteen studies ($n = 1,807$) provided data for hits. Slightly but significantly more hits were obtained for live or videotaped lineups than for photo arrays or line drawings (d = .07, z = 3.13, $p < .05$). Data from ten studies ($N = 1,407$) examined the influence of ITM or cues on false alarms. Live or videotaped lineups produced slightly but nonsignificantly fewer false alarms than did photo arrays or line drawings (d = .17). Cell means for the eleven studies for which hit rates were available and for the seven studies for which false alarm rates were available are displayed in Table 8.9. From these smaller samples, d', a measure of overall sensitivity, and B'', a measure of decision criterion, were computed. Average d' was .10 for all conditions. Average B'' was .09 for live or videotaped lineups and .14 for photo array or line drawings, indicating that subjects in the latter conditions are somewhat more likely to report having recognized a face. In summary, the results for the full sample of available studies (that is, the effect-size analysis) show that live or videotaped lineups produce slightly (but significantly) more hits and nonsignificantly fewer false alarms than do photo arrays or line drawings. The analysis of the subset of studies for which cell means were available did not confirm this pattern. We are inclined to emphasize the results of the effect-size analysis, as it is more complete and less susceptible to selection bias.

Update of the meta-analysis. In an effort to merge the results of Shapiro and Penrod's (1986) meta-analysis of "manipulated studies" with the results of the more recent experiments described above, we conducted a new meta-analysis. As in Shapiro and Penrod (1986), hits and false alarms were analyzed separately. Shapiro and Penrod's meta-analysis of "manipulated studies" was

Table 8.10. *Meta-analysis*

Study	Embellished versus impoverished proportions		Live versus videotape proportions	
	hits	false alarms	hits	false alarms
C, P, & M, 1987	.10	.12		
C & P, 1988	.23	.16		
O, P, C, & S, 1989	−.12	.48		
C, F, & C, 1989			−.09	.59
C & F, 1990	−.04	.52	−.16	.08
E, P, & G, 1977	.45			
S, E, & D, 1982	−.13		−.19	
S & P, 1986	.07	.17		
Average, weighted d	.08	.19	−.15	.20
Average, weighted r	.04	.09	−.08	.10
Significance, p	.07	.01	.40	.41
Total n	2335	1776	124	43

	Hits		False alarms	
	M	(n)	M	(n)
Photoarrays or slides	.54	(1127)	.35	(879)
Live or videotaped lineups	.53	(1208)	.29	(897)
Nonstandardized mean difference	−.01		−.06	
Videotaped lineups	.61	(62)	.23	(34)
Live lineups	.55	(62)	.14	(35)
Nonstandardized mean difference	−.06		−.09	

C, P, & M = Cutler, Penrod, & Martens; C & P = Cutler & Penrod; O, P, C, & S = O'Rourke, Penrod, Cutler, & Stuve; C, F, & C = Cutler, Fisher & Chicvara; C & F = Cutler & Fisher; E, P, & G = Egan, Pittner, & Goldstein; S, E, & D = Shepherd, Ellis, & Davies; S & P = Shapiro and Penrod.

treated as a single study; its results represent the previous research not reviewed here. By virtue of its large sample, their meta-analysis justly will carry disproportionate weight in the averaging of effect-sizes. Effect-sizes (d) from each new experiment reviewed here (except for Cutler, Penrod, O'Rourke, & Martens, 1986, which was included in Shapiro and Penrod's meta-analysis) were added to the analysis. The summary list of effect-sizes is displayed in Table 8.10. Two different hypotheses were tested on both hits and false alarms: Live and videotaped lineups produce comparable identification performance, and live and videotaped lineups produce more accurate identification performance than do photo arrays, slides, line drawings, or videotaped lineups containing impoverished cues. *DSTAT* (Johnson, 1989) was used for all computations. Results are summarized in Table 8.10.

Hypothesis one was supported. The effect of live versus videotaped lineups was small and nonsignificant on both hits ($d = -.15$; $p > .05$) and false alarms ($d = .20$; $p > .05$). Slightly more hits and false alarms were obtained with videotaped lineups. Hypothesis two showed some support. Live and videotaped lineups produced slightly and marginally significantly more hits ($d = .08$, $p < .07$) and significantly fewer false alarms ($d = .19$, $p < .0001$) than did photo arrays, slides, line drawings, or videotaped lineups containing impoverished cues. The average, weighted means are also displayed in Table 8.10. Means from the Shapiro and Penrod meta-analysis represent the subset of studies from which hit rates and false alarm rates were available (see above). It is clear that all mean differences are small, whether statistically significant or not. The largest difference (.09) was also the least statistically reliable.

Conclusions. The updated meta-analysis of the main effects for ITM cues revealed that their effect varies considerably across experiments, although we are unable to associate this variability with specific features of the studies. When averaged across studies, cues produce a trivial effect on identification accuracy. Experiments that showed appreciable main effects for ITM or cue conditions (Egan, Pittner, & Goldstein, 1977; Cutler & Fisher, 1990) on hits or false alarms were met with enough competing null effects from other studies to render the overall effect equivocal. Thus, the finding that live and videotaped lineups (which presumably contain embellished cues) produced comparable identification performances loses its shock value when we consider that both produced identification performances comparable to photo arrays, slides, and line drawings (which presumably contain impoverished cues).

This pessimistic conclusion must be tempered for a variety of reasons. First, the research reviewed here identified some conditions in which the impact of cues varies (Cutler & Penrod, 1988; Cutler, Penrod, & Martens, 1987). These qualifying conditions are not reflected in the meta-analysis, which only considered the effect of cues *averaged* across all experimental conditions. Second, the effectiveness of ITM is likely to depend on the quality of exposure to the perpetrator at the time of the crime. For example, if the witness views only the face of the perpetrator, the additional cues provided by live and videotaped lineups are unlikely to improve recognition accuracy. We are unaware of the cues available at exposure in most of the studies reviewed. Third, the above analyses assume that live and videotaped lineups contained comparable cues and both contained more cues than did the photo arrays and slides. Some experiments (Cutler & Fisher, 1990; Cutler, Fisher, & Chicvara, 1989) deliberately set out to create such differences in the ITM. We have no basis for evaluating the appropriateness of this assumption for the Shepherd, Ellis, and Davies (1982) and Egan, Pittner, and Goldstein (1977) experiments because of a lack of information regarding the behavior of the lineup members. Fourth, most of the experiments that involved videotaped lineups (Cutler &

Fisher, 1990; Cutler, Fisher, & Chicvara, 1989; Cutler & Penrod, 1988; Cutler, Penrod, & Martens, 1987; Cutler, Penrod, O'Rourke, & Martens, 1986; O'Rourke, Penrod, Cutler, & Stuve, 1989) used modest videotaping equipment and unskilled technicians. None of the experiments reviewed thus far made full use of the technologically advanced videotaping equipment available today. Fifth, we do not know the extent to which any of the viewing conditions in these experiments resemble the stimuli used in actual tests of eyewitness identification. It is possible, for example, that the photo arrays used here are of better or worse quality than those used in actual cases. Sixth, it is possible that ITM is confounded with other variables in the existing research.

Implications for further research and practice

How might the pattern of results change with the use of higher quality videotape equipment and sophisticated editing features? There are many things that can be done with videotaped lineups that cannot be done with live lineups (and obviously not with photo arrays). With the use of large monitors, faces can be blown up larger than life. With the use of jog-and-roll dials, lineup members can be shown moving in slow motion, even on a frame-by-frame basis. Videotaped lineups can be paused on a specific frame, showing a lineup member in a specific bodily position. In addition, videotaped lineups can be shown repeatedly and for an unlimited amount of time. The equipment is so simple that eyewitnesses can be placed in control of some of the features, such as the jog-and-roll dial. Thus, it is conceivable that videotaped lineups might improve identification accuracy rates in comparison to live lineups. The potential benefits of these features should be addressed in further research. An attempt should also be made to ascertain the typical quality of videotaped lineups and photo arrays in actual eyewitness cases. These ITMs should be evaluated both for quality and quantity of cues.

Another potentially qualifying factor is the role of stress experienced by the witness at the time of the identification. It is conceivable that eyewitnesses, in some circumstances, experience considerable stress when confronting a perpetrator in a live lineup, and this might affect his or her decision processes or willingness to identify the perpetrator. The stress associated with confrontation might be particularly relevant for children witnesses. Videotaped lineups and photo arrays should be less stressful. Future research attention should concentrate on the conditions likely to qualify the effect of cues and ITM. The interactions described above suggest some possible directions and deserve replication. A final direction for future research would be to examine the impact of ITM in field experiments that better resemble realistic eyewitness cases (for example, Krafka & Penrod, 1985). We suspect that in actual crimes witnesses are able to encode a wider variety of cues, and the effects of ITM might therefore be greater.

With respect to current practices, the conservative conclusion is that, based on available research, there is no reason to believe that live lineups, videotaped lineups, or photo arrays produce substantial differences in identification performance. Based on what is currently known, identifications from photo arrays should therefore not be given less weight in investigations or in trials than identifications from live lineups. Another conclusion is that, given the apparent comparability of live lineups and photo arrays, it is not worth the trouble and expense to use live lineups. Although live lineups, videotaped lineups, and photo arrays apparently produce comparable identification performances, they have different implications for legal procedure, such as the defendant's rights to counsel during the identification test (see, for example, Wells & Cutler, 1990). These differences must be considered in deciding which ITM is appropriate for a given case.

References

Cutler, B. L., & Fisher, R. P. (1990). Live lineups, videotaped lineups, and photoarrays. *Forensic Reports, 3,* 439–448.

Cutler, B. L., Fisher, R. P., & Chicvara, C. L. (1989). Eyewitness identification from live versus videotaped lineups. *Forensic Reports, 2,* 93–106.

Cutler, B. L., & Penrod, S. D. (1988). Improving the reliability of eyewitness identification: Lineup construction and presentation. *Journal of Applied Psychology, 73,* 281–290.

Cutler, B. L., Penrod, S. D., & Martens, T. K. (1987). Improving the reliability of eyewitness identifications: Putting context into context. *Journal of Applied Psychology, 72,* 629–637.

Cutler, B. L., Penrod, S. D., O'Rourke, T. E., & Martens, T. K. (1986). Unconfounding the effects of contextual cues on eyewitness identification accuracy. *Social Behaviour: An International Journal of Applied Social Psychology, 2,* 113–134.

Egan, D., Pittner, M., & Goldstein, A. G. (1977). Eyewitness identification: Photographs v. live models. *Law and Human Behavior, 1,* 199–206.

Johnson, B. T. (1989) *DSTAT: Software for the meta-analytic review of research literatures.* Hillsdale, NJ: Erlbaum.

Krafka, C., & Penrod, S. D. (1985). Reinstatement of context in a field experiment on eyewitness identification. *Journal of Personality and Social Psychology, 49,* 58–69.

Lindsay, R. C. L., Lea, J. A., & Fulford, J. A. (1991). Sequential lineup presentation: Technique matters. *Journal of Applied Psychology, 76,* 741–745.

Lindsay, R. C. L., & Wells, G. L. (1985). Improving eyewitness identifications from lineups: Simultaneous versus sequential lineup presentation. *Journal of Applied Psychology, 70,* 556–564.

O'Rourke, T. E., Penrod, S. D., Cutler, B. L., & Stuve, T. E. (1989). The external validity of eyewitness identification research: Generalizing across subject populations. *Law and Human Behavior, 13,* 385–395.

Shapiro, P. N., & Penrod, S. D. (1986). Meta-analysis of facial identification studies. *Psychological Bulletin, 100,* 139–156.

Shepherd, J. W., Ellis, H. D., & Davies, G. M. (1982). *Identification evidence: A psychological evaluation.* Aberdeen, Scotland: University Press.

Tulving, E., & Thomson, D. M. (1973). Encoding specificity and retrieval processes in episodic memory. *Psychological Review, 80,* 352–373.

Wells, W. P., & Cutler, B. L. (1990). The right to counsel at videotaped lineups: An emerging dilemma. *Connecticut Law Review, 22,* 373–395.

9   Biased lineups: Where do they come from?

R. C. L. Lindsay

Over the past two decades eyewitness researchers have employed staged crimes to investigate the impact of biased lineup procedures on eyewitness identification accuracy. The results have been remarkably consistent. Biased lineups dramatically increase the rate of false identifications of innocent people but have little effect on the rate of correct identification. This pattern has been found for lineups biased because the foils did not resemble the suspects (Lindsay & Wells, 1980), only the suspects wore clothing similar to that worn during the crime (Lindsay, Lea, Nosworthy, Fulford, Hector, LeVan, & Seabrook, 1991; Lindsay, Wallbridge, & Drennan, 1987), or the instructions led witnesses to believe that the guilty person must be in the lineup (Kohnken & Maass, 1988; Lindsay et al., 1991; Malpass & Devine, 1981).

These studies of lineup bias were stimulated by real world examples of highly biased lineups. One of the most notorious is the black suspect in an otherwise all white lineup used by police in Minneapolis (Ellison & Buckhout, 1981). In that case, police explained the use of only white foils by claiming there were no other blacks in the building when the lineup was constructed and that there were few blacks in Minneapolis so the lineup was representative of the population. Neither of these explanations is acceptable. Surely other blacks could have been found with little delay and juries, not lineups, should be representative of the population. This example and others remain inadequately explained.

For the remainder of this discussion, poor lineup foils will be used as the source of lineup bias although there is no reason for the points made to be different if another form of lineup bias were to be considered.

I am concerned here only with extremely biased lineups, where the suspect is very likely to be selected whether guilty or not. Such lineups would fail tests of lineup fairness, having functional or effective sizes of approximately 1.0 (Malpass & Devine, 1981; Wells, Leippe, & Ostrom, 1979). The fact that

Support for this research was provided by the Social Sciences and Humanities Research Council of Canada. I wish to thank Linda Cancelli who collected the data for one of the experiments as an undergraduate research project.

182

all lineups are not "perfect" (whatever that would mean) is not the issue. The problem is that some are atrocious.

How often do police use such biased lineups? It is difficult to answer this question definitively; however, examples are described periodically in the eyewitness literature (for example, Ellison & Buckhout, 1981; Doob & Kirshenbaum, 1973; Wells, Leippe, & Ostrom, 1979) and it is unlikely that every instance has been documented. Wells and Wright (1986) report that many examples of biased lineups can be found (see also Brigham, this volume). Regardless of how common the practice may be, the origin or cause of biased lineups remains an interesting issue. The issue to be addressed here is not how often such lineups are used but rather why they are used. I will conclude that there is no excuse for police ever to use such highly biased lineups so that any frequency of their occurrence is unacceptable. The research reported below confirms that when such extremes of bias occur, they reflect intentional biases designed to elicit identification of the suspect.

Why do police use biased lineups? Three possible answers to this question are examined: ignorance, sloppiness, and deliberate intent.

Ignorance. Police may construct biased lineups because they are unaware of the consequences of their actions.

Sloppiness. Even if police are aware of the effects of biased lineups, they might produce poor identification procedures because they do not care about the consequences, do not think about what they are doing, or are working under an assumption that leads them to disregard their knowledge.

Intentional bias. Police may intentionally use biased lineup procedures because they increase the probability of identification and conviction of the suspect.

Ignorance

There are at least five sources of information that police might be exposed to with regard to the effectiveness and dangers of various lineup procedures: psychological literature, legal literature, police literature (or training), on the job experience (either their own or stories from colleagues), and personal intuitions. Because police are neither psychologists nor lawyers, they cannot be expected to be acquainted with the literature in either of these fields. Police do receive training, however, and some of their instructors ought to be aware of the psychological and legal aspects of identification issues. Some level of knowledge in these fields could thus be expected of and does exist in police forces.

Officers who received their training many years ago or who are members of very small departments may have had substantially less opportunity to be exposed to these issues. Seniority and small departments need not lead to ignorance, however. For example, in the Province of Ontario, Canada, all police officers are trained at a single, central facility, the Ontario Police College. Officers from the smallest towns to the largest cities and the provincial police all receive the same training. Courses are provided on a continuous basis to update the knowledge of experienced officers and those who will be assigned to special duties (such as conducting identification procedures). It is too much to demand, however, that every officer in every department be aware of the most up-to-date procedures for obtaining eyewitness identifications. At least some identification procedures will inevitably be conducted by police with little or no exposure to the specific problems of lineup construction, so ignorance appears to be a plausible explanation for some biased lineup procedures.

Even if an officer conducting an identification procedure is ignorant of the psychological and legal issues and has received no relevant training, this would explain the use of biased lineup procedures only if such procedures are the "natural" or "obvious" ones to use. That is, lack of training can be used as an explanation of poor lineup procedures only if untrained people are prone to construct biased lineups. Is this the case? If so, then average people asked to create lineups should create biased lineups because they have not been trained. To test this notion, an experiment was conducted with introductory psychology students and members of the general public who were asked to construct lineups. Presumably neither of these populations is knowledgeable about eyewitness issues.

Pilot study

Pilot data were collected prior to the experiments to provide ratings of the similarity of eighty photographs of potential lineup members to each of four "suspects" used in the studies. The photographs were of white males between the ages of eighteen and thirty. The men were highly variable in appearance; none was wearing glasses. Ratings were made on a nine-point scale from "not at all similar" (1) to "very similar" (9). Subjects were fourteen female and eleven male Queen's University introductory psychology students aged seventeen to twenty-three.

The mean similarity ratings in the pilot study were used as a measure of the similarity of the "suspects" to each potential "foil" in the subsequent lineup construction tasks. Mean similarity ratings were generally low ($M = 2.29$) but highly variable with a range from 1.16 to 6.12. The mean similarity ratings of the five foils most similar to the four suspects were 4.42, 4.39, 4.26, and 4.01 (suspects one to four respectively). These numbers represent the best six-person lineup (suspect plus five foils or distractors) that could be selected for each suspect from the available pool of pictures.

To produce a uniform scale for each suspect, subjects' choices of foils in the subsequent experiments were first assigned the mean ratings given them by the pilot subjects, then averaged across the five foils selected, and finally expressed as a percentage of the maximum possible value a lineup could have received for the suspect (for example, a lineup for suspect one with a mean similarity score of 3.75 would be converted to a score of 3.75/4.42 = 84.8 percent). Alternative analyses (for example, using unaltered mean ratings) produce exactly the same pattern of results reported below.

Later, another thirty pilot subjects rated eighty additional faces in the same manner for two of the suspects (suspects two and three). The new faces on average were slightly less similar to the suspects (M = 2.03) but had an equally large range of values (from 1.00 to 6.02). The larger combined set of faces (N = 162) was used in Experiment 4 only. The best lineups available for the two suspects using the 160-face pool produced mean similarity scores of 4.48 and 4.36.

The resulting scale of lineup quality has some features worth noting. At the top of the similarity ratings scale, mean similarity ratings decline rapidly from the most similar foil to the second most similar foil, and so forth. As a result, if the most similar foil (according to the pilot ratings) was not selected for the lineup, the score for the best possible remaining lineup decreased rapidly. Substantial disagreement existed in the pilot work concerning the order of most to least similar foils for each suspect. Few subjects, therefore, later selected the five highest rated foils as lineup members. High similarity lineups (like those used as fair lineups in other research) are associated with scores at or above about 60 to 65 percent. Many faces were rated as having little similarity to each suspect and thus creating a poor lineup was easy. Mathematically, the worst possible lineups would result in scores of about 26 percent.

These pilot data are not unusual. Pilot work has often revealed extensive disagreement about the exact degree of perceived similarity of the faces of potential foils to confederates (suspects). Other researchers have described similar experiences during informal discussions at conferences. On the other hand, high rank order correlations of most to least similar faces are common between subjects; thus, the exact order and numerical ratings of the top quarter or third of the distribution may vary considerably from rater to rater but a high level of agreement is still found so a subset of available faces would be much more similar to the targets or suspects than others.

EXPERIMENT 1

Subjects. The subjects were thirty Queen's University undergraduates (thirteen males, seventeen females aged seventeen to twenty-six) recruited by phone numbers provided at the beginning of the academic year and thirty members of the general public (fifteen males, fifteen females aged twenty-two to fifty-seven) recruited by random selection of phone numbers from the City of Kingston, Ontario, telephone directory. All participants were volunteers. (*Note:* All subjects in the studies reported were white. Race is not considered in these studies.)

Procedure. Undergraduate subjects participated in the laboratory. Members of the public had the option of coming to the laboratory or having the experimenter come to their home ($n = 18$ took this option). Only one subject participated in each session.

Subjects were informed that they would be asked to construct a lineup by selecting five photographs from a large pool of pictures to use as foils in a lineup. The eighty photographs were spread out on a table in eight rows of ten each. A photo of a suspect was provided and the subjects were told they could take as long as they felt necessary to select five foils from the eighty-picture array. After the first lineup was completed, the five selected foils were replaced in the pool, a second suspect photo was provided, and the task repeated. A similar procedure was followed for the third and fourth suspects. Subjects were unaware that they were to construct another lineup until they were provided with the second suspect photo; they were then told of the total number of lineups to be constructed. The order of lineup construction for the four suspect photographs was counterbalanced. Lineups constructed when a suspect was presented first did not differ from the lineups constructed when the same suspect was presented later (in other words, constructing multiple lineups did not influence the quality of the lineups).

Following the selection of the fourth set of lineup foils, subjects rated the similarity to the respective suspects of each of the foils they had selected, using the same scale as the pilot study. Finally, the subjects completed a questionnaire including a test of their knowledge of eyewitness issues (Yarmey & Jones, 1983) and items assessing their assumptions as to the guilt of the suspect or other evidence.

Results. There were no significant differences between the students' responses and those of the general public. There were no significant sex effects nor differences across suspects. The data were collapsed across these variables.

Overall, the mean lineup scores were 73.7 percent of the maximum possible values, consistent with some attempt on the part of most subjects to select foils similar to the suspects. When asked on the final questionnaire to rate on a seven-point scale ($1 =$ not at all, $7 =$ very much) the degree to which they attempted to select pictures similar to the suspect, subjects' mean response was 5.92 (s.d. $= 0.48$). No subject gave a response below 4 on the scale. No subject selected a foil that was not one of the twenty-one most similar to the suspect as rated by the pilot subjects. Over 90 percent of choices were of foils rated as the twelve most similar to each of the suspects.

Subjects' ratings of the similarity to the suspects of the foils they selected were compared to the rated similarity of the same foils selected by the pilot subjects. The mean similarity rating for the lineup based on the pilot data was subtracted from the mean similarity rating provided by the lineup constructors and the mean of the resultant values ($M = 1.09$) was significantly greater than zero ($t (58) = 9.63, p < .01$). Every subject rated the foils they had selected as more similar to the suspects than the pilot subjects had rated them.

Postexperimental interviews with the subjects probed their reasons for selecting the pictures they had chosen. Every subject mentioned similarity as one of their criteria for selecting foils. When pressed further to explain why similarity was an important criterion, many responded that it was obvious that lineup foils had to look like the accused or there would be no sense in having a lineup.

Correct responses were given on average to 52.8 percent of the Knowledge of Eyewitness Behavior Questionnaire items. As expected, the subjects indicated no special knowledge of eyewitness issues.

Discussion. Taken together, the findings from Experiment 1 indicate there is no evidence to support the hypothesis that the average person, whether undergraduate or a member of the general public, would produce biased identification procedures if asked to construct lineups. Untrained members of the public and introductory psychology students consistently selected foils that were highly similar to the accused. They sought, perhaps maximized, similarity to the accused.

If extremely biased lineups are relatively rare, it may be that people ignorant of eyewitness issues produce random lineups and these are only occasionally highly biased. The data are not consistent with this view. The fact that every selected foil was similar to the accused (every choice was at or above the 73rd percentile of similarity to the target) illustrates that every individual selected only foils similar in appearance.

The tendency to rate foils selected for lineups as more similar to the suspects than indicated by the pilot data is interesting. One plausible explanation for this finding is that the subjects distorted their perceptions of similarity to coincide with their desire to maximize similarity. The similarity ratings may be inflated to reduce cognitive dissonance associated with a lack of available foils as similar to the suspect as the subjects would have liked. If true, this is also inconsistent with the notion that biased lineups may be produced through simple ignorance of the eyewitness literature. Apparently, people with no special knowledge of eyewitness issues intuitively conclude that lineup foils should resemble the accused to some degree.

Alternatively, the difference in ratings may be an artifact of the method employed. There was considerable disagreement regarding which foils were most similar to each target. Obviously, the five most similar foils selected by a subject would be the five highest rated by that particular lineup constructor. Many of the pilot subjects would not have rated one or more of these five as among the most similar five faces available. Thus, if a subject selected pictures one through five as lineup members and if these five pictures were selected by the subject because they seemed the most similar to the target or accused, then the similarity ratings made by the lineup constructor for this particular set of five faces should be quite high. The average rating of these same five faces based on the pilot data could include similarity ratings made by some subjects who would have selected other faces. As a result, the average ratings of the pilot subjects would be expected to be lower than the average ratings of the lineup constructors. This argument applies only if subjects were maximizing perceived similarity of the foils to the suspects.

Discussions with experienced police officers at the Ontario Police College indicate that they have been aware of the effects of poor lineup foils for some time. It has long been known that the use of poor foils increases the likelihood the suspect will be identified. Experienced officers are aware that this is true even if the suspect is innocent. If ignorance plays any part in the construction of biased lineups, it is likely due to the failure of police to realize that poor foils decrease correct identification rates.

Sloppiness

Police are trained to take great care when collecting evidence so that it will be usable in court. Failure to do so out of indifference is unprofessional. It seems unlikely that officers who create biased lineups would argue that they didn't care how well they did the job.

Police may produce a biased lineup because similar foils are not readily available, and time pressures keep them from searching for adequate lineup members. This excuse was used by the Minneapolis police in the example cited earlier. If adequate foils are not immediately available, however, identification attempts should be delayed until an unbiased procedure can be conducted. If photographic arrays are used instead of live lineups, it is difficult to believe that a reasonable set of foils could not be found quickly for any suspect other than one quite unusual in appearance. Even then, all other lineup members would surely be of the same race and gender and share gross physical similarities.

Sloppiness could occur because an officer fails to appreciate the importance of a properly constructed lineup or because he or she assumes some other factor negates the importance of the lineup procedure. A variety of assumptions about identification procedures and/or eyewitnesses may induce sloppy lineup construction.

Misidentifications unlikely. Police may assume that eyewitnesses are unlikely to identify innocent people. If true, the procedures used are unimportant. Thus, poor lineup procedures might double or triple the rate of false identification in psychological research, but if the rate of false identification in the real world is trivially small to begin with, there is little danger.

The assumption that eyewitness errors occur at a trivially low rate is dispelled quickly for most police with on-the-job experience. Conversations with police indicate a clear appreciation of the potential for eyewitness errors. Most officers with experience in conducting lineups revel in tales of witnesses choosing police officers or other known innocent foils from lineups. Wrongful convictions are more often attributable to identification errors than any other source (Rattner, 1988). Lawyers argue in court that eyewitness reports are unreliable. Traffic officers have an endless supply of stories of eyewitnesses telling conflicting accounts of the same event. Clearly, police know that eyewitnesses are prone to error and most know they might identify innocent people. Police know that biased lineups are potentially dangerous; another assumption might reduce their concern, however.

Lineup procedures irrelevant. Police may assume that the probability of making a false identification is a witness factor unrelated to the lineup procedures employed. Bad witnesses, or those with a poor memory for the criminal, will be prone to make false identifications whereas good witnesses will not, regardless of the characteristics of the lineup.

The assumption that identification errors are made by bad witnesses independently of the quality of the lineup is consistent with the finding that a substantial percentage of eyewitnesses are likely to use relative judgment strategies (Lindsay, Lea, Nosworthy, Fulford, Hector, Levan, & Seabrook, 1991; Wells, 1984). Unfortunately, these studies suggest that such witnesses are particularly prone to make errors when attempting identifications from biased lineups. Police cannot be expected to know these research results, but, it is still not clear how the assumption that witnesses will make false identifications can be used to explain the existence of biased lineups. As discussed previously, selection of similar foils is perceived to be the appropriate way to construct lineups in general. Police have no way of knowing whether or not a particular witness will be prone to error before conducting the lineup. On what basis could he make such a judgment? Even if the witness were not prone to error, why would that negate the necessity to create a fair lineup? Some other assumption would have to justify creating and using a biased lineup.

Presumption of guilt. Police may assume the suspect is guilty and there need be no concern about a false identification resulting from a poor lineup (assuming a single suspect lineup). Biased lineups lead to identification of the suspect and since the suspect is guilty, a false identification cannot occur.

The second and third experiments were conducted, in part, to test the impact of the presumption of guilt on the selection of lineup foils. If the presumption of guilt is important as a preexisting condition for the construction of biased lineups, subjects constructing lineups under a presumption of guilt would be expected to be less concerned about the quality of lineup foils than subjects who presumed the suspect was innocent.

EXPERIMENT 2

Subjects. The subjects were fifty female and thirty-four male Queen's University introductory psychology students ranging in age from seventeen to twenty-seven.

Procedure. Subjects were informed that they would be asked to construct a lineup by selecting five photographs from a large pool of pictures to use as "foils." Before constructing the lineups, they were randomly assigned to one of five conditions. A control group ($n = 28$) was given no special instructions. The remaining groups ($n = 14$ each) were asked to keep in mind one of the following: (1) Assume the suspect is guilty; (2) Assume the suspect is innocent; (3) Be sure to be fair to the witness; (4) Be sure to be fair to the accused. The presumptions under which the subjects were working were repeated before the foils were selected for each of the four suspects. The remainder of the procedure was the same as for Experiment 1 with the addition of manipulation checks assessing the perceived fairness of the lineups constructed to both the accused and the witness as well as the extent to which subjects presumed the suspect guilty or innocent. The same photographs described previously were used.

Results. The manipulations of assumed guilt and innocence were successful. When asked to rate the degree to which they had assumed, during the foil selection task, that the accused was guilty ($1 = $ did not assume to $7 = $ definitely assumed guilt), subjects instructed to assume guilt were more likely ($M = 5.43$) to think of the accused as guilty than were subjects in the control ($M = 3.29$), fair to witness ($M = 2.93$), fair to accused ($M = 2.71$), or presume innocent ($M = 1.79$) conditions ($F(4,79) = 7.89, p < .01$). Ratings of assumed innocence ($1 = $ did not assume to $7 = $ definitely assumed innocence) indicated that subjects instructed to assume the accused was innocent ($M = 5.86$) were more likely to think of the accused as innocent during the task than were subjects in the fair to accused ($M = 4.21$), fair to witness (M

= 2.86), control (M = 2.79), or assume guilt (M = 1.93) conditions (F (4,79) = 10.25, p < .01).

Instructions given to the subjects failed to produce significant differences across conditions in ratings of the degree to which subjects were concerned with fairness to the accused and fairness to the witness. Subjects indicated a uniformly high level of concern for fairness to the accused (M = 5.53 on a seven-point scale) and a moderate level of concern with fairness to the witness (M = 3.17 on a seven-point scale). This manipulation apparently was unsuccessful. However, correlations were calculated between rated concern for fairness to the accused and lineup quality as well as fairness to the witness and lineup quality. Neither correlation was significant (a finding I will return to later when considering another possible reason for sloppiness).

Subjects' selection of lineup foils was consistent with a strategy to maximize similarity to the accused. On average, lineups were 76.9 percent of the maximum similarity values possible (as compared to 77.3 percent for Experiment 1). No significant differences were obtained across instruction conditions or gender. Ironically, the average lineup quality was slightly higher when the accused was presumed guilty (M = 78.8 percent) than when presumed innocent (M = 74.6 percent) although this difference was not significant. Rated assumptions of guilt or innocence were not significantly correlated with lineup quality.

As in Experiment 1, subjects rated the similarity of the foils to the suspects as substantially higher than the ratings provided by the pilot subjects (M = 4.64 versus 3.22, t (82) = 11.52, p < .01). Again, subjects described their strategy as one of seeking foils similar to the accused and selected only those the pilot data would indicate were at least in the top quartile of available photos most similar to the accused. Responses to the Knowledge of Eyewitness Behavior Questionnaire were correct 49.2 percent of the time.

Overall, subjects revealed that the primary concern of untrained lineup constructors with no special knowledge of eyewitness issues is to seek foils similar to the accused. The lineups they produced contained only foils reasonably similar to the accused and the subjects perceived the foils to be more similar to the accused than the pilot data would indicate.

Although the manipulation of concern for fairness to the accused versus the witness was unsuccessful, subjects revealed a high level of concern for fairness to the accused in all conditions. If this pattern is typical, there is no reason to expect that biased lineups result from a lack of concern for the accused unless the lineup constructor has become jaded and intentionally sets aside such concerns. Moreover, the presumption of guilt alone does not appear to be sufficient to lead even untrained people to construct biased lineups. However, the manipulation may have led subjects to respond to the manipulation check in the expected manner without actually influencing their feelings that the accused was or was not guilty. A third experiment was conducted in which subjects believed the accused to be guilty.

EXPERIMENT 3

An attempt was made in this experiment to ensure that subjects really believed the accused was guilty while they constructed the lineup. In the previous experiment, they may have known that they were to assume this, yet not have felt it with the same conviction as a police officer convinced that the accused is the guilty party. Perhaps a stronger (or true) belief that the accused was guilty would lead to decreased concern for lineup quality and thus the selection of inferior foils.

Subjects. The subjects were eighteen male and eighteen female Queen's University introductory psychology students between the ages of eighteen and twenty-three.

Procedure. One of the four suspects had worked as a confederate in a previous staged crime experiment (Lindsay & Wells, 1985). A videotape of the crime (theft of a calculator) was available. All subjects in the current study watched the videotape which had been edited to finish with a "freeze frame" of the criminal just before he left the room. The tape was paused, leaving the criminal visible on the screen, and the subject was informed that he or she was to construct a lineup for a suspect arrested in the case. The subject was then handed a photograph of the guilty confederate or a photograph of an innocent suspect, but also one of the four suspects used in the previous experiments.

The innocent suspect was similar to the criminal in that both were white males in their early twenties with short brown hair and no outstanding distinguishing marks. The two did not closely resemble each other, however (for instance, the innocent suspect had thin eyebrows and parted his hair on the side but the confederate had bushy eyebrows and parted his hair in the middle). An additional group of pilot subjects (nineteen members of a fourth-year psychology-law class) rated the similarity of the innocent suspect to the criminal as 2.38 on the same scale used by the other pilot subjects.

The experimenter delayed for a moment after handing the picture to the subject then explained that the suspect was guilty. To other subjects, he proclaimed the suspect not guilty. In the innocent suspect conditions, every subject spontaneously commented on the fact that he or she had been given a picture of "the wrong man" before the experimenter raised the issue. None of the guilty suspect subjects commented on the photograph they were given. The experimenter then pointed out the guilt or innocence of the suspect to all subjects and commented that "in a real case, sometimes the accused is guilty and sometimes he is innocent. A real police officer constructing a lineup would not know for sure if the suspect was guilty or not." All subjects then constructed a lineup from the same array of eighty photographs used previously.

Results. The manipulation checks in this case produced no variance within conditions. Every subject in the guilty suspect condition circled 7 on the assumption of guilt item and 1 on the assumption of innocence item. Responses in the innocent suspect condition were exactly the reverse. This manipulation of perceived or assumed guilt was thus completely successful. The quality of the lineups for the guilty suspect ($M = 76.2$ percent), however, was not significantly different from the quality of the lineups for the innocent suspect ($M = 74.8\%$), $t < 1$).

Lineups on average were 75.5 percent of the maximum possible values, quite comparable to the results from the first two experiments. Selected foils were rated to be significantly more similar to the suspects by the current subjects than by the pilot subjects (t (35) $= 6.72$, $p < .01$). Average scores on the Knowledge of Eyewitness Behavior Questionnaire were similar to those in previous experiments (56.0 percent).

In this experiment, the spontaneous comment of every subject in the innocent suspect condition that he or she had been given the wrong picture, combined with the total absence of comments from those in the guilty suspect condition, suggests that presumptions of guilt may occur quite readily. Apparently the subjects were surprised when the suspect was not the criminal but not surprised when the suspect was the criminal. The subjects in this experiment clearly believed in the guilt or innocence of the suspect as they constructed the lineups. Even certain knowledge of guilt, however, was insufficient to lead untrained undergraduates to construct biased lineups.

Lineups unfair to witnesses. Police may assume that the use of good foils will make the identification task inordinately difficult for the witness. If true, unbiased lineups might reduce the rate of correct identification. If good foils make the task of witnesses more difficult, police concerned with fairness to the witness may select foils less similar to the suspect than those concerned with fairness to the accused. There is some evidence that people may perceive similar foils as likely to produce such a problem. Lindsay, Nadkarni, and Nemiroff (1992) had introductory psychology students examine lineups that varied widely in similarity of the foils to the suspects and then predict the percentage of eyewitnesses that would identify the suspect from the lineup if the suspect was guilty and again if the suspect was innocent. Anticipated rates of correct identification declined as lineup foils became more similar to the suspect; but the anticipated decline was more rapid when the accused was guilty (from 76.9 to 36.1 percent) rather than innocent (43.7 to 27.5 percent).

Expectations that correct identification rates might suffer from the use of fair lineups thus could lead to the selection of poor foils.

Experiment 2 partially tested this possibility. Although the manipulations of concern for the witness and the accused were unsuccessful, correlations were calculated between individual ratings of concern for fairness to the accused or to the witness and lineup quality. Individual self ratings of concern for the witness or suspect were not significantly correlated with the quality of the lineups produced ($r = .12$ and $-.03$ respectively). Biased lineups were no more likely to be produced by subjects concerned with fairness to the witness than those relatively unconcerned with fairness to the witness.

Conversations with police officers suggest that they fear reductions in correct identification rates only when the foils are unduly similar to the suspect. This would explain the reluctance of police to search extensively for foils nearly identical to the suspect in appearance or to modify the appearance of foils to make them more similar (for example, so they all have the same scar or birthmark). Luus and Wells (1991; also this volume) have raised this concern also. They point out that current available research demonstrates the dangers of highly biased lineups leading to recommendations that lineup foils should resemble the accused and/or the description of the criminal provided by the witness(es). However, no upper limit on similarity of foils is described; thus any lineup other than one composed of clones of the suspect could be described as biased. Obviously any approximation to such high levels of similarity could lead to dramatic reductions in the rate of correct identification. Luus and Wells (this volume) provide a strategy for selecting reasonable lineup foils without producing excessive similarity. Their strategy (matching foils to the description provided by witnesses rather than to the appearance of the suspect) would not lead to highly biased lineups. Concern that all or several lineup members not be identical in appearance to the suspect is not the same as a desire to minimize the resemblance of foils to the suspect. As a result, extremely biased lineups are not required to avoid this problem.

Intentional bias

Biased lineups make it obvious whom the police suspect and put pressure on the witness to identify that person. If the suspect is actually guilty, police may believe this will increase correct identification rates. Research evidence indicates that such biased procedures do not increase correct identifications. Police may dismiss these studies because they fail to take into account factors such as fear of reprisals that may reduce the likelihood of real world eyewitnesses attempting identifications. Some evidence for such an effect could be inferred from Murray and Wells's (1982) finding that eyewitnesses to a staged crime were less likely to identify anyone when they thought the crime was real than when they were aware it had been staged. If the suspect is

innocent, biased lineup procedures will still increase the probability of identification.

Police may construct biased lineups to increase the probability that the
suspect will be identified. Another experiment was conducted to test this
possibility.

EXPERIMENT 4

Subjects. The subjects were twelve males and thirty-six females aged eighteen
to twenty-seven from introductory psychology classes at Queen's University.

Design. The experiment was a two by two factorial design with half the
subjects told the suspect was guilty and the other half that he was innocent.
Half the subjects were instructed to construct a lineup for the suspect. The
remaining subjects were told to "make a lineup that guarantees a witness to
the crime will pick the suspect from your lineup." Three males and nine
females were assigned to each condition.

Procedure. Subjects were shown the videotape described previously, given
the instructions appropriate to their group to construct a lineup, then presented with a photograph of the suspect. Again, the guilt or innocence of the
suspect was obvious but pointed out by the experimenter to all subjects. A
variation in the lineup construction task was introduced in this study. The
pool of potential foils was increased to one hundred and sixty pictures and
the pictures were arranged in four photo albums containing forty pictures
each. Using the pilot ratings of the photos, each album contained approximately the same quality and diversity of potential foils for each suspect.
Subjects were given one album but told that there were many more pictures
in the albums on a shelf (pointed to by the experimenter) and they could get
more albums by asking the experimenter. Only the three additional albums
were on the shelf indicated, so subjects were aware that the supply of photographs was limited. The dependent measures were the similarity of the
lineup foils as in the previous studies and the number of albums examined.

Results. Again, subjects in the innocent suspect conditions tended to comment spontaneously that the suspect was not the criminal (one of twenty-four
failed to do so). No subject in the guilty suspect conditions commented before
the experimenter pointed out the guilt of the suspect. Manipulation checks
indicated that all subjects were aware while constructing the lineup of the
guilt or innocence of the suspect they were given.

The proportion of subjects examining all four albums was higher if the
subjects thought the suspect was innocent ($Z = 1.84, p < .05$). Most subjects

(91.7 percent) in the innocent suspect conditions examined all four albums. The remaining two subjects examined three albums. Only 70.8 percent of subjects in the guilty suspect conditions examined all four albums although most of the subjects (95.8 percent) examined at least three. One subject in the biased, guilty suspect condition examined only two albums. The proportion of subjects examining all four albums when given instructions to create a biased lineup (66.7 percent) was significantly lower than the percentage for subjects not so instructed (95.8 percent; $Z = 2.58, p < .01$).

Quality of lineups (measured as previously described) was significantly influenced by the instructions. Subjects instructed to produce a biased lineup selected foils much less similar to the suspect ($M = 35.6$ percent) than subjects not given such instructions ($M = 80.0$ percent; $F (1,44) = 321.97, p < .01$). In this experiment, belief that the suspect was innocent led to less biased lineups ($M = 61.2$ percent) than belief that the suspect was guilty ($M = 54.5$ percent; $F (1,44) = 7.64, p < .05$). The interaction was not significant ($F (1,44) = 3.28$). However, simple effects analysis indicated that the lineup quality was significantly better for the innocent than the guilty suspect when the subjects had been instructed to create a biased lineup (41.2 percent versus 29.9 percent) but not when the subjects received no such instructions (81.1 percent versus 78.8 percent).

Subjects in the biased instruction conditions rated the foils they selected as no more similar to the suspect than the pilot subjects had ($t < 1$). As before, subjects in the no biased instructions conditions rated the foils as significantly more similar to the suspect than did the pilot subjects ($t = 11.49$, $p < .01$).

Because the suspect had participated in an earlier staged crime experiment (Lindsay & Wells, 1985), descriptions from witnesses were available. As a result, functional size measures could be obtained for lineups (Wells, Leippe, & Ostrom, 1979). The lineup from each condition with a score closest to the condition mean was selected for this purpose. The functional size measures were obtained from four undergraduate classes ($N = 23, 74, 156,$ and 165). Since 240 witnesses had provided descriptions of the confederate in the staged crime experiment, it was possible to provide each mock witness in the functional size task with a copy of an individual description of the confederate provided by a single eyewitness. This method is superior to providing all mock witnesses with a modal description because it preserves the variance of the original descriptions. The functional size of the lineup for the guilty suspect was 1.00 when subjects were told to bias the lineup and 3.66 when no biasing instructions were given. The functional size of the lineup for the innocent suspect was 1.93 with biasing instructions and 4.81 without biasing instructions.

In Experiment 4, at last untrained subjects were induced to generate biased lineups. All that was required was to ask them to do so intentionally. Even then they apparently were reluctant to do so when they knew the suspect was innocent (as indicated by their production of significantly better lineups for the innocent suspect than the guilty suspect when given instructions to construct a biased lineup). Perhaps the source of extremely biased lineups has been found. Lineup constructors must both believe the suspect to be guilty and intentionally create a lineup from which witnesses will not fail to choose the suspect. If this is the true source of extremely biased lineups, then such lineups occur only when police intentionally create a biased lineup to ensure that the suspect is identified by the eyewitness.

Conclusions

A series of four experiments have been presented that demonstrate the following:

When asked to construct lineups, people with no special training or knowledge of eyewitness issues select foils similar in appearance to the suspect.

Concerns about fairness to the witness and fairness to the accused may not alter the tendency to select foils similar to the suspect.

Untrained lineup constructors who know that the suspect is guilty select foils similar to the suspect.

Dissimilar foils are selected for lineups only when the lineup constructor is explicitly attempting to create a lineup that will lead witnesses to identify the suspect.

Does this evidence conclusively demonstrate that highly biased lineups are the result of intentional police misconduct? No. Proof of intent is difficult, if not impossible, to produce. The results of the experiments are consistent with the thesis, however, that highly biased lineups are the product of intentional police misconduct and alternative explanations all reduce to either incompetence or indifference on the part of police.

If no doubt exists about the guilt of the suspect because the police are in possession of conclusive evidence against him or her before conducting the lineup, there is no need for a biased identification procedure. Sufficient evidence to convict is already available. Failure to obtain an identification under such circumstances is not a problem. If doubt exists about the guilt of the suspect because there is insufficient evidence to support a conviction without an identification, the use of a biased identification procedure is inexcusable and dangerous. Thus, use of biased lineup procedures is dangerous if any doubt exists with regard to the guilt of the suspect.

But there must always be doubt until a court has ruled that the accused is guilty beyond a reasonable doubt (and some doubt exists even then, Rattner, 1988). It is never appropriate for police to decide that no doubt exists in a case. For this reason, biased lineups are never acceptable. They indicate that police are usurping the function of the courts. Using highly biased lineups is logically similar to other types of misconduct that police have sometimes been accused of such as manufacturing or fluffing up evidence by planting weapons or drugs in the possession of the suspect or committing perjury while testifying (Barker & Carter, 1990). The only reason to treat these types of misconduct differently is that, when used, dramatically biased lineups are obvious and undeniable. Now that it is clear where biased lineups come from, is there any reason not to prosecute police who engage in this practice?

Postscript

Four issues consistently occur to people when presented with the arguments described in this chapter. It seems worthwhile to address them here.

1. "Where is the evidence that lineup bias occurs frequently, or at all?" I find this issue irrelevant. Several sources could be used to support the claim that the incidence is not zero. Such lineups have been produced in the past (Ellison & Buckhout, 1981). I recently consulted on a case that would fit my criterion of an extremely biased lineup (functional size of one). But frequency is not the issue. If we assume that no highly biased lineups have been used since the last one I saw, is the issue unimportant? No nuclear bombs have been used in warfare since 1945; are nuclear weapons no longer a threat? So long as police use lineups or photo spreads to obtain identification evidence from eyewitnesses, the possibility of extremely biased lineups exists. One of my purposes in writing this chapter was to suggest to police, the courts, psychologists, and lawyers that use of such procedures ought to be viewed even more negatively than in the past because I can no longer believe they are the result of ignorance or sloppiness. This leads to the second concern.

2. "The flavor of the chapter is moralistic and punitive." I started out on this research before I had extensive interactions with the police and expected to demonstrate that biased lineups were the result of ignorance. I would then have recommended superior training as the cure. I was quickly disillusioned. Beyond the experimental data reported, I have had conversations with police officers who told me (off the record, of course) not only that they knew of the effects of lineup biases, but also that they had intentionally used their knowledge to create biased lineups to obtain identifications of people they "knew" were guilty. These discussions, following the completion of all the reported research, helped confirm my belief that highly biased lineups are the result of intentional actions by police. Is it moralistic to disapprove of these actions? Perhaps, but it would certainly be immoral to ignore them. Is it punitive to suggest police should be held responsible for their actions? Falsifying evidence is a felony. What response should police expect if they commit felonies?

3. "Police will be in an impossible situation if they must fear prosecution every time they construct a lineup." Nonsense! Again I emphasize, my ar-

guments are not directed at imperfect lineups but rather at abysmal lineups. Luus and Wells (1991) provide a mechanism that easily avoids gross errors. No police officer who makes a reasonable attempt to construct a fair lineup could possibly produce something like the Minneapolis lineup (black suspect, white foils). Furthermore, sequential presentation of a lineup with mediocre foils will rarely lead to false identification so there are other means to avoid extreme biases (Lindsay et al., 1991; Lindsay & Wells, 1985).

4. "Publishing these notions will make police uncooperative in future research and suspicious of the intent of eyewitness psychologists (that is, make them think we're out to get them)." Possibly. If so, then a price will have been paid for bringing this issue out in the open. Police should realize, however, that this chapter criticizes a very small proportion of their colleagues for engaging in outrageously unprofessional behavior. I hope this is clear to all and will avoid negative responses from police in general.

I make no apologies for the conclusions drawn in this chapter, nor the recommendation that police who produce atrociously biased lineups be treated as dangerous to the public. The few who will fall into this category we can do without. If it is more than a few, we are in serious trouble and had best start to rectify the situation.

References

Barker, T., & Carter, D. (1990). "Fluffing up the evidence and covering your ass:" Some conceptual notes on police lying. *Deviant Behavior, 11,* 61–73.

Doob, A. N., & Kirshenbaum, H. M. (1973). Bias in police lineups—partial remembering. *Journal of Police Science and Administration, 1,* 287–293.

Ellison, K. W., & Buckhout, R. (1981). *Psychology and criminal justice.* New York: Harper & Row.

Kohnken, G., & Maass, A. (1988). Eyewitness testimony: False alarms or biased instructions. *Journal of Applied Psychology, 73,* 363–370.

Lindsay, R. C. L., Lea, J. A., Nosworthy, G. J., Fulford, J. A., Hector, J., Levan, V., & Seabrook, C. (1991). Biased lineups: Sequential presentation reduces the problem. *Journal of Applied Psychology,* in press.

Lindsay, R. C. L., Nadkarni, L., & Nemiroff, L. S. (1992). Perceptions of lineup fairness. Unpublished manuscript.

Lindsay, R. C. L., Wallbridge, H., & Drennan, D. (1987). Do the clothes make the man? An exploration of the effect of lineup attire on eyewitness identification accuracy. *Canadian Journal of Behavioural Science, 19,* 464–478.

Lindsay, R. C. L., & Wells, G. L. (1980). What price justice? Exploring the relationship of lineup fairness to identification accuracy. *Law and Human Behavior, 4,* 303–313.

Lindsay, R. C. L., & Wells, G. L. (1985). Improving eyewitness identifications from lineups: Simultaneous versus sequential lineup presentation. *Journal of Applied Psychology, 70,* 556–564.

Luus, C. A. E., & Wells, G. L. (1991). Eyewitness identification and the selection of distracters for lineups. *Law and Human Behavior, 15,* 43–57.

Malpass, R. S., & Devine, P. G. (1981). Eyewitness identification: Lineup instructions and the absence of the offender. *Journal of Applied Psychology, 66,* 482–489.

Murray, D. M., & Wells, G. L. (1982). Does knowledge that a crime was staged affect eyewitness accuracy? *Journal of Applied Social Psychology, 12,* 42–53.

Rattner, A. (1988). Convicted but innocent: Wrongful conviction and the criminal justice system. *Law and Human Behavior, 12,* 289–293.

Wells, G. L. (1984). The psychology of lineup identifications. *Journal of Applied Social Psychology, 14,* 89–103.

Wells, G. L., Leippe, M., & Ostrom, T. M. (1979). Guidelines for empirically assessing the fairness of a lineup. *Law and Human Behavior, 3,* 285–293.

Wells, G. L. & Wright, E. F. (1986). Practical issues in eyewitness research. In M. F. Kaplan (Ed.), *The impact of social psychology on procedural justice,* 109–134. Springfield: IL: Charles C. Thomas.

Yarmey, A. D., & Jones, H. (1983). Is the psychology of eyewitness identification a matter of common sense? In S. Lloyd-Bostock & B. Clifford (Eds.), *Evaluating witness evidence* (pp. 13–40). Chichester, England: John Wiley & Sons.

10 Evaluating the fairness of lineups

John C. Brigham and Jeffrey E. Pfeifer

Although the accuracy of eyewitness identifications has long been a topic of debate (Levine & Tapp, 1982), only within the last decade have social scientists taken serious steps to empirically investigate this issue. Some years ago Wells, Leippe, and Ostrom (1979, p. 291) suggested that discussions of eyewitness accuracy were "subjective and confusing, with no empirical or scientific base." One could argue that this statement still has the ring of truth to it, although it has been pointed out that incorrect eyewitness identifications appear to be the leading cause of wrongful criminal convictions in the American legal system (Huff, Rattner, & Sagarin, 1986; *U.S. v. Wade,* 1967; Wall, 1965). According to Huff et al. (1986), for example, erroneous eyewitness identifications could produce some three thousand wrongful felony convictions each year in the United States. Given this estimate, it is not surprising that a number of researchers have recently turned their attention to the study of eyewitness identification.

Concepts of lineup size and lineup bias

Early research in this area suggests that the likelihood of eyewitness misidentification is affected by the fairness of the lineup used (Malpass, 1981). In theory, a lineup is fair to the suspect when it contains a sufficient number of distractors (foils) who are similar in appearance to the prior description of the criminal (Doob & Kirshenbaum, 1973). In order to investigate this concept, two dimensions of lineup fairness have been proposed (Malpass, 1981; Malpass & Devine, 1983). First, the concept of lineup size suggests that a lineup should be large enough that the probability of a chance identification of an innocent suspect is relatively low. In the United States, lineups con-

Correspondence regarding this chapter can be sent to John C. Brigham, Department of Psychology, Florida State University, Tallahassee, FL 32306, or to Jeffrey E. Pfeifer, Department of Psychology, University of Regina, Regina, Saskatchewan, Canada S4S OA2. Portions of the research described in this chapter were supported by National Science Foundation Grant SES-8421030 to John C. Brigham and a postdoctoral fellowship awarded to Jeffrey Pfeifer by the Social Sciences and Humanities Research Council of Canada.

taining six members (the suspect and five foils) have generally been viewed as the minimally acceptable lineup size. Although Wells et al. (this volume) have elucidated the rationale for a minimum lineup size of six, not just any six-person lineup is acceptable. It is critical that the five foils be reasonably plausible alternatives for the choice task (that is, similar in appearance to the criminal's description). If three of the foils, for example, are so dissimilar from the description of the perpetrator that they do not represent viable alternatives, it is as if the eyewitness were in reality facing a three-person lineup containing the suspect and the two remaining foils.

Lineup bias, in contrast, refers to the extent to which the suspect is distinctive from the other lineup members. Anything that causes the suspect to stand out from the other lineup members compromises the validity of the lineup, as this distinctiveness may be used by an uncertain eyewitness as a cue to the identification decision. The suspect is the "odd man out" and thus more likely to be chosen. Distinctiveness can involve physical appearance (for example, a blond suspect among five dark-haired foils, a heavyset suspect among five thin foils, and so forth) or characteristics of the lineup itself (dress, positioning, or demeanor of the foils versus that of the suspect in a live lineup, different quality of the suspect's photo versus that of the foils' photos in a photo lineup).

The concepts of lineup size and bias often overlap. To illustrate, suppose the criminal was described as dark-haired and heavyset, and a dark-haired, heavyset suspect were placed in a lineup with five slender blonds. This lineup fails on both criteria. The lineup is of inadequate size because the suspect is the only viable choice in terms of the description of the culprit. The eyewitness, who remembers that the criminal was heavy and had black hair, really has only one possible person to choose from. Thus, in a psychological sense, the size of this lineup is not six members, it is one. From the eyewitness's perspective, this situation is akin to the showup procedure wherein only the suspect is shown to the eyewitness who is asked, "Is this the guy?" United States courts have consistently ruled that showups are impermissibly suggestive because the chance of misidentification is too high (Brigham, 1989).

In addition, the suspect may be the most distinctive lineup member (the only one with dark hair or a heavy build) and hence the lineup is biased toward him. Distinctiveness can also occur on dimensions that were not part of the eyewitness's description, including other personal characteristics or characteristics of the lineup itself. Anything that sets the defendant apart from all the other lineup members in a systematic way compromises the validity of the lineup. In our example, if someone knowing nothing about the crime (hence, not aware that the perpetrator was described as dark-haired and heavy) were asked which lineup member was the suspect, chances are the dark-haired person would be chosen. He is still the "odd man out," the one who stands out from the others.

This does not mean, however, that all lineup members should be virtual clones of each other for the lineup to be considered unbiased. The foils should be similar in characteristics mentioned in the eyewitness's description of the criminal, but can vary on other, unmentioned characteristics. Wells, Seelau, Rydell, and Luus (this volume) discuss the notion of "propitious heterogeneity" among lineup members. This chapter will further address the concept of lineup fairness by reviewing relevant research on these two major dimensions (size and bias). We will present several of our recent studies on these issues and discuss the external validity of the existing research findings and highlight areas in need of further study.

Lineup size measures

As noted above, the concept of lineup size is based on the premise that lineups should be large enough to ensure that the probability of a chance identification of an innocent suspect is low (Malpass & Devine, 1983). A lineup's size is dependent on the number of acceptable foils (that is, foils who are similar in general appearance to the suspect's description) it contains.

Given this concern for adequate size of a lineup, as represented by a sufficient number of acceptable foils, several researchers have introduced statistical measures for calculating the probability of a chance identification of an innocent suspect. To date, lineup fairness has most often been assessed on the basis of responses from "mock witnesses," research subjects who have not observed the crime but who attempt to identify the target (suspect) using only a description of the criminal's general appearance. For example, a maximally fair six-person lineup would be one in which the suspect and the five foils were selected by mock witnesses equally often, based on the general description. Measures of lineup size analyze how many lineup members were acceptable, in terms of being selected relatively often by the mock witnesses. Increasing the nominal size (number of members) of a lineup does not, however, necessarily reduce the risk of a false identification, the erroneous identification of an innocent suspect, if additional lineup members are not similar enough to the suspect to represent plausible alternatives (Malpass, 1981). The relevance of lineup size for investigating eyewitness accuracy is reflected in two measurement techniques reviewed below.

Effective Size technique

The Effective Size (ES) technique is based on the supposition that lineup foils selected by mock witnesses at a level below that expected by chance are unacceptable for inclusion in the lineup. To illustrate how ES is calculated, imagine that forty mock witnesses view a six-person lineup after being given a description of the criminal and that the target (suspect) is picked by fourteen mock witnesses (35 percent), foil number one by twelve mock witnesses, foil number two by eight, foil number three by six, and the remaining two foils are not picked by any mock witnesses. In order to obtain the ES of a lineup, the lineup's nominal size (number of members) is first adjusted to take into account any zero-response cells (two cells in our example). Second, the choice frequencies of those lineup members chosen by mock witnesses less often than expected by chance (based on the adjusted nominal size) are then subtracted from the adjusted chance expectation. Third, those differences are summed, divided by the adjusted chance frequency, and the resulting figure is subtracted from the lineup's nominal size. This procedure adjusts the lineup's nominal size by subtracting from it the degree to which lineup members are chosen at less than chance expectations.

To illustrate, we show below the choice frequencies of forty mock witnesses who were given a general description of the suspect (target person) and viewed a six-person lineup:

	Choice frequency
Suspect	14
Foil #1	12
Foil #2	8
Foil #3	6
Foil #4	0
Foil #5	0

To calculate Effective Size, first take: adjusted nominal size (ANS) = 6 − 2 (subtracting out "null" foils #4 & #5) = 4; in step two, adjusted chance expectation (ACE), based on 40 mock witnesses = 40/4 = 10.0; in step three, [10-8 (foil #2)] + [10-6 (foil #3)] = 6; in step four, 6/10 = .60; and finally we have Effective Size, 4 − .60 = 3.40.

Acceptable Foils technique

Although the ES technique allows for a statistical analysis of lineup size, a potential disadvantage is that it may not be easily understood by laypersons or judicial officials. This disadvantage was noted by Malpass and Devine (1983) who argued that ideally a technique should be understandable to laypersons, should be close to the raw data, with few numerical transformations or manipulations, and should depend on a minimum of statistical assumptions. Further, the measure should not have embedded in it value judgments or decisions not open to inspection and understanding by laypersons. Therefore, in contrast to the ES technique, which can be seen as complex and not easily understood by laypersons, they suggested that the Acceptable Foils (AF) technique better meets these criteria.

The AF measure is derived by counting the number of lineup members selected by mock witnesses with a frequency that exceeds the chance expectation, or some percentage of it (Malpass & Devine, 1983). The minimum percentage of the chance expectation that is considered acceptable may be based on value judgments or empirical standards. Malpass and Devine (1983, p. 93) utilized three different levels (50, 75, and 90 percent of chance expectation) in their analyses, whereas Brigham, Ready, and Spier (1990) adopted a criterion of 75 percent of chance expectation.

To illustrate, if one adopts the criterion that an acceptable lineup member is one chosen at 75 percent or greater of the chance expectation rate (chance is 17 percent in a six-person lineup), then each lineup member chosen by at least 13 percent of the mock witnesses ($.75 \times .17$) would be acceptable. In our example, each lineup member selected by five or more of the forty mock witnesses (13 percent of forty) would be classed as acceptable, resulting in four acceptable members. Malpass argued that this technique ensures a more accurate reflection of the actual size of a lineup because it disregards foils who are not statistically (and therefore probably not physically) similar to the suspect. This technique may thus give the court a better understanding of the fairness of a particular lineup.[1]

Sensitivity and discriminability of lineup size measures

As noted above, Malpass and Devine (1983) argued for the creation of a lineup size calculation technique that was statistically simple and easily comprehensible to the average individual. However, the accuracy of the technique in assessing lineup size is also a crucial factor. To investigate this issue, we conducted a study in which we compared the two lineup size techniques discussed above in terms of their discriminability and sensitivity (Brigham et al., 1990).

Sensitivity refers to an absolute standard of acceptability inherent in, or attributed to, a measure. The concept involves the cutoff point, in terms of the calculated size or degree of bias, at which a given lineup should be classified as unfair. For some measures (for example, the proportions measure of bias to be discussed below) the level of statistical significance provides a natural cutoff point, but for other measures the choice of a cutoff point is somewhat more arbitrary. Wells et al. (1979, p. 289) proposed that researchers should not attempt to specify appropriate levels of sensitivity for fairness measures, arguing that these value-related distinctions should be left to the courts. Other researchers, however (for example, Brigham et al. 1990; Malpass & Devine, 1983) have suggested that appropriate levels of sensitivity can be estimated. In a general sense, a measure has an appropriate level of sensitivity if the criterion is neither too strict, leading to the classification of virtually all lineups as unfair, nor too lenient, leading to the classification of virtually all lineups as fair.

An example of a measure with an unacceptable level of sensitivity is the chi-square "goodness-of-fit" test. Malpass and Devine (1983) proposed this test as a way to evaluate whether the observed frequency distribution of mock witness choices across lineup members significantly differs from the expected frequency distribution. In our above example, the value of X^2 is 57.14 ($p <$ .001), indicating that the distribution of mock witness responses differs significantly from an expected chance distribution of 6.67 choices (40/6) per lineup member. However, it is our experience that the goodness-of-fit X^2 measure is too sensitive to be useful, if statistical significance of the X^2 value is the criterion of unfairness. The X^2 test yielded a highly significant X^2 value ($p <$ .001) on each of twelve lineup analyses from six actual court cases evaluated by Brigham et al. (1990), as well as all ten experimental lineups created for use in this same study. Hence, this measure appears too sensitive to be useful and will not be discussed further here.

Discriminability, in contrast, is defined as the ability of a lineup fairness measure to distinguish between lineups that are fair and unfair, as established by some independent criterion. Suppose, for example, we have ten six-person lineups, five of which are judged as quite fair by police officers (or researchers) and five of which are judged quite unfair. If we assume that these overall fairness judgments have some validity, when the lineups are analyzed in terms of size, a measure that has adequate discriminability should yield substantially different size estimates for the two sets of lineups, with the fair lineups yielding larger size estimates (closer to the nominal size of six) than do the unfair lineups. Discriminability, therefore, refers to the capacity of a measure to discriminate between lineups differing on a relevant characteristic, in this case, fairness.

In order to assess the sensitivity and discriminability of lineup size measures, we created five such "selected" photo lineups (ostensibly fair lineups, as based on ratings of high foil similarity to the target and on police judgments of foil appropriateness) and five less fair random lineups, created by randomly matching with each target photo five foils that had been rated in the middle one-third of similarity ratings and had not been seen as appropriate foils by our police consultant (Brigham et al., 1990). Two hundred and sixteen white students and 148 black students acted as mock witnesses and viewed these lineups. After hearing a description of the target person's sex, race, age, height, weight, hair color, hair style, eye color, and facial hair, mock witnesses were asked to select the suspect from the lineup.

Results of this study indicated that the Effective Size (ES) technique was able to statistically discriminate between the selected (fair) lineups and the random lineups. Analysis of variance across ES scores derived from twenty

Table 10.1. *Discriminability of lineup size techniques*

Measures of lineup size	5 Selected (fair) lineups	5 Random (less fair) lineups
Effective size (mean)	3.33	3.04*
Acceptable foils (mean)	2.60	2.50
Choice distribution (value of χ^2, 5 d.f.)	188.95	212.23

*$p < .05$ for difference between 5 selected and 5 random lineups, ANOVA across 20 samples, $N = 18$ in each, from which ES scores were calculated.

Table 10.2. *Sensitivity of lineup size techniques*

Measures of lineup size	5 Selected (fair) lineups Lineups classified as fair		5 Random (less fair) lineups Lineups classified as fair	
	Number of lineups	Overall analysis across the 5 lineups	Number of lineups	Overall analysis across the 5 lineups
Effective Size	4/5	Fair	3/5	Fair
Acceptable Foils	2/5	Unfair	2/5	Unfair

samples of eighteen subjects each (the rationale for $N = 18$ per sample will be presented subsequently) yielded a significant ($p < .05$) difference between lineup types, with the selected (fair) lineups showing higher ES values. The Acceptable Foil (AF) and choice distribution (X^2) techniques, however, were not able to significantly discriminate between the selected and random lineups (see Table 10.1).

In terms of sensitivity, when the authors established a criterion that an acceptable ES (denoting a fair lineup) should be at least half the nominal size (that is, 3.0 or greater for a six-person lineup), four of the five selected lineups and three of the five random lineups were classified as fair. Malpass (1981) has argued, however, that a six-person lineup should have an ES of at least 5.0 in order to be considered fair. According to this more stringent criterion, none of the ten lineups would have been adjudicated as fair according to the ES measure. Hence, Malpass's criterion appears to make the ES measure too sensitive. Results from the AF technique indicated that two of the five selected lineups and two of the five random lineups were fair in their composition. Based on these results, we suggested that the ES technique appeared to be the more useful size measure. See Table 10.2.

Lineup bias measures

As stated previously, the fairness of a photo lineup is not based solely on the lineup size. Once a fair size is established, the lineup may still be subject to lineup bias (that is, the distinctiveness of the suspect in comparison to the other lineup members). Like the dimension of lineup size, lineup bias has also been examined through differing measurement techniques. These techniques are reviewed below.

Proportions technique

The most widely used measure of lineup bias, originally described by Doob and Kirshenbaum (1973), compares the proportion of the times the suspect is selected by mock witnesses with the proportion of choices expected by chance alone (.17 in a six-person lineup). If the suspect is selected with greater than chance frequency, as determined by the z test for proportions, the lineup is seen as biased toward the suspect. Recall that in our example, the target was chosen by 35 percent of the mock witnesses and z for proportions $= 2.34$ ($p < .02$), indicating a significant degree of bias.

Although the above technique has been widely employed in eyewitness lineup research, Wells, Leippe, and Ostrom (1979) noted two limitations of this hypothesis testing procedure. First, the likelihood of obtaining a significant difference between the chance probability and the proportion of mock witnesses who pick the suspect is affected by the number of mock witnesses (sample size) as well as by the magnitude of the difference between the proportions. That is, the larger the sample size, the smaller the difference needed to achieve statistical significance. Selecting the most appropriate sample size, they proposed, is a value judgment that should not be made by researchers. In our example, if we had used a sample size of twenty mock witnesses, rather than forty, and the same proportion ($7/20 = .35$) had chosen the suspect, the calculated Effective Size would be the same (3.40), but the proportion of mock witnesses who chose the suspect would no longer be significantly different from chance expectations (z for proportions $= 1.71$, $p > .05$ for $N = 20$).

A second point made by Wells et al. (1979) concerns the insensitivity of the hypothesis-testing measure to the addition of irrelevant lineup foils. In the above example, if another four foils were added to the lineup, the expected proportion of mock witnesses who pick the suspect out of a ten-person lineup would be .10 (1/10). If the additional four foils were "bad" foils, however (ones that did not draw any mock witness choices because they were not similar to the description of the perpetrator), the calculated Effective Size of the lineup would still be 3.40 and the proportion of mock witnesses who picked the suspect would remain the same (.35). Yet in this case, the obtained proportion would be compared with an expected proportion of .10 rather than .17, increasing the chances that a significant difference between proportions would occur and the lineup would be labeled unfair. To wit, the z score based on twenty mock witnesses, nonsignificant when calculated for the six-person lineup, would now be significant (z for proportions $= 2.38$, $p <$ .02) when based on the ten-person lineup, even though the Effective Size of the two lineups is the same (3.40).

Functional size

As a result of these potential problems, Wells and his colleagues (1979) advocated the use of a parameter estimation procedure they labeled *Functional Size* (FS). FS is derived by dividing the total number of mock witnesses by the number who chose the suspect from the lineup. In the above examples, the FS would be 2.86 (40/14) for both the six-person and ten-person lineups. In theory, a (biased) ten-person lineup having a FS of 2.86 is no better, from the perspective of protecting an innocent suspect from being falsely identified, than a six-person (or a twenty-person) lineup with a FS of 2.86. All are approximately equivalent to a fair three-person lineup in which everyone fits the description of the criminal.

Both the FS estimate and the Proportions technique can be seen as indicators of lineup bias, rather than lineup size, because they do not take into account the distribution of foil misidentifications (Malpass, 1981). In our example, the same level of statistical significance for the Proportions technique and the same FS value would result whether the twenty-six foil choices were distributed across all five foils, across three foils, or only one.

Suspect Bias technique

In contrast to the Proportions technique, the Suspect Bias technique (labeled the defendant bias technique by Malpass & Devine, 1983) takes the overall distribution of foil choices into account, but uses the calculated Effective Size of the lineup (in our example, 3.40), rather than the lineup's nominal size (six), as the basis for calculating chance expectancies. In our example, because the ES of the lineup is 3.40, the adjusted expected choice frequency is 1/3.40 $= .29$. Apart from using the Effective Size value for calculating the expected frequency, this measurement technique is similar to the Proportions technique. The issue addressed by this measure is: Given that the lineup is equivalent to a lineup with 3.4 appropriate members (ES $= 3.40$), is the proportion of mock witnesses who chose the suspect significantly larger than one would expect by chance from a fair lineup of 3.4 persons? From this perspective, one may conclude that a photo lineup is biased if the observed choice frequency for the suspect is significantly different from the adjusted expected

Table 10.3. *Discriminability of lineup bias techniques*

Measures of bias against suspect	5 Selected (fair) lineups	5 Random (less fair) lineups
Proportion technique (mean proportion)[a]	.285	.432**
Suspect Bias technique (mean value)[b]	− .004	.126*

Note: *p < .05; **p < .01 for difference between selected and random lineups.
[a]Significance of difference in mean proportions assessed by z for proportions test.
[b]Significance of difference in mean suspect bias values assessed by ANOVA across 20 samples of 18 subjects each.

choice frequency. In our example, the choice frequency of the suspect (14/ 40 = .35), does not differ significantly from the expected chance rate of .29 based on the ES value.

Empirical assessment of lineup bias techniques

We also investigated the appropriateness of measurement techniques for evaluating lineup bias along the lines of discriminability and sensitivity utilizing the experimental paradigm described above (Brigham et al., 1990). Both bias measures, Proportions and Suspect Bias, were able to discriminate between the selected and random lineups (see Table 10.3). In terms of sensitivity, the Proportions measure classified three of the five selected lineups as fair; the proportion of mock witnesses choosing the suspect was not significantly greater (z for proportions test) than would be expected by chance for these three lineups. None of the five random lineups was categorized as fair, as for each lineup a significantly greater-than-chance proportion of mock witnesses chose the suspect. Averaged across lineups, the Suspect Bias measure indicated that the selected lineups were, as a whole, fair, whereas the random lineups were unfair (Brigham et al., 1990).

Based on this pattern of results, Brigham et al. (1990) concluded that the Proportions technique appeared to be the most useful measure of lineup bias, showing considerable discriminability and sensitivity. With respect to sensitivity, however, this method shares a limitation common to any measure using statistical significance as a criterion. As noted earlier, the statistical significance of a given difference between proportions is directly related to sample size (McNemar, 1969, p. 62). Brigham et al. (1990) used subsamples of eighteen mock witnesses each in calculating proportions; this appears to be a reasonable sample size from several perspectives. First, it is a manageable number of mock witnesses likely to be obtainable in a field setting (for example, by law enforcement personnel or attorneys). Second, the data from multiple samples indicated that proportions derived from samples of eighteen were quite reliable, more so than those based on samples of twelve or fewer mock witnesses. Third, for a sample of eighteen, a significant degree of bias ($p < .05$ by the z for proportions test) is shown whenever the target person is selected by at least 34 percent of the mock witnesses, producing a Functional Size of 2.94 or less. In practical terms, this statistical criterion could be approximated by using a sample of eighteen mock witnesses and Functional Size of 3.00 or less as the criterion for meaningful bias.

Relationship of fairness measures to evaluations made by law enforcement personnel

The use of the responses of mock witnesses as a source of lineup fairness assessments is often criticized by attorneys and law enforcement personnel who fail to understand, or decline to accept, the rationale underlying the measures. These observers are critical of a technique that utilizes respondents who have no expertise in lineups and are not evaluating the entire lineup's acceptability in any direct way. This same criticism of a lack of experimental realism or mundane realism has been made of other psycholegal research areas, such as jury studies (Pfeifer, 1990).

To address these concerns, we constructed a sample of lineups that could be evaluated by three sets of subjects performing different tasks (Brigham & Brandt, in press). First, as in earlier studies, a sample of college students served as mock witnesses, attempting to identify the target in each lineup based on a physical description. From their responses, measures of lineup size (Acceptable Foils, Effective Size) and bias (Proportions) were calculated for each lineup.

The other two samples, college student evaluators and law officer evaluators, rated the set of lineups in a more direct manner. Presumably, law officers' evaluations of the appropriateness of a lineup will directly affect whether or not that particular lineup will be shown to an eyewitness in a given case. We are not implying, however, that the judgments of law officers are completely valid criteria of lineup fairness. If they were, there would be no need to investigate possible alternative ways of assessing fairness. But if the rather arcane indices derived from college student mock witnesses are to be valued and utilized by those in the criminal justice system, the demonstration that these measures are substantially related to (though not isomorphic with) law officers' direct evaluations of lineups would be an important step. College student evaluators were used to see whether college students' direct evaluations of lineups would be more strongly related to the law officers' direct evaluations than to the college student mock witnesses' responses.

The central research question concerned how closely lineup fairness indices based on college student mock witnesses corresponded to direct evaluations of lineup fairness made by law enforcement personnel. An additional issue was the degree of correspondence between the responses of the two sets of college student subjects. To investigate these questions, we created a new set of twenty-three photo lineups (Brigham & Brandt, in press). The lineups were categorized into three groups – fair, moderately fair, and least fair – based on three measures derived from the responses of thirty college student mock witnesses: Effective Size, Proportions, and number of Acceptable Foils. Cutting points for categorizing whether a given lineup was fair or unfair on each of the measures were established. Lineups were considered fair in terms of the ES measure if the ES score was 3.00 or greater. Lineups yielding Functional Size estimates of 3.0 or greater were categorized as fair in terms of this metric. Finally, for the Acceptable Foils measure, a fair lineup was defined as one in which at least three of the six members were chosen at 75 percent or more of the chance rate (that is, by 13 percent of the mock witnesses). Eight of the twenty-three lineups were designated as fair because they exceeded the fairness cutoffs on all three measures, and eight were designated as moderately fair, as they surpassed two of the three fairness criteria. The remaining seven lineups, classified as least fair, exceeded the fairness criteria on none or one of the three measures. We labeled this categorization as Global Fairness. There were four white and four black lineups at the high and moderate levels of Global Fairness and three white and four black lineups at the least fair level.

Each of forty law officers evaluated eleven or twelve photo lineups, approximately one-third of which had been classified as fair, moderately fair, and least fair. For each lineup, the officer was told which member was the suspect. Officers first assessed the Global Fairness of each of the twelve lineups in terms of three possible responses: I would use this lineup because it is a reasonably good lineup; construct a new lineup because this one is not acceptable – it would be too difficult for the eyewitness to identify the suspect; or construct a new lineup – it would be too easy for the eyewitness to identify the suspect. Respondents then evaluated the acceptability of each of the five foils on a six-point scale ranging from 1 = very acceptable to 6 = very unacceptable as a lineup member. Their instructions read: "Given that lineup member X is the suspect, how acceptable are each of the other lineup members (foils) as members of a *fair lineup* for this suspect (X)?" The college students were given added instructions (deemed unnecessary for the law officers) that "a fair lineup is usually defined as one in which the foils are 'reasonably similar in appearance' to the suspect." Finally, in a question designed to elicit Estimated Proportions scores, respondents were asked: "If 100 persons who had *never seen* the criminal were asked to *guess* who the suspect in the lineup was, based on the descriptive information given on the lineup folder, about how many of those persons do you think would guess that lineup member [the suspect] was the suspect?" A sample of sixty college student evaluators also saw eleven or twelve lineups apiece and responded to the same questions for each lineup.

Four general types of lineup fairness measures were derived from the three samples: Global Fairness, lineup bias (Proportions), and two measures of lineup size (Effective Size and Acceptable Foils). Before investigating the relationship between fairness indices gathered from the different samples, we examined the relationship among the various measures within each sample. The relationship among the four measures was generally strong and positive, with mean correlation values of .81 within the mock witness sample, .64 in the law enforcement evaluator sample, and .39 in the college student evaluator sample. The correlation was expected to be highest in the mock witness sample because the one to three Global Fairness index was created directly from the other three fairness indices yielded by this sample, whereas in the two evaluator samples the Global Fairness variable was dichotomous, derived from their response to the use/don't use question (that is, a "use" response was taken to denote a fair lineup).

Across the twenty-three lineups, law enforcement evaluators were significantly more willing to use the lineups (63.2 percent of all responses said that the lineup should be used) than were the college student evaluators (54.9 percent; z for proportions $= 2.77, p < .01$). With respect to the most central question, whether college student, mock witness responses were predictive of how law officers would evaluate the same lineups, a significant correlation was found across the twenty-three lineups ($r(21) = .42, p < .03$). Those lineups classified as least fair by the college student, mock witness responses also tended to be seen as less useful by the law officers. Stepwise multiple regression analysis yielded a multiple R of .602 for the individual mock witness measures on the law officers' Global Fairness ratings, as the ES and Acceptable Foils mock witness measures contributed significantly to explaining the variance in the law officers' responses.

As Table 10.4 indicates, both sets of respondents more often saw the least fair lineups as "too easy" (31.0 percent of the time) than the moderately fair or fair lineups (15.4 percent) (z for proportions $= 7.80, p < .001$). In addition, the student evaluators perceived fewer least fair lineups as "too hard" (16.3 percent) than moderately fair or fair lineups (27.4 percent) (z for proportions $= 4.39, p < .001$). The law officers did not make this latter distinction, however, as the least fair lineups were just as likely to be rated "too hard" (19.9 percent) as the moderately fair and fair lineups were (16.7%) (z for proportions $= 1.16, ns.$)

When college students completed the same direct lineup evaluation task as the law officers, their Global Fairness responses were even more closely related to the law officers' Global Fairness responses ($r(21) = .62, p < .001$).

Table 10.4. *Overall evaluation of lineup usefulness by law enforcement officers and college students*

Evaluators	Categorization of lineups according to college student mock witnesses	Percent of respondents who "would use" this lineup	Percent of respondents saying lineup is unusable because "too easy" to identify the suspect	Percent of respondents saying lineup is unusable because "too hard" to identify the suspect
Law	Fair[a]	67.0	14.9	18.1
enforcement	Moderately fair[a]	67.8	16.9	15.3
evaluators	Least fair[b]	53.4	26.7	19.9
College	Fair[a]	58.4	14.4	27.2
student	Moderately fair[a]	57.2	15.3	27.5
evaluators	Least fair[b]	48.4	35.3	16.3

[a] Eight lineups.
[b] Seven lineups.

Table 10.5. *Correspondence between the same lineup fairness measures derived from different samples, across 23 lineups*

	CS mock witnesses and LE evaluators	CS evaluators and LE evaluators	CS mock witnesses and CS evaluators
Global Fairness	0.42*	0.62**	0.46*
Bias: Actual/estimated proportions	0.30+	0.48**	0.49**
Size: Mean acceptable ratings	—[a]	0.47*	—[a]
Size: Designated acceptable foils	—[a]	0.51**	—[a]

[a]This measure cannot be derived for individual mock witnesses.
**$p < .01$; *$p < .05$; +$p < .10$ (one-tailed).
CS = college students; LE = law enforcement officers.

As Table 10.5 indicates, each of the individual bias and size measures (Proportions, Mean Acceptability Ratings, Designated Acceptable Foils) were significantly related across the two samples of evaluators, college students and law officers.

The relationships among the individual measures of lineup fairness taken from the various samples are depicted in Table 10.6. Two of the mock witness measures, Proportions and Effective Size, were consistently related to fairness measures derived from the other two samples, yielding significant correlations

Table 10.6. *Correlations between lineup fairness scores derived from mock witness responses and those derived from law enforcement and college student evaluators, across 23 lineups*

	Mock Witness Responses			
Sample that evaluated the 23 lineups	Bias: Proportions	Size: Effective Size	Size: Acceptable Foils	Overall (Global) Fairness categorization (1–3)
Law enforcement evaluators				
Bias: Estimated Proportions	.30+	.38*	.20	.47*
Size: Mean Acceptable ratings	.04	.29+	.14	.41*
Size: Designated Acceptable Foils	.12	.46*	.25	.52**
Global Fairness	.21	.46*	.19	.42*
College student evaluators				
Bias: Estimated Proportions	.49**	.55**	.38*	.59**
Size: Mean Acceptable ratings	.24	.35*	.20	.38*
Size: Designated Acceptable Foils	.24	.30+	−.07	.38*
Global Fairness	.20	.33+	.24	.46*

**$p < .01$; *$p < .05$; + $p < .10$ (one-tailed).

($p < .05$) in six of sixteen comparisons, with another four correlations reaching marginal significance at the $p < .10$ level. The other mock witness size measure, number of Acceptable Foils, was not consistently related to the other fairness measures based on the evaluators' responses. This is consistent with results of the Brigham et al. (1990) study which found that the Acceptable Foils measure showed less ability to discriminate between fair and unfair lineups than did the other two mock witness measures, Proportions and Effective Size.

The law officers' Global Fairness ratings were significantly related to the Effective Size measure derived from the mock witness responses ($r(21) = .46, p < .02$) and, as noted earlier, to the Global Fairness index based on all three mock witness measures ($r(21) = .42, p < .03$). The law officers' Global Fairness ratings were significantly related to two of the individual fairness indices derived from the college student evaluators' responses, ($r(21) = .36, p < .05$ with Mean Acceptability Ratings, and .37 ($p < .05$) with Designated Acceptable Foils, and substantially correlated with the college student-evaluators' Global Fairness ratings ($r(21) = .62, p < .01$).

The effect of race, extent of experience, and racial attitudes on the law officers' responses was also investigated, as previous research on the effect of race on lineup evaluations had not yielded entirely consistent results. Brigham and Ready (1985) found that race affected the way that same-race

Table 10.7. *Proportion of the time that white officers (N = 20) and black officers (N = 20) rated lineups as useful*

	Black lineups (N = 12)	White lineups (N = 11)	All lineups
Black officers	.492	.630	.558
White officers	.638	.728	.681
All officers	.565	.679	

and other-race lineups were constructed, with blacks and whites showing stricter criteria for selecting appropriate foils for target persons of their own race than for other-race lineups. Brigham et al. (1990) found, however, that the race of the mock witness did not have a strong impact on responses in the mock witness paradigm, as blacks and whites in the role of mock witnesses produced values that were very similar to each other for the lineup size and lineup bias measures across the ten lineups evaluated.

In the study under discussion, the race of law officers affected their evaluations of the lineups in a systematic way. As Table 10.7 indicates, the white officers found the twenty-three lineups more useful as a whole (68 percent of the time they were classed as useful) than the black officers did (56 percent useful; z for proportions = 3.86, $p < .001$). The effect of subject race was most evident on evaluations of the black lineups, which were rated as useful more often by the white officers (64 percent of the time) than by the black officers (49 percent of the time; z for proportions = 3.22, $p < .01$). Further, the white lineups were seen as more useful by both groups combined (68 percent) than the black lineups were (57 percent; z for proportions = 3.57, $p < .001$). To see whether there was a significant interaction between race of officer and race of lineup, we utilized the procedure proposed by Langer and Abelson (1972) for detecting interaction effects among proportions in a two by two contingency table via the arc sine transformation (Langer & Abelson, 1972, pp. 28–29). This procedure indicated an interaction effect of borderline significance ($z = 1.73$, $p = .08$). Table 10.7 shows that the black officers' evaluation of the usefulness of the black lineups was considerably more negative than that of any other officer combination of race and lineup.

These findings are somewhat consistent with the previously reported finding that people made finer distinctions in evaluating lineups containing members of their own race (Brigham & Ready, 1985), although this was the case only for black subjects here.

The overall pattern of results indicated that measures of lineup fairness derived when college students play the role of mock witnesses (the source of the fairness measures most commonly utilized by contemporary researchers) are related to direct measures of lineup fairness made by people who evaluate entire lineups in a more straightforward manner. Thus, mock witness-based fairness measures are related to other indices of lineup fairness, including law officers' direct lineup evaluations. The pattern of significant relationships was salient even though practical constraints and theoretical concerns necessitated a research test involving a small N (of lineups) and limited statistical power.

Lineup fairness standards

Can researchers come up with reasonable estimates of what constitutes "fair" and "unfair" lineups? Wells et al. (1979) argued that this distinction should be left to the courts, but this would necessitate that the courts be cognizant of the conceptual underpinnings and empirical characteristics of fairness measures, as well as, perhaps, the approximate distributions of fairness measures across the population of lineups used in actual cases. It seems to us that researchers may be able to suggest rough guidelines that reflect the conceptual and empirical characteristics of various fairness measures. It would be up to the legal system to utilize these guidelines in any way it chose.

As a step in this direction, Brigham et al. (1990) proposed the cutoff points for fairness described earlier, based on the pattern of mock witness responses that was found. A six-person lineup was categorized as fair when the Effective Size was 3.0 or greater, Functional Size was 3.0 or greater (which will result in a significant z for proportions whenever the number of mock witnesses is eighteen or more) or, for the Acceptable Foils measure, when at least three of the six lineup members were chosen by mock witnesses at 75 percent or greater of the chance rate.

Although any fairness criterion will be somewhat arbitrary, some additional support for the appropriateness of these cutoff points is available. We calculated Proportions, Effective Size, and Acceptable Foils values, based on mock witness responses, for lineups that had been used in six actual criminal cases. These lineups were brought to our attention by defense attorneys who thought they were unfair. The six cases permitted twelve analyses because several cases involved more than one eyewitness, yielding more than one description; different sets of mock witnesses were exposed to each description. All three fairness measures demonstrated reasonable levels of sensitivity when the standards suggested above were applied. A statistically significant degree of bias was present in 62 percent of the Proportions analyses, whereas 46 and 38 percent of the analyses indicated inadequate lineup size according to the Acceptable Foils and Effective Size measures. The three least fair lineups in the actual cases yielded a mean Functional Size of 1.59, a mean Effective Size value of 2.19, and a mean (number of) Acceptable Foils score of 2.00. In comparison, the seven least fair lineups derived empirically for the Brigham and Brandt (in press) study yielded similar values, having a mean Functional

Size of 1.55, a mean Effective Size of 2.47, and a mean Acceptable Foils score of 2.00. Hence, the seven least fair lineups utilized by Brigham and Brandt were very similar in fairness (based on these three measures) to the least fair half of a set of lineups used in six actual criminal cases.

A second piece of evidence emerged from findings reported by Nosworthy and Lindsay (1990), who found that when a lineup contained three good foils (similar in appearance to the suspect), the addition of more foils, whether good foils or poor ones, did not appreciably affect the rates of correct or false identifications. The use of additional foils did increase the values of Effective Size and Functional Size, however. These findings suggest that lineup fairness may not have a linear relationship to the likelihood of misidentifications, but may rather be a threshold phenomenon, wherein further increases in the similarity of foils to the suspect beyond a certain point do not affect accuracy. Because concern about identification accuracy is the starting point for interest in lineup fairness, further information about this point of diminishing returns would be most valuable.

If one assumes that, on average, law officers' direct evaluations of lineup fairness are somewhat valid but subject to various biasing influences, then the moderate degree of relationship found by Brigham and Brandt (in press) between the fairness measures derived between law officer evaluators, college student evaluators, and college student mock witnesses seems appropriate. That is, we would predict only a moderate relationship if both samples are responding in terms of the same concept but are affected by different types of external biasing factors.

Additional issues concerning lineup fairness

A number of additional issues are also relevant to the fairness of lineups and the conditions under which they are administered (see, for example, Wells & Luus, 1990; Wells et al., this volume). Wells (1984) proposed that showing an eyewitness a "blank lineup" that does not contain the suspect before a second lineup containing the suspect may enable one to detect a strong response bias in an eyewitness. When witnesses choose someone from the blank lineup, this suggests that they may have been overly eager to choose someone or that their memory of the culprit was poor. Wells (1984) found that use of a prior blank lineup did not detract significantly from the ability of eyewitnesses to identify the culprit in the second lineup, as subjects who were first shown a blank lineup (including those who did and did not choose someone from the blank lineup) identified the target from a second, target-present lineup at a rate (50 percent) not significantly different from the accuracy rate of subjects who were not initially shown a blank lineup (60 percent). The blank lineup procedure may still have drawbacks from the policy perspective, however. In practical terms those witnesses who chose a foil known to be innocent from the blank lineup (37.5 percent of the witnesses in Wells's study) may no longer be acceptable in court as eyewitnesses, because opposing lawyers could seriously question the witness's credibility. Other research has shown that use of a sequential lineup, where eyewitnesses are shown photos one at a time and must make an identification decision after viewing each photo, may decrease the likelihood of false identifications while not depressing the rate of accurate identifications (Cutler & Penrod, 1988; Lindsay & Wells, 1985).

A second concern revolves around the issue of suspect distinctiveness. As noted by Brigham et al. (1990), it can be an arduous task to assemble a lineup that contains a suspect and an adequate number of fair foils. This task is made even more difficult when the suspect is distinctive or unusual in appearance. Indeed, when this situation occurred in the Brigham et al. (1990) study, the researchers were unable to compose a fair lineup for one very distinctive target person.

In one of the handful of U.S. Supreme Court cases that created case law on the utilization of eyewitness evidence, *Neil v. Biggers* (1972), law officers used a one-person showup as the identification task, rather than the usual six- to eight-person lineup. Two detectives walked the suspect past the rape victim, directing him to say, "Shut up or I'll kill you," the phrase uttered by the rapist during the rape seven months previously. The police claimed that they had earlier checked the city jail and the city juvenile home for persons to serve as foils in a live lineup, but could find no one at either place fitting the suspect's unusual physical description. The U.S. Supreme Court upheld Neil's conviction, ruling that although the showup procedure may have been suggestive, under the "totality of circumstances" standard, the victim's identification of the suspect was reliable and was properly allowed to go to the jury. Among the circumstances enumerated by the Court were the facts that the victim earlier failed to make any positive identification from thirty to forty photographs from several photo lineups and photo showups she was shown in the months after the rape, and that she had expressed "no doubt" of the correctness of her identification of Neil from the live showup.

Yet, contrary to the Court's assumption in *Neil,* research has shown that the relationship between an eyewitness's certainty and the accuracy of her or his identification is generally weak. A meta-analysis of thirty-five staged-event studies found a mean r of .25 (Bothwell, Deffenbacher, & Brigham, 1987). The confidence–accuracy relationship is even weaker or nonexistent when the initial conditions of observation are "nonoptimal" (for example, short time duration, high stress, poor opportunity to view). Subsequent research also indicated that the distinctiveness of the target person affected the certainty–accuracy relationship. Brigham (1990) found that the relationship between a witness's confidence in a lineup choice and the accuracy of that choice is significantly stronger when the target is highly distinctive in appearance.

A final relevant issue is the similarity of the foils to each other. Traditional mock-witness-based fairness measures, Proportions and Effective Size, assess the similarity in appearance between the lineup members and the culprit, as represented by the eyewitnesses' descriptions of the culprit. Wells and his colleagues (Luus & Wells, 1991; Wells et al., this volume) have pointed out that these measures do not take into account similarities or dissimilarities in appearance of lineup members on dimensions not included in the eyewitnesses' descriptions. Eyewitness descriptions typically include five to seven characteristics (Brigham et al., 1990) – should lineup members be similar to the suspect on all additional features as well? Luus and Wells (1991) labeled this issue the "clone paradox" and asserted that lineups wherein all members closely resemble each other on all features (that is, are clones of one another) will yield uninformative results. They suggested that lineups should have "propitious heterogeneity" (helpful differences) in the appearance of their members, that is, variations on characteristics not pertinent to the description of the culprit. They argued that lineups with high propitious heterogeneity should increase the likelihood of a correct identification if the suspect is indeed the culprit. Further, they maintain that such heterogeneity should not increase the likelihood of the false identification of an innocent suspect if the real culprit is not in the lineup. This theoretical proposition deserves further investigation.

In addition to their general concern regarding foil similarity, Luus and Wells (1991) also suggested that foils be selected according to their similarity to the witness's description as opposed to their actual similarity to the suspect (see recommendations 3 and 4 in Wells et al., this volume). Although this suggestion appears to make sense, it does raise a number of issues regarding the employment of measuring techniques to evaluate the fairness of a lineup. Specifically, one must now decide whether the Functional Size of the lineup is calculated according to how well the foils match the witness's description of the culprit, or how well they match the suspect's appearance. For example, if a witness describes a suspect as white, short, and balding, and the police arrest a suspect who is white, tall, and balding, what types of foils should be employed in the lineup? Should the foils be tall to match the suspect's appearance or short to match the witness's description?

Continued empirical and theoretical attention to these and other relevant issues should enable us to refine valid techniques for assessing the fairness of lineups and to increase the likelihood that lineup identifications and non-identifications will yield accurate, diagnostic information on whether or not a suspect is the culprit.

Have psychological theorizing and research yielded concepts and data that may be relevant and useful within the legal system? We believe that they have. The concepts of lineup size and bias, and the methods that have been developed for empirically assessing these factors, can enable law officers and attorneys to go beyond the simple "eyeballing," opinion, and guesswork that characterize current methods of evaluating lineups. We also believe that social scientists, law enforcement personnel, and legal professionals, working together, could develop standards of lineup acceptability that would be scientifically defensible, empirically based, legally appropriate, and of practical utility. It is hoped that the ideas presented in this chapter represent a small step in that direction.

Note

1 Though Malpass and Devine argued that measures of lineup fairness should not contain value judgments, it seems that the researchers' decision on what percentage of chance is designated as acceptable could involve value judgments.

References

Bothwell, R. K., Deffenbacher, K. A., & Brigham, J. C. (1987). Correlation of eyewitness accuracy and confidence: Optimality hypothesis revisited. *Journal of Applied Psychology, 72,* 691–695.

Brigham, J. C. (1989). Disputed eyewitness identifications: Can experts help? *The Champion, 8*(5), 10–18.

Brigham, J. C. (1990). Target person distinctiveness and attractiveness as moderator variables in the confidence–accuracy relationship in facial identification. *Basic and Applied Social Psychology, 11,* 101–115.

Brigham, J. C., & Brandt, C. C. (1992). Measuring lineup fairness: Mock witness responses vs. direct evaluations of lineups. *Law and Human Behavior, 16,* 475–489.

Brigham, J. C., & Ready, D. R. (1985). Own-race bias in lineup construction. *Law and Human Behavior, 9,* 415–424.

Brigham, J. C., Ready, D. J., & Spier, S. A. (1990). Standards for evaluating the fairness of photograph lineups. *Basic and Applied Social Psychology, 11,* 149–163.

Cutler, B. L., & Penrod, S. D. (1988) Improving the reliability of eyewitness identification: Lineup construction and presentation. *Journal of Applied Psychology, 73,* 281–290.

Doob, A. N., & Kirshenbaum, H. M. (1973). Bias in police lineups – partial remembering. *Journal of Police Science and Administration, 1,* 287–293.

Huff, C. R., Rattner, A., & Sagarin, E. (1986). Guilty until proven innocent: Wrongful conviction and public policy. *Crime and Delinquency, 32,* 518–544.

Langer, E. J., & Abelson, R. P. (1972). The semantics of asking a favor: How to succeed in getting help without really dying. *Journal of Personality and Social Psychology, 24,* 26–32.

Levine, F. J., & Tapp, J. L. (1982). Eyewitness identification: Problems and pitfalls. In V. J. Konecni & E. B. Ebbesen (Eds.), *The criminal justice system: A social-psychological analysis* (pp. 99–127). San Francisco, CA.: W. H. Freeman.

Lindsay, R. C. L., & Wells, G. W. (1985). Improving eyewitness identifications from lineups: Simultaneous versus sequential lineup presentations. *Journal of Applied Psychology, 70,* 556–564.

Luus, C. A., & Wells, G. L. (1991). Eyewitness identification and the selection of distractors for lineups. *Law and Human Behavior, 15,* 43–57.

Malpass, R. S. (1981). Effective size and defendant bias in eyewitness identification lineups. *Law and Human Behavior, 5,* 299–309.

Malpass, R. S., & Devine, P. G. (1983). Measuring the fairness of eyewitness identification lineups. In S.M.A. Lloyd-Bostock & B. R. Clifford (Eds.), *Evaluating witness evidence* (pp. 81–102). Chichester, England: Wiley.

McNemar, Q. (1969). *Psychological statistics* (4th ed.). New York: Wiley.

Neil v. Biggers, 409 U.S. 188 (1972).

Nosworthy, G. J., & Lindsay, R. C. L. (1990). Does nominal lineup size matter? *Journal of Applied Psychology, 75,* 358–361.

Pfeifer, J. E. (1990). Reviewing the empirical evidence on jury racism: Findings of discrimination or discriminatory findings? *Nebraska Law Review, 69,* 230–250.

United States v. Wade, 388 U. S. 218 (1967).

Wall, P. M. (1965). *Eyewitness identification in criminal cases.* Springfield, IL: Charles C. Thomas.

Wells, G. L. (1984). The psychology of lineup identifications. *Journal of Applied Social Psychology, 14,* 89–103.

Wells, G. L., Leippe, M. R., & Ostrom, T. M. (1979). Guidelines for empirically assessing the fairness of a lineup. *Law and Human Behavior, 3,* 285–293.

Wells, G. L., & Luus, C. A. E. (1990). Police lineups as experiments: Social methodology as a framework for properly conducted lineups. *Personality and Social Psychology Bulletin, 16,* 106–117.

Wells, G. L., Seelau, E. P., Rydell, S. M., & Luus, C. A. (this volume). Recommendations for properly conducted lineup identification tasks. In Ross, D. F., Read, J. D., & Toglia, M. P. (Eds.), *Adult eyewitness testimony: Current trends and developments* (pp. 223–244). New York: Cambridge University Press.

11 Recommendations for properly conducted lineup identification tasks

Gary L. Wells, Eric P. Seelau, Sheila M. Rydell, and C. A. Elizabeth Luus

An eyewitness takes the stand and describes salient aspects of an event that he or she witnessed several months earlier. Then, in the hush of the courtroom, points to the defendant and says "That's him. That's the man I saw." Simple, clean, and convincing. And therein rests the problem; what appears to be a simple identification is in fact the result of a series of complex and potentially unreliable social and cognitive events that began unfolding several months earlier when the event was originally witnessed.

This chapter, and much of the empirical research on which it is based, operates on an assumption that there are two sources of unreliability in eyewitness accounts. First, there are some inherent limitations in human information processing. These limitations exist at sensory levels (for example, Sperling, 1960), attentional levels (for example, Broadbent, 1958; Deutsch & Deutsch, 1963; Triesman, 1964), and memory levels (for example, Miller, 1956; Atkinson & Shiffrin, 1968). But inaccuracies in eyewitness accounts are not entirely attributable to human imperfections in sensation, perception, and memory. The second source of inaccuracy in eyewitness accounts can be attributed to the *methods* the justice system uses to obtain information from eyewitnesses. The work of Elizabeth Loftus on the effects of misleading questions serves to make this point (see Loftus, 1979; and this volume). The account one gets from an eyewitness depends very much on the methods used to solicit the information.

The study of how to improve eyewitness accuracy by manipulating the methods used to obtain information from eyewitnesses is known as a system-variable approach to eyewitness research (Wells, 1978). Unlike studies of the inherent deficiencies of eyewitnesses, system-variable research can inform us of ways to improve the accuracy of eyewitness accounts. The purpose of this chapter is to review what we have learned about the best ways to obtain eyewitness identifications. Our concern is with how to minimize false identification rates and maximize accurate identification rates.

Portions of this chapter were supported by a grant to the first author from the National Science Foundation (#SES-9022182).

We begin with the assumption that there is an identification problem. Wells (1992) argued that there are three observations consistent with this assumption. First, a large number of experiments using simulated or staged crime methods have found that false identifications occur with surprisingly high frequency (for example, Brigham & Cairns, 1988; Brigham, Maass, & Snyder, 1982; Buckhout, 1974; Cutler, Penrod, & Martens, 1987; Davies, Ellis, & Shepherd, 1978; Ellis, Shepherd, & Davies, 1980; Leippe, Wells, & Ostrom, 1979; Lindsay, 1986; Lindsay & Wells, 1980; Lindsay & Wells, 1985; Lindsay, Wells, & Rumpel, 1981; Loftus & Greene, 1980; Malpass & Devine, 1981; Parker & Caranza, 1989; Shepherd, Ellis, & Davies, 1982; Wells, 1984; Wells, Ferguson, & Lindsay, 1981; Wells & Leippe, 1981; Wells, Lindsay, & Ferguson, 1979). Second, there is considerable research evidence indicating that there is a "sincerity" to most of the false identifications observed in these experiments; the eyewitnesses often seem actually to believe that their false identifications are in fact accurate identifications. They express considerable levels of subjective confidence in their identifications and give testimony in a persuasive fashion (for example, see Deffenbacher, 1980; Leippe, 1980; Luus & Wells, 1992; Murray & Wells, 1982; Wells & Murray, 1984). Third, analyses of over a thousand actual cases of wrongful convictions have revealed that eyewitness error was the single largest factor leading to these miscarriages of justice (see Borchard, 1932; Frank & Frank, 1957; Brandon & Davies, 1973; Huff, Ratner, & Sagarin, 1986).

These three observations, two of which are based on experimental research and one on case studies, lead us to believe that there is in fact an important problem to be addressed. Our attempt to address the eyewitness identification problem is guided in a general sense by the system variable approach described earlier. In this chapter we go one step further by proposing a theoretical framework followed by a set of specific recommendations for the best ways to conduct identification tasks.

It might be fair to argue that the eyewitness identification process has not yet been described in a coherent theoretical framework. (By eyewitness identification process we mean the social and cognitive processes involved in the eyewitness's decision to identify or not identify a particular member of a lineup.[1]) We attempt to rectify that deficiency here by showing how we may be able to tie together a number of empirical observations by reference to a small number of propositions and corollaries. We admit from the outset that the result is not a true theory in the sense that a strict theoretician might use the term. Nevertheless, we present what we think is a useful framework for the understanding, prediction, and control of the eyewitness identification process. By pointing out how each recommendation is related back to a proposition or corollary, we hope to show that these recommendations are not just a haphazard collection of observations but instead are parts of an interrelated framework.

Propositions

Our recommendations on how to properly conduct a lineup are tied together by an interrelated set of two propositions and a major corollary. In some cases the recommendations are derivations from the propositions. In other cases, recommendations represent hypotheses that have been tested empirically. The empirical tests of these hypotheses in turn reflect back on the plausibility of the propositions and the corollary. In this section, we introduce the two propositions and the corollary.

Proposition I: *The purpose of a lineup is to uncover information in an eyewitness's recognition memory that was not available in recall.* (Luus & Wells, 1991)

The general truth value of Proposition I is self-evident. If it were the case that an eyewitness's verbal description of a culprit were sufficiently diagnostic of the identity of the culprit, then why would a lineup be conducted at all? In relatively rare cases, a verbal description has this level of diagnostic value. For instance suppose an eyewitness describes a culprit as a Caucasian male, about five feet tall, with a tattoo on his left hand that says "War is Hell," a two-inch scar over his left eye that is shaped like a pear, and a missing eye tooth on the left top side. If the police find a suspect with exactly these features, would a lineup be necessary? No. We conduct lineups because verbal descriptions typically do not contain a level of information that allows us to definitely decide whether our suspect is the culprit or not.

The idea that there is information in eyewitnesses' recognition memories that is not verbally recallable is consistent with the empirical observation that there is little statistical relation between various measures of verbal recall for faces (for example, accuracy, fluency, consistency, completeness) and recognition accuracy (for example, Pigott & Brigham, 1985; Wells, 1985). Statistically, this means that recall and recognition for faces account for different aspects of the variance in accuracy.

A derivation from Proposition I says that the diagnostic value of conducting a lineup increases as the diagnostic value of an obtained verbal description decreases. In other words, if the eyewitness's description is especially useless (the witness can only say that the culprit was a male of average height with medium-length hair), a lineup must be conducted to see if the witness can further reduce that uncertainty by identifying a particular suspect. If that uncertainty has already been reduced to near zero based only on the witness's verbal description, then a lineup task is not likely to further reduce our uncertainty.

Although the plausibility of Proposition I is somewhat self-evident, it is surprising to us how little this proposition has been exploited in certain domains, especially as it relates to the question of how distractors in lineups should be selected. As we describe later in connection with our recommendations for selecting distractors, a good distractor is one who fits the verbal description *but* varies in appearance from the suspect on features that were not a part of that description. This derivation is qualitatively and importantly different from the simple idea that distractors should look like the suspect but not too much like the suspect. We reject the latter idea as rather useless in a practical sense as well as imprecise; it is misleading and unnecessarily damaging to the overall value of the lineup to follow such a strategy.

Proposition II: *The identification process is governed not only by simple memorial factors but also by extramemorial judgment and heuristic processes.*

If proposition II were not true, and identification were a pure and simple memory process, we would not care about certain methods of conducting identification tasks. For example, what would it matter if the police told the eyewitness prior to viewing a lineup that person number three is the suspect and the remaining lineup members are actually police officers? Presumably, this would put considerable social pressure on the eyewitness to identify person number three. The eyewitness would know the police want a positive identification of person number three and must decide whether or not to give them the response they want. This is a way of saying that an eyewitness's identification decision is just that; it is a *decision*. Like all decisions, it can be said to be preceded by a set of judgments. Some of these judgments are perceptual or memorial but are based on external sources of information, social pressures, inferences, and heuristic processes.

One of these heuristics is the relative judgment heuristic (Wells, 1984). The relative judgment heuristic is a strategy for making a positive identification in which the eyewitness chooses the lineup member who most closely resembles the culprit *relative* to the other lineup members. Like other heuristics, the relative judgment heuristic works very well under one set of conditions but leads to error under another. The problem arises when people cannot or do not distinguish between conditions where the heuristic is functional and conditions where it is dysfunctional. In the case of the relative judgment heuristic, it is marvelously efficient and productive when a lineup contains the actual culprit, but it is dangerous and damaging when it does not. As will be evident later in this chapter, the relative judgment heuristic has led to some testable derivations for improving lineup procedures.

Corollary to Proposition II: *A lineup task can be likened to a social psychology experiment: Factors that can confound the interpretation of an experimental outcome can similarly confound the interpretation of the outcome of a lineup task.*

Our corollary can be thought of as a simple analogy between the set of rules that describe a good design and procedure for conducting an experiment on the one hand, and the set of rules that would describe a good design and procedure for conducting a lineup on the other.[2] In this sense our corollary is relatively powerful because it draws on a large and respected body of literature on experimental research methods and sources of threat to validity (for example, Aronson & Carlsmith, 1968; Rosenthal, 1976).

For example, we know from the logic of experimental procedure that a researcher should not reveal the research hypothesis to the subject until all the relevant data are collected. Analogously, if an eyewitness identifies someone from a lineup, the lineup administrator should not tell the witness whether the identified person was the suspect (versus one of the distractors) if he still expects to get a meaningful answer to the question of how confident the witness is in his or her identification. Any lineup administrator who leaks the hypothesis (for example, that number three in the lineup is the culprit) and then collects additional data from the eyewitness has contaminated the meaning of those data. They should thereby be rejected just as surely as any experimenter's data that rested on a similar error should be rejected.

Some fundamental distinctions and assumptions

A lineup might or might not contain the actual culprit. If one thinks of a lineup as an array of persons that includes the culprit, and the task of the eyewitness as one of finding the culprit among the array, one is depicting the situation in a limited and ecologically invalid manner. In actual cases, as well as in our experiments, the culprit is absent from the lineup on at least some occasions. For instance, in actual cases the police might have arrested an innocent suspect and the actual culprit is still at large. We use the terms "culprit present" and "culprit absent" to distinguish between these two states of affairs. The consequences of being in the culprit-present state versus the culprit-absent state are enormously different. Because we cannot be certain in actual cases whether or not the lineup includes the culprit, any claim for a superior lineup identification procedure must be tested under both possible states.

A distinction must also be made between culprits, suspects, and distractors.[3] A suspect is one who is merely suspected of being the culprit, but might in fact be innocent. Hence, when we refer to the identification of a suspect we do not mean that this is an accurate identification; we mean only that the eyewitness identified the lineup member whom the police suspect is the culprit. A distractor is not a suspect. A distractor is a member of the lineup who is known to be innocent of the offense in question. A distractor might be a police officer, someone from a jail cell, or a citizen of the community. If an eyewitness identifies a distractor, the identification is readily dismissed ("I'm sorry Mrs. Miller, but you identified someone who was in a jail cell at the time you were robbed").

With these distinctions in mind, we now impose an assumption. The assumption is that a lineup is composed of only one suspect (who might or might not be the culprit) and the remaining lineup members are innocent distractors. This assumption is not fully grounded in police practices. Wells and Turtle (1986) reported that perhaps as many as one of every three police lineups fails to use distractors but instead uses several suspects. The dangers of this practice in terms of controlling false identification rates have been documented and will not be reviewed in detail here (see Wells & Turtle, 1986). Suffice it to note for current purposes that the likelihood of false identification is additive across the number of suspects in a lineup and that the failure to use innocent distractors in a lineup is akin to giving the witness a multiple-choice test in which there can be no wrong answer. Using distractors known to be innocent, on the other hand, allows the police to use a "grading key" of sorts; if a distractor is identified, the identification can clearly be classified as an error and the eyewitness can justifiably be discredited to some extent.

Finally, we distinguish between an identification error and a false identification. Although a false identification is an error and an error is a false response, we reserve the term false identification for instances in which the eyewitness identifies an innocent *suspect;* if the eyewitness identifies a distractor we call this a foil identification or distractor identification. As already noted, the consequences of identifying a distractor versus a suspect are profoundly different. The former would never result in charges being brought against the identified person whereas the latter usually would.

An integration of these distinctions and assumptions allows us to state that a false identification cannot occur when the actual culprit is a member of the lineup. This follows from our definition of a false identification (identification of an innocent suspect) in conjunction with the assumption that the lineup contains only one suspect. Conversely, false identifications can occur only when the lineup does not contain the actual culprit. Identification errors (that is, distractor identifications), on the other hand, can occur in either a culprit-present or a culprit-absent lineup.

Recommendations on conducting lineups

Having stated our basic propositions, assumptions, and distinctions, we are now prepared to state our recommendations. Each recommendation is accompanied by discussion of its relation to one of the two general propositions and, whenever possible, to empirical data supporting the recommendation. We have organized these recommendations according to the order we think the relevant issue would arise when someone is considering conducting a lineup in a given case.

Recommendation 1: *Verbal descriptions of the culprit should be obtained from all eyewitnesses prior to conducting a lineup.* As will be noted in greater detail later, verbal descriptions of the culprit are essential to making decisions about the selection of appropriate distractors. In general terms, Recommendation 1 follows from the logic of our first proposition, namely that the purpose of a lineup is to uncover information from a recognition memory task that was not available in recall. There are other forensically relevant reasons for this rather obvious recommendation. For example, if the eyewitness is ever brought into court to testify about the witnessed event, she or he will be asked to describe the culprit from memory. If a prelineup description was not obtained earlier one cannot be sure whether the verbal description is being retrieved from the original event or if it is merely a description of the person the witness identified in the lineup. Only if there is a record of what the witness recalled about the culprit prior to viewing the lineup can we be certain about how to interpret the witness's in-court description.

Recommendation 2: *A lineup should contain at least five appropriate distractors for every one suspect.* We define later what makes a distractor "appropriate." The purpose of this recommendation is to set a minimum standard for the number of distractors. The number five is somewhat arbitrary in the same sense that the number six for a minimum sized jury is arbitrary. There is no threshold number below which the dangers of false identification are significant and above which they are not. On the other hand, there are clear theoretical arguments about the rate at which false identifications can be expected to decline as a function of the ratio of distractors to innocent suspects (see Doob & Kirshenbaum, 1973; Lindsay & Wells, 1980; Wells, in press). The decline in false identification rates as a function of the number of good distractors should be a diminishing return function. That is, adding a good distractor when there are only two other good distractors should have more impact than adding a good distractor when there are six or ten other good distractors.

The only empirical data bearing directly on the question of how many good distractors should be used in a lineup or photo spread comes from a study by Nosworthy and Lindsay (1990). Their data indicate that the addition of good distractors beyond a nominal size of three provides little or no additional protection for an innocent suspect. We note, however, that Nosworthy and Lindsay's study selected "good" distractors by using a resemblance-to-suspect criterion rather than a match-to-description criterion. This might have implications for the shape of the function relating the number of good distractors to the risk of false identifications of the suspect.

A critical element of Recommendation 2 is that it specifies a ratio of suspects to distractors rather than a ratio of suspects to total lineup members. Recall that a distractor is a lineup member known to be innocent. Hence, suspects cannot count as distractors for other suspects. For example, if there are two people suspected of being the culprit in question and the police want to conduct a single lineup containing both suspects, each suspect would have to have five separate distractors, resulting in a total of ten distractors. Counting the two suspects, this lineup would have a minimum number of twelve members.

Readers are referred to Wells and Turtle (1986) for a more thorough treatment of the problem of the ratio of suspects to distractors. In general, we agree with Wells and Turtle that a lineup should have only one suspect with the remaining members being innocent distractors. We have worded Recommendation 2, however, to accommodate the practical concern that it might be difficult or perhaps impossible to narrow the range of suspects to only one in a given real-world case. We see no room to compromise on the fact that an adequate ratio of suspects to distractors is critical in controlling the rate of false identifications. This point becomes more obvious when we consider the case of an all-suspect (no distractor) lineup. Suppose there were six suspects and each served as a foil for the others. Suppose now that the eyewitness makes a random choice for his or her identification. In this case chances are at least five in six that the identification would be a false identification.[4] If there were only one suspect and the other five were distractors, however, the chance of a false identification from this, a mere guessing strategy, falls to one in six or less.[5] The remaining five chances out of six represent identification errors, but they are identifications of innocent people who are not at risk of false accusation, and thereby need not fear being charged with the offense.

Recommendation 3: *Distractors should be chosen to match the eyewitness's verbal description of the culprit.* This follows from Proposition I, which states that the purpose of the lineup is to uncover information from recognition memory that was not available in verbal recall. If the suspect is the only one who matches the witness's verbal description, the lineup (recognition) task cannot be said to serve the function stated in our first proposition. Specifically, under such conditions we cannot determine whether an identification of the suspect was something that went beyond what the witness was already able to report (that is, the witness relied on the earlier description) or whether we actually have a process of recognition that went beyond the recall level.

Recommendation 3 has received wide attention among eyewitness identification researchers. Doob and Kirshenbaum (1973) and Malpass (1981) have written extensively about this problem and there are empirical data showing how the innocent suspect is protected (without significant loss in rates of identifying the actual culprit) by following Recommendation 3 (see Lindsay & Wells, 1980; Wells, Seelau, & Rydell, 1992). Wells et al. (1978) as well as Malpass (1981) and Malpass and Devine (1983, 1984) have proposed ways to measure the extent to which Recommendation 3 has been effectively met in a given case.

Recommendation 3 follows not only from Proposition I but also from Proposition II and its corollary. Previous writings have almost exclusively treated the idea in Recommendation 3 as an issue of extramemorial influences on the judgment and decision processes of eyewitnesses. Wells and Luus (1990), for example, argued that violations of Recommendation 3 allow the eyewitness to discern the hypothesis of the police, thus placing social pressures on the witness to choose the only person who matches the description.

Recommendation 3a: *In cases where the eyewitness's description of the culprit does not match the suspect's appearance, the suspect's appearance on the discrepant feature(s) should be used rather than the eyewitness's description of that (those) feature(s).* A discrepancy between the eyewitness's description of the culprit and the appearance of the suspect is not unusual. This could happen for three reasons. First, the suspect might not be the culprit. Second, the eyewitness's description might include errors of recall. Third, the suspect might be the culprit and the eyewitness's description might be accurate, but the culprit might have altered his or her appearance between the time of the witnessed event and the lineup. Recommendation 3a states that the suspect's actual appearance on the discrepant feature(s) constitutes the default descriptor for selecting distractors. This strikes us as the only viable solution to the suspect-description discrepancy. If one were to select distractors who match the description when the suspect does not match the description, then the suspect might stand out as being distinctive in the set of lineup members. It is important to note, however, that the suspect's appearance on given features is used as the default only for those features on which there is a discrepancy between the witness's description and the suspect's appearance.

Recommendation 4: *The set of potential distractors who match the description should exceed the number of distractors needed so that any who show undue resemblance to the suspect can be discarded from the set that is used.* This is our most controversial recommendation and, as far as we know, has never been advocated in print. Hence, we will take extra care to document its rationale.

Recommendation 4 follows generally from our first proposition, that the purpose of a lineup is to uncover information in recognition memory not available in recall. The theoretical underpinnings for Recommendation 4 can be found in Luus and Wells's (1991) article on strategies for selecting distractors for lineups. Here, however, we have taken their developments one step further.

The general idea behind discarding distractors who too closely resemble the suspect is to allow the eyewitness greater levels of perceptual discrimi-

Table 11.1. *Hypothetical set of four lineup members who match the eyewitness's description but vary on nondescribed features*

	Person A	Person B	Person C	Person D
Features part of eyewitness's description of culprit	male Caucasian 5'10"–6' 170–175 lbs mustache short hair brown hair 30–35 yrs old	male Caucasian 5'10"–6' 170–175 lbs mustache short hair brown hair 30–35 yrs old	male Caucasian 5'10"–6' 170–175 lbs mustache short hair brown hair 30–35 yrs old	male Caucasian 5'10"–6' 170–175 lbs mustache short hair brown hair 30–35 yrs old
Features not part of eyewitness's description of culprit	curly hair round chin blue eyes bushy brow round eyes	straight hair square chin green eyes average brow squinty eyes	wavy hair round chin brown eyes thin brow normal eyes	wavy hair angular chin blue-green eyes thick brow squinty eyes

nation among the lineup members. It is critical to keep in mind, however, that the remaining distractors must still match the description of the culprit as recalled by the eyewitness. Hence, Recommendation 4 in no sense violates Recommendation 3, nor in any sense should it produce a bias against the suspect.

Recommendation 4 is an attempt to increase *propitious heterogeneity* (helpful differences) in the appearance of lineup members so that the guilty suspect stands out for the witness but an innocent suspect would not. In general, variation in appearance across lineup members is not inherently bad unless that variation leads to bias against the innocent suspect. Those who have argued that a good lineup is one in which the distractors are selected to resemble the suspect have been promoting a fallacious strategy logic. Distractors must match the witness's description of the culprit, but no further protection to the innocent suspect is logically or theoretically gained by pressing for additional similarity. Instead, the practice of going beyond the witness-description criterion serves merely to reduce propitious heterogeneity and, in effect, protect the guilty suspect.

Potential resistance among psychologists to the idea of maximizing propitious heterogeneity might stem from disbelief that increasing differences in the appearance of lineup members can be done without prejudicing responses against an innocent suspect. We offer Table 11.1 as an illustration of our point that heterogeneity per se is not tantamount to increased risk of an innocent suspect being identified. In this example, the eyewitness described the culprit as a Caucasian male, about thirty or thirty-five years old, with short brown hair and a mustache, five feet, ten inches to six feet tall, and weighing one hundred seventy to one hundred seventy-five pounds. No other information could be recalled. Notice that each of the four lineup members matches this description, thereby satisfying Recommendation 3. Should we go further to make certain that the distractors also match the suspect on additional features such as eye color, shape of chin, and so on? We argue that one should not try to match these additional features. As evidence that this hypothetical four-person lineup in Table 11.1 is not biased against an innocent suspect, we ask at this point that the reader try to guess which person (A, B, C, or D) is the suspect. Notice there is no way for the reader to make this determination. That is exactly our point. If only one of the four members matched the eyewitness's description on the above-the-line features in Table 11.1, then it would be possible to deduce (using only the description) which lineup member is the suspect. But variation below the line in Table 11.1 does not allow such deductions.

Hence, the only reason the eyewitness should prefer one lineup member (member B, for instance) over the others is if that lineup member is the culprit or by chance happens to look like the culprit on the features that were not part of the description. But each lineup member has an equal a priori like-lihood of looking like the culprit by mere chance on the nonrecalled features. Thus, there is no bias against the suspect.

How would we know if an attempt to achieve propitious hetereogeneity somehow inadvertently created a malevolent form of heterogeneity that biased the lineup against the suspect? Luus and Wells (1991) argued that a lineup must still pass tests of having adequate functional size. Readers are referred to the chapter by Brigham and Pfeifer (this volume) for a discussion of the methods for measuring functional size and related measures of the fairness of a lineup.

We put our theory of propitious hetereogeneity to the test in a recent experiment (Wells et al., 1992). We staged thefts for 252 unsuspecting eye-witnesses in groups of two to four in size. There were seven different thieves (thirty-six witnesses per thief) that varied in appearance (two were African American, one was Asian, four were Caucasian; four were female, three were male). Witnesses were separated immediately after the theft and asked to provide a written description of the thief. Eyewitnesses were randomly as-signed to one of three conditions: (1) A low functional size lineup was con-structed in which only the suspect matched the eyewitness's description; (2) a lineup was constructed in which the distractors were chosen to be similar in appearance to the suspect; (3) a lineup was constructed in which distractors matched the eyewitness's description but were otherwise dissimilar to the suspect. Half of the eyewitnesses in each lineup condition viewed a lineup containing the actual thief and half viewed a lineup in which an innocent

Table 11.2. *Percentage of witnesses making correct and incorrect decisions as a function of strategy used for constructing lineups*

	Low functional size	Resemble suspect	Match-to-description
Accurate identifications			
Thief present	71.4	21.4	66.7
Thief absent	X	X	X
False identifications			
Thief present	X	X	X
Thief absent	42.9	11.9	11.9
Distractor identification			
Thief present	7.1	42.9	7.1
Thief absent	11.9	47.6	31.0
"Not there"			
Thief present	14.3	28.6	11.9
Thief absent	31.0	21.4	31.0
"Don't know"			
Thief present	7.1	7.1	14.2
Thief absent	14.2	19.0	26.2

X = cannot occur.

suspect replaced the thief. Eyewitnesses were told that the actual thief might or might not be present.

The data in Table 11.2 show a clear pattern. Accurate identifications were equally high for the low functional size and match-to-description lineups and both were significantly higher than the resemble-suspect lineup. The important point, however, is that the match-to-description strategy held false identification rates down to the same low level that the resemble-suspect strategy was able to achieve.

The strategy of selecting distractors who match the eyewitness's description of the culprit but otherwise do not resemble him or her is an effective strategy for holding false identification rates down to a level comparable to that in strategies that attempt to make the distractors look like the suspect. At the same time, the match-to-description-but-maximize-propitious-heterogeneity strategy manages to secure accurate identification rates comparable to those in a lineup biased against the guilty suspect. Readers are encouraged to read the Luus and Wells (1991) article for a more detailed analysis of the theoretical underpinnings of this important aspect of selecting distractors as well as an analysis of special problems that can arise.

Recommendation 5: *Separate lineups should be conducted for each eyewitness in multiple-witness cases. Minimally, the positioning of the suspect and foils should be different for each lineup; in some cases different distractors should be used.* The primary rationale for conducting separate lineups is to maintain some potentially critical elements of independence in the identification responses of the eyewitnesses.

By separate lineups, we mean not only that the eyewitnesses should not as a group view the lineup, but also that they should not view a lineup at the same time even if they are in separate viewing rooms. The rationale for this concern is that any bias in the lineup that might result from an unusual occurrence or the positioning of the suspect would replicate itself across each of the eyewitnesses. Separately conducted lineups, on the other hand, allow the suspect to be placed in more than one position in the lineup. If several eyewitnesses identify the suspect under conditions where he or she appears in a different lineup position for each eyewitness, then our certainty that the suspect was identified for reasons other than superficial features such as position in the lineup should increase. Changing the position of the suspect in the lineup also helps prevent more direct forms of interwitness influence, such as one witness telling another which person in the lineup is the suspect.

In general, Recommendation 5 follows from Proposition II and more specifically from the corollary to Proposition II. Recall that this corollary likens a lineup to a scientific experiment. In keeping with this analogy, we can have greater confidence in the validity of a conclusion when there is convergence across different measures (Campbell & Fiske, 1959). Changing the position of the suspect and distractors for each witness is a minimum requirement for claiming convergence of evidence.

In a behavioral experiment, there is a concern about the dangers of running several subjects who are assigned to the same experimental condition in the same session. The problem arises when there is a unique event that occurs in a given session, thereby affecting several subjects at once. Because each affected subject was in the same condition, it can appear that there was a large effect for the condition itself rather than merely a peculiar event in a given session. The solution in experiments is to randomly assign subjects to conditions within a session or to run only one subject per session (see Myers, 1972). This same concern applies to the way lineups are conducted. If two or more eyewitnesses view the same lineup in the same session, even if the eyewitnesses are in separate viewing rooms, any peculiar events will affect all the eyewitnesses and their identification responses can be correlated for spurious reasons.

When there are multiple eyewitnesses, there is a strong likelihood that the descriptions of the culprit will vary across those eyewitnesses. When this occurs, each eyewitness might require a different set of distractors. At the very least, it would be unacceptable to use one eyewitness's description of the culprit to select distractors for a second eyewitness if the latter's description were more detailed than that of the former. Suppose, for example, the first eyewitness described the culprit as a white male, twenty to twenty-four years of age, and about six feet tall, whereas the second described the culprit similarly but added that he had dark, curly hair and a mole on his left cheek. Suppose further that the suspect was a twenty-two-year-old Caucasian male, six feet, one inch tall, with dark curly hair and a mole on his left cheek. In this case, it is permissible to use the shorter description to select distractors only for the first witness. The second witness must have distractors who match the second witness's description.

Recommendation 6: *The lineup administrator should not be aware of which person in the lineup is the suspect and which persons are distractors.* We realize this recommendation might be difficult to follow in small police departments, but we see no reason why larger police departments cannot follow this practice. The recommendation follows from Proposition II in general and its corollary in particular. In the experimental analogy, this recommendation parallels the rationale for keeping experimenters blind to experimental conditions (Rosenthal, 1967).

That there are expectancy effects, wherein the experimenters' hypotheses, hunches, or desires for obtaining a particular response from a research subject affect the likelihood of obtaining such responses, is not in doubt. Rosenthal and Rubin (1978) conducted a meta-analysis of 345 studies of expectancy effects and found a mean correlation of r-33 between experimenters' expectations and subjects' behaviors under conditions where the expectations alone were the causal agents.

Fanselow (1975) demonstrated that the lineup administrator's nonverbal behaviors can influence eyewitness identification responses. In Fanselow's study subject witnesses viewed a photo lineup in which the lineup administrator was instructed to smile and show approval of a certain photograph. Although none of the photos was of the person in question, this nonverbal behavior led to an increased rate of selecting that photograph.

Recommendation 7: *The eyewitness should be told explicitly that the perpetrator might or might not be in the lineup. This statement should be made when the eyewitness is initially asked to view a lineup and again just prior to viewing the lineup.* Many eyewitnesses seem to approach a lineup with the assumption that the culprit is in the lineup and that their task is to decide which lineup member is the culprit (Malpass & Devine, 1981; Wells, 1984). This assumption, which we will call the culprit-present fallacy, has very serious consequences. Any lineup, even if it does not include the actual culprit, will have someone who more closely resembles him or her than do the other lineup members. Given that the culprit is not in the lineup, the culprit-present fallacy reinforces the already pervasive tendency to make relative judgments and identify the person who shows the closest resemblance to the culprit relative to the other lineup members.

Although telling the eyewitness that the perpetrator in question might or might not be in the lineup does not fully eliminate eyewitnesses' reliance on relative judgments (Wells, 1984; Wells, 1992), it does reduce the likelihood that they will select someone from a culprit-absent lineup (Malpass & Devine, 1981). This reduction in mistaken identification rates for culprit-absent lineups as a function of the "might or might not be present" instruction does not produce an appreciable decline in the likelihood that the culprit will be identified from a culprit-present lineup (Malpass & Devine, 1981).

The logic behind the "might or might not be present" recommendation is so powerful and important that it seems unlikely that anyone could seriously debate the necessity of including the statement. At the same time, however, police often approach a given lineup task with a firm belief that the suspect is the culprit in question. In a given case, for instance, the police might have definitive evidence against the suspect but be unable to use that evidence for some reason and, hence, need an identification from the eyewitness. In such circumstances, it might be difficult for them to "remember" to tell the eyewitness that the actual culprit might or might not be present. Although understandable perhaps, such forgetfulness is totally unacceptable. The eyewitness must understand the situation as one in which the actual culprit might not be in the lineup.

Recommendation 8: *The eyewitness should first be asked to indicate whether or not the culprit is present in the lineup and only if the eyewitness makes an affirmative response should he or she be asked to indicate which lineup member is the culprit in question.* This recommendation is consistent with Recommendation 7 in that the initial question to the eyewitness does not presume the culprit is among the lineup members. If the lineup administrator were first to tell the eyewitness that the culprit might or might not be present and then immediately ask which person is the culprit, the eyewitness has not been given a proper opportunity to act on a belief that the culprit is not among the lineup members. The lineup situation can have considerable demand characteristics that lead eyewitnesses to feel they are not doing their job or helping the cause of justice if they fail to identify someone. Eyewitnesses need to know that "he's not there" or "I don't know" are acceptable responses. In general, Recommendation 8 can be considered a derivation from the corollary to Proposition II. Recall that this corollary likens a lineup task to a behavioral science experiment; if we are interested in measuring someone's beliefs, we must not imply with our procedures that some responses are better than others.

Recommendation 9: *If an eyewitness identifies someone from the lineup, the eyewitness should be asked how certain he or she is that the identified person is the culprit. This question should immediately follow the identification re-sponse so that no extraneous factors can influence the eyewitness's statement of certainty.* There is a large body of empirical research showing that the certainty expressed by an eyewitness is poorly related to accuracy of identi-fication (for example, Brigham, Maass, Snyder & Spaulding, 1982; Cutler, Penrod, & Martens, 1987a; Cutler, Penrod, & Martens, 1987b; Cutler, Pen-rod, O'Rourke, & Martens, 1987; Fleet, Brigham, & Bothwell, 1987; Gor-enstein & Ellsworth, 1980; Greenberg, Wilson, Ruback, & Mills, 1979; Hilgendorf & Irving, 1978; Hosch & Cooper, 1982; Hosch, Leippe, Mar-chioni, & Cooper, 1984; Jenkins & Davies, 1985; Kassin, 1985; Krafka & Penrod, 1985; Leippe, Wells, & Ostrom, 1978; Lindsay & Wells, 1986; Lind-say, Wells, & Rumpel, 1981; Malpass & Devine, 1981a; Malpass & Devine 1981b; Murray & Wells, 1982; Pigott & Brigham, 1985; Sanders & Warnick, 1980; Sanders & Warnick, 1981; Shepherd, Ellis, & Davies, 1982; Smith, Kassin, & Ellsworth, 1989; Wells, Ferguson, & Lindsay, 1981; Wells & Leippe, 1981; Wells, Lindsay, & Ferguson, 1979; Yuille & McEwan, 1985). Hence, some experts might argue that we should not recommend asking eyewitnesses about their certainty of identification because it has proven to be a misleading index of accuracy.

Nevertheless, we recommend that a confidence statement be secured from the eyewitness for two reasons. First, the empirical literature indicates that an eyewitness's statement of confidence immediately following an identifi-cation can have some diagnostic value, albeit perhaps to a trivial degree. Later, however, an eyewitness is likely to have his or her confidence influenced by extramemorial factors, thereby confusing the issue of how to interpret later statements of confidence. Second, triers of fact are going to use eye-witness confidence to infer something about the accuracy of the eyewitness regardless of whether the confidence statement is taken immediately following the identification or at some later time. Hence, we suggest that a confidence statement be taken at the time of identification so that whatever confidence level the eyewitness expresses is relatively clean of the extraneous influences that can occur later.

In another chapter in this volume (Luus and Wells), the issue of the relation between confidence and accuracy is discussed in greater detail. The general point is that there are numerous, relatively uncontrollable events that can occur subsequent to an eyewitness's identification that serve to confound later statements about how confident he or she is in the identification. For example, if the eyewitness mentally rehearses the image of the identified person and is motivated to resist being influenced by cross examination, his or her ap-parent confidence on the witness stand might increase dramatically even if the identification is incorrect (Wells, Ferguson, & Lindsay, 1981). An eye-witness's confidence in a false identification has been shown to increase dramatically by telling him or her that another eyewitness has identified the same person (Luus & Wells, 1992). Similarly one can imagine the difficulty an eyewitness might have if, following an identification, he or she is told that the identified person's fingerprints were found at the scene of the crime. If the eyewitness were not asked until after receiving this extramemorial information how confident he or she is in his or her identification, can the external information be ignored? What does it mean if the eyewitness now says he or she is highly confident in the identification?

Recommendation 9 follows generally from Proposition II, which states that eyewitness responses can be influenced by extramemorial factors. Although we commonly think about the ways extramemorial factors might influence the identification decision, we must also be concerned with the ways in which extramemorial factors can influence postidentification judgments such as eyewitness confidence.

For these reasons we recommend that any identification decision be followed almost immediately with a question about how confident the witness is in that identification. Under no circumstances would it be appropriate to express pleasure or displeasure to the eyewitness, or "inform" the eyewitness in any way until the confidence statement is secured. Some might argue that it is unrealistic to assume that a lineup administrator can avoid responding nonverbally with pleasure or displeasure following an eyewitness's identification decision. We do not need to presuppose some kind of superhuman quality of a lineup administrator (who is somehow immune to nonverbal leakage), however, as long as Recommendation 6 is followed. Recall that Recommendation 6 states that the lineup administrator should not be aware of which lineup member is the suspect and which are distractors.

Recommendation 10: *All phases and aspects of the lineup should be meticulously recorded, preferably using videotape.* The common practice of merely having a photograph of the lineup (or a copy of the photo spread), with some notes and forms filled out by the lineup administrator, should no longer be considered an acceptable record. These notes are almost always incomplete and there is considerable doubt at times about how such things as oral instructions to eyewitnesses were delivered as later reported in the police officer's notes.

Given the pervasive accessibility and ease of operation of video recording equipment today, there seems little excuse for not videotaping the instructions that were given to the eyewitness, the lineup, the questions asked of the eyewitness, the eyewitness's identification response, and the eyewitness's statement of confidence. Ultimately, it will be up to the courts to decide whether or not a copy of such tapes should be given routinely to defense counsel or whether this should happen only on a case by case basis by petition and argument from defense counsel. There can be no doubt, however, of the potential utility of videotaping lineup procedures.

Acceptable variations in lineup methods

The standard lineup procedure is one in which a suspect is embedded among distractors and the entire set of lineup members is presented at one time to the eyewitness. In recent years, variations on this method have been tested empirically. Wells (1984), for example, proposed a dual lineup procedure in which one lineup contains the suspect and the other does not. Wells argued that the dual lineup procedure is psychologically different from a larger lineup that simply joins these two separate lineups. This is especially true when the eyewitness is unaware that there will be two lineups. Under these conditions, any propensities of eyewitnesses to make an identification based on relative judgments (who looks most like the culprit relative to the other lineup members) will be detected because all members of the first lineup are innocent distractors. The empirical data show that this procedure, called the blank-lineup control, is an effective "lure" or "screen" for weeding out unreliable eyewitnesses.

We endorse the blank-lineup control procedure, but we hesitate to make it one of our explicit recommendations for two reasons. First, it may be unduly costly for police to construct two lineups for each eyewitness. Second, widespread practice of the blank-lineup control procedure could result in the practice becoming known to the general population. We could imagine, for instance, eyewitnesses always skipping over the first lineup because they have somehow learned that the suspect always appears in the second lineup.

Another variation on standard lineup procedures is the sequential lineup, proposed originally by Lindsay & Wells (1985). The sequential lineup presents one lineup member at a time and the eyewitness is asked to make a decision (is this person the culprit?) of yes or no for each person viewed at the time of initial presentation. The theoretical idea behind the sequential procedure stems from Wells's (1984) relative-judgment conceptualization. Specifically, it is argued that the eyewitness who is confronted with the sequential lineup task cannot fall back on mere relative judgments because the set of possible relative comparisons is incomplete. The eyewitness might be able to say that a given person (for example, number three in the sequence) is a relatively better likeness than were the ones previously viewed, but he or she cannot be certain that a yet-to-be-viewed lineup member is not perhaps an even better likeness relative to the one being viewed now. Hence, by forcing the eyewitness to make a yes or no decision for each lineup member without knowing what the remaining members look like, the eyewitness is forced away from relative judgments and made to rely more on an absolute comparison between the lineup member being viewed at the time and his or her memory of the culprit.

There is considerable consistent empirical support for the superiority of the sequential method over the simultaneous method (for example, Cutler & Penrod, 1988; Lindsay et al., in press; Lindsay et al., 1991; Lindsay & Wells, 1985; Parker & Ryan, 1990; Sporer, 1990). Nevertheless, we are not yet prepared to recommend that all lineups be conducted sequentially. Although we anticipate that the sequential procedure will be widely advocated by eyewitness experts within the decade, we worry that police departments that do not or cannot implement Recommendation 6 (lineup administrator kept blind as to which person is the suspect) might create more problems with the sequential procedure than they would with the simultaneous procedure. Our fear is that a lineup administrator might more effectively "communicate" (either intentionally or unintentionally) the identity of the suspect to the eyewitness with the sequential procedure than with the simultaneous procedure. In general, we endorse the sequential lineup whenever the lineup administrator can be kept blind as to which lineup member is the suspect; but if it is impractical, or if it is questionable whether the lineup administrator is truly blind in this regard, we believe that a simultaneous procedure may be safer.

Conclusions

We have argued that eyewitness error is a joint product of inherent human cognitive limitations and the methods that are used to obtain information from eyewitnesses. We now have a number of relatively specific recommendations about the best ways to conduct lineup identification tasks so as to minimize the rate of false identifications and maximize rates of accurate identification. We have tried to show how the principal recommendations we made in this chapter can be tied back to two simple, overreaching propositions: A lineup is conducted for the purpose of obtaining information with a recognition task that was not available using a recall task; the identification process is governed not only by memorial processes but also by extramemorial factors. Recommendations 1 through 9, each of which has empirical support, can be said to derive from one or both of these general propositions. We believe that there are other important recommendations that can be derived from these propositions and tested empirically; we trust these recommendations will be refined and new ones added in the next few years. Meanwhile, it seems that we have a practical body of research that can help reduce what we believe to be a significant problem in police practice.

Notes

1 We use the term lineup here to refer to live presentations of suspects and distractors as well as photographic spreads and videotaped methods of presentation.
2 See Wells & Luus (1990) for a more detailed treatment of the analogy.
3 Police sometimes call distractors "fillers." In the eyewitness literature they are sometimes called foils.
4 The actual odds are higher assuming there is some probability that the culprit is not in the lineup at all.
5 The actual odds are lower assuming there is some probability that the suspect is in fact the culprit.

References

Aronson, E., & Carlsmith, J. M. (1968). Experimentation in social psychology. In G. Lindsay & E. Aronson (Eds.), *The handbook of social psychology* (2d Ed.), (Vol. 2, pp. 1–79). Reading, Mass: Addison-Wesley.

Atkinson, R. C., & Shiffrin, R. M. (1968). Human memory: A proposed system and its control processes. In K. W. Spence & J. T. Spence (Eds.), *The psychology of learning and motivation* (Vol. 2). New York: Academic Press.

Borchard, E. (1932). *Convicting the innocent: Errors of criminal justice*. New Haven: Yale University Press.

Brandon, R., & Davies, C. (1973). *Wrongful imprisonment*. London: Allen & Unwin, 1973.

Brigham, J. C., & Cairns, D. L. (1988). The effect of mugshot inspections on eyewitness identification accuracy. *Journal of Applied Social Psychology, 18*, 1394–1410.

Brigham, J. C., Maass, A., Snyder, L. D., & Spaulding, K. (1982). Accuracy of eyewitness identifications in a field setting. *Journal of Personality and Social Psychology, 42*, 673–681.

Broadbent, D. E. (1958). *Perception and communication*. London: Pergamon Press.

Buckhout, R. (1974). Eyewitness testimony. *Scientific American, 231*, 23–31.

Campbell, D. T., & Fiske, D. W. (1959). Convergent and discrimination validation by the multitrait-multimethod matrix. *Psychological Bulletin, 56*, 81–105.

Cutler, B. L., & Penrod, S. D. (1988). Improving the reliability of eyewitness identification: The role of system and estimator variables. *Journal of Applied Psychology, 73*, 281–290.

Cutler, B. L., Penrod, S. D., & Martens, T. K. (1987). The reliability of eyewitness identification: The role of system and estimator variables. *Law and Human Behavior, 11*, 233–258.

Davies, G. M., Ellis, H. D., & Shepherd, J. W. (1978). Face recognition accuracy as a function of mode of representation. *Journal of Applied Psychology, 63*, 180–187.

Deffenbacher, K. (1980). Eyewitness accuracy and confidence: Can we infer anything about their relationship? *Law and Human Behavior, 4*, 243–260.

Deutsch, J. A., & Deutsch, D. (1963). Attention: Some theoretical considerations. *Psychological Review, 70*, 80–90.

Ellis, H. D., Shepherd, J. W., & Davies, G. M. (1980). The deterioration of verbal descriptions of faces over different delay intervals. *Journal of Police Science and Administration, 8*, 101–106.

Fanselow, M. (1975). How to bias an eyewitness. *Social Action and the Law, 2*, 3–4.

Fleet, M. L., Brigham, J. C., & Bothwell, R. K. (1987). The confidence–accuracy relationship: The effects of confidence assessment and choosing. *Journal of Applied Social Psychology, 17*, 171–187.

Frank, J., & Frank, B. (1957). *Not guilty*. London: Gallancz, 1957.

Gorenstein, G. W., & Ellsworth, P. C. (1990). Effect of choosing an incorrect photograph on a later identification by an eyewitness. *Journal of Applied Psychology, 65*, 616–622.

Greenberg, M. S., Wilson, C. E., Ruback, R. B., & Mills, M. K. (1979). Social and emotional determinants of victim crime reporting. *Social Psychology Quarterly, 42*, 364–372.

Hilgendorf, E. L., & Irving, B. L. (1978). False positive identification. *Medicine, Science and the Law, 18,* 255–262.

Hosch, H. M., & Cooper, D. S. (1982). Victimization as a determinant of eyewitness accuracy. *Journal of Applied Psychology, 67,* 649–652.

Hosch, H. M., Leippe, M. R., Marchioni, P. M., & Cooper, D. S. (1984). Victimization, self-monitoring, and eyewitness identification. *Journal of Applied Psychology, 69,* 280–288.

Huff, R., Rattner, A., & Sagarin, E. (1986). Guilty until proven innocent. *Crime and Delinquency, 32,* 518–544.

Jenkins, F., & Davies, G. (1985). Contamination of facial memory through exposure to misleading composite pictures. *Journal of Applied Psychology, 70,* 164–176.

Kassin, S. M. (1985). Eyewitness identification: Retrospective self-awareness and the confidence–accuracy correlation. *Journal of Personality and Social Psychology, 49,* 878–893.

Krafka, C., & Penrod, S. (1985). Reinstatement of context in a field experiment on eyewitness identification. *Journal of Personality and Social Psychology, 49,* 58–69.

Leippe, M. R. (1980). Effects of integrative memorial and cognitive processes in the correspondence of eyewitness accuracy and confidence. *Law and Human Behavior, 4,* 261–274.

Leippe, M. R., Wells, G. L., & Ostrom, T. M. (1978). Crime seriousness as a determinant of accuracy in eyewitness identification. *Journal of Applied Psychology, 63,* 345–351.

Lindsay, R. C. L. (1986). Confidence and accuracy in eyewitness identification from lineups. *Law and Human Behavior, 10,* 229–239.

Lindsay, R. C. L., Lea, J. A., & Fulford, J. A. (1991). Sequential lineup presentation: Technique matters. *Journal of Applied Psychology, 76,* 741–745.

Lindsay, R. C. L., Lea, J. A., Nosworth, G. J., Fulford, J. A., Hector, J., Levan, V., & Seabrook, C. (in press). Biased lineups: Sequential presentation reduces the problem. *Journal of Applied Psychology.*

Lindsay, R. C. L., & Wells, G. L. (1980). What price justice? Exploring the relationship of lineup fairness to identification accuracy. *Law and Human Behavior, 4,* 303–314.

Lindsay, R. C. L., & Wells, G. L. (1985). Improving eyewitness identifications from lineups: Simultaneous versus sequential lineup presentations. *Journal of Applied Psychology, 70,* 556–564.

Lindsay, R. C. L., Wells, G. L., & Rumpel, C. M. (1981). Can people detect eyewitness identification accuracy within and across situations? *Journal of Applied Psychology, 66,* 79–89.

Loftus, E. F., & Greene, E. (1980). Warning: Even memory for faces may be contagious. *Law and Human Behavior, 4,* 323–334.

Luus, C. A. E., & Wells, G. L. (1991). Eyewitness identification and the selection of distracters for lineups. *Law and Human Behavior, 15,* 43–57.

Luus, C. A. E., & Wells, G. L. (1992). *The malleability of eyewitness confidence: Social influence and perseverance effects.* Manuscript under editorial review.

Malpass, R. S., & Devine, P. G. (1981a). Eyewitness identification: Lineup instructions and the absence of the offender. *Journal of Applied Psychology, 66,* 482–489.

Malpass, R. S. & Devine, P. G. (1981b). Guided memory in eyewitness identification. *Journal of Applied Psychology, 66,* 343–350.

Miller, G. A. (1956). The magical number seven plus or minus two: Some limits on our capacity for processing information. *Psychological Review, 63,* 81–97.

Murray, D. M., & Wells, G. L. (1982). Does knowledge that a crime was staged affect eyewitness performance? *Journal of Applied Social Psychology, 12,* 42–53.

Myers, J. L. (1972). *Fundamentals of experimental design.* Boston: Allyn & Bacon.

Nosworthy, G. J., & Lindsay, R. C. L. (1990). Does nominal lineup size matter? *Journal of Applied Psychology, 75,* 358–361.

Parker, J. F., & Caranza, L. E. (1989). Eyewitness testimony of children in target-present and target-absent lineups. *Law and Human Behavior, 13,* 133–149.

Parker, J. F., & Ryan, V. (1990, March). An attempt to reduce guessing behavior in children's and adults' eyewitness testimony. Paper presented at the meeting of the American Psychology-Law Society, Williamsburg, VA.

Pigott, M. A., & Brigham, J. C. (1985). Relationship between accuracy of prior description and facial recognition. *Journal of Applied Psychology, 70,* 547–555.

Rosenthal, R. (1967). Covert communication in the psychological experiment. *Psychological Bulletin, 67,* 356–367.

Rosenthal, R. (1976). *Experimenter effects in behavioral research.* New York: Irvington Press.

Rosenthal, R., & Rubin, D. B. (1978). Interpersonal expectancy effects: The first 345 studies. *Behavioral and Brain Sciences, 3,* 377–386.

Sanders, G. S., & Warnick, D. (1980). Some conditions maximizing eyewitness accuracy: A learning/memory analogy. *Journal of Criminal Justice, 8,* 395–403.

Shepherd, J. W., Ellis, H. D., & Davies, G. M. (1982). *Identification evidence: A psychological evaluation.* Aberdeen, Scotland: Aberdeen University Press.

Smith, V. L., Kassin, S. M., & Ellsworth, P. C. (1989). Eyewitness accuracy and confidence: Within versus between-subject correlations. *Journal of Applied Psychology, 74,* 356–359.

Sperling, G. (1960). The information available in brief visual presentations. *Psychological Monographs, 74,* 1–29.

Sporer, S. L. (1990, March). Dissecting a witness's choice. Decision times as predictors of eyewitness identification decisions in simultaneous and sequential lineups. Paper presented at the meeting of the American Psychology-Law Society, Williamsburg, VA.

Triesman, A. M. (1964). Verbal cues, language, and meaning in selective attention. *American Journal of Psychology, 77,* 206–218.

Wells, G. L. (1978). Applied eyewitness testimony research: System variables and estimator variables. *Journal of Personality and Social Psychology, 36,* 1546–1557.

Wells, G. L. (1984). The psychology of lineup identifications. *Journal of Applied Social Psychology, 14,* 89–103.

Wells, G. L. (1992). *What do we know about eyewitness identification?* Manuscript under editorial review.

Wells, G. L., Ferguson, T. J., & Lindsay, R. C. L. (1981). The tractability of eyewitness confidence and its implications for triers of fact. *Journal of Applied Psychology, 66,* 688–696.

Wells, G. L., & Leippe, M. R. (1981). How do triers of fact infer the accuracy of eyewitness identifications? Using memory for peripheral detail can be misleading. *Journal of Applied Psychology, 66,* 682–687.

Wells, G. L., Lindsay, R. C. L., & Ferguson, T. (1979). Accuracy, confidence, and juror perceptions in eyewitness identification. *Journal of Applied Psychology, 64,* 440–448.

Wells, G. L., & Luus, C. A. E. (1990). Police lineups as experiments: Social methodology as a framework for properly-conducted lineups. *Personality and Social Psychology Bulletin, 16,* 106–117.

Wells, G. L. & Murray, D. M. (1984). Eyewitness confidence. In G. L. Wells & E. F. Loftus (Eds.), *Eyewitness testimony: Psychological perspectives* (pp. 155–170). New York: Cambridge University Press.

Wells, G. L., Seelau, E. P., & Rydell, S. M. (1992). *Eyewitness identification and the value of propitious heterogeneity.* Manuscript under editorial review.

Wells, G. L., & Turtle, J. W. (1986). Eyewitness identification: The importance of lineup models. *Psychological Bulletin, 99,* 320–329.

Yuille, J. C., & McEwan, N. H. (1985). Use of hypnosis as an aid to eyewitness memory. *Journal of Applied Psychology, 70,* 389–400.

12 Improving eyewitness testimony with the Cognitive Interview

Ronald P. Fisher, Michelle R. McCauley, and R. Edward Geiselman

In a comprehensive study of criminal investigation processes, the Rand Corporation (1975) reported that the principal determinant of whether or not a case is solved is the completeness and accuracy of the eyewitness's account. This official document mirrors the feelings unofficially held by many law enforcement agents (Sanders, 1986). Defense attorneys have made similar claims: The more evidence they can marshal, the better they can defend a client (Visher, 1987). In short, all concerned profit from having more complete and accurate eyewitness evidence. The criminal is more effectively pursued and tried; the innocent person is less likely to be harassed by the police or falsely convicted.

Despite the obvious importance of eyewitness evidence, police receive inadequate training in conducting effective interviews with cooperative eyewitnesses (Sanders, 1986). A poll of American police departments revealed that more than half had no formal training whatsoever for newly appointed investigators (Rand Corporation, 1975). A comparable lack of systematic training was found for British police (Cahill & Mingay, 1986). Most textbooks in police science either completely omit the issue of effective interviewing techniques or provide only superficial coverage (although see Flanagan, 1981, and Wells, 1988, for notable exceptions).

How do police learn to conduct eyewitness interviews? Typically, they either observe and try to emulate the style of a senior officer or they learn by trial and error. Often they are given a checklist of evidence to be gathered and are left on their own, without guidance, to elicit the information. It should not be surprising that police investigators (and others equally untrained, like

The research described herein was supported by grants from the National Institute of Justice (USDJ-83-IJ-CX-0025 and USDJ-85-IJ-CX-0053) and the National Science Foundation (SES-8911146). We should like to thank Chief John Farrell and the participating detectives from the Robbery Division of the Metro-Dade Police Department for assisting in the field study. We should also like to thank our research assistants for their constructive input and hours of time required to interview, transcribe, and score the data: Heidi Holland, David McKinnon, Denise Chin, Kathy Quigley, and Petra Brock.

245

attorneys or accident investigators) frequently make avoidable mistakes and fail to elicit potentially valuable information.

In response to the need to improve police interview techniques, Fisher and Geiselman developed a new procedure based on the scientific literature of cognitive psychology (the Cognitive Interview: CI). This chapter reviews our work in developing the CI and is presented in five stages: I, The original Cognitive Interview; II, revisions of the original procedure; III, tests of the revised Cognitive Interview; IV, use in other investigative interviews; and V, practical applications. We review past research and present work currently in progress in our laboratories.

The original cognitive interview

Over the last two thousand years, persons interested in memory enhancement have developed a variety of mnemonics, ranging from the Greek's use of imagery to the more modern notions of depth of processing and organization. These mnemonics have proven effective in many learning tasks, but they are inappropriate for police investigation because they must be employed at the encoding or acquisition stage. Given the unpredictability of most crimes, the speed at which they occur, and their highly arousing nature, it is difficult to imagine that many eyewitnesses would intentionally employ mnemonics during the commission of a crime. To be used successfully in a criminal investigation, memory enhancing procedures must be applied at the retrieval phase of memory, after the crime has occurred. Only then is the recall task intentional (Klatzky, 1980) and the eyewitness composed enough to control his or her mental operations. Our search through the literature revealed no well documented retrieval mnemonics for meaningful material. As a result we took as our starting point general principles of cognition – and hence the name, Cognitive Interview.

Theoretical background of the Cognitive Interview

Two basic principles of memory guided the development of the CI. First, the effectiveness of a retrieval cue is related to the amount of feature overlap with the encoded event (Flexser & Tulving, 1978; Tulving & Thomson, 1973). Second, there may be several retrieval paths to the encoded event, so that information not accessible with one retrieval cue may be accessible with a different cue (Tulving, 1974).

Cognitive Interview instructions

Based on this theoretical framework, we developed an interview protocol containing four general memory enhancement instructions (Geiselman,

Fisher, Firstenberg, Hutton, Sullivan, Avetissian, & Prosk, 1984). Of these, two attempt to increase the feature overlap between encoding and retrieval contexts: mentally reinstating the environmental and personal context that existed at the time of the original event (Malpass & Devine, 1981; Smith, 1979), and reporting everything, even partial information, regardless of its perceived importance (Smith, 1983). The other two instructions encourage using many retrieval paths: recounting the events in a variety of orders (Whitten & Leonard, 1981), and reporting the events from a variety of perspectives (Anderson & Pichert, 1978). In addition to these general instructions, directions are given to assist recalling specific information (names, numbers, speech characteristics, appearance, and conversations). These specific techniques encourage eyewitnesses to think about particular features of the event. For example, to assist in recalling a name, eyewitnesses are asked to think about whether the name is short or long, common or uncommon; for recalling a number, eyewitnesses are asked to think about whether the number is even or odd, high or low.

Empirical research

Several laboratory experiments were conducted to compare the efficacy of the initial version of the CI to a standard police interview under controlled, yet realistic, conditions. In all these experiments volunteer witnesses observed one of four emotionally arousing films of a simulated crime (liquor store robbery, shoot-out in a bank, family dispute, or search through a warehouse). The films, approximately four minutes long, are the same as those used by the Los Angeles Police Department to train recruits in life-threatening situations.

Two days after viewing the filmed crime, the eyewitnesses returned to the laboratory where they were interviewed by experienced detectives about the persons, objects, and events contained in the crime. These interviews were tape-recorded, transcribed, and then scored for the number of correct and incorrect responses. Accuracy was determined by comparing the eyewitness's responses to the details as portrayed on the film.

The first major study compared the CI with a standard police interview and a hypnosis interview (Geiselman, Fisher, MacKinnon, & Holland, 1985). Eighty-nine college students served as the volunteer eyewitnesses, generating a total of more than one hundred and twenty hours of recorded interviews. The interviewers were seventeen experienced law enforcement agents all of whom had previously received a forty-hour course on forensic hypnosis and had conducted hundreds of field interviews prior to the experiment. Training in the CI consisted of reading a two-page handout and attending a group question-answer session lasting approximately thirty minutes. Eyewitnesses

Table 12.1. *Performance measures for cognitive, hypnosis, and standard interview procedures*

	Interview Procedure		
Variable	Cognitive	Hypnosis	Standard
Number correct	41.15	38.00	29.40
Number incorrect	7.30	5.90	6.10
Question time (minutes)	39.70	28.20	32.10

and interviewers were assigned randomly to one of the three interview conditions.

As seen in Table 12.1, both the CI and hypnosis elicited approximately 30 to 35 percent more correct answers than did the standard interview. The amount of incorrect information was approximately the same across conditions. The CI took somewhat longer to conduct than the hypnosis and standard interviews. Time did not account for the superiority of the CI, however, as the number of correct responses was greater in the CI than in the standard interview even after time was covaried out.

The preceding results were based on the total number of facts, irrespective of their importance to the crime depicted. Thus it is possible that some of the facts recalled were not essential to a police investigation – although note that the interviewers were experienced law enforcement agents whose task was to determine what occurred during the crime. Nevertheless, we rescored the data for only the twenty most important pieces of information about the crime (for example, descriptions of the assailants, weapons, central actions). The pattern of results was similar to the overall analysis. The CI and hypnosis interviews still elicited approximately 30 to 35 percent more correct information than did the standard interview (mean numbers of correct facts = 11.95, 12.35, 9.4 facts, respectively) and again with no significant differences in the number of incorrect facts.

It is interesting to note, especially in light of the superiority of hypnosis over the standard interview, that many of the hypnosis interviewers told the eyewitnesses to "take themselves back to when they first saw the film," an instruction akin to the CI request to reinstate the original context. Surprisingly, although all the interviewers had received training on conducting hypnosis interviews – and presumably on instructing eyewitnesses to "take themselves back" – those in the standard condition did not use this instruction. It is as if they believed the context-reinstatement instruction was an inseparable component of hypnosis and could not be used without first inducing hypnosis. Yuille and Kim (1987) also found that following induction of hypnosis, interviewers often instructed the eyewitnesses to reinstate the original context; they also instructed the eyewitnesses to "imagine the event from different perspectives" and "tell everything that came to mind" (p. 425), again overlapping the instructions of the CI. Although we cannot separate our hypnosis induction from the CI mnemonics in our study, others have suggested that hypnosis induction without the associated mnemonic instructions is of little value (for example, Timm, 1981). As Yuille and Kim concluded, "the cognitive interview is the 'active' memory component of hypnosis" (p. 427).

Several follow-up studies were conducted to examine the generalizability of these initial results to other populations. Geiselman, Fisher, MacKinnon, and Holland (1986) replicated the earlier procedure with adult witnesses who were not students and found essentially the same results (15 percent improvement over the standard police interview, with no increase in the number of incorrect responses). Geiselman and Padilla (1988) examined the technique with children between seven and twelve years of age, and again found the same pattern of results: 21 percent more correct facts recalled with the CI than with the standard interview, and approximately the same number of incorrect facts.

Until recently, all the empirical tests of the CI were conducted in our laboratories. In the past two years Kohnken and his colleagues have conducted independent replications with a German version of the technique. In their first study witnesses observed a film containing an innocuous scene of three men in an amusement arcade. When asked to recall this scene, those subjects given the CI recalled 38 percent more than those given a standard interview (Aschermann, Mantwill, & Kohnken, 1991). The superiority of the CI was greater for open-ended questions (73 percent advantage) than for specific closed questions (18 percent advantage), a pattern similar to that found in Geiselman et al. (1984). As in all our laboratory studies the number of incorrect responses did not differ significantly between the two types of interviews, although, as found by others, there were more errors when responding to closed questions (9.6) than to open-ended questions (3.1), regardless of interview type.

A follow-up study was conducted to eliminate the possibility that the superiority of the CI reflected a substandard quality in the standard interviews. This is especially problematic, as standard police interviews are known to contain a host of errors (Fisher, Geiselman, & Raymond, 1987a). To overcome this potential problem, Kohnken, Thuerer, and Zoberbier (unpublished data) provided extensive training (four hours) in basic principles of interviewing to both standard and Cognitive interviewers, complete with written and videotape materials and a practice session followed by a group discussion. The only difference is that those learning the CI were also instructed on specific memory-enhancement techniques. Despite the equivalent and extensive training provided, those interviewers who used the CI elicited more correct facts (mean = 112.9) than those given the standard training (74.2), again with no significant difference in the number of incorrect facts.

As far as we know, the original version of the CI has been found effective in at least seventeen separate eyewitness experiments, across a variety of events (live intrusions, simulated crimes) and eyewitnesses (adults, children, students, nonstudents, Americans, and Germans). In all but one of these studies, more total correct information was elicited with no increase in incorrect responding. Clearly, applying principles of cognition can enhance eyewitness recollection.

Revisions of the original procedure

The CI was an improvement over standard police procedures, but it still had many shortcomings. Much of the original event information was still unrecalled. In the CI condition of Geiselman et al. (1985), for instance, subjects recalled on the average only twelve of the twenty most important facts from the simulated crimes. The technique had been developed initially for laboratory use and did not take into account some of the practical obstacles faced by police investigators in the field. For example, real victims and witnesses of crime, as opposed to our laboratory subjects, often show symptoms of high anxiety, have poor communication skills, and seem to be unaware of their role in the interview. Given the limitations of the original CI and the differences between laboratory and field conditions, we revised the technique.

Revising the CI for field investigations required that we broaden our scope and provide guidance along a variety of issues in addition to the memory component of eyewitness recall. The revised CI therefore supplements the original version by addressing issues such as controlling the eyewitness's emotional state and improving communication between the eyewitness and the interviewer. Within the cognitive domain, we have also expanded our interests to overcome problems of limited attention and verbal skills.

Reflecting this broader scope, the revised technique has become increasingly eclectic, borrowing liberally from the literature in social psychology, and adopting some practical techniques used by clinical psychologists, journalists, and so forth. In addition to examining the formal literature, we also perused hundreds of hours of tape-recorded interviews conducted by us, by research assistants, or by law enforcement agents either in the laboratory or in the field. In so doing we modeled good and poor interviewers (as defined by the amount of information gathered), building on techniques used by good interviewers and excising those used by poor interviewers (see Fisher et al., 1987a, for an analysis).

The revised CI builds on the four basic techniques of the original version: reinstating the original context, reporting everything, describing the event in a variety of temporal orders, and from different personal perspectives. To minimize the possibility that the latter two techniques (varying order and perspective) might encourage fabrication, and as a general safeguard against guessing, eyewitnesses are explicitly cautioned not to fabricate answers.

Most of the additional principles of the revised CI fall into one of three categories: memory and general cognition, social dynamics between the interviewer and the eyewitness, and communication. Because of space limitations, we include only superficial descriptions of the underlying principles and a sampling of the most important interviewing techniques. A complete description of the revised CI, including a more thorough analysis of the relevant principles and an explanation of how the various techniques instantiate the principles, is provided in Fisher and Geiselman (1992).

Memory and general cognition

Limited mental resources. People have only limited mental resources to process information (Baddeley, 1986; Kahneman, 1973). Therefore any sources of distraction may interfere with the eyewitness's retrieval of events from memory (Johnston, Greenberg, Fisher, & Martin, 1970; Jou & Harris, 1992). Similarly, anything that interferes with the interviewer's mental resources detracts from his or her ability to conduct the interview effectively. Some of the specific interviewing techniques suggested to minimize distractions are: not interrupting in the middle of the eyewitness's response, asking open-ended questions, and conducting the interview in a quiet location.

Multiple coding and guided imagery. Each eyewitness may have several mental representations of the target event (Fisher & Chandler, 1991). Some representations are highly detailed and reflect the minute, sensory properties of an isolated episode within the complex event; others are more generic and reflect a more abstract, meaningful interpretation of the event (compare Paivio's [1971] dual-coding hypothesis). To induce recall based on the more detailed, sensory representations, the interviewer encourages the eyewitness to close his or her eyes and use mental imagery (including nonvisual images), and explicitly requests a detailed response.

Witness-compatible questioning. Each eyewitness's mental representation of an event is unique and depends on his or her particular cognitive, emotional, and physiological context at the time of encoding. The interviewer must therefore tailor the questions to the unique mental representation of the particular eyewitness instead of asking all eyewitnesses the same set of questions. A corollary of this principle is that at any time during the interview, only one of the eyewitness's mental representations is in an activated state (compare Kintsch & van Dijk, 1978). Recollection is facilitated if the interviewer's questions are compatible with the particular mental representation currently activated. For example, if the eyewitness is currently describing the assailant's face then the next several questions must concern the assailant's face. Questions unrelated to the assailant's face (for example, about the gun or get-away car) must be held in abeyance.

Social dynamics between the interviewer and the eyewitness

Knowledge of event-specific content. By definition, the eyewitness has some firsthand knowledge of the crime not available to the interviewer. Therefore the eyewitness, not the interviewer, should be doing most of the mental work entailed in the interview and directing the flow of information. In practice, the roles are often reversed and the eyewitness sits passively waiting for the interviewer to ask the next question. Interviewers can encourage eyewitnesses to become more active by asking open-ended questions, not interrupting during their responses, and permitting eyewitnesses to engage in tangential narration.

Knowledge of crime-relevant information. The eyewitness knows more about the details of the specific crime, but the interviewer knows better which dimensions of the crime are important for the investigation. The interviewer therefore must guide the eyewitness's report to such relevant dimensions without dominating the interview. Techniques to accomplish this are: framing questions to address informative content, asking closed questions strategically (to complete answers to open-ended questions), and explicitly conveying to the eyewitness the interviewer's need for detailed responses.

In addition to the above, the revised CI addresses some of the critical social skills that are particularly important when interviewing victims of crime: developing rapport, maintaining the eyewitness's confidence, and controlling the eyewitness's anxiety.

Communication

Once the conditions for effective information processing and for proper social dynamics between the interviewer and the eyewitness have been established there still remains the problem of the eyewitness communicating his or her recollection to the interviewer. A parallel issue is that the interviewer must convey the investigative needs to the eyewitness. The following principles will assist the eyewitness in providing an extensive, detailed description.

Promoting extensive responses. Speakers often pause during narrative descriptions to organize the remainder of their response (Ford & Holmes, 1978). Any interruption during this pause, even to ask a follow-up question, may cut short additional information that would have been forthcoming. Interviewers may promote more extensive answers by remaining silent during these pauses or by a simple utterance encouraging witnesses to extend their responses (for example, "OK," "continue," "mm-hmm").

Using nonverbal responding. The traditional interview is marked by a series of verbal exchanges between the interviewer and the eyewitness. By relying exclusively on the verbal medium, however, the quality of the interview is limited by the eyewitness's vocabulary. This is particularly so for eyewitnesses whose verbal skills are impoverished. Even articulate eyewitnesses are limited, since some events or objects are difficult to describe verbally (Leibowitz & Guzy, 1990). To overcome this limitation, eyewitnesses should be encouraged to use nonverbal methods to replace or supplement their verbal responses. For instance, eyewitnesses might be asked to draw a sketch of the location, to move an object (for example, a model of a car) to convey its direction of motion, or to act out a movement. The interviewer can videotape the nonverbal response or ask the eyewitness to verbalize what he or she has just portrayed. Ideally, the medium and format of responding should be compatible with the eyewitness's mental representation of the object or event. Such compatibility minimizes the number of transformations required to translate the mental representation into an overt response (compare ideo-motor theory, Greenwald, 1970).

Sequence of the Cognitive Interview

In addition to the specific techniques mentioned above, the revised CI follows an order intended to coordinate the individual techniques. The general strategy of the interview is to guide the eyewitness to those memory codes richest in relevant information and facilitate communication when the codes have been activated. The CI is divided into five sections, each of which makes a unique contribution to attaining the overall goal.

1. The introduction establishes the appropriate psychological states and interpersonal dynamics required to promote effective memory and communication during the remainder of the interview.
2. An open-ended narration permits the interviewer to infer the eyewitness's overall representation of the event and to develop an efficient strategy for probing the various memory codes.
3. The probing stage is the primary information gathering phase during which the interviewer guides the eyewitness to the richest sources of knowledge and thoroughly exhausts them of their contents.
4. In the review stage, the interviewer reviews the information already recorded to check on its accuracy. This also provides the eyewitness with an additional opportunity to recall the events.
5. When closing the interview, the interviewer fulfills any official police requirements, offers a suggestion to extend the functional life of the interview, and tries to leave the eyewitness with a positive, last impression.

Compared to the original version, the revised version of the CI makes many more demands on the interviewer and is more difficult to learn. The current training is covered in two six-hour days and includes lecture, demonstrations, practice exercises, and group feedback. We believe that the greater effectiveness of the revised version is due to both the additional content and the improved training methods (Fisher, Geiselman, Raymond, Jurkevich, & Warhaftig, 1987b; George, 1991).

Tests of the revised Cognitive Interview

Because of its newness, the revised version of the CI has less empirical support than does the original version. In one important way, however, the support for the revised version is of greater practical consequence because the studies have been conducted in both the laboratory and in the field, with real victims and witnesses of crime. We report these completed studies below; in addition we report some ongoing research to expand the technique to other related eyewitness tasks (constructing facial composites and person identification tests).

The first test of the revised CI was a laboratory study under conditions that were similar to the earlier tests conducted by Geiselman et al. (1985, 1986). In this study (Fisher et al. 1987b) undergraduate students saw a videotape of a simulated crime (either a bank robbery or a liquor store robbery). Two days later they returned to the laboratory and were interviewed. Half of the subjects received the original version of the CI and half received the revised version.

The interviewers, high school and college students with no prior experience conducting investigative interviews, were trained to conduct both versions of the CI. Training on the original version entailed listening to several tape recordings conducted by the best police interviewers from our earlier studies. The interviewers received the same thirty-minute training session given to the police interviewers in the earlier studies. Training on the revised version required about ten hours, and entailed studying a list of positive and negative suggestions similar to those described here, and observing demonstrations of the various techniques. In both the original and revised versions, training concluded with the interviewers practicing the appropriate techniques and receiving feedback on their performance. Finally the interviewers conducted two sets of practice interviews, one with the original and one with the revised version, until they felt comfortable with each.

As in the earlier studies, the experimental interviews were tape-recorded and scored by comparing the transcripts with the videotaped crimes. The revised technique yielded approximately 45 percent more correct information than did the original version (mean number of facts = 57.5 and 39.6, respectively), with no significant loss of accuracy (12.0 versus 9.4 errors). The revised CI took somewhat (although nonsignificantly) longer to conduct than the original version (38.5 versus 29.3 min). An analysis of covariance showed the revised version to be superior even after time was covaried out, although the effect was attenuated somewhat.

Compared to a standard police interview (from similar conditions in Geiselman et al., 1985), the revised CI elicited almost twice as much information (96 percent increase), again with no loss of accuracy. This almost twofold increase in information is even more startling when one considers that the standard interview (from Geiselman et al.) was conducted by experienced detectives whereas the revised CI was conducted by high school and undergraduate students with approximately ten hours of training. It has been suggested that perhaps the college-aged subjects felt less intimidated and therefore recalled more when being interviewed by someone their own age (in Fisher et al.) than by older police detectives (Geiselman et al.). This seems unlikely, since performance was almost identical in the condition common to the two studies (original CI).

Fisher et al. (1987b) is the only study that directly compares the original and revised versions of the CI. A more indirect comparison can be made by matching the results from two studies with overlapping conditions, one study comparing the standard and original CI and the other study comparing the standard and revised CI. In two such studies with children as eyewitnesses, the original version of the CI elicited 26 percent more correct facts than a standard interview (Geiselman, Saywitz, & Bornstein, in press), whereas the revised version of the CI elicited 84 percent more correct facts than a standard interview (McCauley & Fisher, 1992). Admittedly this comparison is tenuous as it relies on two different studies. Further, children served as the eyewitnesses. Nevertheless the extent to which the revised CI exceeds the original CI is similar to the 46 percent advantage found in the direct comparison (Fisher et al., 1987b).

Another laboratory study was conducted in England to compare the revised CI with standard (British) police techniques and with another innovative technique currently being used in some British police departments, Conversation Management. According to George (1991) Conversation Management is intended to improve the interviewer's social and communication skills. As currently taught, it covers the following topics in a five-day training program: feedback, body language, respect for the individual, hidden agenda, encouragement, topic changing, conversational styles, question types, probing, obtaining microdetail, effective use of the pause, question pacing, interaction of personality types, resistance, and others (see Shepherd, 1991, for additional information). Some of these topics (for example, pausing, pacing, probing, question types) are also covered in the CI training, whereas others (for example, hidden agenda, body language, resistance, interaction of personality types) are unique to Conversation Management. One important conceptual difference between the two procedures is that the CI is geared exclusively to interviewing cooperative eyewitnesses whereas Conversation Management is directed primarily to interviewing suspects.

In George's study college students observed two actors interrupt a lecture. Two weeks later the student eyewitnesses returned to the laboratory for interviews. Approximately one-third of the eyewitnesses were interviewed by experienced detectives who conducted standard interviews; one-third were interviewed by detectives trained on the CI 1; and one-third by detectives trained on both the CI and Conversation Management.

The recorded responses were scored separately for event information (actions) and for descriptions of the two intruders. The total amount of correct information showed a superiority of the CI (mean number of facts = 67.5) and combined CI-Conversation Management (70.8) over the standard interview (49.8), with no reliable difference between the CI and the combined group. The same pattern held for each of the three measures, with some minor variation. The combined group was slightly better than the CI group for event information, and the CI group was slightly better for one of the intruders. The total number of errors was approximately the same for the standard (mean = 7.75) and CI groups (7.25), and slightly, but nonsignificantly, higher for the combined groups (10.71).

Having demonstrated that the revised CI is effective in a laboratory setting, we conducted a test in the field where conditions may be rather different. One might argue that laboratory studies are biased against standard police interviewing techniques, as these techniques have evolved to meet the realistic conditions found in the field, not the ideal conditions found in the laboratory. If so, the field is the more appropriate venue for testing the CI.

The field study (Fisher, Geiselman, & Amador, 1989) was conducted with sixteen experienced detectives from the Robbery Division of the Metro-Dade Police Department. In the typical case examined, the eyewitness was the victim or witness of a purse-snatching or commercial robbery. In most instances, the eyewitness had been interviewed at least once before, usually by a less experienced uniformed police officer. The follow-up detectives' interviews were conducted between two hours and four days after the crime.

In the initial phase of the study the detectives tape-recorded four to six interviews. Based on their performance in these interviews and on their supervisors' ratings, the detectives were divided into two equivalent groups. One group of seven detectives received training on the revised CI; the other group of nine detectives did not receive this additional training. The training was not so rigorous as that described earlier and currently in use (with practice exercises and group feedback) but consisted of four two-hour sessions of lectures and demonstrations of good and poor interviewing techniques. Following training, the detectives conducted a practice interview in the field and received feedback on their technique. Practice-plus-feedback appears to be an integral part of training, as many of the techniques we described in the lecture-demonstration sessions were not implemented properly in the practice interview. Many detectives denied that they made such errors until they

Table 12.2. *Number of facts elicited by trained and untrained detectives*

Training group	Training phase	
	Before	After
Trained	26.83	39.57
Untrained	23.75	24.21

listened to their taped interviews. After the feedback session, all the detectives again tape-recorded their next several interviews with victims and witnesses. The taped interviews were then transcribed and scored blind for the number of crime-relevant facts.

Qualitatively, the interviews conducted by the untrained detectives resembled those found in an earlier analysis of field interviews (Fisher et al., 1987a; George, 1991). The interview began with the interviewer asking the eyewitness for an open-ended description of the crime. A few seconds into the eyewitness's narration, the format changed and the interview evolved into a succession of closed, short-answer questions on the order of: How tall was he? How much did he weigh? What color was his shirt? and so forth. This staccato style of brief-questions–brief-answers continued until the end of the interview when the interviewer usually asked: Is there anything else you can remember about the event? By comparison, interviewers in the CI asked fewer questions. Of those questions asked a greater percentage were open-ended (for example, Can you describe his clothing?). Not surprisingly, the eyewitnesses' responses tended to be longer and more detailed.

The results can be evaluated by comparing the number of facts elicited before versus after training for only those detectives who received training; in addition, we can compare the number of facts elicited by the trained versus the untrained detectives (see Table 12.2). As a group, the trained detectives collected 48 percent more information after training than before. Of the seven trained detectives, six improved dramatically (34 to 115 percent improvement). Only the detective who did not change his interviewing style – and continued to ask primarily closed questions – failed to improve. A post hoc examination did not reveal any obvious pattern as to why some interviewers improved more than others (compare Fisher et al., 1987b).

The second analysis reflects the phase and training interaction. The trained and untrained detectives were equivalent before training, but the trained group collected 63 percent more information after training.

These analyses reflect the additional information elicited by the posttrained detectives. Perhaps these posttrained interviews were unusually easy cases, the viewing conditions were better, or the eyewitnesses had better verbal skills. If so, this should be apparent in other interviews with the same eyewitnesses, as in the earlier interview conducted by the uniformed police officers. As an unbiased measure of the quality of the detective's interview, we scored the transcripts in terms of how much additional information the detective elicited compared with the uniformed officer. Each statement elicited by the detective was categorized as being either the same as in the uniformed officer's report (*same*), different from that reported by the uniformed officer (*different*), or containing new information not described in the uniformed officer's report (*new*). More facts were elicited in the posttrained interviews, but only for *new* information, facts that the uniformed officer had not uncovered. There were no differences for *same* and *different* information. *Same* information, which duplicates the uniformed officer's report, provides no new insights for the investigation because that information has already been gathered. *Different* information just casts doubt on the reliability of the eyewitness or investigative procedures (although see Fisher & Cutler, 1992, showing that consistency and accuracy are not necessarily strongly related). That the superiority of the posttrained interviews occurred only for *new* information supports the practical utility of the CI.

Another practical concern for using the CI is the amount of time required. In the present study the posttrained interviews of the trained detectives (11.47 minutes) were not significantly longer than their pretrained interviews (10.65 minutes) or than those conducted by the untrained detectives (9.05 minutes). Of the seven trained detectives, four took more time to conduct posttrained than pretrained interviews and three took less time. That interview time was approximately equivalent before and after training seems to rule out interviewer motivation as an explanation of the effect of training. If posttrained detectives were more motivated than pretrained (or untrained) detectives one would expect them to conduct longer interviews. Similarly, one might expect them to ask more questions, which also did not occur. In fact, detectives asked fewer questions after training (see George, 1991, for an analysis of number of questions asked).

In comparison to laboratory research, field studies do not permit us to determine the accuracy of the elicited information. We therefore estimated accuracy by determining the degree to which statements were corroborated by other witnesses to the crimes. In twenty-two cases there was another victim or witness of the crime whose description was recorded on the police crime report. In all there were 325 statements that could be corroborated. Overall, the corroboration rates (percentage of elicited facts corroborated by other witnesses) were extremely high, and were comparable for both the pretrained (93.0 percent) and posttrained (94.5 percent) interviews.

Note that the corroboration rates are extremely high in comparison with the accuracy rates reported in typical laboratory studies (80 to 85 percent).

Table 12.3. *Change in interviewing style from before to after training in the Cognitive Interview*

Measure	Training phase	
	Before	After
Number of questions per minute	4.70 (4.64)	1.53 (4.97)
Proportion of open-ended questions	.05 (.04)	.47 (.07)
Number of pauses[a] per 10 questions	.01 (.00)	.13 (.04)
Number of leading questions per interview	1.55 (1.50)	.12 (.78)

Note: Mean score for the other three conditions (no additional training, CM only, CI + CM) are given in parentheses.
[a]Pause = a minimum of one second of silence after a question or a response.
Source: George, 1991.

High accuracy rates were also reported in field studies by Yuille and Cutshall (1986) and Yuille and Kim (1987). Although not definitive, it is interesting that the accuracy corroboration rates in the three field studies of eyewitness memory are considerably higher than their laboratory counterparts. If this difference between laboratory and field studies is replicated, one may question the validity of citing in court as evidence of the general unreliability of eye-witness testimony the accuracy rates found in the laboratory (compare McCloskey & Egeth, 1983).

An independent field study of the CI was conducted by George (1991) with British police officers. Thirty-two experienced police officers representing different areas of investigation and different police departments were assigned randomly to one of four training conditions: CI only, Conversation Management (CM) only, both CI and CM (CI+CM), or no additional training. Following training, each police officer tape-recorded three interviews with victims or witnesses of street crimes. The tapes were transcribed and scored for type of question (open-ended versus closed), use of specific techniques (for example, pauses, instructions to close eyes), interview time, and amount of information.

The questioning style changed dramatically from before training to after training in the CI group. Compared to their interviewing style before training, the CI group after training asked fewer questions, asked a higher proportion of open-ended questions, injected more pauses, and asked fewer leading questions (this occurred in all four groups, but the largest reduction was for the CI group) (see Table 12.3). Although the questioning style changed, there was no change in the time required to conduct the interview (before training, 20.6 minutes; after training, 17.2 minutes) in the CI group.

As we had done earlier, George examined only those eyewitness statements relevant to the investigation. Unlike us, George is an experienced police officer (Detective Inspector with the City of London Police Department). Thus, whereas critics may question our judgment about the investigative relevance of a statement, they should be reasonably confident with George's evaluations.

George parsed the responses in the field study into whether they addressed a who, what, when, where, why, or how question. The pattern was the same for all categories of information: The CI elicited more information than did the standard police interview, whether comparing trained to untrained interviewers (14 percent advantage) or trained detectives before and after training (55 percent advantage). By comparison, neither CM nor the combined CI + CM group elicited more information than the untrained group. These groups also did not change their interviewing style very much from before to after training. This is especially enigmatic for the combined CI + CM group, as they received training in the CI as part of their training package. It is not apparent to us why additional training on CM would diminish the effects of CI training, particular given George's earlier laboratory study where detectives trained on both CI and CM performed the same as those trained on only CI.

One major advantage of George's field study over ours is that George scored the interviews for specific CI techniques employed by the interviewer. That is, although those trained in the CI were taught all the different techniques not all of them used every recommended technique. By examining the amount of information elicited when various techniques were and were not used, George was able to isolate the effectiveness of various component techniques. In this analysis he found evidence in favor of the recommendations to use more open-ended questions, reinstate context (see also Geiselman et al., 1986), use guided imagery, and instruct eyewitnesses to "work hard and concentrate." Two of the recommended instructions to respondents were used too infrequently by interviewers to evaluate: change perspective and order of responding, and not to edit responses (although see Geiselman et al., 1986, for supportive evidence). No data are reported about any of the remaining techniques.

Thus far, the CI has been used successfully to elicit more information from an eyewitness when describing the perpetrator or the event itself. Typically this marks the initial phase of the police investigation. Following this, police may ask the eyewitness to help construct a facial composite of the perpetrator, and/or identify the perpetrator from a photo array or live lineup. We describe two recent sets of studies examining the CI in these tasks.

Constructing facial composites

Luu and Geiselman (unpublished data) tried to enhance facial composites by using elements of the CI with the Field Identification System (FIS). The FIS is a facial composite system that permits eyewitnesses to examine individual facial features either in the context of other facial features (encouraging holistic processing) or in isolation (encouraging specific-feature processing). Experimental subjects saw a videotape of a simulated purse snatching and then attempted to construct a composite image of the perpetrator using the FIS. Some subjects formed the composite by examining the features in the context of the entire face and others examined features in isolation. Within each of these groups, some subjects were instructed to "think about the face of the suspect" while constructing the composite, whereas others were instructed to use elements of the CI: reconstruct the original viewing context, report everything, search for the best overall image of the target face, think of alternative images of the face, recall the events in reverse order, and change personal perspective. A second group of subjects evaluated the resulting composites by rating them on a one to five scale of likeness to a picture of the target face (1 = not very much like the face; 5 = very much like the face). The results showed that the CI increased the likeness ratings, but only in the face-context condition (mean likeness rating = 2.81; mean rating for the other three conditions = 2.20). Surprisingly, the CI suppressed performance slightly (nonsignificantly) in the isolated-feature condition (mean rating = 2.08). The positive effect with the face-context condition, coupled with Davies and Milne's (1985) finding that instructions to recreate the original viewing conditions enhanced facial composites, suggests the possibility that some variant of the CI might be employed successfully to improve facial composites. At this point the evidence is not extensive enough to make such a claim with much confidence.

Identifying suspects from lineups and photo arrays

Two experiments examined use of the CI for the final stage of the investigative process, identifying the suspect. In the first experiment (Fisher, Quigley, Brock, Chin, & Cutler, 1990) witnesses observed a staged theft. Two days later they tried to describe the suspect and identify him from a four-person lineup. Half the witnesses were given the revised CI before attempting to identify the thief and half were asked simply (unaided) to describe the thief before identifying him. Although witnesses provided better descriptions with the CI than in the unaided interview (mean number of facts correctly recalled = 5.8 versus 3.2, respectively) there were no differences in the identification scores. The CI witnesses were correct on 61 percent of the lineups and the unaided group on 64 percent. We postulated two hypotheses to explain this failure to improve identification: The CI improves access to verbal information, but face recognition is mediated by pictorial information; and the CI facilitates accessing specific features (for example, eye color), but face recognition is mediated by holistic information (overall shape) (Wells & Turtle, 1988).

These hypotheses were tested in a follow-up study in which we altered the CI to encourage witnesses to concentrate more thoroughly on developing pictorial information rather than translating into verbal descriptions, and to think in terms of holistic properties of the face rather than specific features. In this study, two days after viewing a videotape of a robbery witnesses tried to identify the suspect from a five-person lineup. Again, there were no differences: The CI witnesses were correct on 63 percent of the trials and the unaided witnesses on 65 percent. Two additional studies were conducted, and the results remained unchanged: The CI did not improve identification from lineups or photo arrays.

Chin (personal communication) suggested that face recognition cannot be improved substantially by altering the eyewitness's retrieval processes with verbal instructions. This explanation appears to be incompatible with the findings of others that some strategic manipulations (notably, context reinstatement) do improve eyewitness identification (for example, Malpass & Devine, 1981). One possible explanation of the discrepancy is that in our studies, we only encouraged eyewitnesses to reconstruct the original context, whereas others either provided actual physical cues from the original context (Krafka & Penrod, 1985) or provided material information to correct eyewitnesses when they erred in attempting to recreate the original context (Malpass & Devine, 1981). In support of Chin's suggestion, Smith and Vela (1992) showed that verbal instructions to recreate context did not enhance identification, whereas physically recreating the original context did.

The research on the revised CI shows it to be more effective than the original CI, Conversation Management, and standard police interviewing techniques. Perhaps its major asset is that it can and has been used effectively in field investigations by police to elicit more eyewitness information. Furthermore, the field evidence does not seem to be vitiated by either a decrease in accuracy (corroboration) or an excessive increase in the time required to conduct the interview.

The technique appears to be limited to the initial phase of the investigation, when the eyewitness is attempting to describe the perpetrator or the event. Some preliminary evidence suggests that it may also assist in constructing facial composites; however, that evidence is limited to only one study. Thus far, we have no evidence that it can enhance the later stage of investigation, attempting to identify the suspect from a lineup or photo array.

The Cognitive Interview in other investigative interviews

Because the CI is based on general principles of cognition, the technique should be applicable to situations other than interviewing adult eyewitnesses about a crime. We describe briefly some of our research in which the eye-witnesses were children or the event in question was a noncriminal act.

Children as eyewitnesses

In recent years an increasing number of children have been asked to testify, especially about events in which they were alleged to be victims. We therefore examined the revised CI with children, with slight modifications to accommodate their specific processing abilities. Toward this aim we primed children to provide more elaborate responses by practicing giving a detailed response to a well-known activity (brushing their teeth) before describing the experimental event.

In the first experiment (McCauley & Fisher, 1992) seven-year-old children interacted with an adult experimenter by going through a series of actions in the form of a Simon-says game. Two weeks later the children were interviewed about the Simon-says activities either in the standard format used by investigative interviewers or by the revised CI techniques as modified for children. The children who received the CI recalled correctly almost twice as many actions (15.56) as those who received the standard interview (8.44). The number of incorrect facts reported was surprisingly small and similar for the two groups (mean number of errors = 0.55). To ensure that the standard interview was similar to a real interview, in a second experiment we asked members of the local State Attorney's office who are responsible for conducting such children's interviews to construct an interview protocol modeling their own procedures. A preliminary analysis of the first eighteen subjects found that the CI elicited almost twice as many correct actions as the standard interview (14.6 versus 8.3, respectively). As an additional control we asked two experienced interviewers from the children's division of the local State Attorney's office to interview several children. They elicited 7.14 facts per child, comparable to our control and less than half the number elicited with the CI, which was conducted by undergraduate research assistants with minimal training. The number of errors again was low and similar across all three conditions (mean errors per interview = 0.83).

Noncriminal investigations

It seems reasonable to assume that memory and communication processes used by eyewitnesses to describe a criminal event are similar to those used to describe other episodic, but noncriminal, events. If so, the CI ought to extend to a wide variety of investigative interviews. Two such situations are described here: an eyewitness to a car accident and an ill person recalling the foods eaten at an earlier meal.

In the first of these studies (Fisher, Cutler, & Brock, unpublished data) undergraduate students watched a short videotape including a fifteen-second excerpt of a car accident. They were then interviewed either with the revised CI or with a standard protocol modeled after that used by investigators from the National Transportation Safety Board. All the witnesses were interviewed twice: five minutes after viewing the accident and two weeks later. Half the subjects received the same type of interview on the two occasions (both CI or both standard) and half received different types of interviews (standard on the first interview and CI on the second, or vice versa). Because each witness was interviewed twice, we can examine the effectiveness of the CI at each interview and also whether or not there is any carryover effect. That is, if the CI elicits more information than the standard interview on the first interview, will that advantage transfer to the second interview?

The results showed that for each interview almost twice as many correct facts were elicited with the CI as with the standard interview. On the first interview the CI elicited a mean of 25.9 correct facts whereas the standard interview elicited 14.9 correct facts. The scores were almost identical on the second interview: CI = 24.6 and standard = 14.8. It is interesting that there was almost no forgetting from the first (five-minute delay) to the second (two-week delay) interview, perhaps reflecting the memory-enhancing effects of the initial retrieval attempt (Fisher & Chandler, 1991).

As opposed to the findings in all our prior eyewitness studies, we observed here that more errors were elicited with the CI than with the standard interview. For the first interview, the mean number of errors elicited by the CI and the standard interview were 10.4 and 6.1, respectively; for the second, the error scores were 10.5 and 6.8. Note that although the CI elicited more errors than did the standard interview, the rate of inaccuracy (number of errors divided by total number of responses) was approximately the same for the CI (.29) and the standard interview (.30).

Although the CI elicited more correct information than did the standard on the first interview, there was no carryover effect to the second interview. The CI/CI group did not recall significantly more correct information on the second interview (mean = 24.0) than did the standard/CI group (22.9), and the CI/standard (15.0) group did not recall significantly more than did the standard/standard group (14.1). Similarly, the additional errors elicited by the CI on the first interview did not carry over to the second interview. Thus, any advantage conferred by conducting the CI is restricted to that particular interview.

In the second noncriminal study (Fisher & Quigley, 1991) we simulated an investigation of an outbreak of food poisoning, where health officials interview ill people to track down the source of contaminated food. Twenty-six volunteers ate a variety of (uncontaminated) foods and were interviewed four to fourteen days later to determine which foods they had eaten earlier. Half the respondents were not provided with any clues to assist in remembering the foods; the others were given a modified CI that was geared toward the types of activities in selecting and eating foods (for example, How did you decide which foods to select? What did the plate look like?). The CI group correctly recalled twice as many foods as the unaided group (12.22 versus 5.92) with no significant difference in the number of intrusions (1.77 versus 1.69). The CI group also recognized more of the foods from a menu of potential foods (Hit rates = .83 versus .75) with comparable false alarm rates (.03 versus .05).

The CI has now been shown to enhance recollection in both a recognition task (of foods eaten) and in a face construction task (composite images). Nevertheless, it has not been at all effective in a task requiring recognition of faces. Apparently, there is something unique in the face recognition task not found in recognition tasks in general or in other memory tasks using faces.

Practical applications

Research to develop the CI began as a purely applied project with a narrow focus: to enhance the recollection of eyewitnesses to crime. Because it has been successful in this task – or at least more so than other techniques currently available – we recommend that police departments consider its adoption for training investigators (see also George, 1991). Suggested training guidelines are described in Fisher and Geiselman (1992). Further, although we have referred to the CI as an information-gathering device for the prosecution (police), the technique should be equally useful for the defense as it is not biased toward eliciting exculpatory evidence.

Limitations

Although the CI has the potential to be an effective investigative instrument, its utility will vary from one situation to another. Its primary contribution will be in cases like commercial robbery, assault or battery, where the bulk of the evidence comes from eyewitness reports, as opposed to crimes where there is an abundance of physical evidence. Second, the CI was designed to be used with cooperative eyewitnesses. Those who wish to withhold information intentionally will not be "broken" by the CI. Third, a fair amount of time is required to conduct the CI properly. Thus, it cannot be used effectively when time is limited. Finally, the CI requires considerable mental concentration on the part of the interviewer. He or she must make more on-line decisions and show greater flexibility than is typically demanded in police interviews. It is thus more difficult to conduct the CI than the standard interview. Concomitantly, more time and resources will be required to train detectives to use the CI than is currently devoted to interviewer training.

Whether such additional training is worthwhile is a policy decision that only police and other potential users can make.

Legal challenges

We expect that use of the CI to enhance eyewitness recollection will be challenged in court, probably citing the same problems as those attributed to hypnosis (Buckhout, personal communication). One might even argue that the CI is simply hypnosis in disguise.

The major reservations about using hypnosis are that it is unreliable as a memory enhancer (see Smith, 1983 for a review), it leads to increased error or confabulation (for example, Dywan & Bowers, 1984), and it renders eyewitnesses hypersuggestible to leading questions (for example, Putnam, 1979). Fortunately, none of these objections has been found with the CI. In twenty-three of the twenty-four experiments that we are aware of (seventeen by Fisher and/or Geiselman, four by Kohnken, two by George, and one by Memon) the CI has led to more information than has a standard interview. Note that this holds only when eyewitnesses are attempting to describe people or events, not when they are attempting to identify people from lineups or photo arrays. In twenty-two of the twenty-four studies, there were no reliable differences between the number of errors elicited by the Cognitive and standard interviews. If anything, the error rates (percentage of responses that were incorrect) were lower in the CI than the standard interview. Fewer leading questions were asked when police conducted the CI than when they conducted a standard interview in the field (George, 1991). In the one laboratory study where (mis)leading questions were intentionally introduced, those eyewitnesses given the original CI were less influenced by the (mis)leading information than were those given the standard interview (Geiselman, Fisher, Cohen, Holland & Surtes, 1986). Thus, the concern about suggestibility to leading questions argues in favor of, not in opposition to, using the CI.

Conclusion

Research in developing the CI is still in its infancy. It has generally been found successful as a memory enhancer, but only in a limited number of conditions. We have examined retention intervals of up to fourteen days, but obviously many real-life interviews occur after much longer delays. We have tested young adults and children, but oftentimes victims are elderly. More research certainly needs to be done to refine the procedure and to expand and define its domain of effectiveness.

Our bias has been to explore the cognitive end of the task, but clearly, other dimensions could contribute significantly to improving the technique.

Finally, although our initial bias was to rely almost exclusively on theoretical input, we have found repeatedly that many practitioners used idiosyncratic techniques that were as effective as those tied directly to theory. We encourage other researchers and practitioners to apply their insights to develop an improved version of the CI.

References

Anderson, R. C., & Pichert, J. W. (1978). Recall of previously unrecallable information following a shift in perspective. *Journal of Verbal Learning and Verbal Behavior, 17,* 1–12.

Aschermann, E., Mantwill, M., & Kohnken, G. (1991). An independent replication of the cognitive interview. *Applied Cognitive Psychology, 5,* 489–495.

Baddeley, A. D. (1986). *Working memory.* Oxford: Oxford University Press.

Cahill, D., & Mingay, D. J. (1986). Leading questions and the police interview. *Policing,* Autumn, 212–224.

Davies, G. & Milne, A. (1985). Eyewitness composite production: A function of mental or physical reinstatement of context. *Criminal Justice and Behavior, 12,* 209–220.

Dywan, J., & Bowers, K. S. (1983). The use of hypnosis to enhance recall. *Science, 222,* 184–185.

Fisher, R. P., & Chandler, C. C. (1991). Independence between recalling interevent relations and specific events. *Journal of Experimental Psychology: Learning, Memory, & Cognition, 17,* 722–733.

Fisher, R. P., & Cutler, B. L. (1992). *The relation between consistency and accuracy of eyewitness testimony.* Third European Conference of Law and Psychology, Oxford.

Fisher, R. P., & Geiselman, R. E. (1992). *Memory-enhancing techniques for investigative interviewing.* Springfield, IL: Charles C. Thomas.

Fisher, R. P., Geiselman, R. E., & Amador, M. (1989). Field test of the cognitive interview: Enhancing the recollection of actual victims and witnesses of crime. *Journal of Applied Psychology, 74,* 722–727.

Fisher, R. P., Geiselman, R. E., & Raymond, D. S. (1987a). Analysis of police interview techniques. *Journal of Science and Administration. 15,* 177–185.

Fisher, R. P., Geiselman, R. E., Raymond, D. S., Jurkevich, L. M., & Warhaftig, M. L. (1987b). Enhancing enhanced eyewitness memory: Refining the cognitive interview. *Journal of Police Science and Administration. 15,* 291–297.

Fisher, R. P., & Quigley, K. L. (1991). Applying cognitive theory in public health investigations: Enhancing food recall. In J. Tanur (Ed.), *Questions about Questions.* New York: Sage Press.

Fisher, R. P., Quigley, K. L., Brock, P., Chin, D., & Cutler, B. L. (1990). *The effectiveness of the cognitive interview in description and identification tasks.* Paper presented at the American Psychology–Law Society, Williamsburg, Virginia.

Flanagan, E. J. (1981). Interviewing and interrogation techniques. In E. J. Grau (Ed.), *Criminal and civil investigation handbook.* New York: McGraw-Hill.

Flexser, A. J., & Tulving, E. (1978). Retrieval independence in recognition and recall. *Psychological Review, 85,* 153–172.

Ford, M., & Holmes, V. M. (1978). Planning units and syntax in sentence production. *Cognition, 6,* 35–53.

Geiselman, R. E., Fisher, R. P., Cohen, G., Holland, H., & Surtes, L. (1986). Eyewitness responses to leading and misleading questions under the cognitive interview. *Journal of Police Science and Administration, 14,* 31–39.

Geiselman, R. E., Fisher, R. P., Firstenberg, I., Hutton, L. A., Sullivan, S. J., Avetissian, I. V., & Prosk, A. L. (1984). Enhancement of eyewitness memory: An empirical evaluation of the cognitive interview. *Journal of Police Science and Administration, 12,* 74–80.

Geiselman, R. E., Fisher, R. P., MacKinnon, D. P., & Holland, H. L. (1985). Eyewitness memory enhancement in the police interview: Cognitive retrieval mnemonics versus hypnosis. *Journal of Applied Psychology, 70,* 401–412.

Geiselman, R. E., Fisher, R. P., MacKinnon, D. P., & Holland, H. L. (1986). Enhancement of eyewitness memory with the cognitive interview. *American Journal of Psychology, 99,* 385–401.

Geiselman, R. E., & Padilla, J. (1988). Interviewing child witnesses with the cognitive interview. *Journal of Police Science and Administration, 16,* 236–242.

Geiselman, R. E., Saywitz, K. J., & Bornstein, G. K. (in press). Effects of cognitive questioning techniques on children's recall performance. To appear in G. Goodman & B. Bottoms (Eds.), *Understanding and improving children's testimony: Developmental, clinical, and legal issues.* New York: Guilford Publications.

George, R. (1991). *A field and experimental evaluation of three methods of interviewing witnesses/victims of crime.* Unpublished manuscript. Polytechnic of East London, London.

Greenwald, A. G. (1970). Sensory feedback mechanisms in performance control: With special reference to the ideo-motor mechanism. *Psychological Review, 77,* 73–99.

Johnston, W. A., Greenberg, S. N., Fisher, R. P., & Martin, D. W. (1970). Divided attention: A vehicle for monitoring memory processes. *Journal of Experimental Psychology, 83,* 164–171.

Jou, J., & Harris, R. J. (1992). The effect of divided attention on speech production. *Bulletin of the Psychonomic Society, 30,* 301–304.

Kahneman, D. (1973). *Attention and effort.* Englewood Cliffs, NJ: Prentice-Hall.

Kintsch, W., & Van Dijk, T. A. (1978). Toward a model of text comprehension and production. *Psychological Review, 85,* 363–394.

Klatzky, R. L. (1980). *Human memory: Structures and processes.* San Francisco: Freeman.

Leibowitz, H. W., & Guzy, L. (1990). *Can the accuracy of eyewitness testimony be improved by the use of non-verbal techniques?* Paper presented at the American Psychology-Law Society, Williamsburg, Virginia.

Malpass, R. S., & Devine, P. G. (1981). Guided memory in eyewitness identification. *Journal of Applied Psychology, 66,* 343–350.

McCauley, M. R., & Fisher, R. P. (1992). *Enhancing children's eyewitness recollection with the cognitive interview.* Paper presented at the American Psychology-Law Society, San Diego.

McCloskey, M., & Egeth, H. (1983). What can a psychologist tell a jury? *American Psychologist, 38,* 550–563.

Paivio, A. (1971). *Imagery and verbal processes.* New York: Holt, Rinehart, & Winston.

Putnam, W. H. (1979). Hypnosis and distortions in eyewitness memory. *International Journal of Clinical and Experimental Hypnosis, 27,* 437–448.

Rand Corporation (1975). *The criminal investigative process.* Vols. 1–3. Rand Corporation Technical Report R-1777-DOJ. Santa Monica, CA.

Sanders, G. S. (1986). On increasing the usefulness of eyewitness research. *Law and Human Behavior, 10,* 333–335.

Shepherd, E. (1991). Ethical interviewing. *Policing, 7,* 42–60.

Smith, M. (1983) Hypnotic memory enhancement of witnesses: Does it work? *Psychological Bulletin, 94,* 387–407.

Smith, S. M. (1979). Remembering in and out of context. *Journal of Experimental Psychology: Human Learning and Memory, 5,* 460–471.

Smith, S. M., & Vela, E. (1992). Environmental context-dependent eyewitness recognition. *Applied Cognitive Psychology, 6,* 125–139.

Timm, H. W. (1981). The effect of forensic hypnosis techniques on eyewitness recall and recognition. *Journal of Police Science and Administration, 9,* 188–194.

Tulving, E. (1974). Cue-dependent forgetting. *American Scientist, 62,* 74–82.

Tulving, E, & Thomson, D. M. (1973). Encoding specificity and retrieval processes in episodic memory. *Psychological Review, 80,* 352–373.

Visher, C. A. (1987). Juror decision making: The importance of evidence. *Law and Human Behavior, 11,* 1–17.

Wells, G. (1988). *Eyewitness identification: A system handbook*. Toronto: Carswell Legal Publications.

Wells, G. L., & Turtle, J. W. (1988). What is the best way to encode faces? In M. Gruneberg, P. Morris, & R. Sykes (Eds.), *Practical aspects of memory: Current research and issues*. New York: Wiley.

West, R. (1985). *Memory fitness over 40*. Gainesville, FL: Trial Press.

Whitten, W., & Leonard, J. (1981). Directed search through autobiographical memory. *Memory & Cognition, 9*, 566–579.

Yuille, J. C., & Cutshall, J. L. (1986). A case study of eyewitness memory for a crime. *Journal of Applied Psychology, 71*, 291–301.

Yuille, J. C., & Kim, C. K. (1987). A field study of the forensic use of hypnosis. *Canadian Journal of Behavioral Science, 19*, 418–419.

Part III

Whom to believe? Distinguishing accurate from inaccurate eyewitnesses

13   Distinguishing accurate from inaccurate eyewitness identifications: A reality monitoring approach

Lisa Beth Stern and David Dunning

Eyewitness identifications tend to be one of the most compelling types of evidence presented in police investigations and criminal trials. One extensive survey of real-life cases, for example, revealed a 73 percent conviction rate for trials in which the only evidence brought against the defendant was eye-witness identification testimony (Devlin, 1973). Yet psychological research has shown that eyewitness testimony can be unreliable. Human memory is fragile and easily influenced by both external and internal factors.

Given this state of affairs, it is not surprising that social and behavioral scientists have focused on identifying the factors that indicate whether a witness has provided accurate or erroneous testimony. And to a great extent these researchers have been successful in determining the general factors that prompt accuracy and error in eyewitness identification. Many variables, such as the time of day, duration of exposure, presence or absence of a weapon, interrogation procedure, and lineup construction can enhance or impair an individual's memory for an event (for reviews, see Loftus, 1979; Wells, Seelau, Rydell, & Luus, this volume).

In another sense, however, this research leads to disappointment. Ask legal or criminal justice officials what they need from psychological research, and the answer will involve some sort of test or examination they can give to specific witnesses involved with particular cases that establishes the accuracy or inaccuracy of individual identification. Unfortunately, given the necessary focus of behavioral research on general factors, psycholegal researchers have been unable to find or create a test to be used with particular witnesses in specific cases.

In this chapter, we present a first step toward constructing such a test. We propose that individual witnesses, when attempting to identify a perpetrator

The empirical research reported in this chapter was part of Lisa Stern's dissertation, conducted under the supervision of David Dunning. The authors thank David Ross for generously providing the crime stimulus used in the first study. They also thank Jeff Bernstein, Julie Grass, and Lim Li for their able assistance in data coding. Finally the authors extend their gratitude to Steve Ceci, James Cutting, and Barb Finlay for their thoughtful comments while serving on the dissertation committee.

from a lineup, do leave "markers" that indicate whether their identifications have been accurate or inaccurate. These markers will not discriminate accurate from inaccurate witnesses with certainty, but they do allow a criminal investigator to ask a set of questions that may sort correct from erroneous eyewitness identifications. The strategy is inspired in general by cognitive psychological work on reality monitoring and is guided in its specifics by research on face recognition and eyewitness identification. The strategy focuses on the decision process used by the eyewitness. We propose that accurate eyewitnesses employ different strategies from inaccurate witnesses when making a positive identification.

In the discussion below, we examine past research on markers of eyewitness accuracy. We then develop a theory concerning the potentially divergent decision strategies of accurate witnesses and inaccurate witnesses. Subsequently, we describe the results of two studies searching for these differences. The first directly examined decisions made by accurate and inaccurate eyewitnesses. The second studied whether information about witness decision-making strategies would help mock jurors to discriminate accurate from inaccurate witnesses. Finally, we conclude with some caveats and a few suggestions concerning avenues for further research.

Past work on markers of eyewitness accuracy

Much psychological research on eyewitness testimony has focused on determining indicators of eyewitness accuracy. This research can be grouped into two categories. In one category, investigators have searched for personological markers of eyewitness accuracy. Are some types of people more likely to make accurate identifications than others? In the other category, researchers have examined situational factors in eyewitness accuracy. Are some external circumstances more likely to produce accurate eyewitness identifications than others? Each approach has yet to produce a test of eyewitness accuracy that can be used with individual witnesses.

Personological factors

The search for personological markers, traits, or characteristics that would indicate accuracy or error has been largely unsuccessful. For example, one would think that individual differences in memory ability would go a long way toward identifying accurate from inaccurate eyewitnesses. It has often been shown, however, that memory performance in any one circumstance is largely determined by situation-specific expertise or particular situational circumstances (Ceci & Liker, 1986; Gardner, 1983; Neisser, 1982). In addition, it seems intuitive that explicit training in memorizing faces should promote accuracy, yet police officers in facial identification tests perform no better than untrained individuals (Clifford & Scott, 1978; Yarmey 1979). The most obvious personal marker of accuracy, the eyewitness's confidence in his or her eyewitness identification, has also been shown to possess a mercurial relationship at best to actual accuracy and error. In some experiments, confidence is positively related to accuracy. In many, it is not. In a few, confidence is negatively related to eyewitness accuracy (for a review, see Luus & Wells, this volume).

Situational markers

At first blush, research into situational factors associated with accuracy would appear more promising. Several factors have been found, in general, to predict and prompt eyewitness accuracy. Witnesses are more often accurate in their accounts and identifications when queried immediately after witnessing the crime as opposed to much later (Ebbinghaus, 1885/1964; Lipton, 1977). People are generally better able to identify someone of their own race than an individual from a different one (Malpass & Kravitz, 1969; Bothwell, Brigham, & Malpass, 1989). Witnesses are more often accurate when they experience a moderate level of stress as opposed to high or low levels (Loftus, 1979). Witnesses are more likely to be accurate the longer they have observed the perpetrator at the scene of the crime (Laughery, Alexander, & Lane, 1971). In general, the introduction of a weapon degrades memory for everything in the crime scene except the weapon itself (Kramer, Buckhout, & Eugenio, 1990). Asking witnesses to view mug books often hinders their ability to render an accurate identification (Davies, Shepherd, & Ellis, 1979).

Applying these general research findings to specific court cases, however, is often problematic. Take as an example the case of physiological arousal or stress. It is well known (articulated in 1908 as the Yerkes-Dodson law) that people perform better on many cognitive tasks, including facial identification, when under moderate levels of stress. But how can this piece of information be applied to a particular eyewitness case? Suppose a witness has viewed a crime. How are we to determine his or her stress level during the incident? Without having the witness strapped to a polygraph machine at the time of the crime, it may be impossible to tell. Further complicating the issue is the fact that the Yerkes-Dodson curve is different for different people, and varies according to the particular task at hand. The specific moderate level at which people perform optimally tends to vary from one occasion to the next. As a consequence, one never knows whether the witness approached his or her optimal level of stress when witnessing a crime.

The reality monitoring approach

We hypothesize that usable individual markers of eyewitness accuracy and error do exist. Beyond looking toward the person and his or her characteristics, or to the circumstances surrounding the crime, we propose that researchers should focus on characteristics of the testimony itself. By examining how witnesses describe their decisions, it may be possible to distinguish valid identifications from invalid ones.

This analysis begins from work on reality monitoring. At its heart, reality monitoring research is concerned with how people distinguish true memories, those provided by sensory-perceptual experience, from false ones, those produced via imagination and fantasy (Johnson & Raye, 1981). According to this approach, true and false memories (in the researchers' parlance, externally versus internally generated) differ in many qualitative aspects. Externally generated memories are a product of sensory-perceptual experience, and so contain a great deal of contextual information (time and place), sensory and spatial detail (color and shape), along with the core content of the memory. By contrast, reports of internally generated memories reflect the intentional cognitive or reflective work that went into producing them. The research indicates that individuals use these qualities to distinguish memories for events objectively experienced from those they have imagined.

Externally versus internally generated memories do differ on the dimensions proposed, whether they recall pallid laboratory stimuli (Johnson & Raye, 1981) or more complex autobiographical events (Johnson, Foley, Suengas, & Raye, 1988). Evidence for these differences comes from experimental situations in which subjects are induced to make reality monitoring errors. For example, in one study subjects had difficulty distinguishing memories of their own dreams (internally generated) from accounts given by others (externally generated), largely because the creation of dreams occurs with little intentional cognitive effort (Johnson, Kahan, and Raye, 1984). In another example, Johnson, Raye, Foley, and Foley (1981) presented subjects with animal names (for example, penguin) or asked subjects to generate their own (for example, "Name an animal whose first letter is 'p' "). Subsequently, subjects were successful in discriminating the animal names they had generated from those they had been given, presumably because generating animal names required substantive cognitive effort. When the name generation task was easy, however, ("Name an animal whose first letter is 'd' "), people made a larger number of errors when attempting to discriminate given names from internally generated ones. According to the researchers, this likely occurred because the easy task involved less cognitive effort, a characteristic that would mark any memory as internally generated.

The reality monitoring approach, with its description of the differences between real and imagined memories, has already been shown to have direct application to eyewitness testimony. Schooler, Gerhard, and Loftus (1986), for example, used reality monitoring principles in an investigation of the misleading information effect. In work on misleading information (see Loftus, 1979, for a review; also D. S. Lindsay, this volume; Loftus, this volume), subject witnesses are induced to incorporate erroneous information into their testimony by the use of subtle, suggestive questions. For example, witnesses can be prompted to remember, mistakenly, the presence of a yield sign at a traffic accident by being asked a question that presupposes the existence of one ("How fast was the Nissan going when it passed the yield sign?"). Schooler et al. speculated that incorporating this erroneous information, and subsequently reporting it, required the same type of cognitive effort as did imagining the information. Any memory prompted by misleading information would contain references to that cognitive work. By contrast, subjects who accurately reported the same information (that is, the information had indeed been present at the crime scene) would tend to report more sensory and perceptual detail in their accounts, not mentioning much cognitive effort.

Schooler et al. found support for their arguments in a study in which subjects were misled to believe they saw a nonexistent item. They were shown a series of slides depicting an auto-pedestrian accident. Half the subjects were actually shown a yield sign, and half received misleading information only suggesting they had seen one. Later, those subjects who reported seeing the sign were asked to describe it. In their descriptions, misled subjects used more words, mentioned more cognitive processes (for example, what the subject was thinking or paying attention to at encoding), verbal hedges (for example, "I think/ believe," "I'm not sure"), more references to the function of the item, and reported fewer sensory details than did witnesses who actually saw the traffic sign.

Further research echoes these findings and hints even more strongly that accurate and inaccurate eyewitnesses may differ in the characteristics of their accounts. Leippe, Manion, and Romanczyk (1991) asked child and adult witnesses to recount a laboratory session concerning a "touch sensitivity" test, in which witnesses had to judge whether they had been touched on their arms and faces with several different types of materials. After the conclusion of the session, witnesses were asked to provide free recall accounts of the session's events, as well as to identify experimental confederates from photo spreads. From their performances on these memory tasks, two groups of witnesses were identified, those that were highly accurate and those that were highly inaccurate in their testimony. The researchers compared the testimony given by these two groups of eyewitnesses. In contrast to their inaccurate counterparts, accurate witnesses provided more complete and comprehensive free recall accounts, fewer admissions that their memory was faulty, and proffered their accounts in a more powerful speech style that contained fewer hedges and hesitations.

Application to eyewitness identification

Reality monitoring phenomena suggest that there might be differences in the memory processes involved between accurate recognition of perpetrators and mistaken identifications of innocent individuals. The translation between past

work on reality monitoring to the eyewitness identification task is not, however, straightforward. Eyewitness identification is a recognition task. Witnesses are given a set of plausible choices and must make a decision concerning
the individual they believe to be the perpetrator, if they decide to choose
anyone at all. In contrast, past work on reality monitoring has focused on
recall tasks. Subjects are asked to recall whether they saw or imagined a
particular object, and then to describe it, with differences between perceptually experienced and simply imagined objects revealed through open-ended
descriptions of the object. Given that eyewitnesses do not perform this description task at the time of their identifications, how are we to apply the
lessons learned from reality monitoring research? How else will differences
between accurate and erroneous witnesses reveal themselves?

We propose that accurate and inaccurate witnesses will distinguish themselves in particular instances by how they pursue the recognition task. Asking
witnesses how they reached their decisions should reveal some differences.
Past research on facial recognition and eyewitness judgment provides some
hints about potential differences, tendencies that are similar to the distinctions
made in the reality monitoring literature.

Profile of an accurate eyewitness identification

Past research suggests that accurate witnesses, like subjects recalling externally generated memories, should make their identifications automatically,
quickly, without much cognitive effort. Consequently, asking accurate witnesses about their decisions should reveal that the judgment occurred with
little reflective thought, and was based on their memory of the perpetrator.

Supportive evidence for these assertions comes from the work of Hay,
Young, and Ellis (1986), who presented subjects with several famous and
nonfamous faces and later asked the subjects whether the same faces were
contained in another test set of photographs. When dealing with famous faces,
subjects were quick to recognize the relevant face in the test set. Moreover,
the speed of their responses was left unaffected by the number of faces they
had previously been asked to remember. Hay et al. argued that this was
evidence for "facial recognition units," or FRUs, that subjects had extracted
from previous exposure to famous faces. According to the researchers, these
FRUs contained much configural information about the gestalt of the face.
Thus, when asked to recognize the face from a test set, the subjects easily
compared the presented faces to the relevant FRU, and were able to identify
the celebrity in question. Hay et al. argued that this comparison process was
automatic, requiring little conscious thought. Indeed subjects frequently mentioned that famous faces had simply "popped out at them" from the test set.
Research by Sporer (this volume) also provides evidence that accurate identifications occur quickly. In his work, he timed witnesses as they observed

lineups and reached their identifications. He found that accurate positive identifications of the perpetrator were made significantly faster than erroneous identifications of an innocent foil.

Work by Schooler and Engstler-Schooler (1990) also suggests that accurate face recognition is a rapid process. They examined how verbal descriptions of a face tend to overshadow and interfere with a person's visual memory. They found that the ability to recognize a face was degraded by requiring subjects to provide a verbal description of it. This degradation did not occur, however, when subjects were asked to recognize faces rapidly, that is, in an interval of five seconds. From this result, Schooler and Engstler-Schooler argued that an individual's access to any visual code of a face occurred quickly, certainly more rapidly than to any semantic code contained in a verbal description.

The results of these research programs are not surprising considering research on how facial stimuli are retained in memory. Faces are represented as holistic gestalts, that is, as whole configural images (compare Klatzky, 1986). Asking subjects to make holistic judgments of a face, such as making personality trait judgments, thus facilitates later recognition (Bower & Karlin, 1974; Patterson & Baddeley, 1977; Strnad & Mueller, 1977; Wells & Hryciw, 1984), whereas focusing on individual features, as when constructing composite sketches, often produces a greater number of recognition errors (Davies & Christie, 1982; Ellis, Shepherd, & Davies, 1978; Laughery & Fowler, 1980; Schooler & Engstler-Schooler, 1990). Therefore, it seems reasonable to suppose that recognition could involve an immediate and automatic one-to-one matching between a stored gestalt and the external stimulus face. Because faces are never broken down into their constituent components in recognition, and subjects in the studies above seem not to analyze component parts of the faces presented to them at the time of recognition, it seems unlikely that successful facial identification requires much reflective thought.

Profile of an inaccurate eyewitness identification

If a witness is going to provide an inaccurate identification, how is he or she likely to go about it? If work on reality monitoring is any guide, inaccurate witnesses should exhibit a great deal of cognitive work when asked about their decision strategies. The strategies should be deliberate and slow, and include more discussion of the photographs or individuals in the lineup. Specifically, past research suggests that inaccurate witnesses will likely compare and contrast the various faces or persons presented to them until they arrive at the closest match to their memory, no matter how similar that selection is to their memory of the perpetrator. Wells (1984) has termed this strategy the "relative judgment" process, and proposed that this procedure results in many erroneous positive identifications.

Research evidence confirms this deliberative, effortful relative judgment strategy. When people are prevented from employing a relative judgment or process of elimination strategy by being presented with faces in a lineup sequentially (as opposed to simultaneously), the number of false positive identifications is reduced (R. C. L. Lindsay & Wells, 1985). Wells (1984) also discovered this trend toward relative judgment in an experiment in which subject-witnesses viewed two separate lineups, the first of which did not contain the perpetrator, and found that witnesses with the worst memories of the perpetrator were the ones most likely to pursue this process of elimination approach. In his study, witnesses who chose someone erroneously from the first lineup, indicating reliance on a relative judgment strategy, were relatively less accurate when shown a second lineup which contained the perpetrator. Witnesses who refused to select someone from the initial blank lineup, indicating they were not using a relative judgment strategy, were more accurate in their identifications.[1]

STUDY 1: DECISION PROCESSES OF ACCURATE AND INACCURATE EYEWITNESSES

Given these research findings, we can make a few predictions concerning the decision strategies likely to be used by accurate and inaccurate eyewitnesses in their identifications. Accurate witnesses should make their identifications quickly, without conscious thought or strategy. When asked about their explicit decision processes, they should have little to report, stating that they relied on their memory or image of the perpetrator. When asked about any impact that the other pictures in the lineup may have had on their identifications, they should state that the other pictures had little or no influence, or that they looked over the other alternatives to reaffirm their choice. Inaccurate witnesses, on the other hand, should report a relatively higher degree of explicit cognitive effort. They should be slower in reaching their identification judgments. When asked to describe their decision strategies, they should state that they followed a process-of-elimination strategy until they reached the closest choice. They should report that the alternatives had a substantive impact on their decision, or perhaps confused them, since they concentrated on the lineup alternatives in this process. Moreover, because they likely had incomplete or weak memories of the perpetrator's face, they should report focusing on specific facial features when making their identifications.

Thus, we should be able to distinguish accurate from inaccurate eyewitnesses by asking them to describe their experiences when making an eyewitness identification. That was the aim of the first study described below. Witnesses were presented with a videotaped crime and subsequently asked to select the perpetrator from a photo spread. We later queried the subjects on two separate issues. The first was on the decision strategy they had used when making an identification. The second was on the influence of the non-selected photographs on their judgment. The responses of accurate and inaccurate subjects were compared to determine if the groups relied on divergent strategies when making their choices. Note that inaccurate identifications were produced in two different ways. First, we examined the responses of witnesses who selected the wrong photograph when viewing a perpetrator-present lineup. Second, we presented several witnesses with a blank (perpetrator-absent) lineup, in which any positive identification would be incorrect.

Method

Subjects. A total of 126 undergraduates at Cornell University served as subjects in this experiment. They received extra course credit for their participation.

Stimulus film. All subjects were shown a three-minute videotape that depicted a day in the life of a preschool teacher (also used in the work described in Ross, 1990, this volume). The film was composed of various scenes in which three instructors, two males and one female, interacted with small children in several different activities (playing in a sandbox or on a swing set, reading a story, playing games). Each segment was approximately thirty seconds to one and a half minutes in length.

In the final scene, the female instructor (the victim) took a break from her classroom activities. She entered a cafeteria and sat down at a table next to a college-aged man (the perpetrator). The victim took money from her wallet, placed the wallet on the table, and rose to make a purchase from a vending machine. While she was away from the table, the culprit carefully removed money from the wallet, put it in his pocket, and slowly got up and walked out of the cafeteria. This segment lasted approximately thirty-four seconds.

Procedure. Subjects participated individually and entered the laboratory believing they were taking part in a study about education in which they were going to critique a teacher recruitment film. The experimenter told each subject that he or she was going to be shown an unedited film made by the Psychology Department at Cornell University for the National Education Association. The tape was designed to stimulate interest in the teaching profession. Subjects were told to pay close attention to the videotape because they were going to be asked for their comments on the quality of the film.

The film was shown on a nineteen-inch color television monitor. When the film ended, the experimenter shut off the VCR and informed subjects that the study was about eyewitness testimony. They were then given a five-minute distractor questionnaire that asked them to recall information from all the scenes except the last.

After subjects completed the questionnaire, they were shown a photo spread containing five photographs, and asked to identify the perpetrator. Each subject, in random assignment, saw one of two lineups. In the target-present (valid) condition, subjects were shown the suspect and four unfamiliar foils. In the target-absent (blank) condition, subjects were shown five unfamiliar foils.[2] The experimenter provided the same instructions to each subject: "I am going to ask you to make an identification of the perpetrator you saw on the screen. When you do, I would like you to tell me why you made the decision you did." Subjects either identified one of the photographs as the culprit or said he was not there. They were not told initially that the perpetrator's photo might be absent from the lineup. However, if they asked the experimenter if the perpetrator might not be present, the experimenter replied that that was a decision for the subject to reach. Subjects were asked to report their confidence in their decisions, on a scale that ranged from 0 to 100 percent, and to provide an explanation for their judgment. Each subject was tape-recorded while he or she reached a judgment. These tape recordings allowed us to time how long it took the subjects to reach their decisions. In essence, this allowed us an opportunity to examine some of Sporer's (this volume) findings regarding decision speed for accurate and inaccurate identifications.

After reaching their identification judgments, subjects were given another questionnaire which asked them to describe, in several different ways, how they had made their decisions. They were then debriefed and thanked for their participation.

Dependent measures

Decision strategy questions. The first measure was a closed question, aimed at determining the strategy subjects followed as they made their identifications, specifically asking them "How would you best describe your decision process?" Subjects were provided with five responses, and they could check as many of the five as they wished. Two responses were aimed at automatic recognition: "I just recognized him, I cannot explain why," and "I matched the image in my head to the picture in front of me." Two focused on an effortful, relative judgment strategy: "I compared the photos to each other in order to narrow the choices," and "He was the closest person to what I remember, but not exact." One option was designed to examine reliance on specific facial features, "I looked for characteristic facial features."

The next question on decision processes was open-ended, and requested subjects to "briefly describe the strategy you used in making your decision." Raters examined each response according to six categories. Two focused again on automatic recognition: the subject relied only on his or her memory of the assailant, mentioning no other strategy; and the subject-witness relied on his or her memory, but did use other strategies in making the identification.

Three categories focused on a relative judgment strategy: The subject compared the photos to each other; the subject used a process of elimination; and the subject-witness looked at all the photographs before making a decision. A last category noted whether the subject had relied on specific facial features when making an identification.

Questions determining the influence of the photographs in the lineup. The next two questions asked subjects to characterize how important the nonselected photographs were in making their judgments. The first query was "How much influence did the other pictures have on your decision?" Raters coded responses into four potential categories: the pictures served to confirm the subject's decision; the pictures had little or no influence on the subject's decision; the pictures were used in a process of elimination; and the pictures confused the subject and hindered his or her decision process. The first two categories were taken to indicate an automatic recognition decision in which the photos had a negligible impact. The last two categories were taken to indicate an effortful relative judgment strategy.

The final question was "What would you say had a greater influence on your decision, the pictures in the lineup, or your memory of the culprit?" Raters sorted responses into six categories: memory had a greater influence, either positive or neutral; the photographs had a greater positive, neutral, or negative influence; memory and pictures affected the decision equally. These categories were then collapsed into two broader categories: memory had a greater influence; pictures had a greater influence. (There was no difference between accurate and inaccurate subjects' reports that both their memories and the pictures had equal influence.)

The two raters who coded open-ended responses were blind to the hypotheses under investigation. The categories described above were generated by the coders themselves after looking over the open-ended responses that subjects provided. We then specified each to be an indicator of automatic processing or a relative judgment strategy before looking at the data. When formally coding responses, raters achieved 100 percent agreement for all three open-ended questions, with initial disagreements being resolved by discussion.

Results and discussion

Of the one hundred twenty-six subjects, eight were dismissed during the identification procedure because they knew one or more of the lineup members. For those seventy-seven remaining subjects presented with a valid photo spread, fifty-five accurately identified the perpetrator's photo (71 percent), sixteen falsely identified someone else (21 percent), and six incorrectly stated that the perpetrator was absent (8 percent). In the blank photo spread condition, thirty-seven of forty-one subject-witnesses mistakenly identified a photograph (90 percent), and four correctly judged that the perpetrator was absent (10 percent).

These responses left us with three subject groups. The first was the accurate identification group ($n = 55$). The second was the inaccurate-valid group ($n = 16$), that is, those subjects who had viewed the valid lineup yet had identified the wrong photograph. The third group, the inaccurate-blank ($n = 37$), consisted of those individuals who had erroneously selected someone from the perpetrator-absent photo spread.

Reports of decision strategies

To what extent did accurate and inaccurate witnesses report using automatic versus effortful processes when making their identifications? To examine this question, we first examined subject-witness responses to the closed question on this topic. Recall that two responses were presumed a priori to indicate automatic processing; two were assumed to indicate a relative judgment strategy. As can be seen in Table 13.1 accurate and inaccurate witnesses did differ. This was confirmed by submitting their responses to a linear contrast, weighted by number of subjects in each condition, that compared the reactions of accurate witnesses (responses weighted $+2$) to those of inaccurate subject-witnesses (responses weighted -1).

These contrasts, as is evident in Table 13.1, revealed that accurate subjects were more likely to endorse automatic processing responses than were their inaccurate counterparts, $F(1, 105) = 10.72, p < .001$. Compared to their inaccurate peers, accurate subjects were more likely to state that they "didn't know" how they had recognized the perpetrator, $z = 2.71, p < .01$.[3] They were also marginally more likely to state that they had matched the photographs to their image of the perpetrator, $z = 1.73, p < .10$.

Further linear contrasts (see Table 13.1) revealed that inaccurate subjects were more likely to endorse process-of-elimination items than their accurate counterparts, $F(1, 105) = 9.23, p < .001$. Inaccurate witnesses were marginally more likely to state that they had compared the photographs to each other, $z = 1.72, p < .10$, than did subjects making correct identifications. They also were more likely to state that they had chosen the "closest" though "not exact" match, $z = 2.79, p < .01$.

On the open-ended question on decision processes, however, similar analyses failed to produce such clear results. As can be seen in Table 13.1, accurate witnesses overall were neither more nor less likely to articulate an automatic processing strategy, $F = 1.28$, or a process of elimination approach, $F = 1.15$. When we examined the specific responses that most directly indicate either strategy, however, we again found that accurate and inaccurate witnesses differed. When we looked at accurate and inaccurate witnesses whose *only* response was to indicate that they had matched the photograph chosen

Table 13.1. *Proportions of accurate and inaccurate subjects endorsing each type of decision strategy report.*

Measure	Accurate ($n = 55$)	Inaccurate-valid ($n = 16$)	Inaccurate-blank ($n = 37$)	p^a
			Witness type	

Measure	Accurate ($n = 55$)	Inaccurate-valid ($n = 16$)	Inaccurate-blank ($n = 37$)	p^a
Question: "How would you best describe your decision process?" (close-ended)				
Indicators of automatic processing				
I just recognized him, I cannot explain why	.38	.06	.19	<.01
I matched the image in my head to the picture in front of me	.69	.50	.54	<.10
Sum	1.07	.56	.73	<.001
Indicators of process of elimination				
I compared the photos to each other in order to narrow the choices	.60	.75	.76	<.10
He was the closest person to what I remember, but not exact	.47	1.00	.62	<.01
Sum	1.07	1.75	1.38	<.001
Question: "Briefly describe the strategy you used in making an identification." (open-ended)				
Indicators of automatic processing				
Compared memory to photo (only response given)	.33	.06	.14	<.01
Compared memory to photo (other responses cited)	.29	.56	.32	
Sum	.62	.63	.46	
Indicators of process of elimination				
Conducted a process of elimination	.20	.44	.35	<.05
Compared photos to each other	.16	.06	.16	
Looked at all photos before making a decision	.26	.06	.38	
Sum	.62	.56	.89	

[a]Statistical significance of linear contrast comparing accurate witness group to two inaccurate witness groups.

to their image or memory of the perpetrator, we found that accurate subject-witnesses articulated this approach more often than their incorrect counterparts, $z = 2.68$, $p < .01$. In addition, when we focused on subjects who directly described a process of elimination approach, we found that inaccurate witnesses were more likely to endorse such a strategy than were accurate participants, $z = 2.04$, $p < .05$.

Additional analyses explored differences between the two groups of inaccurate witnesses (that is, those who had viewed a valid versus a blank lineup). No systematic differences were found. Accurate and inaccurate witnesses did

Table 13.2. *Proportions of accurate and inaccurate eyewitnesses endorsing responses concerning impact of nonchosen photos*

| Measure | Witness type | | | p^a |
	Accurate ($n = 55$)	Inaccurate-valid ($n = 16$)	Inaccurate-blank ($n = 37$)	
Question: "How much influence did the other pictures have on your decision?"				
Indicators of neglibible impact				
Pictures reinforced decision	.20	.00	.05	<.05
Had little influence/decision was obvious	.36	.31	.30	
Sum	.56	.31	.35	<.05
Indicators of substantive impact				
Used in process of elimination	.20	.31	.24	
Pictures confused witness	.29	.31	.54	<.10
Sum	.49	.63	.78	<.10
Question: "Which would you say had a greater influence on your decision, the lineup, the pictures in the lineup, or your memory of the culprit?"				
Memory of culprit	.66	.38	.41	<.05
Lineup/pictures	.26	.44	.41	<.10

[a]Statistical significance of linear contrast comparing accurate witness group to two inaccurate witness groups.

not differ on how often they reported relying on specific features of the face in their identifications.

Influence of photographs

If accurate witnesses followed a different approach from their incorrect counterparts, they should have made divergent claims about the impact of the non-selected photographs on their identifications. When we examined the responses of accurate versus inaccurate witnesses to the first open-ended question on this issue, again via a series of linear contrasts, we found that accurate subjects were more likely to state that the photographs had a negligible impact, $F(1, 105) = 5.19, p < .05$ (see Table 13.2). This result was driven by the fact that accurate witnesses were more likely to claim that they had used the photographs to "reinforce" an identification already made, $z = 2.59, p < .02$. Accurate and inaccurate subjects were equally likely to state that the photos had "little" or "no" influence on their decisions, $z = .68$, *ns*.

Further analyses revealed that inaccurate witnesses were marginally more likely to state that the photographs had had an impact on their decision, $F(1,$

105) = 3.86, $p < .06$ (see Table 13.2). This result was produced primarily by statements concerning whether the photos had confused the subject. Inaccurate witnesses were more likely to make this assertion than were accurate subject-witnesses, $z = 1.94$, $p < .06$. Surprisingly, accurate and inaccurate subjects did not differ as to how often they mentioned a process-of-elimination strategy on this query, $z = .79$, *ns*.

The final open-ended query asked subjects to report whether their memory of the perpetrator or the photographs they had been shown had a greater influence on their identification decisions. As can be seen in Table 13.2, accurate witnesses were more likely to state that their memory had carried a greater impact than were inaccurate witnesses, $z = 2.69$, $p < .01$. Inaccurate witnesses were marginally more likely to state that the photographs had possessed a greater impact, $z = 1.77$, $p < .10$.

Finally, supplemental analyses that focused on the two groups of inaccurate subjects (had seen a valid versus a blank lineup) revealed no systematic differences between these two groups on the impact of lineup alternatives.

Supplemental measures

Before summarizing, we should note other differences between accurate and inaccurate subjects that took place on two supplemental measures.

First, and perhaps most intriguing, accurate subjects took significantly less time to make their identifications than did inaccurate subjects ($Ms = 13.3$ sec, 18.5 sec, and 17.2 sec, for accurate, inaccurate-valid lineup, inaccurate-blank lineup witnesses, respectively), linear contrast $F(1, 105) = 4.33$, $p < .05$. Again, this indicates that accurate witnesses were recognizing the perpetrator relatively automatically, whereas inaccurate witnesses exerted more effort in their judgments. This also replicates the core of Sporer's (this volume) research on reaction times: Accurate witnesses reach their decisions more quickly than do their inaccurate counterparts.

Accurate subjects were also significantly more confident in their identifications than were inaccurate subjects ($Ms = 76.7$, 61.6, and 65.8 percent, for accurate, inaccurate-valid lineup, inaccurate-blank lineup witnesses, respectively), linear contrast $F(1, 105) = 8.32$, $p < .01$.

Summary

In sum, there do, indeed, appear to be individual markers of accuracy and inaccuracy in eyewitness identification. In the study above, accurate and erroneous eyewitnesses tended to report divergent strategies when making their identifications, though the results of the one open-ended query on this point were somewhat unclear. The reports of accurate witnesses were more likely to indicate an identification derived from automatic recognition, causing them to say they had "just recognized" the perpetrator without being able to give a specific rationale for their choice. The responses of inaccurate subjects revealed more effortful process of elimination strategies in which they chose the person who "most closely" matched their memory of the culprit. Supplemental data on the time subjects took to make their identifications were also consistent with this distinction between accurate and inaccurate subject-witnesses. Accurate witnesses made their identifications more quickly than their inaccurate counterparts.

Responses concerning the impact of lineup photographs also suggested that accurate and inaccurate witnesses had reached their decisions by way of different processes. Consistent with an automatic recognition interpretation, accurate witnesses were more likely than their incorrect peers to state that the other photos had merely confirmed the decision they reached. Accurate witnesses more often reported relying on their memory when making an identification than did inaccurate subjects. Consistent with an effortful, relative judgment strategy, inaccurate subjects were more likely to report that the set of photographs had confused them. They also more often stated that they had relied on the photographs to make their judgment.

A comprehensive analysis

The analyses above indicate that accurate and inaccurate subject-witnesses reacted differently to the individual questions we posed. But, overall, how large was this difference? The best gauge required aggregating the reactions of subjects across the four key questions. Thus, for each subject, we counted how many indicators of accuracy they articulated (up to eight), as well as how many indicators of error they endorsed (again, up to eight). We then compared the extent to which the responses of accurate subjects diverged from their incorrect peers. Linear contrasts, again pitting the responses of accurate subjects against those of inaccurate participants, revealed that accurate witnesses described a very different decision process. Accurate witnesses were more likely to endorse indicators of accuracy ($M = 2.91$) than did either group of inaccurate subjects ($Ms = 1.88$ and 1.95 for inaccurate witnesses viewing valid and blank lineups, respectively), $F(1, 105) = 19.52$, $p < .0001$. These differences were apparent in more specific comparisons of accurate subjects to inaccurate-valid lineup subjects, $F(1, 69) = 9.70$, $p < .005$, and to inaccurate-blank lineup participants, $F(1, 90) = 14.16, p < .001$. In addition, accurate witnesses were less likely to articulate indicators of error ($M = 2.44$) than did either group of inaccurate subjects ($Ms = 3.38$ and 3.46 for inaccurate witnesses viewing valid and blank lineups, respectively), $F(1, 105) = 11.23$, $p < .005$. Again, these differences were apparent in more specific comparisons of accurate subjects to inaccurate-valid lineup subjects,

$F(1, 69) = 4.98, p < .05$, and to inaccurate-blank lineup participants, $F(1, 90) = 9.19, p < .01$.

These differences were apparent when we examined the perhaps most forensically relevant comparison in the data. At its heart, the legal system is interested in distinguishing two situations: one in which witnesses have correctly identified the perpetrator from one where the police have inadvertently arrested a "lookalike" that many witnesses are apt to identify. That second situation was produced by our blank lineup condition. Of the thirty-seven witnesses making a false positive identification, 25 (or 68 percent) identified the photograph replacing the perpetrator's. Given this circumstance, do our indicators of accuracy and error help distinguish accurate identification from specific false identifications of the "lookalike"? The answer is yes. Accurate witnesses were more likely to endorse indicators of accuracy ($M = 2.91$) than were blank lineup witnesses falsely incriminating the replacement photo ($M = 2.04$), $t(68) = 3.04, p < .01$. Correct subjects were also marginally less likely to articulate indicators of inaccuracy than those identifying the replacement ($Ms = 2.44$ and 3.12 for accurate and inaccurate subjects, respectively), $t(68) = -1.87, p < .07$.

Are these indicators useful in distinguishing accurate from inaccurate witnesses?

The study above revealed statistically significant differences between accurate and inaccurate eyewitnesses, but how useful are these indices of accuracy and error? To what extent can they be used to classify accurate and inaccurate eyewitnesses' identifications?

To explore these questions, we conducted a supplemental, computerized analysis of subjects' responses in the study above. From the data collected in this study, could we examine subjects' responses to the postidentification questionnaire and then make predictions concerning who had made accurate and inaccurate identifications? By such a procedure, what proportion of subject-witnesses could we successfully classify as accurate or inaccurate?

To that end, for each subject we summed the number of accurate and inaccurate indicators that he or she had endorsed. Because subjects articulated a greater number of inaccuracy indicators overall, we standardized both scores to equate them in terms of number. We then classified each subject as "accurate" or "inaccurate" on the basis of these separate standardized scores. If a subject's standard score for accuracy was greater than it was for inaccuracy, that subject was classified as accurate. If the standard score for inaccuracy was greater than the one for accuracy, the subject was classified as inaccurate. By this procedure, roughly 66 percent of the subjects in the study above were correctly classified. The procedure allowed us to classify 67 percent of the fifty-five accurate subjects in the study correctly. We also correctly classified 64 percent of the fifty-three inaccurate subjects as being erroneous (69 percent of the inaccurate-valid subjects and 62 percent of the inaccurate-blank subjects). In sum, these indices are potentially useful in determining the veracity of eyewitnesses' identifications.

STUDY 2: CAN AND WILL PEOPLE USE THESE INDICATORS TO DISCRIMINATE ACCURACY FROM INACCURACY?

What about humans (not computers) or, more specifically, criminal justice officials? Would providing interested officials, as opposed to a computer, with information about the decision processes of accurate and inaccurate eyewitnesses help them to discriminate accurate eyewitness identifications from inaccurate ones? To answer that question, we conducted one additional study.

Past research, focusing on the judgments of jurors, suggests that people are not adept at discriminating accurate witnesses from inaccurate ones. People do show some modest facility at making these judgments (Leippe, Manion, & Romanczyk, 1991; Manion, Leippe, & Romanczyk, in press), but such assessments are often guided by faulty heuristics. For example, Bell and Loftus (1989) and Wells and Leippe (1981) found that subject-jurors tended to believe witnesses who recalled more trivial and irrelevant details about a crime than those who remembered only central information, though the basis for this inference is tentative at best. Similarly, research has consistently shown that jurors often base their decisions of witness accuracy on confidence, even though eyewitness confidence has a weak to nonexistent relationship to accuracy and error (for example, Leippe et al., 1991; Luus & Wells, this volume; Manion et al., in press; R. C. L. Lindsay, Wells, Rumpel, 1981; Wells, R. C. L. Lindsay, & Ferguson, 1979).

But what of reality monitoring cues, such as those gathered in the study above? Would jurors and other interested individuals use them successfully if attempting to discern accurate from erroneous memories? Schooler, Gerhard, and Loftus (1986) examined this question directly and found that people do not use reality monitoring cues if left to their own devices. In their work, several groups of subjects looked over eyewitness accounts of accurate and inaccurate subject-witnesses, attempting to judge whether each was correct or incorrect. When given no training regarding the relationship between reality monitoring cues and eyewitness accuracy, subjects were only modestly successful in discerning accurate from inaccurate accounts (that is their performances tended to be only slightly above chance). When subjects were educated about the reality monitoring differences found between accurate and inaccurate witnesses, however, their performances improved significantly. In a related vein, Leippe, Manion, and Romanczyk (1991) reported that subject-jurors tended to be unaware of diagnostic differences between accurate and inaccurate eyewitnesses, such as powerful speech style, length of free recall reports, and decreased hesitation. Subject-jurors tended to rely instead on direct reports of confidence, leading them to have some, but not much, ability to discriminate accurate from erroneous witnesses.

It seems reasonable, therefore, to determine the extent to which interested individuals can determine the veracity of eyewitness identifications, and to assess whether they will or can use reality monitoring differences when making these judgments. To that end, two groups of subjects were given some of the eyewitness identification protocols collected in the study above. One group was asked to judge the accuracy of each eyewitness identification. The second group was given a series of hints about reality monitoring differences before making the same judgments. It was anticipated that untrained subjects would not rely on reality monitoring cues and that their performance level would thus be modest. It was further predicted that informing subjects of reality monitoring principles would improve their ability to perform the given task.

Method

Subjects. Subjects were thirty-one Cornell University graduate and under-graduate students. All subjects were entered in a lottery for the chance of winning fifty dollars as compensation for their participation. Subjects completed the task in groups of three to four.

Materials. Protocols from forty accurate and forty inaccurate witnesses in Experiment 1 were randomly selected, and arranged into four booklets, each containing twenty accurate and twenty inaccurate descriptions. All the booklets included a set of written instructions that briefly described Experiment 1 and the circumstances under which the responses were generated.

Procedure. Subjects were told that they were participating in a jury decision-making study in which they were going to be asked to make judgments about the accuracy of eyewitness identifications, based on witnesses' descriptions of their decision strategies. Each subject was given a booklet and a set of written instructions, which were read aloud by the experimenter. The instructions asked subjects to classify the identification as accurate or inaccurate, and then to provide a reason why they classified it as they did. Subjects in the no hint condition ($n = 15$) were not provided with any additional information. In the hint condition ($n = 16$), subjects were informed about the differences between accurate and inaccurate eyewitnesses. They were told that accurate witnesses tended to make their identifications automatically, without being able to describe how they came to their decisions, to rely more heavily on their memory of the culprit than on the pictures presented to them, to compare their memory to the pictures rather than the pictures to each other, and not to be influenced by other pictures once they recognized the target (the pictures

Table 13.3. *Accuracy of hint and no hint witnesses attempting to classify accurate and inaccurate eyewitness protocols*

	Protocol type		
Condition	Accurate (percent)	Inaccurate (percent)	Overall (percent)
Hint	69.1	67.2	67.9
No hint	59.7	58.7	59.2

serve to confirm their decision). Subjects were further told that inaccurate eyewitnesses tended to go through a great deal of effort before making their choice, using a process of elimination strategy in which they compared the pictures to each other to narrow their choices, to compare their memory of the culprit to the pictures, but still rely more heavily on the pictures than on their memory, to be confused by the pictures, to choose the person who was closest to, but not necessarily identical to, their recollection. In addition, subjects in the hint condition were warned that confidence may or may not be an indication of accuracy.

In both conditions, the experimenter read the instructions aloud, and asked if there were any questions. All subjects were given as much time as they needed to complete the task. Subjects took thirty-five to forty-five minutes to complete the task in both conditions.

Results and discussion

It can be seen in Table 13.3 that subject-judges in both conditions were able to differentiate accurate from inaccurate identifications above chance accuracy levels, $Ms = 67.9$ and 59.2 percent, $ts = 7.77$, and 6.06, $ps < .001$, for hint and no hint conditions, respectively. However, and as predicted, providing hints to subject-judges significantly improved their ability to classify identifications. A two by two mixed model ANOVA (hint versus no hint condition; accuracy of protocol being judged), revealed the improvement ($+8.7$ percent) to be highly statistically significant, $F(1, 27) = 18.07$, $p < .001$. There was no significant interaction between hint condition and accuracy of the protocol being judged.

Judgmental strategies

What did subject-judges use when making the decisions concerning the accuracy of the eyewitness protocols? How did the strategies of subjects in the hint and no hint conditions differ? To address these questions, each subject's

Table 13.4. *Reported instances of use of reality monitoring cues when assessing accuracy of eyewitness protocols*

	Condition		
Reality monitoring cue	Hint	No hint	*p*
Indicators of accuracy			
Witness reports automatic decision	4.2	1.1	<.001
Witness compared memory to pictures	5.0	1.6	<.01
Witness relied on memory	9.8	8.0	
Witness not affected by pictures	1.7	.3	<.001
Indicators of inaccuracy			
Witness used process of elimination	5.4	.3	<.001
Witness chose "closest" photo	2.1	2.0	
Witness relied on pictures	4.5	2.7	<.05
Witness confused by pictures	4.3	2.6	<.05

explanation for his or her decision on each of the forty protocols was examined. We then assessed the number of times each subject mentioned any number of possible factors in his or her decision. See Table 13.4.

This analysis revealed that subjects in the no hint condition predominantly relied on eyewitness confidence when making their decisions. Participants in the no hint condition used eyewitness confidence an average of 10.3 times, whereas those in the hint condition relied on it an average 3.1 times (per set of forty descriptions), t (29) = 3.18, p < .005. This reliance on confidence probably led to the above-chance performance level that no hint participants exhibited in this study, since confidence was significantly related to eyewitness accuracy (r = .27, p < .05) in the first experiment.

Further analyses revealed that no hint subjects did not in general articulate and rely on reality monitoring cues, such as those provided to subjects in the hint condition. It is clear that no hint subjects mentioned these cues many fewer times than did hint condition subjects (Ms = 19.6, and 36.9, respectively, t (29) = −6.65, p < .001). As can be seen in Table 13.4, no hint subjects tended to mention "relies on memory" frequently in their explanations (M = 8.0), at a rate equivalent to subjects in the hint condition (M = 9.2). For virtually all other reality monitoring cues (with the exception of "chose closest, but not exact picture," which subjects cited infrequently), the untrained subjects relied on reality monitoring factors significantly less often than their educated counterparts.

Some subjects in the no hint condition misapplied the reality monitoring information contained in the eyewitness protocols. A few stated that automatic processing was an indication of inaccuracy. For example, one judge wrote, "Poor memory, chose 'a' [I just recognized him, I cannot explain why] for Question #2 [How would you best describe your decision process?] – seems illogical and unconfident." Another no hint judge incorrectly thought a witness was inaccurate, and explained, "Subject doesn't really say much about decision process; maybe was more of a passive decision." In comparison, when judges were provided with guidelines, they correctly used effortless recognition as an indication of accuracy. For example, one informed judge indicated a belief that a witness was accurate because the decision was based on "instinct – can't explain why," whereas many others said they identified (correctly) an accurate witness simply because it was "an automatic decision."

In sum, this second study revealed much about the ability of the interested individual to distinguish accurate from inaccurate eyewitness identifications. People exhibit some facility at this task. The performances attained by most subjects were above chance levels. Subjects did not, however, intuitively use reality monitoring cues when making these decisions. They often misread the significance of automatic processing cues, taking them to indicate error as opposed to accuracy. When educated about reality monitoring differences between accurate and inaccurate eyewitnesses, they tended to report using information about decision-making strategy more frequently, and as a consequence revealed a much improved ability to discern accurate identifications from inaccurate ones.

Caveats and future directions

At the beginning of the chapter, we asked whether the testimony given by individual eyewitnesses would display characteristics that might indicate potential accuracy or error. The two studies described above suggest that, indeed, there are markers that distinguish accurate identifications from erroneous ones. In the first study, accurate witnesses tended to describe their decisions as automatic or effortless. They also took less time to reach their identification judgments. In contrast, inaccurate witnesses tended to characterize their decisions as an effortful process of elimination strategies. They also reported relying more heavily on the photographs placed before them when reaching their judgments. In the second study, in which subjects attempted to discern accurate eyewitness identifications from inaccurate ones, subjects who were informed about these reality monitoring differences showed an improved facility to discern accurate from inaccurate eyewitness identifications relative to uneducated peers.

We should note, however, that the two studies described above serve only as first steps in determining potential differences displayed by accurate and inaccurate witnesses. These studies, like all individual pieces of research, leave open questions that must be addressed. For example, one could raise the issue of demand characteristics with the first study we described above. It could be argued that the results we obtained in that study occurred because subjects felt compelled to select someone from the lineup (fewer than 10 percent of subjects in the study refused to make a positive identification) and that the differences between accurate and inaccurate eyewitnesses would not have arisen if people felt less pressured to make a choice.

We believe this issue to be important, but that it should not, for three separate reasons, temper our interpretation of the results we obtained. First, there is ample evidence suggesting that witnesses are biased toward choosing someone out of a lineup, even when explicitly warned that the culprit may not be present (see Cutler & Penrod, 1987; Deffenbacher & Horney, 1981; R. C. L. Lindsay & Wells, 1985). Second, any pressure to choose someone out of the lineup would most likely obscure differences between accurate and inaccurate witnesses, not create them. Consider subjects' responses when viewing a valid lineup. In the first study, any pressure to choose would probably have led subject-witnesses to choose the perpetrator's photograph, since they tended to choose his replacement in the blank lineup condition. Those decisions would only occur, however, after subjects had pursued a relative judgment strategy, thus creating accurate witnesses who would look like inaccurate ones. Third, we have since replicated these findings in a study in which we took great pains not to pressure subjects into making positive identifications. In this study, only 66 percent of subject-witnesses provided positive identifications, yet the reality monitoring differences found here were once again observed (Dunning & Stern, 1992).

There are many other questions these two studies leave open. What would happen if there was a week's delay before witnesses were asked to make an identification, when witness memory would be bound to have decayed? What would happen if the lineup were particularly biased? What if a sequential lineup procedure were used (compare R. C. L. Lindsay & Wells, 1985), or if the identification task were easy or difficult? Can identifications of innocent bystanders (see Read, this volume; Ross, this volume) be distinguished from correct identifications of perpetrators? And given the increased reliance of the legal system on child witnesses, are there developmental differences in the decision strategies pursued? Are children's metacognitive abilities sophisticated enough to allow them to describe their cognitive processes, revealing any differences between accurate and inaccurate accounts? Future research could profitably pursue any of these areas.

Most specifically, future research could be designed that examined witness reactions to showups, in which criminal justice authorities present a single individual to an eyewitness for identification. Would witnesses making an accurate positive identification of the accused in a showup describe a different decision process than those making wrongful positive identification? It seems likely that accurate witnesses in showups would describe an automatic process much like that of the witnesses in the study above (for example, "Yes, it's him. I don't know why I know, but it's him"). But what would inaccurate witnesses say? In a showup, there are no alternatives to compare in a process of elimination. If erroneous showup witnesses expend cognitive effort in their identifications, what form will that effort take?

Implications for reality monitoring

The studies described above also have implications for theoretical work on reality monitoring. In past work on the differences between accurate and imagined memories, the focus has been on recall tasks in which subjects describe their memory. Here, the focus was on a recognition task, and we found that accurate versus inaccurate memories garnered via a recognition report show some of the same characteristics as those obtained in a recall format. Accurate witnesses (reporting an externally generated memory of a face) made their identifications without much cognitive effort, as evidenced by the reaction time data and reports of decision-making processes. By comparison, inaccurate witnesses (who reported an internally generated "false" memory) used a recognition strategy that required more effort and time. In short, whether the memory is articulated by way of a recall or recognition format, the same characteristics that distinguish externally from internally generated memory appear to hold.

Moreover, our studies reaffirm the findings of Schooler et al. (1986; in a related vein, see Leippe et al., 1991; Manion et al., in press) that people are generally not aware of reality monitoring processes when assessing the validity of other people's memories. It appears that people use confidence as the prime indicator of veracity of eyewitness testimony. Consequently, the ability of people to discriminate accuracy from inaccuracy is measurable, yet poor. People can be educated about reality monitoring principles, however, with concomitant improvements in their detection abilities.

Concluding remarks

For more than a century, psychologists have studied human cognition to achieve a better understanding of the way it operates. In 1908, Munsterberg proposed that American jurisprudence could be improved by the application of psychologists' empirical findings (Blau, 1984). For nearly a century, psycholegal research has demonstrated that eyewitness memory is quite fragile and can be unreliable, yet the legal system has been hesitant to accept these findings. To many lawyers and judges, the conclusions drawn from empirical research, focused on general principles and tendencies, are too vague and uncertain to be of use. The findings do not "prove" anything. They cannot provide specific information about a particular case. They are therefore forensically irrelevant.

In our studies, we have taken the first steps toward providing information about specific individuals that can be useful to the legal system. We have shown there are measurable differences between accurate and inaccurate witnesses. When informed about these differences, the criminal justice official or trier of fact may be better able to assess the validity of individual eyewitness identifications. Although more work needs to be done, these results suggest that the validity of identification procedures could be improved by asking witnesses how they came to their decisions. They also suggest that educating interested individuals about such processes could lead to more accurate judgments about the facts of a case.

Such work is crucial, for although the American judiciary system was designed to protect the innocent, in practice it has the potential to find the innocent guilty. It seems apparent that this possibility can be reduced by learning more about the underlying mechanisms of eyewitness memory, and applying the lessons learned to the individual witnesses the criminal justice system deals with every day. It is hoped that, as researchers begin to tailor their findings to situations involving individual witnesses, the relevance of such behavioral scientific work will become more apparent, and the work more frequently applied in legal settings.

Notes

1 The fact that some witnesses in Wells (1984) positively identified a photograph from the initial blank lineup does not imply, with certainty, that they were following a relative judgment strategy. Nor does it conclusively imply that these witnesses deliberately followed a relative judgment strategy that tended to lead them toward erroneous identifications. What is important, for our purposes, is that Wells argued that wrongful identifications appeared to correlate with behavior suggestive of a relative judgment strategy. It is this correlation that we examine and document, in a more straightforward way, in this chapter.

2 The two lineups were also taken from Ross (1990; this volume). All foils tended to be rated (by a sample of seventy-six Cornell University students) as somewhat dissimilar in appearance from the perpetrator, mean ratings = 2.48 to 2.65 on a seven-point scale. This includes the photograph of the person used to replace the perpetrator when constructing the blank lineup.

3 These linear contrasts on the proportions of subject-witnesses endorsing each individual item were conducted after those proportions underwent arcsine transformations, as by the procedure outlined by Langer and Abelson (1972) and Winer (1971). We should note that the results obtained by all linear contrasts differed only negligibly from analyses in which we simply collapsed data from the two inaccurate witness groups into one, and then compared their responses with those of accurate subjects.

References

Bell, B. E., & Loftus, E. F. (1989). Trivial persuasion in the courtroom: The power of (a few) minor details. *Journal of Personality and Social Psychology, 56,* 669–679.

Blau, T. H. (1984). *The psychologist as expert witness.* New York: John Wiley & Sons.

Bothwell, R. K., Brigham, J. C., & Malpass, R. S. (1989). Cross-racial identification. *Personality and Social Psychology Bulletin, 15,* 19–25.

Bower, G.H., & Karlin, M. B. (1974). Depth of processing pictures of faces and recognition memory. *Journal of Experimental Psychology, 103,* 751–757.

Ceci, S. J., & Liker, J. K. (1986). A day at the races: A study of IQ, expertise, and cognitive complexity. *Journal of Experimental Psychology: General, 115,* 255–266.

Clifford, B.R., & Scott, J. (1978). Individual and situational factors in eyewitness testimony. *Journal of Applied Psychology, 63,* 352–9.

Cutler, B. L., & Penrod, S. D. (1988). Improving the reliability of eyewitness identification: Lineup construction and presentation. *Journal of Applied Psychology, 73,* 281–290.

Davies, G., & Christie, D. (1982). Face recall: An examination of some factors limiting composite production accuracy. *Journal of Applied Psychology, 67,* 103–109.

Davies, G., Shepherd, J., & Ellis, H. (1979). Effects of interpolated mugshot exposure on accuracy of eyewitness identification. *Journal of Applied Psychology, 64,* 232–237.

Deffenbacher, K. A., & Horney, J. (1981). Psycho-legal aspects of face perception. In D. Davies, H. Ellis, & J. Shepherd, *Perceiving and remembering faces.* London: Academic Press.

Devlin, Hon. L. P. *Report to the secretary of state for the home department of the departmental committee on evidence of identification in criminal cases.* London: Her Majesty's Stationery Office.

Dunning, D., & Stern, L. B. (1992). *Distinguishing accurate from inaccurate eyewitness identifications via inquiries about decision processes.* Unpublished manuscript, Cornell University.

Ebbinghaus, H. E. (1885/1964). *Memory: A contribution to experimental psychology.* New York: Dover.

Ellis, H. D., Shepherd, J. W., & Davies, G. M. (1979). Identification of familiar and unfamiliar faces from internal and external features: Some implications for theories of face perception. *Perception, 8,* 431–439.

Gardner, H. (1983). *Frames of mind: The theory of multiple intelligences.* New York: Cambridge University Press.

Hay, D. C., Young, A.W., & Ellis, A. W. (1986). What happens when a face rings a bell?: The automatic processing of famous faces. In H. D. Ellis, M. A. Jeeves, F. Newcombe, & A. Young (Eds.), *Aspects of face processing.* Dordrecht, The Netherlands: Nijhoff.

Johnson, M. K., Foley, M. A., Suengas, A. G., & Raye, C. L. (1988). Phenomenal characteristics of memories for perceived and imagined autobiographical events. *Journal of Experimental Psychology: General, 117,* 371–376.

Johnson, M. K., Kahan, T.I., & Raye, C. L. (1984). Dreams and reality monitoring. *Journal of Experimental Psychology: General, 133,* 329–344.

Johnson, M. K., & Raye, C. L. (1981). Reality monitoring. *Psychological Review, 88,* 67–85.

Johnson, M. K., Raye, C. L., Foley, J. H., & Foley, M. A. (1981). Cognitive operations and decision bias in reality monitoring. *American Journal of Psychology, 94,* 37–64.

Klatzky, R. L. (1986). Levels of representation and memory for faces. In H. D. Ellis, M. A. Jeeves, F. Newcombe, & A. Young (Eds.), *Aspects of face processing,* Dordrecht, The Netherlands: Nijhoff.

Kramer, T. H., Buckhout, R., & Eugenio, P. (1990). Weapon focus, arousal, and eyewitness memory: Attention must be paid. *Law and Human Behavior, 14,* 167–184.

Langer, E. J., & Abelson, R. P. (1972). The semantics of asking a favor: Or how to succeed in getting help without really dying. *Journal of Personality and Social Psychology, 24,* 26–32.

Laughery, K. R., Alexander, J. F., & Lane, A. B. (1971). Recognition of human faces: Effects of target exposure time, target position, and type of photograph. *Journal of Applied Psychology, 59,* 490–496.

Laughery, K. R., & Fowler, R. H. (1980). Sketch artist and identikit procedures for recalling faces. *Journal of Applied Psychology, 65,* 307–316.

Leippe, M. R., Manion, A. P., & Romanczyk, A. (1991). *Eyewitness persuasion: How and how well do factfinders judge the accuracy of adults' and children's memory reports?* Unpublished manuscript, Adelphi University.

Lindsay, D. S. (this volume). Memory source monitoring and eyewitness testimony (pp. 27–55).

Lindsay, R. C. L., & Wells, G. L. (1985). Improving eyewitness identifications from lineups: Simultaneous versus sequential lineup presentation. *Journal of Applied Psychology, 70,* 556–564.

Lindsay, R. C. L., Wells, G. L., & Rumpel, C. M. (1981). Can people detect eyewitness-identification accuracy within and across situations? *Journal of Applied Social Psychology, 66*, 79–89.

Lipton, J. P. (1977). On the psychology of eyewitness testimony. *Journal of Applied Psychology, 62*, 90–93.

Loftus, E. F. (1979). *Eyewitness testimony.* Boston: Harvard University Press.

Luus, C. A. E., & Wells, G. L. (this volume). Eyewitness identification certainty: Its causes and persuasive impact.

Malpass, R. S., & Kravitz, J. (1969). Recognition for faces of own and other race. *Journal of Personality and Social Psychology, 13*, 330–334.

Manion, A. P., Leippe, M. R., & Romanczyk, A. (in press). Discernibility of discrimination? Understanding jurors' reactions to accurate and inaccurate child and adult eyewitnesses. In G. S. Goodman & B. Bottoms (Eds.), *Understanding and improving children's eyewitness testimony.* New York: Guilford Press.

Munsterberg, H. (1908). *On the witness stand.* New York: Doubleday, Page.

Neisser, U. (1982). *Memory observed: Remembering in natural contexts.* San Francisco: W. H. Freeman.

Patterson, K. E., & Baddeley, A. D. (1977). When face recognition fails. *Journal of Experimental Psychology: Human Learning and Memory, 3*, 406–417.

Read, J. D. (this volume). Understanding bystander misidentifications: The role of familiarity and contextual knowledge (pp. 56–79).

Ross, D. F. (1990). *Unconscious transference and mistaken identity: When a witness misidentifies a familiar but innocent person from a lineup.* Unpublished doctoral dissertation, Cornell University.

Ross, D. F., Ceci, S. J., Dunning, D., & Toglia, M. P. (this volume). Unconscious transference and lineup identification: Toward a memory blending approach (pp. 80–100).

Schooler, J. W., & Engstler-Schooler, T. Y. (1990). Verbal overshadowing of visual memories: Some things are better left unsaid. *Cognitive Psychology, 22*, 36–71.

Schooler, J. W., Gerhard, C. A., & Loftus, E. F. (1986). Qualities of the unreal. *Journal of Experimental Psychology: Learning, Memory, and Cognition, 12*, 171–181.

Sporer, S. L. (this volume). Decision times and eyewitness identification accuracy in simultaneous and sequential lineups (pp. 300–327).

Strnad, B. N., & Mueller, J. H. (1977). Levels of processing in facial recognition memory. *Bulletin of the Psychomonic Society, 9*, 17–18.

Weingardt, K. R., Toland, H. K., & Loftus, E. F. (this volume). Reports of suggested memories: Do people truly believe them? (pp. 3–26).

Wells, G. L. (1984). The psychology of lineup identifications. *Journal of Applied Social Psychology, 14*, 89–103.

Wells, G. L., & Hryciw, B. (1984). Memory for faces: Encoding and retrieving operations. *Memory & Cognition, 12*, 338–344.

Wells, G. L., & Leippe, M. R. (1981). How do triers of fact infer accuracy of eyewitness identification? Using memory of peripheral details can be misleading. *Journal of Applied Psychology, 66*, 682–687.

Wells, G. L., Lindsay, R. C. L., & Ferguson, T. J. (1979). Accuracy, confidence and juror perceptions in eyewitness identifications. *Journal of Applied Psychology, 64*, 440–448.

Wells, G. F., Seelau, E. P., Rydell, S. M., & Luus, C. A. E. (this volume). Recommendations for properly conducted lineup identification tasks (pp. 223–244).

Winer, B. (1971). *Statistical principles in experimental design.* New York: McGraw-Hill.

Yarmey, A. D. (1979). *The psychology of eyewitness testimony.* New York: The Free Press.

Yerkes, R. M., & Dodson, J. D. (1908). The relation of strength of stimulus to rapidity of habit-formation. *Journal of Comparative and Neurological Psychology, 18*, 459–482.

14 Decision times and eyewitness identification accuracy in simultaneous and sequential lineups

Siegfried Ludwig Sporer

Learning from common sense psychological assumptions in the history of legal decision making

For a long time legal scholars have recognized that mistaken identifications have been and continue to be a major source of miscarriages of justice (for example, Sello, 1911; Hirschberg, 1960; Peters, 1972; Sobel, 1983; see Lipton, in press, for a recent review of the legal literature on this topic). Considering the fact that problems with identification seem to have been realized time and again, the judiciary should be equipped to meet this problem, and the occasional reoccurrence of false identifications should not be that surprising or unusual. The crucial issue seems to be, however, that triers of fact do not notice or know how to tell when an identification attempt is in error. The question we have to address is why identification decisions are so difficult to evaluate and what means might be available to improve assessment of identification decisions in individual cases.

The particular problem with identification evidence has been pointed out by the judiciary and psychological researchers alike. As Lord Devlin has phrased it most succinctly:

[T]he problem peculiar to evidence of visual identification is that this evidence, because of its type and not because of its quality, has a latent defect that may not be detected by the usual tests. The highly reputable, absolutely sincere, perfectly coherent, and apparently convincing witness may, as experience has quite often shown be mistaken. (Devlin, 1976, cited in Shepherd, Ellis, & Davies, 1982, p. v).

Shepherd et al. (1982) have elaborated on this point by drawing attention to the binary nature of an identification decision that may be right or wrong:

The major problem with identification evidence is that, unlike verbal testimony, which can be submitted to the scrutiny of cross-examination for internal consistency and general plausibility, and can be compared with other testimony and circumstantial evidence, the witness in an identification simply asserts that the accused is the person he has identified as having been at a particular place on a certain occasion. There is

This research was supported by grants from the Deutsche Forschungsgemeinschaft to Prof. Dr. D. Meurer (Me 272/2-2) and to the present author (Sp 262/1-2).

300

no story to dissect, no inconsistencies to be reconciled, and usually little contradictory evidence to challenge the identification. For even if the defence can produce witnesses who were not able to identify the suspect, the jury can make little of this except to infer that perhaps these witnesses were not very observant or have poor memories. (Shepherd, Ellis, & Davies, 1982, pp. 2–3)

We need additional cues that allow us to discriminate between accurate and inaccurate statements. Most research on eyewitness testimony has been designed to explore the conditions likely to determine its accuracy. With this approach we have learned a lot about situational factors influencing eyewitness accuracy (so-called estimator variables: Wells, 1978) and about control variables likely to improve identification accuracy (for example, Cutler & Penrod, 1988; Malpass, in press; Wells, 1978). On the other hand, some researchers have attempted to investigate individual differences in eyewitness identifications as a function of personality differences, albeit generally with little success (see Shapiro & Penrod, 1986, for review). Dent and Stephenson (1979, Experiment 5) have analyzed different processing strategies of witnesses at photographic lineups and their relative efficiency.

Most recently, several attempts have been made to gain additional information about an identification decision which can be used to evaluate the likelihood of the decision being accurate. For example, Stern and Dunning (this volume) argue that real memories, in this case correct identifications, would be associated with certain "markers" that characterize these statements and thus make them distinguishable from incorrect testimony. They have gained some insights into the nature of the underlying decision processes by questioning subjects after their decisions. Ross, Toglia, Hopkins, Hanson, and Devenport (1992; also, Ross, Ceci, Dunning, & Toglia, this volume) have similarly questioned witnesses after their decisions to pin down theoretical alternatives in the explanation of the unconscious transference effect.

Another approach has been followed by Sporer (1992a) who has proposed so-called *assessment variables* as a class of variables that may be used in the assessment of individual cases. Assessment variables are those verbal and nonverbal behaviors that can be observed directly in connection with the identification procedure or through additional questioning or assessment techniques. They include a variety of variables that have traditionally been investigated as estimator variables such as personality measures (for example, self-monitoring: Hosch, Leippe, Marchioni, & Cooper, 1984; see also Hosch, this volume), a witness's recognition ability (Hosch, Bothwell, Sporer, & Saucedo, 1989), the accuracy or amount of detail of prior descriptions of the perpetrator (for example, Pigott & Brigham, 1985; Sporer, 1992b, in press), or the witness's confidence in his or her decision (see the reviews by Bothwell, Deffenbacher, & Brigham, 1987; Cutler & Penrod, 1989; Deffenbacher, 1980; Leippe, 1980; Wells & Murray, 1983). As assessment variables are partially under the control of the investigator, through the form in which person descriptions are elicited or the way confidence is scaled, they overlap Wells's (1978) distinction between estimator and control variables (Sporer, 1992a).

Eyewitness confidence, which has been debated as the major candidate for "pre-dicting," or more precisely, "post-dicting" identification accuracy, is probably the most prominent example of a typical assessment variable (for critical reviews, see Bothwell, Deffenbacher, & Brigham, 1987; Cutler & Penrod, 1989; Deffenbacher, 1980; Leippe, 1980; Wells & Lindsay, 1985). Other assessment variables include the quantity and quality of prior descriptions (for example, Pigott, Brigham, & Bothwell, 1985; Sporer, 1992b; Wells, 1985; for review, see Sporer, in press) or the reasons given for an identification as proposed by Stern and Dunning (this volume). All these indicators focus on the witness's verbal utterances. To the extent that verbal and visual memorial processes are likely to be unrelated (Tulving, 1985), only low correlations between measures drawing from these different memory modes should be expected (Sporer, 1989). This is most evident for the low correlations typically obtained between person descriptions – a verbal recall task – and identification accuracy – a visual recognition task (Pigott, Brigham, & Bothwell, 1985; Sporer, 1992b; Wells, 1985).

One particular subgroup of assessment variables is a witness's nonverbal behavior accompanying his or her identification decision. For example, it is conceivable that certain patterns of eye movements might be related to the accuracy of a witness's choice. Although the variety of potential nonverbal indicators is large, there is almost no empirical research on this topic. The only variable in this group that only most recently has received some attention is decision time, that is, the time a witness takes to arrive at a recognition judgment.

The idea to use the expressive (hence observable) form of an identification response as well as the reasons stated for an identification decision as potential indicators of its evidentiary value is by no means new in the history of criminal law. In 1838, Henke, the author of a *German Handbook of Criminal Law and Criminal Politics,* alluded to this possibility in his lucid recommendation on how to conduct an identification procedure:

Above all, the identification procedure has to be preceded by a comprehensive interrogation of the witness, wherein he is to describe the characteristic features which could facilitate recognition of the persons or objects to which his testimony or statements refer. Thereafter, in the identification procedure itself, he is, whenever possible, to be confronted with several persons or objects resembling the one to be identified. He should be urged to point out, for example, the identified, *without hesitation,* and also to give the reasons why he had identified this one as the real one instead of the others. . . . On the one hand, the investigator has to take care, to the best of his ability, to remove any changes that may have occurred in the object to be recognized and that may thus impair recognition: therefore, for example, he must not present the accused in his prison clothes, or with a distorting beard, etc. On the other hand, the investigator must beware of drawing the witness's attention to the correct object through facial expressions, gestures, or external signs that differentiate the object in question from others. (Henke, 1838, pp. 705–706, trans. in Sporer, 1982, p. 324; italics ours)

We interpret the phrase "without hesitation" to imply that a spontaneous (quicker) response should be judged to be more credible than one uttered after some delay. This interpretation flies counter to an observation by Dent and Stephenson (1979, Experiment 5) who have observed that a strategy of "slow procession," used more frequently by women, was less effective than the "quick procession" strategy. In slow procession, subjects proceeded from left to right along the line looking slowly at each set of photographs in turn whereas in quick procession they did so quickly. Here, the speed of these processing strategies refers to the change between alternative persons in the lineup (compare the comparison strategies used by other witnesses in that study). This may not necessarily indicate a contradiction to our analysis of decision time which refers to the time taken from seeing a lineup person to choosing or rejecting him or her (for example, in a sequential lineup procedure: Sporer, 1992a). Note also that Stern and Dunning's approach (this volume) corresponds to Henke's (1838) recommendation that witnesses are supposed to present the reasons underlying their decision, that is, why they have chosen a particular "object."

Before we review some empirical studies relating decision times to the accuracy of recognition judgments we undertake a brief historical excursion on the use of decision times as an indicator of psychological processes. Thereafter, we present some laboratory findings on the use of reaction times in basic memory research, particularly on facial recognition. Finally, we present the results of a series of new staged event and filmed scenario experiments, most of them conducted at our university, that demonstrate the usefulness of decision times as an assessment variable. The latter is further subdivided into studies employing a simultaneous versus a sequential lineup presentation mode. A distinction between choosers and nonchoosers is proposed as a crucial mediating variable for the relationship between decision time and accuracy. We conclude with some practical recommendations for the conduct of lineup procedures and the assessment of decision times as well as for the evaluation of eyewitness identifications by triers of fact.

Decision time as an indicator of mental processes

Mental chronometry and the personal equation

According to standard textbooks on the history of psychology, the speed of reaction as a research problem was first noted in astronomy in the late eighteenth century when an astronomer's assistant was dismissed for making errors in recording the times at which stars crossed the meridians (Boring, 1950; Watson, 1978). A few years later, the Prussian astronomer Bessel (1784–

1846) realized that there were systematic differences among astronomers in observing stellar events. They developed "personal equations," that is, constants specific for individual observers that could be added or subtracted to make observations comparable. With technological advances such as the Hipp chronoscope, individual observers' times could be measured precisely in absolute terms (Watson, 1978). The Dutch physiologist Donders (1818–1889) applied this approach to physiological tasks, and the method since then has been called reaction time. Donders developed this method further, differentiating between simple discrimination and choice reaction times using the subtractive procedure. Performing more complex mental tasks (for example, discriminating two stimuli), it was reasoned, would take longer than a simple predetermined response to a stimulus.

This paradigm became one of the major foci of research in Wundt's laboratory in Leipzig (Boring, 1950). Other mental processes were investigated using additive and subtractive procedures, hoping to establish a chronometry of the mind (Watson, 1978). As it became apparent, however, that the "times for a separate process were constant neither from person to person nor from study to study" (Watson, 1978, p. 283), and that – as the Würzburg School demonstrated – the elements could not be considered additive, the high hopes in reaction time experiments vanished (Boring, 1950; Watson, 1978). Nonetheless, cognitive psychology remembered its predecessors when it succeeded in its attack against the dominating behaviorist paradigm in the 1960s (for example, Neisser, 1967).

Response latencies in basic and applied memory research

In basic memory research, reaction times have been a popular measure both of recall and recognition. Although this may be even more true for short-term (for example, Murdock, 1980; Sternberg, 1969) than for long-term memory studies (for example, Theios, 1973, 1975), many current memory models utilize response latency data to support their claims. In short-term recognition studies the notion of the accuracy-speed tradeoff has received much attention (see Murdock, 1982). This would indicate that accuracy will be sacrificed by arriving at a decision quickly. Under different circumstances, however, and in different paradigms, shorter reaction times will be indicative of accuracy (for example, in the study-test procedure: see Murdock, 1980). Within other domains of memory research, for instance on semantic memory, response times are used as an indicator of the stages of processing a subject must go through to achieve certain goals.

For example, in Anderson's (1983) spreading activation theory of memory, reaction times serve as a central indicator of retrieval processes. In his ACT model, reaction times are even considered a purer measure of interference than percent recall. Response latencies illustrate well the fan effect in sentence recognition, that is, the inverse relationship between the time required for association to spread to associated nodes and the number of associated nodes being activated (for example, Anderson, 1976). Latencies are the major measures in lexical decision, semantic and episodic memory priming, and sentence verification tasks (for example, Collins & Quillian, 1969; Meyer & Schvaneveldt, 1971; compare Best, 1989; Matlin, 1989). The underlying assumption common to most of these studies seems to be that response latencies covary with the number of individual steps postulated for certain decision-making processes.

There are also several face recognition studies that have employed response latencies as dependent measures. For example, Peris and Tiberghien (1984; compare Tiberghien, 1986) distinguished slow and fast responses associated with hits as a function of various context manipulations (changing name and/ or voice with which the name was announced). Ellis, J. W. Shepherd, Gibling, and J. Shepherd (1988) reported consistently faster responses to memorable than to nonmemorable faces over fifteen learning trials. All mean latencies were well below one second.

Sporer (1988, Experiment 2) showed that response latencies allowed finer discriminations among the effects of various forms of visual and verbal rehearsal with face stimuli than pure recognition measures. Responses to rehearsed faces were made faster than to nonrehearsed faces and hits ($M = 6.48$ sec) were made faster than the time taken for false alarms ($M = 10.11$ sec). Here, response latencies were in general substantially larger than those of the studies reported previously due to the procedure used. The yes–no recognition test more closely resembled a photo spread task conducted in the sequential lineup mode (for example, Lindsay & Wells, 1985; Sporer, 1992a) than the recognition tasks presented electronically in the typical laboratory studies.

Hay, Young, and A. W. Ellis (1986) based their claims about so-called face recognition units on reaction times. Subjects' decisions about familiarity were quicker than semantic decisions (classifying them as politicians versus nonpoliticians). This is seen as an indication that face recognition based on familiarity can be characterized as an automatic process that requires little if any conscious thought. By contrast, semantic decisions go beyond the use of face recognition units and demand access to identify-specific semantic codes, a process that takes more time (see also Bruce, 1986).

We should be cautious in generalizing from studies with familiar faces (of famous people) to the processes involved for recognizing strangers. Although the recognition of unfamiliar and familiar faces should be considered on a continuum (Bruce, 1988; Sporer, 1992c), the relevance of the former for eyewitness identifications in criminal cases involving strangers is questionable.

Also, practically all laboratory studies have generally measured latencies as a complement or an alternative to performance measures, without relating these two measures to each other, that is, without reporting their correlation. Thus we cannot know whether latency is predictive of accuracy in an individual case even though the two measures may covary as a function of experimentally induced manipulations. In other words, knowing that a response was made quickly is not necessarily an indicator that this particular response is more likely correct or not.

In memory research applied to the eyewitness arena the use of response latencies as indicators of memory strength or other cognitive processes is the exception. Loftus, Donders, Hoffman, and Schooler (1989) employed confidence ratings and response times to argue that "memories" for suggested events are held as confidently and are produced as swiftly as recollections of real events. Smith, Kassin, and Ellsworth (1989) explored the utility of response latencies as a predictor of accuracy both between and within subjects. They reported very low but significant correlations ($r = -.05$ and $-.09$, respectively) between latencies of responses to alternative-forced-choice questions regarding an auto-pedestrian accident and the accuracy of these responses.

In the following, we focus on studies that have measured decision times in connection with eyewitness identifications in forensically relevant paradigms. All the experiments reported have staged a live event or showed a filmed event before subjects and had them later identify the target in a photo (or live) lineup.

Studies using staged or filmed event paradigms

On the relationship between confidence and decision time

Before we review studies that have used decision times as a complement (or an alternative) assessment variable next to eyewitness confidence, we should first address the relationship between these two variables.

In line with common sense psychological assumptions expressed by jurors and higher courts alike (for example, *Neil v. Biggers,* 1972), most eyewitness identification studies using a staged event or filmed event paradigm have questioned witnesses as to their confidence as an assessment variable to postdict accuracy. Generally, confidence–accuracy relationships have been quite low and occasionally moderate in magnitude (see the reviews by Bothwell, Deffenbacher, & Brigham, 1987; Deffenbacher, 1980; Leippe, 1980; Wells & Murray, 1983). Although some recent studies have pointed to important mediating variables (for example, distinguishing between pre- and postdecision confidence: Cutler & Penrod, 1989; Fleet, Brigham, & Bothwell, 1987), or between choosers and nonchoosers (Brigham, 1988; Fleet, Brigham, & Bothwell, 1987; Sporer, 1992a, 1992b; see below) experts have generally agreed that confidence should be treated with extreme caution in evaluating witness evidence.

To what extent may decision times serve as an alternative or a complementary assessment variable? First, it should be noted that most studies that have measured confidence and decision times have shown these two variables to be more or less strongly negatively related. Thus, to some extent both measures may tap the same underlying construct. Alternatively, response latencies may serve to mediate self-attributions of confidence (Turtle, 1988). This typical negative relationship holds, however, only for the relationship between decision time and postdecision confidence, not for predecision confidence.

For example, Kassin (1985) reported an average correlation of $-.25$ between postdecision confidence and decision time in his four experiments. Sporer (1992a) found that predecision confidence was only marginally significantly related to postdecision confidence ($r = .19, p < .10$) and unrelated to decision time ($r = -.06$, *ns.*). Postdecision confidence showed the predicted negative relationship with decision time ($r = -.33, p < .01$) but this relationship was not so high as to render these variables redundant predictors for the accuracy of lineup decisions. Sporer (1992b) observed an even higher negative relationship between accuracy and postdecision confidence ($r = -.55, p < .001$) but not with predecision confidence ($r = .00$, *ns.*). In this study, partial correlations showed that the predictive value of decision time was substantially diminished when postdecision confidence was controlled for. Nonetheless, both variables jointly accounted for considerably more variance than either variable by itself. Thus, decision time may at times convey information to the trier of fact that is redundant with postdecision confidence, and at times it may add a new aspect that will help to evaluate an identification decision more adequately.

Decision times in simultaneous lineups

We will first review several studies that have tested recognition with a simultaneous lineup procedure. Next, we introduce choice as an important mediating variable and report some of our own studies, first with the simultaneous and finally with the sequential lineup presentation mode, in which decision times have been particularly useful as an assessment variable. In all cases, correlations between identification accuracy and decision time are *point-biserial* correlations which may actually underestimate the true relationship between these two constructs. These correlations are expected to be negative, that is, correct witnesses should arrive at a decision more quickly than incorrect ones.

Bothwell, Brigham, and Pigott (1987) exposed students to a live target under varying levels of arousal (for example, by placing a syringe package on a table in front of the subject). Following presentation of the target, subjects were asked to identify him in a target-present or a target-absent lineup. For the total sample of 128 subjects, reaction time was negatively related to identification accuracy ($r = -.28, p < .05$). In Stern and Dunning's (this volume) experiment, subjects watched a videotape that showed an assailant stealing money from a wallet. In line with the postulated decision strategies predominantly followed by accurate witnesses who rely more on their memories of the culprit and arrive at their recognition judgments automatically, they found reliably shorter response times for correct identifications ($M = 13.3$ sec) than for foil identifications in target-present ($M = 18.5$ sec) or false identifications in target-absent photo spreads ($M = 17.2$ sec). The observed F-value for the linear contrast between these correct and incorrect positive choices can be transformed into a (point-biserial) correlation coefficient of $-.20$.

Kassin (1985) conducted four studies using a videotape of a staged vandalism or burglary. The purpose of the study was to arrive at a more detailed understanding of the accuracy–confidence relationship by employing a retrospective self-awareness manipulation based on Bem's (1972) self-perception theory. In the first three experiments, recognition was tested in a simultaneous presentation mode with a six-person photo array in which the target was always present. Besides confidence Kassin also measured reaction times during the identification task as a predictor variable.

The correlations between response latencies and identification accuracy were $-.37$, $-.16$ and $-.10$ (all *ns.*) in the first three experiments. In Experiment 4, that used a sequential lineup procedure, a marginally significant relationship ($-.23, p < .06$) was obtained. Only in two control conditions of Experiment 4, that is, without the thinking aloud procedure, significant relationships in the retrospective awareness ($r = -.62, p < .01$) and in the standard condition ($r = -.50, p < .05$) were observed. This was also the only experiment in which latency could be demonstrated (via partial correlations: see Kassin, 1985, p. 888, note 9) to serve a mediating function between accuracy and confidence.

Due to the absence of target-absent conditions in all four experiments, however, Kassin could not have observed the mediating effect of choosing which seems to be crucial for obtaining substantial relationships (Sporer, 1992a, 1992b; see below).

An important extension of Kassin's retrospective self-awareness approach has been advanced by Turtle (1988, Study 3) who proposed a causal link between witnesses' impressions of their decision time and their estimates of confidence and accuracy. Providing witnesses with false feedback suggesting that they had been rather fast compared to the average respondent led to higher confidence ratings when the target was present in the lineup, but with target-absent lineups, confidence ratings were lower. More important for the assessment of individual decisions was the finding that decision times for hits in target-present lineups were made significantly faster than for correct rejections in target-absent lineups (almost a forty-second difference according to his figure). Unfortunately, Turtle did not calculate the difference between hits and false identifications which we argue should be most crucial (about a fifteen-second difference according to his figure).

Choosing as a mediating variable in our studies

Bothwell and Thomas (in press) cite Bothwell's 1985 doctoral dissertation in which he

was able to account for all of the variance in accuracy of confident choosers by taking into account *reaction time.* Four of five confident male choosers were accurate. However, the inaccurate male choosers had a reaction time on the lineup task that was longer than 20 s, whereas all of the accurate choosers had reaction times less than 20 s. Therefore, accuracy could be predicted using the following rule: confidence greater than 6 or 7 on the 7-point scale *and* reaction time less than 20 s. (Bothwell & Thomas, in press, pp. 22–23, italics in the original)

This appears to be very compelling evidence for the use of decision times as an assessment variable, at least for highly confident choosers. Another way to interpret this finding is to postulate that choosers should be considered differently from nonchoosers (see also Brigham, 1988; Sporer, 1992a, 1992b). Consequently, the correlation between decision time and accuracy should not be considered for the total sample but separately for these two subgroups of witnesses. We will discuss several studies that have explicitly taken choosing as a mediating variable into account.

STUDY 1

Probably one of the first studies – carried out in 1983 – that used decision times as an indicator of decision accuracy was conducted by Sporer (1992b). This study involved a staged incident in a university classroom, in which a confederate entered the classroom and got into an altercation with the experimenter about who was to use the slide projector the experimenter was setting up. During the incident, the target was visible to the audience for only about twenty seconds. In this experiment, the memory of the subjects was tested unexpectedly after one week, using a video lineup in which the intruder was present or absent. In addition to the response alternatives provided in most experiments that only permit a positive identification of one of the persons in the lineup or a not present alternative, thus forcing witnesses to make one decision or another, this experiment also allowed for a don't know response if subjects could not make up their minds.

These last subjects took particularly long ($M = 26.7$ sec) before they finally

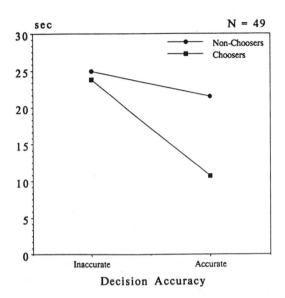

Figure 14.1: Mean decision times for correct and incorrect decisions of choosers and non-choosers (data from Sporer, 1992b, *European Journal of Social Psychology, 22,* 157–180).

decided not to commit themselves to one of the more definitive response options (selecting somebody from the lineup or rejecting the lineup by indicating that the target was not present). Correct decisions ($M = 14.3$ sec) were made significantly faster than incorrect decisions ($M = 24.1$ sec). Although this difference was reliable (the F-value corresponding to an $r = -.36, p < .05$), the most compelling evidence is obtained when we consider choosers, that is, witnesses who positively identified somebody in the lineup – the forensically most relevant group – separately from nonchoosers who asserted that the target is not present. (The don't know subjects were dropped from this analysis.)

Using choice (choosers versus nonchoosers) and decision accuracy (correct versus incorrect) as classifying variables in a two by two ANOVA with decision times as the dependent variable, the a priori contrast between correct (hits: $M = 10.7$ sec) and incorrect choosers (false identifications: $M = 23.8$ sec) was highly reliable. Comparing correct and incorrect rejections ($Ms = 21.5$ versus 24.9 sec, respectively) revealed no significant effect. Figure 14.1 illustrates these differential outcomes for choosers and nonchoosers.

The corresponding accuracy–decision time correlations which statistically correspond to the a priori contrast were $-.43$ ($p < .05$) for choosers and $-.20$ (*ns.*) for nonchoosers, respectively. Despite the small sample size, these data indicate that accurate identifications may result from a more spontaneous recognition decision than false identifications, which seem to result from a slower deliberation process.

Multiple discriminant analyses. In the preceding paragraphs we have summarized the results of Sporer's (1992b) univariate correlational analyses and the analysis of variance on decision time. From an applied perspective, the relevant question is: Can we discriminate between witnesses who make correct or incorrect identification decisions on the basis of their decision behaviors?

In the following, we present some additional analyses of Sporer's data not reported in that paper. We wanted to see to what extent it would be possible to predict correct versus incorrect identification decisions from a multivariate combination of four predictor variables analyzed in this study: number of descriptors (that is, the number of descriptive details contained in the person descriptions), pre- and postdecision confidence, and decision times. We computed three multiple discriminant analyses with decision accuracy as the outcome to be predicted, and these four variables as predictors, first for the sample of subject-witnesses who had arrived at a decision ($N = 49$), and separately for choosers ($n = 33$) and nonchoosers ($n = 16$).

For the whole sample, the canonical correlation between these four variables and decision accuracy was .50 (*Wilk's Lambda* $= .75, p = .013$), with all but predecision confidence contributing significantly to this discrimination. On the basis of the obtained discriminant function equation actual group membership (correct versus incorrect decisions) could be predicted correctly in thirty-four (69.4 percent) of the forty-nine cases.

Prediction outcomes were more successful when we restricted our analyses to choosers only ($n = 33$). Here, twenty-eight (84.9 percent) of the thirty-three cases were predicted accurately. Of the five misclassifications, two were false positives and three were false rejections. The canonical correlation was .60 (*Wilk's Lambda* $= .641, p = .012$), with postdecision confidence and decision time as significant univariate contributors.

Results for nonchoosers ($n = 16$) should be treated with caution due to the small sample size. Twelve (75 percent) of the sixteen cases could be classified correctly which does not exceed chance level, considering there were four predictor variables. None of the predictor variables discriminated significantly in the univariate analyses.

In sum, when choice is considered as a mediating variable it seems possible to use these predictor variables to classify individual cases within a multiple discriminant analysis. Although we would find it precocious to use the discriminant functions derived from such an analysis for the post-dictive classification of real cases we suggest these analyses and their cross-validation on a larger sample as a useful supplement to the correlational analyses generally reported. Surely, the percentage of correctly versus incorrectly classified cases

– here 84.9 percent correctly classified for choosers – can be communicated much more easily to the legal community which we ultimately want to reach with this research.

Encouraged by these results, we have (re-)analyzed the results of several other studies in the same way to see whether or not they replicate these findings.

STUDY 2

Hosch, Bothwell, Sporer, and Saucedo (1989) attempted to evaluate the predictive value of several variables to post-dict eyewitness identifications after exposure to a target under optimal viewing, delay, and retrieval conditions. The experimenter entered the laboratory and explained to the subjects an impending slide recognition task. Subjects saw the target in a well lighted room (face-to-face) for approximately thirty-seconds. The experiment was then continued by a confederate. About fifteen minutes after initial exposure the identification of the target occurred from a stack of photographs in which the target was present or absent. For the total sample, decision time showed a moderately negative relationship to identification accuracy ($r = -.29$, $p < .10$). Again, breaking the sample down into choosers and nonchoosers was more revealing: Decision time was more strongly (but only marginally significantly) related to identification accuracy with choosers ($r = -.48$, $p < .10$), and nonsignificantly with non-choosers ($r = -.11$, $ns.$).

Decisions after receiving misleading postevent information

STUDY 3

Loftus (1979) and her colleagues, as well as other researchers, have amply demonstrated that witnesses may be misled by postevent information. This misinformation effect has generally been demonstrated with misleading verbal information followed by a verbal (seldom visual) recall or recognition test. In our studies (Franzen & Sporer, in press-a, in press-b) we focused exclusively on the visual mode. First we presented the original information in a film (a staged theft of a pair of expensive sunglasses in an optometrist's store). Second, after a one-week delay, we exposed subjects to a newspaper article that contained either a good computer-generated facial composite, a misleading composite resembling one of the foils, or no composite of the target. Third, we tested recognition of the target in target-present or target-absent photo spreads.

In addition, we explored various countermeasures that should reduce, or even inoculate against, the distorting effects of misleading information. In the first experiment, we hypothesized that rereading their own prior description of the perpetrator, as a form of reinstatement of context, should help witnesses in their identification (Cutler, Penrod, & Martens, 1987) and reduce the errors occurring from the suggestive information.

In the first experiment (Franzen & Sporer, in press-a; $N = 154$), a few but significantly more mix-ups (that is, false identifications of the suspect depicted in the misleading composite) occurred as a function of the misleading post-event information. But there were also a great number of foil identifications of other members in the lineup – which some authors consider legally irrel-evant. Rereading of subjects' own prior description of the thief did not reduce either kind of error nor increase correct identifications.

The recognition test was conducted as a photo spread in a simultaneous presentation mode. Decision times that were collected for 149 subjects showed no relationship to identification accuracy ($r = .03$, *ns.*). Breaking down the sample into choosers and nonchoosers did not alter this conclusion ($r = -.02$ for choosers and $r = .06$ for nonchoosers, both *ns.*). Additional comparisons among misled subjects revealed that decision times for falsely identifying the suspect resembling the misleading composite were as fast ($M = 19.0$ sec) as for correct choices of the target ($M = 24.0$ sec) in that condition.

This could mean that misled witnesses may indeed not be able to distinguish between their false memory trace and the alternative implanted by the sug-gested misleading postevent information (Loftus, Donders, Hoffman, & Schooler, 1989). We should also note, however, that in this experiment the overall rate of false identifications was very high whereas that of the particular misleading foil (the mix-up) was too small to make statistical inferences mean-ingful. Apparently, memory for the perpetrator was not very good and sub-jects found it very hard to arrive at a decision.

One of the reasons for the difficulties subjects had with this task was the highly homogeneous lineup which made it very difficult for them to pick the right person, even in target-present lineups. Consequently, we attempted to replicate this experiment, systematically varying lineup similarity by using a homogeneous and a heterogeneous lineup.

STUDY 4

In this follow-up experiment by Franzen and Sporer (in press-b; $N = 178$), false identifications of the misleading foil were substantially higher, particu-larly in the heterogeneous photo spread. Visualization of the target – as an imagery-based method of reinstatement of context (compare Bekerian, Den-nett, Hill, & Hitchcock, 1990) – before the identification task did not improve performance or counteract the misinformation effect. Testing with a homo-geneous lineup, however, led to significantly fewer false identifications of the misleading foil than a low similarity lineup.

Decision times were negatively related to accuracy in the total sample

($N = 165$) for which response latencies had been measured ($r = -.15, p <$ .10), but the effect was only marginally significant. For choosers, this relationship was reliably negative ($r = -.25, p < .05$) whereas for nonchoosers a nonsignificant positive relationship was observed ($r = .09, ns.$). In analysis of variance terms, this result corresponds to a significant choice by decision outcome interaction.

As in the first experiment, we compared decision times for correct choices and those for the mix-ups in the misleading postevent condition. The pattern of means was in the expected direction but did not differ reliably (probably due to the small n's): Hits ($M = 68.9$ sec) were made faster than mix-ups ($M = 84.2$ sec) which in turn were faster than foil identifications ($M = 96.7$ sec). Note that the means for decision times between hits and mix-ups were reversed to those in the first experiment where no reliable differences had been observed. Again, this may indicate that the identification decisions made as a function of misleading postevent information may not be internally distinguishable by the subject.

Unfortunately, the results of both experiments are not consistent. Nonetheless, the findings of the second study are encouraging. They indicate that decision times should not be used as a predictor in absolute terms but should be looked at separately for choosers and nonchoosers, that is, depending on whether or not a witness has positively chosen someone in the lineup. The inconsistency in findings across the two experiments may place a restriction on the generality of this effect. Decision times may not always be indicative of correct positive decisions, especially when the conditions are particularly difficult as was the case in the first study (that is, an incidental learning situation and testing with a high similarity lineup). The pattern of correlations in the second study, however, did not differ between the homogeneous and the heterogeneous conditions. This gives us hope that this finding is not restricted to easy lineup tasks only.

One of the assumptions guiding the second experiment was that the imagery mnemonic (visualizing the target prior to the identification) should lead to a clearer internal image of the perpetrator in the witness's mind which in turn should speed up the decision process as well as increase his or her confidence.

To answer these questions, we gathered additional data on the vividness of the image of the perpetrator which should shed light on the role imagery played in the identification process. The imagery technique employed should lead the witness step by step to a recollection of the target's face: A witness was asked to create successively an image of the interior of the store, the persons entering the store, the actions of the target, his stature, and finally his face. This would presumably lead to an optimal representation of the target in the witness's mind which should be helpful in the identification task. This reasoning corresponds with two alternative theoretical views: According to Bekerian et al. (1990), the cognitive interview owes its success to an imagery component which is a key ingredient for reinstating the encoding context. Alternatively, a vivid image of the perpetrator as a basis for an identification also follows one of the predictions derived from the reality monitoring approach applied to eyewitness identifications (Stern & Dunning, this volume).

As a manipulation check, one group of subjects was asked to rate for vividness on a five-point scale (averaged over the five ratings: $M = 3.20$) the successive images occurring to them; another group rated the vividness of the obtained images at the end of these successive steps in a single rating ($M = 3.07$). Correlations between the vividness of these images and identification accuracy were slightly negative at chance level ($r = -.11$ and $r = -.05$, respectively). Vividness ratings were also not correlated with decision times ($r = -.05$ and $r = -.14$, both *ns.* for these two groups). However, the vividness of these images did show very high correlations with predecision confidence, that is, the witness's belief that he or she would be able to identify the target in a lineup ($r = .56$ and $.71$, respectively, both $p < .001$). Postdecision confidence was also related to these imagery ratings ($r = .24$, $p < .10$, and $.54$, $p < .001$).

We propose that the vividness of the imagery may be used by a witness for metacognitive aspects of the decision, like gauging one's confidence, but not as the basis of the decision process itself. Hence, the reported vividness of the imagery of the target does not predict the accuracy of the recognition judgment. For the latter, decision time seems to be a better indicator, at least in case of a positive choice.

Decision times in showup identifications

Most recently, Yarmey (1992) has presented data from a field experiment on showup identifications. Citizens were approached by one of two young adult females who spoke to them for a total of fifteen seconds. Two minutes later, the experimenter approached the witnesses and asked questions about the personal appearance of the target. Half the subjects were presented with a showup, that is, a single photograph which displayed the target or a similar looking foil, the other half with a tape recording of the target or a foil. Surprisingly, subjects were better (84 percent correct) in rejecting the foil than in recognizing the target (55 percent correct) on the photograph. In addition, the average time taken to arrive at a decision about the foil ($M = 2.91$ sec) was significantly faster than that to decide about a target ($M = 3.95$ sec). Unfortunately, the author did not indicate whether the respective correct decisions differed from the respective incorrect decisions for targets or foils. For voice identifications, no reliable difference in decision times for target voice ($M = 13.1$ sec) or foil voice ($M = 12.5$ sec) was observed.

Decision times under the influence of social factors

Decision times may not only be an indicator of cognitive processes. At times they may reflect the influence of social factors such as the pressure exerted on witnesses by the police to make a positive identification, particularly with live lineups. For example, using a staged event paradigm involving a classroom theft Kohnken and Maass (1988) manipulated the pressure exerted on witnesses through biased (versus unbiased) instructions. In addition, half the witnesses were told the identification took place within the context of a psychological experiment, the other half were not. Decision times were not only prolonged by biased instructions but witnesses in the biased instruction condition were extremely slow when they had been led to believe that their testimony would actually be part of a criminal prosecution.

Unfortunately, Kohnken and Maass did not report the correlations of decision times with the accuracy of lineup decisions. Considering the strong influence instructional bias exerted on decision times, however, it should be clear that the strength of these correlations was probably masked by the variables.

Comparing the mean values in their first (all cell means between 41.5 and 102.2 sec) and their second experiment (between 23.0 and 37.2 sec) also demonstrated that decision times may vary widely under different conditions even within the same study. Although the authors did not address this issue, we suspect that the difference may have resulted from the presence of the don't know option in the first but not in the second experiment. Sporer (1992b; see above) had also found the slowest responses among witnesses who refused to arrive at a positive or negative decision by checking the "don't know – can't remember" option.

Instructional bias, the pressure perceived by a witness to arrive at a decision, and other social factors will have to be taken into account if decision time is to be used as an assessment variable of identification accuracy. In the next section, we will review studies employing sequential lineup presentation modes that allow multiple assessments of decision times (and confidence), and consequently allow comparisons of decision times both between and within witnesses.

Decision times in sequential lineups

Sequential lineup presentation modes have been suggested by Wells (1984) and Lindsay and Wells (1985) as an alternative to the common simultaneous testing procedures. The rationale of a sequential mode of testing is to lead the witness away from the relative judgment strategy prevalent with simultaneous testing to an absolute judgment strategy. By inducing witnesses to make successive identification decisions and individual comparisons of each lineup member with their internal representation of the culprit, cognitive aspects of the decision process are stressed (Sporer, 1992a). One of the major advantages of the sequential lineup mode, which has been repeatedly replicated, is that it seems to lead to fewer false identifications in target-absent lineups without losing the power to detect the culprit when he is present (for example, Cutler & Penrod, 1988; Lindsay, Lea, & Fulford, 1991; Lindsay & Wells, 1985; Melara, DeWitt-Rickards, & O'Brian, 1989; Parker & Ryan, 1990; Sporer, 1992a; Sporer, Eickelkamp, & Spitmann-Rex, 1990).

With sequential lineups where response latencies can be assessed for each individual decision separately (that is, for each of the six lineup faces) we can employ more refined methods of analysis that take the relative times for choices versus nonchoices and for accurate versus inaccurate choices into account. In research studies, these measures can be compared both between and within subjects – the latter for choosers only. In an individual case, decision times (and confidence judgments) can be assessed repeatedly for each individual decision. This strategy has been followed by Sporer (1992a) as well as in a new unpublished study (Sporer, in preparation) to be summarized below.

STUDY 5

In Study 5 (Sporer, 1992a), eyewitness identification accuracy was investigated in simultaneous and sequential lineups. Seventy-two subjects watched a film of a robbery in a public park under incidental learning conditions, supposedly to judge its artistic quality. They returned to the laboratory the following day to answer questions about the film. Sequential lineup procedures led to significantly fewer false identifications than the simultaneous lineup mode, with comparable performance in identifying the perpetrator when he was present in the lineup.

A more traditional analysis, as most researchers have generally reported the relationships between accuracy and decision time (and/or confidence), would have led to the conclusion that accuracy showed only a low correlation with predecision confidence ($r = .23, p < .05$) and decision time ($r = -.22, p < .05$), and a fairly high correlation with postdecision confidence ($r = .53, p < .001$).

The subsidiary analyses, however, that focused on a distinction between choosers and nonchoosers revealed quite a different picture. For choosers, the relationship between accuracy and postdecision confidence was boosted to .58 ($p < .001$) as compared to only .34 ($p < .05$) for nonchoosers. The importance of choice as a mediating variable that has recently been found to boost the accuracy–confidence relationship was again confirmed (Sporer, 1992b; see above). Choosing turned out to be an even more crucial mediator for the relationship between decision time and accuracy. For choosers, this relationship was significantly negative as predicted ($r = -.36$, $p < .01$) whereas for nonchoosers it was nonsignificantly positive ($r = .17$, *ns.*).

These relationships are best expressed in ANOVA terms as an interaction between choosing and decision outcome that was highly reliable. As a dependent variable the average time taken for a decision of individual lineup members was used. These results are collapsed across lineup type. For simultaneous lineups, the total decision time was divided by the number of members in the lineup (six). In the sequential lineup, in case of a positive choice, the time for that individual choice was taken. For rejections, the average across all six decision times was computed.

An alternative method would have been summing up the decision times in the sequential lineup to make them comparable to the simultaneous lineup. Summing up decision times for individual faces in the sequential lineup mode may overestimate the actual time taken, as the verbalization time for each choice enters the total six times whereas it will only enter decision time once in the simultaneous mode. On the other hand, once subjects had made a positive choice in the sequential lineup they would be more likely to reject the subsequent faces more quickly. (Some authors argue that they should not even be shown at all.) Overall decision time also depended on the position of the target which was systematically varied from Position 1 to Position 6 in the target-present lineups. Therefore, in case of a positive choice in sequential lineups, the time taken for this particular choice was used for analysis instead of the average time for all six lineup decisions.

Figure 14.2 displays the mean decision times for correct and false identifications as well as for correct and false rejections.

Additional within-subjects analyses of choosers in sequential lineups are even more telling. For subjects who had made a positive choice, a two by two mixed model ANOVA was performed that compared average rejection and positive identification time for the particular face chosen within subjects (repeated measures factor) as a function of the accuracy of the underlying decision (between-subjects factor). Again, the crucial interaction was most telling (see Figure 14.3). One way to look at this interaction is to compare the decision time for a hit that was much faster than for a false identification. This is a between-subjects comparison, however, usually not available in real cases. Another way to look at this interaction is to note that a false identification occurred after a much longer deliberation time than the average rejection time for the other lineup faces. Thus, with sequential lineups, decision time can be indicative of accuracy in a dual sense.

Although the data presented by Sporer (1992a) are statistically reliable despite the small number of subjects, conclusions drawn from the study must be treated with caution. Subjects in that study had been exposed to a film they thought they would later judge for its artistic quality. An incidental learning situation may be analogous to unexpectedly witnessing a crime as a

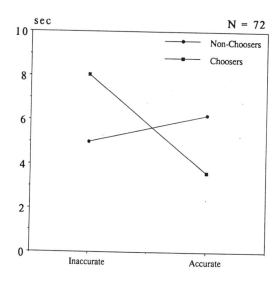

Figure 14.2: Mean decision times for correct and incorrect decisions of choosers and non-choosers (data from Sporer, 1992a, *Journal of Applied Psychology*).

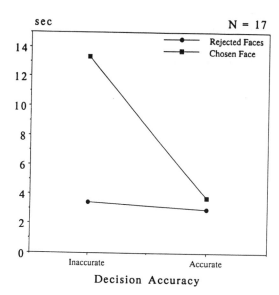

Figure 14.3: Mean decision times for correct and incorrect individual choices and average rejection times for nonchosen faces of choosers in sequential lineups (data from Sporer, 1992a, *Journal of Applied Psychology*).

bystander, but the filmed event paradigm is still a far cry from the involvement (and arousal) of witnesses in real crimes. Consequently, we launched a large scale study with a staged event paradigm featuring an incident likely to focus the subjects' attention on the target.

STUDY 6

The major purpose of this study was to compare the viability of sequential and simultaneous lineup procedures with live and representational (video and photo) lineups (see Sporer, in preparation). We will not discuss those aspects of that study but only present the results of the data on decision times and their relationship to identification accuracy. Five different lineup modes were employed:

1. Sequential black-and-white photo lineup ($n = 46$)
2. Sequential color photo lineup ($n = 25$)
3. Sequential live lineup ($n = 23$)
4. Sequential color video lineup ($n = 28$)
5. Simultaneous live lineup ($n = 28$)

A policeman interrupted ongoing teaching sessions in different university departments, stating that "something had happened" and he would have to check for something in the room. One week later, 150 volunteer subjects participated in an attempt to identify the target via one of the five different modes with the target present or absent. Decision times were measured unobtrusively by the experimenters or judged from a video or audio recording of the subjects at the time of identification.

Decision times varied tremendously across different lineup procedures as well as across subjects within the different lineup presentation modes. Means for the photo lineups (black-and-white: 14.74 sec; color: 16.51 sec) were rather low, the live sequential lineup took substantially longer (24.19 sec), and responses to the video lineup were slowest (30.35 sec). The shortest average decision time was for the live simultaneous condition (6.27 sec) perhaps because we divided the total decision time by the number of lineup members (six); apparently, this correction was not necessary. The important point is that there were no interactions between lineup presentation mode and any of the other variables (all F's < 1, ns.), which makes the conclusions generalizable across these modes.

On average, choosers took significantly longer ($M = 18.6$ sec) than nonchoosers ($M = 16.5$ sec) whereas overall correct decisions ($M = 15.6$ sec) were not made significantly faster than incorrect decisions ($M = 20.4$ sec). Individual comparisons made clear that there was no difference in decision times between correct and incorrect nonchoosers but the times for hits and false identifications again differed reliably. This pattern of results corresponds to the data we have found in previous studies (Sporer, 1992a, 1992b). In terms of the

Table 14.1. *Correlations between decision times and identification accuracy for choosers and nonchoosers in studies 1 to 6*

Lineup type	Total N	Choosers only	Nonchoosers only	All subjects
Simultaneous				
Sporer (1992b)	49	−.43*	−.20	−.36*
Hosch, Sporer, Bothwell, & Saucedo (1989, Exp. 1)	33	−.48°	−.11	−.29
Franzen & Sporer (in press-a)	149	−.02	.06	.03
Franzen & Sporer (in press-b)	165	−.25*	.09	−.15°
Simultaneous/sequential				
Sporer (1992a)	72	−.36**	.17	−.22*
Sporer (in prep.)	150	−.29*	.05	−.16*

*p < .05; **p < .01; °p < .10.

more familiar correlation coefficients usually reported (see Table 14.1), there was a small but negligible negative correlation between decision time and accuracy in the total sample ($r = -.16, p < .05$). This relationship was again stronger among choosers ($r = -.29, p < .01$) as compared to nonchoosers, for whom it was nonsignificantly positive ($r = .05, ns.$).

Within-subjects analyses of this experiment analogous to those by Sporer (1992a) replicated these findings. The only exception was the video lineup condition in which response latency could not be used as an indicator of accuracy. This may have been a function of the procedure used (each lineup member paraded back and forth and displayed himself in three different facial poses).

Summary

In the last sections we have reviewed studies that employed a staged or filmed event paradigm and measured decision time as a correlate of decision accuracy. Overall, there seems to be a small but reliable negative relationship between decision time and accuracy. This relationship can be boosted in studies employing both target-present and target-absent lineups when choosing is considered as a mediating variable. Table 14.1 summarizes six of our own studies that have followed this criterion.

The relationship among choosers becomes consistently stronger whereas for nonchoosers the correlation is generally not different from zero or even slightly positive in some cases. A potential exception may be studies in which misleading postevent information has contaminated the memory of witnesses. Here, accurate identifications are generally made no faster than mix-ups with another person suggested by a misleading facial composite. Within a sequential lineup mode, within-witness comparisons of the decision time for a positive choice and average rejection times have been particularly revealing. Overall, these findings point to the utility of decision times as an assessment variable for the evaluation of individual cases. We should not forget, however, that a host of other, particularly social, factors are also likely to affect both decision accuracy and decision times and hence will obscure this postulated relationship.

Practical implications

With respect to the forensic utility of decision time, we must still clarify under which conditions decision time may or may not serve as a useful predictor. For example, Kohnken and Maass (1988) have demonstrated that decision times may be prolonged by the pressure exerted on witnesses through biased instructions. In live lineups, witnesses may also attempt to escape the aversiveness of the situation by arriving at a decision quickly, "to get it over with." These potential mediating variables must be taken into account if decision times (or any other lineup behaviors) are to be used in assessing a witness's identification decision.

At this point it remains unclear whether decision time and postdecision confidence may or may not be (jointly) influenced by the same types of variables other researchers have posited as influential for the accuracy–confidence relationship (for example, Deffenbacher's [1980] optimality hypothesis).

Despite these caveats we are optimistic that measuring decision times and considering other verbal and nonverbal behaviors in an identification decision will be a worthwhile undertaking. Stern and Dunning (this volume) have pointed out reality monitoring aspects of identification decisions that could help us to arrive at a better understanding of the underlying decision process. Although some of these approaches may still be more intriguing to theoreticians than to practical decision makers, we nonetheless point out some conclusions about the way lineups should be conducted to make optimal use of these assessment variables. We stress that these conclusions are tentative and reflect admittedly personal views in light of our most recent findings. As more research along these lines becomes available these conclusions may be subject to change.

In the following, we spell out some practical guidelines which should help the investigator to optimally conduct lineups and the trier of fact to use as much information as possible to arrive at an assessment of lineup testimony.

Lineups should be conducted with a sequential (as opposed to a simultaneous) procedure. Sequential lineups not only offer the advantage of reducing the likelihood of false identifications but also allow multiple measurements of decision times.

It is essential to observe certain rules in conducting a sequential lineup, not giving witnesses a second guess, not instructing them as to the number of people in the lineup (see Lindsay, Lea, & Fulford, 1991; Parker & Ryan, 1990; Sporer, 1992a; Sporer, Eickelkamp, & Spitmann-Rex, 1990).

When assessing the probative value of a lineup decision on the basis of decision time (and confidence) it is necessary to distinguish between choosers, who have made a positive identification, and nonchoosers. Only for the former can decision time serve as an indicator of accuracy.

Situational and social factors (for example, pressure exerted by the investigator to arrive at a positive decision) should be taken into consideration. They may invalidate the predictive value of the assessment variables. Misleading postevent information may be a source of error.

In sequential lineups, analyses of decision times of choosers allow for a within-witness comparison between the time taken for the person chosen and the (average) time for rejection of the other lineup members. Presumably, only the rejection times for the lineup members shown prior to making a choice should be considered in this analysis. This obviously requires that the suspect not be placed as the first person in the lineup.

To render measurements of decision times (and other lineup behaviors) as objective as possible not only should the lineup members be documented through photographs or videotapes, but the entire witness testimony should be videotaped (unobtrusively). This videotape should include not only the decision process as the major focus of analysis but also the investigatory interview, for example, questions about the perpetrator's appearance, about predecision confidence, the exact wording of unbiased lineup instructions, and postdecision utterances of the witness. This last should include a postdecision confidence judgment, particularly in case of a positive choice, as well as reasons for the choice taken (see Stern and Dunning, this volume). The decision times can be measured unobtrusively by an officer observing the witness (for example, from behind; Sporer, 1992a) or from the videotape (Sporer, in preparation).

Although some of these variables may not be useful predictors in assessing the accuracy of a witness choice (in particular, person descriptions and predecision confidence), others may be more valid under some circumstances (for example, confidence and decision times). We hope that this individual-differences approach to eyewitness identifications will produce other potentially useful variables in our search to discriminate right from wrong identification decisions. Ultimately, a multivariate approach should help us to clarify the interrelationships between these predictor variables and their relative importance.

References

Anderson, J. R. (1976). *Language, memory and thought.* Hillsdale, NJ: Erlbaum.
Anderson, J. R. (1983). A spreading activation theory of memory. *Journal of Verbal Learning and Verbal Behavior, 22,* 261–295.
Bekerian, D. A., Dennett, J. L., Hill, K., & Hitchcock, R. (1990). *Effects of detailed imagery on simulated witness recall.* Unpublished manuscript, MRC Applied Psychology Unit, Cambridge.
Bem, D. J. (1972). Self-perception theory. In L. Berkowitz (Ed.), *Advances in experimental social psychology* (Vol. 6, pp. 1–34). New York: Academic Press.
Best, J. B. (1989). *Cognitive psychology* (2d ed.). St. Paul, MN: West.
Boring, E. G. (1950). *A history of experimental psychology.* New York: Appleton.
Bothwell, R. K., Brigham, J. C., & Pigott, M. A. (1987). An exploratory study of personality differences in eyewitness memory. *Journal of Social Behavior and Personality, 2,* 335–343.
Bothwell, R. K., Deffenbacher, K. A., & Brigham, J. C. (1987). Correlation of eyewitness accuracy and confidence: Optimality hypothesis revisited. *Journal of Applied Psychology, 72,* 691–695.
Bothwell, R. K., & Thomas, C. E. (in press). *The confidence–accuracy relationship in eyewitness identifications.*
Brigham, J. C. (1988). Is witness confidence helpful in judging eyewitness accuracy? In M. M. Gruneberg, P. E. Morris, & R. N. Sykes (Eds.), *Practical aspects of memory* (Vol. 1, pp. 77–82). Chichester: Wiley.
Bruce, V. (1986). Recognising familiar faces. In H. D. Ellis, M. A. Jeeves, F. Newcombe, & A. Young (Eds.), *Aspects of face processing* (pp. 107–117). Dordrecht/Boston/Lancaster: Nijhoff.
Bruce, V. (1988). *Recognising faces.* Hove/London: Erlbaum.
Collins, A. M., & Quillian, M. R. (1969). Retrieval time from semantic memory. *Journal of Verbal Learning and Verbal Behavior, 8,* 240–247.
Cutler, B. L., & Penrod, S. D. (1988). Improving the reliability of eyewitness identifications: Lineup construction and presentation. *Journal of Applied Psychology, 2,* 281–290.
Cutler, B. L., & Penrod, S. D. (1989). Forensically relevant moderators of the relation between eyewitness identification accuracy and confidence. *Journal of Applied Psychology, 74,* 650–652.
Cutler, B. L., Penrod, S. D., & Martens, T. K. (1987). Improving the reliability of eyewitness identifications: Putting context into context. *Journal of Applied Psychology, 72,* 629–637.
Deffenbacher, K. A. (1980). Eyewitness accuracy and confidence: Can we infer anything about their relationship? *Law and Human Behavior, 4,* 243–260.
Dent, H. R., & Stephenson, G. M. (1979). An experimental study of the effectiveness of different techniques of questioning child witnesses. *British Journal of Social and Clinical Psychology, 18,* 41–51.
Ellis, H. D., Shepherd, J. W., Gibling, F., & Shepherd, J. (1988). Stimulus factors in face learning. In M. M. Gruneberg, P. E. Morris, & R. N. Sykes (Eds.), *Practical aspects of memory: Current research and issues. Volume 1: Memory in everyday life* (pp. 136–144). New York: Wiley.
Fleet, M. L., Brigham, J. C., & Bothwell, R. K. (1987). The confidence–accuracy relationship: The effects of confidence assessment and choosing. *Journal of Applied Social Psychology, 17,* 171–187.
Franzen, S., & Sporer, S. L. (in press-a). Personenverwechslungen durch irreführende Rekonstruktionsbilder: Zum Einfluß nachträglicher Informationen und der Wiederherstellung des Wahrnehmungskontextes. In S. L. Sporer & D. Meurer (Eds.), *Die Beeinflußbarkeit von Zeugenaussagen.* Marburg, Germany: N. G. Elwert.
Franzen, S., & Sporer, S. L. (in press-b). Personenverwechslungen und Möglichkeiten ihrer

Vermeidung: Können Augenzeugen durch Visualisierung gegen den Einfluß von irreführenden Rekonstruktionsbildern immunisiert werden? In S. L. Sporer & D. Meurer (Eds.), *Die Beeinflußbarkeit von Zeugenaussagen.* Marburg, Germany: N. G. Elwert.

Fraser, I. H., Craig, G. L., & Parker, D. M. (1990). Reaction time measures of feature saliency in schematic faces. *Perception, 19,* 661–673.

Hay, D. C., Young, A. W., & Ellis, A. W. (1986). What happens when a face rings a bell: The automatic processing of famous faces. In H. D. Ellis, M. A. Jeeves, F. Newcombe, & A. Young (Eds.), *Aspects of face processing* (pp. 136–144). Dordrecht/Boston/Lancaster: Nijhoff.

Henke, E. (1838). *Handbuch des Criminalrechts und der Criminalpolitik. Vierter Teil.* Berlin: Nicolai.

Hirschberg, M. (1960). *Das Fehlurteil im Strafprozeß.* Stuttgart: Kohlhammer.

Hosch, H. M. (1993). Individual differences in personality and eyewitness identification. In D. Ross, J. D. Read, & M. P. Toglia (Eds.), *Adult eyewitness testimony: Current trends and developments.* New York: Cambridge University Press.

Hosch, H. M., Leippe, M. R., Marchioni, P. M., & Cooper, D. S. (1984). Victimization, self-monitoring, and eyewitness identification. *Journal of Applied Psychology, 69,* 280–288.

Johnson, M. D., & Raye, C. L. (1981). Reality monitoring. *Psychological Review, 88,* 67–85.

Kassin, S. M. (1985). Eyewitness identification: Retrospective self-awareness and the accuracy–confidence relationship. *Journal of Personality and Social Psychology, 49,* 878–893.

Kohnken, G., & Maass, A. (1988). Eyewitness testimony: False alarms on biased instructions? *Journal of Applied Psychology, 73,* 363–370.

Leippe, M. R. (1980). Effects of integrative memorial and cognitive processes on the correspondence of eyewitness accuracy and confidence. *Law and Human Behavior, 4,* 261–274.

Lindsay, R. C. L., Lea, J. A., & Fulford, J. A. (1991). Sequential lineup presentation: Technique matters. *Journal of Applied Psychology, 76,* 741–745.

Lindsay, R. C. L., & Wells, G. L. (1985). Improving eyewitness identifications from lineups: Simultaneous versus sequential lineup presentation. *Journal of Applied Psychology, 70,* 556–564.

Lipton, J. P. (in press). Legal aspects of eyewitness testimony. In S. L. Sporer, R. S. Malpass, & G. Kohnken (Eds.), *Psychological issues in eyewitness identification.* Hillsdale, NJ: Erlbaum.

Loftus, E. F. (1979). *Eyewitness testimony.* Cambridge, MA: Harvard University Press.

Loftus, E. F., Donders, K., Hoffman, H. G., & Schooler, J. W. (1989). Creating new memories that are quickly accessed and confidently held. *Memory & Cognition, 17,* 607–616.

Malpass, R. S. (in press). Enhancing eyewitness memory. In S. L. Sporer, R. S. Malpass, & G. Kohnken (Eds.), *Psychological issues in eyewitness identification.* Hillsdale, NJ: Erlbaum.

Matlin, M. W. (1989). *Cognition* (2d ed.). New York: Holt, Rinehart and Winston.

Melara, R. D., DeWitt-Richards, T. S., & O'Brien, T. P. (1989). Enhancing lineup identification accuracy: Two codes are better than one. *Journal of Applied Psychology, 74,* 706–713.

Meyer, D. E., & Schvaneveldt, R. W. (1971). Facilitation in recognizing pairs of words: Evidence of a dependence between retrieval operations. *Journal of Experimental Psychology, 90,* 227–234.

Murdock, B. B., Jr. (1980). Short-term recognition memory. *Attention and Performance, 8,* 497–519.

Murdock, B. B., Jr. (1982). Recognition memory. In C. R. Puff (Ed.), *Handbook of research methods in human memory and cognition* (pp. 1–26). New York: Academic Press.

Neil versus Biggers (1972). 409 U.S. 188.

Neisser, U. (1967). *Cognitive psychology.* Englewood Cliffs, NJ: Prentice-Hall.

Parker, J. F., & Ryan, V. (1990). *An attempt to reduce guessing behavior in children's and adults' eyewitness identifications.* Paper presented at the biennial meeting of the American Psychology-Law Society in Williamsburg.

Peris, J. L., & Tiberghien, G. (1984). Effet de contexte et recherche conditionelle dans la reconnaissance de visages non familiers. *Cahiers de Psychologie Cognitive, 4,* 323–334.

Peters, K. (1972). *Fehlerquellen im Strafprozeß: Vol. 2. Eine Untersuchung der Wiederaufnahmeverfahren in der Bundesrepublik Deutschland.* Karlsruhe: C. F. Müller.

Pigott, M. A., & Brigham, J. C. (1985). Relationship between accuracy of prior description and facial recognition. *Journal of Applied Psychology, 70,* 547–555.

Pigott, M. A., Brigham, J. C., & Bothwell, R. K. (1985). *A field study of the relations between description accuracy and identification accuracy.* Unpublished manuscript, Florida State University.

Ross, D. F., Ceci, S. J., Dunning, D., and Toglia M. P. (1993). Unconscious transference and lineup identification: Toward a memory blending approach. In D. Ross, J. D. Read, & M. P. Toglia (Eds.), *Adult eyewitness testimony: Current trends and developments.* New York: Cambridge University Press.

Ross, D. F., Toglia, M. P., Hopkins, S., Hanson, E., & Devenport, J. (1992). *Lineup identification and mistaken identity: Evidence for a memory blending approach to unconscious transference.* Paper presented at the 1992 meeting of the American Psychology-Law Society, San Diego.

Sello, E. (1911). *Die Irrtümer der Strafjustiz und ihre Ursachen* (Vol. 1). Berlin: R. v. Decker's Verlag.

Shapiro, P. N., & Penrod, S. (1986). Meta-analysis of facial identification studies. *Psychological Bulletin, 100,* 139–156.

Shepherd, J. W., Ellis, H. D., & Davies, G. M. (1982). *Identification evidence: A psychological examination.* Aberdeen: Aberdeen University Press.

Smith, V. L., Kassin, S. M., & Ellsworth, P. C. (1989). Eyewitness accuracy and confidence: Within- versus between-subjects correlations. *Journal of Applied Psychology, 74,* 356–359.

Sobel, N. R. (1983). *Eyewitness identification. Legal and practical problems.* New York: Boardman.

Sporer, S. L. (1982). A brief history of the psychology of testimony. *Current Psychological Reviews, 2,* 323–339.

Sporer, S. L. (1988). Long-term improvement of facial recognition through visual rehearsal. In M. M. Gruneberg, P. E. Morris, & R. N. Sykes (Eds.), *Practical aspects of memory* (pp. 182–188). London: Wiley.

Sporer, S. L. (1989). Verbal and visual processes in person identification. In H. Wegener, F. Lösel, & J. Haisch (Eds.), *Criminal behavior and the justice system: Psychological perspectives* (pp. 303–324). New York: Springer.

Sporer, S. L. (1992a). Eyewitness identification accuracy, confidence and decision-times in simultaneous and sequential lineups. *Journal of Applied Psychology, 78,* 32–46.

Sporer, S. L. (1992b). Post-dicting eyewitness accuracy: Confidence, decision-times and person descriptions of choosers and non-choosers. *European Journal of Social Psychology, 22,* 157–180.

Sporer, S. L. (1992c). *Das Wiedererkennen von Gesichtern.* Weinheim: Psychologie Verlags Union.

Sporer, S. L. (in prep.). *Quick but accurate? Response latency as an indicator of accuracy in face recognition judgments.* Unpublished manuscript, University of Marburg, Germany.

Sporer, S. L. (in press). Describing others: Psychological issues. In S. L. Sporer, R. S. Malpass, & G. Kohnken (Eds.), *Psychological issues in eyewitness identification.* Hillsdale, NJ: Erlbaum.

Sporer, S. L., Eickelkamp, A., & Spitmann-Rex, D. (1990). Gegenüberstellungen vs. Lichtbildvorlagen. In D. Meurer & S. L. Sporer (Eds.), *Zum Beweiswert von Personenidentifizierungen: Neuere empirische Befunde* (pp. 48–105). Marburg: Elwert.

Stern, L. B., & Dunning, D. (in press). Distinguishing accurate from inaccurate eyewitness identifications: A reality monitoring approach. In D. Ross, J. D. Read, & M. P. Toglia (Eds.), *Adult eyewitness testimony: Current trends and developments.* New York: Cambridge University Press.

Sternberg, S. (1969). Memory-scanning: Mental processes revealed by reaction-time experiments. *American Scientist, 57,* 421–457.

Theios, J. (1973). Reaction time measurements in the study of memory processes. In G. H. Bower (Ed.), *The psychology of learning and motivation* (Vol. 7, pp. 43–85). New York: Academic Press.

Theios, J. (1975). The components of response latency in simple human information processing tasks. *Attention and Performance, 5,* 418–440.

Tiberghien, G. (1986). Context effects in recognition memory of faces: Some theoretical problems. In H. D. Ellis, M. A. Jeeves, F. Newcombe, & A. Young (Eds.), *Aspects of face processing* (pp. 88–104). Dordrecht/Boston/Lancaster: Nijhoff.

Tulving, E. (1985). How many memory systems are there? *American Psychologist, 40,* 385–398.

Turtle, J. W. (1988, June). *Does eyewitness-identification behavior provide cues to improve judgments of identification accuracy?* Paper presented at the NATO Advanced Study Institute in Maratea, Italy.

Watson, R. I. (1978). *The great psychologists* (4th ed.). New York: Lippincott.

Wells, G. L. (1978). Applied eyewitness research: System variables and estimator variables. *Journal of Personality and Social Psychology, 36,* 1546–1557.

Wells, G. L. (1984). A reanalysis of the expert testimony issue. In G. L. Wells & E. F. Loftus (Eds.), *Eyewitness testimony: Psychological perspectives* (pp. 304–314). New York: Cambridge University Press.

Wells, G. L. (1985). Verbal descriptions of faces from memory: Are they diagnostic of identification accuracy? *Journal of Applied Psychology, 70,* 619–626.

Wells, G. L., & Lindsay R. C. L. (1985). Methodological notes on the accuracy–confidence relation in eyewitness identifications. *Journal of Applied Psychology, 70,* 413–419.

Wells, G. L., & Murray, D. M. (1983). What can psychology say about the Neil vs. Biggers criteria for judging eyewitness accuracy? *Journal of Applied Psychology, 68,* 347–362.

Yarmey, A. D. (1992, March). *Accuracy of eyewitness and earwitness showup identifications in a field setting.* Paper presented at the American Psychology-Law Society conference, San Diego.

15 Individual differences in personality and eyewitness identification

Harmon Hosch

Although much empirical research has been conducted during the last decade evaluating variables that influence the accuracy of eyewitness identification, the majority of studies have focused on the effects of situational variables (see the other chapters in this volume). In contrast, little is understood about the influence of individual differences in personality and their effects on identification.

There are two primary reasons for this dearth of research. First, most researchers in the eyewitness field have earned their degrees in social or cognitive psychology. They continue to do research from these perspectives, neither of which focuses on individual differences, and have historically treated such differences as experimental error (see Cronbach, 1957) to be eliminated with tighter experimental control.

The second reason relates to a belief articulated in a seminal paper by Wells on the difference between system and estimator variables in eyewitness identification (Wells, 1978). System variables are those that can be manipulated in actual criminal cases, such as the structure of lineups, the time lapse between the crime occurrence and identification, or the use of techniques designed to elicit maximal recall of information (compare Geiselman, Fisher, MacKinnon, & Holland, 1985, 1986).

Estimator variables are those that cannot be controlled in criminal cases and the effects of which must therefore be estimated after the fact. Estimator variables include characteristics of defendants such as their race or attractiveness, characteristics of the crime such as its perceived seriousness, and characteristics of eyewitnesses such as individual differences in personality.

Wells argued that psychologists should focus on system variables to increase the practical utility of their research. Experts who can testify only about the general impact of estimator variables are not able to explain thoroughly the potential interactions among variables. Given the complexity of research required to assess all possible variable interactions, expert testimony would lend little to court proceedings (see also McCloskey & Egeth, 1983, for a similar argument). Further, Wells argued that even general statements are risky in that our research literature is built on potentially biased investigations where, for example, the subjects are typically university students, witnessing staged crimes, with no consequences to the criminal if witnesses identify them. Finally, the impact of estimator variables cannot be changed in efforts to improve identification accuracy.

More recent research suggests that many of Wells's concerns were unfounded. Using a very complex design to simultaneously study the main effects and two-way interactions among some thirteen independent variables, Cutler, Penrod, and Martens (1987) did much to alleviate the concern with the interactions among estimator variables and their effects on eyewitnesses' identification accuracy. Only one significant interaction was obtained, suggesting that we need not be overly concerned about the complicating effects of interactions among predictors of eyewitness identification accuracy.

A different position is taken here. If a variable can be theoretically linked to differential performance in eyewitness identification tasks, it is worth studying that variable. For example, if it is known that individuals who differ along a personality dimension also differ in their identification accuracy, would that information not be potentially useful? Although it is not possible or ethically permissible to attempt to change the degree to which individuals possess personality characteristics, one could still assign people who are good at certain tasks (by virtue of their personalities) to work in situations where they can capitalize on their advantageous characteristics. If, for example, we know that some characteristics make one an accurate witness, psychologists could help owners of stores, particularly those at greater risk for robbery, to identify clerks with those characteristics.

In this chapter we will explore personality variables that are biologically based and that focus on individual differences in cognitive processes and are theoretically linked to face identification. The foci of this exploration will be three variables my colleagues and I have studied over the course of the last decade. First, the social psychological variable self-monitoring (Snyder, 1979) and its relation to eyewitness identification will be reviewed. Second, we will discuss facial recognition ability as measured by the neuropsychological Benton Facial Recognition Test (BFRT; Benton, Hamsher, Varney, & Spreen, 1983) and present studies relating individual differences in facial recognition to witness identification. Third, we will present data from two of our studies that suggest there are individual differences in cognitive or decision-making style. Finally, other personality variables or cognitive styles related to differences in modes of attending, perceiving, remembering, and recognizing faces that should prove fruitful as predictors of accuracy in eyewitness identification will be presented.

Self-monitoring

Self-monitoring as developed by Mark Snyder (Snyder, 1979, 1987), refers to the extent to which people observe, regulate, and control their public presentation of self in social situations and in their interpersonal relationships. People who monitor and control to a great extent the images they project are referred to as *high self-monitors* (HSMs). *Low self-monitors* (LSMs) in contrast, are not very concerned with assessing the social climate within which they interact. Whereas HSMs deliberately attempt to be the right person at the right time, the LSMs value congruence between their attitudes, their true self, and what they do. The prototypical HSM is particularly sensitive to cues indicative of the situational appropriateness of his or her social behavior and uses them as guidelines for controlling and regulating his or her expressive behavior. LSMs are less attentive to social cues and do not have an extensive repertoire of self-presentational skills. LSM individuals are controlled by their own attitudes, dispositions, and values, rather than the constraints of others in social situations (Snyder, 1987).

We have explored the differences between HSMs and LSMs in eyewitness identification in four studies (Hosch & Cooper, 1981; Hosch, Leippe, Marchioni, & Cooper, 1984; Hosch & Platz, 1984; Zimmerman, 1982). In each of these, we hypothesized: If HSMs are more keenly sensitive to the behavior of others as they would need to be to appropriately regulate their own behavior in social situations, they should learn and remember more about salient people within social situations. Research had indicated that HSMs are not more attentive to people than are LSMs, in the sense that they do not spend more time looking at others (Berscheid, Graziano, Monson, & Dermer, 1976; Dabbs, Evans, Hopper, & Purvis, 1980). Berscheid and her colleagues discovered, however, that despite equal levels of attention to others, HSMs, in comparison to LSMs, later recalled more about the most relevant person in a situation. It seems likely that HSMs are biologically set to process human social information, and faces in particular, differently from LSMs. This hypothesis will be discussed in greater detail below.

EXPERIMENT 1

In the first of our experiments (Hosch & Cooper, 1981), subjects were exposed to the theft of a calculator that was lying on a table in the experimental laboratory, or to the theft of their own wristwatch, or they participated in a no-theft control condition (for complete details of the study, see Hosch & Cooper, 1982). Self-monitoring scale (SMS) scores significantly predicted eyewitness accuracy across all three treatment conditions, $r (64) = .26, p < .05$. The higher the SMS, the more likely they were to be accurate in their identifications.

EXPERIMENT 2

Zimmerman (1982) compared HSM and LSM subjects on a face recognition and unexpected photo lineup identification task. Subjects were greeted as they arrived at the laboratory by an experimental assistant who led them to a cubicle and left them alone. A second experimenter arrived and ran the subjects through two phases of a facial recognition task. In the first phase, they were told to concentrate on the faces because they would be tested for recognition accuracy. The second phase was the recognition task. The experimenter then asked the subjects to look at a photo lineup and see if the person who had greeted them and led them to the cubicle was depicted. Zimmerman's results showed no difference between the self-monitoring groups in their performance on the facial recognition task, but a significant difference in favor of the HSM subjects in accuracy of identifying the experimental confederate. These data suggest that when a situation is structured so that the explicit demand of the task asks subjects to focus their attention on faces, all subjects do so and no behavioral differences in recognition accuracy are obtained. On the other hand, when processing facial information is incidental to the task, HSMs and LSMs differ in the degree to which they perceive and remember faces.

EXPERIMENT 3

Hosch and Platz (1984) conducted a field study in which convenience store clerks were tested for their ability to remember confederates who had visited the store no more than two hours earlier. The confederates enacted predetermined routines designed to force the clerks to look at them and to maximize the duration of the interaction between them.

The SMS scores of the clerks and the number of correct photo identifications they made were correlated. A significant association was obtained, $r(84) = .51$, $p < .001$. As predicted, clerks who were high in self-monitoring were more likely to be correct in their identifications. Indeed, when the clerks were split into those in the upper and lower quartiles of the distribution of SMS scores, striking differences emerged. Clerks in the upper quartile were correct on 73 percent of their attempted identifications whereas those in the lower quartile were correct on only 25 percent.

EXPERIMENT 4

In another study (Hosch et al., 1984) HMS and LSM subjects participated in an experiment in which they were exposed to a staged crime. In addition to expecting differences in identification accuracy between the HSM and LSM witnesses, we expected differences between the two groups as a function of lineup instructions. We reasoned that because HSMs are more sensitive and responsive to social cues to appropriate behaviors than LSMs, they should be more influenced by biased lineup instructions. Bias in lineup instructions occurs when police officers suggest to the witness that the thief is present in the lineup and their task is to identify the correct person. Unbiased instructions communicate that the thief may or may not be present.

In addition, we expected differences in the degree to which HSMs and LSMs would be confident in their lineup choices. LSMs are guided by their attitudes and internal states so they may be more introspective and should be more sensitive to the strength or weakness of their memories.

The results of this study indicate that the association between self-monitoring and witness accuracy is not necessarily a simple one. HSMs were more accurate in identifying the thief when they were the victim (when their watch was the stolen object) than when they were bystanding eyewitnesses (other people's property was stolen). The reverse pattern was true for LSMs. They were more accurate when they were bystanding witnesses than when they were victims. If one assumes that arousal is greater for victims than for bystanding witnesses, it may be that the increased arousal interacts with the type of self-monitoring to augment or narrow the subjects' attention to the cues they are stylistically set to focus on. That is, HSMs will attend even more to faces when highly aroused, whereas LSMs in the same circumstances may focus more on their internal states.

As expected, instruction type and self-monitoring interacted to influence subjects' behavior. HSMs were more likely to attempt an identification under biased instructions than they were under unbiased instructions. LSM witnesses were virtually identical in their propensity to make a choice following the two types of instructions.

The studies reviewed above indicate that individual differences in self-monitoring are useful in predicting identification accuracy, but not confidence in those identifications, in forensically relevant contexts. Our most recent efforts have been toward understanding more clearly the fundamental differences between HSM and LSM people – that is, how and why they differ.

Theoretical work focusing on the underlying causes of individual differences in self-monitoring has recently evolved. Self-monitoring was originally seen as a clearly social psychological concept grounded in sociologically oriented theory. The more contemporary notion is that individual differences in self-monitoring are likely to be biologically based (Gangestad & Snyder, 1985; Snyder, 1987).

EXPERIMENT 5

Evidence for biologically based differences between the processing of facial information by HSMs and LSMs was obtained in a study recently conducted by Pannell, Hosch, and Sands (1992). Fifteen HSMs and fifteen LSMs participated in a facial recognition study. All subjects were shown a random block of forty faces for a period of five seconds each with a five-second intertarget interval. Subjects were told to attend to each face, as they would be tested later on facial recognition.

After a five-minute rest period during which subjects were told to "think about the faces you have just seen," they were tested for recognition of the target faces and foils. During both the acquisition and recognition phases of the study, evoked potentials were recorded from a cap containing twenty-eight electrodes.

No differences in overall facial recognition accuracy rates were expected because of the nature of this task nor were any obtained. Significant differences in the correlation between response latency and identification accuracy were obtained. HSMs' correlation was .23, whereas LSMs' correlation was $-.39, z = 1.58, p = .06$. This finding indicated that the classic speed–accuracy tradeoff obtained for HSMs; the faster they responded, the fewer the number of faces they correctly recognized; the slower their responses, the more accurate. The opposite was true for LSM subjects, however. As they responded more quickly, their accuracy increased. This suggests there are stylistic response differences between high and low self-monitors even when the task is structured so that (on average) they respond correctly equally often.

More intriguing were the neurophysiological data. Recall that the patterns of cortical electrical activity were recorded while the subjects searched their memories to decide if a target face was one they had seen previously or not. Of interest are the amplitude and latency of the spikes of electrical activity (evoked potentials) after the facial stimulus is presented. Dramatic differences in amplitudes of evoked potentials between HSMs and LSMs were obtained at 175, 300, 500, and at 600 milliseconds after the stimuli. In each case, the HSM subjects exhibited greater peak amplitude than did the LSM subjects.

Peak latencies were significantly different for the two groups at P200 and P600. Here, the HSMs were responding more slowly at 200 milliseconds after stimulus presentation and the LSMs more slowly at 600 milliseconds. Discriminant analysis using evoked potentials as independent variables allowed correct categorization of 80 percent of the HSMs and 86.6 percent of the LSMs.

These data suggest important differences in the ways that HSMs and LSMs search memory and decide whether they have or have not seen a face previously. The next studies in this series will reincorporate the more forensically relevant paradigm while measuring evoked potentials. For example, we will elaborate on the study above by testing subjects' recognition of faces they have been warned they will be tested on as well as for faces they have seen but have not been told to remember. We expect to see group differences in recognition accuracy favoring HSMs for the faces they were not warned to remember. The patterns of evoked potentials obtained while the two groups search their memories for the faces should help us understand these groups of people.

Neuropsychologically based facial recognition ability

Robert Bothwell, Siegfried Sporer, Carlos Saucedo, and I have been interested in assessing generalized, traitlike individual differences in facial recognition ability to determine whether or not such differences might influence eyewitness accuracy. We have examined these differences by using the Benton Facial Recognition Test (BFRT; Benton, Hamsher, Varney, & Spreen, 1983). The test was designed as part of a neuropsychological assessment battery to detect potential damage to the right cerebral hemisphere (Benton, 1980).

Clinical studies have shown that damage to the posterior right hemispheric areas of the brain can impair facial recognition for relatively unfamiliar faces (Benton, 1985; Dricker, Butters, Berman, Samuels, & Carey, 1978; Warrington & James, 1967). Visual field studies (see Sergent & Bindra, 1981, for a review) have also suggested that right hemispheric processing is important in facial recognition especially for recognition involving unfamiliar faces, degraded stimuli, and highly discriminable faces. Finally, Benton and Gordon (1971) found that facial recognition was significantly correlated with visuospatial abilities such as brightness pattern discrimination.

The ability to utilize visuospatial cues such as shades of gray and of color should affect an individual's ability to process salient facial cues (Shepherd, Davies, & Ellis, 1981) such as eye and hair color, and may also help persons make accurate age estimates. We wanted to determine whether individual differences on the BFRT between nonpathological (or nonclinical) subjects and those who score within the normal range on the BFRT, would be predictive of eyewitness accuracy.

Five experiments have now been conducted where individual differences in facial recognition and eyewitness accuracy have been assessed. These will be discussed below.

EXPERIMENT 1

In the first study (Hosch, Bothwell, Sporer, & Saucedo, 1990), subjects arrived at the laboratory individually and were greeted by a male experimenter (the target) who briefly described a slide recognition task that was to follow. Subjects saw the target face-to-face in a well lighted room for about thirty seconds. A confederate then started a projector that presented thirty color slides of ten- to thirteen-year-old males in frontal pose. The slides were presented for five seconds each with a five-second interstimulus interval. Subjects were told that we were interested in memory for faces and instructed to attend closely to the stimuli because their recognition would be tested later. The delay between the acquisition and retrieval phases of the slide recognition test was approximately five minutes.

During the retrieval phase, subjects viewed slides of sixty (thirty target and thirty distractor) faces, randomly arranged, for fifteen seconds each with a fifteen-second interstimulus interval. For each face, they indicated whether it had been seen before and their certainty in that decision.

A lineup task was presented to subjects approximately forty minutes after they had seen the target. They were led to another room where they were asked to see if the experimenter they had seen earlier was or was not pictured in a stack of photographs (the lineup). Whether the target was or was not present was determined randomly.

The subjects' final task was to complete the BFRT (Benton, Hamsher, Varney, & Spreen, 1983). The BFRT is a twenty-two-item scale. For the first six items, subjects are required to find a match to a target face by comparing it with six other faces. The final sixteen items require the subject to find three matches among a set of six photographs. The test involves matching identical front-view photographs of a face, matching a front view with views from different angles, and matching front-view photographs taken under different lighting conditions.

Identification accuracy on the lineup was strongly and positively related to BFRT performance, $r(31) = .54$, $p < .01$. When the data were separated for subjects who chose someone from the lineup and those who correctly rejected the target-absent lineup, accuracy was still strongly and positively related to BFRT scores ($r = .50$ for choosers and $r = .57$ for nonchoosers). Data from the slide task will be discussed in the next section of this chapter.

EXPERIMENT 2

In a second study (Hosch, Bothwell, Sporer, & Saucedo, 1991) we again examined the accuracy of identifications as it related to BFRT scores. The general procedure was similar to that described above with two exceptions. First, a more forensically likely delay interval was used between the time the witnesses saw the target and the time they attempted an identification. Second, the target was presented via videotape rather than live.

Groups of subjects watched the videotape of a young white male walking down a narrow forty-foot hallway. The target walked toward the camera for six seconds, turned left, and exited the building. Subjects then viewed either a photograph of the target or a decoy, randomly determined. This task simulated a "showup," a frequently used identification procedure in which police detain a suspect and bring that person to the witness to identify. Subjects made their decisions in private.

Subjects returned after a one-week delay and individually viewed either a target-present or target-absent photographic lineup. The target-absent lineup was comprised of the decoy and five other photos from the target-present lineup. After the lineup task, all subjects were given the BFRT (Short Form). Two weeks later they returned to the laboratory and participated in the slide recognition task described above.

Subjects were correct in their initial identification (showup) 67 percent of the time. Neither signal sensitivity (A'; $r = .06$), nor response style on the slide task (B''; $r = -.21$), nor scores on the Benton Test ($r = .05$) succeeded in predicting accuracy on the showup.

With respect to identification accuracy on the photo lineup after a one-week delay, subjects made a correct identification decision 64 percent of the time. Of those initially correct in their showup identification decision, 75 percent were also correct in their identification decision on the lineup. Overall, a significant positive correlation was obtained between the BFRT and the accuracy on the lineup decision (r(36) = .39, p <.01) and accuracy on the showup ($r(36) = .33, p = .03$).

EXPERIMENT 3

Bothwell recently completed two studies that elaborate our understanding of BRFT and eyewitness identification. The first of these was a partial replication of the second study above with a new group of twenty-seven subjects. These subjects were shown the same videotape as were the subjects in the previous study. They were divided into one-week or eight-week delay interval groups. Subjects were tested with a target-present or a target-absent photo lineup and completed the BRFT Short Form.

Again the BRFT was significantly and positively related to identification accuracy, $r(25) = .41, p < .05$. Subjects with greater facial recognition ability were more likely to be accurate in their photo identification.

EXPERIMENT 4

In his second study, Bothwell wanted to learn if feedback on the accuracy of identifications would influence the identification accuracy/BFRT relationship. Forty-seven subjects participated in this study. As before, they saw the videotape of the target walking toward them down a hallway. Two days later subjects were asked to look at a target-absent or target-present lineup. Bothwell reasoned that when police administer a lineup, they have a suspect present. The suspect will either be the target or a similar decoy. He wondered what impact on performance there might be if lineup choosers were told they were correct in making either of these choices and if nonchoosers were told they failed to choose the target (in a target-present lineup) or the decoy (in the target-absent one).

The manipulation was that the experimenter provided feedback for the choices. Subjects were told they were correct if they identified the target in the target-present lineup or a highly similar looking decoy in the target-absent lineup. They were given negative feedback if they failed to make either of these choices. All subjects completed the BFRT.

The results failed to show the usual positive association between BFRT and identification accuracy, r (45) = − .06, *ns*.

Experiment 5

An interesting additional study has now been completed (Bothwell, personal communication, February 1992). In this study, the same videotape of the stimulus person was seen as in the experiments above. In this case, the photo identification was made from a serially presented set of photographs seen by each subject on a computer screen. This computer lineup occurred one week after exposure to the stimulus. The subjects saw a target-absent or target-present lineup and responded either yes or no to each of six faces to indicate whether the person was or was not the target person originally seen. The dependent measure of interest was the number of false alarms which were scored 0 if the subjects made none, 1 if they made one, and 2 if they made more than one.

For the subjects who made a choice, number of false alarms was correlated with their BFRT score. The relationship was again strong and significant, $r(14) = − .51, p < .05$. As before, high scores on the BFRT were associated with correct identification decisions (fewer false alarms). In this case, it appears that the BFRT distinguishes between those subjects who correctly identify the target or make only one false alarm and those subjects who make two or more false alarms. These data must be explored further to see how decision-making style and BFRT scores are related.

In summary, we have data from five studies collected in different locations using different methods of presentation of target and photo lineup. For four of the five studies, the correlation between facial recognition ability as measured by the BFRT and eyewitness identification accuracy was strong. Those with higher scores on the BFRT were better at identifications.

The outcomes of these studies were combined using two different methods discussed by Rosenthal (1984). Using a p of .5 for the nonsignificant fourth study, the combined probability of obtaining the results of these five studies by chance alone was $p = .0008$. Adding logs resulted in a χ^2 (10) = 30.48. The associated p for the set of studies was < .001.

As researchers in facial recognition have previously argued (for example, Ellis, 1984), our data show that there are general differences in facial recognition ability. Our data also show that these differences can be assessed psychometrically and may account for differences in eyewitness accuracy.

Scores on the Benton Facial Recognition Test are predictive of eyewitness identification accuracy. This is true for accuracy in a photographic lineup following exposure to the live target or after exposure to a target via videotape.

In summary, we have identified a generalized individual differences measure that is useful in evaluating the accuracy of eyewitness identifications. Additional research evaluating the BFRT as a predictor of identification accuracy and methods for using it in actual investigations is encouraged. Unlike the work with self-monitoring, BRFT scores have never been tested as predictors of accuracy of identification in less constrained or naturally occurring situations. Laboratory experiments are by their very nature socially constraining situations. It may be that when people are free to behave in ways that demonstrate their individual differences, the observed relationship may change. Some evidence that this might be true in the case of the Benton is that in all of our studies that have successfully related BFRT to identification accuracy, the subjects have made their decisions in private and therefore were under a minimum of social pressure. Data suggest that the relation can be masked if situational pressures during the identification are strong (Bothwell, personal communication, February 1992). A field study similar to those conducted by Brigham, Maass, Snyder, and Spaulding (1982) and by Platz and Hosch (1988) would go a long way to increasing our confidence in the degree to which the BFRT will help us understand individual differences in identification accuracy.

Breadth of categorizing style

During the mid-1960s and the 1970s, psychologists began investigating individual differences in modes of information processing. These individual differences were construed to be components of personality and were labeled cognitive styles (Kogan, 1971). There are several cognitive styles or strategies that are logically related to eyewitness identification, but which have not been extensively researched or researched in this context.

One of these cognitive styles that might fruitfully be explored in researching individual differences in eyewitness identification is called breadth of categorizing (Kogan & Wallach, 1967; Messick & Damarin, 1964). Breadth of categorizing refers to a preference for being inclusive, rather than exclusive, when establishing an acceptable range for specified categories. There appear to be individual differences in the kinds of risks we are willing to tolerate. For example, categorizing requires that we decide if an event or an individual is of type A or type B. Air Defense Artillery Batteries must decide if an incoming aircraft is a friend or foe (IFF). A pathologist must decide if a cell in her microscope is cancerous or not. More pertinent to the focus of this book, eyewitnesses must decide if a photograph represents the likeness of the person whom they saw commit a crime. It should be readily apparent that miscategorization in any of these examples carries potentially serious consequences. If the IFF decision incorrectly classifies a friend (recall the Persian Gulf incident when the *USS Vincennes* misidentified a neutral target) as a foe, lives can be lost. On the other hand, if a foe is incorrectly misclassified as a friend, dire consequences may await one's compatriots. In the case of the eyewitness, if a person's style is to tolerate overinclusiveness in a category (that is, to use a lax criterion for inclusion in the category of previously seen perpetrators), innocent foils will be incorrectly identified. In contrast, if a person's categorizing style is overly exclusive, guilty suspects will fail to be identified. In laboratory tasks, subjects are usually asked to decide whether an event is a member of category A, or not-A. The investigator can thereby index the range of instances or values that are acceptable for membership in that category (Kogan, 1971). Broad categorizers prefer to risk being overly inclusive whereas narrow categorizers prefer to risk being overly exclusive.

Some evidence exists suggesting that breadth of categorizing is related to facial recognition accuracy. Messick and Damarin (1964) found that narrow categorizers were better in remembering faces than were broad categorizers.

In addition to individual differences in facial recognition, recent data from studies I conducted with my colleagues (Hosch, Bothwell, Sporer, & Saucedo, 1990; Hosch, Bothwell, Saucedo, & Sporer,) 1991 suggest that response biases related to breadth of categorizing are predictive of eyewitness accuracy. Recall that in both studies, we assessed categorizing style differences with a laboratory facial recognition task. Subjects were shown a set of critical faces and later their recognition ability was tested by examining responses to a larger set of critical and distractor faces. Previous research suggests, however, that performance on this type of task is not related to performance on a lineup task (Deffenbacher, Brown, & Sturgill, 1978; Shepherd, Davies, & Ellis, 1980).

Four different measures were computed for the face recognition test. The number of hits (the proportion of correctly recognized faces) and false alarms (the proportion of times subjects incorrectly identified a face they had not previously seen) were calculated and used to compute two other measures: A' and B''.

A' presents the nonparametric equivalent to d' and is a measure of sensitivity to a signal (discrimination ability) that is independent of response bias. B'' indicates the tendency of a subject to respond more or less cautiously when presented with a given test item (Coren, Porac, & Ward, 1984). It varies in magnitude and direction from -1 (indexing an extreme tendency to say "Yes I've seen that person" or to use a lax criterion) to $+1$ (indexing an extreme tendency to say "No I have not seen that person" or a stringent criterion). These measures were then used as predictors of accuracy on a photo lineup task described more completely earlier in this chapter.

STUDY 1

For the first study, the nonparametric measure of sensitivity (A') yielded values of $M = .89$, and $s = .05$. The values for the index of response bias (B'') were $M = .40$, and $s = .33$. A' was not predictive of identification accuracy for the whole sample, $r(31) = .07$, ns, or for choosers or nonchoosers separately. In stark contrast, the nonparametric measure of response bias B'' correlated significantly with identification accuracy, $r(31) = .50$, $p < .01$, particularly with choosers, $r(13) = .73$, where it emerged as a strong correlate. Subjects who committed false alarms in the photo lineup were much less cautious $(B''$, $M = -.01)$ in the slide recognition task than subjects who identified the target correctly $(M = .59)$.

STUDY 2

In the second study we presented subjects with a showup almost immediately after they had been exposed to the target and either a target-present or a target-absent lineup after a one-week delay. Neither signal sensitivity $(A'$; $r = .06)$ nor response style on the slide task $(B''$; $r = -.21)$ was associated with identification accuracy at the showup.

Again, A' was unrelated to identification accuracy on the photographic lineup $(r = -.21)$. B'' was, however, related to accuracy on the lineup task $(r = .28$, $p = .05)$. As with the first study, this result indicates that those subjects who were most cautious on the slide task were more likely to be correct in identifying a target from a photo lineup.

As with previous research (Deffenbacher et al., 1978; Shepherd et al., 1980), our data suggest that sensitivity to a signal (that is, discrimination ability), measured as d' or A' in a typical facial recognition task may not be related to performance on a photographic lineup task. In both experiments, however, the nonparametric measure of response bias, B'', on photo recognition was a significant predictor of identification accuracy for witnesses who made a choice at the lineup.

Recall that B'' indexes the subject's tendency to employ a lax or a stringent criterion in deciding whether a stimulus has been seen previously; in this context, responding yes in a lineup, irrespective of the subject's true memory strength, is a lax style. This finding also instructs us on the importance of distinguishing the cognitive aspects of a lineup task such as may be indexed by the BFRT from the social determinants of choosing such as the influence of lineup instructions on high self-monitors discussed above, and a cautious response style that can be assessed in both laboratory and field studies (compare Malpass & Devine, 1984, for a general discussion of the importance of making a choice for lineup identifications).

It seems logical to reason that lineup construction is another forensic task that should benefit from research on categorization. Based on the cross-ethnic/racial identification findings that persons have difficulty distinguishing among members of other racial or ethnic groups (see Bothwell, Brigham, & Malpass, 1989 for a meta-analysis of cross-racial studies), Brigham has argued that persons who construct lineups should be of the same race or from the same ethnic group as the suspects (see Brigham, this volume). The own-race effect occurs in facial recognition studies when the ratio of hits to false alarms is greater for facial stimuli from one's own group than for those from another racial or ethnic group. If an Anglo-American constructing a lineup sees all African-Americans as looking alike, he would tend to create an overly inclusive lineup, that is, one of large nominal size but low functional size. If this same logic were applied to lineup constructors prone to be either broad or narrow categorizers, the difficulty of the lineups they construct should be affected.

The functional size of a lineup will be affected even if lineup constructors follow the argument of Wells et al. (this volume) that lineup foils should only satisfy the criterion that they fit the verbal description of the suspect rather than matching the physical appearance of the suspect as closely as possible. Persons who differ in categorizing style will generate lineups of different functional size no matter what criterion they are given. Additional research pursuing the effects of categorizing style on lineup construction and eyewitness identification should prove to be informative and exciting.

Other cognitive styles related to identification

We now briefly explore the cognitive styles of field independence (Wapner & Demick, 1991; Witkin, Dyk, Faterson, Goodenough, & Karp, 1962), reflection-impulsivity (Kagan, Rosman, Day, Albert, & Phillips, 1964), and leveling-sharpening (Gardner, Holzman, Klein, Linton, & Spence, 1959).

Two excellent reviews have been done by Clifford and Bull (1978) and by Yarmey (1979) so I will concentrate on work that has been done since those reviews were published.

Field independence–field dependence

The most heavily researched of the cognitive styles is usually called field independence versus field dependence or an articulated versus global psychological differentiation. This construct refers to the ability to discriminate parts from the whole in which they are embedded. For example, persons who are faster at isolating a simple geometric figure from a more complex one that includes it would be more field independent. Individuals who take longer to disembed the simple figure are more field dependent or global in style.

Witkin noted that persons with a global cognitive style rely on external sources for definitions of their attitudes, judgments, sentiments, and views of themselves, whereas persons with a more articulated style experience themselves as separated from others and rely on internal frames of reference to guide their definitions of the self (Witkin, 1965). He reasoned that field dependent people should be better at recognizing faces than field independent people because they are more attentive to faces in their environment. Konstadt and Forman observed that children with a global cognitive style tended to look at the face of an adult examiner about twice as often as did field independent children when the children were taking a test under stress. More important for research in eyewitness identification, Crutchfield, Woodworth, and Albrecht (1958) and Messick and Damarin (1964) discovered that field dependent subjects were more likely to remember faces of people they had previously seen. In sharp contrast to the studies supporting Witkin, when Clifford and Bull (1978, pp. 176–178) and Yarmey (1979, pp. 128–130) reviewed this literature, they discovered other studies that found that field independent subjects were better at recognizing faces (Adcock & Webberley, 1971; Baker, 1967; Beijk-Docter & Elshout, 1969; Hoffman & Kagan, 1977). The findings at this point do not support any clearcut conclusions.

More recently, it was hypothesized that field independent subjects would have a better memory for objects and people's actions, whereas field dependent subjects would be better at recalling people's physical appearance (Christiaansen, Ochalek, & Sweeney, 1984). To test these hypotheses, Christiaansen et al. had a female and a male experimenter stand in front of a class and request volunteers to participate in an upcoming study. After a one-day delay, the subjects responded to the Group Embedded Figures Test (GEFT), a measure of field independence, and answered questions about the appearance and behavior of the experimenters they had seen the day before.

Subjects' recall of objects and actions, and of appearances were not related to field independence. This study has a number of limitations, however. First, subjects were tested for their recall of verbal descriptions of the previously seen experimenters' actions and appearances. Subjects were not asked to identify the faces of the targets, so this research tells us little about field dependence and facial recognition. Second, the investigators reported a gender difference in accuracy. Females were more accurate than males in their recall of items in general and of items related to the female target in particular. It is well established that women are more likely to be field dependent than men. Moreover, because there were nearly three times as many female subjects as males (124 versus 46), it seems that subject gender and field independence are hopelessly confounded. Further, Christiaansen et al. did not report data, such as the mean and standard deviations of GEFT scores for subjects of the two genders, that could assist us in teasing these variables apart or allow us to make sense of the results (or lack of support for the hypotheses).

In summary, field independence is a cognitive personality dimension that has been theoretically linked with facial identification accuracy. Empirical evidence in support of the hypothesis is conflicting. A more direct test of the Christiaansen et al. hypothesis would be helpful in deciding if there is additional value in continuing this line of inquiry.

Reflection–impulsivity

Individual differences in reflection-impulsivity (Kagan, Rosman, Day, Albert, & Phillips, 1964) have been extensively explored among children. Differences on this dimension refer to individual consistencies in the speed with which hypotheses are selected and information processed. Impulsive children tend to offer the first answer that occurs to them whereas reflective children ponder alternatives before deciding. As Drake (1970) indicated, impulsive youngsters do not scan all the alternatives before responding whereas reflective youngsters search all possibilities before they offer a response. It is not surprising that high levels of impulsivity are associated with more frequent errors in choices.

Whether one is reflective or impulsive should influence accuracy of identifications on a variety of eyewitness tasks including looking for suspects in mug books and deciding if a member of a lineup was a previously seen perpetrator of a crime. Whereas there seems to be a real advantage to having a more reflective style in the context of academic tasks, this may not, however, be advantageous in eyewitness identification. A recent study (Bothwell, Brigham, & Pigott, 1987) suggested that there is a negative association between decision time on a lineup task and accuracy of choice. Individuals who deliberated for relatively longer periods of time were more likely to falsely identify someone they had never seen before than were individuals who made rapid selections. Two other studies by Sporer (1989a, 1989b; this volume; see also Stern & Dunning, this volume) further explored this relation as a function of making a lineup choice. Witnesses to staged incidents who made correct lineup identifications did so much faster than witnesses who misidentified foils. For witnesses who rejected the lineup, correct and incorrect decisions took approximately equal amounts of time. For nonchoosers, the relation between accuracy and decision time was not significant.

Leveling–sharpening

Leveling–sharpening refers to reliable individual variations in assimilation in memory (Gardner, Holzman, Klein, Linton, & Spence, 1959). Levelers have been described as tending to blur similar memories and to merge perceived objects or events with similar but not identical events recalled from previous experience. Sharpeners tend not to merge memories and they see the present as dissimilar from the past. In the eyewitness arena, we might expect to see differential susceptibility to unconscious transference (wrongly categorizing familiar faces; see for example, Ellis, 1984; see also Read et al., 1990, and this volume; Ross et al., this volume) and the misinformation effect (misleading postevent information modifying recollection for an event; Williams, Loftus, & Deffenbacher, 1992; Weingardt et al., this volume; Lindsay, this volume) as a function of reliable individual differences in leveling–sharpening.

Summary

In this chapter we have presented recent experimental research that focuses on individual differences in personality and their relation to eyewitness identification accuracy. We have discovered consistent differences between high and low self-monitors and their accuracy in identification. High self-monitors concern themselves to a greater extent than low self-monitors with social information informing them how their interactions with others are proceeding. The human face is a rich source of such social information. As predicted, high self-monitors, when they are in situations where this natural tendency is allowed to be expressed, are better able to remember the faces of people they have met. It appears that they process information differently than do low self-monitors based on differences in amplitude and latency of their cortical evoked potentials.

In addition, reliable individual differences in identification accuracy are related to individual differences on the neuropsychological Benton Facial Recognition Test. Future research along this line should identify people at the extremes of the normal range to provide a strong test of hypothesized differences in an eyewitness identification task. In particular, field studies should be conducted to determine the generalizability of the current findings.

The third promising area for exploring the relation between eyewitness identification accuracy and individual difference variables comes under the general theme of cognitive styles. We have begun to explore differences in decision-making style related to categorizing. It appears that whether an individual's decision criterion is strict or loose, as indexed by the nonparametric signal detection value B'', is predictive of accuracy in identification. Because there are only two studies extant of which I am aware, much more needs to be done to determine the circumstances under which this relation holds. It appears, however, that effort expended along this line will bear fruit.

Finally, three other cognitive styles theoretically related to identification accuracy have been reviewed. The first was field independence versus field dependence. Several studies have been done looking at the relation between this style and facial recognition; the results to date are mixed. Future research to clarify the conditions under which this dimension does or does not predict accuracy of eyewitness identification would be valuable.

Two other cognitive styles, leveling–sharpening and impulsivity–reflectivity, seem to me to be predictive of individual differences in performance on a variety of forensic tasks including lineup construction. Research along the lines of either of these styles will facilitate our understanding of the phenomena underlying the process of eyewitness identification.

References

Adcock, C., & Webberley, M. (1971). Primary mental abilities. *Journal of General Psychology, 84,* 229–243.

Baker, E. (1967). Perceiver variables involved in the recognition of faces. Unpublished doctoral dissertation, University of London.

Beijk-Docter, M. A., & Elshout, J. J. (1969). Veldfhankelijkheid en geheugen met betrekking tot sociaal relevant en sociaal niet-relevant materiaal. *Nederlands Tijdschrift voor de Psychologie en haar Grensgebieden, 24,* 267–279.

Benton, A. L. (1980). The neuropsychology of facial recognition. *American Psychologist, 35,* 176–186.

Benton, A. L. (1985). Visuoperceptual, visuospatial, and visuoconstructive disorders. In K. M. Heilman & E. Valenstein (Eds.), *Clinical neuropsychology* (2d Ed.), Oxford University Press.

Benton, A. L., & Gordon, M. C. (1971). Correlates of facial recognition. *Transactions of the American Neurological Association, 96,* 146–150.

Benton, A. L., Hamsher, K. de S., Varney, N. R., & Spreen, O. (1983). Facial recognition: Stimulus and multiple choice pictures. *Contributions to neuropsychological assessment.* New York: Oxford University Press.

Berschied, E., Graziano, E., Monson, T., & Dermer, M. (1976). Outcome dependency: Attention, attribution, and attraction. *Journal of Personality and Social Psychology, 34,* 978–989.

Bothwell, R. K., Brigham, J. C., & Malpass, R. S. (1989). Cross-racial identification. *Personality and Social Psychology Bulletin, 15,* 19–25.

Bothwell, R. K., Brigham, J. C., & Pigott, M. A. (1987). An exploratory study of personality differences in eyewitness memory. *Journal of Social Behavior and Personality, 2,* 335–343.

Brigham, J. C., Maass, A., Snyder, L. S., & Spaulding, K. (1982). The accuracy of eyewitness identifications in a field setting. *Journal of Personality and Social Psychology, 42,* 673–681.

Christiaansen, R. E., Ochalek, K., & Sweeney, J. D. (1984). Individual differences in eyewitness memory and confidence judgments. *Journal of Genetic Psychology, 10,* 47–52.

Clifford, B. R., & Bull, R. (1978). *The psychology of person identification.* Boston: Routledge & Kegan Paul.

Coren, S., Porac, C., & Ward, L. M. (1984). *Sensation and Perception.* Orlando, FL: Academic Press.

Cronbach, L. J. (1957). The two disciplines of scientific psychology. *American Psychologist, 12,* 671–684.

Crutchfield, R. S., Woodworth, D. G., & Albrecht, R. E. (1958). Perceptual performance and the effective person. *U S A F W A D C Technical Note,* no. 58–60, Lackland AFB, Texas.

Cutler, B. L., Penrod, S. D., & Martens, T. K. (1987). The reliability of eyewitness identification: The role of system and estimator variables. *Law and Human Behavior, 11,* 233–258.

Dabbs, J. M., Jr., Evans, M. S., Hopper, C. H., & Purvis, J. A. (1980). Self-monitors in conversation: What do they monitor? *Journal of Personality and Social Psychology, 39,* 278–284.

Deffenbacher, K. A., Brown, E. L., & Sturgill, W. (1978). Some predictors of eyewitness memory accuracy. In M. M. Gruneberg, P. E. Morris, & R. N. Sykes (Eds.), *Practical aspects of memory* (pp. 219–226). London: Academic Press.

Drake, D. M. (1970). Perceptual correlates of impulsive and reflective behavior. *Developmental Psychology, 2*, 202–214.

Dricker, J., Butters, N., Berman, G., Samuels, I., & Carey, S. (1978). The recognition and encoding of faces by alcoholic Korsakoff and right hemispheric patients. *Neuropsychologia, 16*, 683–695.

Ellis, H. D. (1984). Practical aspects of face memory. In G. L. Wells & E. F. Loftus (Eds.), *Eyewitness testimony: Psychological perspectives* (pp. 12–37). New York: Cambridge University Press.

Gangestad, S., & Snyder, M. (1985). "To carve nature at its joints": On the existence of discrete classes in personality. *Psychological Review, 92*, 317–349.

Gardner, R. W., Holzman, P. S., Klein, G. S., Linton, H. B., & Spence, D. P. (1959). Cognitive control: A study of individual consistencies in cognitive behavior. *Psychological Issues, 1* (Monograph 4).

Geiselman, R. E., Fisher, R. P., MacKinnon, D. P., & Holland, H. L. (1985). Eyewitness memory enhancement in the police interview: Cognitive retrieval mnemonics versus hypnosis. *Journal of Applied Psychology, 70*, 401–412.

Geiselman, R. E., Fisher, R. P., MacKinnon, D. P., & Holland, H. L. (1986). Enhancement of eyewitness memory with the cognitive interview. *American Journal of Psychology, 99*, 385–401.

Hoffman, C., & Kagan, S. (1977). Field dependence and facial recognition. *Perceptual and Motor Skills, 44*, 119–124.

Hosch, H. M., Bothwell, R. K., Sporer, S. L., & Saucedo, C. (1990). The accuracy of witness' choice: Facial recognition ability, reaction time, and confidence. Southwestern Psychological Association, Houston, TX.

Hosch, H. M., Bothwell, R. K., Sporer, S. L., & Saucedo, C. (1991). Assessing eyewitness identification accuracy: An individual differences approach. Southeastern Psychological Association, New Orleans, LA.

Hosch, H. M., & Cooper, D. S. (1981). Victimization and self-monitoring as determinants of eyewitness accuracy. Unpublished manuscript, University of Texas at El Paso.

Hosch, H. H., & Cooper, D. S. (1982). Victimization as a determinant of eyewitness accuracy. *Journal of Applied Psychology, 67*, 649–652.

Hosch, H. M., Leippe, M. R., Marchioni, P. M., & Cooper, D. S. (1984). Victimization, self-monitoring, and eyewitness identification. *Journal of Applied Psychology, 69*, 280–288.

Hosch, H. M., & Platz, S. J. (1984). Self-monitoring and eyewitness accuracy. *Personality and Social Psychology Bulletin, 10*, 283–289.

Kagan, J., Rosman, B. L., Day, D., Albert, J., & Phillips, W. (1964). Information processing in the child: Significance of analytic and reflective attitudes. *Psychological Monographs, 78*, (1, Whole No. 578).

Kogan, N. (1971). Educational implications of cognitive styles. In G. S. Lesser (Ed.), *Psychology and Educational Practice* (pp. 242–292). Glenview, IL: Scott, Foresman.

Kogan, N., & Wallach, M. A. (1967). Risk taking as a function of the situation, the person, and the group. In G. Mandler, P. Mussen, N. Kogan, & M. A. Wallach (Eds.), *New Directions in Psychology, III* (pp. 111–278). New York: Holt, Rinehart and Winston.

Konstadt, N., & Forman, E. (1965). Field dependence and external directedness. *Journal of Personality and Social Psychology, 1*, 490–493.

Malpass, R. S., & Devine, P. G. (1984). Measuring the fairness of eyewitness identification lineups. In S. Lloyd-Bostock & B. R. Clifford (Eds.), *Evaluating witness evidence* (pp. 81–102). Chichester: Wiley.

McCloskey, M. E., & Egeth, H. E. (1983). Eyewitness identification: What can a psychologist tell a jury? *American Psychologist, 38*, 550–563.

Messick, S. & Damarin, F. (1964). Cognitive styles and memory for faces. *Journal of Abnormal and Social Psychology, 69*, 313–318.

Pannell, W. K., Hosch, H. M., & Sands, S. (1992). Self-monitoring and event related potentials as predictors of facial recognition. Manuscript submitted for publication.

Platz, S. J., & Hosch, H. M. (1988). Cross-racial/ethnic identification: A field study. *Journal of Applied Social Psychology, 18,* 972–984.

Read, J. D., Tollestrup, P., Hammersley, R. H., McFadzen, E., & Christensen, A. (1990). The unconscious transference effect: Are innocent bystanders ever misidentified? *Applied Cognitive Psychology, 4,* 3–31.

Rosenthal, R. (1984). Meta-analytic procedures for social research. Beverly Hills, CA: Sage.

Sergent, J., & Bindra, D. (1981). Differential hemispheric processing of faces: Methodological considerations and reinterpretation. *Psychological Bulletin, 89,* 541–554.

Shepherd, J. W., Davies, G. M., & Ellis, H. D. (1980). Identification after delay. Unpublished manuscript, University of Aberdeen, Aberdeen, Scotland.

Shepherd, J. W., Davies, G. M., & Ellis, H. D. (1981). Studies of cue saliency. In G. M. Davies, H. D. Ellis, & J. W. Shepherd (Eds.), *Perceiving and remembering faces* (pp. 105–131). London: Academic Press.

Snyder, M. (1979). Self-monitoring processes. In L. Berkowitz (Ed.), *Advances in experimental social psychology* (Vol. 12, pp. 85–128). New York: Academic Press.

Snyder, M. (1987). *Public appearances/Private realities.* New York: W. H. Freeman.

Sporer, S. L. (1989a). Eyewitness identification accuracy, confidence and decision-times in simultaneous and sequential lineups. University of Marburg, Manuscript submitted for publication.

Sporer, S. L. (1989b). Psychologische Aspekte der Personenbeschreibung. In G. Kohnkan & S. L. Sporer (Eds.), *Zeugenidentifizierungen: Psychologisches Wissen, Probleme und Perspektiven.* Göttingen: Hogrefe.

Wapner, S., & Demick, J. (1991). *Field dependence-independence: Bio-psycho-social factors across the life span.* Hillsdale, NJ: Erlbaum.

Warrington, E. K., & James, M. (1967). An experimental investigation of facial recognition with unilateral cerebral lesions. *Cortex, 3,* 317–326.

Wells, G. L. (1978). Applied eyewitness testimony research: System variables and estimator variables. *Journal of Personality and Social Psychology, 36,* 1546–1557.

Williams, K. D., Loftus, E. F., & Deffenbacher, K. A. (1992). Eyewitness evidence and testimony. In D. K. Kagehiro & W. S. Laufer (Eds.), *Handbook of Psychology and Law,* (pp. 141–166). New York: Springer-Verlag.

Witkin, H. A., Dyk, R. B., Faterson, H. F., Goodenough, D. R., & Karp, S. A. (1962). *Psychological differentiation.* New York: Wiley.

Yarmey, A. D. (1979). *The psychology of eyewitness testimony,* New York: The Free Press.

Zimmerman, S. (1982, April). *Photo recognition accuracy.* Presented at the meeting of Southwestern Psychological Association, El Paso, TX.

16   Eyewitness identification confidence

C. A. Elizabeth Luus and Gary L. Wells

The production has been staged many times over the last decade. Although the plot and cast of characters have often varied, the story always involves a crime, a number of unsuspecting eyewitnesses, and an attempt to identify the criminal. Despite these variations, the ending usually remains the same: Some eyewitnesses feel certain they have identified the perpetrator; others lack that certainty. The accuracy of a witness's testimony cannot, however, necessarily be garnered from the certainty he or she expresses. Eyewitness confidence has been found to account for less than 10 percent of the variance in eyewitness identification accuracy (Wells & Murray, 1984).

Eyewitness confidence and eyewitness accuracy are often poorly calibrated (for example, Bothwell, Deffenbacher, & Brigham, 1987; Deffenbacher, 1980; Leippe, 1980; Wells & Murray, 1983, 1984). However, jurors tend to rely heavily on eyewitness confidence to infer witness accuracy (for example, Cutler, Penrod, & Stuve, 1988; Lindsay, Wells, & Rumpel, 1981; Wells, Lindsay, & Ferguson, 1979). For example, Wells, Lindsay, and Ferguson found that subject-jurors' ascriptions of eyewitness confidence accounted for 50 percent of the variance in their assessments of eyewitness accuracy. Furthermore, the United States judiciary recognizes confidence as a key factor to be considered in deciding the accuracy of eyewitness testimony (*Neil v. Biggers*, 1972). Given the persuasive power that eyewitness confidence can have in the criminal justice system, it is important to understand the factors that influence eyewitness confidence, particularly those factors that can weaken or destroy an existing confidence–accuracy relationship.

To date, four separate reviews of the accuracy–confidence relationship have concluded that we should not necessarily expect a relationship between eyewitness accuracy and confidence (Bothwell, Deffenbacher, & Brigham, 1987; Deffenbacher, 1980; Leippe, 1980; Wells & Murray, 1984). These reviews offered suggestions as to why eyewitness accuracy and confidence are often

Preparation of this chapter was supported in part by a grant to the first author from the Social Sciences and Humanities Research Council of Canada, and by a grant to the second author from the National Science Foundation (SES 9022182).

poorly related. Wells and Murray (1984) suggested that the variation in accuracy–confidence correlations across studies might reflect variation in the researchers' procedures and statistical analyses. Deffenbacher (1980) and Bothwell et al. (1986) suggested that the confidence–accuracy relationship is moderated by the quality of the encoding conditions existing at the time an eyewitness observes a crime; the better the encoding conditions, the stronger the accuracy–confidence relationship. Leippe (1980) proposed that eyewitness accuracy and confidence could be controlled by different mechanisms. That is, some factors could influence accuracy while having no effect on confidence and other factors could influence confidence but not accuracy.

In this chapter, we will review each of these suggestions. More specifically, we will review literature concerning methodological issues involved in assessing confidence–accuracy relationships, moderators of the confidence–accuracy relationship, and the malleability of eyewitness confidence independent of eyewitness accuracy. In addition, we will present some of our recent findings concerning confidence malleability.

Eyewitness confidence can be broadly defined to include witnesses' beliefs in the accuracy of their judgments concerning various aspects of a witnessed event (for example, what was said, the sequence of events, the perpetrator's appearance and attire, the victim, the duration of the event). We will restrict our review to studies of eyewitnesses' confidence in their lineup identification decisions. Furthermore, our discussion is restricted to forensically relevant situations rather than a general confidence–accuracy relation. This focus reflects the differences that exist between lineup identification tasks and other tests of recognition memory (see Wells, in press).

For example, whereas subjects in some memory experiments might attempt to recognize an array of previously encountered stimuli, eyewitnesses faced with a lineup identification task typically attempt to identify only one individual from the lineup. Hence, in contrast to many other recognition memory tests, the eyewitness confidence–accuracy relation is derived from an interindividual (between-subjects) rather than an intraindividual (within-subjects) analysis. Each witness contributes only two data points to the correlation; one accuracy score and one confidence rating. The analysis then compares the identification decisions and confidence ratings of different witnesses rather than the responses of a single witness across a number of face recognition trials. It cannot, therefore, separate individual differences in confidence among eyewitnesses from the identification decisions those witnesses make (see Smith, Kassin, & Ellsworth, 1989). Yet researchers interested in the confidence–accuracy relation will likely remain committed to an interindividual focus given its forensic relevance. In actual cases, the court is concerned with a witness's ability to recognize one particular individual rather than his or her facial recognition performance across a number of identification tasks.

Methodological considerations in assessing the confidence–accuracy relationship

The need for target-absent lineups

Wells and Murray's (1984) review identified thirteen studies that found a significant positive correlation between eyewitness accuracy and confidence and eighteen studies that found a negative or no relation between accuracy and confidence. They suggested that methodological factors might account for the inconsistencies in the literature. In particular, they noted that some studies included a target-absent lineup and others did not.

Target-absent conditions must be included in order to make a true assessment of the confidence–accuracy relation, because this assessment does not depend on an analysis of whether witnesses who choose the target are more confident in their choice than witnesses who instead choose a foil. (In actual cases, the police cannot know whether the perpetrator is present in the lineup.) Instead, the relevant comparison is between witnesses who choose the target when he or she is present in the lineup and witnesses who choose an innocent replacement for the target in a target-absent lineup (Wells & Lindsay, 1985). This reasoning follows from the premise that there is (or ought to be) only one suspect in real lineups and therefore the choice of a foil in a target-present lineup is a "known error" (see Wells & Turtle, 1986). A witness's confidence in a known error is forensically irrelevant because such an identification would never lead to prosecution of the individual identified.

In comparing studies that yielded a significant accuracy–confidence correlation with those that did not, Wells and Murray noted that many of the former investigations used only target-present lineups. Studies that include target-present and target-absent lineups commonly obtain a significant relation between confidence and accuracy when the target is present, but yield no such relation when the target is absent from the lineup. "This suggests that any positive relationship between confidence and accuracy with perpetrator-present lineups may be cancelled by a negative relationship that obtains with perpetrator-absent lineups!" (p. 163).

Errors of commission versus errors of omission

Wells and Lindsay (1985) also stressed the importance of discerning between incorrect choices from lineups (that is, errors of commission) and incorrect rejections (that is, errors of omission). Collapsing across errors of choosers and nonchoosers in calculating the confidence–accuracy correlation obscures the forensic value of such an analysis. Consider, for example, the possibility that choosers are more likely to be correct than nonchoosers and that choosers are more confident than nonchoosers (or the reverse). An overall analysis (collapsed over choosers and nonchoosers) would indicate a significant confidence–accuracy relation even if those witnesses who make false identifications are as confident as those who correctly identify the target and those who make incorrect rejections are as confident as those who correctly make no choice. In other words, the confidence–accuracy relation in the overall analysis would be misleading from a forensic perspective. Practically speaking, it is of no value to determine whether confident choosers are more accurate than nonconfident nonchoosers, particularly if the relation is based on witnesses' status as choosers or nonchoosers rather than their status as confident or nonconfident.

The confidence main-effect issue

There is one further methodological issue that is important from an applied perspective. The issue (not previously discussed in the literature) is as follows. Every time a researcher conducts an eyewitness identification study, the average confidence of witnesses tends to vary. In one experiment, for instance, the mean confidence might be 3.8 on a seven-point scale whereas in another experiment the mean confidence might be 5.3. Sources of this variance are innumerable, including such factors as the subject population, the nature of the witnessed event, and so on.

If we look within experiments, we might find a confidence–accuracy relation. Suppose, for example, the mean confidence of an accurate witness is 4.1 in the first experiment and the mean for an inaccurate witness is 3.5. Similarly, suppose that the means for accurate and inaccurate witnesses in the second experiment are 5.6 and 5.0, respectively. Suppose that the confidence–accuracy correlation is .30 within each experiment. Suppose further that we wish to apply our knowledge of a .30 correlation to a given real world case. Consider the case where we have a real world witness who is 4.8 in confidence. Do we consider that level of confidence to be high or low? In the context of the first experiment, we would consider this a high level of confidence and tend to believe this witness's identification decision. In the context of the second experiment, we would consider this low confidence and tend not to believe the eyewitness.

In reality, the witness is from neither experiment, and herein lies the critical issue. Without some idea of the role played by main effects on mean confidence and the factors that govern it, it is impossible to know how to read the confidence of a witness in a real case in isolation. Our analyses in experiments are better suited to a special real world case in which there are multiple witnesses (who had comparable views of the culprit) who disagree in their identifications of the culprit. In such a case, to the extent that we have established a confidence–accuracy relation in our experiments, we would tend to believe the confident witnesses over the nonconfident witnesses. In cases where there is only one eyewitness, there can be no mean confidence estimate of accurate versus inaccurate witnesses and thus no clear anchor with which to compare the confidence of this particular witness.

Perhaps another way to consider this issue is to note that in an experiment we use statistics uninfluenced by the mean level of confidence obtained from the subjects. In real cases, however, we must contend with this issue while being in the dark. Consider, for example, an experiment that produces a mean confidence rating of 6.1 on a seven-point scale among witnesses who identify someone from the lineup. Assume virtually no witnesses fell below 5.0 in confidence and yet 45 percent of the witnesses have made false identifications. Suppose we find a correlation of .40 between confidence and accuracy. What then will we do in a real case if we encounter a witness whose self-rated confidence is 6.0? Can we consider this witness highly confident, even though his or her confidence falls below the mean in this most recently conducted experiment?

The general point of these observations is that a cutoff on a confidence scale wherein higher levels suggest the witness is accurate and lower levels suggest the witness is inaccurate will vary from one experiment to the next. Undoubtedly, such variation would also occur from one real world case to another. Accordingly, it is difficult to assess the validity of eyewitnesses' confidence in actual cases.

Moderators of the confidence–accuracy relationship

Recent research has sought to develop an understanding of the conditions that foster or inhibit accuracy–confidence relationships. This research has progressed in accordance with two different perspectives, emphasizing a focus on either encoding (that is, witnessing) or retrieval (that is, identification) conditions. These two different approaches represent the distinction Wells (1978) has articulated between estimator and system variables. Estimator variables operate at the encoding stage of memory (viewing conditions) and are outside the control of the legal system. Although estimator variables can be controlled in research experiments, in actual cases their effects can only be estimated. System variables, on the other hand, are postwitnessed event variables (for example, lineup identification instructions) that are under at least some control by the legal system. They can be manipulated to maximize the correspondence between eyewitness accuracy and confidence.

Estimator variables as moderators of
confidence–accuracy relationships

Deffenbacher (1980) advanced one of the first proposals concerning possible estimator variable moderators of the confidence–accuracy relationship, which he called the "optimality" hypothesis. According to Deffenbacher, the confidence–accuracy relationship is moderated by the quality of the encoding conditions at the time an eyewitness observes a crime; the better the encoding conditions, the stronger the accuracy–confidence relationship. Characteristics of the encoding conditions could potentially involve qualities of the situation, the target person, and/or the witness (Brigham, 1990; Hosch, this volume). We will review each of these variables in turn.

Characteristics of the situation. Empirical tests of the optimality hypothesis have been largely restricted to studies of the role of situational characteristics (for example, target exposure time) in confidence–accuracy relations. Consistent with the notion that optimal encoding conditions should enhance the confidence–accuracy relation, a recent meta-analysis indicated that variation in exposure time to the target person's face accounted for "as much as 27 percent of the variation in the predictability of accuracy from confidence" (Bothwell, Deffenbacher, & Brigham, 1987, p. 694).

In contrast to the findings of this meta-analysis, however, and the intuitive appeal of the premise, the optimality hypothesis has received little support from studies that have manipulated witnesses' opportunities to view the target (Brigham, 1990; Lindsay, Wells, & Ferguson, 1979). For example, Lindsay, Wells, and Ferguson (1979) varied witnessing conditions and determined that changes in eyewitness accuracy were not associated with changes in eyewitness confidence or with the magnitude of the confidence–accuracy relation. In this study, eyewitness accuracy was varied by exposing subject-witnesses to a staged theft under one of three types of viewing conditions that varied in terms of how good a view they afforded of the thief (for example, varying such factors as the amount of viewing time and whether or not the thief wore a hat that masked his hair). This manipulation produced significant differences in accuracy among groups. Changes in accuracy, however, were not accompanied by changes in confidence or by changes in the confidence–accuracy relation.

Characteristics of the target. One dimension along which the quality of encoding conditions can vary is the target person's appearance. People's faces vary in attractiveness and distinctiveness. Unattractive or distinctive looking faces are typically easier to remember or identify than attractive or unexceptional faces (for example, Mueller, Heesacker, & Ross, 1984; Shapiro & Penrod, 1986; Brigham, 1990). Brigham (1990) tested the idea that distinctive looking or unattractive targets afford the witness an optimal viewing situation and thus should be associated with strong positive accuracy–confidence correlations. Consistent with this prediction, he found that the confidence–accuracy relation was stronger when the target's face was distinctive rather than nondistinctive and unattractive rather than attractive.

Characteristics of the witness. A small number of studies have sought to determine whether there are individual differences that moderate the confidence–accuracy relation (see Hosch, this volume, for a more extensive discussion of individual differences between witnesses). This research suggests two factors that might moderate the confidence–accuracy relation: the willingness of witnesses to choose someone from a lineup or photo spread (Fleet, Brigham, & Bothwell, 1987; Pigott & Brigham, 1985; and public self-consciousness, that is, a dispositional focus on the outward, observable aspects of oneself (Kassin, Rigby, & Castillo, 1991).

The former studies have found stronger accuracy–confidence correlations among witnesses who chose someone from the lineup they viewed than among nonchoosers. The reliability and forensic value of this finding, however, must be considered questionable given the recommendations of Wells and Lindsay (1985) discussed previously. Recall that Wells and Lindsay noted that a forensically relevant assessment of the confidence–accuracy relationship derives from a comparison of witnesses who choose the target from a target-present lineup and witnesses who choose an innocent replacement for the target from a target-absent lineup.

System variable moderators of confidence–accuracy relationships. The one successful investigation of system variables that might moderate the accuracy–confidence relationship was conducted by Kassin (1985). In a series of four experiments, Kassin demonstrated that the accuracy–confidence relation could be improved by allowing witnesses to view videotapes of themselves making their identifications from a photo spread before asking them to rate their confidence in their identifications. Kassin claimed that witnesses gained "retrospective self-awareness" (RSA) from this procedure.

Kassin suggested two reasons for the success of RSA in improving the accuracy–confidence relation. First, from a self-perception perspective, it may have provided witnesses with an opportunity to make relevant inferences based on their overt behavior. Witnesses may, for example, have inferred that the quicker they made a decision, the more likely they were to be accurate. Second, RSA may have allowed witnesses to reexperience the thoughts they had when they first viewed the lineup and made an identification decision.

Follow-up research (Kassin, Rigby, & Castillo, 1991) suggests that RSA enhances the confidence–accuracy relation primarily because of a modified self-perception hypothesis, that is, one that applies to witnesses high but not low in public self-consciousness. "Specifically, people who are predisposed to focus on their public behavior and appearance are uniquely sensitive to subtle cues that betray the ease or difficulty with which they made their decision" (Kassin et al., 1991, p. 704).

Researchers concerned with moderators of the confidence–accuracy relation should consider the forensic value of their findings. Here, the distinction between system and estimator variables is important. Findings concerning estimator variable moderators of confidence–accuracy relationships are forensically valuable insofar as they can be incorporated into either expert testimony or jury instructions and then used by jurors to decide how much weight to assign to a witness's identification testimony. Such findings cannot be used, however, to increase the actual confidence–accuracy relation. Knowledge of system variable moderators, on the other hand, can be used to develop procedures designed to optimize the confidence–accuracy relation in actual cases. Given the forensic value of such knowledge, we recommend that future research be devoted to first identifying system variable moderators of the CA relation and then using these data to develop procedures designed to maximize the correspondence between confidence and accuracy.

The malleability of eyewitness confidence

Leippe (1980) suggested that we should not necessarily expect a relationship between eyewitness accuracy and confidence because the human information processing systems seem "capable of altering memory and confidence in orthogonal directions, especially in the context of powerful and rich social situations" (p.271). Leippe suggested that eyewitness accuracy and confidence could be controlled by different mechanisms. That is, some factors could influence accuracy but have no effect on confidence and other factors could influence confidence but not accuracy.

For example, in judging the likelihood that their memories are accurate, witnesses presumably use a heuristic in which the vividness of their recollections serves as a cue to the accuracy of the underlying memory. A vivid recollection is considered indicative of an accurate memory. To the extent that witnesses are unaware of encoding or witnessing conditions that can cause memory inaccuracies, however, such as short target exposure time (Shapiro & Penrod, 1986) and low perceived crime seriousness (Leippe, Wells, & Ostrom, 1978), they might vividly recall a distorted or inaccurately encoded memory. Alternatively, social influences, such as discussion with other people present at the scene of a crime might "corroborate" a witness's memory and thus enhance the strength of his or her belief in the accuracy of the recollection of what happened, rather than influence the vividness of the recollection.

Although numerous studies have confirmed the malleability of eyewitness memory, there has been little theorizing or research devoted to confidence malleability. Only two studies (Luus & Wells, 1991; Wells, Ferguson, & Lindsay, 1981) have investigated Leippe's (1980) suggestion that certain factors might influence eyewitness confidence but have no effect on accuracy. In both these studies, manipulations designed to alter witnesses' confidence were introduced after they had made their identifications, thereby isolating confidence and eliminating any possibility that changes in accuracy might accompany changes in confidence.

Wells, Ferguson, & Lindsay, 1981

Drawing on Tesser's (1978) finding that people's attitudes tend to polarize with postexposure thought about a stimulus, Leippe (1980) proposed that the confidence of eyewitnesses might increase with postidentification thought about their lineup choices. Wells et al. (1981) tested Leippe's suggestion by staging thefts for unsuspecting witnesses who first attempted to identify the thief from a photo spread and then were cross-examined. Prior to the cross-examination, half the witnesses were induced to think about their lineup choices. They were briefed about the types of questions they could expect under cross-examination and were encouraged to rehearse possible answers to these questions. The remaining witnesses received no such instruction. The briefings were expected to increase thinking about the witnessed event (including lineup choice) and thus bolster eyewitness confidence. Elevated confidence was expected to enhance perceived eyewitness credibility.

The results indicated that witnesses who had been briefed expressed more confidence in their identifications than did those who were not briefed. The elevated confidence associated with the briefing manipulation was primarily attributable to increased certainty on the part of eyewitnesses who misidentified the perpetrator. The briefing manipulation produced statistically significant increases in expressed confidence for inaccurate but not accurate eyewitness identifications. Subject-jurors who viewed the witnesses' videotaped testimony were unable to distinguish accurate from inaccurate eyewitnesses. Subject-jurors were also significantly more likely to convict the accused if he had been identified by eyewitnesses who had been briefed rather than by an eyewitness who had not been briefed.

Briefing witnesses before they take the stand is a common courtroom practice. It augments the difficulty of the task faced by jurors of distinguishing accurate from inaccurate eyewitness accounts. Unfortunately, the practice of briefing eyewitnesses is probably not the only source of inflated eyewitness confidence. In actual criminal cases, there are numerous events that might occur after an eyewitness makes an identification, but before giving testimony, that could affect the certainty with which that identification testimony is delivered.

We have recently initiated a program of research designed to enhance our understanding of this issue. Our findings to date indicate that eyewitnesses can become more or less confident about their lineup choices as a function of social comparison information obtained after they have made their identifications. This research investigated the effects of informing witnesses of the identification decision of a co-witness (Luus & Wells, 1991).

Luus & Wells, 1991

Our (1991) research tested the idea that eyewitness confidence might be influenced by knowledge of the identification decision made by a co-eyewitness. It is not uncommon for more than one eyewitness to view a criminal event. Although modern eyewitness procedural guidelines firmly recommend that eyewitnesses be separated prior to and during lineup iden-tification tasks (Wells, 1988), there are no prohibitions against discussing their identification decisions after the task.

We noted that the role of social influence (the influence of other people) on the confidence of eyewitnesses has been limited to research and theory on the malleability of eyewitness memory with no attempt to examine its impact on eyewitness confidence. Furthermore, dominant theorizing about memory malleability has not adopted a social influence (for example, con-formity, compliance, persuasion) perspective, but rather has operated from a reconstructive memory or other purely cognitive framework (Loftus, 1974). Recently, a social influence perspective, involving concepts such as conform-ity, compliance, and source credibility has been advocated in the memory malleability research literature (for example, see McCloskey & Zaragoza, 1987), but the role of social influence in eyewitness certainty has remained conspicuously absent.

In addition, little attention has been paid to the processes that influence the genesis and expression of eyewitness identification confidence. We rea-soned that given the weak relationship between eyewitness accuracy and confidence, it is unlikely that eyewitness identification confidence is a simple function of ecphoric similarity. Ecphoric similarity is the judged degree of resemblance between a memory trace and an external stimulus (Tulving, 1981). Within the realm of an eyewitness identification task, a decision based on ecphoric similarity would derive from a comparison of the eyewitness's memory for the culprit and the physical appearance of the person chosen from the lineup. We do not believe that this is the type of judgment process that operates in eyewitness identification situations. Instead, we believe that eyewitness identification confidence is determined at least to some degree by factors that are not related to ecphoric similarity.

To test this assumption, we staged thefts for pairs of unsuspecting witnesses, then had the witnesses attempt to identify the thief from a target-absent photo lineup. Biased instructions were used to induce false identifications. More specifically, we did not caution witnesses that the thief might not be present in the photo lineup (see Malpass & Devine, 1981). Instead, we instructed witnesses to indicate which of the lineup members they saw steal our equip-ment. Following the identification task, witnesses were given randomly de-termined information concerning the alleged identification decision of their co-witness. Some witnesses were led to believe that the co-witness identified the same person they had. Others were informed that the co-witness had made a different decision when shown the lineup (either identifying a different individual or asserting that the thief was not present). All witnesses were then questioned (and videotaped) about their memory for the theft. The video-taped interviews were later shown to subject-jurors who evaluated the wit-nesses' credibility.

Our results indicate that eyewitness confidence can be both raised and lowered by information concerning a co-witness's identification decision and that manipulated confidence can influence jurors' assessments of eyewitness credibility. Compared to a control condition in which witnesses received no information concerning their co-witness, co-witness agreement produced a robust inflation of confidence (mean = 8.77 on a ten-point scale) whereas co-witness disagreement produced a precipitous decline in confidence (mean = 4.67 on a ten-point scale). Note that this confidence deflation did not derive from the mere fact that the co-witness allegedly identified a different person from the lineup. *Who* the co-witness was said to have identified played a critical role in shaping the confidence of witnesses. Subject-witnesses who were led to believe that the co-witness identified someone who bore no re-semblance to the culprit became more confident about the accuracy of their identifications (mean = 7.87 on a ten-point scale). Furthermore, witnesses whose confidence was either raised or lowered by information concerning the alleged identification decision of a co-eyewitness generally persevered in those levels of confidence. Their confidence ratings did not shift if they were sub-sequently told that the co-witness information they had received was in error (see Table 16.1). In addition, the effects of the identification feedback ex-tended beyond eyewitnesses' self-rated confidence to subject-jurors' ratings of perceived credibility. Subject-jurors' credibility ratings generally paralleled the witnesses' confidence ratings.

Our findings suggest one reason why eyewitness confidence and eyewitness identification accuracy are not likely to be well correlated by the time witnesses take the stand in actual cases. Specifically, eyewitnesses might learn about the identification decisions of other witnesses prior to the trial or learn about other evidence consistent or inconsistent with their identification decision. An eyewitness, for example, might make an identification and later learn that the suspect was in possession of stolen goods or that he or she had committed a similar offense in the past.

Concluding remarks

Eyewitnesses who claim to be very confident about their identifications prob-ably believe that the person they identified matches their memory for the culprit. Does this belief on the part of an eyewitness serve as a reliable cue to his or her accuracy? Given the large number of studies that have found

Table 16.1. *Luus and Wells's confidence malleability study*

Postidentification information	Witnesses' self-rated confidence
No information (control)	
Witness receives no information regarding the identification decision of co-witness	6.90_a
Same information	
Co-witness allegedly IDed the same person	8.77_b
Not present	
Co-witness allegedly did not believe the suspect was present in the photo spread	3.57_c
Different identification	
Co-witness allegedly identified a different person (a person who looks similar to the one he/she identified)	4.67_c
Implausibly-different identification	
Co-witness allegedly identified a different person (one who looks dissimilar to his/her choice)	7.87_b
Different/same	
Witness is told that the co-witness IDed a different person (one who looks similar to his/her choice); the experimenter later corrects the information, stating that the other witness identified the same person	4.60_c
Same/different	
Witness is told that the co-witness IDed the same person; experimenter later corrects that information, stating that the co-witness IDed a different person (one who looks similar to the one he/she identified)	8.33_b
Same/withdraw	
Witness is told that the co-witness identified the same person; the experimenter later withdraws that information, stating that she is not sure who the co-witness identified	8.53_b
Different/withdraw	
Witness is told that the co-witness identified a different person; the experimenter later withdraws this information, stating that she is not sure who the co-witness identified	6.13_a

Note: Means not sharing a common subscript differ at $p < .05$ using a Newman-Keuls analysis.

little relation between confidence and accuracy, we caution against assuming that such reliability exists. Eyewitnesses' statements of confidence in their identifications might be only partly determined by how similar the identified person is to their memories of the culprit. The research reviewed in this chapter suggests that, in many cases, a statement of confidence could derive from social influences as well as individual differences across witnesses. These additional influences may sometimes overshadow the similarity between the identified person and the eyewitness's memory of that person.

This is problematic to the extent that these additional determinants of confidence are unrelated to eyewitness accuracy because the eyewitness identification problem is not a question of false identifications per se but rather one of credible or persuasive false identifications (Wells et al., 1979). Hence, the danger is that eyewitnesses who make false identifications might also firmly believe they have identified the culprit. This combination of false identification testimony with a confident belief in its validity creates the potential for miscarriage of justice.

References

Bothwell, R. K., Deffenbacher, K. A., & Brigham, J. C. (1987). Correlations of eyewitness accuracy and confidence: Optimality hypothesis revisited. *Journal of Applied Psychology, 72,* 691–695.

Brigham, J. C. (1990). Target person distinctiveness and attractiveness as moderator variables in the confidence–accuracy relationship in eyewitness identifications. *Basic and Applied Social Psychology, 11,* 101–115.

Cutler, B. L., Penrod, S. D., & Stuve, T. E. (1988). Juror decision making in eyewitness identification cases. *Law and Human Behavior, 12,* 41–56.

Deffenbacher, K. (1980). Eyewitness accuracy and confidence: Can we infer anything about their relationship? *Law and Human Behavior, 4,* 243–260.

Fleet, M. L., Brigham, J. C., & Bothwell, R. K. (1987). The confidence–accuracy relationship: The effects of confidence assessments and choosing. *Journal of Applied Social Psychology, 17,* 171–187.

Kassin, S. M. (1985). Eyewitness identification: Retrospective self-awareness and the accuracy–confidence correlation. *Journal of Personality and Social Psychology, 49,* 878–893.

Kassin, S. M., Rigby, S., & Castillo, S. R. (1991). The accuracy–confidence correlation in eyewitness testimony: Limits and extensions of the retrospective self-awareness effect. *Journal of Personality and Social Psychology, 61,* 698–707.

Leippe, M. R. (1980). Effects of integrative and memorial cognitive processes on the correspondence of eyewitness accuracy and confidence. *Law and Human Behavior, 4,* 261–274.

Leippe, M. R., Wells, G. L., & Ostrom, T. M. (1978). Crime seriousness as a determinant of accuracy in eyewitness identification. *Journal of Applied Psychology, 63,* 345–351.

Lindsay, R. C. L., Wells, G. L., & Rumpel, C. M. (1981). Can people detect eyewitness identification accuracy within and across situations? *Journal of Applied Psychology, 66,* 482–489.

Loftus, E. F. (1974, April). Reconstructive memory: The incredible eyewitness. *Psychology Today,* pp. 116–119.

Loftus, G. R. (1972). Eye fixations and recognition memory. *Cognitive Psychology, 3,* 525–557.

Luus, C. A. E., & Wells, G. L. (1993). The malleability of eyewitness confidence: Social influence and perseverance effects. Manuscript submitted for publication.

Malpass, R. S., & Devine, P. G. (1981). Eyewitness identification: Lineup instructions and the absence of the offender. *Journal of Applied Psychology, 66,* 482–489.

McCloskey, M., & Zaragoza, M. (1985b). Postevent information and memory: Reply to Loftus, Schooler, and Waegnaar. *Journal of Experimental Psychology: General, 114,* 375–380.

Mueller, J. H., Heesacker, M., & Ross, M. J. (1984). Likability of targets and distractors in facial recognition. *American Journal of Psychology, 97,* 235–247.

Neil v. Biggers, 409 U. S. 188 (1972).

Pigott, M. A., & Brigham, J. C. (1985). Relationship between accuracy and prior description and facial recognition. *Journal of Applied Psychology, 70,* 547–555.

Shapiro, P. N., & Penrod, S. (1986). Meta-analysis of facial identification studies. *Psychological Bulletin, 100,* 139–156.

Smith, V. L., Kassin, S. M., & Ellsworth, P. C. (1989). Eyewitness accuracy and confidence: Within versus between-subject correlations. *Journal of Applied Psychology, 74,* 356–359.

Tesser, A. (1978). Self-generated attitude change. In L. Berkowitz (Ed.), *Advances in experimental social psychology,* Vol. 11. New York: Academic Press.

Tulving, E. (1981). Similarity relations in recognition. *Journal of Verbal Learning and Behavior, 20,* 479–496.

Wells, G. L. (1978). Applied eyewitness-testimony research: System variables and estimator variables. *Journal of Personality and Social Psychology, 36,* 1546–1557.

Wells, G. L. (1988). *Eyewitness identification: A system handbook.* Toronto: Carswell Legal Publications.

Wells, G. L. (1993). What do we know about eyewitness identification? *American Psychologist, 48,* 553–571.

Wells, G. L., Ferguson, T. J., & Lindsay, R. C. L. (1981). The tractability of eyewitness confidence and its implications for triers of fact. *Journal of Applied Psychology, 64,* 440–448.

Wells, G. L., & Lindsay, R. C. L. (1985). Methodological notes on the confidence–accuracy relationship in eyewitness identifications. *Journal of Applied Psychology, 70,* 413–419.

Wells, G. L., Lindsay, R. C. L., & Ferguson, T. J. (1979). Accuracy, confidence, and juror perceptions in eyewitness identification. *Journal of Applied Psychology, 64,* 440–448.

Wells, G. L., & Murray, D. M. (1983). What can psychology say about the Neil v. Biggers criteria for judging eyewitness identification accuracy? *Journal of Applied Psychology, 68,* 347–362.

Wells, G. L., & Murray, D. M. (1984). Eyewitness confidence. In G. L. Wells & E. F. Loftus (Eds.), *Eyewitness testimony: Psychological Perspectives* (pp. 155–170). Cambridge, England: Cambridge University Press.

Wells, G. L., & Turtle, J. W. (1986). Eyewitness identification: The importance of lineup models. *Psychological Bulletin, 99,* 320–329.

17   Expectations of eyewitness performance: Jurors' verdicts do not follow from their beliefs

R. C. L. Lindsay

Eyewitness identification has been cited as perhaps the single most persuasive source of evidence (for example, Loftus, 1979; Woocher, 1977), but also as the most frequent cause of wrongful convictions (Rattner, 1988). Generally speaking, eyewitnesses are considered by jurors to be a credible source of evidence. Wells, Lindsay, and colleagues found that eyewitness confidence was a major determinant of witness credibility, accounting for as much as 50 percent of the variability in mock juror belief of eyewitness testimony (Lindsay, Wells, & Rumpel, 1981; Wells, Ferguson, & Lindsay, 1981; Wells, Lindsay, & Ferguson, 1979). An extensive literature exists indicating that there is a small positive association between confidence and accuracy probably, but not one of sufficient size to make confidence a reliable criterion of identification accuracy (for example, Wells & Murray, 1984). Even if the confidence–accuracy relationship is reliable immediately following identification, there are many reasons to believe that this relationship will not exist in the courtroom (for example, Wells, Lindsay, & Tousignant, 1980). Leippe (1980) provides a particularly thorough and insightful discussion of these issues.

Other factors that might influence juror belief of eyewitness testimony include the internal consistency of the evidence given, agreement or disagreement among multiple witnesses, and physical features of the situation that might reasonably be expected to influence eyewitness accuracy (such as lighting, length of exposure, and so forth; Wells & Lindsay, 1983). Work in my laboratory has continued to support the importance of eyewitness confidence (for example, Lindsay, Wells, & O'Connor, 1989), but has produced inconsistent evidence in support of other factors as determinants of mock juror

The research reported in this chapter was supported by grants from the Social Sciences and Humanities Research Council of Canada. Some of the studies described in this chapter have been or will be reported in greater detail elsewhere. Others are reported only here. Many were conducted first as undergraduate thesis projects with additional data added later. I am indebted to the following students for their efforts: Linda Cancelli, Deborah Cully, Daphne Drennan, Jennifer Fulford, Julia Hector, Jim Lea, Virginia LeVan, Robert Lim, Glenn Nosworthy, Paula MacDonald, Louis Marando, Susan McGarry, Lavita Nadkarni, Lisa Nemiroff, Catherine Richmond, Renee Roberts-Brauer, Caroline Seabrook, and Harold Wallbridge.

belief of eyewitness testimony (reviewed below). Cutler and Penrod provide further evidence not only that confidence influences mock jurors, but also that witness confidence has a greater impact on evaluations of witness credibility than other factors; including many of the variables that determine identification accuracy (Cutler, Penrod, & Dexter, 1990; Cutler, Penrod, & Stuve, 1988).

In this chapter, studies are described that were designed to determine what factors, in addition to eyewitness confidence, influence belief of eyewitnesses. First, survey/prediction studies are described. In these studies, I wanted to determine what factors people felt were important determinants of eyewitness accuracy and, for that reason, would be expected to influence attributions of witness credibility and thus belief of eyewitness testimony. Second, mock jury studies were conducted to examine the degree to which highly rated variables actually influenced mock juror decision making. Finally, the impact of the lineup procedure used to collect identification evidence was assessed in terms of the effect it has on the perceived credibility and believability of the witness. Lineup variables are important determinants of the probative value of eyewitness testimony and therefore ought to be determinants of juror belief of eyewitnesses. I conclude that jurors may not know how they make decisions, or what information is useful to them. A corollary to that conclusion is that eyewitness errors are unlikely to be corrected in court.

Perceived importance of eyewitness variables

In previous research, subjects have been asked to indicate the most likely effect of variables on identification accuracy. The methods of these prediction studies were a starting point for my research. For example, Deffenbacher and Loftus (1982) and Yarmey and Jones (1983) presented four alternative, multiple choice questionnaires to various populations to determine the extent to which knowledge of eyewitness issues was a matter of common sense. Their primary concern was to determine if knowledge of factors influencing eyewitness accuracy was a proper subject for expert testimony in court. If the average person were aware of the factors determining eyewitness accuracy, then expert testimony would not be required to educate triers of fact. On the other hand, any substantial discrepancy between the opinions of the experts and others, particularly potential jurors, would indicate that eyewitness memory is a proper subject for expert testimony. The multiple choice method was adequate for this purpose. However, accuracy was a problem. The experts failed to agree on the appropriate responses. For example, the percentage of experts giving the response considered correct by Yarmey and Jones varied from 44 to 100 percent. Only one of sixteen "correct" responses was unanimously endorsed. Obviously there is room for debate in any scientific domain. The relatively small amount of data available on some of the issues at the time (and still in some cases) suggests that differing opinions should be expected. All that was required for the purpose of supporting the use of expert testimony was a demonstration that the experts were largely in agreement among themselves and that the responses of prospective jurors were substantially different from those of the experts. Both these goals were met as the experts gave the "correct" responses 78 percent of the time on average whereas members of the general public gave "correct" responses only 41 percent of the time (Yarmey & Jones, 1983).

Although these results were interesting, many questions remained unanswered. The multiple choice nature of the questions did not reveal how strong the respondents felt the effects were nor how important they perceived the variables to be as determinants of eyewitness accuracy. For example, respondents may state that they believe child eyewitnesses will be less likely than adults to correctly identify a criminal from a lineup. This finding would not indicate, however, how important witness age is perceived to be as a determinant of identification accuracy either in absolute terms (how large the difference between the accuracy rates would be for adults versus children) nor in relative terms, that is, in comparison with other variables that might influence eyewitness accuracy (is witness age a more or less important determinant of accuracy than arousal level of the witness during the crime?).

SURVEYS 1 AND 2

In my first two attempts to assess the perceived importance of variables influencing witness accuracy, respondents were asked how likely a witness would be to make an accurate identification decision under various conditions. Each person responded to thirty-eight items by circling a number on a scale from one (almost certain to be inaccurate) to nine (almost certain to be accurate). The thirty-eight items described nineteen variables with two statements indicating different levels of each variable (for example, "the witness knew the accused prior to the crime" versus "the witness had never seen the criminal before the crime" or "the crime was" versus "the crime was not very stressful for the witness"). The thirty-eight items were presented in one of several random orders with the restriction that the two items defining any particular variable were separated by at least three other items.

Before starting the survey, respondents were provided with a sample question and told that there were no correct answers to the questions. The researchers were described as interested only in the respondent's opinions. Because the two items representing a variable did not appear together, contrast effects may have been reduced. Demand characteristics could be invoked as an explanation if every variable had produced significant effects; however, this did not happen. It is not clear how demand could explain why some variables revealed significant and substantial differences although others did not.

The absolute importance of the individual variables as determinants of identification accuracy could be inferred from the difference between the mean ratings for the two items for each of the nineteen variables. For example, a small difference in mean anticipated accuracy of witnesses who did versus did not experience the crime as stressful would indicate that witness experiences of stress are not perceived as an important determinant of identification accuracy. A large (statistically significant) difference between these means would suggest that stress is an important determinant of witness accuracy (at least in the opinion of the respondents) and should be an important factor in evaluating witness credibility.

The relative importance of the variables in comparison to each other might crudely be assessed by rank ordering the size of the absolute differences between the means for the two items representing each variable. If the difference in anticipated accuracy of witnesses who did versus did not experience stress is greater than the difference in the anticipated accuracy of children versus adults as eyewitnesses, then stress would rank higher than age as a determinant of identification accuracy and could be inferred to be a more important determinant of attributions of witness credibility.

The variables tested and results of these two surveys, conducted three years apart, are presented in Table 17.1 (N = 120 Queen's University undergraduates in each survey). Some of the results were encouraging. First, there was considerable agreement across the first survey and the replication. The rank order correlation of the absolute differences between the means for pairs of questions across the two samples was .74, $p < .001$. Thus the relative importance of the variables was quite similar for both samples. Nine variables were expected to significantly influence identification accuracy (means of the two items defining the variable differed by t test at the .05 level) in the first survey and eight in the replication with six common to both. The same five variables resulted in the five largest absolute differences for both samples.

Variables perceived as determinants of eyewitness accuracy

Attention to the criminal. The highest ranking variable (largest difference between the two items defining the variable) for both samples was attention paid to the criminal during the crime. Witnesses were expected to be accurate if they had paid "attention to the criminal during the crime" (Ms = 6.75, 6.78) but quite unlikely to be accurate if they had "not paid attention to the criminal during the crime" (Ms = 1.71, 1.73).

Opportunity to view the criminal. The opportunity to view the criminal during the crime ranked second in both surveys. Responses to the item stating that

Table 17.1. *Rated likelihood of accurate identification decisions as a function of crime, criminal, and witness factors*

Variable	Study 1		Study 2	
	High	Low	High	Low
Paid attention to criminal	6.75	1.61*	6.68	1.67*
Opportunity to view criminal	6.95	2.17*	6.87	1.90*
Confidence of witness	6.52	3.10*	6.74	3.03*
Memory for peripheral detail	3.59	6.32*	2.97	7.44*
Interval between crime and ID	6.43	3.81*	6.49	3.36*
Appearance of the accused (tidy, well groomed vs. not)	7.23	4.87*	5.37	4.83
Accused had a prior record	7.28	5.16*	5.18	5.19
Original description fits in court appearance	5.80	3.87*	6.03	3.81*
Appearance of witness (tidy, well groomed vs. not)	7.08	5.37*	5.48	5.36
Witness knew accused before crime	6.59	5.17	6.69	5.19*
Lineup foil similarity	4.28	4.10	5.37	6.87*
Stress or arousal level	5.03	5.79	4.68	5.93
Witness had prior record	5.06	5.57	5.26	5.36
Same vs. cross race ID	5.52	5.18	5.72	5.06
Victim vs. bystander	5.46	5.80	5.32	5.84
Alibi (stranger vs. relative)	4.83	5.11	4.67	4.88
Lineup instructions	5.26	5.49	5.27	5.60
Charges against witness (dropped vs. not for ID)	4.86	5.06	4.94	5.01
Same vs. cross sex ID	5.51	5.50	5.42	5.57

*The difference between means is significant at the .05 level.
"High" refers to items expected to produce higher accuracy.
Higher numbers indicate greater rated likelihood of accuracy.

the witness had "a good opportunity to view the criminal" led to high expectations of identification accuracy (Ms = 6.95, 6.87) whereas the item stating that the witness "did not have a good opportunity to view the criminal" led to low expectations of accuracy (Ms = 2.17, 1.90).

Confidence. Confidence of the eyewitness was considered an important criterion of identification accuracy by both samples (ranking third and fourth). Confident eyewitnesses (Ms = 6.52, 6.74) were expected to be significantly more accurate than nonconfident eyewitnesses (Ms = 3.10, 3.03). The results of many mock jury studies indicate that witness confidence is heavily relied upon by mock jurors. As discussed previously, confidence is not a good criterion or "post-dictor" of eyewitness accuracy and thus heavy reliance on this variable as a determinant of witness credibility is unlikely to improve jury performance.

Peripheral detail. Memory for peripheral detail was also consistently perceived to be related to identification accuracy (ranking fourth and third). Witnesses with superior memory for peripheral details ($Ms = 6.32, 7.44$) were expected to make more accurate identification decisions than witnesses with poor memory for peripheral details ($Ms = 3.59, 2.97$). Unfortunately, studies on this topic have demonstrated that witnesses with superior memory for peripheral detail are less likely to make correct identification decisions than those with poorer memory for peripheral detail (Cutler, Penrod, & Martens, 1987; Wells & Leippe, 1981), perhaps because one sacrifices attention to critical details of the person in order to encode peripheral information. To the extent that these data generalize to real jurors, this would indicate that a factor appropriately deemed important as a determinant of accuracy probably leads to less rather than more accurate verdicts because the direction of the effect is misunderstood.

Delay between crime and identification. Delay between the crime and the identification attempt was also considered important, ranking fifth in both surveys. Higher accuracy was expected after short delays between the crime and identification attempt ($Ms = 6.43, 6.49$) than if there was a long delay ($Ms = 3.81, 3.36$). Note that the actual length of short and long delays was not specified so that it is only clear that delay in general is perceived as a potentially important variable.

Description. Fit between the original description provided by the witness and the in-court appearance of the accused was also expected to be a reliable criterion of identification accuracy by both samples (ranked eighth and sixth). A good fit between the original description of the criminal provided by the eyewitness and the accused's appearance in court was expected to be associated with relatively high accuracy ($Ms = 5.80, 6.03$) whereas substantial discrepancies between the original description and in-court appearance were believed to be associated with poorer identification performance ($Ms = 3.87, 3.81$). Again, the available evidence suggests that accuracy of description is not strongly related to accuracy of identification making this variable a questionable criterion of identification accuracy (for example, Wells, 1985).

Prior acquaintance with criminal. The means for both samples were almost identical for this variable, but the difference in the ratings was significant for one sample only (marginally so for the other, $p < .10$). In both cases, a witness who "had met the criminal before the crime" ($Ms = 6.59, 6.69$) was expected to be more accurate than a witness who had not met the criminal prior to the crime ($Ms = 5.17, 5.19$). The rankings for this variable were 10 and 7.5. Note that witnesses were expected to be relatively accurate in either case.

These are intuitively sensible variables that the courts agree could be important determinants of identification accuracy (*Neil v. Biggers*, 1972). This does not guarantee that these variables are actually useful criteria of eyewitness accuracy (Wells & Murray, 1983). Frequently intuitions about factors that influence eyewitness accuracy are in error and could lead to serious miscarriages of justice.

Several other variables were judged to influence eyewitness accuracy significantly by only one of the samples.

Appearance of the accused. Eyewitness identification was rated as less likely to be accurate if the accused appeared tidy and well groomed in court ($M =$ 4.87) than if the accused was untidy and not well groomed ($M = 7.23$). However, this difference was significant only for the first sample. The results for the second sample were in the same direction but did not approach significance ($Ms = 4.83$ versus 5.37). Apparently, some subjects felt a neat, well groomed person was unlikely to be a criminal. It is disturbing to think that some jurors may be highly influenced by the grooming of the accused.

Appearance of the witness. The first sample also felt that the appearance of the witness was a meaningful criterion of eyewitness accuracy; tidy, well groomed witnesses were seen as more likely to be accurate ($Ms = 7.08$ versus 6.37). These data certainly reinforce the long held folk wisdom of lawyers that in court appearance may be an important determinant of witness credibility in some cases or for some jurors.

Prior record. The same sample that was concerned with appearance felt that the eyewitness was more likely to make a correct identification if the accused had a prior record (7.28) than if the accused had no prior record (6.16). Because the questions did not specify whether or not the accused was guilty, this result may reflect an inference that the accused is more likely to be guilty if he or she has a prior record. If this was the inference made, the predicted difference conforms to the data collected in staged crime studies. Correct identification decisions are more common when the criminal is present in rather than absent from the lineup (for example, Lindsay & Wells, 1980; 1985; Malpass & Devine, 1981). Thus the reasoning could be that an eyewitness is more likely to identify a guilty person than an innocent one and someone with a prior record is more likely to be guilty. This potential confound was eliminated in a subsequent survey described below by specifying the guilt or innocence of the accused.

Variables not perceived to be determinants of eyewitness accuracy

Somewhat encouraging were the findings that respondents indicated little anticipated effect of the status of the witness, whether victim or bystander, with similar findings regarding the sex of the criminal and witness; variables few researchers expect to influence identification accuracy. Unfortunately, concerns are raised because some other variables were not perceived as important determinants of accuracy. Substantial evidence exists that false identification rates can be dramatically influenced by lineup structure, instructions, attire, and simultaneous versus sequential presentation (Buckhout, Alpern, Chern, Silverberg, & Slomovits, 1974; Buckhout, Figueroa, & Hoff, 1975; Cutler & Penrod, 1988; Cutler, Penrod, & Martens, 1987; Malpass & Devine, 1981; Lindsay, Lea, & Fulford, 1991; Lindsay, Lea, Nosworthy, Fulford, Hector, LeVan, & Seabrook, 1991; Lindsay, Wallbridge, & Drennan, 1987; Lindsay & Wells, 1980; 1985; Wells, 1984). Lineup procedures ought therefore to influence attributions of witness credibility; but they do not, or at least not in the appropriate direction. These results are described below.

Foil similarity. High similarity of lineup foils to the accused was not expected to influence accuracy by the first sample (rank of 11); but was expected by the second sample (rank of 7.5) to decrease identification accuracy significantly (Ms = 6.37 and 6.87 for similar versus dissimilar foils respectively). Lindsay and Wells (1980) and Lindsay, Lea, Nosworthy, et al. (1991) found that identification decisions were more accurate if the foils resembled the suspect. The respondents may have assumed the criminal was present in the lineup and that similar foils would decrease accuracy by interfering with memory for the criminal. Even this conclusion is not supported by the data; correct identification rates are not significantly influenced by foil similarity.

Lineup instructions. Lineup instructions were not expected to influence identification accuracy significantly, ranking seventeenth and thirteenth. Not only were the differences small, but the means for both samples indicated that, if anything, biased instructions ("he's in there, all you have to do is pick him out") were expected to lead to higher accuracy than fair instructions ("remember, the guilty person may not be in the lineup"). Research results indicate that biased instructions do not influence correct identification rates but significantly increase false identification rates (for example, Lindsay et al., 1991; Malpass & Devine, 1981).

These results support the conclusion drawn from the earlier prediction studies that people do not understand the impact of many variables on the accuracy of eyewitness identifications (Deffenbacher & Loftus, 1982; Yarmey & Jones, 1983). Whether expert testimony is the answer to this problem is debatable (Lindsay, MacDonald, & McGarry, 1989; Loftus, 1983a; 1983b; 1986; Loftus & Monahan, 1980; McCloskey & Egeth, 1983a; 1983b; McCloskey, Egeth, & McKenna, 1986; Wells, 1986; Yarmey, 1986). I will return to this issue later.

Methodological limitations

There are several methodological issues relevant to interpreting the findings from the surveys. The absolute importance of the variables could not easily be derived from the ratings of likely accuracy. How large would the anticipated difference in accuracy have to be before the variable was considered to be influential? When the respondents gave a rating of one or nine, did this mean they expected eyewitnesses under such conditions to be accurate 0 or 100 percent of the time? How large could an expected difference in accuracy be without being considered important? Are differences in the rate of correct and false identifications weighed equally in making such decisions? Returning to the example of subjects believing that child witnesses would be less accurate than adults, does this tell us whether they expect the difference in accuracy rate to be quite small (for example, 85 versus 90 percent) or very large (for example, 25 versus 90 percent)? Clearly not. Both patterns indicate the same expected effect of age in terms of the direction of the effect. The first pattern would be compatible with the view that witness age is a trivial determinant of accuracy, however, whereas the second pattern suggests that witness age may be a critical factor in determining witness credibility. This problem is present in the multiple choice format as well.

Even the relative importance of the variables is not necessarily clear from the surveys. Are variables with the largest differences between the mean rated accuracy levels considered the most important determinants of identification accuracy? The results may have been highly dependent on the exact wording of the items and/or respondents' interpretations of them. For example, how long is a "long delay between the crime and attempt to identify the criminal"? The respondents may have thought of a short delay as a matter of minutes and a long delay in terms of several months, thus accounting for the strong and consistent effects expected for this variable. If the short versus long delay were specified to be one day versus one week, the anticipated effects on accuracy may be less and other variables might be considered more important. Specifying exact values of the relevant variables and asking respondents to directly rate the importance of the variables could reduce these problems.

Direct ratings of importance

Respondents could be asked to estimate the actual rate (percent) of accurate identification decisions under various conditions. Brigham and Bothwell (1983) used such a method to demonstrate that people were poor predictors of the results of specific staged event experiments (Brigham, Maass, Snyder, & Spaulding, 1982; Leippe, Wells, & Ostrom, 1978). Once again, their purpose was to demonstrate that expert testimony was required to correct misunderstandings about the probable accuracy of eyewitnesses. My starting point was an interest in perceptions of factors believed to influence eyewitnesses and their potential influence on attributions of witness credibility.

SURVEY 3

The sample in this case consisted of a large number of members of the general public from Kingston, Ontario ($N = 836$) sampled via direct approach either on the street or in shopping malls over a relatively long period (about six years). An additional 477 undergraduate students participated over the last three years. The majority of respondents for each item were drawn from the general public with two exceptions. Two questions concerning the effects of mug shots were added to the data only recently and the data for those two items were obtained only from students.

To examine people's intuitions about factors influencing identification accuracy, a version of the prediction strategy employed by Brigham and Bothwell was used. Each respondent was asked to consider one issue. Before responding, they were asked to examine several levels of the variable to be considered and think about its possible impact on identification accuracy. A sample question was provided to illustrate that respondents were free to indicate large or small differences and they were explicitly told that the correct answer should reflect their intuitions and that no difference across conditions was an acceptable response. Next they rated the importance of the variable on a nine-point scale from one (not at all important) to nine (very important) as a determinant of eyewitness accuracy. Finally, respondents estimated eyewitness accuracy under the previously examined levels of the variable (these estimates are not discussed in this chapter). The design was entirely between subjects, with each person asked to rate and estimate the effects of only one variable.

The anticipated effects of twenty-five different variables were examined. Several variables were included to test the sensitivity of the samples of relevant versus irrelevant variables. For example, "prior record" may be diagnostic of guilt or innocence, but should have no effect on identification accuracy (unlike the previous survey, guilt or innocence of the suspect was always specified). The actual prediction of accuracy rates will not be discussed in this chapter; only the importance ratings are discussed here.

The mean importance ratings across twenty-five variables were compared. There were no significant gender effects in the data. The opinions of the general public and those of students differed at the .05 level for only one of the twenty-five variables, a frequency that would be expected by chance. The results of this analysis and a description of each of the variables examined is presented in Table 17.2.

The direct importance ratings produced results quite comparable to the indirect calculations performed on the data from the previous surveys. Only

Table 17.2. *Mean rated importance of 25 variables as determinants of
eyewitness identification accuracy.*

Variable	Rated importance	N
Delay between crime and identification	8.19	67
Witness prior acquaintance with criminal	8.15	48
Attention paid to criminal during crime	7.98	47
Duration of crime	7.95	56
Illumination during crime	7.88	58
Appearance different	7.77	56
Victim versus bystander	7.60	65
Memory for peripheral details	7.55	58
Similarity of lineup foils to suspect	7.46	63
Level of witness intoxication during crime	7.39	51
Stress or arousal level during crime	7.30	53
Witness confidence*	7.04	53
Weapon focus	6.98	48
Number of lineup foils	6.91	47
Prior exposure to suspect in mug shots	6.80	15
Charges against witness dropped	6.73	49
Lineup instructions	6.65	48
Age of witness	6.52	61
Lineup attire	6.50	62
Source of alibi	6.17	47
Race of witness and criminal	5.77	66
Accused's appearance (ugly, average, attractive)	5.48	60
Witness previously examined mug shots	5.40	15
Accused has prior record	4.81	56
Sex of witness and criminal	3.80	64

*Means differing by .18 or more are different at the .05 level by Neuman-Kuels test (Kirk, 1982).

fourteen items overlap the first surveys and the explicit ratings of importance. The rank order of the mean importance ratings correlated significantly with the rank order of the absolute differences in anticipated accuracy for the previously reported samples ($r = .56$ and $.75$), indicating that the difference between the means was a reasonable measure of perceived importance.

Delay between the crime and attempted identification, attention paid to the criminal during the crime, and change in appearance from the original description ranked first, third, and sixth in mean importance. These three variables were thus consistently touted as important determinants of identification accuracy. Attention to the criminal during the crime, prior acquaintance with the criminal, duration of the crime (exposure time), illumination during the crime, status as victim versus bystander, memory for peripheral details, similarity of lineup foils to the suspect, and the witness's levels of stress and intoxication during the crime were all rated as significantly more important than witness confidence as determinants of eyewitness identification accuracy. The number of lineup foils was considered equal in importance to witness confidence (data indicate the number of lineup foils may be irrelevant, Nosworthy & Lindsay, 1990). Weapon focus was also considered equal to confidence as a predictor of witness accuracy (but other data revealed that the anticipated effect was in the direction opposite to the weapon effect as demonstrated in the literature; Kramer, Buckhout, & Eugenio, 1990; Maass & Kohnken, 1989).

All other variables were considered significantly less important than witness confidence. These include procedural variables demonstrated to influence identification accuracy such as lineup instructions and lineup attire and ex-amination of mug shots prior to attempting an identification from a lineup. Race, gender, and age of the witness and suspect were also considered less important than witness confidence. The appearance of the accused, whether or not he had a prior record, source of alibis (relative versus stranger), and whether or not charges against the witness were dropped in exchange for his or her testimony were considered relatively unimportant.

Eyewitness experts are aware that some variables viewed as important by the respondents have little or no probative value whereas others deemed unimportant have substantial impact on identification accuracy. Despite this, the results seem to make intuitive sense. In general, people believe that a variety of variables associated with the nature of the crime, characteristics of the criminal, and characteristics of the witness ought to matter. They are not convinced that police procedures are particularly important.

The data to this point demonstrate that potential jurors have consistent intuitions about factors that will lead to high versus low levels of identification accuracy. The highest importance ratings could be seen as dividing roughly into three groups. The most important variables are directly related to the crime (duration, illumination), witness factors that would influence encoding (prior acquaintance with the criminal, attention to the crime or criminal, witness intoxication, witness stress, witness status as victim), and factors that would interfere with retrieval (delay between the crime and identification attempt, changes in the criminal's appearance since the crime). Two other variables, memory for peripheral detail and witness confidence, may be viewed as important because they are seen as direct indications of the quality of the witness's memory.

Police lineup and mug shot procedures were viewed as moderately impor-tant. Only the similarity of lineup foils to the criminal was viewed as more important than witness confidence and then the direction of the relationship was misunderstood. Characteristics of the criminal and witness such as sex, race, and physical attractiveness were seen as relatively unimportant.

Although people's expectations of eyewitness accuracy are often in error, many of the findings are reflected in the reasoning of the courts (for example,

Neil v. Biggers). Knowing this, it seemed reasonable to argue that mock jurors' perceptions of witness credibility should be influenced by those variables consistently rated as important determinants of eyewitness accuracy. In cases solely based on identification, the variables rated as important may also determine verdict. In the final section of this chapter, mock jury studies are reported that manipulated many of the variables from the surveys to examine their impact on eyewitness credibility and verdicts in mock trials. My simplistic (and inaccurate) prediction was that variables rated as important would influence belief of eyewitness testimony more than variables rated as unimportant.

Mock jury studies

Do the data reported so far allow us to predict the credibility of eyewitness testimony? If they do, then differences in the identification procedures employed should have relatively little impact on witness credibility whereas other variables such as delay between the crime and identification, attention paid to the criminal during the crime, and discrepancy between the original description of the criminal and the in-court appearance of the accused should have substantial impact on attributions of identification accuracy and thus trial verdicts.

Lineup procedures. The first attempt I made to test the impact of lineup variables on eyewitness credibility was conducted more than a decade ago. Gary Wells and I had published one of our early studies demonstrating, to no one's surprise, that the use of poor lineup foils (faces not remotely resembling the suspect) substantially increased the rate of false identifications of an innocent suspect who resembled the true criminal (Lindsay & Wells, 1980). Poor foils did not result in a significantly increased rate of correct identifications (a less obvious finding), so the use of poor foils produced lineups with low diagnosticity (Wells & Lindsay, 1980). Because many people commented that this finding was intuitively obvious, it seemed almost certain that jurors would discount, at least to some extent, identifications from lineups containing only foils quite dissimilar to the suspect. Obviously such identification procedures lead to evidence of low probative value. From a legal perspective, the lack of probative value of biased lineups suggests that identifications from such procedures should be treated as a questionable, perhaps inadmissible, source of evidence. Jurors ought to look on identifications from biased lineups with considerable skepticism.

The first six experiments described below examined the impact of identification procedures on belief of eyewitness testimony. Based on studies of identification accuracy, we know that the lineup procedures described in the mock trials are important determinants of eyewitness accuracy. The surveys just described indicated that the importance of these variables is poorly understood at best. One possible solution to this dilemma is to expose juries to expert testimony on the issues (Loftus, 1983). Several of the studies included expert testimony conditions to explore the possibility that the understanding and perceived importance of lineup procedures could be altered with a resultant improvement in jury decision making.

EXPERIMENT 1

Lindsay and Wells (1980) presented videotapes of witnesses to a staged crime giving testimony about the event and their identification of someone from a six-picture photographic array. The witnesses were drawn from those exposed to the lineups containing foils either high or low in similarity to the confederate who had staged the crime or his innocent replacement (in criminal-absent lineups). As part of the evidence, the mock jurors were shown one of the lineups used to obtain identifications with some seeing the fair lineups and others the biased lineups. Lineup quality did not significantly influence verdicts.

EXPERIMENT 2

Queen's University undergraduates watched a videotaped mock trial. The students knew that the witness they saw testify had participated in a staged crime experiment and that the witness had attempted to answer all questions honestly and to the best of her ability. The trial included the testimony of the experimenter who described conducting a lineup (a six-picture photographic array) using fair instructions. The testimony of the eyewitness indicated that she had identified the suspect and was moderately certain that she had made the correct decision. The mock jurors were presented with "the" photographic array as part of the evidence. Half the mock jurors saw a fair lineup (similar foils). The remaining mock jurors were shown a biased lineup in which none of the five foils resembled the description of the criminal but the suspect closely resembled the description. Additional conditions also included expert testimony.

Manipulation checks indicated that the dissimilar foils were perceived to be significantly less similar to the suspect than the similar foils and that the suspect was the only lineup member in the biased lineup matching the description provided by the eyewitness. Otherwise, the mock jurors' responses were startling! They were more likely to vote guilty when shown the biased lineup (82 percent of twenty-two subjects) than when shown the fair lineup (73 percent). After deliberating, this difference was much greater (77 versus 33 percent of twenty-one). Equally striking was a postverdict measure of perceived lineup fairness. Mock jurors rated the biased lineup as significantly fairer than the fair lineup. An open-ended question asking why they felt the lineup was or was not fair indicated that a substantial proportion of the subjects felt the high similarity lineup was unfair to the witness and had not even considered the possibility that a lineup could be unfair to the accused. Many felt that the ease with which they could select the suspect from the biased lineups indicated that the witness would also find it easy to identify the accused. The possibility that the suspect was innocent was not a prominent concern which may reflect a general presumption of guilt.

Expert testimony could be the cure for this failure of mock jurors to respond appropriately to relevant variables. The study contained expert testimony conditions that presented a general discussion of the limitations of eyewitness reliability based on the illustration provided by Loftus (1979) at the end of her book. Consistent with McCloskey and Egeth's (1983a) claim that expert testimony on eyewitness issues produces only a discrediting effect, belief declined for both the biased (68 percent) and the fair (50 percent) lineup conditions. A competent expert, however, would tailor his or her testimony to the facts of the case. Additional expert testimony conditions were included in which the expert explicitly discussed the effects of high versus low similarity of lineup foils to the suspect. The procedures and results of the Lindsay and Wells (1980) study were described and interpreted for the jury. This resulted in no further decline in belief for the biased lineup condition (72 percent) but further reduced belief in the fair lineup condition (36 percent). Explaining this failure of expert testimony to aid mock jurors is not the purpose of this chapter (nor within the author's capabilities); the effect is intriguing, however, and replicable as demonstrated in the studies described below.

Experiment 3

Another study was conducted with a more elaborate videotaped trial. Once again, manipulation checks confirmed that the difference in similarity of the foils to the suspect was apparent to the subjects. Again, identifications from a biased lineup were not discounted. Guilty votes were given by 43 percent of sixty mock jurors in each lineup quality condition (biased versus fair). Although the objective lineup structure did not influence verdicts, jurors voting guilty rated the lineup as significantly fairer to the accused ($M = 6.53$ on a nine-point scale) than jurors voting not guilty ($M = 4.75$), regardless of the quality of the lineup they had seen.

Experiment 4

A study was conducted manipulating the fairness of lineup instructions. Research has clearly demonstrated that instructions leading witnesses to believe that the guilty person is in the lineup increase the rate of false, but not correct, identifications (for example, Cutler, Penrod, & Martens, 1987; Lindsay, Lea, Nosworthy, et al., 1991; Malpass & Devine, 1981). A person playing the part of a police officer described the procedures used to obtain the identification. Half the mock jurors were informed that fair instructions were used whereas the remaining subjects heard that the witness was told "We've got the guy, all you have to do is pick him out."

Manipulation checks indicated that the subjects were aware of the difference in instructions. Guilty votes were given by 73 percent (of forty-eight subjects) when the lineup instructions were biased and 52 percent when the instructions were fair. Jurors who voted guilty ($M = 6.18$ on a nine-point scale) rated the lineup instructions as significantly fairer to the accused than jurors who voted not guilty ($M = 3.47$), regardless of the instructions given the witness.

EXPERIMENT 5

In this study, instructional bias, foil bias, and the presence or absence of expert testimony were orthogonally manipulated. Guilty votes were obtained from 38 percent (of sixty) mock jurors exposed to a lineup containing poor foils and 25 percent from a fair lineup. Similarly, biased instructions resulted in 38 percent guilty votes and fair instructions produced 25 percent guilty votes. A significant interaction resulted as 73 percent guilty votes were obtained in the expert testimony condition combining both biased instructions and poor foils! All other conditions were significantly different from this one and not different from each other ($M = 23$ percent guilty votes across the other conditions). Once again, jurors who voted guilty rated the lineups and lineup instructions as significantly fairer to the accused than did jurors who voted not guilty.

EXPERIMENT 6

In this experiment, expert testimony was provided that clearly invaded the province of the triers of the facts. The expert in each of the fair and biased lineup conditions (good versus poor foils) drew conclusions regarding the credibility of the eyewitness: When the lineup was biased, the expert concluded explicitly that the witness was not a credible source of information under the circumstances and should be ignored. When the lineup was fair, the expert testified that under such conditions eyewitness identification could be highly reliable and the jurors should consider the identification as strong evidence of the guilt of the accused. This testimony was presented by an expert described as a friend of the court requested to testify by the judge (an unlikely story in North America to be sure, although a desirable one in comparison to a battle of experts, Lindsay, MacDonald, & McGarry, 1989).

Control conditions (no experts) produced the, now expected, higher rate of belief for the biased lineup (65 percent of twenty) than for the fair lineup (50 percent). The expert testimony conditions eliminated this nonsignificant difference by reducing belief to 35 percent for either lineup. Other conditions were presented with the same expert testimony but it was given by experts hired by the defense or prosecution as appropriate. This produced similar results (40 percent belief in the biased lineup condition, 35 percent in the fair lineup condition). A final pair of conditions presented the testimony as a battle of competing experts who disagreed about the quality of the lineups (for these conditions a less extreme version of the biased lineup was used to permit the prosecution expert to argue that the foils were similar enough though not highly similar to the accused). Again, there was no significant difference in the rate of belief for the biased (30 percent) versus the fair (35 percent) lineups. A measure of respect for psychology as a profession was taken in this last experiment (Adair & Fenton, 1971). The only difference found was less respect for psychology in the battle of experts conditions than in any of the other conditions, again as predicted by McCloskey and Egeth (1983). Once again, the lineup procedures were rated as significantly fairer to the accused by mock jurors who voted guilty as compared to those who voted not guilty.

Summary

Consistent with rating lineup procedures as being of little importance as determinants of witness accuracy, variations in identification procedures were generally ignored by mock jurors. When lineup procedures influenced verdict, the effect was in the direction opposite to the desirable outcome as identifications from biased lineups were more convincing than identifications from fair lineups. Expert testimony did not help (and possibly hurt). This pattern of results raises serious concerns about the ability of juries to appropriately evaluate testimony of eyewitness identification. To the extent that these data represent typical reasoning about eyewitness accuracy, judges may be no better than jurors as evaluators of eyewitness accuracy. Apparently errors made by police in identification procedures are unlikely to be understood by jurors and thus such errors are unlikely to be corrected in court.

Characteristics of the crime, criminal, or witness. Few undergraduates have ever been asked to identify someone from a lineup; however, all have seen people for long or short intervals, in well lit or dimly lit settings. Perhaps people would do better with factors they directly experienced. This series of experiments is similar to the previous set; mock trials were presented to undergraduates who were asked to indicate (among other things) whether they would vote guilty or not guilty. Various factors associated with the crime, the criminal, and/or the eyewitness were the focus of attention.

EXPERIMENT 7

In this study, eyewitness confidence and the level of stress reported by the eyewitness were manipulated. The identification accuracy literature indicates a small but significant relationship between confidence and accuracy. A significantly negative relationship has been found between stress/arousal and accuracy (Shapiro & Penrod, 1986). When stress was high, 48 percent of jurors voted guilty whereas only 38 percent voted guilty if stress was low, a nonsignificant difference. Jurors rated themselves as being significantly more likely to be accurate as witnesses under conditions like those presented in the trial if they had been exposed to the high rather than the low stress conditions. Confident witnesses (43 percent) were no more likely to be believed than nonconfident witnesses (43 percent), a rare failure to replicate the confidence–belief effect. This may have occurred because the witness was perceived to be relatively high in confidence even in the low confidence conditions.

EXPERIMENT 8

In another study, witness confidence (high versus low), status of the witness (victim or bystander), and delay between the crime and the identification (two versus thirty-five days) were manipulated. The literature indicates that victims and bystanders are equally good witnesses (for example, Hosch & Cooper, 1982). In general, long delays between the crime and the identification attempt are expected to reduce identification accuracy although exceptions are known (for example, Cutler, Penrod, & Martens, 1987). Confident witnesses were believed by 63 percent of jurors, significantly more than nonconfident witnesses (32 percent). Victims were believed by 47 percent of jurors and bystanders by 47 percent. A short interval between the crime and identification led to 52 percent belief whereas a long interval resulted in 42 percent belief. Neither of the latter two differences was significant. Compared to those voting not guilty, jurors who voted guilty rated (on seven-point Likert scales) the witness as significantly more confident and the delay as significantly shorter.

EXPERIMENT 9

A study was conducted manipulating confidence of the eyewitness (high versus low) and level of intoxication of the witness at the time of the crime (described as having consumed one, eight, or twenty-four bottles of beer in the four hours preceding the crime). In the twenty-four beer condition the witness admitted to being extremely drunk, in the eight beer condition he described himself as slightly drunk, and in the one beer condition claimed the alcohol had no noticeable effect on him. If the eyewitness was confident, state of intoxication had no effect on belief: 75, 80, and 75 percent of twenty mock jurors voted guilty in each of the low, moderate, and high intoxication conditions, respectively. If the witness was not confident, however, intoxication significantly reduced belief: 85, 55, and 20 percent guilty votes, respectively. Again, compared to those voting not guilty, jurors who voted guilty rated the witness as more confident and less impaired regardless of manipulated condition.

EXPERIMENT 10

This experiment (from Lindsay et al., 1986) involved manipulating the physical attractiveness of the accused and the consistency of the eyewitness's testimony. In the inconsistent testimony conditions, the in-court appearance of the accused was dramatically different from the original description provided by the witness immediately after the crime. Under cross-examination, the witness acknowledged the discrepancy, agreed that the appearance of the accused when identified was similar to the in-court appearance (that is, inconsistent with the original description), and had no explanation for the discrepancy. The witness maintained she was certain the identification was correct. In the consistent testimony conditions, the original description was consistent with the in-court appearance of the accused.

Manipulation checks confirmed that the inconsistency in the testimony was accurately perceived as was the difference in defendant attractiveness. Attractiveness significantly influenced verdict with the attractive defendant more likely to be convicted than the unattractive defendant (60 versus 33 percent, respectively). It is not clear why the attractive defendant was more likely to be convicted. Consistent with previous research on attractiveness, recommended sentence was shorter for the attractive defendant if convicted. Not only did inconsistency of testimony fail to significantly influence verdict, but inconsistent testimony actually led to slightly higher rates of guilty votes than consistent testimony (50 versus 43 percent, respectively).

EXPERIMENT 11

Mock jurors in this study heard the testimony of an eyewitness who had seen the criminal either in full daylight or outside, at night, with no nearby source of light (Lindsay et al., 1986). The exposure to the criminal lasted either five seconds or thirty minutes, and an additional pair of conditions described the witness as interacting with the criminal repeatedly during the thirty-minute period (the witness was not aware that a crime was in progress). Guilty votes

were more often made for the daytime conditions (57 percent) than for the
night conditions (37 percent), although this difference was only marginally
significant. Length of exposure to the criminal and interaction with him did
not significantly influence verdict. A five-second exposure (45 percent) led to
slightly more guilty votes than a thirty-minute exposure (40 percent) and
slightly less than the long exposure combined with extensive interaction (55
percent). Jurors who voted guilty rated the lighting conditions as better and
the interaction as both lasting longer and involving more contact between the
witness and criminal than jurors who voted not guilty regardless of condition.

Summary

Many of the variables rated as important determinants of eyewitness accuracy
failed to influence verdict (stress and status of the witness as victim or bystander; lighting and duration of the crime; delay between the crime and
identification attempt). Despite the fact that the manipulation of these variables failed to influence verdict, mock jurors tended to rate conditions as
more positive for the witness if the verdict was guilty rather than not guilty.
The best explanation of this pattern may be that the jurors were justifying
or rationalizing their decisions rather than explaining the basis on which the
decisions were made. The variables that influenced verdict significantly were
not encouraging either. Witness intoxication only influenced belief if the
witness was not confident and attractiveness of the accused was rated as not
important and as generally irrelevant.

Conclusions

Jurors may not be aware of the factors that actually influence their decisions
to believe versus not believe the testimony of an eyewitness (Nisbett & Wilson,
1977). Asking them to explain their decisions results in post hoc rationali-
zation.

Expert testimony on eyewitness issues easily meets the legal criteria of
admissibility; most people have little idea of how to evaluate the accuracy of
an eyewitness identification, underestimate the importance of many relevant
variables, and apply significantly wrong expectations regarding other variables.

Unfortunately, it is not clear that expert testimony on eyewitness issues
assists the trier of fact if the criterion of assistance is that superior decisions
are made.

Lineup procedures can be altered to reduce dramatically the probability of
false identification (Cutler & Penrod, 1988; Lindsay, Lea, & Fulford, 1991;
Lindsay, Lea, Nosworthy et al., 1991; Lindsay, Wallbridge, & Drennan, 1987;

Lindsay & Wells, 1980; 1985; Malpass & Devine, 1981). This fact in combination with the first three conclusions suggests the following:

The most important contributions that psychologists can make in the eyewitness area will result from developing techniques that increase the accuracy of eyewitness reports (for example, the Cognitive Interview, Geiselman, Fisher, MacKinnon, & Holland, 1985) or the accuracy of eyewitness identifications (for example, sequential lineups, Cutler & Penrod, 1988; Lindsay, Lea, & Fulford, 1991; Lindsay, Lea, Nosworthy, et al., 1991; Lindsay & Wells, 1985).

The best way to reduce the tragedy of wrongful convictions based on eyewitness errors is to prevent those errors from occurring. Once the case is before the courts, it is probably too late!

References

Adair, J. G., & Fenton, D. C. (1971). Subject's attitudes toward psychology as a determinant of experimental results. *Canadian Journal of Behavioral Science, 3,* 268–275.

Brigham, J. C., & Bothwell, R. K. (1983). The ability of prospective jurors to estimate the accuracy of eyewitness identifications. *Law and Human Behavior, 7,* 19–30.

Brigham, J. C., Maass, A., Snyder, L. D., & Spaulding, K. (1982). Accuracy of eyewitness identifications in a field setting. *Journal of Personality and Social Psychology, 42,* 673–680.

Buckhout, R., Alpern, A., Chern, S., Silverberg, G., & Slomovits, M. (1974). Determinants of eyewitness performance on a lineup. *Bulletin of the Psychonomic Society, 4,* 191–192.

Buckhout, R., Figueroa, P., & Hoff, E. (1975). Eyewitness identification: Effects of suggestion and bias in identification from photographs. *Bulletin of the Psychonomic Society, 6,* 71–74.

Cutler, B. L., & Penrod, S. D. (1988). Improving the reliability of eyewitness identifications: Lineup construction and presentation. *Journal of Applied Psychology, 73,* 281–290.

Cutler, B. L., Penrod, S. D., & Dexter, H. R. (1990). Juror sensitivity to eyewitness identification evidence. *Law and Human Behavior, 14,* 185–191.

Cutler, B. L., Penrod, S. D., & Martens, T. K. (1987). The reliability of eyewitness identification: The role of system and estimator variables. *Law and Human Behavior, 11,* 233–258.

Cutler, B. L., Penrod, S. D., & Stuve, T. E. (1988). Juror decision making in eyewitness identification cases. *Law and Human Behavior, 12,* 41–55.

Deffenbacher, K. A., & Loftus, E. F. (1982). Do jurors share a common understanding concerning eyewitness behavior? *Law and Human Behavior, 6,* 15–30.

Geiselman, R., Fisher, R., MacKinnon, D., & Holland, H. (1985). Eyewitness memory enhancement in the police interview: Cognitive retrieval mnemonics versus hypnosis. *Journal of Applied Psychology, 70,* 401–412.

Hosch, H. M., & Cooper, D. S. (1982). Victimization as a determinant of eyewitness accuracy. *Journal of Applied Psychology, 67,* 649–652.

Kirk, R. E. (1982). *Experimental design* (2d ed). Monterey, CA: Brooks/Cole.

Kramer, T. H., Buckhout, R., & Eugenio, P. (1990). Weapon focus, arousal, and eyewitness memory: Attention must be paid. *Law and Human Behavior, 14,* 167–184.

Leippe, M. R. (1980). Effects of integrative memorial and cognitive processes on the correspondence of eyewitness accuracy and confidence. *Law and Human Behavior, 4,* 261–274.

Leippe, M. R., Wells, G. L., & Ostrom, T. M. (1978). Crime seriousness as a determinant of accuracy in eyewitness identification. *Journal of Applied Psychology, 63,* 345–351.

Lindsay, R. C. L., MacDonald, P., & McGarry, S. (1989). Perspectives on the role of the eyewitness expert. *Behavioral Sciences & the Law, 8,* 457–464.

Lindsay, R. C. L., Lea, J. L., & Fulford, J., (1991). Sequential lineup presentation: Technique matters. *Journal of Applied Psychology, 76,* 741–745.

Lindsay, R. C. L., Lea, J. L., Nosworthy, G. J., Fulford, J., Hector, J., LeVan, V., & Seabrook, C. (1991). Biased lineup procedures: Sequential presentation reduces the problem. *Journal of Applied Psychology, 76,* 796–802.

Lindsay, R. C. L., Lim, R., Marando, L., & Cully, D. (1986). Mock-juror evaluations of eyewitness testimony: A test of metamemory hypotheses. *Journal of Applied Social Psychology, 16,* 447–459.

Lindsay, R. C. L., Wallbridge, H., & Drennan, D. (1987). Do the clothes make the man? An exploration of the effect of lineup attire on eyewitness identification accuracy. *Canadian Journal of Behavioural Science, 19,* 463–478.

Lindsay, R. C. L., & Wells, G. L. (1980). What price justice? Exploring the relationship of lineup fairness to eyewitness identification accuracy. *Law and Human Behavior, 4,* 303–313.

Lindsay, R. C. L., & Wells, G. L. (1985). Improving eyewitness identifications from lineups: Simultaneous versus sequential lineup presentation. *Journal of Applied Psychology, 70,* 556–564.

Lindsay, R. C. L., Wells, G. L., & O'Connor, F. J. (1989). Mock-juror belief of accurate and inaccurate eyewitnesses: A replication and extension. *Law and Human Behavior, 13,* 333–339.

Lindsay, R. C. L., Wells, G. L., & Rumpel, C. M. (1981). Can people detect eyewitness identification accuracy within and across situations? *Journal of Applied Psychology, 66,* 79–89.

Loftus, E. F. (1979). *Eyewitness testimony.* Cambridge, MA: Harvard University Press.

Loftus, E. F. (1983a). Silence is not golden. *American Psychologist, 38,* 550–563.

Loftus, E. F. (1983b). Whose shadow is crooked? *American Psychologist, 38,* 576–577.

Loftus, E. F. (1986). Experimental psychologist as advocate or impartial educator. *Law and Human Behavior, 10,* 63–78.

Loftus, E. F., & Monahan, J. (1980). Trial by data: Psychological research as legal evidence. *American Psychologist, 35,* 270–283.

Maass, A., & Kohnken, G. (1989). Eyewitness identification: Simulating the "weapon effect." *Law and Human Behavior, 13,* 397–408.

Malpass, R. S., & Devine, P. G. (1981). Eyewitness identification: Lineup instructions and the absence of the offender. *Journal of Applied Psychology, 66,* 482–489.

McCloskey, M. E., & Egeth, N. E. (1983a). Eyewitness identification: What can a psychologist tell a jury? *American Psychologist, 38,* 550–563.

McCloskey, M. E., & Egeth, N. E. (1983b). A time to speak or a time to keep silence? *American Psychologist, 38,* 573–575.

McCloskey, M. E., Egeth, N. E., & McKenna, J. (1986). The experimental psychologist in court: The ethics of expert testimony. *Law and Human Behavior, 10,* 1–10.

Neil v. Biggers, 409 U.S. 188 (U.S. Tenn., 1972).

Nisbett, R. E., & Wilson, T. D. (1977). Telling more than we can know: Verbal reports on mental processes. *Psychological Review, 84,* 231–259.

Nosworthy, G. J., & Lindsay, R. C. L. (1990). Does nominal lineup size matter? *Journal of Applied Psychology, 75,* 358–361.

Rattner, A. (1988). Convicted but innocent: Wrongful conviction and the criminal justice system. *Law and Human Behavior, 12,* 283–293.

Shapiro, P., & Penrod, S. D. (1986). Meta-analysis of the facial identification literature. *Psychological Bulletin, 100,* 139–156.

Wells, G. L. (1984). The psychology of lineup identifications. *Journal of Applied Social Psychology, 36,* 89–103.

Wells, G. L. (1985). Verbal descriptions of faces from memory: Are they diagnostic of identification accuracy? *Journal of Applied Psychology, 70,* 619–626.

Wells, G. L. (1986). Expert psychological testimony: Empirical and conceptual analyses of effects. *Law and Human Behavior, 10,* 83–96.

Wells, G. L., Ferguson, T. J., & Lindsay, R. C. L. (1981). The tractability of eyewitness confidence and its implications for triers of fact. *Journal of Applied Psychology, 66,* 688–696.

Wells, G. L., & Leippe, M. R. (1981). How do triers of fact infer the accuracy of eyewitness identifications? Using memory for peripheral detail can be misleading. *Journal of Applied Psychology, 66,* 682–687.

Wells, G. L., & Lindsay, R. C. L. (1980). On estimating the diagnosticity of eyewitness nonidentifications. *Psychological Bulletin, 88,* 776–784.

Wells, G. L., & Lindsay, R. C. L. (1983). How do people infer the accuracy of eyewitness memory? Studies of performance and a metamemory analysis. In S. Lloyd-Bostock and B. R. Clifford (Eds.), *Evaluating witness evidence.* Chichester, England: John Wiley and Sons.

Wells, G. L., Lindsay, R. C. L., & Ferguson, T. J. (1979). Accuracy, confidence, and juror perceptions in eyewitness identifications. *Journal of Applied Psychology, 64,* 440–448.

Wells, G. L., Lindsay, R. C. L., & Tousignant, J. (1980). Effects of expert psychological advice on human performance in judging the validity of eyewitness testimony. *Law and Human Behavior, 4,* 275–285.

Wells, G. L., & Murray, D. M. (1983). What can psychology say about the Neil v. Biggers criteria for judging eyewitness accuracy? *Journal of Applied Psychology, 68,* 347–362.

Wells, G. L., & Murray, D. M. (1984). Eyewitness confidence. In G. L. Wells & E. F. Loftus (Eds.), *Eyewitness testimony: Psychological perspectives.* New York: Cambridge University Press.

Woocher, F. D. (1977). Did your eyes deceive you? Expert psychological testimony on the unreliability of eyewitness identification. *Stanford Law Review, 29,* 969–1030.

Yarmey, A. D. (1986). Ethical responsibilities governing the statements experimental psychologists make in expert testimony. *Law and Human Behavior, 10,* 101–116.

Yarmey, A. D., & Jones, H. P. T. (1983). Is the psychology of eyewitness identification a matter of common sense? In S. Lloyd-Bostock and B. R. Clifford (Eds.), *Evaluating witness evidence.* Chichester, England: John Wiley and Sons.

18   The appraisal of eyewitness testimony

Michael R. Leippe

With emphasis bordering on the dramatic, dozens of important articles and books on eyewitness testimony have begun by emphasizing the central, indeed pivotal, role that eyewitness testimony plays in criminal cases. This chapter will be no exception. An eyewitness report, confidently delivered, has swayed many a jury. Even more profoundly, an eyewitness influences the legal process even before the witness takes the stand in court. If there is an eyewitness, especially one who makes a positive impression, the police and prosecutor's office are more likely to pursue a case. And what the witness reports will influence the course of an investigation. When we add to these facts the research evidence that eyewitness memory is often inaccurate, we have a real potential for frequent misfires of the justice process, errors that cost money, time, and, in some cases, the freedom of an innocent person.

It is, however, decisions about eyewitness testimony, rather than the testimony itself, that lead to errors in the delivery of justice. They occur when a fact finder (a police officer, clinical interviewer, juror, or judge) believes an inaccurate witness or doubts an accurate one. As Wells (1985a) has noted, "if jurors and judges were able to discriminate meaningfully between accurate and inaccurate eyewitness testimony, our concerns about inaccurate testimony would be lessened considerably" (p. 45). In this chapter, I will be concerned with how fact finders appraise eyewitness reports. I will review research and lay some theoretical groundwork concerning how and how well people evaluate memory reports. What factors influence judgments of witness credibility and how valid are these judgments? Can eyewitness testimony be extracted, and can fact finders be trained, in ways that improve ability to make the right decision about the witness's accuracy? At a theoretical level, what principles of persuasion, communication, and judgment characterize decisions about a communicator's memory? This chapter assesses what we know and can reasonably speculate about as we set about answering these critical questions.

There are two components to credibility: trustworthiness and expertise

Some of the research described in this chapter was supported by a grant from the National Science Foundation (Grant SES-8711659) to the author.

385

(McGuire, 1985). Trustworthiness involves perceptions that a communicator is being honest, whereas expertise involves perceptions of knowledgeability, ability, and accuracy. This chapter focuses on the latter component of credibility – expertise – as it applies to eyewitness communication. The concern is with sincerely offered reports of genuine memories and what determines whether fact finders believe them and can tell with any certainty whether they are accurate. Although fact finders may automatically weigh testimony for both accuracy and honesty, the current analysis restricts itself to accuracy judgments made when fact finders have concluded that there is little or no reason to suspect that the memory report includes fabricated lies. The concern is with judging testimony in terms of its memory accuracy, not in terms of its honesty. Accordingly, I will not discuss judgments of deception (for example, Brown, 1986; Miller & Burgoon, 1982; Zuckerman, DePaulo, & Rosenthal, 1981) or recent work on "statement credibility analysis" (Raskin & Yuille, 1989; Stellar & Kohnken, 1990; Undeutsch, 1982). The latter is a systematic procedure for determining the truthfulness of eyewitness testimony. In contrast to this chapter's focus, it deals primarily with detecting conscious memory fabrication (versus accuracy of a genuinely offered memory) and with analysis of written (versus orally delivered) testimony.

A communication/persuasion approach to eyewitness testimony

Eyewitness testimony is aptly described as a persuasive communication – an appeal to an audience (for example, a jury) to believe one's account of an event (Leippe & Romanczyk, 1987; 1989; Saks & Hastie, 1978). The witness, in essence, is an influence agent delivering what we might call a "memory message." The fact finding audience, in its turn, decides whether or not to accept, or be persuaded by, the message, just as would the audience to, say, a speech concerning some sociopolitical issue. Persuasion researchers have found that a number of factors may influence acceptance of a message (see Zimbardo & Leippe, 1991, for a review). Both source, or communicator, characteristics, such as attractiveness (for example, Chaiken, 1979) and expertise (for example, Petty, Cacioppo, & Goldman, 1981), and audience characteristics, such as preexisting attitudes (for example, Lord, Ross, & Lepper, 1979) and knowledge (for example, Wood, 1982) about the message topic, may contribute to the persuasive impact of the message. In addition, and quite intuitively, persuasion may vary positively with the logic and strength of message arguments, especially if the audience is highly motivated to hold an informed opinion on the issue (Petty & Cacioppo, 1984). Finally, the delivery style of the communicator may contribute to persuasive impact. Fast speech rate (Miller, Maruyama, Beaber, & Valone, 1976) and steady eye contact (Mehrabian & Williams, 1969), for example, may increase a speaker's persuasiveness.

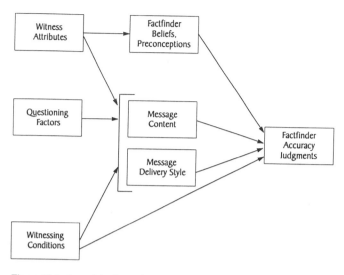

Figure 18.1: A model of eyewitness persuasion.

The four categories of persuasion-relevant factors – source, audience, message, and delivery characteristics – all play a role in eyewitness persuasion. Testimony has some unique features, however, that compel us to consider a more complex model than one that simply views these factors as additive contributions to a memory message's persuasive impact. Figure 18.1 presents a descriptive model of eyewitness persuasion that incorporates these considerations.

The model depicted in Figure 18.1 identifies fours sets of direct influences on fact finders' judgments of a memory message. The major influences, not surprisingly, are what the witness says (message content) and how he or she says it (message delivery style). The memory report, both style and substance, is influenced by at least three other sets of variables, which, via their effects on the memory report, have indirect influences on fact finder judgments. The conditions of witnessing will naturally affect what is remembered and thus what is said. In addition, in an important departure from the typical "persuasion setting," memory reports are often delivered in an interactive context. A police officer or lawyer may question the witness, and that questioning may influence both the content and delivery style of the report. Finally, the memory report may be influenced by static attributes of the witness, such as his or her age and status. Witness attributes affect memory reports because they are correlated with memory and communication abilities and motivation.

Figure 18.1 shows that, beyond the content and delivery of the testimony, a third set of direct influences on fact finder appraisals includes the fact finders' preexisting beliefs, biases, and stereotypes about eyewitness memory. Witness attributes, besides having an indirect effect on final appraisals through their effects on the memory message, may also have an indirect effect through fact finder preconceptions. A child witness's testimony, for example, may be judged low in credibility because jurors believe children are highly suggestible and have poor recall. The fourth category of direct influences on fact finder appraisals is knowledge of witnessing conditions. Jurors (typically) and police interviewers (often) may have information about the memory event gained independently of the witness. They can be expected to enter this information into their calculation of how accurate the witness's report is (Wells & Lindsay, 1983).

Determinants of memory believability

Jurors and other fact finders: Beliefs about believing

Before adult eyewitnesses utter a word, they may have a head start on establishing that their memories are accurate. Surveys, mock trials, and studies of reactions to eyewitness testimony about staged crimes suggest that people often overbelieve memory reports (compare Wells, 1984). A good illustration of overbelief is a study conducted by Brigham and Bothwell (1983). Jury-eligible Floridians read descriptions of experiments in which a crime or crime-like event was staged and the unwitting witnesses were asked to identify the perpetrator from a photo spread lineup. When asked to estimate the percentage of witnesses who made a correct identification in these experiments, the respondents consistently overestimated in comparison to the actual percentages. For one experiment, the estimate was 78 percent, and the actual identification rate was less than 20 percent (Leippe, Wells, & Ostrom, 1978).

A similar overbelief in eyewitness memory, at least for a culprit's face, is evident when fact finders watch actual testimony. Wells and his colleagues established this using a two-phase procedure in which, first, subject-witnesses observed a staged theft, attempted a photo spread identification of the thief, and provided a verbal report in the form of responses to questions about what they saw. Subject-jurors then watched videotapes of the reports and guessed at the accuracy of the identification. In one of these studies, subject-jurors postulated an accurate identification by two-thirds of the subject-witnesses although only one-third of the subject-witnesses had been accurate (Lindsay, Wells, & Rumpel, 1981). In several other studies, inaccurate subject-witnesses have been guessed accurate by anywhere from 40 to 80 percent of the subject-jurors (Wells, Ferguson, & Lindsay, 1981; Wells & Leippe, 1981; Wells, Lindsay, & Ferguson, 1979).

It is reasonable to conclude from this research that people believe human memory for faces and significant events is better than it is. As Wells et al. (1979) have observed, we often experience a sense of recognition of a seldom-seen face ("I know her from somewhere"), and this sense is seldom disconfirmed. In the absence of disconfirmation, people may develop a strong belief in their ability to recognize faces. In turn, they may generalize this (potentially false) belief in the accuracy of their personal memories to others, including eyewitnesses.

However it arises, generalized positive expectations about eyewitness memory may have important effects on how a memory report is processed. For example, fact finders may selectively attend to belief-confirming aspects of the memory report. Alternatively, testimony that is considerably less adept than the positive expectations allow may lead to greater disbelief than it warrants. The testimony may look worse by comparison with the standard implied by those expectations (cf. Leippe & Romanczyk, 1989).

Fact finders do not extend their optimistic expectations to all eyewitnesses indiscriminately. For one thing, generalized beliefs about human memory appear to take into account the age of the eyewitness. In survey studies, respondents as diverse as college students, lawyers, research psychologists, and the parents in parent-teacher organizations have indicated the belief that children under nine or ten years of age typically have poorer memories and are more suggestible than adults (Leippe, Brigham, Cousins, & Romanczyk, 1989; Leippe & Romanczyk, 1987; Yarmey & Jones, 1983). Further evidence that adults have preconceived negative beliefs about children's memory comes from mock-trial studies in which mock jurors read a narrative summary of a criminal trial. The principal prosecution eyewitness is either a child or an adult, but all other case information is identical. These studies have found consistently that the child witness (especially if as young as six years) is rated lower in credibility than the adult witness (Goodman, Golding, Helgeson, Haith, & Michelli, 1987, Experiments 1 and 2; Leippe & Romanczyk, 1989, Experiments 1, 3, and 5). In two studies, mock jurors were also less likely to convict the defendant on the word of a child than on that of an adult (Leippe & Romanczyk, 1989, Experiments 2 and 5).

Yet, when the trial is presented as a video- or audiotaped simulation, or as a printed transcript containing verbatim witness statements, mock jurors' reactions have covered the spectrum of possibilities. Under these circumstances, child witnesses have been perceived less (Goodman et al., 1987, Experiment 3), equally (Johnson & Grisso, 1986), or more (Leippe & Romanczyk, Experiments 4 and 5; Ross, Dunning, Toglia, & Ceci, 1990) positively than adult witnesses who say essentially the same thing. The negative stereotype of children's memory appears to depend on how the child behaves. The usual childlike difficulties in communicating complex matters, even if unrelated to memory accuracy, may draw more attention because of the stereotype and/or otherwise confirm the stereotype and lead to reduced belief. If the child is exceptionally articulate, however, his or her testimony may so strikingly disconfirm the stereotype that belief in the child is augmented (much as we have seen that disbelief in a flawed adult report may be augmented).[1]

Once again, we see the role of fact finder beliefs concerning witness attributes in how testimony is perceived and interpreted.

This effect of beliefs about children is also evident in mock-trial studies, where younger children are more readily believed and trusted than older ones and adolescents when they deliver testimony as alleged victims of sexual abuse – even when written, third-person summaries are presented, not the verbatim words of the child (Duggan, Aubrey, Doherty, Isquith, Levine, & Scheiner, 1989; Goodman, Bottoms, Herscovici, & Shaver, 1989). Part of the child-as-witness stereotype seems to be that young children are less able or willing to fabricate sexual accusations; as a result, their testimony is greeted with less skepticism.

Leippe, Manion, and Romanczyk (1992) employed the two-phase procedure to examine reactions to children's testimony about a real event. Children, aged five and six and nine and ten, and adults spent about six or seven minutes with a male experimenter who administered a test of touch sensitivity, made small talk, and conversed with a female who briefly entered the room. They then provided a memory report about this experience that included a narrative description and responses to numerous questions concerning the activities, people, and surroundings involved. Videotapes of the reports were presented to subject-fact finders. The five- and six-year-olds were judged less consistent and less believable than the adults, and were estimated to have answered fewer recall questions accurately. This occurred even when the memory reports of the children and adults were equally accurate, and when objective analyses revealed no age differences in the inconsistencies contained in the reports. Stereotypes about children's memory apparently color perceptions of testimony.

Besides their beliefs about children and adults, fact finders' beliefs about other witness attributes may affect their judgments. Elderly people appear from some research to have low credibility as memory sources (Yarmey, 1984), as do people who communicate low status by their actions (O'Barr, 1982). In both cases, beliefs about overall intellectual competence appear to generalize to beliefs about memory. On the other hand, people may tend to believe that police officers are highly competent witnesses, presumably because of their training and experience.

In sum, jurors and other fact finders are likely to be influenced in their judgments of eyewitness accuracy by preconceived beliefs about memory and the relationships between memory and static attributes of the eyewitness such as age and apparent intelligence.

Witness attributes and the message:
Who may affect how and what

Witnesses with various static and ascribed qualities may communicate in ways that make them look less or more accurate. Police officers may convey a compelling sense of certainty. Young children may have trouble communicating their memories in a logically sequential or internally consistent fashion (Goodman, Golding, & Haith, 1984), and may be less accurate in some cases than are adult witnesses (for example, Leippe, Romanczyk, & Manion, 1991). And people from lower status backgrounds are more likely than more socially privileged individuals to emit negative credibility cues in their speech (O'Barr, 1982). Relationships between witness attributes and communication will be examined further in the next section, which moves us squarely into consideration of what communication qualities define the look and sound of accuracy.

The memory message: Substance and style

Social-psychological approaches to persuasion broadly conceive of two ways of evaluating a message (Chaiken, 1980; Petty & Cacioppo, 1986). Message recipients may take a central route of carefully scrutinizing the arguments-based central content of the message. Alternatively (or in addition), recipients may respond primarily to information outside of or peripheral to message content – such as who the source is, nonverbal qualities of how the source looks and speaks, and how other recipients are responding. In taking this peripheral route, recipients may decide to accept or reject the message on the basis of a heuristic decision rule suggested by one of the peripheral cues. If the source is an expert, for example, the message may be uncritically accepted because "experts can be trusted." Or the failure of the speaker to make eye contact may encourage disagreement because "she must be hiding something if she can't even look me in the eye." Typically, peripheral-route processing is more likely than central-route processing to the extent that the peripheral cues are strong and attention getting (compare Chaiken, Liberman, & Eagly, 1989) and/or the recipient is unmotivated or unable to carefully evaluate the message (compare Chaiken et al., 1989; Petty & Cacioppo, 1986).

It is easy to conceive of possible peripheral cues in a memory message. We have already seen how fact finders may make assumptions about an eyewitness's credibility based on his or her age or status. In addition, facial (for example, eye contact) and paraverbal (for example, hesitation) cues are as prominent in a memory message as in any other type. The central content of a memory message, however, is another matter. In the typical persuasive communication, content is comprised of arguments (Petty & Cacioppo, 1986). A strong, high quality message has compelling arguments because of their logic, the degree to which they withstand counterarguing (Petty & Cacioppo, 1984), the linkage between what they advocate and audience-desired outcomes (Hovland, Janis, & Kelley, 1953), or the amount of new information they add to the issue in question (Morley, 1987). *But what constitutes a strong memory message?* A memory report usually does not contain arguments whose reasoning can be logically or subjectively evaluated. Nor does it contain much information that can be documented independently of the communicator. (If it did, the issue of eyewitness accuracy would be moot.) A memory report contains a description of events and/or people. The real question is what makes a description compelling. Independent of peripheral cues, what qualities of the verbal content of the report make it a strong message – a report fact finders buy as accurate?

The content of the report

An intriguing place to begin consideration of this question is to examine how people decide the accuracy or reality of their own memories. According to reality monitoring research and theory (Johnson & Raye, 1981), memories of actual, externally derived experiences differ in systematic ways from memories of internal experiences or imagination. Typically, a memory of an event actually seen (versus imagined) will include more sensory attributes, more detail, more contextual information (that is, "when" and "where"), and less of a sense of the cognitive operations going on during the stimulus event and retrieval (because perception is more automatic than imagination) (see Johnson, 1988). Moreover, people tend to use these qualities to decide whether they saw something or just imagined it.

Written descriptions of real and imagined stimuli appear to differ, to an extent, in terms of the reality monitoring variables. In a series of studies by Schooler, Gerhard, and Loftus (1986), some subjects actually saw a yield sign during a slide presentation of an auto accident whereas others were led through suggestive questioning to believe they had seen a stop sign. Subjects who actually saw the sign wrote descriptions of it that were briefer, mentioned more stimulus attributes, and made less reference to cognitive operations than the descriptions of subjects with suggested memories. In addition, the real memories were delivered more confidently and contained fewer verbal hedges.

Details. If people look for certain qualities in deciding whether to trust their own memories, it makes sense that they might look for the same qualities in evaluating someone else's eyewitness report. Consistent with this, fact finders seem more impressed with eyewitnesses who provide a lot of details in their testimony, whether the details are about surrounding context (Wells & Leippe, 1981) or simply vividly depict the central focus of attention (Bell & Loftus, 1989). Bell and Loftus (1989) found that mock jurors who read a summary of a grocery store robbery trial ascribed higher credibility to an eyewitness when he volunteered a description of exactly what the robber allegedly purchased ("Milk Duds and a can of Diet Pepsi") than to an eyewitness who said he was carrying "a few store items." Similarly, using the two-phase procedure, Wells and Leippe (1981) observed that subject-jurors' belief in subject-witnesses' lineup identifications was greater the more complete their memory for peripheral details of the crime setting (for example, number of chairs, color of walls).

Verbal confidence. It will be recalled that Schooler et al. (1986) found that real memories were expressed more confidently than suggested memories. This is consistent with a reality monitoring account in that the memory for something actually seen should be stronger or more vivid to the individual. Thus, verbal assertions of confidence represent a message content that should signal to fact finders that the eyewitness is experiencing a strong recollection. In an empirical demonstration of this, Whitley and Greenberg (1986) presented subjects with a videotape of one of several variants of the scripted eyewitness testimony in a simulated robbery trial. In one version, the witness, on two occasions, asserted high confidence ("I'm certain that's him"), whereas in another version the witness expressed low confidence ("I'm pretty sure that's him"). Ratings of the witness's description and accuracy of identification were higher in the high confidence condition. Moreover, this held true whether nonverbal indicators of nonconfidence (for example, hesitation) were present or absent.

Admissions of memory failure. In addition to variables explicitly identified by reality monitoring studies, there are other qualities of memory-message content that fact finders can be expected to use to judge eyewitnesses, qualities that fit laypeople's intuitive theories of how memory works. One of these is the frequency of memory failure admissions. In an interview, or during courtroom examination, the eyewitness who answers "I don't know" to a high percentage of the questions is apt to look bereft of memory (cf. Loftus & Goodman, 1985). Judging from Wells and Leippe's (1981) research, described earlier, the negative impression may be a global one – generalizing into heightened skepticism about affirmative answers to other questions. On the other hand, the total absence of "I don't knows" in the memory report may also signal low credibility. As Wells and Lindsay (1983) have suggested, fact finders may conclude that the "I-didn't-forget-a-thing" witness has an inappropriately low threshold for accepting his or her memory as accurate.

Little research has examined how admissions of memory failure affect fact finder decisions. Leippe et al. (1992) found that the credibility ratings given to witnesses of an actual event were unrelated to the frequency of don't-knows, despite the fact that don't-knows were negatively related to witness accuracy. It is possible, however, that a higher frequency of don't-knows than occurred among these witnesses is necessary to gain the notice of fact finders.

Consistency. Another aspect of message content that may influence credibility is consistency (Wells & Lindsay, 1983). If, within a single memory report, the witness makes contradictory statements, most fact finders will take notice. Especially in the absence of a challenging questioner, glaring inconsistencies in the same report are highly unlikely and thus unexpected. Unexpected behaviors, especially when they are undesirable, have great perceptual salience and typically lead to a correspondent inference about the actor's disposition (for example, "This witness doesn't have it straight and is not credible") (Jones & Davis, 1965). To date, studies have not evaluated intrareport consistency. The clear expectation would be that fact finders will question the credibility of witnesses who are inconsistent in this fashion.

More common than intrareport inconsistencies are inconsistencies between statements in two different reports given by the witness. Perceptive and logical fact finders privy to both memory messages may lower their belief in the face of interreport inconsistency. But, in contrast to the intrareport case, it is possible they will attribute the inconsistency to delayed improvement in memory or to misleading questioning tactics and hence may not question the accuracy of the newer report. This could explain why the few mock-trial studies that have manipulated the interreport inconsistency of the principal eyewitness have failed to find a consistency–credibility relationship, at least when the witness is an adult (Leippe & Romanczyk, 1989; Lindsay, Lim, Marando, & Cully, 1986). Leippe and Romanczyk (1989) had jurors read a summary of a mugging/murder case that included the prosecution eyewitness's original report to the police as well as excerpts from the witness's courtroom testimony. There were none to three clear discrepancies between what the eyewitness said in the report and what he said at trial. When the witness was an adult, the number of inconsistencies did not influence either verdicts or ratings of the witness's credibility. It is interesting, however, that greater inconsistency lowered credibility ratings when the witness was a six-year-old child. Perhaps a few inconsistencies only create general doubt when fact finders already have some skepticism (for example, a negative child witness stereotype).

Signal-to-noise ratio. A final quality (at least in the present analysis) of memory-message content that may connote credibility is what might be called the "signal-to-noise ratio." This is related to the reality monitoring notion that imagined or internally generated memories are more likely to include mention of cognitive processes, descriptions of what the witness recalls "thinking or paying attention to" (Schooler et al., 1986) while viewing or remembering the event. For example, a report based on a poor or mistaken or confabulated memory may include a relatively large number of comments such as "I remember thinking to myself..." and "The scene reminded me of..." In addition, poor memories may force people to make logical inferences ("Let's see, if I was standing there, the thief must have been facing the rear exit"), or what Wells and Lindsay (1983) refer to as constructive invocations (that is, statements indicative of reconstructive memory such as "I think he had a hat . . . yes, he had a blue hat"). If people recognize that their own memory reports have these qualities when they are unsure, they may be sensitive to how much another's memory report reflects this noisy "thinking out loud," relative to the credibility-suggestive signals of crisp and vivid descriptions (recall Schooler et al.'s finding that real memories of a stimulus were more briefly described than suggested ones).

Thus there are at least five aspects of memory-message content that may influence the credibility judgments of fact finders. There is empirical evidence for only two of these (amount of detail and assertions of confidence), whereas the other three have been studied insufficiently (consistency and memory failure admissions) or not at all (signal-to-noise ratio). The present account is thus tentative, but it suggests conceptually reasonable leads for research.

The delivery of the report

Confidence (again). When we turn from what is in a memory message to how it is delivered, witness confidence requires immediate and preeminent mention. Wells (1985a) has opined that "there is little doubt that eyewitness confidence is the most powerful single determinant of the credibility ascribed to eyewitnesses" (p. 58). We have already seen that explicit statements of confidence within the memory message contribute to perceived credibility. In addition, confidence and nonconfidence are communicated nonverbally, with potent effect.

Survey studies indicate that the majority of jury-eligible adults believe there is a positive relationship between eyewitness accuracy and confidence (Wells, 1984; Yarmey & Jones, 1983). The implications of this belief for judgments of witness credibility are most clearly seen in research employing the two-phase procedure. In Wells's seminal research using this procedure, after watching subject-witnesses' testimony, subject-jurors not only predict whether the witness's identification was accurate, but also rate the witness's apparent confidence. Perceived confidence is invariably highly positively correlated with judgments of identification accuracy (see Wells & Murray, 1984, for a review). Perceived confidence accounts for as much as 50 percent of the variance in subject-jurors' judgments of witness accuracy (Wells et al., 1979).

Leippe et al. (1992) found that the strong positive relationship between perceived confidence and perceived accuracy is also evident when the memory report is about a relatively lengthy participatory experience (rather than a brief theft), witnesses are children (as well as adults), and judgments are made about overall believability and the accuracy of the recall offered in a structured interview (as well as the accuracy of face recognition).

A causal link from apparent confidence to apparent credibility can be inferred from studies in which the demeanor of the witness is manipulated

experimentally. Wells, Ferguson, and Lindsay (1981) briefed half their subject-witnesses about the difficult cross-examination they would soon face and
suggested they rehearse in advance their responses to likely questions. The
result was that, among witnesses who made inaccurate identifications, briefed
(versus nonbriefed) witnesses self-rated themselves as more confident, and
were rated as more confident and more often judged accurate by subject-
jurors. In another two-phase experiment, Wells and Leippe (1981) found that
both accurate and inaccurate witnesses became less believable when grilling
cross-examination questions disrupted their confident demeanor. Thus it
seems that, as impressions of confidence about memory go, so goes belief in
the memory.

Not surprisingly, witnesses' sense of confidence and fact finders' perceptions
of their confidence are related. In the Wells et al. (1981) study, the correlation
between witnesses' self-ratings and subject-jurors' ratings was $r = +.53$. It
is surprising that this correlation is not larger, given that subject-jurors heard
witnesses rate their confidence on a seven-point scale. This clearly suggests
that there are cues to confidence beyond (or instead of) verbal claims – cues
that are nonverbal.

Almost no research has attempted to identify these confidence cues by
isolating the communicative behaviors that distinguish eyewitnesses who are
rated as confident from those rated as unconfident. Instead, researchers have
manipulated behavioral cues in a single speech or statement and then examined how the audience rates the speaker's confidence. This research has
found that the impression of confidence is associated with fast speech rate
and increased loudness of voice (Sherer, London, & Wolf, 1973; Seidel &
Kimble, 1990), as well as an absence of hedges and hesitations (O'Barr, 1982;
Whitley & Greenberg, 1986). Leippe et al. (1992) found that subject-fact
finders' ratings of witnesses' hedging and hesitation were highly negatively
correlated with their ratings of witnesses' confidence ($-.73 < r < -.45$).

The nonverbal behaviors identified in these studies fit our intuitive image
of what might be called the "confident look." They do not conclusively show,
however, that these behaviors are the critical ones that differentiate naturally
occurring confident and nonconfident eyewitness testimony. A mysterious
finding in the Leippe et al. experiments was that perceived confidence was
unrelated to an index of speech qualities in which, among other things, trained
raters quantified the frequencies of objectively observable hedges and hesitations. Perhaps the correlations among the purely subjective ratings reflect
mainly people's stereotype of the confident look. Alternatively, the confident
look may be more holistic. The mixture of all the paraverbal and verbal
qualities may matter more than a high or low count on any one dimension.

Powerfulness of speech. One way or another, apparent confidence is multiply
determined by a number of paralinguistic behaviors. For this reason, apparent

confidence can be called a metavariable. A second metavariable critical to the credibility ascribed to memory messages is what O'Barr (1982) has labeled "powerless speech" and I will refer to as speech powerfulness. According to O'Barr (1982), speech style is related to social status and education level. Individuals with low social status are more likely to have a powerless speech style characterized by high frequency of verbal hedges (word forms such as "sort of" or "maybe" that avoid commitment and reduce the force of an assertion), intensifiers (word forms such as "very" and "definitely" that make an assertion more dramatic), hesitations (unfilled pauses punctuated with "uh" or meaningless fillers such as "you know"), and gestures (indications of direction or action that accompany words, such as pointing to one's wrist and saying "He touched me here"). In contrast, higher status people tend to use these stylistic forms infrequently in speech. They speak powerfully, avoiding unnecessary hedges, intensifiers, hesitations, and redundant gestures. O'Barr documented the powerless–powerful dimension and its correlation with status by studying samples of courtroom testimony.

The power of powerfulness to influence fact finders is suggested by two studies. In one study, by Nigro, Buckley, Hill, and Nelson (1989), the speech powerfulness of written statements was manipulated. It was found that both an adult and a child prosecution witness were judged less credible and elicited fewer guilt ratings when their testimony contained numerous powerless verbalizations than when it contained none.[2] Even more telling is research by Erickson, Lind, Johnson, and O'Barr (1978). Mock jurors listened to audiotaped testimony (adapted from an actual courtroom appearance) that included over one hundred and ten powerless speech forms, or to the same testimony edited to pare down the powerless speech to fewer than twenty instances. Mock jurors who heard the powerless testimony judged the witness to be less convincing and truthful, as well as less competent and intelligent, than those who heard the latter, powerful version.

Erickson et al.'s findings, in particular, suggest that, although powerful speech has some of the same qualities as confident-appearing testimony, it communicates much more than just confidence. As O'Barr and his colleagues have suggested, powerfulness seems to communicate something about the witness's social status which, in turn, suggests a level of competence and intelligence. In other words, speech powerfulness is a cue to expertise, and in the case of memory messages, it may suggest something about the ability of the witness to piece together from memory a complicated event. Alternatively, a blatantly powerless or powerful style may communicate overall incompetence or competence so strongly that the impression generalizes to a decision about the memory report in a more or less automatic fashion, without much conscious consideration for overall competence as a cue to competence as a rememberer. Impact of this sort is possible if speech style is such a well learned credibility cue that it can trigger a heuristic decision rule, much as the trappings of authority can lead to rather mindless obedience and similarity leads to heightened positive affect (compare Cialdini, 1988).

To quote O'Barr (1982), powerless and powerful speech "result from and reflect the speaker's social prestige" (p. 76). The "result from" side of this assertion suggests that various witness groups, based on their social class or communicative skills, may come across as more or less credible than others – not only because of who they are, but of how they talk. For example, women who were raised in and occupy traditional societal roles may be particularly likely to speak "powerlessly" (Lakoff, 1975; O'Barr, 1982). Might children's speech style also be relatively powerless? Leippe, Romanczyk, and Manion (1991) content-analyzed the testimony (about a laboratory event) of college students and children ranging in age from five to ten years, and found almost no age differences in powerless verbalizations. The only exception to this was that the youngest children used an intensifier about twice as frequently as adult witnesses. Perhaps it is noteworthy, however, that nearly all the children in this study were from at least middle class families.

Narrativeness. O'Barr and his colleagues have identified other speech dimensions besides powerfulness that vary among the myriad witnesses who appear in courts of law. Among them, the narrative versus fragmented dimension seems particularly relevant to the appraisal of memory messages. This refers to the tendency to give loquacious, highly elaborate answers to questions as opposed to brief, fragmented answers. There is some experimental evidence that greater credibility is ascribed to memory accounts given in a more narrative (versus fragmented) style (Lind, Erikson, Conley, & O'Barr, 1978).

Other variables. Research on persuasion suggests other aspects of the communication style of a memory report that may contribute to fact finders' belief in the report. A high level of eye contact by communicators as they speak tends to enhance persuasive impact (Beebe, 1974; Mehrabian & Williams, 1969). Speech rate tends to be associated with the perceived credibility of the speaker, with an above average rate increasing and a below average rate decreasing credibility (Miller, Maruyama, Beaber, & Valone, 1976). Fast speech may also disrupt ability to critically evaluate message content (Smith & Shaffer, 1991). Finally, people who speak a bit louder than others within a setting tend to be perceived as more influential and even more logical (Robinson & McArthur, 1982). In large part, these nonverbal qualities of communication appear to influence credibility judgments because they are, through social learning, associated with being knowledgeable and intelligent, in addition to (as we saw previously) self-confident. In the case of a memory message, cues to this effect may add information to one or the other side of the belief ledger, they may distract (or excuse) fact finders from careful scrutiny of the memory report itself, or they may compel fact finders to selectively attend to the report content with greater or lesser skepticism.

Questioning factors: Shaping memory messages by inquiry

Unlike the usual persuasive communication, the most important memory messages occur in an interactive context in which the eyewitness is being questioned. Initially, an eyewitness to a crime is questioned by police officers, at the crime scene and then at the police station. If the case goes further, there will be more questioning by law officers, attorneys preparing their cases, and ultimately, by attorneys in a courtroom in front of a judge and jury. Questioning is essential to gaining information. Eyewitnesses typically do not give a clear and complete account of what they saw in response to the gentle request to "tell me everything that happened." Even if they did, questioners, representing (and looking for) all angles of a case, need to be convinced in a way that only further, and more specific, questioning can satisfy.

The downside to specific questioning is that the questions may influence the answers. There is rather compelling evidence that memory itself is influenced by how a question is asked. In one well-known study, for example, laboratory witnesses gave higher estimates of the speed of a car crash (and even were more likely to report seeing broken glass) when the questioner inquired about when the cars "smashed" as opposed to "hit" (Loftus & Palmer, 1974). Other studies show that what a question implies at Time A may show up in a witness's memory at Time B. Thus, if an early question falsely suggests the presence of a stop sign, the witness may later remember seeing a stop sign (Loftus, Miller, & Burns, 1978); if informed early on that the perpetrator was a truck driver, witnesses estimate him to be heavier than if informed he was a dancer (Christiaansen, Sweeney, & Ochalek, 1983). Chances are strong that these subtle influences of suggestion go unnoticed by fact finders (compare Wells, 1985), a fact that has important implications for the ability of fact finders to discern eyewitness accuracy (see the last section of this chapter). Let us focus here on how questioning can affect the content and style aspects of a memory report that fact finders tune into in judging accuracy.

Repeated questioning. Psycholegal scholars since Whipple (1909) have speculated that repeated offering of a memory report may lead to increased commitment to and confidence in that report. As Leippe (1980) has observed, this would be consistent with a number of social-psychological phenomena, including the greater resistance to change that follows a public espousal of an attitude position, the tendency for people to avoid self-inconsistency, and the self-perception process by which people acquire beliefs by stating them. As yet, research has not demonstrated that self-reported confidence does increase with repeated questioning, or that heightened confidence becomes evident in the style and statements of the memory report. But it is hard to imagine that some such effects of repeated questioning do not occur. At the very least, a memory report delivered for, say, the third time should be more smoothly delivered than the initial offering. Given the persuasive impact of apparent confidence, and the fact that smoothness (that is, few hedges, speedy speech) helps make confidence apparent, it would be surprising if later memory reports are not, on average, more convincing than initial ones – especially to fact finders who are unaware the report has been rehearsed.

Repeated questioning may also affect the internal consistency of the memory message, with potential effect on its persuasive impact. Inconsistencies noted by questioners or by the witness in earlier interviews, will be reconciled and removed from later reports, for example.

Against these effects of repeated questioning on the memory message that could mislead fact finders, there may also be a beneficial effect, the inclusion of additional, accurate memories. Recent research suggests that repeated questioning can yield gains in total accurate recall without badly inflating errors of commission (Dunning & Stern, 1991; Scrivner & Safer, 1988).

Biased lineup instructions and forced choices. A well established finding in the eyewitness literature is that eyewitnesses are less likely to reject a lineup ("I don't recognize the perpetrator from among these individuals") under biased lineup instructions, that is, when the administering law officer presents the lineup with verbal assertions that the perpetrator is in the lineup and without explicitly offering a "none of the above" option. In these circumstances, the rate of false identifications is higher (Malpass & Devine, 1981). Witnesses, in effect, are forced to make a choice. A lineup identification is a memory message to a subset of fact finders, including the police who administer the lineup and the jurors who may be told about the identification. Wells (1984) found that subject-jurors presented with positive identifications given under biased and unbiased instructions were insensitive to the possible effect of the instructions. They gave the same (low) estimates that a false identification occurred in both cases. Thus, we have a questioning device that influences the content (a positive identification) of the memory message in a fashion that may be invisible to fact finders.

More generally, a questioning style that discourages admissions of "I don't know" – that forces choices – should increase the believability of the report to the extent that fact finders cue into the relative absence of memory failure admissions and the witness does not show discomfort with the implied constraint on response options.

Eliciting memory failure admissions. The flip side of this is the questioning style that seeks to get the witness to admit, as much as possible, to not knowing or not remembering. This strategy may be pursued at trial by the cross-examining attorney. Loftus and Goodman (1985) cite courtroom strategists who attest to the effectiveness of this technique in making a witness look discreditable. And who would argue, judging from Wells and Leippe's (1981) demonstration of the potent discrediting effect of grilling eyewitnesses about even patently unimportant details of an event?

Creating fragmentation. If we stay in the courtroom, and keep the eyewitness on the stand, other questioning tactics that will influence the memory report are evident. It was noted previously that highly fragmented, curt responses appear to convey low accuracy, whereas lengthy, narrative ones enhance credibility. Lawyers have it in their power to create fragmentation or to minimize it. The general practice is for attorneys to allow their own witnesses to talk at some length and so display a narrative style, but try to induce a fragmented style in opposing witnesses (for example, by interrupting frequently and insisting the witness "just answer the question").

These styles may lead to the intended effect on the jurors. In addition, as O'Barr (1982) has reasoned, the questioning lawyers' behavior in allowing or fostering a given style may contribute to those impressions. In letting the witness talk at length and "be narrative," the attorney may be perceived as relinquishing some control of the courtroom to the witness. In turn, jurors may assume that the attorney has a very high opinion of this witness's competence, and accept this appraisal as their own. On the other hand, questioner impatience leading to witness fragmentation conveys a negative opinion of the witness's ability that may rub off on jurors – although the opposite impression may be made if jurors see the fragmenting questioning as a deliberate and desperate effort to derail strong testimony.

The cross-examination shake-up. In general, cross-examination can influence both the substance and style of a memory report. Skilled lawyers can highlight inconsistencies as well as use verbal trickery to lead the eyewitness to make statements that appear inconsistent (Bailey, 1985; Saks & Hastie, 1978). Perhaps the most likely effect of cross-examination is to make the witness appear less confident. Turtle and Wells (1989) employed the two-phase procedure to empirically establish this. A day after watching a videotape of an abduction, adult and child subject-witnesses were subjected to direct questioning by a familiar experimenter followed by cross-examination by a second experimenter whom they had not previously met. The cross-examination included challenging queries (for example, "You claimed . . . " "Isn't it true, though . . . ") and falsely leading questions (for example, although there had been no visible wallet, the witnesses were asked "In which hand was the man carrying his wallet?"). Subject-jurors later viewed videotapes of the testimony. Of most interest here, subject-jurors rated witnesses (of all ages) as less confident and as less accurate when they observed them under cross-examination than when they observed them under direct examination.

The power of (suggested) consensus. It is not unusual for more than one person to witness the same crime. This introduces a potential for the testimony of one witness to influence the questioning of a second witness. Based on what the first witness reports, a police officer may form a theory of what happened, making certain inferences about what "must have been." Consciously or unconsciously, the police officer may communicate these inferences as facts while questioning the second witness. The second witness may incorporate these into his or her own memory, or become more certain of (and willing to offer) memories that seem to agree with the officer's inferences. At the very least, the stories of previously interviewed witnesses may influence what aspects of the event the questioner dwells on with the current witness.

Knowing the content of another's memory report may affect the content of a witness's own report. If the other report agrees with his or her memory, the witness is apt to feel more confident and to convey that confidence to fact finders. If there is disagreement, confidence stands to be deflated. Depending on the status or number of other witnesses, conformity pressures may operate to compel the witness toward outward agreement with what is contained in the other testimony (compare Zimbardo & Leippe, 1991).

A recent experiment by Luus and Wells (1991; see also this volume) dramatically illustrates how the confidence of an eyewitness may be affected by another's testimony. Subject-witnesses made a lineup identification of the perpetrator of a staged crime. After this, but before rating their confidence in the accuracy of their identification, they were told that a second eyewitness identified the same man from the lineup, that a second eyewitness identified a different man, or nothing about a second eyewitness. Confidence ratings were profoundly influenced by the feedback. Knowing that the other witness identified the same man led to an increase in confidence from 6.9 to 8.8 on a ten-point scale, whereas knowing that the other identified someone else led to a decrease in confidence of the same magnitude (down to 4.7). More dramatic (and disturbing), both the inflated and the deflated confidence persisted when witnesses learned that the information they had been given was mistaken (an error in recording). This result is consistent with social-psychological research demonstrating that beliefs and attitudes may persist even when the information on which they were originally based is discredited, because, in thinking about their beliefs, people develop additional cognitive support for them that is outside the scope of the discrediting (Anderson, Lepper, & Ross, 1980; Cialdini, 1988).

Who's asking. That it matters to the memory report whether the witness is facing supportive direct examination or tricky cross-examination is not surprising. What may be surprising, or at least more subtle and thus less likely to be taken into consideration by fact finders, is the effect of the knowledge of which side has requested a memory report. In a study by Vidmar and Laird (1983), subjects witnessed (on film) a barroom brawl and later received a mock subpoena asking them to testify on behalf of either the defense, the prosecution, or the court. Individually and under oath, the subject-witnesses gave statements to judges who were blind to the source of the subpoena. Both the judges and similarly uninformed subject-jurors rated the statements of witnesses subpoenaed by the prosecution as more incriminating than the statements of witnesses subpoenaed by the defense, with the statements of those called by the neutral court falling in between. Vidmar and Laird (1983) describe the basis of these differences: "Whereas the witnesses in neutral roles relayed relatively objective accounts, the adversary witnesses tended to describe the factual events with words or phrases that were not affectively neutral but biased in favor of their adversary role" (p. 895). And so it is that a memory message may be subtly shaped by the witness's knowledge of "who's asking" – probably without even realizing it, judging by their own ratings in the Vidmar and Laird experiment.

Interviewing technique. A laudable goal of memory interviewing is to change only the content of the memory report, and to change it on only one dimension and in one direction – an increase in quantity of accurate details. It is generally accepted by memory investigators that memory interviews should begin with a free recall, narrative report prompted by an open-ended request such as "Tell me everything that happened" (Hilgard & Loftus, 1979; Loftus & Goodman, 1985). More specific open-ended questions can then be asked such as "Can you tell me anything else about . . . ?" followed finally by closed questions that probe for more specific information while avoiding suggestion and implication. This format creates a memory report that includes (in the narrative) what is most salient and memorable to the witness, as well as details (in response to structured questions) that the witness may not spontaneously think to mention, is likely to include a structure and focus dictated mainly by what the witness believes is important, and minimizes errors of commission and suggestion by using carefully worded specific questions designed to elicit more open-ended responses.

During the past decade, Geiselman and Fisher have developed a yet more sophisticated interviewing technique known as the Cognitive Interview (Fisher et al., this volume; Fisher, Geiselman, & Amador, 1989; Geiselman, Fisher, MacKinnon, & Holland, 1986). This technique superimposes on the rough format described above several retrieval methods that are based on general principles of memory established by experimental psychologists. Briefly, witnesses are asked to mentally reconstruct the crime context, to report everything, even partial information, without regard to subjective importance, to recount the events in varying orders, and to report the events from several differing perspectives. Witnesses are also given suggestions by empirically validated methods for conjuring recall of names, faces, and other stimuli. Properly executed, the Cognitive Interview elicits appreciably more details than standard police interviewing methods without increasing commission errors. Research has not yet addressed how fact finders' impressions of a memory report are influenced by watching a Cognitive Interview of testimony by a witness interviewed with this method.

Witnessing conditions, memory messages, and perceived accuracy

As depicted in Figure 18.1, the conditions under which an event was observed will influence fact finders' judgments of a memory message both indirectly and directly. The indirect route is through the memory message itself. Physical and temporal conditions (for example, light level, physical distance from the perpetrator, presence of an attention-riveting weapon, duration of exposure to the perpetrator, pace of action) naturally should be related to the strength of the memory trace or, more specifically, the ease, clarity, and amount of recall. In turn, differences in these aspects of recall may show up in content and delivery qualities of the memory message – in numbers of details and memory failure admissions, consistency, apparent confidence, and so on.

The condition of the witness during questioning, such as his or her stress or emotional level, may also affect memory (Deffenbacher, 1983). In addition, the witness's emotions while viewing the event might affect the memory message if those emotions are stirred anew during testimony. Conceivably, strong emotion during testimony could decrease believability by making the report less articulate and full of negative credibility cues. Or the opposite could occur. Strong emotion could create a heightened belief in the witness by increasing sympathy for him or her enforcing plausibility, ("She must really remember well to give such a thorough and confident account even when it is so upsetting to her to think about what happened"; see Kelley, 1972), or activating the assumption of some fact finders (about 40 percent in a survey by Yarmey and Jones, 1983) that "such a traumatized person could never forget the transgressor's face." The role of emotion in communicating credibility deserves research attention. Some research indicates that, at least for child victim-witnesses of sexual abuse, high emotionality is positively correlated with credibility judgments (Goodman, 1989).

The direct effect on fact finders' judgments of witnessing conditions concerns the overall decrement or increment in skepticism about a memory report that may arise from independent knowledge of those conditions (Wells & Lindsay, 1983). If fact finders know that witnessing conditions were poor, they may be more predisposed to counterargue the report (for example, find alternative reasons for a statement other than good memory) or selectively look for problems with the testimony. This is analogous to the biased processing that occurs among recipients of sociopolitical messages that are highly counterattitudinal (Brock, 1967; Lord, Ross, & Lepper, 1979), especially when recipients have independent experience with the issue (Wu & Shaffer, 1987). Alternatively, knowledge of witnessing conditions may be one piece of information that, like information items gleaned from the memory report itself, is assigned a believability-implication value and an importance weight. In turn, all the information, so valued and weighted, may be averaged to create an overall believability judgment (compare discussions of information integration theory in legal decision making by Anderson, 1974, and Kaplan & Kemmerick, 1974).

Of crucial importance to the issue of accuracy discernment (which will be addressed in the next section) fact finders may not take into sufficient account the witnessing conditions (Wells, 1985a). Lindsay, Wells, and Rumpel (1981) manipulated witnessing conditions in a staged crime along a poor-to-good continuum, and found that the manipulation influenced eyewitness identification accuracy in the predicted way. Even when apprised of these conditions, however, subject-jurors did not adjust their beliefs in the eyewitness as much as they should have. They believed eyewitnesses in the poor witnessing conditions less frequently than those in the good witnessing conditions, but this reduction in belief fell well short of what the reduction in actual accuracy warranted. There are at least two plausible reasons for this insensitivity to witnessing conditions. First, even though it is likely that witnessing conditions are considered on the basis of self-referencing ("Would I have remembered under these conditions?"; Wells & Lindsay, 1983), fact finders still may not be aware of the degree to which witnessing conditions influence perception and memory (or the direction, as in the case of witness stress). Second, the influence of witnessing conditions on the memory report may not be very large. As suggested elsewhere (Leippe, 1980), certain variables may influence memory without our awareness and without shaking our confidence in our memory.

Discernibility: Judging eyewitness accuracy

One conclusion is quite clear from the foregoing analysis of eyewitness persuasion. There is no shortage of information available to fact finders in a memory report. Theoretically, they may pick up on a number of communicative and memorial qualities of the report as they make the crucial decision: Do I believe it or not? But is the information available to fact finders valid in terms of making this decision correctly? Can and do fact finders discriminate between accurate and inaccurate eyewitnesses based on the available cues to accuracy? This is the focus of the remainder of this chapter.

Evidence against discernibility

We have seen some indications that fact finders may not be very good at discerning accuracy. Subject-jurors do not seem sufficiently sensitive to the effects on identification accuracy of biased lineup instructions (Wells, 1984) or witnessing conditions (Lindsay et al., 1981). They become less likely to believe accurate lineup identifications when the witnesses admit their ignorance about trivial details concerning the witnessed event (Wells & Leippe, 1981), yet seem to underuse the frequency of memory failure admissions when this is a valid cue to recall accuracy (Leippe et al., 1992). Fact finders also seem overwhelmed by the apparent confidence of the witness, which bodes ill for accuracy discernibility, given extensive evidence that eyewitness confidence and eyewitness accuracy typically are only weakly correlated (Bothwell, Deffenbacher, & Brigham, 1987; Wells & Murray, 1984). Not only is confidence partly a matter of personality and style, it is also affected by questioning and other social factors. Because memory accuracy does not covary isomorphically with these variables, it does not covary much with confidence (Leippe, 1980).

Wells's experiments employing the two-phase, staged crime procedure have painted the most pessimistic picture of fact finders' ability to discern accuracy. After watching subject-witnesses respond to anywhere from fifteen to twenty-five direct and cross-examination questions, subject-jurors do no better than chance at guessing whether the witness correctly identified the thief in the staged crime. The same lack of correlation between predicted and actual identification accuracy has been observed in at least five experiments (see Wells & Lindsay, 1983, for a review).

Evidence for a discerning fact finder

As pessimistic as these results sound, let us not throw in the towel yet on fact finders' ability to tell right from wrong (memory). In part, the lack of discernibility found in the early two-phase studies may be due to the methodology. Subject-fact finders in these studies watched a memory report consisting of directed or cued recall – responses to direct and cross-examination questions about the perpetrator's attributes and actions and the details of the crime scene. From this, they were asked to predict the witness's accuracy in picking out the thief from a lineup – an event they never observed. It is noteworthy that face recognition tends to be poorly correlated with descriptive recall of perpetrator characteristics and actions (Pigott, Brigham, & Bothwell, 1990; Wells, 1985b) and may be negatively correlated with recall of peripheral details (Wells & Leippe, 1981). Accordingly, the fact finders in these studies may have received few cues from the recall report that were relevant to judging face recognition. Had they been asked to judge the overall accuracy of the recall report itself, however, perhaps they would have made more discerning judgments.

Some support for this prediction can be found in the study by Turtle and Wells (1989) in which subject-jurors rated the overall accuracy of the recall responses subject-witnesses gave to both direct questions and cross-examination. Both perceived accuracy ($r = .40$) and perceived confidence ($r = .39$) of the witness under cross-examination (but not under direct examination) were significantly correlated with the actual accuracy of the witness's responses (that is, percentage correct) over the entire testimony. A plausible explanation of these departures from past research is that a recall report includes some valid cues about its own accuracy, particularly when cross-examination questions are included. Content and delivery qualities such as memory failure admissions, inconsistencies, hesitations, and hedges are more likely to be prompted by challenging questions. And, if they are at all related to the actual accuracy of responses to those questions, they will occur more often among those with poorer memories.

Recent progress in the application of reality monitoring theory to the delivery of memory reports also suggests the possibility of accuracy discernment. It was noted earlier that Schooler et al. (1986) found that written descriptions of a stimulus actually seen differed in several ways from written descriptions of a stimulus that subjects did not see yet thought they recalled as a result of suggestive questioning. The real memories included fewer words, fewer verbal hedges, more stimulus attributes, more confidence, and less mention of cognitive processes operative at acquisition and retrieval. In three subsequent experiments, Schooler et al. found that, to a limited extent (60 percent accuracy), people were able to distinguish between the "real" and "unreal" memory reports. When provided with hints about what variables distinguished the two types of reports, subjects improved a bit in their discernibility. Though limited, this discernibility is impressive when one considers that the memory report was about a very specific and somewhat familiar stimulus (a red yield sign) and delivered in the relatively impoverished medium of print.

Lineup recognition accuracy has also been found to be somewhat discernible on the basis of reality monitoring variables. Stern and Dunning (this volume) found that witnesses who correctly identified from a photo spread the perpetrator in a staged crime tended to report that they "just recognized" the face and that they used a "match-to-memory-trace" strategy as they examined the faces. In contrast, incorrect witnesses reported using a ruminating process of elimination in which they used a "compare-to-each-other" strategy of comparing the photographs until they found the most familiar one. Thus, correct identifications were quick and involved a remembering strategy indicative of a rich, detailed memory trace, whereas false identifications were hesitating and indicative of extensive cognitive operations involving a suboptimal comparison process. These differences map nicely onto Johnson and Raye's (1981) external-versus-internal distinctions. They are also consistent with research demonstrating that correct identifications from sequential lineups tend to be fast (Sporer, 1992) and involve a match-to-memory strategy (Lindsay & Wells, 1985).

Most important for present purposes, Stern and Dunning also found that subjects exposed to witnesses' reports of how they made their identifications exceeded chance in their ability to separate the correct from the incorrect witnesses, slightly without (59 percent accurate) and better with (68 percent) instructions about the general differences between the correct and false identifications.

Yet more evidence that fact finders can discriminate (at least modestly) between accurate and inaccurate eyewitness reports comes from my own research (Leippe et al., 1992). In this research, briefly described earlier in this chapter, children and adults gave memory reports of a laboratory experience in which they were administered a bogus test of their sense of touch while a number of other activities also occurred. The memory reports were delivered in the context of an interview. The participant-witnesses first gave an uninterrupted, free recall response to the question "What happened?" and then added to this narrative in response to five open-ended questions (for example, "Can you remember anything else about ———?"). Witnesses then answered up to forty specific, cued-recall questions about various aspects of their experience and finally attempted to identify from photo spreads the male experimenter (the "toucher") and a briefly seen female "intruder."

Leippe et al. (1992) ordered the twenty-six-or-more memory reports within each age group from most-to-least accurate and used various subsets of the extremes at each end as stimulus witnesses in three experiments. Subject-fact finders in these experiments watched videotapes of the free recall and cued-recall portions of the memory reports of either high-accurate (usually 75th percentile or above) or low-accurate (usually 25th percentile or below) subject-witnesses and rated them on believability, confidence, consistency, and other variables. They also estimated the percentage of cued-recall questions an observed witness had answered correctly and judged whether the witness had correctly identified the toucher and the intruder.

Subject-fact finders demonstrated some accuracy discernment in all three experiments and for witnesses of all ages. Compared to low-accurate witnesses, high-accurate witnesses were judged more believable, estimated to have answered more recall questions accurately, and more confidently predicted to have made correct identifications. In addition, in two experiments, high-accurate witnesses were rated more confident and more consistent than low-accurate witnesses. Table 18.1 presents a summary of these results.

These results clearly demonstrate a modest level of accuracy discernment. Additional analyses revealed some important footnotes to this conclusion, however. We objectively scored the memory reports on several dimensions,

Table 18.1. *Credibility judgments of witnesses' memory reports in three experiments*

Witness accuracy	Experiment 1		Experiment 2		Experiment 3	
	Low	High[e]	Low	High[e]	Low	High[e]
Believability[a]	4.58	4.98 m	4.63	5.14 s	4.89	5.51 s
Confidence[a]	4.04	4.29 n	3.97	4.49 m	4.26	4.91 s
Consistency[a]	4.56	4.74 n	4.41	4.94 s	4.70	5.32 s
Estimate of cued recall[b]	.66	.70 n	.66	.73 s	.66	.74 s
Confidence in ID accuracy[c]						
of toucher	0.65	2.20 s	1.11	2.44 m		
of intruder	0.36	1.64 s	−0.67	−0.51 n		
Percent predicting ID[d]						
of toucher					.67	.79 s
of intruder					.44	.53 s

[a]Ratings were made on a 7-point scale in which a higher number indicates more of the attribute.
[b]Mean proportion of cued-recall questions subject-fact finders estimated the witness answered correctly.
[c]Subjects indicated whether they believed the witness would (+1) or would not (−1) make an accurate identification (ID) and rated their confidence in this prediction on a 7-point scale. Multiplying these two values together yields a "confidence-in-accuracy" score ranging from −7 (maximum confidence in an incorrect ID) to +7 (maximum confidence in a correct ID).
[d]Proportion of subjects indicating belief that the witness would make an accurate ID.
[e]Letter indicates the significance level of the difference between the two halves to the left of the letter (i.e., the main effect of accuracy on a measure): s = significant ($p < .05$), m = marginal ($.05 < p < .10$), n = nonsignificant.
Source: Leippe, Manion, & Romanczyk, 1992.

including number of words in the free recall portion of the report, number of memory admission failures in the cued-recall portion, and the speech powerfulness of the testimony coded in terms of O'Barr's (1982) criteria (see above). These variables, along with the subjective ratings of subjects, were regressed on a composite measure of witnesses' actual accuracy in two of the experiments. For adult witnesses, longer free recall reports (indicative of including more sensory details), fewer don't-knows, and (in one experiment) more powerful speech style were all associated with greater actual accuracy, indicating they were valid cues to accuracy. Yet when the same variables were regressed on believability ratings and a measure of perceived accuracy, none of these objective indexes emerged as significant predictors. Apparent confidence and apparent consistency were the only consistently reliable predictors of credibility perception. And between rated confidence and rated consistency, only confidence was associated with both perceived (strongly) and actual (weakly) accuracy. Thus, it seems that fact finders can discern accuracy, but it is not clear how they do it (aside from using – in fact, overusing

– their impressions of witness confidence) and it is clear, consistent with Schooler et al.'s and Stern and Dunning's research, that they are not spontaneously using cues from the witness's behavior that could help them do it better.

Nevertheless, we have now seen several demonstrations that fact finders can discern, to an extent, eyewitness accuracy. The ability seems to be present especially when fact finders judge the component of memory that is reported to them, the questioning style encourages emission of accuracy-relevant cues, and at least some of those cues are valid barometers of good memory. It also helps if fact finders are educated about what the valid cues might be.

A discerning theory: The validity-intuition model
of eyewitness persuasion

There are two problems for the fact finder, however. First, there are so many cues. Given the research findings, some must be valid or diagnostic of memory accuracy, others must be invalid or misdiagnostic. Which ones? The second problem is that valid cues do not always surface. Our inclination to believe our own inaccurate memories suggests a rather poor sensitivity to our own memory processes, and limits the extent to which we will communicate accurate and inaccurate memories differently.

The present analysis looks to the possibility of accuracy discernment within this limit. It is proposed here that the accuracy cues in a memory message fall somewhere along two dimensions. The validity dimension refers to the extent to which the cue actually is diagnostic of memory accuracy. A cue can range from completely invalid (that is, it varies independently of memory accuracy) through various levels of validity defined in terms of how much of the memory report it is diagnostic of and how frequently it is related to memory accuracy in the population of memory reports. The intuitiveness dimension refers to the degree to which people have preconceived beliefs that the cue is related to memory accuracy. Table 18.2 lists the memory message variables we have encountered in this chapter, and classifies them, somewhat speculatively, as high, medium, or low on each dimension.

It can be seen in Table 18.2 that the accuracy cues that score high on validity generally are message content variables based at least tentatively on reality monitoring. That is, they are behaviors (for example, hedges and hesitations) or statements (for examples, detailedness, assertions of confidence, memory failure admissions) that imply qualities of memory that would lead people to suspect the reality of their own memories. Cues that are high on intuitiveness, by contrast, tend to include some of the presumably valid cues (for example, detailedness) as well as communicative behaviors in the message delivery that have learned associations with source attributes such as expertise, knowledgeability, status, and trustworthiness (for example,

Table 18.2. *Accuracy cues in memory messages: A scorecard based on the validity-intuition approach to accuracy discernment*

Accuracy cue	Message locus	Intuitiveness	Validity	Stylistic interference	Discernibility value
Detailedness					
Central/sensory	Content	High	High	Low	High positive
Peripheral	Content	High	Low	Low	Misleading
Confidence					
Verbal	Content	High	Medium	High	Pot. misleading
Nonverbal	Delivery	High	Medium	High	Pot. misleading
Memory failures	Content	Medium	Medium	Low	Positive
Consistency	Content	Medium	Medium	Medium	Pot. misleading
Signal-to-noise	Content	Low	Medium	Low	Low positive
Speech rate	Delivery	Medium	Low	High	Misleading
Loudness of voice	Delivery	Medium	Low	High	Misleading
Hedges/hesitations	Delivery	High	Medium	High	Pot. misleading
Speech powerfulness	Delivery	Medium	Medium	High	Pot. misleading
Narrativeness	Delivery	Medium	Low	High	Misleading
Eye contact	Delivery	Medium	Low	High	Misleading

Note: Pot. misleading = potentially misleading.

speech rate, eye contact, speech powerfulness). The associations (for example, fast speech indicates knowledge about this issue) are learned through experience with other persuasion contexts and generalize, consciously or unconsciously, to eyewitness persuasion (for example, fast speech indicates knowledge about what she or he witnessed).

From this it would seem that the presence of cues that are both intuitive and valid will increase the ability of fact finders to discern memory accuracy, whereas the presence of intuitive but invalid cues will badly hinder this ability. This should be true in general. However, a critical third variable must also be considered: the extent to which the cue behavior is susceptible to stylistic interference. We have seen that the content and delivery of a memory message are not only a product of what is in memory. A message may be influenced by how the witness is questioned. Just as important, a memory message is undoubtedly affected by the traits of the witness. As a function of status, training, and personality, people differ in their characteristic communication styles. Thus, a witness may hedge and hesitate more because he is shy and inarticulate than because he is having trouble recalling. The consistency of a witness's report may reflect her personal skill at organizing a presentation more than her coherent memory. It may also reflect a more general human tendency to impose consistency on one's thoughts and beliefs (compare Zimbardo & Leippe, 1991). To the extent that witness traits also influence the emission of credibility cues – even valid ones – those cues effectively become noncues; they may even become misleading.

Apparent confidence is the quintessential example of this interference effect. Confidence correlated with real-versus-suggested status of written memories (Schooler et al., 1986) and modestly discriminated between highly accurate and highly inaccurate structured memory reports (Leippe et al., 1992). Yet perceived and asserted confidence are often uncorrelated with identification accuracy. From the present vantage point we can see why. Confidence is intuitively valid and has a modicum of actual validity. But there are also individual differences in how much confidence people chronically express in their voices and in how self-confident they are of their memories in general. Fact finders are unlikely to be able to determine the reasons for witness confidence. Instead, given the salient task at hand of judging memory, fact finders tend to relate all signs of confidence or nonconfidence to the likely accuracy of the witness's memory.

Table 18.2 includes a column in which the accuracy cues are assigned a value of high, medium, or low in susceptibility to stylistic interference. These assignments, once again, are somewhat speculative. But they are also testable. In general, it makes some sense to expect the message content variables (other than verbal confidence and consistency) to be the least susceptible to interference, especially those that are more grounded in reality monitoring processes and less relevant to witnesses' daily communication styles (such as detailedness and the signal-to-noise ratio).

The right-most column indicates, for each cue, a "discernibility value." For simplicity, let us equate "medium" and "high" as we quickly work through some of the possibilities concerning the three variables now at hand. A high-valid/low-interference cue should make a positive contribution to accuracy discernment, the more so if it is also highly intuitive. The amount of sensory or central details in a memory report is an example of such a good cue, judging by its performance as a correlate of accuracy in Leippe et al.'s (1992) and Schooler et al.'s (1986) research. Low-valid cues will be misleading regarding accuracy whether they are high or low in interference, and especially if they have high intuitiveness. Hence, impressive accounts of peripheral details led to mistaken belief in face recognition in Wells and Leippe's (1981) research. A high-valid/high-interference cue will have weakened discernibility value at the least, and is potentially misleading if the stylistic impact is in the opposite direction of what the impact of the memory should be. Apparent confidence falls squarely in this category. A low-valid/high-interference cue – such as eye contact – is an unequivocally bad cue. Especially if it is highly intuitive, such a cue, orthogonal as it is to accuracy, will mislead fact finders.

Then there is the category of accuracy cues that are low or moderately low on intuitiveness yet at least somewhat valid. What I have called the signal-to-noise ratio exemplifies this category. So does the frequency of memory admission failures, which proved to be correlated with accuracy in the Leippe et al. (1992) experiments yet was not related to perceived accuracy or believability. Even though I have assigned it "medium" intuitiveness, frequency of don't-knows seems underintuitive relative to its potential diagnostic value. Because they are present in a memory report but unused by fact finders, underintuitive-but-valid cues are a latent resource for discernibility that might be tapped simply by informing fact finders about them.

In general, information or instruction about all accuracy cues seems necessary if accuracy discernment is to reach a satisfactory level. Both Schooler et al. and Stern and Dunning found that being instructed about the valid cues improved fact finders' discernibility skill from very modest to modest. And Leippe et al.'s (1992) fact finders were decidedly underappreciative of the fact that the amounts of details, don't-knows, and powerlessness-related communicative behaviors – all seemingly at least somewhat intuitive – were reliably related to accuracy.

But why do intuitive cues go unused? There are at least two reasons. First, we are really dealing with the relative use and visibility of many cues. Some intuitive cues are more visible than others and thus more likely to be used. These may in fact overwhelm the less visible or salient ones, which then either go unnoticed or receive little weight in the final credibility judgment. Stylistic confidence in the Leippe et al. (1992) experiments probably had this kind of impact. Apparent confidence was weakly related to accuracy but subject-fact finders were strongly swayed by it – and thus missed better credibility cues and failed to disentangle stylistic and memory determinants of confidence.

Second, a memory message may not easily be parsed into all these different cues. Fact finders hear and see an entire report and often must render a holistic, overall believability judgment. Perhaps it is combinations of cues that cohere into distinct impressions of the witness, rather than a single dominating cue or a cumulative checklist. Even if judgments are holistic, however, it should help fact finders to have individual dimensions of accuracy-relevant cues explained to them.

Conclusions

The typical eyewitness memory report is a richly textured persuasive communication. Conceptual analysis of its anatomy, guided by a relevant research literature in persuasion and nonverbal communication and a growing research literature tuned specifically to testimony, reveals a plethora of factors that contribute to its believability in the eyes of fact finders. The communication-persuasion framework is an attempt to organize these factors in a conceptually coherent fashion that informs criminal justice practitioners who solicit and evaluate memory reports and also guides new research. A thorough understanding of eyewitness persuasion is an important theoretical and practical goal, and we are well on the way to attaining it. This goal is a necessary first step to what is, arguably, an even more important goal – learning how and how well fact finders can potentially discern witness accuracy. If accuracy discernment does prove possible and improvable beyond a token amount, the body of research that does the proving will take its place among the most valuable contributions of empirical psychology, for it will increase the validity of decisions, some of which have life and death ramifications, required of thousands of fact finders every day. The validity-intuition model of discernibility, high on conjecture and low on empirical backing as it is, offers a point of departure for this critical research challenge.

Notes

1 In child sexual abuse cases, heightened belief in the child victim-witness may also occur because fact finders assume that young children do not have the knowledge, cognitive skills, or motivation to fabricate a sexual accusation (Goodman, Bottoms, Hescovici, & Shaver, 1989).
2 Empirical evidence for the sensible notion that powerless speech raises a red flag about confidence is provided by the Nigro et al. (1989) study. Content analysis of mock-jury deliberations revealed that jurors who read the powerless version of the eyewitness's testimony discussed the eyewitness's confidence more than did jurors who read the powerful version.

References

Anderson, C. A., Lepper, M. R., & Ross, L. (1980). Perseverance of social theories: The role of explanation in the persistence of discredited information. *Journal of Personality and Social Psychology, 39*, 1037–1049.

Anderson, N. A. (1974). Cognitive algebra. In L. Berkowitz (Ed.), *Advances in experimental social psychology*. New York: Academic Press.

Bailey, F. L. (1985). *To be a trial lawyer*. New York: Wiley.

Beebe, S. A. (1974). Eye contact: A nonverbal determinant of speaker credibility. *The Speech Teacher, 23*, 21–25.

Bell, B. E., & Loftus, E. F. (1989). Trivial persuasion in the courtroom: The power of (a few) minor details. *Journal of Personality and Social Psychology, 56*, 669–679.

Bothwell, R. K., Deffenbacher, K. A., & Brigham, J. C. (1987). Correlation of eyewitness accuracy and confidence: The optimality hypothesis revisited. *Journal of Applied Psychology, 72*, 691–695.

Brigham, J. C., & Bothwell, R. K. (1983). The ability of prospective jurors to estimate the accuracy of eyewitness identifications. *Law and Human Behavior, 7*, 19–30.

Brock, T. C. (1967). Communication discrepancy and intent to persuade as determinants of counterargument production. *Journal of Experimental Social Psychology, 3*, 296–309.

Brown, R. (1986). *Social psychology: The second edition*. New York: The Free Press.

Chaiken, S. (1979). Communicator physical attractiveness and persuasion. *Journal of Personality and Social Psychology, 37*, 1387–1397.

Chaiken, S. (1980). Heuristic versus systematic information processing and the use of source versus message cues in persuasion. *Journal of Personality and Social Psychology, 39*, 752–766.

Chaiken, S., Liberman, A., & Eagly, A. H. (1989). Heuristic and systematic processing within and beyond the persuasion context. In J. S. Uleman & J. A. Bargh (Eds.), *Unintended thought* (pp. 212–252). New York: Guilford.

Christiaansen, R. E., Sweeney, J. D., & Ochalek, K. (1983). Influencing eyewitness descriptions. *Law and Human Behavior, 7*, 59–65.

Cialdini, R. B. (1988). *Influence: Science and practice* (2d ed.). Glenview, IL: Scott-Foresman.

Deffenbacher, K. (1983). The influence of arousal on reliability of testimony. In S. M. A. Lloyd-Bostock & B. R. Clifford (Eds.), *Evaluating witness evidence: Recent psychological research and new perspectives* (pp. 235–251). Chichester, England: Wiley.

Duggan, L. M., Aubrey, M., Doherty, E., Isquith, P., Levine, M., & Scheiner, J. (1989). The credibility of children as witnesses in a simulated child sexual abuse trial. In S. J. Ceci, D. F. Ross, & M. P. Toglia (Eds.), *Perspectives on children's testimony* (pp. 71–99). New York: Springer-Verlag.

Dunning, D., & Stern, L. B. (1991). Examining the generality of eyewitness hypermnesia: A close look at time delay and question type. Manuscript, Cornell University.

Erickson, B., Lind, E. A., Johnson, B. C., & O'Barr, W. M. (1978). Speech style and impression formation in a court setting: The effects of "powerful" and "powerless" speech. *Journal of Experimental Social Psychology, 14,* 266–279.

Fisher, R. P., Geiselman, R. E., & Amador, M. (1989). Field test of the cognitive interview: Enhancing the recollections of actual victims and witnesses of crime. *Journal of Applied Psychology, 74,* 722–727.

Geiselman, R. E., Fisher, R. P., MacKinnon, D. P., & Holland, H. L. (1986). Enhancement of the eyewitness memory with the cognitive interview. *American Journal of Psychology, 99,* 385–401.

Goodman, G. S. (1989). *The emotional effects on child sexual assault victims of testifying in criminal court.* Final report to the National Institute of Justice, U.S. Department of Justice.

Goodman, G. S., Bottoms, B. L., Herscovici, B. B., & Shaver, P. (1989). Determinants of the child victim's perceived credibility. In S. J. Ceci, D. F. Ross, & M. P. Toglia (Eds.), *Perspectives on children's testimony* (pp. 1–22). New York: Springer-Verlag.

Goodman, G. S., Golding, J. M., & Haith M. M. (1984). Jurors' reactions to child witnesses. *Journal of Social Issues, 40,* 139–156.

Goodman, G. S., Golding, J. M., Helgeson, V., Haith, M. M., & Michelli, J. (1987). When a child takes the stand: Jurors' perceptions of children's eyewitness testimony. *Law and Human Behavior, 11,* 27–40.

Hilgard, E. R., & Loftus, E. F. (1979). Effective interrogation of the eyewitness. *International Journal of Clinical and Experimental Hypnosis. 27,* 342–357.

Hovland, C. I., Janis, I., & Kelley, H. H. (1953). *Communication and persuasion.* New Haven, CT: Yale University Press.

Johnson, M. K. (1988). Discriminating the origin of information. In T. F. Oltmanns & B. A. Maher (Eds.), *Delusional beliefs: Theoretical and empirical perspectives.* New York: Wiley.

Johnson, M. K., & Grisso, T. J. (1986, August). *On the credibility of child witnesses: The jury is still out.* Symposium paper presented at the meeting of the American Psychological Association, Washington, D.C.

Johnson, M. K., & Raye, C. L. (1981). Reality monitoring. *Psychological Review, 88,* 67–85.

Jones, E. E., & Davis, K. E. (1965). From acts to dispositions: The attribution process in person perception. In L. Berkowitz (Ed.), *Advances in experimental social psychology* (Vol. 2). New York: Academic Press.

Kaplan, M. F., & Kemmerick, G. D. (1974). Juror judgment as information integration: Combining evidential and nonevidential information. *Journal of Personality and Social Psychology, 30,* 493–499.

Kelley, H. H. (1972). Attribution in social interaction. In E. E. Jones, D. E. Kanouse, H. H. Kelley, R. E. Nisbett, S. Valins, & B. Weiner (Eds.), *Attribution: Perceiving the causes of behavior.* Morristown, NJ: General Learning Press.

Lakoff, R. (1975). *Language and woman's place.* New York: Harper and Row.

Leippe, M. R. (1980). Effects of integrative memorial and cognitive processes on the correspondence of eyewitness accuracy and confidence. *Law and Human Behavior, 4,* 261–274.

Leippe, M. R., Brigham, J. C., Cousins, C., & Romanczyk, A. (1989). The opinions and practices of criminal attorneys regarding child eyewitnesses: A survey. In S. J. Ceci, D. F. Ross, & M. P. Toglia (Eds.), *Perspectives on children's testimony* (pp. 100–130). New York: Springer-Verlag.

Leippe, M. R., Manion, A. P., & Romanczyk, A. (1992). Eyewitness persuasion: How and how well do fact finders judge the accuracy of adults' and children's memory reports? *Journal of Personality and Social Psychology, 63,* 181–197.

Leippe, M. R., & Romanczyk, A. (1987). Children on the witness stand: A communication/ persuasion analysis of jurors' reactions to child witnesses. In S. J. Ceci, M. P. Toglia, & D. F. Ross (Eds.), *Children's eyewitness memory* (pp. 155–177). New York: Springer-Verlag.

Leippe, M. R., & Romanczyk, A. (1989). Reactions to child (versus adult) eyewitnesses: The influence of juror's preconceptions and witness behavior. *Law and Human Behavior, 13,* 103–132.

Leippe, M. R., Romanczyk, A., & Manion, A. P. (1991). Eyewitness memory for a touching experience: Accuracy differences between adult and child witnesses. *Journal of Applied Psychology, 76,* 367–379.

Leippe, M. R., Wells, G. L., & Ostrom, T. M. (1978). Crime seriousness as a determinant of accuracy in eyewitness identification. *Journal of Applied Psychology, 63,* 345–351.

Lind, E. A., Erickson, B., Conley, J. M., and O'Barr, W. M. (1978). Social attributions and conversational style in trial testimony. *Journal of Personality and Social Psychology, 36,* 1558–1567.

Lindsay, R. C. L., Lim, R., Marando, L., & Cully, D. (1986). Mock-juror evaluations of eyewitness testimony: A test of metamemory hypotheses. *Journal of Applied Social Psychology, 16,* 447–459.

Lindsay, R. C. L., & Wells, G. L. (1985). Improving eyewitness identifications from lineups: Simultaneous versus sequential lineup presentation. *Journal of Applied Psychology, 70,* 556–564.

Lindsay, R. C. L., Wells, G. L., & Rumpel, C. (1981). Can people detect eyewitness identification accuracy within and between situations? *Journal of Applied Psychology, 66,* 79–89.

Loftus, E. F., & Goodman, J. (1985). Questioning witnesses. In S. M. Kassin & L. S. Wrightsman (Eds.), *The psychology of evidence and trial procedure* (pp. 253–279). Beverly Hills, CA: Sage.

Loftus, E. F., Miller, D. G., & Burns, H. J. (1978). Semantic integration of verbal information into a visual memory. *Journal of Experimental Psychology: Human Learning and Memory, 4.* 19–31.

Loftus, E. F., & Palmer, J. C. (1974). Reconstruction of automobile destruction: An example of the interaction between language and memory. *Journal of Verbal Learning and Verbal Behavior, 13,* 585–589.

Lord, C. G., Ross, L., & Lepper, M. R. (1979). Biased assimilation and attitude polarization: The effects of prior theories on subsequently considered evidence. *Journal of Personality and Social Psychology, 37,* 2098–2109.

Luus, C. A. E., & Wells, G. L. (1991, June). *Eyewitness confidence: Social influence and belief perseverance.* Symposium paper presented at the meeting of the American Psychological Society, Washington, D. C.

Malpass, R. S., & Devine, P. G. (1981). Eyewitness identification: Lineup instructions and the absence of the offender. *Journal of Applied Psychology, 66.* 345–351.

McGuire, W. J. (1985). Attitudes and attitude change. In G. Lindzey & E. Aronson (Eds.), *The handbook of social psychology* (Vol. 2, pp. 233–346). New York: Random House.

Mehrabian, A., & Williams, M. (1969). Nonverbal concomitants of perceived and intended persuasiveness. *Journal of Personality and Social Psychology, 13,* 37–58.

Miller, G. R., & Burgoon, J. K. (1982). Factors affecting assessments of witness credibility. In N. L. Kerr & R. M. Bray (Eds.), *The psychology of the courtroom* (pp. 169–194). New York: Academic Press.

Miller, N., Maruyama, G., Beaber, R., & Valone, K. (1976). Speed of speech and persuasion. *Journal of Personality and Social Psychology, 34,* 615–624.

Morley, D. D. (1987). Subjective message constructs: A theory of persuasion. *Communication Monographs, 54,* 183–203.

Nigro, G. N., Buckley, M. A., Hill, D. E., & Nelson, J. (1989). When juries "hear" children testify: The effects of eyewitness age and speech style on jurors' perceptions of testimony.

In S. J. Ceci, D. F. Ross, & M. P. Toglia (Eds.), *Perspectives on children's testimony* (pp. 57–70). New York: Springer-Verlag.

O'Barr, W. M. (1982). *Linguistic evidence: Language, power, and strategy in the courtroom.* New York: Academic Press.

Petty, R. E., & Cacioppo, J. T. (1984). The effects of issue involvement on responses to argument quantity and quality: Central and peripheral routes to persuasion. *Journal of Personality and Social Psychology, 46,* 69–81.

Petty, R. E., & Cacioppo, J. T. (1986). The elaboration likelihood model of persuasion. In L. Berkowitz (Ed.), *Advances in experimental social psychology* (Vol. 19, pp. 123–205). New York: Academic Press.

Petty, R. E., Cacioppo, J. T., & Goldman, R. (1981). Personal involvement as a determinant of argument based persuasion. *Journal of Personality and Social Psychology, 41,* 847–855.

Pigott, M. A., Brigham, J. C., & Bothwell, R. K. (1990). A field study on the relationship between quality of eyewitnesses' descriptions and identification accuracy. *Journal of Police Science and Administration, 17,* 84–88.

Raskin, D. C., & Yuille, J. C. (1989). Problems in evaluating interviews of children in sexual abuse cases. In S. J. Ceci, D. F. Ross, & M. P. Toglia (Eds.), *Perspectives on children's testimony* (pp. 184–207). New York: Springer-Verlag.

Robinson, J., & McArthur, L. Z. (1982). Impact of salient vocal qualities on causal attributions for a speaker's behavior. *Journal of Personality and Social Psychology, 43,* 236–247.

Ross, D. F., Dunning, D., Toglia, M. P., & Ceci, S. J. (1990). The child in the eyes of the jury: Assessing mock jurors' perceptions of the child witness. *Law and Human Behavior, 14,* 5–23.

Saks, M. J., & Hastie, R. (1978). *Social psychology in court.* New York: Van Nostrand Reinhold.

Schooler, J. W., Gerhard, D., & Loftus, E. F. (1986). Qualities of the unreal. *Journal of Experimental Psychology: Learning, Memory, and Cognition, 12,* 171–181.

Scrivner, E., & Safer, M. A. (1988). Eyewitnesses show hypermnesia for details about a violent event. *Journal of Applied Psychology, 73,* 371–377.

Seidel, S., & Kimble, C. E. (1990, June). *Speed and loudness of vocal responses indicate confidence.* Paper presented at the meeting of the American Psychological Society, Dallas, TX.

Sherer, K. R., London, H., & Wolf, J. J. (1973). The voice of confidence: Paralinguistic cues and audience evaluation. *Journal of Research in Personality, 7,* 31–44.

Smith, S. M., & Shaffer, D. R. (1991). Celerity and cajolery: Rapid speech may promote or inhibit persuasion through its impact on message elaboration. *Personality and Social Psychology Bulletin, 17,* 663–669.

Sporer, S. L. (1992). Eyewitness identification accuracy, confidence and decision-times in simultaneous and sequential lineups. *Journal of Applied Psychology,* in press.

Stellar, M., & Kohnken, G. (1990). Statement analysis: Credibility assessment of children's testimonies in sexual abuse cases. In D. C. Raskin (Ed.), *Psychological methods for criminal investigation and evidence.* New York: Springer-Verlag.

Turtle, J. W., & Wells, G. L. (1989). Children versus adults as eyewitnesses: Whose testimony holds up under cross-examination? In Gruneberg et al. (Eds.), *Practical aspects of memory.* London: Wiley.

Undeutsch, U. (1982). In A. Trankell (Ed.), *Reconstructing the past: The role of psychologists in criminal trials* (pp. 27–56). Stockholm: Nostedt & Soners.

Vidmar, N., & Laird, N. M. (1983). Adversary social roles: Their effects on witnesses' communication of evidence and the assessments of adjudicators. *Journal of Personality and Social Psychology, 44,* 888–898.

Wells, G. L. (1984). How adequate is human intuition for judging eyewitness testimony. In G. L. Wells & E. L. Loftus (Eds.), *Eyewitness testimony: Psychological perspectives* (pp. 256–272). New York: Cambridge University Press.

Wells, G. L. (1985a). The eyewitness. In S. M. Kassin & L. S. Wrightsman (Eds.), *The psychology of evidence and trial procedure* (pp. 43–66). Beverly Hills, CA: Sage.

Wells, G. L. (1985b). Verbal descriptions of faces from memory: Are they diagnostic of identification accuracy? *Journal of Applied Psychology, 70,* 619–626.

Wells, G. L., Ferguson, T. J., & Lindsay, R. C. L. (1981). The tractability of eyewitness confidence and its implications for triers of fact. *Journal of Applied Psychology, 66,* 688–696.

Wells, G. L. & Leippe, M. R. (1981). How do triers of fact infer the accuracy of eyewitness identification? Using memory for detail can be misleading. *Journal of Applied Psychology, 66,* 682–687.

Wells, G. L. & Lindsay, R. C. L. (1983). How do people infer accuracy of eyewitness memory? Studies of performance and a metamemory analysis. In S. M. A. Lloyd-Bostock & B. R. Clifford (Eds.), *Evaluating witness evidence: Recent psychological research and new perspectives* (pp. 41–55). Chichester, England: Wiley.

Wells, G. L., Lindsay, R. C. L., & Ferguson, T. J. (1979). Accuracy, confidence, and juror perceptions in eyewitness identification. *Journal of Applied Psychology, 64,* 440–448.

Wells, G. L. & Murray, D. M. (1984). Eyewitness confidence. In G. L. Wells & E. L. Loftus (Eds.), *Eyewitness testimony: Psychological perspectives* (pp. 155–170). New York: Cambridge University Press.

Whipple, G. M. (1909). The observer as reporter: A survey of the psychology of testimony. *Psychological Bulletin, 6,* 153–170.

Whitley, B. E., Jr., & Greenberg, M. S. (1986). The role of eyewitness confidence in juror perceptions of credibility. *Journal of Applied Social Psychology, 16,* 387–409.

Wood, W. (1982). Retrieval of attitude relevant information from memory: Effects on susceptibility to persuasion and on intrinsic motivation. *Journal of Personality and Social Psychology, 42,* 798–810.

Wu, C., & Shaffer, D. R. (1987). Susceptibility to persuasive appeals as a function of source credibility and prior experience with the attitude object. *Journal of Personality and Social Psychology, 52,* 677–688.

Yarmey, A. D. (1984). Age as a factor in eyewitness memory. In G. L. Wells & E. L. Loftus (Eds.), *Eyewitness testimony: Psychological perspectives* (pp. 142–154). New York: Cambridge University Press.

Yarmey, A. D., & Jones, H. P. T. (1983). Is the psychology of eyewitness identification a matter of common sense? In S. M. A. Lloyd-Bostock, & B. R. Clifford (Eds.), *Evaluating witness evidence: Recent psychological research and new perspectives* (pp. 13–40). Chichester, England: Wiley.

Zimbardo, P. G., & Leippe, M. R. (1991). *The psychology of attitude and social influence.* New York: McGraw-Hill.

Zuckerman, M., DePaulo, B., & Rosenthal, R. (1981). Verbal and nonverbal communication of deception. In L. Berkowitz (Ed.), *Advances in experimental social psychology* (Vol. 14, pp. 1–59). New York: Academic Press.

Name index

419

Subject index